The Quest for Unity

First published by Fanele, an imprint of Jacana Media (Pty) Ltd, in 2023

10 Orange Street
Sunnyside
Auckland Park 2092
South Africa
+2711 628 3200
www.jacana.co.za

ISBN 978-1-77634-588-5

Also available as an ebook.

Cover design by Hothouse Specialist Graphic Designers
Editing by Glenda Younge
Proofreading by Megan Mance
Index by L-P Content & Curation
Set in Ehrhardt MT Std 10.5/14.5pt
Printed by Inside Data
Job no. 004028

See a complete list of Jacana titles at www.jacana.co.za

The Quest for Unity

An Appraisal of Regional Integration in Africa

Edited by Sizo Nkala and David Monyae

This book is dedicated to Professor Gilbert Khadiagala. Professor Khadiagala is a widely respected scholar who holds a doctorate in international studies from the Paul H. Nitze School of Advanced International Studies (SAIS), Johns Hopkins University, Washington, D.C. Professor Khadiagala currently serves as the Jan Smuts Professor of International Relations and Director of the Centre for the Study of the United States (ACSUS) at the University of the Witwatersrand, in Johannesburg, South Africa. His research interests encompass comparative politics, African politics, and international relations in Kenya, Canada and the United States. He is the recent editor of War and Peace in Africa's Great Lakes Region *(New York: Palgrave-MacMillan, 2017) and author of* Regional Cooperation on Democratization and Conflict Management in Africa *(Washington D.C.: Carnegie Endowment for International Peace, 2018). Professor Khadiagala has worked long and hard throughout his academic career nurturing upcoming scholars and making major contributions to African scholarship.*

Contents

PART 3: CONTINENTAL INTEGRATION MECHANISMS

PART 4: THE AFRICAN CONTINENTAL FREE TRADE AREA: CHALLENGES AND PROSPECTS

PART 5: INFRASTRUCTURAL INTEGRATION IN AFRICA

PART 6: THE MEDIA AND EXTERNAL ACTORS IN REGIONAL INTEGRATION

Foreword

Rob Davies

Regional integration was identified many years ago as being critical to Africa's quest to overcome its colonially induced underdevelopment. The idea of integrating the balkanised countries and economies inherited from colonialism into larger regional entities dates back to the pioneers of Pan-Africanism. Many of the founding leaders of independent Africa saw regionalism as a central component of strategies to break from their countries' structural dependence on the production and export of primary commodities used in industrial processes elsewhere.

The record of regional integration in Africa has been a mixed one, however. On the one hand, several potentially significant programmes or projects have been stillborn or have been inadequately implemented. On the other hand, a network of relatively stable Regional Economic Communities (RECs) has been established, and one of its most ambitious initiatives – the African Continental Free Trade Area (AfCFTA) – is now being 'operationalised'.

All of this takes place against a background where intra-African trade remains low compared to that in other regions. According to the former Executive Secretary of the United Nations Economic Commission for Africa, intra-African exports, as a percentage of the continent's total exports, rose from 10 per cent in 1995 to around 17 per cent in 2017, but this is still low compared to intraregional exports of 31 per cent of the total in North America, 59 per cent in Asia and 69 per cent in Europe.[1]

---

1   Songwe, V. (2019). 'Intra-African trade: A path to economic diversification and inclusion'. Washington, DC: Brookings Institute, February 2019.

Efforts to promote regional integration, and construct the AfCFTA in particular, are now taking place in the context of important changes in the global order that are set to add new challenges. The global economy is now enmeshed in stagflation – a combination of stagnation and inflation – not seen since the 1970s. The unipolar world order with its undisputed global hegemon, established at the end of the Cold War, is now giving way to a world that will be more multipolar with several competing and contesting centres of power. The project of hyper-globalisation and neoliberalism, which was promoted in the era of unipolarity with an overwhelming sense of self-confidence in its universality, is now being halted in its tracks, as processes like 'nearshoring' and the recovery by the developed world of 'industrial policy' look likely to lead to what some are calling 'de-globalisation'. At the same time, an accelerated transition to a lower carbon economy (driven by the threat of catastrophic climate change) is underway. This follows on the heels of the so-called Fourth Industrial Revolution (the mining, management and application of 'big data'), which is set to have disruptive effects on all existing economic activities across the world.

While both these mega trends are increasingly recognised as likely to widen inequalities, both within and between countries, they have also led to increasing competition between transnational corporations, which has spilled over into increasing contestation and rivalry between different developed countries and blocs, as well as between these and China and other 'emerging economies'. A new, more inclusive and development-orientated multilateralism, called for by many in the developed world, is but one – and not necessarily the most likely – scenario for the reconstruction of a more multipolar global order. Ongoing processes of bloc formation and pressures to 'reform' or 'reset' global institutions in the interests of the already powerful could equally shape a very different global order. As several of the largest and most advanced countries are recovering their focus on 'industrial policy', some are selectively opting out of the global rules, which they consider no longer serve their needs, while imposing new unilateral obligations on trading partners (including those from Africa). The latter includes, among other things, the implementation of measures requiring exporters to demonstrate that their products have met defined 'net zero' carbon emission targets or face costly penalties for not doing so. All of this has led a growing cohort of analysts and observers to suggest that the next few decades will be characterised by growing uncertainty, widening inequality and long-running multiple crises – economic, social, health, security and environmental – leading some to suggest that we are entering an era of 'polycrisis'.[2]

While all of this adds to the imperative to advance regional integration in Africa, with particular emphasis on the AfCFTA, many discussions, both within and about the continent, have, in my view, proceeded with insufficient consideration of the relevance or otherwise of conventional trade-integration models derived from the realities of other regions. Arguments have been advanced that ambitious tariff liberalisation would lead to huge increases in intraregional trade, without any serious reflection on either non-tariff regulatory barriers or 'real economy' constraints. Adopting formal arrangements (deriving from orthodox trade integration theory) has sometimes been prioritised over realistic considerations of concrete realities on the ground, leading to the proclamations of customs unions or common markets that simply do not exist in reality. Some have even argued for tariff liberalisation within the continent to become a stepping-stone towards ambitious tariff liberalisation with the world at large – on the grounds that this is the royal road to 'integrating' the continent into the world economy.

All of this ignores the fundamental reality that, under colonialism, African economies were, in fact, integrated into the global economy, but at a particular location in the global division of labour, that is, as producers and exporters of primary commodities (the least lucrative location in value chains). This reality – which, with few exceptions, has continued to be reproduced to this day – is in the view of many heterodox economists and historians the fundamental reason why Africa remains under (not un) developed and poor. It is also this reality that constitutes the fundamental structural barrier to increasing intraregional trade to levels similar to those reached in other areas with more diversified productive sectors. Economies based on the production of raw materials, with little or no industrial capacity, have a serious real economy limit to what they can trade with each other. Thus, if country X is a producer and exporter of some unprocessed mineral commodity, it has little to trade with the next-door country Y, which produces and exports the same or another primary commodity. This is further exacerbated if the communications infrastructure is skewed (as it is in Africa) towards moving raw materials from their point of production to the nearest port for shipping out of the continent, rather than linking up

---

2   A term coined in the World Economic Forum's Global Risks Report 2023.

the continent's different countries and regions.

From this, proponents of development integration or developmental regionalism have argued that the biggest barriers to intraregional trade are not so much tariffs as underdeveloped production structures and inadequate infrastructure. This, in turn, suggests that any trade integration arrangements need to be complemented, and indeed shaped, by programmes of cooperation to overcome infrastructure backlogs and to promote both economic diversification and industrial development.

Fortunately, there is now a growing consensus that the AfCFTA cannot be seen as a narrow trade-integration arrangement. Rather, its trade and tariff arrangements need to be complemented by – and indeed spur – a significant push to develop infrastructure to link the different countries and regions, and advance a profound economic structural transformation that would lead to a higher level of value-added production, more equitably spread across the continent's various countries and regions. More precisely, the larger continental market created by the AfCFTA (which begins to match the size of larger Asian economies) needs to become a vehicle to construct regional value chains (RVCs) in which African-based enterprises would produce higher-value products. Under this scenario, AfCFTA's real prize would be not only a quantitative increase in intraregional trade, but also the qualitative change in the character of that trade brought about by this arrangement. This would occur as RVCs supported the production of components and other intermediate inputs in a number of countries before being assembled into 'products of Africa' consumed by the citizens of the continent, but also exported. This would, in turn, lead to a greater absolute and relative intratrade in components and intermediate products – which is in fact the largest and fastest growing part of global trade in goods.

Such an outcome is doubly urgent in the face of the challenges being posed by the emerging global conjuncture. The threat of catastrophic climate change, as indicated earlier, is leading to an accelerating transition to a lower-carbon economy. Even if this threat is averted (and climate science tells us that we are not on track to achieve this yet), more frequent and damaging extreme weather events are inevitable, suggesting an urgent need for a massive programme of adaptation, including 'climate proofing' social and economic infrastructure.

A key question that arises in this regard is, will Africa be able to emerge as a producer and exporter of low-carbon, value-added products or will it be left in the position, once again, of being a mere supplier of raw materials and a consumer of so-called green products, technologies and 'solutions' developed elsewhere? What is certain is that a positive answer to this question is not inevitable. In fact, the 'default' scenario of what happens if nothing changes is probably negative. A developmental outcome will depend on the implementation of active industrial policy and clarity that regional integration arrangements like the AfCFTA will be vehicles to advance the continent's industrialisation.

The chapters in this volume, authored as they are by researchers from across the continent, are a valuable resource for policy-makers, analysts and scholars grappling with these issues. Individually and collectively, they offer a deep dive into pertinent conceptual and theoretical issues, and provide case studies of several of the RECs, as well as the processes involved in constructing the AfCFTA. This is an important and timely contribution towards a better understanding of the matters of vital importance to Africa's development.

Acknowledgements

This book would not have been possible were it not for the selfless support we received from many people during the process of its development. The support has been overwhelming. We are deeply indebted to the various authors who took the time out of their very busy schedules to contribute the outstanding chapters that make up this book. We would also like to express our sincere gratitude to the reviewers who went through the various chapters in this book and whose feedback immensely improved the quality of the contributions. The administrators at the University of Johannesburg Centre for Africa-China Studies (CACS), Ms Lebo Mosebua and Ms Zizipho Masiza, worked tirelessly to ensure that due process was observed, and adequate resources were allocated towards this book project. Without their hard work and dedication, this project would not have been successful. Glenda Younge was kind enough to agree to edit our manuscript. Her meticulous and impeccably thorough work ensured that the quality of writing and the organisation of the book were of the highest standard. We thank the publishers, Jacana Media, and particularly Bridget Impey, who saw value in our proposal and handled the production of this book with consummate professionalism. We hope that the book will be a source of pride to all those who played a role in its making.

Acronyms and abbreviations

ACDEG	African Charter on Democracy, Elections and Governance
ACP	Caribbean and Pacific states
AEC	African Economic Community
AEEP	Africa–EU Energy Partnership
AEP	African Economic Platform
AfCFTA	African Continental Free Trade Area
AfDB	African Development Bank
AFISMA	African-led International Support Mission in Mali
Afreximbank	African Export–Import Bank
AFRICOM	Africa Command (United States of America)
AfSEM	African Single Electricity Market
AGOA	African Growth and Opportunity Act (United States)
AMA	African Media Agency
AMIB	African Mission in Burundi
AMIS	African Union Mission in Sudan
AMISEC	African Union Mission Support to Elections in Comoros
AMISOM	African Union Mission to Somalia
AMR	antimicrobial resistance
AMU	Arab Maghreb Union
APF	African Peace Facility
APO	African Press Organisation
APRM	Africa Peer Review Mechanism
APSA	African Peace and Security Architecture (African Union)
ARTIN	African Regional Transport Infrastructure Network

ASEAN	Association of Southeast Asian Nations
ASF	African Standby Force
ASTF	Africa Sustainable Transport Forum
ASWJ	Ahlu Sunnah Wal Jammah (al-Shabaab)
AU	African Union
AUB	African Union of Broadcasting
AUC	African Union Commission
AUDA	Africa Union Development Agency
AU-PSO	AU-Peace Support Operations
AUYVC	African Union Youth Volunteer Corp
AVAT	African Vaccine Acquisition Trust
BACI	Database for International Trade Analysis
BDEAC	Development Bank of Central African States
BEAC	Bank of Central African States
BRI	Belt and Road Initiative (Chinese)
CAPP	Central African Power Pool
CAR	Central African Republic
CCU	Continental Customs Union
CDC	Centres for Disease Control and Prevention
CEAO	West African Community (Communuaté économique de l'Afrique de l'ouest)
CEEAC	Communuaté économique des États de l'Afrique centrale (Economic Community of Central African States)
CEMAC	Central African Economic and Monetary Community (Communauté Economique et Monetaire de l'Afrique Centrale)
CEN-SAD	Community of Sahel-Saharan States
CEPGL	Economic Community of the Great Lakes Region
CET	common external tariff
CEWARN	Conflict Early Warning and Response Mechanism (IGAD)
CEWS	Continental Early Warning System
CFA	African Financial Community (Communauté financière africaine
CGM	Compagnie Générale Maritime
CMP	Continental Master Plan
COBAC	Banking Commission of Central Africa

COMELEC	Comité Maghrébin de l'Electricité
COMESA	Common Market for Eastern and Southern Africa
CPA	Comprehensive Peace Agreement (Sudan)
CPA	Cotonou Partnership Agreement
CPHIA	Conference on Public Health in Africa
DCA	Designated Competent Authority (AfCFTA)
DIE	Department of Infrastructure and Energy
DRC	Democratic Republic of the Congo
DSB	Dispute Settlement Body (AfCFTA)
DSM	digital single market
DSM	Dispute Settlement Mechanism (AfCFTA)
DSR	Digital Silk Road
DTS	Digital Transformation Strategy
EAC	East African Community
EACJ	East African Court of Court of Justice
EACMO	East African Common Market Organisation
EAHC	East African High Commission
EALA	East African Legislative Assembly
EAPP	East African Power Pool
EBID	ECOWAS Bank for Investment and Development
ECA	Economic Commission for Africa
ECA	Economic Cooperation Agreement
ECCAS	Economic Community of Central African States
ECOMOG	ECOWAS Monitoring Group
ECOSACC	Economic, Social and Cultural Council
ECOWAS	Economic Community of West African States
ECPF	ECOWAS Conflict Prevention Framework
ECREEE	ECOWAS Centre for Renewable Energy and Energy Efficiency
ECSC	European Coal and Steel Commission
EDCTP	European and Developing Countries Clinical Trials Partnership
EDF	European Development Fund
EDZ	economic development zones
EEC	European Economic Community
EEZ	exclusive economic zone
EIJ	Eritrean Islamic Jihad

EMCP	ECOWAS Monetary Cooperation Programme
EOM	election observation mission
EPA	economic partnership agreement
EPF	European Peace Facility
ERERA	ECOWAS Regional Electricity Regulatory Authority
ETLS	ECOWAS Trade Liberalisation Scheme
EU	European Union
EU-CDC	European Union Centre for Disease Control and Prevention
EuroMeSCo	Euro-Mediterranean Study Commission
FANR	Food Security, Agriculture and Natural Resources Sector (SADC)
FAO	Food and Agricultural Organization (UN)
FDI	foreign direct investment
FEDOM	European Overseas Development Fund
FLS	Front Line States
FMP	Free Movement of Persons
FOCAC	Forum on China–Africa Cooperation (formerly Colonies françaises d'Afrique)
FTA	free trade area
GDP	gross domestic product
GEA	Ghana Employers' Association
GIABA	Inter-governmental Action Group against Money Laundering and Terrorist Financing in West Africa
GIEWS	Global Information and Early Warning System (Food and Agriculture Organization, UN)
GIZ	Gesellschaft für International Zusammenarbeit
GPT	generalised preferential tariff
HPE	Hewlett Packard Enterprise
HRW	Human Rights Watch
HS	Harmonised System (UNCTAD)
ICA	Infrastructure Consortium for Africa
ICAO	International Civil Aviation Organisation
ICBT	informal cross-border trading
ICM	Integrated Committee of Ministers (SADC)
ICPAC	IGAD Climate Prediction and Applications Centre
ICPALD	IGAD Centre for Pastoral Area and Livestock Development

ICT	Information and communications technology
IESE	Instituto de Estudos Sociais e Económicos (Mozambique)
IFI	international financial institutions
IGAD	Intergovernmental Authority on Development
IGADD	Intergovernmental Authority on Drought and Development
IGNU	Interim Government of National Unity (Liberia)
IHR	International Health Regulation
IHSTN	Integrated High-Speed Train Network
IMF	International Monetary Fund
IMS	Integrated Maritime Strategy (IGAD)
INGO	international non-governmental organisations
IOM	International Organisation for Migration
IRAPP	IGAD Regional Aids Programme
IRIMP	IGAD's Regional Infrastructure Master Plan
IS	Information and Science
ISCAP	Islamic State of Central Africa
ISGS	Islamic State of the Greater Sahara
ISS	Institute for Security Studies
ISSP	IGAD Security Sector Programme
ISWAP	Islamic State of West Africa Province
ITU	International Telecommunications Union
JAES	Joint Africa–EU Strategy
JBP	Joint Border Posts (ECOWAS)
JICA	Japanese International Cooperation Agency
LDC	Least-Developed Country
LMIC	low and middle-income countries
LNA	Libyan National Army
LPA	Lagos Plan of Action
LRA	Lord's Resistance Army
MAPROBU	African Prevention and Protection Mission in Burundi
MDC	Movement for Democratic Change (Zimbabwe)
MFN	most favourable nation
MINUSCA	United Nations Multidimensional Integrated Stabilisation Mission in the Central African Republic
MINUSMA	United Nations Multidimensional Integrated Stabilisation Mission in Mali

MIP	Minimum Integration Programme (African Union)
MISCA	African-led International Support Mission in the Central African Republic
MNC	multinational company
MONUSCO	United Nations Organisation Stabilisation Mission in the DRC
MoU	Memorandum of Understanding
MRU	Mano River Union (West Africa)
MSC	Mediation and Security Council (ECOWAS)
NAFTA	North American Free Trade Agreement
NC	National Committee
NCDC	Nigeria Centre for Diseases Control
NCP	National Contact Point (SADC)
NEPAD	New Economic Partnership for Africa's Development
NPHIs	national public health institutes
NTB	non-tariff barrier (AfCFTA)
NWICO	New World Information and Communication Order
OAU	Organisation of African Unity
ODA	Official development assistance
OCAM	Union for Economic Cooperation of Africa and Malagasy (Union africaine et malgache de cooperation économique)
OECD	Organisation for Economic Co-operation and Development
ONUB	United Nations Operation in Burundi
OPAAC	Observatory of Abnormal Practices along the main Central African corridors
PAIGC	African Party for the Independence of Guinea and Cape Verde
PANA	Pan-African News Agency
PAP	Pan-African Parliament
PEPFAR	*President's Emergency Plan for AIDS Relief (United States)*
PHE	Public Health England (now defunct)
PHI	public health institutes
PIDA	Programme for Infrastructure Development in Africa
PPE	personal protective equipment
PPP	public–private partnerships
PRIDA	Policy and Regulatory Initiative for Africa

PSC	Peace and Security Council
PTA	Preferential Trading Agreement for Eastern and Southern Africa (PTA),
REC	Regional Economic Community
RISDP	Regional Indicative Strategic Development Plan (SADC)
RMI	Road Management Initiative
ROE	Regional Operations Envelope (AfDB)
RoO	rules of origin (AfCFTA)
RPP	regional power pools
RRRP	Regional Refugee Response Plan
RTA	regional trade arrangement
RVC	regional value chains
SAATM	Single African Air Transport Market
SACU	Southern African Customs Union
SADC	Southern African Development Community
SADCC	Southern African Development Coordination Conference
SAP	structural adjustment programme
SAPP	Southern African Power Pool
SCF	Stabilisation and Cooperation Fund (WAMZ)
SCT	Single Customs Territory
SCU	Sectoral Coordinating Units (SADC)
SDG	Sustainable Development Goal
SDM	Single Digital Market (for Africa)
SDR	Special Drawing Right
SE4ALL	Sustainable Energy for All
SETC	Suez Economic and Trade Cooperation Zone
SHD	Social and Human Development
SIPO	Strategic Indicative Plan for the Organ (SADC)
SITC	Standard Industrial Trade Classification (UNCTAD)
SME	small and medium-sized enterprise
SNC	SADC National Committee
SPLA	Sudan People's Liberation Army
SPLM	Sudan People's Liberation Movement
SSA	Sub-Saharan Africa
SSATP	Africa Transport Policy Programme
TAC	Trans-African Corridor
TAF	Technical Assistance Facility (EU)

TB	tuberculosis
TDCA	Trade, Development and Co-operation Agreement
TFA	trade facilitation agreement (AfCFTA)
TFTA	Tripartite Free Trade Agreement
TICAD	Tokyo International Conference on African Development
TIFI	Trade, Industry, Finance and Investment Sector (SADC)
TST	Transnational Security Threats programme (IGAD)
TTC	Trade and Technology Council (EU–US)
TVWS	Television White Spaces
UDEAC	Customs and Economic Union of Central Africa (Union douanière et économique de l'Afrique centrale)
UDEAO	Union douanière de l'Afrique de l'Quest (Customs Union of West African States)
UEA	University of East Africa
UEAC	Central African Economic Union
UEMOA	West African Economic and Monetary Union (Union Economique et Monétaire Ouest Africaine)
UEMOA	West African Monetary and Economic Union
UMA	Arab Maghreb Union (Union du Maghreb Arabe)
UMAC	Central African Monetary Union
UNCTAD	United Nations Conference on Trade and Development
UNDP	United Nations Development Programme
UNECA	United Nations Economic Commission for Africa
UNESCO	United Nations Educational Science and Cultural Organization
UNFPA	United Nations Populations Fund
UNHCR	High Commission for Refugees
UNMIS	United Nation Mission in Sudan
UNMISS	United Nation Mission in South Sudan
UNOCHA	United Nations Office for the Coordination of Humanitarian Affairs
UNPKO	United Nations Peacekeeping Operations
URTNA	Union of National Radios and Televisions of Africa
USAID	United States Agency for International Development
USCDC	United States Centre for Diseases Control
VAT	value added tax
WACB	West African Central Bank

WACH	West African Clearing House
WAEMU	West African Economic and Monetary Union
WAGP	West Africa Gas Pipeline
WAHO	West African Health Organisation
WAMA	West African Monetary Agency
WAMI	West African Monetary Institute
WAMZ	West African Monetary Zone
WAPP	West African Power Pool
WAUA	West African Unit of Account
WHO	World Health Organization
WIDER	World Institute for Development and Economic Research
WIPO	World Intellectual Property Organisation
WNBF	West Nile Bank Front (Uganda)
WTO	World Trade Organization
ZANU-PF	Zimbabwe African National Union–Patriotic Front
ZTE	Zhonging Telecommunication Equipment

Regional Economic Communities

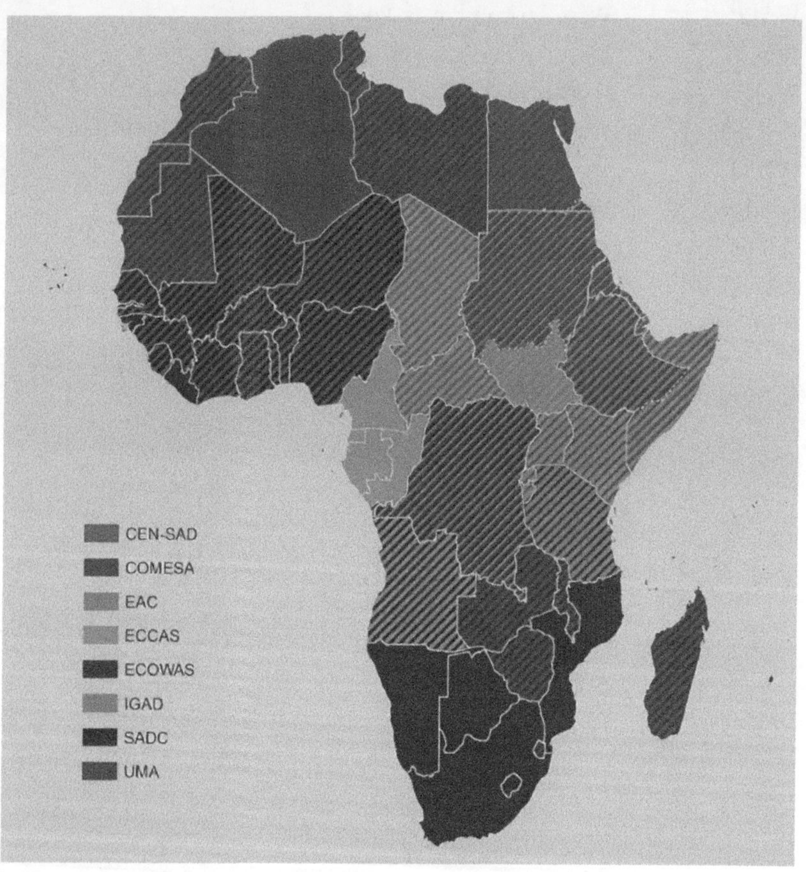

Source: https://archive.uneca.org/oria/pages/regional-economic-communities

Regional integration in Africa's development

SIZO NKALA AND DAVID MONYAE

Introduction

Regional integration has been an evergreen theme in postcolonial African political discourse (Aniche, 2020). The dawn of the post-independence era in the 1960s was greeted by widespread optimism about Africa's socioeconomic future, free of the shackles of colonialism. One of the most devastating legacies of colonialism for Africa's economic and political development was the geographic fragmentation of the continent, orchestrated by the colonising powers through the imposition of arbitrary and artificial borders in the late 19th century. The redrawn political map produced a multitude of small and landlocked polities, ill-suited for and incapable of any socioeconomic development (see Uzodike, 2009). The resultant states proved to be little more than accessories to the large-scale extraction and underdevelopment. As more and more African colonies attained political independence in the 1960s, the widely shared wisdom of the day was that for Africa to overcome its economic malaise, regional integration was indispensable (Mistry, 2000; Gibb, 2009). The utility of regional integration was appreciated beyond Africa's shores, as witnessed by the coming into existence of the European Economic Community (EEC) in 1957, the Latin America Free Trade Association (1960), the Central American Common Market (1961) and the Caribbean Free Trade Association (1968) (Adedeji, 2002). The United Nations Economic Commission for Africa (ECA) made regional integration in the continent one of its priorities following its establishment in 1958. The commission divided Africa into subregions with a view to advancing economic links between the countries within the subregions (Tavares and Tang, 2011). Founding leaders of the first independent countries, such as Kwame Nkrumah of Ghana, Julius Nyerere of Tanzania and Sékou Touré of Guinea, among others, bought into and vigorously promoted the idea of regionalism. In his speech at the first Organisation of African Unity (OAU) Summit on 24 May 1963, Nkrumah was under no illusions about the importance of unity, asserting that 'Our objective is African union now. There is no time to waste. We must unite now or perish. I am confident that by our concerted effort and determination, we shall lay here the foundations for a continental Union of African States' (*New African*, 3 May 2013). Regional integration has been trumpeted throughout the post-independence era. Africa's many development plans from the Lagos Plan of Action in 1980 to the New Economic Partnership for Africa's Development (NEPAD) in 2002 and the 2013 Agenda 2063 have all stressed the importance of regional integration in Africa's development (Gibb, 2009).

In the six decades since the demise of colonialism, Africa has evolved various regional integration arrangements in the form of Regional Economic Communities (RECs), preferential trade agreements, and continental institutions in different spheres of Africa's political economy. By 2012, African governments had concluded agreements on 17 RECs of various sizes and ambitions, including the eight recognised by the African Union (AU) as the building blocks for the African Economic Community (AEC) envisaged by the 1991 Treaty on the Establishment of the African Economic Community (Hartzenberg, 2011). Moreover, Africa is home to 47 of the world's 355 regional trade agreements. In a bid to intensify regional integration, the African Union launched the African Continental Free Trade Area (AfCFTA), which seeks to eliminate tariff and non-tariff barriers to trade and promote the movement of capital and labour across national borders. At the time of writing, 48 out of 54 states in the continent had ratified the AfCFTA agreement, thus paving the way for its implementation. This volume takes stock of the state of regional integration in Africa today. The various sections in this book address different facets of regional integration in the continent, including its conceptual and theoretical underpinnings, the RECs, continental governance institutions, macroeconomic convergence, infrastructural integration, and the roles of the media, civil society and external actors on regional integration. This book offers an incisive and comprehensive review of regional integration in Africa with a view to identifying the challenges and effective strategies to accelerate progress towards integration.

The history of regional integration in Africa

The idea and first phase of regional integration can be traced back to the rise of Pan-Africanism in the 19th century. Pan-Africanism was an ideology that sought to inculcate a sense of solidarity and collective identity among people of African descent, living in or outside Africa, in response to slavery and colonialism. It became the basis for envisaging an African political and economic union. Although Pan-Africanism was started by the Africans in the diaspora in the 19th century, it was later dominated by Africans in Africa as the decolonisation campaign gained momentum in the second half of the 20th century. African leaders participated in the 1945 Pan-African Congress in Manchester and used the platform to mobilise support for African unity.

The second phase of regional integration was inadvertently pursued by the colonising powers to maximise the exploitation of their colonies. The French colonial administration created two federations: French West Africa and French Equatorial Africa. The first comprised Mauritania, Senegal, Mali, Guinea, Benin, Niger, Burkina Faso and Côte d'Ivoire. The latter included Central Africa, Chad, Congo, Gabon and Cameroon. While these federations were more administrative unions than economic unions, they had tremendous potential for economic development. The French also created the African Financial Community (CFA), which saw their colonies use the same currency in 1945, with a central bank in Dakar, Senegal overseeing the French West Africa federation, and a central bank in Cameroon managing French Equatorial Africa (Aniche, 2020). Even when these federations were disbanded in 1958, with each territory becoming independent, they continued to use the CFA franc.

In British West Africa, the British colonisers established a common currency through the West African Currency Board and common services like research institutes and the West African Airways Company (Aniche,

2020). In East Africa, a customs union between Kenya and Uganda was established in 1917, and Tanganyika was added in 1927. This union was aimed at creating free trade, common external tariffs, a common currency and common services (such as telecoms, railways and postal services).

The third phase of regional integration came in the immediate post-independence era in the 1960s and 1970s. Numerous intergovernmental single-sectoral and multisectoral cooperation organisations emerged to promote economic integration. The former member states of the French West Africa federation (Côte d'Ivoire, Senegal, Benin, Burkina Faso, Mauritania and Niger) tried to promote economic cooperation by creating the West African Customs Union in 1959. The Conseil de l'Entente was established in 1959 to promote economic cooperation between Côte d'Ivoire, Benin, Burkina Faso and Niger. Central African states, which were part of the French Equatorial Africa federation, also tried to promote integration after the dissolution of their federation in 1958.

The Organisation of African Unity (OAU) was established by 32 newly independent African states in Addis Ababa, Ethiopia, in 1963. Germane to the formation of the OAU was the creation of a continental political framework that would serve as the basis of the unity of African states. Article 2(1)(a) and (b) of the OAU Charter stated that the organisation exists 'to promote the unity and solidarity of African states' and 'to coordinate and intensify their cooperation and efforts to achieve a better life for the peoples of Africa'. Article 2(2) further implored the member states to 'coordinate and harmonize their general policies' across the political, diplomatic, economic, defence and security, educational, social welfare, and scientific research spheres (OAU, 1963). Although the OAU Charter lacked specific and concrete details on how the unity on a continental scale was going to be achieved, it did set the ideological tone, which has kept the quest for African unity alive through the decades.

The West African Economic Community (CEAO) was established in 1973 by six Francophone countries – Côte d'Ivoire, Niger, Senegal, Mali, Mauritania and Burkina Faso – to rekindle the economic relations they had enjoyed during the French West Africa federation. In the same year, Liberia and Sierra Leone agreed to form the Mano River Union (MRU) with a view to intensifying economic cooperation. The MRU was paralysed and rendered stagnant, however, by the internal conflicts experienced by the founding states. It was reactivated and expanded in 2004 with the addition of Côte d'Ivoire and Guinea-Conakry. After years of failed attempts to bring West African states under one organisation, the Economic Community of West African States (ECOWAS) Treaty was signed and ratified by all 16 states in 1975 in a matter of a few weeks. The ECOWAS finally brought the Francophone and Anglophone countries under one umbrella.

The success of ECOWAS inspired other initiatives in Eastern and Southern Africa and Central Africa, pushed by the ECA. In 1981, the Preferential Trade Agreement for Eastern and Southern Africa (PTA) was signed, and in 1983 the Economic Community of Central African States (ECCAS) was established. Although the UDEAC did not make significant headway in economic integration in Central Africa, 11 states from the region formed the ECCAS in 1983 with a much broader scope of cooperation. The objectives of the ECCAS included sectoral policy coordination, macroeconomic policy coordination, social integration and reinforcing the common currency.

The Arab Maghreb Union (UMA), comprising Libya, Algeria, Tunisia and Morocco, which had been established in 1965 but disbanded later, was revived in 1989. Burundi, Rwanda and the Democratic Republic of the Congo (DRC) created the Economic Community of the Great Lakes Countries in 1976. This was tasked with ensuring the security of the member states, coordinating development policies, and facilitating trade and the movement of people across borders. In short, between 1975 and 1983, four regional organisations were established (consisting of 16, 22, 10 and three countries).

Further thinking about African unity and integration evolved into the Lagos Plan of Action, which was adopted by the OAU in 1980 (Heidhues and Obare, 2011; Bawa and Ateku, 2020). The Lagos Plan of Action emphasised the need to enhance economic cooperation within Africa in sectors such as industry, agriculture, infrastructure and transport, among others. This, it was reasoned, would help boost intracontinental trade and reduce Africa's excessive dependency on the export markets of the developed countries, which was brutally exposed by the 1970s global oil crisis. The Lagos Plan identified six areas of integration, namely integration of the physical, institutional and social infrastructure, integration of production structures, market integration, the resolution of inter-country conflicts, peace and security at national and international levels, and an enabling environment for entrepreneurship and cross-border movements (Adedeji,

2002). The Final Act of Lagos presented a stage-by-stage agenda for regional integration, which included strengthening the existing regional groupings, promoting continental sectoral integration, and improving harmonisation and coordination among regional organisations. The Act also authorised the drafting of the treaty for the establishment of the African Economic Community (hereinafter the Treaty), which was eventually signed in 1991 in Abuja.

The Treaty was a 34-year plan to be implemented in six stages, which would culminate in the formation of an African Economic Community (AEC) as the end goal. This would see African states adopting a common economic policy in monetary, financial and fiscal areas, as well as trade tariffs. It was the most detailed and comprehensive plan by the continental body, mapping out the path to continental economic and political integration. The process towards realising the AEC was to be anchored in regional integration. The first stage in establishing the AEC involved the strengthening of the existing RECs, and establishing them in regions where they did not exist within the first five years of the Treaty coming into force. In the second stage, the RECs were implored to prepare for the removal of tariff and non-tariff barriers to enhance intra-REC trade, including strengthening sectoral integration at the regional level within eight years of the Treaty coming into force. The establishment of a free trade area (FTA) and a customs union with a common external tariff in each REC within 10 years was the chief aim of the third stage. The fourth stage called for the harmonisation and coordination of tariff and non-tariff systems between the RECs within two years, which would pave the way for a continental customs union. The fifth stage would see the creation of an African Common Market and common trade and economic policies. Finally, stage six involved establishing a host of institutions such as the African Monetary Union, the African Central Bank and the Pan-African Parliament, and setting up the executive structure of the AEC within five years (OAU, 1991).

The Treaty set in motion a new wave of regional integration. In 1994, the CEAO was replaced by the West African Monetary and Economic Union (UEMOA), which added the monetary integration dimension. The UEMOA made significant progress by establishing a customs union in 2000, introducing a common trade policy and conducting macroeconomic surveillance. Six members of the ECCAS, namely Gabon, Cameroon, the

Central African Republic (CAR), Chad, the Republic of the Congo and Equatorial Guinea, went on to establish the Central African Economic and Monetary Community (CEMAC) in 1994. Its main objective was to achieve a common market among the member states.

The Southern African Development Coordination Conference (SADCC), which was formed in 1981 to reduce economic dependency of southern African countries on apartheid South Africa, was transformed into a fully-fledged REC and renamed the Southern African Development Community (SADC) in 1992. Although South Africa was initially not part of the SADC, it joined the organisation following the downfall of the apartheid regime in 1994. The 1981 PTA for Eastern and Southern Africa was renamed the Common Market for Eastern and Southern Africa (COMESA) following a treaty signed in Kampala, Uganda, in 1993. The goals of COMESA were to expand trade, secure an energy supply and accelerate regional integration overall. Both the SADC and COMESA have made progress in establishing free trade areas, although this has not been easy.

The Intergovernmental Authority on Development (IGAD) was a 1996 reconstitution of the Intergovernmental Authority on Drought and Development (IGADD), which had been established in 1986. The founding members of IGAD included Kenya, Ethiopia, Sudan, Djibouti, Somalia and Uganda. While the 1986 IGADD was formed to address the drought that affected the region, the IGAD had a broader mandate of expediting regional integration in all its aspects. The East African Community (EAC), comprising Kenya, Tanzania and Uganda, was established in 1967. However, it was terminated in 1977 as a result of hostilities between Tanzania and Uganda, which saw the two countries going to war in 1978. The three countries revived the EAC through a 1993 treaty with a view to accelerating and deepening economic integration. In 2006, Rwanda and Burundi were admitted as new members of the EAC.

The Community of Sahel and Saharan States (CEN–SAD) was formed in 1998 and is now the largest regional body with 28 member states covering North Africa, the Horn of Africa and even West Africa. The Southern African Customs Union (SACU) was formed in 1910 with South Africa, Lesotho, Botswana and Swaziland as the founding members. Namibia, then known as South West Africa, joined the SACU after the First World War. Having survived political changes for almost 100 years, in 2004 the SACU was transformed into a regional integration organisation and established a secretariat in Namibia. SACU members developed a method of pooling tariff and excise revenues and a mechanism for sharing the revenue equitably. Moreover, the five members of the SACU have a common trade policy, which makes their membership of the SADC relatively less problematic. To accelerate the establishment of the AEC, African governments signed the Constitutive Act establishing the African Union in 2000. The vision of a continental political union was motivated by the spirit of Pan-Africanism.

Why regional integration?

There are several reasons why African leaders have expended so much effort and energy on realising regional integration in the continent. Economic logic has been the dominant factor in the rationale as regional integration is seen as a remedy to Africa's development impasse. It was strongly believed that regional integration would create the impetus for Africa's industrialisation and structural economic transformation. Forging economies of scale by creating trade pathways and opening channels for the movement of labour and capital between African countries would attract foreign direct investment, encourage indigenous entrepreneurship and innovation, and make African firms more competitive in the global economy (Johnson, 1991; Kayizzi-Mugerwa *et al.*, 2014). Regionalism could also boost Africa's participation in the global economy. Foreign enterprises could take advantage of the economies of scale and make Africa their production and export base to access both the regional and global markets. African enterprises could be roped in through forward and backward linkages, thus plugging them into the global value chains (Dinka and Kennes, 2007). With almost a third of Africa's population living in landlocked countries, regional integration would help reduce transport costs and bring these countries closer to global markets. Johnson (1991) also points out that economies of scale in research, encouraged by integration, can increase factor productivity and cushion African countries from the fluctuations in commodity prices, which can be debilitating for their economies. Further, regional integration promotes technology transfer, which would enable African economies to compete with more advanced economies. It also has the potential to alleviate Africa's food security problems by enhancing intra-African trade in food products and forging regional value chains with greater value addition taking place in Africa (Uzodike, 2009; Kayizzi-Mugerwa *et al.*, 2014). It has also been reported that the national power systems of almost 20 countries in Africa are inefficient. Regional power pools, through infrastructure sharing, could help improve the efficiency of power generation. Although it has been argued that regional integration would not benefit the continent because of low intra-African trade, it has been shown that there is high potential for intra-African trade, which could be actualised within the RECs frameworks.

From a geopolitical standpoint, a more industrialised Africa would expand intra-African trade through increased productive and supply capacity, and drastically reduce the continent's dependence on American, Chinese, European and Russian markets, thirsty for Africa's raw materials (Gibbs, 2009). The same European markets outcompete African producers by supplying African consumers with manufactured articles. Africa's dependency on European markets, the foundation of which was laid in the colonial era, suppressed the continent's potential for independent and internal development. Hence, regional integration would be an effective way to redress Africa's harmful dependency on, and exploitative relations with, the West (Nkrumah, 1965; Rodney, 1972). Other scholars have pointed out that the expected growth in economic size as a result of regional integration would reinforce Africa's bargaining power in its relations with external actors (Jalloh, 1976; Johnson, 1991). If African countries shared economic interests, they would be better able to negotiate agreements that would benefit the continent and its people on platforms such as the World Trade Organization (WTO).

There is also a security dividend in regional integration. The increased interdependence that it entails not only reduces the probability of interstate conflicts but of intrastate ones as well. Regional institutions provide a platform for countries to dialogue and resolve differences peacefully. These institutions are also likely to act quickly in the case of domestic conflicts because of their regional implications (Thonke and Spliid, 2012). For example, the Economic Community of West African States through the ECOWAS Monitoring Group (ECOMOG) and the Intergovernmental Authority on Development (IGAD) in the Horn of Africa are playing an increasingly important role in conflict resolution and prevention in their respective regions. Regional integration can also provide an institutional framework to address transnational threats such as human trafficking, climate change and the management of public goods such as energy and water. The African Union developed the African Peace and Security Architecture (APSA) to address the security threats in the continent. The APSA consists of the Peace and Security Council, a Continental Early Warning System, the Panel of the Wise, its Peace Fund and five regional African Standby Forces in southern, eastern, central, western and northern Africa. Its structure is set to be mirrored in the eight AU-recognised RECs.

Challenges to regional integration

However, as the contributions in this book will show, regional integration has faced daunting challenges, which have undermined its progress in Africa. Mkandawire (2014) notes that Africa's huge geography is one of the basic hindrances to regional integration because of the huge distances between markets and the lack of infrastructure to connect them. Disconnected and disjointed infrastructure has been the missing link in regional integration. Transport and communications infrastructure still reflects the colonial heritage of being oriented towards European capitals rather than to African capitals. Electricity and telecommunications infrastructure fails to achieve minimum efficiency because it was built with national interests in mind and failed to take advantage of the economies of scale at the regional level (Mistry, 2000; Aniche 2020).

Second, ideological differences between member states and their leaders within the same regional organisation have hindered regional integration. As Johnson (1991: 12) notes, 'ideological differences and personal dislikes are a reality among African leaders' (see also Mkandawire, 2014). For example, the East African Community (EAC) was destabilised by tensions between Uganda and Tanzania, and the mutual dislike between Julius Nyerere and Idi Amin, the former leaders of Tanzania and Uganda, respectively. The Arab Maghreb Union (AMU) is immobilised by the hostility between Morocco and Algeria over the Western Saharan independence, and members of the Economic Community of Central African States (ECCAS) have found themselves on different sides of regional conflicts (Thonke and Spliid, 2012).

Moreover, differences in levels of development between member states are a challenge to the development of regional organisations. Some member states, especially the more developed ones, may stand to gain more than others, which leads to a lack of unity of purpose to achieve regional integration. For example, in addition to the hostilities between

Tanzania and Uganda, the perception that Kenya was benefitting more from the arrangement than other members, because of its advanced supply capacity, also contributed to the tensions that led to the EAC's collapse in 1977 (Johnson, 1991; Dinka and Kennes, 2007). It has been argued that in COMESA, South Africa, Egypt and Kenya are likely to benefit more than other member states because of their well-developed productive capacity. The three countries are also likely to be the preferred destinations of the vast majority of investors attracted by the free trade regime. This will drive the trade and development gap between them and their fellow member states even further (Khandelwal, 2004). The smaller and less well-developed economies, which often rely on trade taxes for a significant part of their revenue, lose out while the relatively developed economies gain more. Since countries may have different comparative advantages, the tariff structure may also cost some more than others (Johnson, 1991). Robust and equitable compensation mechanisms are needed so that members do not lose out or have the perception that they are losing from being part of a regional integration arrangement.

The implementation of free trade agreements has been a challenge, with most member states failing to implement the agreements, resulting in the private sector not benefitting from free trade. This failure to implement agreements is a reflection of the low-level of state-building at the national level, with most African countries characterised by significant institutional deficiencies (Mistry, 2000). It is also a result of the lack of political will on the part of the national elites and their failure to forge a national consensus on regional integration, involving policy-makers, civil society and the private sector, with a clear understanding of the pros and cons of participating in the regional integration arrangement in question (Mkandawire, 2014).

The lack of education on the alignment of regional and national interests is another major obstacle to regional integration. Member states tend to be wary of ceding part of their sovereignty to regional institutions and hence grow cold feet when faced with implementing agreed-on regional initiatives (Mistry, 2000; Dinka and Kennes, 2007). Losing autonomy over trade policy in a customs union, and monetary and fiscal policy in an economic union, may be too much for some countries to stomach (Johnson, 1991). Gibb (2009) observes that Africa's neo-patrimonial states are only interested in regional organisation to boost their regional and international legitimacy, and not to pursue regional integration. Since neo-patrimonial states are based on patronage and the personal control of resources, many states in Africa are not willing to lose any part of their sovereignty to regional institutions.

Further, overlapping membership of different regional organisations is an impediment to regional integration. Tavares and Tang (2011) indicate that about 95 per cent of members of the RECs in Africa are also members of another organisation. This makes it hard for them to pay their membership fees and implement the agreements of the various regional organisations to which they belong. In a survey, over 25 per cent of policy-makers in African countries say that belonging to multiple memberships makes it difficult for them to meet their obligations, while 23 per cent cite it as the reason for the poor implementation of regional initiatives. Interestingly, more than half of the respondents said political and strategic interests were the reason behind joining multiple RECs, while only 35 per cent cited economic interests (Tavares and Tang, 2011). According to Adedeji (2002), the lack of sanctions for non-performance, low participation by the private sector and civil society, an overreliance on tariffs for revenue and the weak rule of law in member states have hampered effective regional integration. The dependent and neocolonial nature of African economies has made them vulnerable to external shocks and kept them in a crisis mode, which has also undermined integration. In an economic crisis, the common policy is to protect the national economy from intruders. Africa's lost decade of the 1980s reversed whatever gains had been made in regional integration.

The failure of nation-building in many African states that are bedevilled by ethnicism and other internal hostilities has also contributed to the failure of regional integration. 'Endemic instability and conflict have forced regional economic groups to focus on peace and security matters or to put "integration at a standstill"' (Uzodike, 2009: 36). Leaders have to pay attention to political and security cooperation to create stable nation states. Hard and soft infrastructure deficiencies have also been a major obstacle to regional integration. Poor and dilapidated road and rail networks, minuscule productive capacity, non-tariff barriers such as the rules of origin and incompatible regulatory regimes, time-consuming customs processes at border posts, and the exclusion of the private sector have hindered progress in regional integration. Businesses find it very difficult to operate in regions with underdeveloped and fragmented financial infrastructure and regulatory systems (Dinka and Kennes, 2007). Developing countries, especially the least developed countries, which make up the majority of states in Africa, lack a robust private sector and entrepreneurial class that is capable of taking advantage of free trade agreements. Hence, there is a need for African countries to build an environment that is conducive to the growth and expansion of the private sector.

Outline of the book

This volume strives to tackle the question of regional integration in a systematic manner. The first section deals with the theoretical and conceptual underpinnings of regional integration. In Chapter 1, Gilbert Khadiagala traces the conceptual evolution of regionalism that has been at the centre of regional integration programmes in Africa from the 1960s through the 1990s. It calls for a revision of the conceptual frameworks that have hitherto underpinned regionalism. Such a revision would help Africa formulate realistic practices and programmes that would make headway in taking regional integration forward. Rich Mashimbye examines the ideological roots of regional integration in Pan-Africanism in Chapter 2 and details how ideology has been central to the regionalism processes in Africa. In Chapter 3 Muxe Nkondo explains how an African lingua franca such as Swahili can be a catalyst for regional integration in the continent.

Part 2 examines Africa's regional economic communities as instruments of regional integration. In Chapter 4, Siphamandla Zondi zooms in on the progress of regional integration in southern Africa through an analysis of the performance of the Southern African Development Community (SADC), which is the major REC in the region. While the chapter acknowledges the progress that has been made in the political and security realms, it laments the lack of implementation of the SADC protocols and initiatives by member states, which has undermined integration in the region. Chapter 5, by John Akokpari and Emmanuel Ampomah, takes stock of how the Economic Community of West African States (ECOWAS) has fared in terms of promoting integration in West Africa. While ECOWAS has been effective in conflict resolution – insisting on good governance principles and facilitating the free movement of people in the region – this REC has met with limited success in boosting intraregional trade, ensuring macroeconomic convergence and mending the Francophone–Anglophone divide. Moreover, the region still faces frequent coups d'état, overlapping memberships and divided loyalty to ECOWAS. The East African Community (EAC) is the focus in Chapter 6 by Emmanuel Matambo. This chapter takes us through the history and evolution of the EAC and, despite some failures, a shared history, language and culture can create a strong foundation for regional integration in East Africa. However, the reluctance to implement regional integration initiatives, such as the issuance of a common passport, has been a stumbling block.

In Chapter 7, Joseph Makanda evaluates the performance of the Intergovernmental Authority on Development (IGAD) in the Horn of Africa, which comprises Ethiopia, Djibouti, Eritrea, Somalia, South Sudan, Sudan, Kenya and Uganda. The IGAD succeeded the Intergovernmental Authority on Drought and Development in 1996. The latter was founded in 1986 to deal with droughts and natural disasters that affected the region. While drought mitigation is still central to IGAD's policies, the organisation has an expanded mandate compared to its predecessors with its priority areas encompassing infrastructure development, peace and security, trade, economic cooperation and social development, among other things. Teniola Tayo and Michael Odijie focus on the Central African Economic and Monetary Union (CEMAC) in Chapter 8. CEMAC has succeeded in establishing a relatively stable monetary union, expediting the free movement of persons and creating strong supranational institutions. However, regional integration has not realised its full potential due to lack of political will, corruption, and the weak monitoring and enforcement mechanisms.

Chapter 9 is the first chapter in Part 3 on continental governance mechanisms. Here, David Monyae and Sizo Nkala assess the potential of the Pan-African Parliament (PAP) to play the role of a catalyst in regional integration. They argue that the legislative dimension of the PAP makes the African Union more people-centred as it holds the AU executive arm accountable. Moreover, the PAP, which brings the AU member states' legislatures together, can speed up the ratification of continental legislation, which is the responsibility of national legislatures, thus accelerating the implementation of continental initiatives. However, its limited powers have rendered it ineffective in performing its mandate of promoting democracy, peace and security. Thus, institutional reforms in the form of direct elections, real legislative powers and budgetary independence are necessary to make the PAP a catalyst of regional integration. Chapter 10 by Bhaso Ndzendze and Anslelm Aduminay is an appraisal of the AU's Peace and Security Council's (PSC's) performance since its inception in 2003. The authors acknowledge the importance of the PSC in facilitating regional integration in the continent. However, they contend that the institution's impressive performance in its earlier years has since been undermined by incompetence, structural shortcomings and a chronic lack of resources.

In Chapter 11, Kingsley Orievulu analyses the Africa Centre for Disease Control and Prevention (Africa CDC), which has come to prominence since the advent of the COVID-19 pandemic. The Africa CDC came into existence in 2015, tasked with improving and coordinating Africa's response to infectious diseases. Africa's regional integration agenda can only go forward in a healthy environment, free of pandemics that limit the movement of people and goods across borders. This chapter identifies various issues that will have to be addressed in the next five years to enhance the effectiveness of the Africa CDC. These include stability, autonomy, handling partnerships with various actors and pushing for the manufacturing of vaccines in Africa. Khabele Matlosa tackles the important topic of the free movement of persons and African integration in Chapter 12. While highlighting the obvious benefits of the free movement of people, the chapter laments that not much progress has been made towards realising open borders in the continent.

The African Continental Free Trade Area (AfCFTA) is the subject of Part 4. In Chapter 13, Rod Alence zooms in on the patterns and dynamics of intraregional trade in Africa, tracing the geography and product composition of this trade. In so doing, he not only reveals the extent to which the continent has achieved regional integration but also spotlights opportunities for growing the trade volume. Chapters 14 and 15 address various aspects of the AfCFTA, namely the institutionalisation of the new free trade area and its Protocol on Trade in Goods, respectively.

Infrastructural integration is examined in Part 5. Chapter 16 by Ekeminiabasi Eyita-Okon examines regional electricity infrastructure, while Sikanyiso Masuku looks at transport infrastructure in Chapter 17. Chapter 18 by Odilile Ayodele deals with digital infrastructure, and Thokozani Simelani and Francis Mwailande examine the potential for a Blue Economy in Africa in Chapter 19. Regional integration and intra-African trade cannot grow without cross-border infrastructure connecting

African countries. In Part 6, chapters 20 and 21 explore the roles of the media and external actors in regional integration in Africa respectively.

References

Adedeji, A. (2002). 'History and Prospects for Regional Integration in Africa'. The Third Meeting of the African Development Forum, Addis Ababa, 5 March 2002.

Aniche, E.T. (2020). 'From Pan-Africanism to African regionalism: A chronicle', *African Studies*, 79(1): 70–87.

Dinka, T. and Kennes, W. (2007). *Africa's Regional Integration Arrangements: History and challenges*. European Centre for Development Policy Management, Discussion Paper No. 74. Available at: http://www.ecdpm.org/dp74 (Accessed 20 December 2022).

Gibb, R. (2009). 'Regional integration and Africa's development trajectory: Metatheories, expectations and reality', *Third World Quarterly*, 30(4): 701–20.

Hartzenberg, T. (2011). *Regional Integration in Africa*. World Trade Organization, Staff Working Paper No. ERSD-2011-14. Available at: https://www.wto.org/english/res_e/reser_e/ersd201114_e.pdf (Accessed 20 December 2022).

Heidhues, F. and Obare, G. (2011). 'Lessons from structural adjustment programmes and their effects in Africa', *Quarterly Journal of International Agriculture*, 50(1): 55–64.

Jalloh, A.A. (1976). 'Regional integration in Africa: Lessons from the past and prospects for the future', *Africa Development*, 1(2): 544–57.

Johnson, O.E.G. (1991). 'Economic integration in Africa: Enhancing prospects for success', *Journal of Modern African Studies*, 29(1): 1–26.

Kayizzi-Mugerwa, S., Anyanwu, J.C. and Conceicao, P. (2014). 'Regional integration in Africa: An introduction', *African Development Review*, 26(1): 1–6.

Khandelwal, P. (2004). *COMESA and SADC: Prospects and challenges for regional trade integration*. IMF Working Paper No. WP/04/227. Available at: https://www.imf.org/external/pubs/ft/wp/2004/wp04227.pdf (Accessed 20 January 2023).

Mistry, S. (2000). 'Africa's record of regional cooperation and integration', *African Affairs*, 99: 553–73.

Mkandawire, T. (2014). On the Politics of Regional Integration. Tralac

Annual Conference, 15–16 May 2014, Cape Town, South Africa.

New African. (2013). 'We must unite now or perish' – President Kwame Nkrumah, 3 May 2013. Available at: https://newafricanmagazine.com/3721/ (Accessed 20 January 2023).

Nkrumah, K. (1965). *Neo-colonialism: The last stage of imperialism*. New York: International Publishers.

Organisation of African Unity (OAU). (1991). *Treaty Establishing the African Economic Community*, 3 June. Abuja, Nigeria.

Organisation of African Unity (OAU). (1963). *The OAU Charter*, 25 May, Addis Ababa, Ethiopia.

Rodney, W. (1972). *How Europe Underdeveloped Africa*. Dar es Salaam: Bogle-L'Ouverture Publications.

Tavares, R. and Tang, V. (2011). 'Regional economic integration in Africa: Impediments to progress?' *South African Journal of International Affairs*: 18(2): 217–33.

Thonke, O. and Spliid, A. (2012). 'What to expect from regional integration in Africa', *African Security Review*, 21(1): 42–66. https://doi.org/10.1080/10246029.2011.629452.

Uzodike, U.O. (2009). 'The role of regional economic communities in Africa's economic integration: Prospects and constraints', *Africa Insight*, 39(2): 26–42.

PART 1
THEORIES AND CONCEPTS OF REGIONAL INTEGRATION

Chapter One

Theories and concepts of regional integration in Africa

GILBERT KHADIAGALA

Introduction

In postcolonial Africa, policy-makers and scholars have proposed regional integration because of its potential to overcome political fragmentation and economic fragility. Furthermore, both the mantra of 'global competitiveness' and forging 'economies of scale' have been the impetus for regional integration since the early 1960s. In the same breath, integration in Africa has remained hostage to theories and concepts that often do not reflect the patterns and practices on the ground. Wholesale borrowing of concepts, primarily from Europe, has resulted in the creation of institutions that have largely underperformed. To a large extent, this underperformance stems from the inability of African states to reconcile national and regional priorities, the fixation with narrow nationalisms, and the unresolved tensions between continental and subregional commitments. All these factors have continued to militate against effective regional cooperation and collaboration.

This chapter analyses the record of integration, first by analysing the dominant scholarship of functionalism, which dominated the study of regionalism in the 1960s and 1970s, and second, the literature of new regionalism that emerged in the early 1990s. In highlighting the conceptual turns in African regionalism, the chapter illuminates the struggles by African states to build meaningful systems of regional cooperation. My main proposal is that to construct realistic visions and practices of regional integration would require acknowledging the limits of the theoretical and conceptual frameworks that have had a stranglehold on understanding African regionalism. Regional integration is critical to Africa's economic and political needs, but to overcome the current scourge of ineffective regionalisms, Africa would need to rethink the foundations of states that anchor these negative trends. If regionalism is the deliberate political project of pooling sovereignties, Africa's penchant to cling to the postcolonial weak state forms will merely reproduce equally weak regionalisms. In the absence of more shared political sovereignties at subregional levels, African integration schemes will continue to be dysfunctional. This chapter proceeds in a chronological order; first, it reviews the formative debates on regionalism in the 1960s and 1970s, then it examines the trends since the 1990s. It concludes with brief and random musings about the future of regionalism in the face of the persistence of the current African state forms.

The first decades of African integration, 1960–1990

In the formative phases of African integration, European ideas of functionalism dominated the field of international relations. Scholars and policy-makers, borrowing from the seminal works of David Mitrany, captivated both the academic and policy arenas with the propositions of pooling sovereignties to manage economic and political challenges (Mitrany, 1933). Writing in the inter-war period in Europe, Mitrany envisaged new political forms that could 'make frontiers meaningless' in an increasingly interdependent global order. To Mitrany, functionalism was the process of rendering states obsolescent through international cooperation that would pre-empt interstate wars and foster socioeconomic interactions. Mitrany's strategy aimed at capitalising on the common problems that all nations shared, particularly security and welfare. Thus, if all states sought cooperative solutions to social and economic problems, this would obviate the need for war by 'rooting out the material causes' of conflicts (Mitrany, 1965: 119–49; Harrison, 1976: 200–02). Operating almost like private entities, the new systems of cooperation would put emphasis on the practical needs of economic and social development at the expense of divisive political ideologies (Anderson, 1998: 577–92; Rosenboim, 2013: 2–25).

Building on Mitrany, Haas (1958) introduced the concept of neofunctionalism to underline the fact that, unlike private entities, states needed to muster the political will to design regional institutions. He thus defined regional integration as 'the process whereby political actors in several distinct national settings are persuaded to shift their loyalties, expectations and political activities toward a new centre, whose institutions possess or demand jurisdictions over the pre-existing national states' (Haas, 1958: 16). In a later elaboration, Haas (1970: 607–08) stated that the study of regional integration was concerned 'with explaining how and why states cease to be wholly sovereign, how and why they voluntarily mingle, merge, and mix with their neighbors so as to lose the factual attributes of sovereignty while acquiring new techniques for resolving conflict between themselves'.

Both functionalism and neofunctionalism had a profound influence on integration theory, which constituted a core part of the 'European Ideal' popularised by Robert Schuman and Jean Monnet, the architects of European integration. Since the early 1950s, the European Coal and Steel Commission (ECSC), the European Economic Community (EEC) and the current European Union (EU) have exemplified the spirit of integration that seeks wide-ranging cooperation in political and socioeconomic spheres. For Schuman, European integration entailed a more gradual approach, premised on incrementalism, pluralism and functionalism. According to him, 'European integration would be … indispensable to the maintenance of peace, but Europe will not be made all at once, as a single whole: it will be built by concrete achievements which first create de facto solidarity' (cited in Alting von Geusau, 1969: 22).

At the inception of the EEC through the Treaty of Rome in 1957, the process of integration unleashed in Europe had decisive influence on determining the trajectory of Africa's regionalism. In spearheading European integration, France convinced its European partners to provide aid, technical assistance and trade preferences to its former colonies. The Treaty of Rome allowed for the association linking the EEC to a number of former colonies in Africa and created the first European Overseas Development Fund (FEDOM) to meet their economic needs. Europe subsequently formalised the association membership in the Yaoundé Agreements of 1963 and 1969. Alongside these agreements, France galvanised its former colonies to form new regional blocs, such as the Union douanière économique de états l'Afrique de l'Ouest (UDEAO) (the Customs Union of West African States) and the Union africaine et malgache de coopération économique (OCAM) (the Union for Economic Cooperation of Africa and Malagasy). With the United Kingdom's accession to the EEC membership in the early 1970s, more African countries, plus the Caribbean and Pacific states (ACP), came together to sign the Lomé Convention in 1975, which advocated for economic and trade benefits. The other objective of these conventions was to deepen integration in Africa by strengthening trade and aid relationships and, in essence, tethered Africa to the European practices and dynamics of integration (Zartman, 1971; Khadiagala, 2008: 67–82).

Prior to the formal inauguration of the European-inspired regionalism, colonial regimes had, through regional economic schemes, tried to overcome the deficiencies of fragile and fragmented economies and polities, undoing the territorial and political tapestry established during the partition of Africa. Questions of economies of scale and political viability framed these integration arrangements, as well as the colonial regimes' desire to pool resources. One of the largest colonial initiatives was the French bid to group 13 territories into two federations – the French West Africa Federation (Afrique – Occidentale française or AOF, made up of Côte d'Ivoire, Dahomey, French Guinea, French Soudan, Mauritania, Niger, Senegal and Upper Volta), and French Equatorial African Federation (Afrique-Équatoriale française, made up of Chad, Central African Republic, Congo, Gabon and Cameroon). Similarly, the Southern African Customs Union (SACU), the Central African Federation and the East African Common Market Organisation (EACMO) were colonial bids to exploit geographical proximities to lay the foundations for trade, monetary, industrial and infrastructural cooperation (Green and Krishna, 1967; Robson, 1967; Roland, 1967; Green and Seidman, 1968).

The hegemony of the European-centred regionalism was compounded by the fact that the framers of integration in Africa borrowed the classical economic characterisation of integration associated with Jacob Viner and Bela Balassa (Viner, 1950; Balassa, 1961). This depiction identifies five sequential stages: a preferential trade area; a customs union; a common market; economic union; and complete economic integration. According to Balassa:

The various forms of economic integration represent varying degrees of integration. In a free trade area, tariffs (and quantitative restrictions) between the participating countries are abolished, but each country retains its own tariffs against non-members. The establishment of a customs union involves, besides the suppression of discrimination in the field of commodity movements within the union, the creation of a common tariff wall against non-member countries. A higher form of economic integration is attained in a common market, where not only trade restrictions but also restrictions on factor movements are abolished. An economic union, as distinct from a common market, combines the removal of restrictions on commodity and factor movements with a degree of harmonization of economic, monetary, fiscal, social, and countercyclical policies. Finally, total economic integration presupposes the unification of economic, fiscal, etc. policies and requires the setting up of a supranational authority whose decisions are binding for the member states (Balassa, 1961: 5–6).

In this conceptualisation, the gradual and incremental stages in the trade arena would build the momentum and foundations for substantive forms of integration, particularly as states lost autonomy and sovereignty over economic policy and, thus, would be more willing to share collective political and economic decisions (Viner, 1950; Balassa, 1961: 3–14; Robson, 1998).

Africa's adoption of integration driven by the functional and neocolonial, subregional imperatives generated a countermovement from Pan-Africanists led by Ghana's Kwame Nkrumah, who saw the dangers in the balkanisation of Africa. Instead, Nkrumah mobilised several African countries to promote a grand Continental Union Government that would reduce colonial fragmentation, promote political unity by diminishing sovereignty, and fostering economic development. Nevertheless, most African states, protective of their newly found independence, challenged the maximalist vision of integration, and gravitated towards the minimalist integration vision of gradualism and incrementalism. The gradualists saw economic integration beginning at the subregional level and proceeding in progressive stages until the attainment of a common market. The contest between continentalism and subregionalism was resolved in the formation of the Organisation of African Unity (OAU), when African states opted for both continental institutions for security and political integration, based on respect for sovereignty and territorial integrity, and coexisting parallel subregional economic institutions and arrangements (Green and Seidman, 1968; Asante, 2016: 127–31). Over the years, although a tenuous compromise has emerged to simultaneously deepen integration at subregional and continental levels, tensions persist.

In the 1960s and 1970s, the UN Economic Commission for Africa (UNECA) became the foremost institution in African integration debates. From the outset, it brought with it dominant incrementalism and gradualism perspectives. At the OAU Heads of State and Government conference in 1963, the UNECA prescribed a pragmatic and gradualist approach to integration in Africa:

> There are two main forms which an integration scheme can take. It may either be intended to solve certain specific problems and perhaps lead to increasingly intense and intimate cooperation. Or else it may aim from the beginning at the creation of an economic union, where labour and capital will be free to move as well as goods, and where the economic and social policies of member governments will be harmonized to a high degree. Integration of the first kind starts by building up habits of cooperation; integration of the second kind starts by creating the forms of highly intense cooperation. Under African conditions, an integration scheme of the first type would seem especially important. Certainly, it seems that the economic background is not yet ripe for a full economic union, quite apart from the political obstacles. An economic union presupposes a high degree of economic interdependence among the countries concerned, which can be conveniently measured by the ratio of their mutual trade to their total trade. The main purpose of an integration scheme in Africa at this stage would be to pave the way for fuller economic union later, that is, to create conditions which would lead to a growing interdependence of African countries and lessen their dependence on those outside the region, in the context of accelerated development (UNECA, 1963: 397–98).

In proposing a 'large-scale import substitution based on larger subregional markets', the UNECA, nonetheless, pointed to the major obstacles that Africa would confront on the path to integration:

> For obvious reasons, the desire for national planning in countries that

have only recently acceded to independence tends to be very strong; besides, due to the poor state of intra-Africa communications in the past, African countries have had little opportunity to learn about each other. Moreover, while markets must be widened, it must not be forgotten that at the same time the national markets of African countries are also in need of internal integration; in many cases, a true national market has still to be created (UNECA, 1963: 398).

Despite these reservations, the UNECA and African actors embarked on wide-scale initiatives to construct integration along geographical and functional lines. Influenced by functionalism and gradualism, UNECA experts proposed no alternatives to the conventional wisdom. As the gradualist vision became increasingly hegemonic, African subregions became the critical locus for experiments with regional cooperation. Starting from the mid-1960s, subregional organisations, such as the East African Community (EAC), the Economic Community of West African States (ECOWAS), the Inter-Governmental Authority on Development (IGAD), the Southern African Development Community (SADC), plus multiple others in West and Central Africa evolved to articulate the economic vision that came to define regionalism in Africa (Meyers, 1974; Legum, 1975).

Building on the inherited colonial trade and services institutions, Kenya, Uganda and Tanzania led the process of East African integration by creating the East African Community (EAC) in 1967. However, although it was hailed as one of the most successful models of regional organisations on the globe, strains of nationalism appeared towards the late 1970s, which were to impair integration. Starting with political, personality and economic conflicts, the three countries strayed away from the objectives of integration, leading to the collapse of the EAC in 1977 (Mugomba, 1978; Mazzeo, 1984).

The disintegrative trends in East Africa belied the renewed momentum for integration in West Africa. Since the 1950s, West Africa had been a theatre of competing regional institutions, most of them with duplicative memberships. For a long time, UDEAO – formed in 1959 and comprising most of the Francophone countries – dominated attempts to expand trade in the region. In 1972, however, Dahomey, Côte d'Ivoire, Mali and Mauritania replaced UDEAO with the Communauté économique de l'Afrique de l'ouest (CEAO) or the Economic Community of West Africa, whose objectives were the improvement of infrastructure, the acceleration of joint industrialisation and the expansion of trade (Yansane, 1977: 43–59; Adejumobi, 2016: 213–30). Parallel initiatives culminated in the formation of the most comprehensive economic cooperative framework in Africa, the Economic Community of West African States (ECOWAS) in May 1975. With the formation of ECOWAS, regional states started to confront ways of diminishing the debilitating Francophone–Anglophone divide that had long dominated the region (Yansane, 1977: 43–59; Ojo, 1980: 571–604). In conception and modalities, ECOWAS echoed the gradualist and functionalist intentions of Africa's regional integration schemes, putting emphasis on cooperation and harmonisation in agriculture, trade, industry, transportation, finance and labour mobility.

Beyond ECOWAS, Africa witnessed a spurt of integration schemes in the 1980s, most of which built on subregional proximities and sought limited functional objectives. In Central and Equatorial Africa, where the Union douanière et économique de l'Afrique centrale (UDEAC), with a common currency and central bank, had dominated regionalism since 1964, there were moves to set up a comprehensive organisation. This was crucial because of the existence of a competing organisation, the Communuaté économique des Pays des Grands Lacs (CEPGL) or the Economic Community of the Great Lakes Region, which Burundi, Rwanda and Zaire had formed in 1976. The search for a new institution produced the Communuaté économique des États de l'Afrique centrale (CEEAC) (or the Economic Community of Central African States, ECCAS), incorporating UDEAC and CEPGL, plus Equatorial Guinea and São Tomé and Príncipe (Lemarchand, 2016: 231–44).

In eastern and southern Africa, a new organisation, the Preferential Trading Area for Eastern and Southern Africa (PTA), the precursor to the Common Market for Eastern and Southern Africa (COMESA) was formed in 1981 to promote trade among 18 countries, spanning from Egypt to Swaziland. In southern Africa, the efforts by the Frontline States neighbouring minority regimes led to the formation of the Southern African Development Coordination Conference (SADCC) to reduce dependence on South Africa and foster sectoral collaboration, mainly in transport and communications (Nagar, 2016: 119–212; Taylor, 2016: 157–74).

Despite the growth in regional institutions, Africa's economic crises, which started in the 1970s, had a profound effect on the trajectory of integration. Thus, as the crisis forced many countries to be more inward looking, it became increasingly difficult to translate lofty conceptual ideals of regionalism into practice. Amidst the disappointing economic performance and Africa's deepening economic dependence on external actors, the UNECA, under the leadership of Nigeria's Adebayo Adedeji, advised the OAU to adopt a new blueprint for Africa's self-reliance and industrialisation, geared toward the domestic market. Unveiled in the Lagos Plan of Action for the Development of Africa, 1980–2000, the OAU tried to recommit Africa to the objectives of 'promoting economic and social development and integration to achieve an increasing measure of self-sufficiency, self-sustainment and self-reliant development'. Thus, as the plan noted, given the small size of African domestic markets, regional organisations would enlarge the market by protecting infant industries and attracting foreign direct investments (OAU, 1980: 100). The Plan of Action also envisioned strengthening the existing regional economic communities and establishing other economic groupings in all the regions of Africa with the goal of creating a continental African Economic Community (AEC) by the year 2000 (OAU, 1980: 99). Throughout the 1980s, UNECA and the OAU convened a series of exploratory meetings, which culminated in the 1991 Abuja Treaty for the Establishment of the African Economic Community. Consistent with the dominant functionalist logic, the OAU expected the establishment of the AEC to occur in progressive stages over a 34-year period. Article 8(3) of the Abuja Treaty conferred on the Assembly of Heads of State and Government – the supreme organ of the AEC – the power to 'give directives, coordinate, and harmonise the economic, scientific, technical, cultural, and social policies of member states' (OAU, 1991: 17). Through the Abuja Treaty, African countries tried once more to reconcile the three-decade-long contest between continentalism and subregionalism.

Toward the end of the 1980s, the proliferation of regional integration schemes along functional and geographical lines underscored the dominance of theories of functionalism on Africa. Yet, these arrangements faced profound questions of effectiveness and relevance. Although African countries pursued integration for the purposes of market enlargement, industrialisation, sustained development and growth, and increased international competitiveness, it was difficult for these arrangements to translate these lofty commitments into substantive outcomes. Many critics of European-inspired integration continued to be sceptical about the contribution of regional integration to African development. Omotunde Johnson summarised the prevailing view:

> African countries seem unable to surmount the associated difficulties that have arisen in all their attempts at economic integration of the type that is supposed to end with the formation of a customs union – whether the defunct East African Economic Community, or any of those still in existence, such as ECOWAS, the Mano River Union, the Communuaté économique des États de l'Afrique centrale (CEEAC), the Union douanière et économique de l'Afrique centrale (UDEAC), or the PTA. The precise structure and details of the actual schemes being promoted have been unrealistic in the light of the costs and sacrifices that African governments and their citizens are willing to bear (Johnson, 1991: 3).

Similarly, in a review of ECOWAS, Peter Robson pointed to the ills facing integration across Africa:

> The principal achievement of ECOWAS to date has been to build up the necessary institutional framework that is required for establishing a customs union, including a tariff nomenclature and the basic common customs documentation. A range of important protocols has been adopted to give operational content to some of the more general provisions of the Treaty as regards both trade and customs... Nevertheless, there are crucial weaknesses in the present strategy of the Community that will have to be overcome if concrete progress is to be made and if real benefits are to be realized. These defects substantially contribute to the central problem for which ECOWAS is notorious: that decisions adopted by the Heads of State or by Ministers almost invariably fail to be implemented by action at the national levels (Robson, 1985: 616).

Other critics cast doubts on the applicability of the European-style trade liberalisation approach to integration, noting that it was not feasible in the African context because of the economic disparities among African countries and their dependence on foreign trade. Besides, the European model hinged on high levels of political and economic convergence. In a trenchant critique of the European model, Domenico Mazzeo proposed that African integration should serve primarily to reinforce autonomous national productive capacities rather than to create intercountry interdependence at the productive level. Unlike Europe, where strong and sturdy states anchored integration, Mazzeo contended that Africa needed to prioritise boosting nation- and state-building capacities before contemplating regional integration (Mazzeo, 1984).

The new regionalism in African integration

The post-Cold War period in the 1990s, and the growing prominence of globalisation, prompted new conceptualisations on regionalism that were relevant to African debates on regional integration. The impetus for the new wave was the growth in regional institutions in Africa, North America, Southeast Asia and Latin America, pointing to what scholars called 'the turn of regionalization in global politics' (Goldstein, 2002). The new vistas in the post-Cold War order seemed to stem from the emergence of diverse and pluralistic forms of regional institutions drawing from local contexts, but increasingly responding to the global competitive forces. More vital, scholars of new regionalism suggested that there was a marked transition from state-centred regionalism towards the incorporation of multiple voices and actors in integration. As Fredrik Söderbaum argued, new regionalism embraced a wide range of academic strands:

> The new regionalism referred to a number of new trends and developments, such as the spectacular increase in the number of regional trade agreements, an externally oriented and less protectionist type of regionalism, an anti-hegemonic type of regionalism which emerged from within the regions themselves instead of being controlled by the superpowers, the rise of a more multi-dimensional and pluralistic type of regionalism, which was not primarily centered around trading schemes or security cooperation and with a more varied institutional design, and the increasing importance of a range of business and civil society actors in regionalization (Söderbaum, 2015: 16).

An equally suggestive component of this new wave was the concept of developmental regionalism, which emphasised the move away from trade and trade facilitation associated with the previous decades towards cooperation in a broad range of areas, such as investment, research and development, as well as policies aimed at accelerating regional industrial and infrastructural development (Sloane, 1971: 142). In Africa, developmental regionalism gained prominence with the publication of the 2013 *Economic Development in Africa Report* by the UN Commission Conference on Trade and Development. The report emphasised that regional schemes ought to nurture and coordinate proactive economic policies, as opposed to politically passive approaches of trade liberalisation (Scholvin, 2018: 118).

New regionalism has benefitted from the wide-ranging economic and political reforms that African countries have adopted since the early 1990s to overcome decades of authoritarian rule and economic mismanagement. At the domestic level, the shift towards democratisation, transparency and accountability in governance, poverty eradication, gender equality, and civil society building provided the foundations for political renewal. As these reforms gathered pace, analysts saw the opportunities for economic similarities and convergence that would be conducive to frontal approaches to revitalised forms of cooperation and coordination. As Mistry pointed out:

> In principle, the new approach has abandoned the ossified, static, protected-fortress approach to integration among closed, state-run economies. It lays more emphasis on development of thematic integration (i.e., cooperating to save on large-scale infrastructure costs and achieving economies of scale) and open, rather than protected, market enlargement as a means of consolidating national economic policy shifts towards greater liberalization, market orientation, competitiveness, and efficiency (Mistry, 2000: 559–60).

Southern Africa paved the way for new regionalism by transforming the 1980s SADCC, which focused on reducing dependence on South Africa, to the Southern African Development Community (SADC), created in 1992 to address comprehensive goals. South Africa's accession to SADC membership in 1994 enhanced the viability of the organisation because of its large economy and contribution to the region's GDP (Söderbaum, 2004). From the outset, South Africa sought developmental regionalism, which emphasised the promotion of regional trade through market integration, infrastructure rehabilitation and industrial policy initiatives in the SADC (Adejumobi and Obi, 2020). In 1996, the SADC signed a trade protocol that phased out barriers among members as a preliminary step in the establishment of a Free Trade Area in 2008. The expansion of institutions around the SADC, for instance the SADC Parliamentary Forum, and the involvement of business groups and civil society actors seemed to reinforce the participatory assumptions of new regionalism (Godsäter, 2015; Mukumba and Musiwa, 2016).

In East Africa, Kenya, Tanzania and Uganda re-established the East African Community (EAC) in 1999, along the old functionalist lines. Under the new arrangement, the EAC committed to a common market by 2010, a monetary union by 2012, and eventually a political federation. Amidst disagreements on the feasibility of political federation, the EAC appointed a committee in 2017 to consider a political confederation as an interim phase before a federation. In December 2006, the EAC admitted Rwanda and Burundi, followed by South Sudan in 2016. The EAC also inaugurated a joint legislative assembly to handle regional policy matters, and a regional court to settle cross-border disputes. The EAC adopted several regional development plans to expand cooperation in infrastructure and industrial development, but the main thrust of integration has remained trade promotion. Even on this score, although the EAC established a customs union and made progress in areas such as the free movement of people, issues such as political and personality differences, trade wars, and competing infrastructural and industrial visions, have continued (UNECA, 2019).

The 1990s also witnessed the revitalisation and expansion of the PTA through the formation of COMESA in 1994, with the objective of deepening regional integration through trade and investment. An innovative initiative in African regionalism, which dovetailed with developmental regionalism, was the launching of negotiations in 2008 for a COMESA–SADC–EAC Tripartite Free Trade Agreement (TFTA) with a combined population of over 527 million people and a GDP of US$624 billion. Formalised in 2011, the TFTA seeks to strengthen the economic integration of the three blocs through joint planning, design, coordination, and the implementation of policies and programmes. In addition to the focus on trade, customs, infrastructure development and industrialisation, the TFTA provides a platform on which to address the overlapping memberships of countries to the three organisations. As Scholvin argues, South Africa has advocated for the TFTA as 'a means of "developmental regionalism", which is expected to facilitate region-wide industrialisation based on value addition in regional value chains (RVCs). For this purpose, South Africa seeks to coordinate industrial policies within the TFTA and rehabilitate infrastructure jointly with regional states' (Scholvin, 2018: 116; see also Lwanda, 2011: 4–38).

Elsewhere in Africa, old and new regional integration frameworks continued to operate largely within the trade-based logic, even though a few, such as ECOWAS, started to incorporate civil society voices in regional deliberations. Overall, even as analysts looked optimistically at the possibilities of new regionalism, two major threats confronted regional integration in Africa. First, the civil wars, which started in the 1990s, exacted a heavy toll on regional integration schemes as almost all of these institutions increasingly took on conflict resolution, peacemaking and peacebuilding roles. Despite the emergence of multiple institutions for peace and security (including the reinvigorated African Union and regional mechanism), the established economic institutions (now characterised by the African Union as Regional Economic Communities – RECs) bore a disproportionate burden of these security roles. The escalation of mandates invariably weakened these institutions and distracted from their core functions of economic integration.

Second, Africa's negotiations for the Economic Partnership Agreements (EPA) with Europe, mandated under the Cotonou Partnership Agreement, compromised regional institutions in Africa. Signed in 2000, the Cotonou Agreement envisaged the removal of the trade arrangements by January 2008 and their replacement by EPAs that would fulfil the requirements of the World Trade Organization (WTO) and better coordinate EU aid programmes. With some countries forced to negotiate in new regional configurations, critics castigated the EPAs for undermining the existing regional blocs (Murray-Evans, 2018). Although the EPAs are supposed to expand intraregional trade and trade links with Europe, Christopher Stevens observed that they may erect new trade barriers among African countries, thus defeating the objective of integration: 'By increasing the stakes, EPAs may make regional liberalisation less likely. Some countries willing to remove barriers to imports from their neighbours with similar economies may be unwilling to offer the same terms to highly competitive (and possibly dumped) EU imports. Regional groups may splinter between those willing to liberalise towards the EU and the others' (Stevens, 2006: 447). Europe, on the other hand, has argued for EPA negotiations in subregional contexts, where members have proximate relationships and closer economic interactions (Draper, 2007; Krapohl and Van Hutt, 2020: 565–82). After more than a decade of negotiations, the EU has concluded an EPA with ECOWAS, while the rest remain in progress (European Commission, 2020).

Perhaps, the major glimmer of hope in African integration in the 21st century was the unveiling of the African Continental Free Trade Area (AfCFTA) in January 2021. This agreement creates the largest free trade area in the world, connecting 1.3 billion people across 55 countries, with a combined gross domestic product (GDP) valued at US$3.4 trillion. Proponents have hailed the AfCFTA as providing an opportunity for Africa to integrate competitively into the global economy, reduce poverty and promote inclusion. In bringing the continental aspirations of the Lagos Plan of Action and the Abuja Treaty closer to reality, the AfCTA potentially builds on the momentum unleashed by the COMESA–SADC–EAC TFTA to broaden trade while engendering development across all sectors. As Ismail has proposed:

> African states should adopt a 'developmental regionalism' approach to trade integration under the AfCFTA, to ensure that it promotes inclusive economic growth and development and benefits all African countries. These four pillars of developmental regionalism have begun to gain traction across Africa and are on their way to becoming mutually reinforcing in practice. This approach to regional integration in Africa has great potential to catalyze and accelerate a virtuous circle of regional trade integration, transformative industrialization, cross-border infrastructure, democracy, inclusivity, and good governance across the continent (Ismail, 2020).

However, as the World Bank has cautioned, although AfCFTA can provide an anchor for long-term reform and integration, implementation will require determined political efforts and substantial policy reforms at the national level to enable goods, capital and information to flow freely and easily across the African borders (World Bank, 2021). Similarly, the United Nations Conference on Trade and Development (UNCTAD) suggests that trade policies alone are inadequate to support inclusive economic growth and need to be backed by other measures, such as cooperation in promoting investment and competition policies, accelerating financing of infrastructure, and providing equal access to socioeconomic opportunities and productive resources (UNCTAD, 2021).

Conclusion

Is African integration fated to remain brittle, even in light of the overwhelming need for cooperation and coordination to manage the crisis of multiple small states? Should African regionalism await the next grand theory that accurately explains the structural constraints of integration? Is the AfCFTA eventually going to consign the smorgasbord of regional economic institutions to history? Ravenhill (2016: 42), one of the leading sceptics of integration, has contended that:

> Economic regionalism in Africa has often combined a commitment to very ambitious integration agenda (notably customs unions and common currencies), with a very shallow institutional framework, in which few regional responsibilities are delegated to regional institutions. This lack of correspondence between institutional design and the purported mission of regional collaboration has been a major factor in the credibility gap that regional regionalism has faced. To observers, it often appears that African regional institutions have been 'designed to fail'.

Although this may sound overly pessimistic, the sorry state of African integration needs to be acknowledged and steps initiated to redress the predicament. Throughout the four decades, African states have rigidly adhered to narrow forms of sovereignty, defying the prescriptions for ceding some forms to supranational institutions to realise the gains from integration. Yet, rather than bemoaning the absence of 'political will' to integrate, the debate should shift to how some regional economic communities could potentially initiate processes to re-engineer the political foundations of existing states. If, as is widely suspected, African states are stubbornly beholden to their sovereignty and incapable of achieving any sustainable measure of integration, new social movements and the African publics at large need to agitate for political, economic and security communities that build on the synergies of culture, proximity and common destiny. The energy expended on programmes such as the AU Agenda 2063 – which merely reinforce weak intergovernmentalism – are not going to gain traction in the resolve to transcend the Westphalian contraptions that are no longer fit for the purpose of integration.

There has been sufficient theorising and conceptualisation about African integration. No new theories will help to unravel what has remained a constant – the inability of regionalism to thrive in the throes of fundamental state- and nation-building chores. The experience since the 1990s has shown that attempts by African regional institutions to rebuild states through peacemaking and peacebuilding are unlikely to make a difference when the very architecture of these states is deficient and flawed. Besides, while there is consensus on the problems around integration, this has not translated into measurable solutions to deal with them. The AfCFTA could potentially broaden the geographical reach of regionalism by removing the perennial conflicts between subregionalism and continentalism in African integration. Nonetheless, the celebrations and triumphalism about the AfCFTA have ignored the fact that implementation depends primarily on the same states and regional institutions that have disappointed Africa in the past.

References

Adejumobi, S. (2016). 'Region-building in West Africa', in D.H. Levine and D. Nagar (eds). *Region-Building in Africa: Political and economic challenges*. London: Palgrave Macmillan, pp. 213–304.

Adejumobi, S. and Obi, C. (eds). (2020). *Developmental Regionalism and Economic Transformations in Southern Africa*. London: Routledge.

Alting von Geusau, F. (1969). *Beyond the European Community*. Leiden: A.W. Sijthoff.

Anderson, D. (1998). 'David Mitrany (1888–1975): An appreciation of his work and ideas', *Review of International Studies*, 24: 577–92.

Asante, S.K.B. (2016). 'The political economy of Africa's region-building and regional integration', in Levine and Nagar (eds). *Region-Building in Africa: Political and economic challenges*. London: Palgrave Macmillan, pp. 231–44.

Balassa, B. (1961). 'Toward a theory of economic integration', *Kyklos*, 14: 1–17. https://doi.org/10.1111/j.1467-6435.1961.tb02365.x

Börzel, T.A. and Risse, T. (2009). *The Transformative Power of Europe: European Union and the diffusion of ideas*, KFG Working Paper No. 1. Berlin: Freie Universität.

Draper, P. (2007). *EU–Africa Trade Relations: The political economy of economic partnership agreements*. Jan Tumlir Policy Essays No. 02/2007.

Brussels: European Centre for International Political Economy (ECIPE).

European Commission. (2020). 'Commission Reports on Negotiating Round with Five Eastern and Southern African Countries', November. Brussels: European Commission.

Godsäter, A. (2015). 'Civil society and regional governance: Knowledge production and issue-framing around SADC', *Journal of Civil Society*, 11(1): 100–16.

Goldstein, A. (2002). *The New Regionalism in Sub-Saharan Africa: More than meets the eye?* Paris: OECD Development Centre, Policy Brief No. 20.

Green, R.H. and Krishna, K.G. (1967). *Economic Cooperation in Africa: Retrospect and prospects.* London: Oxford University Press, 1967.

Green, R.H. and Seidman, A. (1968). *Unity of Poverty? The economics of pan-Africanism.* London. Penguin.

Gruhn, I.V. (1979). *Regionalism Reconsidered: The Economic Commission for Africa.* Boulder, CO: Westview.

Haas, E. (1970). 'The study of regional integration: Reflections on the joy and anguish of pre-theorizing,' *International Organization*, 24(4): 607–47.

Haas, E. (1958). 'The challenge of regionalism', *International Organization*, 12(4): 440–58. DOI: https://doi.org/10.1017/S0020818300031349

Harrison, R.J. (1976). 'Review of David Mitrany's *The Functional Theory of Politics*', *Millennium*, 5: 200–02.

Ismail, F. (2020). 'A call for the developmental regionalism approach to the Continental Free Trade Area (AfCFTA)', *Great Insights Magazine*, 9(1). Available at: https://ecdpm.org/work/the-african-continental-free-trade-area-from-agreement-to-impact-volume-9-issue-1-2020/a-call-for-a-developmental-regionalism-approach-to-the-african-continental-free-trade-area-afcfta (Accessed 27 October 2021).

Johnson, O.E. (1991). Economic Integration in Africa: Enhancing prospects for success. *The Journal of Modern African Studies*, 29(1): 1–26.

Khadiagala, G.M. (2016). 'Region-building in East Africa', in D.H Levine and D. Nagar (eds). *Region-Building in Africa*. London: Palgrave Macmillan, pp. 175–90.

Khadiagala, G.M. (2008). 'The evolution of Euro–African relations', in T. Lyons and G.M. Khadiagala (eds). *Conflict Management and African Politics: Ripeness, bargaining, and mediation*. London: Routledge, pp. 67–82.

Krapohl, S. and Van Hutt, S. (2020). 'A missed opportunity for regionalism: The disparate behaviour of African countries in the EPA negotiations with the EU', *Journal of European Integration*, 42(2): 565–82.

Legum, C. (1975). 'The Organization of African Unity: Success or failure?' *International Affairs*, 51(2): 208–19. DOI:10.2307/2617233

Lemarchand, R. (2016). 'Region-building in Central Africa', in D.H. Levine and D. Nagar (eds). *Region-Building in Africa*. London: Palgrave Macmillan, pp. 231–44.

Lwanda, G. (2011). *Can EPAs Strengthen Regional Integration in Southern Africa: A qualitative analysis.* DBSA Working Paper Series No. 27. Johannesburg, Development Bank of Southern Africa, pp. 4–38.

Mazzeo, D. (ed). (1984). *African Regional Organizations.* Cambridge: Cambridge University Press.

Meyers, D.B. (1974). 'Intra-regional conflict management by the Organization of African Unity', *International Organization*, 28(3): 345–73.

Mistry, P. (2000). 'Africa's record of regional cooperation and integration', *African Affairs*, 99: 553–73.

Mitrany, D. (1965). 'The prospect of integration: Federal or functional', *Journal of Common Market Studies*, 4(2): 119–49. https://doi.org/10.1111/j.1468-5965.1965.tb01124.x

Mitrany, D. (1933). *The Progress of International Government.* New Haven, CT: Yale University Press.

Mugomba, A.T. (1978). 'Regional organizations and African underdevelopment: The collapse of the East African Community', *Journal of Modern African Studies*, 2(2): 261–72.

Mukumba, C. and Musiwa, M. (2016). 'Civil society role in the SADC integration: A missed opportunity', *Great Insights Magazine*, 5(4), July/August.

Murray-Evans, P. (2018). *North–South EPAs and the Multilateral System: Contesting the EPAs.* London: Routledge.

Nagar, D. (2016). 'COMESA and SADC: The era of convergence', in D.H. Levine and D. Nagar (eds). *Region-Building in Africa*. London: Palgrave Macmillan, pp. 119–212.

Ojo, O.J.B. (1980). 'Nigeria and the formation of ECOWAS', *International Organization*, 34(4): 571–604.

Organisation of African Unity (OAU). (1991). *The Abuja Treaty Toward the Establishment of the African Economic Community.* Addis Ababa: OAU, July.

Organisation of African Unity (OAU). (1980). *The Lagos Plan of Action for African Development, 1980–2000*. Addis Ababa: OAU, February.

Ravenhill, J. (2016). Regional integration in Africa: Theory and practice', in D.H. Levine and D. Nagar (eds). *Region-Building in Africa*. London: Palgrave Macmillan, pp. 37–52.

Robson, P. (1998). *The Economics of International Integration*. London: Routledge.

Robson, P. (1985). 'Regional integration and the crisis in sub-Saharan Africa', *Journal of Modern African Studies*, 23(4): 603–22.

Robson, P. (1967). 'Economic Integration in Southern Africa', *Journal of Modern African Studies*, 5(4): 469–90.

Roland, J. (1967). 'The experience of integration in French-speaking Africa', in A. Hazelwood (ed). *African Integration and Disintegration*. New York: Oxford University Press.

Rosenboim, O. (2013). 'From the private to the public and back again: The international thought of David Mitrany, 1940–1949', *Les Cahiers européens de Sciences Po*, 2: 2–25. Available at: https://www.sciencespo. fr/centre-etudes-europeennes/sites/sciencespo.fr.centre-etudes-europeennes/files/02_2013%20from-the-private-to-the-public-and-back-again-the-international-thought-of-david-mitrany-1940-1949.pdf (Accessed 21 October 2021).

Scholvin, S. (2018). 'Developmental regionalism and regional value chains: Pitfalls to South Africa's vision for the tripartite free trade area', *Africa Spectrum*, 53(3): 115–29.

Sloan, J.W. (1971). 'The strategy of developmental regionalism: Benefits, distribution, obstacles, and capabilities', *Journal of Common Market Studies*, 10(2): 138–62.

Söderbaum, F. (2015). *Early, Old, New and Comparative Regionalism: The scholarly development of the field*, KFG Working Paper Series No. 64. Berlin: Freie Universität.

Söderbaum, F. (2004). *The Political Economy of Regionalism: The case of southern Africa*. London: Palgrave Macmillan.

Stevens, C. (2006). 'The EU, Africa, and economic partnership agreements: Unintended consequences of policy leverage', *Journal of Modern African Studies*, 44(3): 441–58.

Taylor, S. (2016). 'Region-building in southern Africa', in D.H. Levine and D. Nagar (eds). *Region-Building in Africa*. London: Palgrave Macmillan, pp. 157–74.

United Nations Conference on Trade and Development (UNCTAD). (2021). *Economic Development in Africa Report 2021*, 8 December. Available at: https://unctad.org/webflyer/economic-development-africa-report-2021 (Accessed 25 October 2022).

United Nations Economic Commission for Africa (UNECA). (2019). 'Assessing the status of regional integration in Africa'. Addis Ababa: UNECA.

United Nations Economic Commission for Africa (UNECA). (1963). 'Approaches to African economic integration', *Journal of Modern African Studies*, 1(3): 397–98.

Viner, J. (1950). *The Customs Union Issue*. New York: Carnegie Endowment for International Peace.

World Bank. (2021). *The African Continental Fee Trade Area*. Washington, DC: The World Bank, 27 July.

Yansane, A.Y. (1977). 'West African economic integration: Is ECOWAS the answer?' *Africa Today*, 24(3) September: 43–59.

Zartman, W. (1971). *The Politics of Trade Negotiations Between Africa and the Economic Community: The weak confronts the strong*. Princeton, NJ: Princeton University Press.

The ideological roots of regional integration in Africa

RICH MASHIMBYE

Introduction

Regional integration is regarded as important because of the benefits it offers to states, such as preferential trade arrangements, ease of movement of goods and people, and opportunities to pool resources and work with others to advance peace and security. All the continents of the world have some level of integration, or aspire to achieve greater regional integration. Indeed, Africa is one of these continents that considers regional integration as crucial for intra-African trade and the achievement of effective cooperation to respond to a multitude of issues, including the security and political crises that affect peace and stability of the continent. Since regional integration and regionalism presuppose the creation of transboundary governance structures to act in the interest of all – structures that are then devolved by certain powers traditionally associated with the sovereign state – it has tended to generate resistance. This is also a problem in Africa.

Against this background, ideologies become pivotal instruments that can be used to sustain the impetus for integration. In Africa, ideologies that anchor regional integration emanate from anti-colonial struggle, Pan-Africanism and the thinking of nationalist leaders. Africa is one of the most poorly integrated regions in the world and this, in turn, has contributed to the persistence of poverty on the continent. This chapter explores the ideological foundations of regionalism in Africa and seeks to examine the extent to which this has ensured that integration remains on the agenda of states on the continent.

This chapter starts by exploring and analysing the concept of ideology, and links this to a discussion of regionalism and regional integration. It examines Pan-Africanism as a political ideology and its call for the unity of Africa, and focuses on political actors that attempted to marry Pan-Africanism with regional integration. It explores the thinking of Kwame Nkrumah, Sékou Touré and Amilcar Cabral on Pan-Africanism and integration, as the three are considered to have been prominent in the efforts to implement the ideology of Pan-Africanism in Africa. The chapter then moves on to the balkanisation of post-independence Africa into regions configured in terms of former colonial relations, and the issue of sovereignty as a challenge to regional integration.

The concept of ideology in the African context

Throughout the political history of human societies, ideology has been one concept that has featured as a dominant *motif*. In fact, it is impossible to imagine a country or civilisation without some kind of ideology. Nonetheless, and despite its preponderant presence throughout history, ideology remains quite a broad concept (Eagleton, 1994). However, in this chapter ideology is taken to refer to general views or perspectives that are political in character and concern matters such as how society should be organised, and what role the state ought to assume. One distinguishable aspect of ideology is its 'political connotations'. Johnson (2012: 5) contends that 'political ideas have a tendency to focus around specific issues'. Hence, for Johnson, an ideology is political in nature and helps people understand 'how society came to develop the ideas it has' and it also 'seek[s] to justify either the society or itself, or how society can be changed' (2012: 5). From this perspective, an ideology, by nature, has a sort of totality – it can lead to fundamental and wholesome social and political transformations, or it can be used to sustain an entire system, whether a social, political and/or economic system. It is a powerful social construct and has propensity to gravitate towards dominance. It is this power of ideology that is of particular relevance here, to understand whether the ideologies behind the political imperative of regional integration in Africa are powerful enough to sustain the desire for integration.

In the context of regional intergovernmental organisations, ideology would be composed of worldviews and convictions, mainly in the character of regional integration and unity, that have influenced states to form and join inter-state organisations in the first place. In terms of its nature, an ideology is not composed of a single idea but draws from and is made up of an array of related ideational units which, when considered collectively, form a particular ideology. For example, Marxism as a political ideology is composed of many ideas, including dialectic materialism, the productive forces, the economic structure, and the role of the bourgeoisie and the proletariat, and it offers ideas on how the capitalist system could be overthrown (Donham, 1999).

In reality, ideologies can achieve hegemonic status in the sense of being preponderant in society or in an interstate milieu or, alternatively, give rise to contestations. On the one hand, and in relation to regional integration, ideologies that are hegemonic in nature would be able to spur the impetus for regional integration, thus compelling member states to take steps towards integration, notwithstanding the obstacles that may exist. It is a tool that can be used to mobilise states towards certain political goals and objectives (Schwrzmantel, 2008). On the other hand, ideologies that meet serious opposition or contestation can generate a paralysis in terms of initiating the practical measures necessary for regional integration.

Of course, pertinent to the discourse on hegemony, and its tendency to drive major political and social processes, is the Italian Marxist theorist, Antonio Gramsci, who tackled the concept through his many treatises discussed in his *Prison Notebooks*. Gramsci, who was also a former leader of the Italian Communist Party that attempted and failed to overthrow the Benito Mussolini regime immediately after the First World War – a crime that landed him in prison – theorised about hegemony, as expressed through ideational domination in the context of Fascist Italy while in incarceration. Gramsci's solitary intellectual engagement with hegemony while in prison led him to define the concept as entailing the 'formation and organisation of consent' (Ives, 2004: 3). Therefore, an ideology or ideologies that underpin regional integration would be considered to have become hegemonic once they are able to solicit society-wide consent on a particular course that was aimed at furthering integration.

Gramsci grapples with the relationship between ideology and social and political change, arguing that revolutions are not only determined by changes in the 'economic structure' and the material conditions obtained on the ground, but also at the ideological level (Hawkes, 2003: 113). For Gramsci, ideas are closely linked with power, and those ideas that are able to dominate will determine the direction society takes. This is related to what has been termed 'dominant ideology thesis', which posits that the dominant class always seeks to impose its own worldview on society as a whole. With regard to regional integration, the effectiveness of ideological hegemony builds consciousness in the actors/states to whom it is applicable – this consciousness being crucial to influence the actors to undertake fundamental social and political changes. To this effect, Gramsci refers to what he calls 'national-popular collective will' – a condition of ideological hegemony that emerges as a result of the ruling elites' ability to satisfy the needs and interests of major groups in society. Again, in the case of a regional environment, a national-popular will would necessarily have to be replaced by a 'regional-popular collective will' for the ideology of regional integration to achieve hegemony. The ideologies that drive integration in Africa are rooted in the history of the liberation struggle, Pan-Africanism and the political thought that was developed primarily by African nationalists leading the anti-colonialism struggle on the continent.

Pan-Africanism and African unity

People who have been subjugated and oppressed, as African people were through colonialism, tend to develop a sense of brotherhood and sisterhood generated out of their unfortunate experience. In their common suffering, a common interest emerges – the interest or need to rip asunder the shackles of oppression. Indeed, the struggle against colonialism and imperialism in the 20th century in Africa produced a continent-wide solidarity. This solidarity was underpinned by the conviction that African peoples' experience of oppressive European domination was similar and, as such, their fate was similar, which required some form of unity among the oppressed to organise effective resistance. Therefore, it was not surprising that people of African origin in the diaspora also identified with their kith and kin in Africa, as they, too, had suffered persecution and marginalisation on the basis of their skin pigmentation (Feagin, 2006). The African diaspora was located mainly in the Caribbean and the Americas, having been brought to these places as a result of slavery in the 16th and 17th centuries. Like their African counterparts, they, too, agitated for freedom from oppression.

Pan-Africanism is the political ideology that has anchored the vision of African integration. Based on notions of African brotherhood and sisterhood, it proceeded from the idea that Africans, regardless of geographic location, have had a common experience of European colonialism and racism, and their dislocating and dehumanising effects. Accordingly, a sense of solidarity, informed by recognition that Africans have a common destiny, took hold. In 1963, Ghana's founding statesman, Kwame Nkrumah, gave a seminal speech to an Organisation of African Unity (OAU) Summit of Heads of State wherein he passionately argued for the unification of African states, as underscored by his famous statement that 'we [Africa] must unite now or perish' (*New African*, 2013; AU, n.d). This speech popularised the idea of a 'United States of Africa' – the unification of African states to become one sovereign and independent state. Among the reasons advanced by Nkrumah was that the division of Africa into different states was a consequence of European colonialism, a system that partitioned different African territories into 'independent' units and distributed these among European imperial powers. Nkrumah observed that the reasons advanced for why Africa could never be united were that the continent lacked 'a common race, culture and language' (Nkrumah, 1963: 132). However, he argued that what united Africa was much stronger than the aforesaid hurdles, and stretched beyond the common history and similar goals that Africans share: it is their very being – their Africaness.

Nkrumah was at the centre of an international Pan-African movement, created and driven by prominent thinkers of African descent, which included William Edward Burghardt Du Bois, with whom Nkrumah served as the general secretary of a working committee on Pan-African nationalism, while the former became its chairman (Nkrumah, 1963). This committee emanated from the Fifth Pan-Africanism Congress, which was convened in Manchester, Britain, in 1945. As an ardent disciple of Pan-Africanism, Nkrumah became the champion of the ideals that the ideology of Pan Africanism stands for in Africa. Therefore, it was not surprising that, once Ghana achieved independence, Nkrumah used the country as both an instrument and platform for the advancement of African independence and unity. As Nkrumah says in his book, 'while our independence celebrations were actually taking place, I called for a conference of all the sovereign states of Africa, to discuss plans for the future of our continent' (Nkrumah, 1963: 136). What followed were a succession of Pan-African conferences convened mainly in Ghana and attended by independent African states and liberation movements: the Conference of Independent African States in April 1958 in Accra, Ghana; the All-African People's Conference in December 1958 in Accra, Ghana; and the All-African People's Conference in March 1961 in Cairo, Egypt. These conferences, and others of a similar nature, were driven primarily by a concern to rid the continent of all the vestiges of colonial and imperial domination, a Pan-Africanism of a sort. The thread that ran through them was the cognisance that Africans were essentially 'one people' and that their unity was important.

While the idea of African unity appealed to some, others did not support it, as the earlier disagreement between the so-called Casablanca and Monrovia blocs on the issue of unification highlights. The Casablanca bloc was composed of pro-unification states such as Algeria, Egypt, Ghana, Guinea, Libya, Mali and Morocco. The grouping was referred to as the 'Casablanca bloc' because the political meeting that resolved on complete integration was convened in the Moroccan city of Casablanca in 1961. This collection of states advocated for political unification of the African continent (Kloman, 1962). Hardcore Pan-Africanists like Gamal Abdel-Nasser (Egypt), Kwame Nkrumah (Ghana) and Sékou Touré (Guinea) held that it was only through profound integration that Africa could exorcise the spectre of colonialism, and enter the interstate system in the postcolonial period as a strong political, economic and military force. For these leaders, the colonially created African states should cease to exist, and national power should be transferred to a supranational authority, a form of central government that would be in charge of the continent.

The rival bloc, the Monrovia bloc, sternly countered the idea of political unification or federation, and instead called for the recognition and sustenance of the colonial states and their territorial boundaries (Kloman, 1962: 393). This does not necessarily imply that the states that constituted the Monrovia bloc did not believe in the Pan-Africanist idea of unity – they were merely opposed to integration as it had been conceived by the Casablanca bloc. In this sense, while this grouping believed in the importance of integration, it nonetheless opposed total integration, as called for by the Casablanca bloc, which would have seen a supranational authority created and assuming the roles normally associated with the nation-state. Like the Casablanca bloc, the Monrovia bloc was created in 1961, through the Conference of Independent African states, in the Liberian city of Monrovia. The conference was attended by leaders from North and West Africa.

The border discourse in Africa arises whenever regional integration is discussed. This discourse occurs mostly at the political level and involves scholars and leaders of various African countries. It is focused on the historicity of prevailing state borders in Africa. There are those who contend that because state boundaries were drawn by colonial marauders, these borders are not a reflection of African peoples' conception of political polity and how African societies ought to be organised (Deng, 1993). In terms of this view, the African state, as it is presently configured, is undesirable and all borders should be reconsidered. The discourse on the historicity and originality of the borders of the African state, transpiring at a philosophical–ideational level, has paradoxically stimulated an interest in regional integration. While on a state visit to South Africa in 2021, the Kenyan President, Uhuru Kenyetta, called for the expedition of efforts to integrate Africa. He argued that state borders in Africa were a creation of Europeans to separate Africans and exploit the continent's resources and, as such, they were arbitrary. Although he did not call for the abolition of the state, he charged that the integration of different African states through the removal of travel restrictions, increasing trade among Africans, building continental transport and trade infrastructure, among other things, would result in the deepening of integration and, thus, render the colonially imposed boundaries redundant.

The strong arguments against the African colonial state are also informed by fear that the state continues to be dominated by outside powers, hence the idea of the state being trapped in 'neocoloniality'. This concept comes from neocolonialism, and refers to a situation in which former colonial powers continue to wield influence indirectly, especially in the form of economic domination, in the countries they controlled during colonialism (Touré, 1962; Nkrumah, 1965; Makgetlaneng, 2011). This clearly links with the thinking of Amílcar Cabral, Kwame Nkrumah and Sékou Touré on the subject of colonialism (the thinking of these figures is examined later in this chapter). At the centre of the neocolonial thesis is that former colonial powers were able to retain control over the state even after colonialism. In his seminal book on neocolonialism, *Neo-Colonialism: The last stage of imperialism*, Nkrumah observes that:

> Faced with the militant peoples of the ex-colonial territories in Asia, Africa, the Caribbean and Latin America, imperialism simply switches tactics. Without a qualm it dispenses with its flags, and even with certain of its more hated expatriate officials. This means, so it claims, that it is 'giving' independence to its former subjects, to be followed by 'aid' for their development. Under cover of such phrases, however, it devises innumerable ways to accomplish objectives formerly achieved by naked colonialism. It is this sum total of these modern attempts to perpetuate colonialism while at the same time talking about 'freedom', which has come to be known as *neo-colonialism* (Nkrumah, 1965: 20).

The (weak) African state is a product of the anti-black colonial process and, as such, it is antithetical to the interests of Africa. Since it is an alien imposition, the sentimental attachment to the notion of nation-state, as formed and institutionalised during colonialism, is misguided and certainly should not stand in the way of regional integration. Notwithstanding the disagreement on the kind of political shape that the African continent ought to assume, both the Casablanca and Monrovia blocs were cognisant of the need for integration and unity in the continent. It was primarily because of this understanding by the leaders of both groups that the independent African states decided to create the Organisation of African Unity (OAU) in 1963. The OAU was to be the middle ground between unification and the absence of relations. It sought to coordinate sovereign states' cooperation on issues of common interest, including the total liberation of Africa. As a matter of fact, the ideological position of the Casablanca and Monrovia blocs was similar in that they both viewed integration as crucial for Africa's socioeconomic development, security and international clout. This perhaps explains why states belonging to both blocs supported the idea of the creation of an intergovernmental organisation in the character of the OAU.

Towards the end of the 20th century and the beginning of the 21st century, modern Pan-Africanist leaders like Thabo Mbeki of South Africa and Ologun Obasanjo of Nigeria set in motion fundamental processes that were aimed at deepening integration in Africa (Ezeoha and Uche, 2005). Mbeki's famed 'I am an African' speech was to shape South Africa's foreign policy posture towards the rest of the African continent. Mbeki resuscitated the idea of African renaissance, at the core of which is the rebirth of the continent. It was under Mbeki that South Africa increased its involvement in continental initiatives – especially conflict resolution, peacekeeping and peacemaking – which saw the country being prepared to commit personnel and financial resources to help resolve conflicts in Africa. South Africa's conflict resolution efforts in the Democratic Republic of the Congo (DRC), Sudan, Côte d'Ivoire and many other countries on the continent need to be understood as driven by the ideational anchoring of an African Renaissance.

Equally, under Obasanjo, Nigeria became a leader on issues concerning the resolution of conflicts and economic integration in the continent (Ezeoha and Uche, 2005). Central to the notion of the African Renaissance is the conviction that Africans must have the capacity, will and determination to resolve the challenges and problems that confront the continent without necessarily seeking the assistance of the outside world. The African Renaissance, as an ideology of a sort, partly gave rise to the idea of 'African solutions to African problems' – an approach underpinned by the principle of self-reliance. Perhaps the highlight for both Mbeki and Obasanjo and their efforts to deepen integration in Africa was the creation of the New Economic Partnership for Africa's Development (NEPAD) in 2001 – a Pan-African development agency aimed at facilitating intra-African trade, mainly through the financing of infrastructure projects, the promotion of manufacturing and capacity building in Africa.

One of the obvious implications of the commitment to rely on oneself is that capacity would have to be created to do this. In the context of African integration, this entailed reforming the existing OAU to create supranational structures that would be able to confront many of the challenges that Africa faced. Accordingly, the renaissance or rebirth of Africa spurred efforts at the continental level to create institutions or to reform the existing ones to ensure that they best serve the imperative of regional integration. Thus, in 2002, the OAU was formally disbanded and replaced with the more broad and wide-ranging African Union (AU) to tackle the complex problems that spanned poor economic development and integration, limited continental infrastructure, conflicts and political instabilities.

In light of the historical and recent dynamics explored here, and despite scant progress having been made on integration in Africa, the idea of regional integration remains strong and appealing to most heads of state, being viewed as imperative to correct historical injustice. The following section discusses the thinking and writings of prominent Pan-Africanist leaders – Kwame Nkrumah, Sékou Touré and Amílcar Cabral – leaders whose pioneering works on African unity and integration continue to be influential on the continent.

The thought leaders of African integration

When Nkrumah landed in Ghana in 1947, just two years after the Fifth Pan-African Congress in Manchester in 1945, he immediately formed the Convention People's Party and built it into a mass movement that agitated for an end to British dominion over the Gold Coast, as Ghana was called then (Nkrumah, 1963: 36). This resistance culminated in Ghana attaining its political independence from imperial Britain in 1957. As the country seized its independence, its founding president, Nkrumah, proclaimed that the independence of his country would be hollow if other African countries remained entrapped in colonialism and/or white minority rule (Nkrumah, 1963: 136; Asare-Nuamah, 2017: 54). At this point, it became abundantly clear that, under the presidency of Nkrumah, Ghana was likely to play an important role in the continent-wide anti-colonial campaign that was beginning to gather pace, as marked by Ghana's attainment of independence. Nkrumah, with his grounding in the Pan-Africanism, immediately immersed himself in the struggle for the liberation of the rest of the continent. He specifically called for the unity of African people and was one of the critical figures in the establishment in 1963 of the OAU, Africa's first intergovernmental organisation. In Article II of its founding Charter (OAU, 1963, Article II), the OAU proclaimed commitment to the expulsion of colonialism on the continent. In addition, it also undertook to promote unity and solidarity in Africa.

Certainly, Nkrumah imprinted his ideas on decolonisation and unity of the continent into the OAU. He was influenced by his Pan-Africanist convictions and, being a strong proponent of African unity, he steadfastly held the view that the division of Africa into different states was a ploy by European colonialists to render the continent weak, especially in relation to the international system of states. He charged that Africa should disavow the territorial borders imposed on her by colonial powers and form a single, united states of Africa, similar to the United States of America (Nkrumah, 1963). This would make Africa a great power and, as such, unassailable.

Although his ideas never saw the light of day, they shaped how African leaders and states relate to one another. Interestingly, Nkrumah was convinced that Africa should build a single army, which is indicative of his awareness of the primacy of military power in international affairs, as was the case during the Cold War, a form of international military and diplomatic standoff hinged mainly on the Soviet Union–US rivalry from the 1960s onwards. The idea of self-reliance, and a wariness of the neocolonial tendencies of foreign businesses and powers in Africa, also influenced Nkrumah's thinking about the army. He regretted that Africa could not provide military aid to Patrice Lumumba's government in the DRC when it was facing a secession challenge by the mineral-rich Katanga Province in 1960 (Nkrumah, 1963: 138). Nkrumah was particularly dismayed by the refusal of the United Nations, itself influenced by Western businesses that had interests in the minerals of Katanga, to deploy peacekeepers to repel the secessionists. In his own words, Nkrumah said that if 'the independent states of Africa had been united, or had at least a joint military high command and a common foreign policy, an African solution might have been found for the Congo [crisis]' (Nkrumah, 1963: 38).

Indeed, Nkrumah was, and continues to be, recognised by the slogan 'Africa Must Unite', which underscores his ideas about the type of integration that Africa should strive for (Nkrumah, 1963; 1965). As the current generation of African leaders navigate the complex and difficult journey of regional integration, they are often reminded by history that the continent's founding fathers, Nkrumah included, wanted an Africa that was united and certainly thoroughly integrated.

Sékou Touré was another African intellectual and leader devoted to Pan-Africanism and its commitment to African unity. He became the first president of 'French Guinea' in 1958 when the country won its independence from France. In terms of his ideas, Touré argued that 'African unity is no more a goal [in] itself than was independence. It simply is a means of development, a force of inter-African cooperation' (Touré, 1962: 147). It is clear from the aforesaid that he regarded unity as a requirement for (socioeconomic) development, which in turn requires and results in the deepening of integration among African countries. Furthermore, Touré identified what could be considered an anomaly in relation to colonialism. He observed that while colonial powers had control over several countries, there was no economic relationship between the colonies under the same colonial power; the economic activity was directed towards the development and welfare of the colonising power. This was a strange situation, indeed, and indicated that African states were nothing but chattels of the colonial powers. In light of this, Touré strongly advocated for economic integration of the countries that had just acquired independence, firmly believing that these states could use their vast natural resources and raw materials to spearhead industrialisation in Africa (Touré, 1962). His thinking on the question of integration in Africa, especially economic integration, contributed significantly to the broader ideologies that have ensured socioeconomic and political integration remains firmly on the agenda of African states today.

At a broader international level, Touré charged that the relationship between Africa and other states in the world was problematic, arguing that it was characterised by exploitation and economic domination of Africa by powerful Eurocentric states. This economic domination had evolved to a point where it was no longer facilitated through direct colonial control but via the use of multinational companies (MNCs) located in the West to extract raw materials and 'crude products' from Africa. Ironically, the resources extracted in Africa are then exported to the countries from which these MNCs originate, to create industrialisation and development, which lead to serious socioeconomic revolutions. Of course, the irony is that this happened while Africa remained grossly poverty-stricken.

Touré was critical of the lack of meaningful trade and economic relationships among African states. As an example, he argued that it was regrettable that Guinea was not permitted to sell its products like coffee and palm kernels to countries such as Côte d'Ivoire and Ghana, simply because of the absence of substantive integration and multilateral trade agreements conducive to intra-African trade. Rendering this situation anomalous was that while African states did not trade with one another, they had economic relations with overseas powers. Accordingly, Touré saw industrialisation at the continental level as crucial if Africa were to take its rightful place in the international political economy. He contended that Africa could not enter the international trade space without first developing within the continent, because doing so would be nothing but integration without substance (Touré, 1962).

A cursory look at Africa's current international trade position would reveal that Touré's thinking on continental/regional economic integration was prescient. Reflecting on current international trade, it is apparent that Africa's participation in the international political economy is extremely marginal and somewhat meaningless. The continent accounts for a meagre 3 per cent of total global trade, constituted of both imports and exports, and the paradox is that the continent has a share of about 18 per cent of the world's population, nearly twice that of Europe (10 per cent), which has more than of 30 per cent of international trade. To what degree are the poor levels of intra-African trade and integration accountable for the dismal share of international trade attributable to Africa? Drawing on Touré's thinking, one could argue that the reason Africa derives so little value from its participation in the international political economy is because of the abysmal extent of regional economic integration and industrialisation at the continental level. The regions or continents that extract the most value return from international trade appear to be those that are substantively integrated at the regional level, that is, Europe and Asia. In light of this, Touré's philosophy on continental economic integration, and the related thesis that there is a link between extensive regional integration and high levels of economic development, is more pertinent today than ever before, as African states grapple with the challenge of how to increase economic integration and intra-African trade.

Amílcar Cabral, who was a Guinea-Bissau-born revolutionary, a Pan-Africanist scholar and Marxist theorist, contributed significantly to the liberation of the Portuguese-controlled colonies of Angola, Cape Verde, Guinea-Bissau, Mozambique and Príncipe and São Tomé. In 1956, Cabral and a few colleagues established the African Party for the Independence of Guinea and Cape Verde (PAIGC), a liberation movement formed for the purpose of waging an anti-colonial struggle (Rabaka, 2014). The PAIGC's name may give an incorrect impression as to its goals, in that it includes only Guinea (-Bissau) and Cape Verde, because its liberation struggle was not confined to these two countries. As mentioned earlier, the PAIGC was concerned with the liberation of all African states that were under Portuguese rule.

As a scholar who was actively involved in the liberation struggle, Cabral was deeply immersed in Marxist theory and used it to understand and articulate how the oppressed can fight colonialism. Paradoxically, this duality in his character – Cabral the theorist and Cabral the liberation fighter – contributed to his thinking that intellectual endeavour (to understand colonialism, oppression and racism) must be connected with practical immersion in the struggle for decolonisation (hence the idea of *praxis*) (Ahmad, 1973). He contended that, like other societies in the world, African polities were composed of different social classes and the unity of these classes was crucial for the realisation of national liberation. Clearly, Cabral viewed African unity as pivotal, not only for the attainment of self-rule but also as necessary for the success of an independent Africa.

Like his contemporaries such as Nkrumah and Touré, Cabral grappled with the possibility of continued domination of African societies by erstwhile colonial powers. He advanced the argument that Africa and its people would only achieve true liberation when the exploitative relations between the continent and her former colonial masters were eradicated. To this effect, he contended that 'national liberation exists when, and only when, the national productive forces have been completely freed from all and any kind of foreign domination' (Chabal, 1981: 36). While Cabral's work stretches across many themes from colonialism, imperialism, politics, language and culture, to national liberation and colonial economic exploitation, he also paid attention to the productive forces of the African colonial state and how this continued to be dominated by former colonial powers through neocolonialism. He argued that neocolonialism was characterised by a situation in which a former colonial power creates a bourgeoise class or fake bourgeoisie in its erstwhile colony and uses this class to facilitate the continuation of the exploitation of resources, even after the termination of colonisation. Clearly, the phenomenon of neocolonialism was diametrically opposed and incompatible with the imperative of socioeconomic development in the former colonies, and was a stumbling block to regional economic integration. It is for this reason that Cabral charged that complete decolonisation would be identifiable by the elimination or absence of neocolonial, exploitative relations. Thus, considered collectively, the works and political thought of Cabral, Nkrumah and Touré are crucial to understanding the ideational factors that make regional integration a political theme that current African leaders, and indeed future ones, cannot escape.

The identification of African regions as 'Anglophone', 'Francophone' and 'Lusophone'

European colonial powers divided Africa into different regions, with each power given a group of polities to control, so as to maximise their exploitation of the continent's natural resources and markets. This led to the emergence of an interpretation of the colonial division of Africa as comprising 'Anglophone', 'Francophone' and 'Lusophone' regions, where Africa's regions were viewed in terms of the colonial powers that were in charge. However, this description of regions did not end with the defeat of colonialism; it continues in the post-independence period. This presents both challenges and advantages (which is ironic given that colonialism was a crime against Africans) for regional integration.

Concerning the challenges, the prolonged configuration of the African continent in terms of these colonial geopolitical-demarcation-generated divisions among states on the continent, whereby some view themselves as first belonging to the Anglophone, Francophone or Lusophone regions, and only identifying themselves as African thereafter. This identity stifles efforts aimed at achieving political unity. This division is also reflected in how states approach continental initiatives. An example is the Pan-African Parliament, where members have demonstrated a propensity to consider themselves in terms of the colonially defined regions from which they come. Consequently, they vote on issues, including those relating to the election of leadership of the Parliament, in line with the regions from which they hail, instead of continental and commonly shared interests. Another challenge pertains to the influence that erstwhile colonial powers continue to wield, through imperialism, on countries that were previously under their control. This is particularly pronounced in the so-called Francophone region, where France continues to have untrammelled political and economic clout to the detriment of continental integration (Taylor, 2019). This is a problem that Sékou Touré alluded to in his writings about the political, economic and social situation in Africa that existed during the 1950s, 1960s and 1970s, and in fact still persists. States in the Anglophone, Francophone or Lusophone regions have no intraregional trade integration, but the same states have strong trade links with their former colonial powers (economic exploitation). It is the same neocolonialism and economic domination that Nkrumah and Cabral theorised about many decades ago.

Of course, the colonial partitioning of Africa also presents opportunities for regional integration, however inadvertently this may be. The 1991 Abuja Treaty, which called for the creation or formalisation of subregional intergovernmental organisations, was informed mainly by the realisation that starting integration at the subregional level would serve the goal of creating and achieving continental integration (Kouassi, 2007). Historically, liberation movements located in African states that shared geographic proximity tended to cooperate with one another in their pursuit of their various yet interlocking anti-colonial struggles. Necessarily, this created and fostered political rapport and solidarity and, more crucially, a sense of common political identity, which would later be important for integration in post-colonial Africa. Indeed, some of Africa's subregional organisations, like the SADC, trace their origins to the colonial efforts to coordinate anti-colonial campaigns by liberation movements and certain newly independent African states. Related to the aforesaid, the division of Africa into Anglophone, Francophone and Lusophone also created commonly shared cultural identities at a subregional level, which would, theoretically, contribute to the ease with which states in any given region unite and integrate. In addition, in recent years, a sentiment has emerged, and is gradually gathering pace, which is characterised by a negative attitude towards the colonial connection.

In consideration of the above, the existence of colonial cultural and political identities that are confined in terms of regions stands as a stumbling block to political, social and economic integration on the continent. However, the positive dimension is that the same may be good for integration, especially at a subregional level. In this sense, the continued preponderance of the colonial-era division of Africa in terms of Anglophone, Francophone and Lusophone regions generates certain ideational facts that have a bearing on integration on the continent.

Sovereignty and the question of integration in Africa

Just as the question of state sovereignty and independence loomed large during the early 1960s, as framed in terms of the Casablanca–Monrovia ideological 'rivalry' marked by sharp disagreement on the form of integration the newly independent African states should pursue, integration and sovereignty continue to be perceived as somewhat incompatible (Söderbaum, 2004). Sovereignty regards the nation-state as the final authority that cannot be dictated to by any other entity; other states or intergovernmental organisations cannot impose their will on the sovereign state. A state's right to sovereignty and independence is codified in international law, which asserts that all states shall have the privilege to administer their internal affairs without interference. Necessarily, the status of being a sovereign is conferred on states, defined as constituting those political entities that have a given territory, a population and a functioning government, and are recognised as being legitimate states by peers in the interstate system. Accordingly, the power that a state possesses, that is, its military and economic power, is immaterial in the determination and conferment of the prestige of statehood.

Nearly every inch of Africa was colonised by European powers. As the phenomenon of colonialism was extractive in nature, the states that littered the African continent in the post-independence period were weak and, to a certain degree, this situation persists (Jackson and Rosberg, 1982). Therefore, their sovereignty is more juridical than substantive, and is propped up primarily by international law. This obviously has implications for socioeconomic development; intra-African trade in particular, and continental integration in general. Logic dictates that a region that has a concentration of states that have poor economies and are impoverished is likely to be less integrated, especially economically integrated, as this requires an extensive capital injection into setting up the infrastructure necessary for intra-regional trade, such as roads, rails, manufacturing and the economic competitiveness of each and every country to avoid huge trade imbalances. An often, rather laboured point is that Africa is the least integrated region, and the abovementioned challenges have certainly contributed to the low levels of integration. Ironically, this makes integration appealing in that it would offer countries an opportunity to fast-track the growth of their economies and, as a consequence, develop a competitive edge in relation to the broader international trade environment.

Notwithstanding the oft-intense disagreement on the ideas of sovereignty, non-intervention and intervention, at some level African states appreciate the seemingly inescapable reality of integration, that integration is unavoidable, as was the case during the 1960s. There is a strong sentiment from within Africa and among politicians and researchers that the continent cannot hope to prosper and 'catch-up' with the rest of the world if it continues to be characterised by the absence of unity and integration, particularly economic integration (Jones, 2002). To this end, and as previously argued, African states have introduced a raft of initiatives borne out of multilateral agreements, such as the creation of a continental free trade area and the removal of barriers to the travel and business activities of Africans in order to deepen continental and subregional integration. The African Union's Agenda 2063 also encapsulates the urgency of integration on the continent as a way of overcoming underdevelopment and poverty.

While the existence of vast differences in the economic competitiveness of African states is a problem that threatens economic integration, there is the political will to forge ahead with integration, as the statements of President Kenyetta and others highlight. African leaders are familiar with the colonial history of the continent, including its economic exploitation by colonial powers, and this renders the idea of integration politically irresistible. Integration could result in the elimination of neocolonial and imperial economic relations that many African states have with their erstwhile colonial masters. Indeed, Africa's foremost Pan-Africanist thinkers such as Nkrumah, Touré and Cabral identified the problem of African states maintaining neocolonial economic relations with their former colonisers while failing to establish economic relations among themselves.

Sadly, the situation described earlier still exists to an extent, and the example of the so-called 'African Financial Community' (CFA), set up by France in 1945 for its African colonies, was problematic in that it was, inter alia, an instrument of economic domination. The CFA compelled the African states concerned, such as Equatorial Guinea, Côte d'Ivoire, Mali, Senegal and Togo, among others, to deposit half of their foreign exchange reserves with the French central bank, the Banque de France, in Paris. As a consequence, these African states could not exercise control over national monetary issues, like policy, as the responsibility for monetary policy resided with the French government. This case is an apt practical depiction of neocoloniality, as theorised by Nkrumah, Touré and Cabral. A country's complete control over its currency and monitory policies is the hallmark of sovereignty and independence; the states that were under the CFA lacked this control.

Fortunately, after 75 years of the CFA, this arrangement was terminated in 2020, when France formally ratified an agreement calling for its cancellation. More positively for regional integration, there is a high possibility that a new regional currency will emerge to replace the colonial CFA. The Economic Community of West African States (ECOWAS) has proposed that the region adopts its own currency, to be called the Eco (*Africa News*, 2020). This bodes well for regional integration, intra-regional trade, and interconnection of the West African region. Although this idea of a regional common currency has been formally adopted by the ECOWAS, the Eco is yet to be introduced. Hopefully states will move beyond plans and political speeches on the issue to a stage of actual implementation.

As expected, once states agree to the formation and accept membership of an intergovernmental organisation, the assumption is that they transfer some of their sovereignty to the organisation – a pooling of sovereignty – thus allowing the organisation to act in the common interests of its members (Schimmelfennig, 2014). Intergovernmental organisations perform a wide array of functions, including intervening in a member state to resolve conflicts and political crises that may have a negative impact on regional peace, security and stability. States approach this aspect of regional integration with some trepidation and uncertainty, as no one state wants to find itself in a situation that appears to undermine their sovereignty. This has been particularly pronounced in Africa, where autocratic governments that transgress human rights and stoke political instabilities are often at loggerheads with the African Union and/or the Regional Economic Communities (RECs) regarding issue around the treatment of their citizens and the possibility of intervention by intergovernmental organisations. This is so because these states – and indeed the majority of states – interpret sovereignty as precluding external intervention, hence the uneasiness around the subject of intervention and external interference.

In consideration of the above, and insofar as the African continent is concerned, the seeming tension between sovereignty and intervention has stymied the deepening of regionalism and integration. For instance, the case of disbandment of the SADC Tribunal in 2011 after Zimbabwe rejected the rulings of the Tribunal on land-related disputes highlighted this. While states may agree to form and/or join intergovernmental organisations, they are often resistant to substantive integration, especially political integration. A consummate analysis of the disagreements that existed among African nationalist leaders in the 1950s and 1960s on the question of integration would reveal that they diverged most on the question of political integration, not necessarily on economic and social integration. Thus, the possibility of enhancing and deepening economic integration is real and limitless.

Conclusion

This chapter examined the historical events, processes and figures that provided the ideological basis of integration in Africa. It argued that colonialism and its antithesis, liberation, was the setting within which African nationalist leaders developed political thought that projected the unity and integration of Africa as pivotal for the eradication of all forms of external domination of the continent, and for the actualisation of its potential political and economic power. Neocolonialism is able to thrive where there is poor integration, as the state retains its colonial orientation. In this sense, the end of colonialism ought not to be mistaken for complete independence – however, integration would eliminate or weaken whatever influence that erstwhile colonial power may still wield. As African states and leaders pursue the agenda of regional integration, the thinking of Cabral, Nkrumah and Touré act as a reminder that the unity of Africa is, in fact, a historical mission that the present and future generations must take all steps possible to achieve.

Pan-Africanism remains an appealing ideology in Africa and African leaders continue to use it to rally the people of the continent to unite and embrace integration. Continental and subregional initiatives, such as the African Union's Agenda 2063 and the free trade area programmes of the RECs, indicate that Africa is marching towards integration. Just as the forefathers of Pan-Africanism in Africa recognised, recent and present African leaders appreciate that the integration of the continent, especially the social and economic aspects of it, holds significant potential to transform Africa from being the least developed continent to a thriving one. However, full political integration characterised by a substantive transference of national sovereign privileges to a supranational authority would be difficult, if not impossible, to achieve, at least in the foreseeable future. Nonetheless, a united position on issues of international relations and a mutually shared determination and political will by African states to address some of the security challenges that confront the continent would be sufficient, on the more political side of regional integration.

References

Africa News. 2020/05/21. 'France ratifies law officially ending 75 years of West Africa CFA', *Africa News*. Available at: https://www.africanews.

com/2020/05/21/france-ratifies-law-officially-ending-75-years-of-west-africa-cfa// (Accessed 21 November 2021).

Ahmad, A. (1973). 'Thought of Amilcar Cabral', *Pakistan Forum*, 3(5): 8–10.

Asare-Nuamah, P. (2017). 'Understanding African integration from African perspective', *Ethiopian e-Journal for Research and Innovation Foresight (Ee-JRIF)*, 9(2): Research on Challenges on African Integration. Available at: https://journals.bdu.edu.et/index.php/eejrif4/article/view/224/0 (Accessed 21 November 2021).

African Union (AU). (n.d.) 'Speeches and statements made at the first Organisation of African Unity (O.A.U.) summit'. Available at: https://au.int/sites/default/files/speeches/38532-sp-oau_summit_may_1963_speeches.pdf (Accessed 21 November 2021).

Chabal, P. (1981). 'The social and political thought of Amilcar Cabral: Reassessment', *Journal of Modern African Studies*, 19(1): 31–56.

Deng, F. (1993). 'Africa and the New World dis-order: Rethinking colonial borders', *The Brookings Review*, 11(2): 32–35.

Donham, D. (1999). *History, Power, Ideology: Central issues in Marxism and anthropology*. Berkely, CA: University of California Press.

Eagleton, T. (1994). *Ideology*. New York: Longman.

Ezeoha, A. and Uche, C.U. (2005). *South Africa, NEPAD and the African Renaissance*. ASC Working Paper Series No. 64. Available at: https://hdl.handle.net/1887/4648 (Accessed 21 November 2021).

Feagin, J. (2006). *Systemic Racism: A theory of oppression*. New York: Routledge.

Hawkes, D. (2003). *Ideology*, 2nd edition. London: Routledge.

Ives, P. (2004). *Language and Hegemony in Gramsci*. London: Pluto Press.

Jackson, R. and Rosberg, C. (1982). 'Why Africa's weak states persist: The empirical and the juridical in statehood', *World Politics*, 35(1): 1–24.

Johnson, M. (2012). *Everything You Need to Know about Political Ideology*. Newmarket, ON: BrainMass Inc.

Jones, B. (2002). 'Economic integration and convergence of per capita income in West Africa', *African Development Review*, 14(1): 18–47.

Kloman, E. (1962). 'African Unification Movements', *International Organisation*, 16(2): 387–404.

Kouassi, R. (2007). 'The itinerary of the African integration process: An overview of the historical landmarks', *African Integration Review*, 1(2): 1–23.

Makgetlaneng, S. (2011). *Kwame Nkrumah and the Complex Continental Agenda: A critical analysis*. AISA Occasional Paper No. 12. Pretoria: Africa Institute of Africa.

New African. (2013). '"We must unite now or perish' – President Kwame Nkrumah', *New African*. Available at: https://www.newafricanmagazine.com/3721/ (Accessed 21 October 2022).

Nkrumah, K. (1965). *Neo-Colonialism: The last stage of imperialism*. London: Thomas Nelson & Sons.

Nkrumah, K. (1963). *Africa Must Unite*. New York: Frederick A. Paeger.

Organisation of African Unity (OAU). (1963). 'OAU Charter'. Available at: https://au.int/sites/default/files/treaties/7759-file-oau_charter_1963.pdf (Accessed 24 October 2022).

Rabaka, R. (2014). *Concepts of Cabralism: Amilcar Cabral and Africana Critical Theory*. Lanham, MD: Lexington Books.

Schimmelfennig, F. (2014). 'European integration in the Euro crisis: The limits of postfunctionalism', *Journal of European Integration*, 36(3): 321–37.

Schwarzmantel, J. (2008). *Ideology and Politics*. London: SAGE Publications.

Smith, A.W. and Jeppesen, C. (eds). (2017). *Britain, France and the Decolonization of Africa: Future imperfect?* London: UCL Press.

Söderbaum, F. (2004). 'Modes of regional governance in Africa: Neoliberalism, sovereignty boosting, and shadow networks', *Global Governance*, 10(4): 419–36.

Taylor, I. (2019). 'France à fric: The CFA zone in Africa and neocolonialism', *Third World Quarterly*, 40 (6): 1064–88. https://doi.org/10.1080/01436597.2019.1585183

Touré, S. (1962). 'Africa's future and the world', *Foreign Affairs*, 41(1): 141–52.

Chapter Three
African lingua francas and African knowledge systems: A framework for regional integration
MUXE NKONDO

Introduction

This chapter explains the rationale behind the integration of African lingua francas and knowledge systems in regional integration processes. It describes the various dimensions of regional integration in order to review the various forms of integration, consider their dynamic nature and relate these to contingent circumstances. The assumption behind regional integration is that decision-making is based on mutual benefit and mutual recognition, and that it seeks to maximise complementary differences and minimise conflict; but in the real world these assumptions may not be justifiable. It would probably be more productive when discussing the rationale and strategy for regional integration to move away from simple alternatives, such as decentralisation or centralisation, since these dichotomies do not capture the fluid but clear objective of regional integration, so as to get dispersed activities, such as disaggregated departments and diplomacy units, to work together. The configuration and coordination of the activities of regional institutional arrangements is a more daunting and complex task than it is on a purely national scale. However, implicit in the concept of regional integration is the wide range of options and choices of contingencies compared to those available to a national department. This calls for strategic flexibility when it comes to planning.

This chapter has three interrelated objectives: to examine the concept of regional integration and its implications for Pan-Africanism; to elucidate and elaborate on the concepts of African lingua francas and epistemic complementarity; and to reflect on the key social and political issues for Pan-Africanism posed by regional integration.

However, certain factors have to be considered. Governments will only buy into the concept of the regional integration of African lingua francas and knowledge systems if they believe this would help them to achieve greater efficiency, manage risk or enable innovation and learning. The relationships between the various governments and how they manage this integration are critical to its success. This will determine what activities should be carried out in each state and which would need to be coordinated and controlled in order to become efficient integrative structures in a region that is becoming increasingly globalised.

I consider regional integration as a historical process, which involves the widening and deepening of continent-wide interconnectedness, and consider its potential impact and implications for Pan-Africanism. This process is highly uneven, however, and far from implying the evolution of a more cooperative continent, it has the potential to generate powerful sources of tension, conflict and fragmentation. This is why I explore how transformation could be brought about by the integration of African knowledge systems and the promotion of African lingua francas. These two forces could bring about a conceptual shift in our thinking, which is required to grasp the nature of the envisaged changes. This conceptual shift involves embracing the idea of African lingua francas and knowledge systems – the politics of epistemic diversity and complementarity – as being integral to regional relations and diplomacy. In this process, many of the traditional assumptions about language policy and knowledge would require rethinking since power would no longer be organised along Eurocentric lines. Furthermore, the persistence of Western hegemony has created a distorted African politics in which the interests of the few more often than not take precedence over the interests of the majority. Whether a more just and democratic regional politics can be fashioned out of contemporary regional conditions is a matter of intense debate among development economists, diplomats and activists alike.

Regional integration – simply the widening, deepening and speeding up of Pan-African interconnections – is a coordination issue involving the management of regional politics. Some argue that it will bring about the demise of the sovereign nation state as regional and global forces undermine the ability of governments to control their own economies. They argue that states and geopolitics remain the principal forces shaping the regional and global order (Gilpin, 2001). This chapter takes a rather different approach – an integrative perspective – arguing that regional integration would lead not so much to the demise of the sovereign state but to the regionalisation of African politics, where the traditional distinction between national and regional affairs is no longer valid. Understanding these conditions, politics in a nation-state, it would seem, are related to politics everywhere in the region such that orthodox approaches to the management of the regional relations – which are constructed on this very distinction – provide at best only a partial insight into the real nature of the functioning of the current regional and global order.

Framing regional integration in Ubuntu principles

This chapter is a practical initiative aimed at framing regional integration in ubuntu principles. Ubuntu provides a powerful normative impetus to take the ideals of mutual recognition, and responsibility to and for the other, seriously, to mobilise social cohesion and solidarity in a world of differences. Ubuntu offers a better alternative to the current liberal capitalist tradition, grounded in individualism and competition, by ensuring that policy aims are tested for their impact on the actual lives of people (Nkondo, 2007). Ubuntu philosophy is optimistic at its core, supplying the impetus for fundamental change and development in social, economic and political relations. This could be achieved by reshaping the malleable aspects of the human psyche in accordance with universally justifiable Ubuntu values.

African governments will face greater challenges as a result of deepening poverty, widening unemployment, enduring inequality, systemic and subjective violence against women, and the global flow of capitalist forces. To enhance regional integration and solidarity and achieve Agenda 2063: The Africa We Want, concerted efforts must be taken to integrate Ubuntu principles into national, regional and global development plans to facilitate development programmes. This imperative encompasses the following critical thrusts:

- Building caring and cohesive communities within and across state borders; recognising the humanity of the other, and deepening our understanding of being human and our reverence for life;
- Developing an economic order based on the eradication of Western hegemony and eliminating structural inequalities; pursuing a regional policy that inculcates the love and feeling for the continent as a home, and setting out regional integration as the condition in which caring for and about others arises as an ethical imperative – and doing this by grounding policy and legislation in an indigenous African philosophy.

This Ubuntu imperative incorporates the critical thrusts of previous Pan-African strategies, namely, Back-to-Africa, Africa Unite, negritude, indigeneity, back to basics, authenticity, African socialism, African humanism, Ujaama, return-to-roots, Black Consciousness and the African Renaissance. This would lead to innovative public reasoning, which will have significant implications for diplomacy and interstate relations. Fortunately, Ubuntu is not limited to Africa, but has become important in most discourses on human relations the world over (Ricouer, 1990). Thus, it is a critical resource for the African Union, which is grappling to find African solutions to African problems as the foundation of freedom and justice.

Accordingly, I examine and interrogate the dominance of Western languages and knowledge systems in interstate relations in Africa. The focus is on the epistemological, social and ethical underpinnings, and the attendant regional relations policy and political consequences of the Eurocentric approach to the interrelated areas of current concern in decolonisation discourse, namely, the reliance on Western languages as lingua francas in Africa, and the hegemony of Western science and technology. My argument about the vital importance of African lingua francas and knowledge systems in the integration of the various nation states that it:

- is guided by the objective to focus policy on the complex relationship between language, knowledge, power and ethics;
- appreciates the need to provide a critical overview of the limitations of Western hegemonic approaches, replacing them with fundamentally transformative ways of knowing and doing;
- notes that linguistic and cognitive justice has been at the core of the decolonisation discourse since the 1950s, a field of study that has always

taken stances in support of linguistic and epistemic diversity, and has worked in solidarity with Pan-Africanism to overcome linguistic and epistemic inequalities;

- recognises the deeply rooted nature of these inequalities in African political economies, as well as the need to develop a more responsive understanding of the intricate relationship between language, knowledge systems and power;

- recognises, further, the need to shift away from the idea of knowledge systems and languages as bounded and separate objects, towards languaging and knowledging as indeterminate processes that are constantly in motion and continually becoming something else, with the aim of opening up spaces for the legitimation of new subjectivities and inter-subjectivities;

- realises the importance of revealing how the investigation of linguistic and epistemic systems in regional politics enables us to gain a deeper understanding of the origins and the foundations of social and economic inequality in Africa, and so define linguistic and knowledge systems as key resources that, under certain political conditions, can be exchanged for other symbolic or material resources;

- realises, further, how language and knowledge systems have become instrumental in the regulation of an individual's access to the production and consumption of resources, and how language and knowledge systems are evaluated, as well as the logics and technologies regulating an individual's access to resources, where a price is placed on language and knowledge systems;

- is mindful of the fact that concern about the importance of language and knowledge system entails a problematisation of the consequences of the language and the knowledge system we use, mediated through communication and cognition, and the costs implied in terms of who benefits or loses from the various forms of knowledge and language, and so argue for an increased reflection on the effect that language and knowledge systems have under current political, social and economic conditions, and how they nourish and authorise those practices that allow forms of linguistic and epistemic difference to be viewed as appropriate, and thus become invisible; and

- draws lessons about the integrative power of African lingua francas from the Swahili experience.

Functions of African lingua francas and knowledge systems in regional integration policies and practices

There are so many functions and contexts of African lingua francas and knowledge systems that cataloguing them is daunting. How can we make use of this diversity? These functions appear to range from the individual (a strong sense of identity can affect the way we feel and the way we relate to others and manage our lives) to the social (they can facilitate the coordination of large numbers of people and help to forge a sense of collective identity). They also cover a vast middle ground in which relationships between the self and the other or between the individual and the collective are played out. In addition, they contribute to the continuity and stability of cultures, as well as to the resilience of societies. The individual is implicated in the social and the social in the personal, and a strong sense of identity provides, in this case, a tool for negotiating and mediating regional integration across the continent. These functions cannot be reduced to one: it is not simply that one is incapable of specifying the functions of a strong sense of identity; a sense of self depends for its efficacy on the indeterminacy of its functions and value.

Since the concept of regional integration, in current discourses, functions as a metonym of Pan-Africanism, we should think of Africa as a community of meanings, a social and political imaginary, in the rich web of human relations. By social and political imaginary, I mean the normative order underlying African political society, derived from the nature of its constitutive members. People are rational, sociable agents who are meant to collaborate in peace to their mutual benefit. Starting from ancient, precolonial times, this idea has come more and more to dominate our political thinking, and the way in which we imagine our society, what it is in aid of and how it came to be. It offers an idea of moral order, and tells us how we ought to live together in society. It stresses the obligations and responsibilities we have as individuals towards one another (Mudimbe, 1988; Nabudere, 2011).

Political authority itself is legitimate only because it was consented to by individuals (the original social contract), and this contract creates binding obligations and responsibilities by virtue of the pre-existing principle that obligations have to be met (Taylor, 2007). Thus, whatever its 'truth' in terms of its scientific validity, it is through its discursive operations that the social and political imaginary gives meaning to Pan-Africanism and makes sense to regional integration. It constructs a regional order of intelligibility, provides an archaeology of values and principles, organises our social, economic and political practices within the region and, thus, has come to acquire real social and political significance (Foucault, 1972; 1980).

This affirmation of African languages and knowledge systems signals a break with the discourse of Western hegemony against which liberation struggles were predicated. Through this, Western languages and knowledge systems are seriously dislocated and put permanently 'under African eyes', by the discourse on African languages as languages of knowledge, and African knowledge systems as science and technology grounded in the principles of probability and verification (Wolfreys, 2004; Ndlovu-Gatsheni, 2018).

The capabilities approach: The pragmatic turn

In light of this, I explore a set of interrelated ideas concerning the foundations and the possibilities of African lingua francas and knowledge management systems in a multicultural, multilingual and polyepistemic world, and in particular about the assessment of their capacity to advance a person's capability to function in the Fourth Industrial Revolution. In other words, I explore what a person can do or can be as a direct result of a strong sense of African capabilities, and argue against the more standard concentration on authenticity (as in prevalent Afrocentric formulations). Insofar as authenticity has a role (and it certainly does), this can be seen in terms of its direct connection to happiness and wellbeing; in particular, the political importance of authenticity and, second, the socio-psychological importance of authenticity (in its various forms, such as self-pride, personal dignity and integrity).

The current discourse on 'Africanness' is concerned with culture and identity. The capabilities approach investigates how Africans, through African languages and knowledge systems, are able to make commodities, how they are able to establish command over commodities, and what they get out of these commodities. The determination of whether a person would be better off supplied with all the resources of African lingua francas and knowledge systems is the starting point of this investigation into the power and political economy of African epistemology in our time.

Different approaches can be used to assess the possibilities of a particular cultural, linguistic and knowledge system in the knowledge economy: is a person better off as a result? Can this person compete successfully with others using different cultural, linguistic and knowledge systems? These distinct questions provide an interesting focus on current and future challenges facing Pan-Africanism. The discourse on Africanness has tended to eschew the distinctions implied in these questions and make do with a limited assessment of African heritage. The terms 'happiness', 'wellbeing' and 'advantage' do, of course, have a range of meanings, defined by both neoliberal and development economists. They are used here in the sense in which Amartya Sen uses them – quite rigorously – in his monograph, *Commodities and Capabilities:*

> 'Well-being' is concerned with a person's achievement: how 'well' is his or her 'being'? 'Advantage' refers to the real opportunities that the person has, especially compared with others. The opportunities are not judged only by the results achieved, and therefore not just by the level of well-being achieved. It is possible for a person to have genuine advantage and still to 'muff' them. Or to sacrifice one's freedom to achieve a high level of well-being. The notion of advantage deals with a person's real opportunities compared with others. The freedom to achieve well-being is closer to the notion of advantage than well-being itself (Sen, 1999).

The example of Swahili as a lingua franca

The major challenge is how to deal with a multiplicity of languages and has created problems for interstate relations in Africa. Because of this, we have been forced to use Western languages – English, French, German and Portuguese – as lingua francas.

In what ways can Swahili provide us with an interesting case study of a lingua franca? Fortunately, the history of Swahili – as it moved from North Africa through East Africa to Central Africa – points to opportunities and possibilities in the development of African lingua francas in other parts of the continent (Alexander, 2015).

What has been the impact of Swahili literacy in regional relations? What are its distinguishing features as a lingua franca? How have governments, civil society and markets worked together, sharing responsibilities and using a common language? How has it affected the way in which people in those regions relate to one another? Would this help to erase the sense that African languages are bounded and territorialised entities, which the West has used to categorise and divide people and communities, and impose a Eurocentric hegemonic order?

The concept of African lingua francas is potentially a powerful regional integrative force. A regional, African language commons would be a shared pasture, a regional language learning site inscribed concretely as a social, political and ethical coordinate of an alternative, fundamentally transformative, interstate order. An African lingua franca commons would not be a narrow, exclusive space for an inner circle – for 'sons and daughters of the soil' or for members only narrowly conceived – it would be a linguistically and politically produced space of an inner, responsive, hospitable disposition to difference. A sense of transnational, transterritorial citizenship could then be inculcated and so expand the site of Pan-African solidarity. This could stabilise our understanding of ourselves as belonging together, brought together by the contingency of history and geography. An African-language commons would allow us to insert ourselves into discourses on Pan-Africanism and decolonisation: this undertaking could be ensured by tracing and watching Swahili as it moves across time and place. The use of Swahili as a case study is experimental and pragmatic in the sense that we seek to bring regional integration into the space of diplomacy and interstate relations. It serves to explore concrete trajectories through which regional integration could be negotiated and mediated.

On the premise that language has the power to make and remake worlds, the African Union should follow Swahili in motion to highlight the possibility of using African languages as lingua francas to ground regional integration in a common language. This approach is consciously empirical and experimental, in that in rigorously developing African lingua francas across state borders, it would mobilise, at ground-level, mutual recognition and solidarity. There is no better guide than Swahili of how lingua francas could be used as a resource for regional integration and, in the process, demonstrate the political and social power of language (Gluck and Tsing, 2009). Lessons could also be drawn from how African languages have functioned in other environments – in migration, urbanisation, cosmopolitisation and in the diaspora (Gluck and Tsing k, 2009; May, 2017; Ndlovu, 2017).

The standard ideological framework that came with industrialisation, over and above the imposition of the Eurocentric state system, makes the development of African lingua francas urgent and necessary. The idea of promoting African lingua francas challenges the basic tenets that have informed language policy, even beyond the demise of colonialism in its overt structural forms. Instead, it assumes a post-structuralist perspective that questions colonial definitions of African languages and speech communities, revealing the sociopolitical context that led to the misleading, yet dominant, socio-linguistic concepts and, instead, offers a framework for the development of African lingua francas. Neville Alexander's work on the possibilities of an African lingua franca in South Africa is illuminating (Alexander, 2015).

The education of Ubuntu and the advantage of pragmatism

Much of the scholarship around African languages and knowledge systems has focused on the philosophical, cultural and psychological aspects of language and knowledge, rather than a pragmatic consideration of the ways in which language and knowledge systems can be used within particular social, economic and political contexts (Nabudere, 2011). Being pragmatic in the discourse on linguistic and epistemic systems means, in this instance, assessing how African languages and knowledge systems can function in interstate relations in Africa. To address this question, we need to develop a practical and analytical framework that helps us to assess the capabilities of African languages and knowledge systems in the concrete business of addressing existential needs, such as food and health security, comfortable accommodation, communication, reliable and affordable public transport, free quality education for the poor, and so on. In this way, African languages and knowledge systems become tools that we could use to make things happen in our lives (Rorty, 1989; Morris, 2013).

One way of coming to terms with regional integration could be by patiently working through the hegemonic Eurocentric language policy and epistemology. As indicated earlier, this has to do with the recognition of the strategic political importance of African lingua francas and knowledge systems – their capabilities. Following on from this is the acknowledgement of the question of complementary differences and equivalences before any political account. What are the specific capabilities of African lingua francas and knowledge systems? This would be a significant improvement on the Western approach, and would help to construct a template for governments on the complementary possibilities of African lingua francas and knowledge systems.

As a first step, we have to expose a number of conceptual confusions. We have to demonstrate, in analytical detail, the interpenetration of reason, the body and the imagination in African design, crafts, art and agro-processing. Western philosophers and social scientists have a deep-rooted difficulty in comprehending the creative process that characterises the work of African scientists and technologists, embodied in African languages. They have failed to comprehend the intimate connections between hand and head. Every African scientist, builder, artist, chef, musical instrument maker, and so on, conducts a dialogue between perception and reason, fact and imagination, analysis and justification, and these habits establish a rhythm between problem-identification and problem-solving. Western scholarship on African science and technology drew fault lines between practice and theory, technique and process, technique and expression, crafts and art, and maker and user, and we still suffer from this historical inheritance (Sennett, 2008).

What the capabilities approach calls for is a complex, many-levelled struggle – intellectual, social and political – in which the debates about the language of science and technology interlink with those in a host of political, social and economic institutional settings. One such feature is that the issues of enframing science, technology and African languages are being lived through in concrete forms. Another feature is that these disputes, in turn, feed on and are fed by various attempts to define, in theoretical and practical terms, the place of African languages in science and technology and the demands of an integrated multilinguistic and inter-epistemic epistemology and, beyond this, the shape of curricula and pedagogy and their relation to democratic politics.

This would serve to eradicate the Eurocentric disconnection of linguistic and knowledge systems, which kills the vitality of our inter-epistemic, multicultural and multilingual world. This is not just a hypothetical undertaking. Some information and knowledge institutions spend a major portion of their time exploring possibilities: libraries, archives, museums, innovation hubs, and research institutes are developing systems for organising the knowledge of the world so that people have a wide frame of reference. What they are doing is opening a new system of more flexible epistemic identities, structures and functions.

Encounters with African lingua francas and knowledge systems in concrete environments

In an inter-epistemic, multilingual system, diplomacy would involve a community of shared capabilities, with the ultimate purpose of gaining and constructing shared meanings, generated from a multiplicity of linguistic knowledge systems. It would be the application of the inter-epistemic, multivocal intelligence and imagination to social and economic realities – a shift from the bounded, territorialised epistemology. The hegemonic model has failed to make full use of the complementary capabilities across various linguistic knowledge systems. Once the inter-epistemic mode of addressing social and economic problems occurs in diplomatic settings, classrooms, workplaces and markets, regional integration is concretised and institutionalised in the process. It is correct, therefore, to assert that the inter-epistemic and African lingua francas practices have to be enacted to be experienced, encountered in particular places and moments. This will serve to make inter-epistemicism and African lingua francas less abstract. Gradually, deliberately, people will begin to question the familiar Eurocentric paradigm. Without realising it, they will enact regional integration, moving from antagonistic to supplementary difference. This is decolonisation and Pan-Africanism in their dramatic form. The encounter with African lingua francas and knowledge systems across state borders would be a shortcut, a social and political education strategy, that governments could rely on, and it could be a brilliantly effective device for regional integration learning – often when the very status of Western languages and knowledge systems is questioned.

Challenges of regional integration

The fact that human experiential space, in Africa and elsewhere in the world, is being subtly changed through globalisation should not lead us to assume that we are all becoming globalised citizens. Even the most positive conceivable development and transformation – an erosion of frontiers and borders between cultural horizons and a growing sensitivity towards unfamiliar geographies of life and mutual recognition – does not necessarily demand a sense of global responsibility. The question of how such a sense might become a possibility, with all its implications for Pan-Africanism, has been investigated in-depth.

Africa is failing, and crises in global politics and Pan-African relations have only recently begun to be explored in the literature. There is a forced migration crisis in Africa, with people moving around the continent in unprecedented numbers, driven by hunger, poverty and conflict. There is an environmental crisis, and climate change is merely the most widely debated aspect of this (Jonas, 1984). There is a crisis in human rights with some governments unwilling to honour human dignity and justice. There is also the clash of beliefs, faiths and political ideologies, which raise regional and global tensions (Huntington, 1996; Caputo, 2001). Because of globalisation, African governments have a part to play in addressing problems of regional and global governance, the maintenance of peace, intercultural tolerance, and mutual recognition and respect. Accordingly, we need to develop a regional and global ethics through which governments can articulate and exercise their regional and global responsibilities. The aim of this chapter is to suggest a normative framework for resolving complex issues of regional and global governance, which require the creation and management of international law through bodies such as the African Union and the United Nations.

Communication networks have become so immediate that events anywhere in the region and the world can be brought into our living rooms as they happen. As a result of the media, many brands are also recognisable all over the world, and there is a growing realisation that we live in a regional and world community. We are citizens of specific nation-states, but we are also citizens of the continent and the world. We should be concerned not only for our compatriots, but also for all human beings, especially those on the margins, suffering from poverty, unemployment, socioeconomic inequality and gender-based violence. What I hope will emerge from this is a fully articulated conception of the politics, economics and ethics of regional integration in the global context (Singer, 1981; Amstutz, 1999; Gaita, 1999; Van Hooft, 2009).

Regional integration is a demanding and contentious political and moral position that urges us to include the whole continent in our social, economic, political and moral concerns, to apply the standards of mutual recognition, obligation and solidarity across territorial and cultural boundaries. It is a case for transnational, trans-territorial citizenship in a world of differences and contradictions.

The challenge of nationalism

Nationalism – as both an ideology and social movement – has been one of the formative processes of Africa as we know it today. This has many implications for regional integration. Regional integration creates a market for the flow of goods, but it also provokes responses and resistance from those who feel that their interests are threatened, which is often the case in cross-border conflicts and xenophobia. Nationalism can also be a product of regional integration and globalisation, and the link between nationalism and the modern international state systems is more than historical. It is also normative, in other words, it is also concerned with values, with ideas of how people should live and to whom they owe allegiance. Nationalism has been spreading across the continent and the world, and it has become the main justifying or legitimising doctrine of the international state system.

Prior to the modern period, borders in Africa were justified by allegiance and reference to royal leaders and their dynasties. The spread of nationalism has removed this justification, however, and produced a system in which states are justified on the grounds that they represent their peoples. There is also the principle of the sovereignty of the people, citizenship and self-determination, according to which every nation has the right to decide its own fate, to be independent or, if it chooses, to be part of a happy state. Nationalism has become the ethical basis of regional and international relations, so much so that the international body grouping of the states in the world is called the United Nations, and the one in Africa is called the African Union. Nationalism is now the political basis of nation states and the international state system (Halliday, 2001).

Globalisation brings into sharp focus the centrality of managing regional integration. The problems presented by integration are as pervasive as they are challenging. Governments are confronted by new bases of working together, the redefinition of regional relations, and the establishment of innovative practices. While globalisation and new technologies offer a platform for new ways of communication and interaction, they have also led to the redrawing of diplomatic maps and the abandonment of long-established protocols: change and speed have become the watchwords of the era. Governments have to be ready at all times to respond to the challenges. The ability to handle the implications of such disturbance is highly prized, at the level of both government and the African Union. However, there is a concern about the lack of regional organisational skills, as well as leadership and management competencies. The focus is on facilitation rather than a common, centralised control approach because the essential problem arises from the non-linear nature of regional integration. The entire process is resistant to centralised control and categorisations, rooted as these are in the Eurocentric hegemonic attitude and practice.

One thing that the African Union has to acknowledge, however, is the manifold forms of resistance that often accompany such radical policy shifts. Eurocentric organisations, fearful of losing their current power and influence, will try to subvert the development of lingua francas and the integration of African knowledge systems. As always, they will attempt to block this change, most likely through indirect methods. This calls for vigilant management. The more regionally integrated these operations are, or the more important they are to regional integration needs, the greater the need for vigilant, flexible and adaptive organisation and management. According to contingency theory, knowing how contingencies and structures fit together provides the organisation with firm rules for structural design (Milgrom and Roberts, 1995; Stopford and Wells, 1995; Pettigrew et al., 2002).

Whether from the point of contingencies or configurations, the basic takeaway is clear: flexible management of the web of factors will be key. Organisational structure will be the key element in the AU's tool kit. Without the right structure, regional integration will fail – but there is no categorical model. It will take leadership and managerial judgement, always appreciating the changing contingencies over time. Addressing the dynamics of the structure should be high on the agenda of the African Union (Whittington, 2003).

The institutional and structural approach to regional integration in the era of globalisation is very much of its time and place. Dissatisfaction with simplistic Pan-African recipes containing crude monitoring and evaluation criteria – which have assumed a sizeable scope since the establishment of the African Union – stimulates a search for more nuanced approaches. This opens a space for revelatory diagnosis, followed by design proposals. There is also the realisation that the social and political construction of appropriate institutional arrangements has to be acknowledged through acceptance of the structured nature of interstate relations.

Institutional reconfiguration also offers a degree of certitude to governments, civil society and corporations faced with a rapidly changing environment, and provides for comparison in assessing national and regional capabilities in a globalising marketplace. This would enhance reciprocity in interstate relations, and help to deal with power asymmetries between states. Interstate networks may help to deal with problems of equity, which make it difficult to mobilise power. They would also serve to coordinate interstate relations, in which every state will have to work within 'the rules of the game', but the need for a regional institutional framework is paramount to enable regional relations and diplomacy to be developed. Once in place, the embeddedness of institutional patterns of behaviour within complex independent nation states, and within individuals and communities sharing the same institutional field, will tend to ensure continuity and coherence in approach (Loveridge, 2003; Tolbert, 1996; Powell and Maggio, 1991).

The plan to adopt Ubuntu as a normative framework for regional integration will force some of the malaises of postcolonial African culture. The first concern is with the effects of the corporate system of African culture, of values and outlooks, on 'the ways of life'. By 'incorporation' is meant a more general process of change – the reorganisation of perceptions, as well as of enterprise and institutions; not only the expansion of an industrial system across the continent, or systems of transport and communication, or the spread of the market economy into all regions of African society, but also, and even predominantly, the remaking of cultural perceptions that this process entails. The real project is to educate citizens, who will champion Ubuntu values and the full development of intellectual, social and ethical capabilities, and who will have the disposition for a symbolic existence across differences and borders to solve pressing social, economic and political problems.

A related concern is individualism, of course. Individualism is the value that the Western-educated African elite consider the finest achievement of liberal democracy. We live in societies where people have a right to choose their own way of life, to decide in good conscience what beliefs to espouse, and to determine the form and direction of their lives in a whole host of ways their colonial forbears couldn't control. What complicates matters more is the primacy of instrumental reason that has emerged over time. Now, African educational institutions are preoccupied with producing and transmitting exploitable technical knowledge, not grounded in ethics. But Ubuntu education seeks to ensure that students are equipped with qualifications in the area of social competencies and extra-functional abilities. In this connection, extra-functional refers to all the competencies and attitudes relevant to the pursuit of holistic education in a democratic society, which are not contained per se in exploitable technical knowledge.

There is also the problem of cynicism and the decline in public trust and confidence. We do not know which buttons to push, in our cynical and sceptical consciousness, to get regional integration going. Current cynicism and public distrust present themselves as that of consciousness and sensibility that follows after a naive nationalism and Pan-Africanism. Regional integration, based on Ubuntu, seeks to facilitate the sort of development that has, in fact, occurred since independence – a Pan-African consciousness and trans-territorial citizenship. It emphasises respect for an empathic imagination, the common core of humanity, as the only motive that is not empirical nor contingent or dependent on the vagaries of history.

Concern about the vibrancy and governability of Pan-Africanism is evident in incessant strikes, border wars and contested sovereignties. A cynical perception has emerged that in Africa, the more laws there are, the greater the disorder (Comaroff and Comaroff, 2006; Oluwu, 2012). What's more, the material and political culture in African states presupposes the exploitation of the masses. The purity of liberal democratic principles not only tolerates but also requires systemic violence. Thus, there seems to be a mystification in liberal democracy. Judging from events across the continent in recent years, ideas and practices of liberal democracy belong to a system of violence, of which it could be said, they are the general basis of justification (Merleau-Ponty, 1967; Thompson, 1987; Rawls, 1995; Sennett, 1998; Bird, 1999; Seabrook, 2004; Žižek, 2010; Kotz, 2017; Grayling, 2018; Deneen, 2018).

The internet and social media: Possibilities and opportunities

The potential role that the internet and social media could play in promoting regional integration is enormous. We are actually on the cusp of something exhilarating. Every day, regional integration messages could be propped up on phone screens and passed on to others. This could become empowering and integrative. The internet could ignite debate across borders like never before and decision-making could gradually shift into the hands of more people.

The future of regional integration looks bright – and it could flicker into life in far-flung communities across interstate borders. This would happen if there was a common purpose and an instinctive understanding that everyone matters. The internet and social media would enable people to be more informed: the click of a button would throw up information that previously took time and energy to discover. This would help to operationalise direct inclusive democracy in real time. Public ignorance and fake news are around, but the difference today is the internet's capacity to provide 'alternative facts', to an extent that was not possible before.

The possibilities of direct democracy are not to be taken lightly. The internet has the capacity to distribute power to the people on the ground and this will weaponise them. The internet and social media are not perfect, so it follows that regional integration will always be imperfect. But if governments, the private sector and people rally around the internet as a force for the creation of democratic institutions across borders and at all levels of society, regional integration is possible (Scott, 2019).

References

Alexander, N. (2015). 'History, politics, and the language question', *South African Journal of* Science, 111(7-8): 1–2. http://dx.doi.org/10.17159/SAJS.2015/A0113

Amstutz, M.R. (1999). *International Ethics: Concepts, theories, and cases in global politics.* Lanham, MD: Rowman and Littlefield.

Bird, C. (1999). *The Myth of Liberal Individualism.* Cambridge: Cambridge University Press.

Caputo, J.D. (2001). *On Religion.* London: Routledge.

Comaroff, J. and Comaroff, J. (eds). (2006). *Law and Disorder in the Postcolony.* Chicago, IL: Chicago University Press.

Deneen, P.J. (2018). *Why Liberalism Failed.* New Haven, CT. Yale University Press.

Foucault, M. (1980). *Power/Knowledge: Selected interviews and other writings, 1972–79.* (Ed. C. Gordon). New York: Pantheon Books.

Foucault, M. (1972). *The Archaeology of Knowledge.* Trans. A.M. Sheridan Smith. London: Travistock.

Gaita, R. (1999). *A Common Humanity: Thinking about love and truth and justice.* Melbourne: Text Publishing.

Gilpin, R. (2001). *Global political economy: Understanding the international economic order*. New Jersey: Princeton university press.

Gluck, C. and Tsing, A.L. (eds). (2009). *Words in Motion: Toward a global lexicon*. Durham, NC: Duke University Press.

Grayling, A.C. (2017). *Democracy and its Critics*. London: Oneworld Publications.

Halliday, F. (2001). 'Nationalism', in J. Baylis and S. Smith (eds). *The Globalisation of World Politics: An introduction to international relations*. Oxford: Oxford University Press: 521–38.

Huntington, S.P. (1996). *The Clash of Civilisations and the Remaking of World Order*. New York: Simon and Schuster.

Jonas, H. (1984). *The imperative of responsibility: In search of an ethics for the technological age*. Chicago: University of Chicago Press.

Kotz, D.M. (2017). *The Rise and Fall of Neoliberal Capitalism*. Cambridge, MA: Harvard University Press.

Loveridge, R. (2003). 'Institutional approaches to business strategy', in A. Campbell and D.O. Faulkner (eds). *The Oxford Handbook of Strategy*. Oxford: Oxford University Press, pp. 104–37.

Maloka, E. (ed.). (2001). *A United States of Africa*. Pretoria: Africa Institute of South Africa.

Marquard, D. (2004). *Decline of the Public: The hollowing out of citizenship*. Cambridge: Polity Press/Wiley.

Marx, K. and Engels, F. (1974). *The German Ideology*. London: Lawrence and Wishart.

May, S. (2017). 'Language, Imperialism, and the Modern Nation-State System: Implications for Language Rights'.

Merleau-Ponty, M. (1967). *Humanism and Terror: An essay on the Communist problem* (Trans. John O'Neill). Boston, MA: Beacon Press.

Milgrom, P. and Roberts, J. (1995). 'Complementarities and fit: Strategy, structure and organisational change in manufacturing', *Journal of Accounting and Economics*, 19: 179–208.

Morris, I. (2013). *The Measure of Civilisation: How social development decides the fate of nations*. Princeton, NJ: Princeton University Press.

Mudimbe, V.Y. (1988). *The Invention of Africa: Gnosis, Philosophy, and the Order of Knowledge*. Indiana: Indiana University Press.

Murithi, T. (2014). *Routledge Handbook of Africa. International relations*. London: Routledge.

Mutasa, C. (2018). 'The African Union's socio-economic challenges in Africa', in T. Karbo and T. Murithi (eds). *The African Union: Autocracy, diplomacy, and peacebuilding in Africa*. London: I.B. Taurus, pp. 183–204.

Nabudere, D.W. (2011). *Afrikology, philosophy and wholeness. An epistemology*. Johannesburg: Africa Institute of South Africa.

Nagar, D. and Nganje, F. (2018). 'The African Union and its relations with subregional economic communities', in T. Karbo and T. Murithi (eds). *The African Union*. London: I.B. Taurus.

Ndlovu, F. (2017). 'Language Migration, Diaspora: Challenging the Big Battalians of Groupism, in O. Garcia, N. Flores and M. Spotti (eds). *The Oxford Handbook of Language and Society*. Oxford: Oxford University Press, pp. 141–59.

Ndlovu-Gatsheni, S. (2018). *Epistemic Freedom in Africa: Deprovincialisation and decolonisation*. London: Routledge.

Nkondo, G.M. (2007). 'Ubuntu as national policy in South Africa: A conceptual framework', *International Journal of African Renaissance Studies*, 2(1): 88–100.

Oluwu, D. (2012). 'Public Administration in Africa', in B.G. Peters and J Pierre (eds). *The SAGE Handbook of Public Administration*. Thousand Oaks, CA: SAGE Publications, pp. 543–61.

Parker, M.E. and Maggio, D. (eds). (1991). *The New Institutionalism in Organizational Analysis*. Chicago, IL: University of Chicago Press.

Pettigrew, A. Whittington, R. Van Den Bosch, E. Melin, L. and Ruigrok, W. (2002). *Innovative Forms of Organising: Complementarities and dualities*. Thousand Oaks, CA: SAGE Publications.

Powell, W.W. and Maggio, P.J. (1991). *The New Institutionalism in Organisational Analysis*. Chicago, IL: University of Chicago Press.

Rawls, J. (1995). *Political Liberalism*. New York: Columbia University Press.

Ricouer, P.R. (1990). *Oneself as Another*. Chicago, IL: University of Chicago Press.

Rorty, R. (1989). *Contingency, Irony, and Solidarity*. Cambridge: Cambridge University Press.

Roy, W. G. (1997). *Socialising Capital*. Princeton, NJ: Princeton University Press.

Scott, A. and Markes, A. (2019). *Power and the People: Five lessons from the birthplace of democracy*. Riverrun.

Seabrook, J. (2004). *Consuming Cultures: Globalisation and local lives*.

Sen, A. 1999). *Development as Freedom.* New York: Random House.

Sennet, R. (1998). *The Corrosion of Character: The personal consequences of work in the new capitalism.* New York: W.W. Norton and Company.

Singer, P. (1981). *The Expanding Circle: Ethics and sociobiology.* New York: Farrar, Straus and Giroux.

Stopford, J.M. and Wells, L. (1972). *Managing the Multinational Enterprise.* London: Longman.

Taylor, C. (2007). *A Secular Age.* Cambridge, MA: Belknap Press, an Imprint of Harvard University Press.

Thompson, D.F. (1987). *Political Ethics and Public Office.* Cambridge, MA: Harvard University Press.

Tolbert, P.S. and Zucker, L.G. (1996). 'The Institutionalisation of Institutional Theory', in S.R. Clegg, C. Hardy, and W.R. Nord (eds). *Handbook of Organizational Studies.* Thousand Oaks, CA. SAGE Publications.

Van Hooft, S. (2009). *Cosmopolitanism: A philosophy for global ethics.* London: Routledge.

Whittington, R. (2003). 'Organizational structure', in A. Campbell and D. Faulkner (eds). *The Oxford Book of Strategy.* Oxford: Oxford University Press, pp. 811–40.

Wolfreys, J. (2004). *Thinking Difference: Critics in conversation.* New York: Fordham University Press.

Žižek, S. (2010). *Violence.* London: Profile Books.

PART 2

AFRICA'S REGIONAL ECONOMIC COMMUNITIES AS INSTRUMENTS OF REGIONAL INTEGRATION

Chapter Four

The Southern African Development Community's pursuit of developmental integration

SIPHAMANDLA ZONDI

Introduction

The Southern African Development Community (SADC) is regarded by some as an example of a developmental regional integration scheme because its stated primary goal is to eradicate poverty. The organisation adopted two overarching policies in the SADC's Regional Indicative Strategic Development Plan (RISDP) and the Strategic Indicative Plan for the Organ (SIPO) focused on economic and social development, both as an end in itself (RISDP) and as a means to ensure security and stability (SIPO). It also has many protocols in various policy areas of development cooperation with a potential to stimulate a high level of regional development.[1] The SADC has also tried to open policy space for civil society participation in its programmes through public participation and stakeholder engagement initiatives, such as the SADC National Committees, with a view to place citizen's well-being at the centre of the regional integration process. Even the institutional reforms that took place at the SADC in the late 1990s, and again in 2003–2004, were meant to enhance the organisation's ability to

---

1   See SADC Protocols at https://www.sadc.int/sadc-protocols

achieve its overarching goal of eradicating poverty. Therefore, these were reforms in pursuit of improving the lives of people of the region.

This integration scheme can be traced to the establishment of the Frontline States by Botswana, Lesotho, Tanzania and Zambia in 1975 to reduce their economic dependence on a hostile apartheid South Africa. This solidarity transformed in 1980 into a more institutionalised regional cooperation in the form of the Southern African Development Cooperation Conference (SADCC) when the Frontline States were joined by Lesotho, Swaziland and newly independent Zimbabwe. In 1992, the SADCC leaders decided to replace the memorandum that established the SADCC with a more formal and enforceable treaty. Thus, the organisation morphed into the SADC, established by the SADC Treaty, which made development central to integration. The SADC now included Mauritius, Madagascar and Malawi. Today, the SADC bears hallmarks of both phases of its evolution, a complex balance between political solidarity and a comprehensive agenda for developmental integration.

This chapter argues that the SADC has evolved into a particularly developmental model of regional integration by shifting its primary focus from dealing with South Africa to overcoming development challenges posed by ubiquitous poverty, underdevelopment and uneven development among southern African countries. Today, South Africa is no longer the common enemy, although concerns about its economic and political dominance in the region persist and impact the development of a regional identity. In the process, the SADC becomes an example of an evolving developmental model of regional integration, not just because it has prominent social and economic goals, but because it has, over the years, developed a comprehensive developmental agenda for the region, including trade, infrastructural development, and human development – an agenda it is yet to fully realise.

From the SADCC to the SADC: Cooperation to integration

Regional integration in southern Africa shifted in 1992 from cooperation to integration with the birth of the SADC. Regional cooperation refers to any form of working together by various countries to achieve common objectives without sacrificing their diverse individual interests (Akokpari,

2008: 87). The Frontline States Initiative and the SADCC are examples of these loose cooperative arrangements that allow pronounced nationalism to thrive. Both allowed all key decisions to be made at national capitals rather than at a shared central place.

When the SADCC was replaced by the Southern African Development Community (SADC) in 1991, the SADCC had instituted a major drive to boost food production and build a regional food reserve, liberalise agriculture and agricultural trade and enhance the regional transport infrastructure. Ironically, this progress was also an outcome of South Africa's regional destabilisation campaigns, which tended to disrupt economic activities between the country and its markets in the region, forcing regional countries to look for alternative sources of goods and services. In the process, the profile of investors in the region diversified somewhat. But South Africa's economic dominance continued with the country accounting for 30 per cent of imports in the region, while the region was the source of only 7 per cent of the country's imports by 1991 (on continued South African dominance, see Lee, 2003).

The SADCC founders appreciated that their body had helped in 'forging a regional identity and a sense of common destiny among countries and peoples of southern Africa'. This found expression in such initiatives as a regional food-security framework, transport infrastructure, the promotion of hard-core industries and services, and encouraging responsible exploitation of natural resources. The SADC built on these foundations in pursuit of an explicitly integrationist agenda. The intention to root cooperation in popular ownership was present in 1980, as expressed in the SADCC founding Lusaka Declaration of 1 April 1980 (entitled *Southern Africa: Towards economic liberation*) in which leaders called on the peoples of the region to partner with the SADCC by participating fully in its activities (SADCC, 1980). Of course, the SADCC and member states failed to provide space for people and their organisations to play a part. The SADC was bequeathed this commitment and has been trying various ways of actualising it, as we shall discuss.

The SADC was given a legal status as a regional organisation, duly mandated to represent the region in international relations in terms of international law by the SADC Treaty. Article 3 (1) of the SADC Treaty stipulated that the organisation 'shall have legal personality with capacity and power to enter into contract, acquire, own or dispose of movable or immovable property and to sue and be sued' (SADC, 1992: 5). This raised reasonable expectations that member states would cede to it sufficient sovereignty so that the organisation could be an effective international organisation (on this general expectation, see Klabbers, 2002: 41–58). The SADC Treaty established an additional sixth organ to the five that existed under the SADCC, namely, the Tribunal. This was established to help interpret the treaty, adjudicate disputes over the application of the treaty and the functioning of the organisations when political solutions fail. However, the organ has only recently started functioning properly (for a fuller discussion on this, see Oosthuizen, 2006: 71–72). The intention was clearly to move beyond loose cooperation towards a more integrated response to shared challenges of governance, security and development in the region.

The SADC and developmental integration: The substantive agenda

The SADC's vision and mission directed the organisation towards a holistic and developmental approach to regional integration. Expressly, its mission is to 'promote sustainable equitable economic growth and socio-economic development through efficient productive systems, deeper co-operation and integration, good governance and durable peace and security, so that the region emerges as a competitive and effective player in international relations'. Its overall goal is to eradicate poverty. This is to be achieved through several objectives, which include enhancing the standard and quality of life of the peoples of the region; promoting self-sustaining development and collective self-reliance; ensuring productive utilisation of natural resources; achieving complementarity between national and regional policies and strategies; and strengthening the affinities between the peoples of the region.

The guiding principles outlined are sovereign equality of member states; solidarity, peace and security; human rights, democracy and the rule of law; equity, balance and mutual benefit; and peaceful settlement of disputes. While these principles were common, the SADC did not adopt the principle of non-intervention, even though it did not support non-indifference either. But this allowed space for regional states to act decisively against violations of human rights and aggression. Of course, the SADC has only used this space sparingly, such as in the case of a military intervention to prevent a coup in Lesotho in 1997 and the support that its members provided to the beleaguered Laurent Kabila government in the Democratic Republic of the Congo (DRC).

The development content of the SADC integration is to be found in its eight priority areas of intervention, namely:

1. Food security, land and agriculture
2. Economic development and poverty alleviation
3. Infrastructure and services
4. Industry, trade, investment and finance
5. Human resource development, science and technology
6. Natural resources and environment
7. Social welfare, information and culture
8. Politics, diplomacy, international relations, peace and security.

This constitutes the SADC's development agenda, what it calls a 'common agenda'. This agenda is comprehensive and broad, covering every major area of life and normal policy areas. There was a deliberate focus on the developmental question, limiting political and security issues. This is contrary to typical market integration schemes where the focus is on narrow issues of trade and economic growth at the exclusion of matters of social development. The same could be said of regional integration initiatives that have a strong emphasis on security cooperation. In this sense, the SADC is particularly developmental in its approach to regional integration. If fully implemented, its common agenda has the potential to address the felt needs of the peoples of the region. But a comprehensive development agenda runs the risk of prioritising everything and achieving nothing because of a shortage of resources and capacity to implement these grandiose ideas and plans. This is precisely one of the major shortcomings of the SADC: implementation capacity and impact.

The broad strategies employed by the SADC in its pursuit of its mission are various. Some draw from the paradigm of market integration such as progressively eliminating tariffs and quotas; the removal of obstacles to the free movement of labour, capital and factors of production; mastery of technology and innovation; and improving economic management and performance through cooperation. The idea is to create conditions for free market activity that should help reduce poverty and underdevelopment.

Other strategies seek to deepen development through an efficient distribution of growth dividends; enhanced institutional capacity to provide services; measures to improve human capability through human resource development; and the harmonisation of economic and social policies among member countries. The idea of the SADC playing a primary role in coordinating the conduct of international relations, with a view to mobilising international resources in support of regional development, is a noble strategy, but one that is much less prominent in practice.

The SADC recognised that development would not happen in conditions of conflict, political instability and oppression. The SADC's Organ on Politics, Defence and Security Cooperation is arguably the most powerful organ. It is driven at the highest level by heads of state/government. The Inter-State Defence and Security Committee, established in 1995 to replace the old one formed as part of the Front Line States (FLS), rivals the SADC's Council of Ministers in its powers and influence. In 2004, the SADC Protocol on Politics, Defence and Security Cooperation entered into force, thus providing a policy framework for this area of operation.

The implementation framework and reforms

The SADC has typical political organs to provide direction to its work. The highest decision-making body is the Summit of Heads of State and Government. The Council of Ministers oversees the functioning of the SADC and advises the summit on policy matters and the development of the SADC. It develops the organisation's substantive agenda and sets its strategic priorities and targets. The Integrated Committee of Ministers (ICM) was created in 2003 to replace the sectoral committees of ministers. Its responsibility is to direct the work of the four directorates at SADC charged with socioeconomic issues. This committee also replaced the original commissions. The Standing Committee of Officials functions as a technical advisory committee to guide the council on its responsibilities, as well as to form a link between the council and the ICM.

The Secretariat and the Executive Secretary are the principal administrative and executive institutions of the SADC. The Secretariat is tasked with providing strategic planning and management for the organisation, implementing its decisions and coordinating the policies and strategies of member states to ensure synergy with regional policy positions. As the head of the Secretariat, the Executive Secretary manages the consultation between governments and the SADC, the SADC interface with other regional organisations, organising the meetings of the summit and council, and overseeing the public administration machinery at the SADC.

The bulk of the implementation and coordinating work in relation to the substantive agenda of the SADC was conducted by the Sectoral Coordinating Units (SCUs) until the reforms did away with the SCUs. The SCUs coordinated the implementation of the policies and plans of each sector and a sector implied each priority area of intervention. The SCUs were hosted by different member states, giving such states coordinating powers over the sectors they hosted. For instance, South Africa hosted and, therefore, drove the implementation of programmes of the trade, industry, finance and investment sector, while Zimbabwe coordinated the food security, agriculture and natural resources sector. Each member state had SADC National Contact Points (NCPs) for communication with the Secretariat, as well as a national secretariat on the SADC for coordination of the national SADC agenda. By 2002, there were 22 SCUs as a big sector had been sub-divided, and 14 NCPs spread over the entire membership of the SADC.

Have institutional reforms improved the SADC?

As early as 1993, SADC members were aware that the organisation was institutionally weak and inefficient. This arose from various assessment reports released in 1993, 1994 and 1997. The latter was commissioned by a committee of four member states to consider what these reports found as weaknesses in the Secretariat, the NCPs and the SCUs. All these reports came to the same conclusions, namely: the SADC's decentralised structure was not working well; there were significant gaps in the management and the capacity of different SCUs; the national status of the SCUs made it difficult for the Secretariat to pull these institutions together in a concerted regional response to a common mandate; the Secretariat lacked management capacity to clearly articulate and monitor common goals, strategies and time frames; national policies and strategies lacked a regional dimension; and there was poor communication and cooperation between the SCUs and the Secretariat.

Further review confirmed the fact that the performance of the SCUs varied considerably, with some even outperforming the Secretariat itself, while others barely functioned. Each SCU was managed and run differently, depending on the resources and expertise the host country was able to invest in it. For this reason, the SCUs tended to encourage disintegration and incoherence in the implementation of the SADC agenda. They also tended to develop their own separate agendas, often linked to the national priorities of the host countries, thus weakening the common SADC agenda. There was considerable disjuncture between the plans at the centre and the programmes and projects implemented by the SCUs.

The further audits also confirmed that the Secretariat itself was institutionally weak and ineffective in carrying out its mandate. Weak strategic management, administrative systems and technical competence weakened the Secretariat's capacity to coordinate national policies and implement regional policy positions. It was inadequately and inappropriately staffed and underfunded. The staff morale was found to be very low, and the staff turnover was high. The relationship with the Council of Ministers and the Committee of Officials was also found to be fragile. This meant that the centre of SADC business was generally weak and ineffective. This undermined the entire business of the SADC.

Internal assessments also discovered that there were many problems pertaining to the role of national governments as the key implementers of the SADC agenda. The original idea was that the SADC, as a supranational authority, would provide policy guidance and direction in pursuit of regional integration and development by developing regional policies, adopting regional agreements and designing regional programmes of action. The actual implementation of these was meant to happen at the national level and the member states' governments were expected to put measures in place and drive the implementation of regional policies through national service-delivery machinery. They also needed to mainstream the regional agenda through a deliberate process of ensuring that there was harmony between national and regional policies. Besides this, national governments were expected to allow the SADC space to influence their national agendas (for a more complete analysis of the details of the reviews between 1994 and 2001, see Le Pere and Tjonneland, 2005; and Tjoneland, Isaksen and Le Pere, 2005). The national secretariats were responsible for coordinating a concerted national effort to implement the SADC's programmes, but many of these were either non-functional or weak. Where they existed, they consisted of small desks in departments of foreign affairs and/or regional cooperation. They did not include civil society and business, as required. Member states had neglected a major element of realising the common goals they adopted at the SADC summits. They allowed the process to be state led, even when the SADC had opened space for the participation of non-state actors and the people.

As a result, although the SADC had developed many laudable programmes and projects, they remained unimplemented. As many of these depended on donor funding and technical support, the SADC's approach was thus transformed into project-driven implementation. These tended to be narrow and short-term in nature. It is difficult to measure the impact of such disjointed efforts, even if well meant.

By 2004, the SADC had a plethora of treaties and protocols as the legal basis of its common position. These covered virtually every priority sector and plan at the SADC. Many of these legal instruments were signed after protracted negotiations, spanning years in some cases. The all-important Trade Protocol was negotiated over a period of four years before it came into force in 2000. The Trade Protocol was aimed at boosting intraregional trade, which until 1995 amounted to a mere 5 per cent of all trade among member states, excluding South Africa. The SADC members needed to agree on the formula for the elimination of tariffs, but this was a very difficult matter particularly regarding the sensitive sugar and textile industries.

Once signed, the Trade Protocol implementation was complicated by trade negotiations between South Africa and the European Union, which culminated in the signing of the Trade, Development and Co-operation Agreement (TDCA). The TDCA strained relations between South Africa and other SADC member states. The Southern African Customs Union (SACU) members automatically became members of this agreement, even though they were not part of negotiations, by virtue of being members of the SACU with South Africa. They were aggrieved because free access to the South African market for EU goods meant there would be lower SACU revenues. Non-SACU members were worried about the possible infiltration of their goods by illegal EU goods due to poor border and customs controls.

The challenge was that most of these protocols had not been implemented. The internal reviews in 2000 had found that this was partly to do with the institutional weaknesses at the SADC that accounted for weak implementation of other SADC policies, plans and programmes. The greatest challenge was, and still is, the failure of member states to translate these protocols into binding national laws, as agreed.

Table 4.1: Select SADC protocols

1. Select SADC Protocols
2. Treaty of the Southern African Development Community 1993
3. Protocol Combating Illicit Drugs 1996
4. Protocol on Forestry 2002
5. Protocol on the Control of Firearms, Ammunition and Related Material 2001
6. Protocol against Corruption 2001
7. Protocol on Culture, Information and Sport 2001
8. Protocol on Fisheries 2001
9. Protocol on Development of Tourism 1998
10. Protocol on Education and Training 1997
11. Protocol on Energy 1996
12. Protocol on Health 1999
13. Protocol on Legal Affairs 2000
14. Protocol on Mining 1997
15. Protocol on Trade 2000
16. Protocol on Transport, Communications and Meteorology 1998
17. Protocol on Shared Watercourses 2003
18. Protocol on the Facilitation of Free Movement of People 2005
19. Protocol on Politics, Defence and Security Co-operation 2004
20. Protocol on Immunities and Privileges 1993
21. Protocol on Wildlife Conservation and Law Enforcement 2003
22. Other Treaties
23. SADC Mutual Defence Pact 2003
24. MoU on Macroeconomic Convergence 2002
25. MoU on Co-operation in Taxation and related Matters 2002
26. Charter of Fundamental Social Rights 2003

Based on these reviews, the SADC decided to overhaul the institutions that had been found wanting by the assessments, that is, the Secretariat, the SCUs and the NCPs. The main thrust of these reforms was to collapse the

SCUs by consolidating them into four directorates within the Secretariat to coordinate the region-wide implementation of clustered sectoral plans. These directorates were Trade, Investment, Finance and Industry (TIFI), Food Security, Agriculture and Natural Resources (FANR), Social and Human Development (SHD), and Information and Science (IS). To enhance the management capacity within the Secretariat, two new positions of Deputy Executive Secretary were created and a division on strategic planning was also established. One deputy was to be dedicated to the process of driving the implementation of the integration commitments and plans, while the other was to support institution-strengthening. To complete the overhaul, the SADC replaced the NCPs and secretariats with new entities known as National Committees (NCs). Guidelines on these NCs were elaborated and circulated after consultation. One of the amendments was that NCs should not be made up of government departments only, but should also include non-state actors like civil society and the private sector. Their primary role was to develop national implementation strategies and plans, as well as oversee national responses to the SADC's policies, programmes and decisions. The principle was to ensure public participation in all SADC business, thus bringing the SADC closer to the grassroots.[2]

The governing structures of the SADC were also transformed. The sectoral committees of ministers, which had mirrored the SCUs, were dissolved and replaced by the Integrated Committee of Ministers (ICM), which was to attend to substantive policy issues by sector and to give guidance and direction to the Secretariat. The SADC also created a troika system, whereby the current chairperson of the SADC was to work together with the outgoing and incoming chairs in a troika. The SADC troika was given the responsibility to provide overall direction to the work of the SADC in between SADC Summits, deal with major challenges and crises that might arise, and act on behalf of the SADC in major international meetings and events. This troika was mandated to meet regularly to consider whatever matter may need their attention. The same governing structure was established for the SADC Organ. The two troikas combined, called the Double Troika, were mandated to take overall responsibility for the organisation and regional matters on behalf of the organisation.

The 2008 amendment to the SADC Treaty effected changes arising

---

2   Author's interview with SADC Secretariat Officials in Gaborone, Botswana, 23–25 August 2006.

from the post-2000 reviews and internal discussions, which had not been fully implemented via administrative action after 2001. The amendment provided for sectoral ministerial committees to better coordinate the political support for the integrated implementation of the SADC's plans and programmes. The new executive roles that follow the structure of the Secretariat mentioned earlier are included in the 2008 amendments too. The amendments for 2009 were meant to strengthen the process by which SADC executives are appointed to promote meritocracy and to have a competitive process of recruitment.

These were drastic changes. They helped in many ways to modernise and plug obvious gaps in the SADC's bureaucracy. The new governing structures have helped to ease the role of the chairpersons of the SADC and of the Organ. In fact, the troika system encourages consultation to deal with critical matters that arise in the region and thus ensures a quicker response by the region to these issues than before. The case in point is the Double Troika's response to the degeneration of the political situation in Zimbabwe in March 2007. Within a week, the Double Troika had met, consulted and appointed a mediator to facilitate talks between the ruling ZANU-PF and the opposition Movement for Democratic Change (MDC). This helped avert a violent meltdown of the political situation in that country and assisted the parties to reach a power-sharing settlement.

However, the institutional reforms have failed to overcome the problems of institutional inefficiency and ineffectiveness at the SADC and the attendant challenges of weak implementation capacity. The new SADC Secretariat, reflecting the new comprehensive institutional framework, is yet to make a telling difference in resolving the age-old problem of a lack of capacity to coordinate and implement regional agreements. Although the new organogram was adopted and new posts created, the purpose for which reforms took place remain unachieved. The SADC's central organs remain hamstrung by its normative and political framework. The SADC is an intergovernmental organisation with very limited power and capability to intervene to ensure that states implement collective decisions. The inter-ministerial committee, which is meant to assist in managing the clash between national sovereignty and shared regional sovereignty, remains relatively ineffectual when nation capitals call the shots, based largely on their national interests rather than the common public good of the region.

By 2008, the wise decision to establish national committees made up of the various stakeholders impacted by the SADC's decisions, including citizens' organisations, was found to have been undermined, either by the failure of member states to establish these committees or by their failure to ensure that they operated optimally (Nzewi and Zwane, 2008). This report concluded:

> What this means is that national discussions and decisions on SADC regional programmes and policies, when they are taken, are usually at the level of government functionaries, and not within the participatory parameters of the treaty provisions in terms of SADC national implementation (Nzewi and Zwane, 2008: 47).

The aspiration to have a developmental regional integration, which presupposed an inclusive and people-focused integration process, remained a pipe dream more than 16 years after the SADC Treaty, which made that claim, was signed. The preamble of that treaty had made ensuring the wellbeing of the peoples of the region a primary focus. It had also expressed 'the need to involve the people of the Region centrally in the process of development and integration'.[3] Objective 2(b) expressly invites the people of the region to develop and strengthen regional ties and, most importantly, to participate fully in the implementation of the SADC's plans and programmes.

The second significant reform initiative was the formulation of the Regional Indicative Strategic Development Plan exactly as the process of institutional reform, referred to earlier, began in 2001. But it was only in 2003 that the SADC leaders formally adopted this as 'a comprehensive development and implementation framework guiding the regional integration agenda of the Southern African Development Community (SADC) over a period of fifteen years'.[4] It finally came into force in 2005, with 2020 as the goal to fully achieve the objectives. The idea was that this plan would give direction to the work of the restructured SADC

---

3   SADC. (1992). The Treaty of the Southern African Development Community (latest amendment 2015). Available at: https://www.sadc.int/documents-publications/sadc-treaty/ (Accessed 31 November 2021).

4   SADC Website. Regional Indicative Strategic Development Plan (RISDP). Available at: https://www.sadc.int/about-sadc/overview/strategic-pl/regional-indicative-strategic-development-plan/ (Accessed 13 December 2021).

Secretariat and new institutional linkages between the SADC organs and the member states. If implemented fully, it would focus the region on the long-term social and economic goals for regional integration, including the eradication of poverty, and entrenching democratic governance, anchored in citizen participation in nation and region-building processes. Civil society formations appreciated the comprehensiveness of the plan in that it covered detailed milestones and targets towards trade and economic integration, the development of infrastructure and services, food security, and social and human development. Even cross-cutters like gender, science and innovation, sustainable development, ICTs and statistics were broken down into milestones and targets that are measurable and verifiable (SAPRN, 2005).

At the same time, the SADC unveiled the Strategic Indicative Plan for the Organ to guide its work on political governance and security matters, formally adopted in 2004. It sought to operationalise the Protocol on Politics, Defence, and Security Cooperation through the milestones, targets and specific actions required of the SADC and its member states. On this basis, SIPO led to several laudable achievements in the first five years, namely: the SADC Mutual Defence Pact, the launch of the SADC Standby Force, the inclusion of the Southern African Regional Police Chiefs Cooperation Organisation, the establishment of a regional Early Warning Centre and the SADC Electoral Advisory Council. But it, too, encountered problems that impeded the implementation of the RISDP, namely, poor coordination between the SADC organs and member states, and the poor resourcing of plans and structures. The end of the five-year period for the SIPO led to the development of a second SIPO called SIPO II. This review and revision process was criticised for excluding non-state stakeholders. As a result, the actual run up to the launch in November 2012 included very public consultations with civil society because of the political pressures civil society exerted on the SADC. A study of the SIPO II makes a telling conclusion: that while SADC is evolving a sophisticated security apparatus, it is not becoming a community where strong democratic norms are shared at national and regional levels (Van Nieuwkerk, 2013).

In 2018, the SIPO II was the subject of a review to understand its implementation, involving two major ministerial conferences and several other technical meetings, some of which were open to civil society. This would suggest that institutional effectiveness, weak coordination and the inadequate inclusion of stakeholders remained binding constraints to full realisation of SIPO II's aspirations (Ngwawi, 2018).

Five years after the RISP was adopted, a review of the RISDP became necessary because of various glaring failures. The RISDP target for a customs union had not been met by 2010, as envisaged. The SADC Free Trade Area (FTA), launched in 2008, had not fully matured to allow the progression to a customs union, so the latter was deferred to a later date in 2011. An FTA required a common tariff among SADC states but allowed individual states to set their own tariffs for trade with non-SADC countries; a customs union would have required a common external tariff regime. This was a difficult point to reach, given highly uneven economic and industrial development between South Africa and most other SADC economies. The SADC opted to rather pursue a grand trilateral FTA with the Common Market for Eastern and Southern Africa (COMESA) and the East African Community (EAC). Quickly this tripartite FTA led to the launch of one-stop borders by 2011, including the one between Tanzania and Kenya, and the one between Zambia and Zimbabwe (SARDC, 2011: 1–2).

As the SADC turned 30 in 2021, the reflections about the 'SADC We Want' noted that these targets had not been realised, partly because insufficient institutional capacity and political currency had been given to the implementation of the RISDP and the SIPO.

In the light of the impact of the global financial crisis that began in 2008, and the COVID-19 pandemic in 2020–2021 in southern Africa, the SADC leaders decided to focus on strengthening the SADC's resilience against crises.

But this had been done in 2008 and again in 2012 without changing much in the institutional capacity and political currency that had caused failure to implement previous decisions. In 2012, they decided to reflect and lead all stakeholders to develop a SADC Vision 2050 (SARDC, 2012). This evolved into what became popularly known as the 'SADC We Want' campaign, when citizen organisations protested that the future would not be decided without their inputs and convened civil society forums to register popular aspirations for the SADC. Countries that were oil exporters and those that were heavily dependent on imports had experienced significant economic impacts. This inclusive process of developing a long-term scenario would happen in parallel to the commissioning of a comprehensive review of the

RISDP implementation. This review identified the following challenges, among others: the weak implementation of the RSDP at member state level; ineffective structures for coordinating national actions; ineffective coordination by the SADC Secretariat; inadequate consultation among stakeholders at national levels; inadequate monitoring and evaluation of implementation; and resource constraints (Nagar and Malebang, 2016).

As in previous reviews and research, the picture that emerged was of a SADC founded on laudable goals and expansive visions – renewed and refreshed every now then – but one that did not have the wherewithal to translate these into reality. The story of the SADC National Committees (SNC), which form the nerve-centre of a people-focused developmental regional integration framework is sobering in this regard. As in the 2008 study referred to earlier, the RISDP review in 2014 found that many member states had not set up this multi-stakeholder national structure to coordinate and oversee the translation of the regional agenda into an integral part of their national plans and programmes. Where SNCs were set up, they were not designed to be inclusive of non-state actors but had become platforms for government officials to discuss matters among themselves. This weakened the oversight and the championing of the implementation of the RISDP, protocols and programmes of the SADC at national level. This suggested that member states did not embrace the notion of a shared sovereignty, which they seemed to see as a threat to the sacrosanct nature of their national sovereignty. They did not accept the import of the SNC modus operandi as it enforced a partnership between state and non-state actors, almost as equals, thereby changing the limited democratic culture at national level.

Alongside the review of the RISDP, the SADC was again initiating another initiative in the hope of catalysing progress towards its vision, the *Regional Industrialisation Strategy and Roadmap*, partly inspired by the RISDP. It was partly motivated by the adoption of Agenda 2063 by the African Union, which emphasised the need to urgently accelerate industrialisation to enable Africa to use global value chains to their advantages. This coincided with the re-energised President Mugabe, who had come out of the SADC-mediated government of national unity processes with more energy to push for indigenisation and industrialisation. It was, indeed, at the Extra-Ordinary Summit of the SADC in Harare, Zimbabwe, on 29 April 2015 that the strategy was adopted with much fanfare (SADC, 2015). This decision restored some energy on the part of states, but by 2020 this had fizzled out as the attention turned to crisis management and surviving the COVID-19 pandemic.

The strategy was premised on specific measurable actions to harness domestic, regional and global value chains, and the use of special economic zones to support logistical infrastructure, such as ports and industrial parks.

By 2015, the SADC was focusing on two priorities: to realise the ideals in the RISDP by 2020, and to implement the new agenda, which was called the Regional Industrialisation Strategy and Roadmap (2015–2063). The SADC also needed to respond to a new strategic orientation that was taking place at the continental level with the adoption of the AU Agenda 2063. This agenda required regions to align their own plans with the continental and international obligations. But the SADC was failing to implement its own RISDP so the likelihood of it implementing Agenda 2030 (the Sustainable Development Goals) and the AU Agenda 2063 at the same time was slim. A ministerial retreat in 2017 on the 'SADC We Want' found that many SADC initiatives had not been domesticised or translated into national programmes for implementation, which included most of the protocols.[5]

Conclusion

Following a SADC summit decision in 2019, the SADC Secretariat commissioned a desktop review of the implementation of the RISDP (2005–2020), one year before the lapse of its period. This review covered the SIPO as well. The main finding was that the RISDP was implemented unevenly from country to country. However, the review found that there had been some progress on the political and security fronts: there had been regular elections and smooth changes of government, and few incidents of full-scale conflict, and successful mediation when there was conflict. The review was damning about the failure of SADC member states – which are the real engine for the implementation of the SADC's decisions – to ratify, domesticise and implement protocols, including the trade protocol. The SADC institutional framework, fixed in 2000 and 2008, had produced less than impressive outcomes. The SADC used the recommendation

---

5   SADC. Strategic Ministerial Retreat of the SADC We Want. Available at: https://www.sadc.int/news-events/news/sadc-strategic-ministerial-retreat-work-sadc-we-want-commences-ezulwini-kingdom-swaziland/ (Accessed 20 January 2022).

to extend the RISDP by developing the RISDP 2020–2030 to guide the SADC, alongside the SADC's Vision 2050 (Imani Development, 2020). It seems the member states have not understood the messages repeatedly made about the impediments to the translation of the SADC's ideals into a lived reality, the stumbling blocks to developmental regional integration. They are in denial about the fact that the framework on which they are founded (national sovereignty) and the framework for their cooperation (regional integration) clash at a deep level. They lead to a stalemate in the implementation of the RISDP. This prevents the emergence of a people-centred region founded on shared sovereignty and developmental regional integration for the common good of the peoples of the region.

References

African Development Bank. (1993). *Economic Integration in Southern Africa*, London: Biddles.

Akokpari, J. (2008). 'Dilemmas of regional integration and development in Africa', in J. Akokpari, A.N. Muvumba and T. Murithi (eds). *The African Union and its Institutions*. Cape Town: Centre for Conflict Resolution, pp. 85–110.

Asante, S.K.B. (1997). *Regionalisation and Africa's Development: Expectations, reality and challenges*. London: Macmillan.

De Lombaerde, P. and Van Langenhove, L. (2007) 'Regional integration, poverty and social policy', *Global Social Policy*, 7(3): 377–83.

DeRosa, D.A. (1998). 'Regional integration arrangements: Static economic theory, quantitative findings and policy guidclines'. Unpublished background paper to the World Bank Policy Research Report, 1999.

Edo, F. (1997) *Globalisation and the World Order: Promises, problems, and prospects for Africa in the 21st century*. New York: Praeger.

Hettne, B., Inotai, A. and Sunkel, O. (eds). (1999). *Globalism and the New Regionalism*. London: Macmillan, pp. 1–19.

Ikome, F.N. (2007). 'From the Lagos Plan of Action to the New Partnership for Africa's Development: The political economy of African regional initiatives'. Johannesburg: Institute for Global Dialogue (IGD).

Imani Development. (2020). 'RISDP 2020–2030 Blueprints'. Available at: https://imanidevelopment.com/wp-content/uploads/2020/03/4th-Draft_RISDP-2020-30-Blue-Prints2.pdf (Accessed 30 January 2022).

Klabbers, J. (2002). *An Introduction to International Institutional Law*.

Cambridge: Cambridge University Press, pp. 41–58.

Le Pere, G. and Tjonneland, N. (2005). *Which Way SADC? Advancing co-operation and integration in southern Africa*. IGD Occasional Paper No. 50. Johannesburg: Institute for Global Dialogue.

Lee, M.C. (2003). *The Political Economy of Regionalism in Southern Africa*. Cape Town: UCT Press, pp. 50–51.

Nagar, D. and Malebang, G. (2016). 'Region-building and peacebuilding in Southern Africa Report.' Cape Town: Centre for Conflict Resolution.

Ngwawi, J. (2018). 'SADC to review implementation of development blueprint', *Southern African News Features*, No. 18, 17 August. Available at: https://www.sardc.net/en/southern-african-news-features/sadc-to-review-implementation-of-development-blueprint/ (Accessed 12 November 2021).

Nzewi, O. and Zwane, L. (2008). *Democratising Regional Integration in Southern Africa: SADC National Committees as Platforms for Participatory Policy-Making*. Johannesburg: Centre for Policy Studies.

Oosthuizen, G.H. (2006). *The Southern African Development Community: The organization, its policies, and prospects*. Johannesburg: Institute for Global Dialogue (IGD), pp. 71–72.

Schneider, G, (2006). 'Comparative regional integration: European co-operation and integration', Paper presented at Konstanz Conference on Globalism and Regionalism. Personal copy.

Southern African Development Community (SADC). (2017). 'Strategic Ministerial Retreat of the SADC We Want', 12–14 March, Ezulwini, Swaziland. Available at: https://www.sadc.int/news-events/news/sadc-strategic-ministerial-retreat-work-sadc-we-want-commences-ezulwini-kingdom-swaziland/ (Accessed 20 January 2022).

Southern African Development Community (SADC). (2015). 'Communiqué of the Extra-Ordinary Meeting of the SADC Summit of Heads of State and Government', Harare, Zimbabwe, 29 April. Available at: https://www.sadc.int/files/2714/3037/3905/Communiqu_of_the_Extraordinary_Meeting_of_the_SADC_Summit_of_Heads_of_State__Government.pdf (Accessed 26 January 2022).

Southern African Development Community (SADC). (2015). *The Treaty of the Southern African Development Community* (latest amendment). Available at: https://www.sadc.int/documents-publications/sadc-treaty/ (Accessed 31 November 2021).

Southern African Development Community (SADC). (1997). 'Review and rationalisation of the SADC's Programme of Action', SADC Library.

Southern African Development Community (SADC). (1994). The

Management of Regional Co-operation Report, SADC Library.

Southern African Development Community (SADC). (1993). *A Framework and Strategy for Building the Community*, SADC Library.

Southern African Development Community (SADC). (1992). The Treaty of the Southern African Development Community, signed by the majority of Heads of State and Government on 17 August 1992, Windhoek, Namibia, p. 5.

Southern African Development Community SADC. (1980). 'Southern Africa: Towards economic liberation', April 1980. Lusaka, Zambia, SADC Archives.

Southern African Development Cooperation Conference (SADCC). (1980). 'Southern Africa: Towards economic liberation', Lusaka, Zambia, 1 April 1980. SADC Library.

Southern Africa Poverty Review Network (SAPRN). (2005). On the Implementation of RISDP. A briefing. Author's copy.

Southern African Research and Documentation Centre (SARDC). (2018). 'SADC to review implementation of development blueprint', *Southern African News Features*, 18, No. 3, 17 August. Available at: https://www.sardc. net/en/southern–african–news–features/sadc–to–review–implementation– of–development–blueprint/ (Accessed 12 November 2021).

Southern African Research and Documentation Centre (SARDC). (2012). 'Vision 2050: SADC ponders future', *SADC Today*, 14(4), June: 1–2.

Southern African Research and Documentation Centre (SARDC). (2011). 'Strengthening regional integration', *SADC Today*, 13(2), February: 1–2.

Tjøneland, E., Isaksen, J. and Le Pere, G. (2005). 'SADC's Restructuring and Emerging Policies'. A report commissioned by the Embassy of Norway in Zimbabwe, May 2005, available at CHR, Michelsen Institute on request.

Ujupan, A. (2006). 'Reconciling theories of regional integration: A third way approach'. Unpublished paper presented at Widening and Deeping Integration Conference, Istanbul, Turkey, October 2006.

Van Nieuwkerk, A. (2013). 'SIPO II: Too little, too late', *Southern African Strategic Review*, 35(1): 246–52.

Winter, A. (1999). 'Regionalism versus multilateralism', in R. Baldwin, D. Cohen, D, Sapir, and A. Venables (eds). *Market Integration, Regionalism and the Global Economy*. Cambridge: Cambridge University Press.

Chapter Five

The Economic Community of West African States (ECOWAS)

JOHN AKOKPARI AND EMMANUEL AMPOMAH

Introduction

The Economic Community of West African States (ECOWAS), now comprising 15 states,[1] has evolved over the past four decades to establish itself as an active participant in the politics of the region, yet its operations have been fraught with challenges. ECOWAS has broad objectives, including promoting economic integration, good governance and security in the region, and so far it has demonstrated a capacity to adjust to new realities in the midst of challenges. This chapter argues that, in spite of some success in mitigating conflicts and promoting integration, ECOWAS still has much to do if it is to fulfil its set objectives of engineering socioeconomic integration in the West African subregion. To substantiate this argument, this chapter assesses the achievements of ECOWAS, by highlighting the progress made towards attaining its objectives, including promoting economic integration, facilitating the free movement of goods and persons, developing infrastructure, ending conflicts, and promoting peace and security in the region.

---

1 ECOWAS includes Benin, Burkina Faso, Cabo Verde, Côte d'Ivoire, The Gambia, Ghana, Guinea, Guinea-Bissau, Liberia, Mali, Niger, Nigeria, Senegal, Sierra Leone and Togo.

Evolution of ECOWAS

Regional integration in Africa took inspiration from the quest of the first-generation Pan-Africanists, especially Kwame Nkrumah, who believed that the prosperity of the continent could only be secured if it was politically integrated. He argued further that the sovereignty and territorial integrity of African states was guaranteed only through a political union. While Nkrumah's radical integration idea was denounced in certain quarters as overly ambitious, the eventual formation of the Organisation of African Unity (OAU) in 1963 was a tacit admission by African leaders of the need for some form of integration. However, Nigeria, among some conservative states, argued that subregional integration should precede a continental union and should be a precursor to the establishment of the United States of Africa and a common African market (Okolo, 1983). Nigeria thus became a leading architect of ECOWAS. Yet, Nigeria's leadership in the formation of ECOWAS needs to be understood within the context of the regional politics and, in particular, the unhealthy rivalry that had emerged between it and Côte d'Ivoire for dominance in the region. While it was clear that by virtue of its population and the size of its economy, Abuja was the undisputed hegemonic power in the region, Yamoussoukro was openly supported by France to rival the former's status. Under colonial rule, Côte d'Ivoire became an ipso facto province of France. For Nigeria, a way to limit the influence of France in the politics of the region was to instigate the formation of a subregional body that would assert autonomy from external control. Thus, under Nigerian-led initiatives, ECOWAS was officially launched on 28 May 1975 at a meeting of 16 regional leaders in Lagos, Nigeria.[2]

The 1975 ECOWAS Treaty states that:

The aims of the Community are to promote co-operation and integration, leading to the establishment of an economic union in West Africa in order to raise the living standards of its peoples, and to maintain and enhance economic stability, foster relations among Member States and contribute to the progress and development of the African Continent (ECOWAS Treaty, Article 3).[3]

---

2   Mauritania withdrew from the community in December 2000.
3   Article 3, ECOWAS Treaty. Available at: chrome-extension://efaidnbmnnnibpca-jpcglclefindmkaj/viewer.html?pdfurl=https%3A%2F%2Fwww3.nd.edu%2F~ggoertz%2Frei%2Frei260%2Frei260.23tt1.pdf&clen=242997&chunk=true (Accessed 20 October 2021).

Cooperation, integration and development are the underlying objectives of ECOWAS. In addition, ECOWAS is expected to serve as a stepping stone to materialising the objectives of the Lagos Plan of Action, which 'sought to promote the long-term economic development and industrialization of Africa through the creation of a large sub-regional market, followed by a continent-wide market through merging the sub-regional markets' (AU, 1980). In this way, ECOWAS aimed to establish a common market through trade liberalisation, harmonised economic policies, the removal of trade barriers and facilitation of the free movement of people, goods and services in the region. The preferred approach to economic integration is through a gradual process starting with the creation of a free trade area, the establishment of a customs union and the adoption of full economic integration. Under the ECOWAS Treaty, the community further proposed to undertake sectoral infrastructural development in areas such as transport, communication and energy. To ensure that countries are not disadvantaged by trade liberalisation in the integration scheme, the treaty established a fund for cooperation, compensation and development, commonly referred to as the ECOWAS Fund.

In 1993, however, the ECOWAS Treaty was revised, following the impact of internal and external factors. Internally, the movement towards integration has been frustrated by myriad structural challenges, including schisms and fissures among member states, the tendency for states to guard against any undermining of their sovereignty, security threats posed by incessant and intractable conflicts, and the continuous extroverted trade postures of member states. Externally, adversities such as those posed by the ubiquitous structural adjustment programmes (SAPs) of the 1980s, whose effects in undermining industrialisation were still visible, left telling effects on the community. Together, these regional and external factors undermined effective cooperation among member states and forced a revision of the ECOWAS Treaty in 1993. The revised treaty, often referred to as the Cotonou Treaty, aimed at encompassing a greater number of issues, especially those related to security. The treaty thus broadened the mandate of ECOWAS beyond economics and trade.

Consistent with the expanded objectives under the 1993 treaty, new institutions were created, including an Economic and Social Council, a Community Parliament, a Community Court of Justice, a Commission for Political, Judicial, Regional Security and Immigration, and the

ECOWAS Bank for Investment and Development (EBID), among others. The community further established specialised agencies to aid the integration process. These included the West African Health Organisation (WAHO); the West African Monetary Agency (WAMA); the West African Monetary Institute (WAMI); the Inter-governmental Action Group against Money Laundering and Terrorist Financing in West Africa (GIABA); the ECOWAS Gender and Development Centre; the ECOWAS Youth and Sports Development Centre; and the ECOWAS Water Resources Coordination Centre, among others. In the light of the new challenges facing ECOWAS, the objective of the revised treaty was to reposition the community in the face of new realities, by enhancing its capacity to effectively respond to the development, governance and security demands of the region (Bach, 2004: 75).

In addition, ECOWAS institutionalised its engagements with non-state actors, particularly civil society organisations and the private sector in West Africa in a bid to enhance participatory and collective decision-making. To accelerate development in the region, the community adopted the ECOWAS Vision 2020, a framework aimed at transforming the bloc from an ECOWAS of states to an 'ECOWAS of people'. The community's long-term development plan seeks to 'create a borderless, peaceful, prosperous and cohesive region, built on good governance and where people have the capacity to access and harness its enormous resources through the creation of opportunities for sustainable development and environmental preservation' (ECOWAS, 2010).

To consolidate the gains from the ECOWAS Vision 2020 and redress the challenges that undermine regional integration in West Africa, the ECOWAS Commission adopted the Community's Vision 2050 in August 2021 (Traoré, 2021). The organisation's new vision is underpinned by five fundamental pillars: 'a secure, stable and peaceful region; a region endowed with strong institutions, and that complies with the rule of law and fundamental freedoms; a fully integrated and prosperous region; a region mobilized for transformation, inclusive and sustainable development; a community of peoples fully inclusive of women, the youth and children' (ECOWAS, 2022). The new policy framework is holistic, progressive and people-centred, and it places women and the youth at the heart of the policy. Unfortunately, however, the reality with such frameworks in the subregion has been the half-hearted approach to their implementation. For Vision

2050 to materialise, member states of the bloc have to take ownership of its implementation at the local, national and regional levels. This requires the integration and aligning of the instruments of the framework with national development plans, priorities and policies of each member state.

Despite challenges, some of which will be noted later, ECOWAS represents the hope for integration in the West African subregion. It has been hailed as 'being ahead of the continental integration curve' (Vanheukelom, 2017: 4). So far, it remains the largest Regional Economic Community (REC) and brings together 15 of the 16 sovereign states in the region. Moreover, the organisation epitomises one of the few RECs in the developing world with a membership drawn from countries with different historical experiences and colonial traditions. For example, of the 15 countries in the community, nine are Francophone, five are Anglophone and one is Lusophone. In addition, ECOWAS contains countries of varying sizes in terms of land areas and populations, as well as cultural and religious diversity – Christianity, Islam and traditional African religions. Francis Ikome (2006: 338) could not have been more apt in noting that differences among West African states exceed their similarities. This reality has impacted negatively on the cohesion of the community and especially on the implementation of crucial security decisions. One of these divisions is the Francophone–Anglophone divide, which is discussed later.

Achievements of ECOWAS

Conflict resolution and post-conflict reconstruction

One of ECOWAS's most trumpeted successes is in conflict resolution and peacekeeping. Its success in Liberia, Sierra Leone and the Guinea-Bissau conflicts are remarkable. These successes have elevated ECOWAS as the only REC in Africa that has demonstrated a capacity for peacekeeping. The key to ECOWAS's success in this regard has been the formation of the ECOWAS Monitoring Group (ECOMOG), which initially comprised 16 000 troops, 12 000 of which were supplied by Nigeria. ECOMOG was deployed in Liberia in 1991–1997 and again in 2000–2006; in Sierra Leone in 1997–2000; in Guinea-Bissau in 1999 and in Côte d'Ivoire in 2000–2006, during the years of conflicts in these countries. In Liberia, for instance, although the outcome of ECOMOG's peacekeeping and peace enforcement operations was mixed, the intervention allowed for the Interim

Government of National Unity (IGNU) to be installed while paving the way for international humanitarian organisations to operate. ECOMOG's presence further contributed to a modest level of stability in Monrovia, as well as securing an uneasy cease-fire between 1990 and 1992 (Ampomah, 2019). The Nigerian-led ECOMOG intervention similarly succeeded in restoring power to Sierra Leone's constitutionally elected government after the 1996 military putsch. However, in the intervention in Guinea-Bissau, the ECOMOG force was drawn almost entirely from francophone members of the community while the operation was financed by France.

Nigeria played a marginal role in ECOWAS's intervention in Côte d'Ivoire in 2010, when conflict erupted in the country following President Laurent Gbagbo's refusal to cede power after losing that year's presidential poll to opposition leader Alassane Ouattara. This was not surprising as Nigeria had come under heavy public criticism for sacrificing Nigerian lives and financial resources in regional peacekeeping operations without tangible benefits to the country (Akokpari, 2016). Even more constraining, however, was the growing threat posed by Boko Haram, the al-Qaeda-linked fundamentalist group, to the Nigerian state and the need for the latter to direct its military energy against the insurgents. For reasons of political expediency, Abuja could not afford to be involved in any peacekeeping operations under its prevailing security conditions. Gbagbo was eventually arrested in April 2011 with the assistance of French troops (Nossiter, Sayare and Bilefsky, 2011).

The success of ECOWAS was further evident in its contribution to the post-conflict reconstruction of the war-ravaged states of Liberia, Sierra Leone, Guinea-Bissau and, to some extent, Côte d'Ivoire. It has to be noted though that ECOWAS states are ill-placed to offer any substantial development assistance for post-conflict reconstruction. Nigeria, the richest country in the region, is no exception. It is saddled with external indebtedness, and poverty among a large proportion of its population. With the exception of Nigeria, Ghana and Cape Verde, all ECOWAS members are classified as low-income countries, which are barely able to maintain balanced financial budgets. ECOWAS assistance for post-conflict reconstruction in the region has thus largely been limited to the promotion of post-conflict peace rather than to the rebuilding of infrastructure. In spite of this constraint, ECOWAS has assisted these countries in their post-conflict reconciliation, negotiations and elections. The organisation was involved in the negotiations that ended the first Liberian war in 1997, which paved the way for national elections. The community's efforts were also evident in the run-up to the second post-conflict elections in November 2005, won by Ellen Johnson Sirleaf, who became the first popularly elected female president in Africa. ECOWAS monitored the peace in the run-up to these elections and sent observers to the polls. It also sent observers to the Sierra Leonean elections in 2002 and 2007. It further encouraged the establishment of the Sierra Leone Truth and Reconciliation Commission in 1997 to help heal the wounds of society, as well as the rehabilitation and integration of child soldiers into society. Post-conflict election observation was also undertaken in Guinea-Bissau in 1999, which led to some degree of tranquility in the country.

The successes of ECOWAS's conflict resolution mechanisms have been due to the organisation's mediation abilities. The community's mediation capacity has evolved over time and served not only as a reactive measure to containing conflicts, but also as a proactive response to threats of conflict. In Liberia, for instance, ECOWAS's peacemaking efforts resulted in the signing of the Comprehensive Peace Agreement in 2003, bringing the protracted conflict between the government and the Charles Taylor-led insurgency to an end. Similarly, the Lomé Peace Accord contributed to the resolution of the Sierra Leone civil war. The regional body's mediation further averted large-scale conflicts in Guinea-Bissau (1997/98), Côte d'Ivoire (2002–2007 and 2010–2011), Niger (2009), Mali (2012 and 2020) and, most recently, Guinea in 2021. These peacemaking efforts have resulted in the containment of potentially devastating conflicts in the subregion.

ECOWAS's conflict management has been underpinned by the organisation's robust conflict frameworks and protocols, which have provided justifiable grounds, both morally and legally, for the community's intervention efforts. Essentially, the body of mechanisms adopted by ECOWAS reflects the organisation's thinking on conflicts. These institutional frameworks further provide guidelines on the required approaches to preventing and resolving conflicts. Key among these frameworks is the 1999 Mechanism for Conflict Prevention, Management, Resolution, Peacekeeping and Security (the Mechanism) and the supplementary protocol on democracy and good governance (the Protocol) adopted in 2001. The Mechanism is aimed at ensuring the institutionalisation and strengthening of norms on the collective management of regional security. Accordingly, the framework provided for the creation of the Mediation and Security Council (MSC), the Defence and Security Commission, and the Council of Elders. These organs have contributed to enhancing ECOWAS's capabilities in early warning, mediation, reconciliation and peacekeeping (Lucey and Arewa, 2016). To further strengthen ECOWAS's capacity in conflict management, the bloc adopted the ECOWAS Conflict Prevention Framework (ECPF). This framework was aimed at redressing the structural and operational causes of conflicts in the subregion by adopting a long-term preventative approach. The ECPF details ECOWAS's strategy for conflict prevention, peacebuilding and peacekeeping. Collectively, these frameworks have rendered ECOWAS the most advanced regional economic community in Africa, in terms of designing and nurturing structures and institutions to respond to the myriad security challenges in the region.

The free movement of persons and goods

The eradication of stringent frontier regulations provides a viable basis for effective regional integration. The Protocol on Free Movement of Persons, Right of Residence and Right of Establishment adopted by ECOWAS in May 1979 has become pertinent to the attainment of the community's objectives. Effective economic integration would be an illusion without the free movement of community citizens within the region. Member states became cognisant of the need to enhance transborder mobility to facilitate regional trade and integration. To this end, the protocol evinced efforts at repudiating existing colonial borders that undermined the development of the subregion. Importantly, the protocol enhanced the mobility of labour across the region.

The first phase of the protocol allowed for visa requirements to be waived for intraregional travel for up to 90 days (Opanike and Aduloju, 2015). The second, relating to the right of establishment is, however, yet to come into force. If operationalised, the right of establishment would allow for community citizens to settle in other countries in the region while enjoying the right to engage in economic activities. The free movement protocol is being facilitated by the adoption of a common ECOWAS passport and recent efforts at institutionalising a regional identity document. In realising the provisions of the initial protocol, four supplementary protocols were adopted between 1985 and 1990. These protocols required, among others, that member states of the community commit to providing valid travel document(s) to their citizens; granting community citizens the right of residence for the purpose of seeking and carrying out income-earning employment; ensuring appropriate treatment for persons being expelled; limiting the grounds for individual expulsion to reasons of national security, public order or morality, public health or the non-fulfilment of an essential condition of residence (Agyei and Clottey, 2007: 14–15).

To ease the movement of community citizens, moreover, restrictions on the movement of private and commercial vehicles have equally been removed, subject to drivers meeting basic requirements such as being in possession of a valid driver's license from a member state and an insurance policy. Moreover, private vehicles are allowed to remain in ECOWAS member states for up to 90 days, and 15 days for commercial vehicles. Further, to enhance intraregional mobility, the ECOWAS brown card has been instituted as an insurance scheme for road transport. The policy on the free movement of persons has led to increased intraregional migration. It was estimated that about 7.6 million West Africans resided in other countries in the subregion as of 2020, up from 2.5 million prior to the adoption of the Protocol on Free Movement (UN, 2020). Intraregional migration constitutes about 64 per cent of migration in the subregion and is estimated to be at least seven times greater than migration to Europe. According to the United Nations, over 97 per cent of migrants from Burkina Faso reside within West Africa, similar to 90 per cent of migrants from Niger and 75 per cent from Benin, Côte d'Ivoire, Mali and Togo (UN, 2020). Thus, the protocol has arguably facilitated free movement in the subregion.

On the flip side, however, the free movement of people has met with challenges. A mix of economic pressures and xenophobia has led host communities to view migrants with suspicion and hatred. In 1982 and 1983, Nigeria expelled West African migrants – including over a million Ghanaians – as its economic crises deepened (Akokpari, 2000: 79). Earlier, in 1969, the 'Alien Compliance Order', issued by the Ghana government, led to the expulsion of thousands of West African migrants, including Nigerians, from the country. The expulsion of community citizens has also taken place in Côte d'Ivoire (1999), Senegal (1990), Liberia (1983) and Benin (1998).

Tension has been building up since 2018 between Ghanaian local traders and their Nigerian counterparts in Accra. The latter are accused of engaging in economic activities reserved exclusively for Ghanaians. Tension has escalated in recent years, requiring the intervention of Abuja to diffuse them (Anokam, 2021). Indeed, Human Rights Watch (HRW) (2018) reported that 50 West African migrants bound for Europe, including 44 Ghanaians, were murdered in The Gambia in July 2005, with the complicity of Yahya Jammeh's government. In spite of the spill-over of communities across borders, tensions and skirmishes have frequently characterised the relations between migrants and host communities, making integration of the former difficult. Intraregional conflicts have further limited the freedom of movement within the subregion (Opanike and Aduloju, 2015). These disconcerting developments have marred the efficacy of an otherwise progressive protocol.

Promoting transport infrastructure

ECOWAS has made significant strides in developing key regional road networks as a way of promoting faster integration, with a unique focus on landlocked countries. Of the seven principal regional arteries, five are sea corridors, providing the three landlocked countries in the community – Burkina Faso, Mali and Niger – access to the sea. These landlocked countries have more than one gateway to the sea, compared to other landlocked countries in Africa (Ranganathan and Foster, 2011). Intraregional transportation has been boosted further by the existence of two crucial corridors, the Coastal corridor, stretching from Abidjan (Côte d'Ivoire) to Lagos (Nigeria) and the Sahelian corridor, stretching from Nouakchott (Mauritania) to N'Djamena (Chad). These regional road networks have been almost completely paved, with most of these arteries in relatively good or fairly good conditions (Efobi and Osabuohien, 2016). ECOWAS has also established the National Road Transport and Transit Facilitation Committees, with membership comprising crucial private and state actors involved in transport facilitation in member states. Together with key development partners, ECOWAS has embarked on significant road projects including the six-lane dual-carriage Abidjan–Lagos Corridor Development Programme, aimed at connecting the capital cities of Côte d'Ivoire, Ghana, Togo, Benin and Nigeria. Furthermore, as part of the ECOWAS Joint Border Posts (JBP) programme, the Noepe JBP between Ghana and Togo, and the Seme-Krake JBP between Benin and Nigeria have been completed. These road networks will facilitate movement and boost intraregional trade.

However, railway networks in the subregion are yet to be harnessed. Of the 10 188 kilometres of railway lines in West Africa, only half are tailored to subregional purposes (Bayane, Yanjun and Bekhzad, 2020). These include the transnational railway lines linking Burkina Faso and Côte d'Ivoire (Sitarail) as well as Mali and Senegal (Transrail) (Bayane, Yanjun and Bekhzad, 2020). The existing railway networks in the subregion are mostly used for freight, largely due to the exploitation of mineral and natural resources in West Africa. While the bloc's accomplishment in this sector has been unimpressive, member states have recently initiated projects geared to advancing railway transport in the subregion. In this regard, plans are underway in Ghana to construct a Trans-ECOWAS railway line linking Ghana to Côte d'Ivoire and Togo. Similarly, plans are underway for the construction of a joint railway line that will connect Tema (Ghana) to Ougadougou (Burkina Faso). To foster regional interconnectivity and trade, ECOWAS has approved a railway development master plan for 11 of its member states. ECOWAS's West Coast High Speed Rail project seeks to connect Nigeria, Benin, Togo, Ghana and Côte d'Ivoire. The project revolves around the construction of railway terminals, stations, tunnels and administrative facilities in member states (Timetric, 2017). Thus, the harmonisation of regional railway projects is gradually advancing, despite the many challenges that saddle these efforts. ECOWAS has equally supported member states in the provision of a safe, coordinated and reliable air transport system. The bloc has made significant gains with liberalising the aviation industry in the region. This has contributed substantially to reversing the market collapse in the aviation sector, particularly following the demise of Ghana's and Nigeria's national airlines.

The ECOWAS Department of Transport and Telecommunications has further advanced regional institutional structures in the area of information communication and technology (ICT). This has been realised through the establishment of a single liberal market and the harmonisation of ICT policies and regulatory frameworks in the subregion (Beecroft *et al.*, 2020). Member states have similarly made efforts to improve and modernise existing ICT infrastructure. The establishment of a regional regulatory agency has been instrumental in this regard. To this end, the West Africa Telecommunications Regulators' Association coordinates dialogue on telecommunications policy and regulations in the subregion while disseminating information among member states. The existence of this regional regulatory association has advanced mobile roaming arrangements within the subregion. The telecommunications sector in West Africa has been enhanced further through the 'development of reliable and modern regional Telecoms broadband infrastructure including the INTELCOM II programme and alternative broadband infrastructures' (UNECA, 2021). Furthermore, 11 coastal states in the community have been connected to submarine cables, while three landlocked countries have two access routes to the submarine cables (ECOWAS, 2016). This and other ECOWAS initiatives have made access to ICT services easy and less costly.

Furthermore, the ECOWAS Regional Electricity Regulatory Authority (ERERA) has been established to regulate cross–border electricity connections in West Africa. ERERA has been established within the framework of the Energy Protocol and the West African Power Pool (WAPP) Programme. Through WAPP, an Information Coordination Centre has been established to promote the collation and dissemination of best practices within the subregion. To promote renewable energy and energy efficiency, the ECOWAS Centre for Renewable Energy and Energy Efficiency has been established (Davidson *et al.*, 2017). This institutional structure is aimed at improving energy production, distribution and utilisation in the subregion. Currently, the activities of electricity regulatory institutions in member states have been harmonised, pending the implementation of the second phase of the ECOWAS Regional Electricity Market (AEP, 2021). This electricity market will augment the bloc's effort at promoting industrialisation and development in the subregion. The harmonisation of efforts in the power sector has made it possible for ECOWAS to provide financial assistance to member states experiencing power challenges. To this end, ECOWAS's emergency electrical energy supply programme has provided funding to support countries struggling in the electricity sector, including The Gambia, Guinea, Mali and Sierra Leone (ECOWAS, 2016).

Democracy and good governance

ECOWAS has seen a dramatic improvement in governance fortunes as a result of global developments and regional initiatives. Democratically elected governments have emerged within the region, once dominated by military dictators and self-styled life-presidents. The resolve to move to democratic governance has been strengthened by the adoption of a number of protocols on governance, including the ECOWAS Declaration on Political Principles (1991); the ECOWAS Protocol on Governance and Human Rights (2001); and the ECOWAS Protocol on Democracy and Governance (July 2001). These protocols seek to protect human rights, especially press freedom and the rights of opposition parties (Akokpari, 2008: 7). The ECOWAS Parliament and the Court of Justice have given credence to the community's resolve to promote good and democratic governance.

Unfortunately, the military's intrusion into politics in Guinea in December 2008 marred the democratic credentials of the region. However, consistent with its adopted zero-tolerance stance on unconstitutional changes in government, ECOWAS suspended Guinea from the organisation until democratic rule was restored. In January 2017, ECOWAS forces entered the The Gambia and forced strongman, Yahya Jammeh, out of office. Jammeh was refusing to cede power to the victorious opposition candidate, Adama Barrow, following his defeat in the December 2016 presidential polls (Hartmann, 2017). Moreover, following the occurrence of two military coups in less than a year, ECOWAS took a bold stance and expelled Mali from the organisation on 31 May 2021 until the restoration of constitutional rule (Al-Jazeera, 31 May 2021). In promoting democracy and constitutional rule in Mali, ECOWAS took a position that the Southern Africa Development Community (SADC), for example, would not take on Zimbabwe.

ECOWAS is further credited for encouraging the formation of civic groups as part of its aim to engage civil society. These civil associations include those for the youth (the West African Youth Union), and those based on industry such as the Federation of West African Manufacturers (Ikome, 2006: 338). The proliferation of a number of ECOWAS-inspired civil associations, however, raises concerns about the multiplicity and duplication of these groups. ECOWAS has the added task of rationalising these civil groups to ensure that such multiplicity and possible overlap of membership does not undermine the very purposes of their existence. In spite of these laudable achievements, ECOWAS faces challenges, an issue to which we now turn.

Challenges and failures of ECOWAS

The Anglophone–Francophone rivalry and the failure to adopt a common currency

The absence of a common regional currency presents an impediment to ECOWAS's free trade agenda. The use of different currencies, with varying exchange rates, complicates commercial exchanges and financial transactions. Thus, on 20 April 2000, ECOWAS members established the West African Monetary Zone (WAMZ), as part of the renewed commitment to adopt a common currency, in line with a process that had begun in the 1980s under the auspices of the ECOWAS Monetary Cooperation Programme (Talabi, 2020). WAMZ was established to facilitate the adoption of a common currency, to be called the Eco, among the Anglophone countries. The West African Monetary Institute was subsequently created by WAMZ member states in 2001 to facilitate the creation of the West Africa Central Bank and the introduction of a common currency. It was envisaged that the eco would eventually be adopted by member states of WAMZ (predominantly Anglophone countries in West Africa), as well as Francophone members under the auspices of the West African Economic and Monetary Union (WAEMU, also known under the French acronym, UEMOA) by 2020 (Xuba, 2021).

However, the adoption of a common currency has been postponed five times – in 2003, 2005, 2009, 2015 and 2020 (Egbuna, 2018). The delay in launching the Eco has been largely due to the failure of members of WAMZ to meet the convergence criteria and structural benchmarks required to establish the monetary union (Egbuna, 2018: 8). The macroeconomic convergence criteria, one of the five strategic pillars of WAMZ, includes exchange rate stability, budget deficits and financing, reserves, and an acceptable debt-to-GDP ratio (Talabi, 2020: 5). In turn, WAMZ has been unable to meet the convergence criteria because of a combination of internal and external factors, including insecurity, epidemics and viruses, drought, the global financial crisis, and food and fuel crises, among others (Xuba, 2021). Moreover, member states have not incorporated WAMZ programmes into their national development plans. As a consequence, the timelines set for the implementation of the Eco remain unmet. The divide, even suspicion, between UEMOA and the rest of ECOWAS was amplified when, in December 2019, Alassane Ouattara, the Ivorian president, announced that Francophone (UEMOA) member states were reforming the CFA franc and were changing the name of the CFA franc to the Eco. This move received widespread condemnation from Anglophone members, who accused the WAEMU bloc of hijacking the single currency project, in contravention of the provisions of the ECOWAS currency scheme. The difficulty in adopting a common currency in the region has been attributed to France, which supports its former colonies against Nigeria. Akinterinwa (2020) argued that, 'the controversy over the Eco as a regional currency appears to be the crescendo of the mutual suspicions on which the ties between Abuja and Yamoussoukro are currently based. It is a direct manifestation of Franco-Nigerian rivalry by proxy.'

The origins of the Franco–Nigerian rivalry goes back to the Biafran War (1967–1970) when Paris openly supported Biafra, which was seeking secession from Nigeria. Nigeria thereafter viewed French–ECOWAS foreign policy with considerable suspicion. French–Nigerian rivalry was manifested, moreover, in the ECOMOG interventions in West Africa's conflicts. As noted already, in the ECOWAS intervention in Liberia, ECOMOG forces were drawn exclusively from the four Anglophone countries, plus Guinea. Mali only joined later in 1991, while Senegal, which also joined in 1991, pulled out two years later in 1993, criticising the conduct of Nigeria. It was noted that while ECOMOG was working hard to subdue Charles Taylor's rebels, the latter's mercenaries were being trained in Burkina Faso under Blaise Campaore. In addition, Burkina Faso served as a conduit for the supply of Libyan arms to Charles Taylor's forces (Kajee, 2014). Similarly, only Anglophone members of the community participated in the ECOMOG intervention in the Sierra Leonean conflict, while only Francophone members of the community were involved in the intervention in Guinea-Bissau. On the flip side, Nigeria's conspicuous absence in the intervention to dislodge intransigent Laurent Gbagbo, with the assistance of French forces in November 2011 (Smith, 2011), was due partly to Abuja's internal problems, but also to the involvement of Paris in the regional anti-Gbagbo campaign. These developments were a manifestation of the Abuja–Paris rivalry, which became a de facto Anglophone–Francophone impasse.

Political turmoil and instability

The West African subregion is notorious for unconstitutional changes of governments. A study by the African Development Bank (AfDB) revealed that out of the 200 successful and failed military coup attempts occurring on the continent between 1960 and 2012, the West African subregion accounted for 104 (Barka and Ncube, 2012). The trend of unconstitutional changes of government has changed in the 21st century. Until 2020, the frequency of military takeovers had been significantly reduced, attributable to the modest triumph of liberal democracy in the region. Generally, military interventions, such as have recently occurred in Mali (2012, 2020 and 2021), Guinea (2008 and 2021), Niger (2010) and Guinea-Bissau (2012), threaten democracy and political stability, and ultimately regional integration. Effective regional integration is hardly possible under conditions of instability and insecurity. As a rule, countries in political turmoil tend to be introverted and less inclined to implement regional programmes.

In other cases, political instability is spawned by elected governments seeking to hold on to power beyond their constitutionally mandated terms. This tendency generates at least two implications. First, it leads to disputes over electoral outcomes and, second, to conflicts. Either scenario is inimical to peace, stability and regional integration. In Togo, the reign of the Gnassingbé Eyadéma family – Gnassingbé Eyadéma and Faure Gnassingbé Eyadéma – has been entrenched for over five decades amidst consistent accusations of election rigging. The family shows no sign of relinquishing power, with every presidential election marked by protests and a heavy-handed response from the state. In Côte d'Ivoire, Lauren Gbagbo's refusal to cede power after losing the 2010 presidential polls, Yahya Jammeh's intransigence after suffering defeat in the December 2016 Gambian presidential elections, Alassane Ouattara's controversial election for a third term in November 2020 Ivorian polls, and the highly unpopular bid of Blaise Campaoré to extend his 27-year rule by five more years in Burkina Faso in 2014 all led to violent protests, political turmoil and instability. In the latter case, the unfolding political uncertainty provided an auspicious pretext for the intervention of the military, a phenomenon highly disdained by ECOWAS. Inexplicably, the high-profile bids by presidents to remain in power and the highly disputed electoral outcomes occur mostly in Francophone countries.

Low intraregional trade

ECOWAS has developed ambitious policy frameworks to facilitate trade. Yet, intraregional trade remains pathetically low. Through the ECOWAS Trade Liberalisation Scheme (ETLS) and the common external tariff

(CET) frameworks, ECOWAS has made efforts to expand trade among member states (Bankole, Olasehinde and Raheem, 2012). Operationalised since 1990, the ETLS is an instrument geared to promote a regional Free Trade Area by eliminating trade barriers. Initially, the policy allowed for unhindered market access to agricultural commodities and artisanal handicrafts. Subsequent revisions allowed for industrial products originating from West Africa to be included in the scheme, albeit under certain conditions. The launching of the CET in 2013, after 10 years of negotiations, was instrumental in ensuring uniformity in customs duties and import quotas across the subregion. The CET is structured along five tariff bands of 0 per cent, 5 per cent, 10 per cent, 20 per cent and 35 per cent (Torres and Seters, 2016). More goods are anticipated to be available for trading with the implementation of the CET. This tariff is further envisioned to guarantee predictability and stability to make the subregion attractive to foreign direct investment. Domestic markets in ECOWAS would subsequently be enlarged through the creation of a single market for imported goods (GIZ, 2016). In spite of these innovative regional policies, intra-ECOWAS trade remains minimal, estimated at between 8 and 11 per cent (Torres and Seters, 2016: 17). The paltry intra-ECOWAS trade mirrors a bigger continental picture. Intra-African trade stands at around 17 per cent. This figure pales in comparison with 60 per cent in Europe, 40 per cent in North America, and 30 per cent in the Association of Southeast Asian Nations (ASEAN) (AU, 2021).

Explanations for the low intra-ECOWAS trade abound, but two related arguments are most popular: first, the majority of ECOWAS states rely heavily – but also precariously – on the production and exportation of primary agricultural products for foreign exchange. With limited irrigation, West Africa's agriculture is mainly rain-fed. Second, and related to the first, is what Callaghy (1994: 241) euphemistically referred to as the 'fallacy of agricultural composition'. In this fallacy, similar goods are produced by member states of the RECs. Importantly, such homogeneity in production makes the marketing of products difficult and thus limits intraregional trade. Among ECOWAS members, Benin, Côte d'Ivoire, Ghana and Togo all have cocoa as a major export commodity, while Nigeria and Ghana export crude oil. The Gambia and Senegal are leading producers of peanuts. Under these conditions, ECOWAS members cannot trade among themselves but rather have to find extraregional and, in fact, extra-African markets (Akokpari and Bimha, 2021: 122). Homogeneity in production is also the situation in the East African Community (EAC) where tea and coffee are the main agricultural export commodities of Kenya, Uganda and Tanzania, while oil dominates the exports of Gabon, Equitorial Guinea and Cameroon, among members of the Economic Community of Central African States (ECCAS). Only SADC has a fairly diversified export base. Accordingly, its intra-community trade was the highest in Africa with a value of US$34.7 billion in 2016 compared to ECOWAS's figure of US$11.4 billion in that same year (UNCTAD, 2019). Thus, the very structure of production truncates intraregional trade in ECOWAS. The recently adopted African Continental Free Trade Area (AfCFTA), to which nearly all AU members have committed, offers opportunities for increased intra-African and intra-ECOWAS trade. ECOWAS will have a bigger African market to access and thereby mitigate the trappings of the agricultural fallacy.

Poor regional infrastructure

Infrastructure deficits undermine free trade and faster integration in ECOWAS (Bjornlund *et al.*, 2020). Deficits in infrastructure are visible in the areas of energy supply and transport. While access to electricity in the region varies widely from country to country, the ECOWAS Centre for Renewable Energy and Energy Efficiency (ECREEE), noted that generally, the region suffers from 'energy poverty', with only 42 per cent of its citizens and a paltry 8 per cent of its rural population having access to electricity (Reiss, 2015). These statistics place the community among the bottom RECs in the global ranking in electricity access. Even in countries with sufficient energy infrastructure, the supply of electricity is often erratic. In Nigeria, the economic powerhouse of ECOWAS, for example, it is a luxury and an exception, never the rule, to have an uninterrupted two-hour electricity supply in a day. The ECREEE projects that poor electricity delivery will persist in the region until the West Africa Power Pool (WAPP) project and the AU's Grand Inga Dam hydroelectric project, powered by the DRC's Congo River, are fully operational. This hydroelectric project, one of the flagship projects under the AU's Agenda 2063 programme, is expected to provide Africans with clean, reliable and sustainable access to electricity (AU, 2021). The West Africa Gas Pipeline (WAGP), which transports natural gas from Nigeria's oil field to Benin, Ghana and Togo, began supply in 2009. In spite of the supply, the recipients have continued to experience power outages. The WAGP and the WAPP are two leading energy infrastructure projects for power supply in the region.

In the mean time, inadequate electricity supply has damning consequences for local economies, regional integration and development. The health delivery system and educational outcomes become victims. Further, poor electricity supply negatively affects local industries. Private businesses – from large to small scale – come under pressure to retrench staff in a region where unemployment disturbingly stands at over 25 per cent (Mbaye and Gueye, 2018: 7). In addition, an inauspicious climate is created for investments. In the midst of power shortages that hit Ghana between 2013 and 2016, the Ghana Employers' Association (GEA) noted at a job summit in Accra on 15 April 2015 that almost 13 000 jobs were lost in the private sector within the four-month period between January and April 2015 alone (Tornyi, 2015). The Employers' Association warned further that the regular power outage was a disincentive for new investments. Under conditions of irregular power supply, innovative entrepreneurs resort to the use of portable electric generators, which increases the cost of production. At the continental level, Africa loses between 2 and 3 per cent of GDP due to the lack of reliable energy. Generally, an irregular electricity supply slows down business and adversely impacts the fight against poverty.

Poor transport infrastructure, a further challenge for ECOWAS, hinders trade and the free movement of persons within the community. Road, rail and transport in the region remain inefficient compared to other African RECs. Road transport is slow and expensive because of the quality of roads and administrative delays. While efforts have been made to improve regional corridors, some sections of the international highways, especially in landlocked areas of coastal countries, are poorly maintained. Access to all-season road networks in rural areas within the community is by far the lowest in the developing world (Torres and Seters, 2016: 38). Widespread bribery and corruption among customs officials at border posts significantly undermines intraregional trade, and increases the cost of doing business in the community. Numerous yet unnecessary roadblocks and checkpoints are erected on regional corridors (Bala, 2017). For instance, there are no fewer than seven checkpoints per 100 kilometres between Lagos and Abidjan, and two roadblocks per 100 kilometres between Accra and Ouagadougou (Chete and Adewuyi, 2012).

An interregional rail transportation network is non-existent within ECOWAS. This particular transport deficiency will be rectified with the implementation of the Integrated High-Speed Train Network (IHSTN) system envisioned under the AU's Agenda 2063. The IHSTN system will connect all African capitals and commercial centres (AU, 2020). While air transportation has improved over the last decade, safety remains a concern (World Bank, 2011). The Single African Air Transport Market (SAATM), another of AU's Agenda 2063 projects, is meant to ensure intra-African connectivity and facilitate the creation of a unified air transport market for the continent. In spite of its critical importance as a route by which ECOWAS members conduct trade with one another and with extraregional partners, marine transportation remains inefficient. Most ECOWAS ports are plagued with old equipment, low levels of automation and cargo theft. Together, these lapses slow down economic activities, but also undermine ECOWAS's protocol on free trade and movement of persons.

Multiple and overlapping membership in RECs

Overlapping membership of states in the RECs in Africa has been considered an impediment to effective continental integration. ECOWAS has not been spared this phenomenon. All eight Francophone members of ECOWAS are members of UEMOA, while Côte d'Ivoire, Guinea, Liberia and Sierra Leone are simultaneously members of ECOWAS and the Mano River Union (MRU). Worse yet, while members of UEMOA remain in ECOWAS, they also have membership in the CFA franc zone, along with Cameroon, the Central Africa Republic, Chad, the Congo, Equitorial Guinea and Gabon, which belong to the Central African Economic and Monetary Community (CEMAC) located within ECCAS (UNCTAD, 2009: 12). Similarly, Gambia, Ghana, Guinea, Liberia, Nigeria and Sierra Leone are members of the West Africa Monetary Zone (WAMZ). Such multiple membership in RECs undermines integration if there is conflict in the objectives of the parallel bodies. Conflicting objectives make groups pull in opposite directions. Moreover, there is a tendency for energies and loyalty to be divided if states hold membership in multiple organisations, even in cases where the two competing formations have similar objectives. The AfCFTA may help mitigate the challenges associated with overlapping memberships in the RECs.

The imposition of import and export restrictions

An additional impediment to intraregional trade within ECOWAS is the frequent adoption of protectionist policies by some member states, which involve the imposition of import and export restrictions on agricultural products, aimed at protecting the sector. Food imports that are being controlled include cassava, maize, rice, vegetable oil, sugar, wheat flour, beef, poultry, and frozen and chilled fish (Torres and Seters, 2016: 34). Similarly, export restrictions have affected cereals, especially maize, millet and rice, and are often imposed during periods of food shortage. In response to the 2007/08 food crisis, the Guinean government prohibited food export to neighbouring countries, while Burkina Faso restricted the exportation of local cereal (Engel and Jouanjean, 2013). ECOWAS members have, in some instances, controlled the exportation of subsidised products to avoid leakage. Countries within the subregion thus implement community agreements only when it advances their national interest. This approach, however, is detrimental to free trade and undermines broader economic integration in the region. Thus a major challenge to intraregional trade has been the unwillingness of countries to implement ambitious regional programmes if these do not serve their national interest. This was evinced in Nigeria's closure of its borders in 2019 in the bid to protect local industries. ECOWAS members thus need to strike a careful balance between the protection of national interest and the promotion of free trade.

Conclusion

The importance of ECOWAS for integration, peace and security in the West African subregion cannot be overemphasised. This subregional body has championed the process of economic integration and has acquired the enviable reputation for effectively terminating conflicts alongside promoting regional integration. The backdrop to this was ECOWAS's demonstrated ability to adapt to changing regional situations by the adoption of the revised ECOWAS Treaty in 1993. This revised treaty was aimed at strategically repositioning the organisation to address sociopolitical issues beyond economic integration. In furtherance of this new imperative, novel institutions were created to enhance the community's capacity to achieve its objectives. While conflicts and political turmoil have not been completely eliminated from the region, ECOWAS has developed the instrumentalities and the will to address them timeously in a way that no REC has done in Africa. In fairness, however, conflict resolution has not been the only achievement credited to ECOWAS – the community has also instituted good governance principles, including establishing and enforcing the disdain for unconstitutional changes in government, the defiance of which attracts suspension from the organisation. Human rights are now better respected by states than during the pre-ECOWAS years. Moreover, greater integration has been achieved in the region with the harmonisation of trade policies and the adoption of the Protocol on the Free Movement of Persons. This has, in turn, led to the adoption of a common ECOWAS passport, which has eased restrictions on movement of community members. The development of regional infrastructure in energy and transport are additional areas of credit to the organisation, although much still needs to be done in these areas.

Yet, the challenges militating against the comprehensive attainment of ECOWAS's objectives have been egregious and threaten the very foundation of the organisation. The Franco–Nigerian rivalry, the persistence of conflicts, military coups and political instability in countries, the ever-present rivalry between ECOWAS and UEMOA, multiple and overlapping membership of states in rival regional bodies, which tends to divide loyalty to ECOWAS, failure to adopt a common currency after numerous attempts, and the generally low intra-community trade, resulting from the production of similar commodities, have combined to present a formidable challenge to ECOWAS. This situation has not been helped by the existence of poor infrastructure in transport and in the supply of energy. The launch of the AfCFTA in January 2021 is expected to alleviate most of the challenges currently facing ECOWAS. The removal – or at least the reduction – in tariffs will promote inter-REC trade, while the African Union's broader continental infrastructure development programmes in transport and energy would offset the current deficits seen in ECOWAS. With the introduction of the AfCFTA, optimism can prevail over pessimism about ECOWAS truly meeting its objectives.

References

Abimbola, O., Ayodeji, A.A. and Lawrence, O.A. (2015). 'ECOWAS Protocol on Free Movement and Transborder Security in West', *Journal of Civil and Legal Sciences*, 4(3): 1–3.

Africa Energy Portal (AEP). (2021). Phase II of ECOWAS Regional

Electricity Market starts in 2022/2023. Available at: https://africa-energy-portal.org/news/phase-ii-ecowas-regional-electricity-market-starts-20222023 (Accessed 3 November 2021).

African Union (AU). (2021a). 'BIAT – Boosting Intra-African Trade'. Available at: https://au.int/en/ti/biat/about (Accessed 6 December 2021).

African Union (AU). (2021b). 'Africa Single Electricity Market (AfSEM)'. Available at: https://au.int/en/videos/20210604/africa-single-electricity-market-afseM (Accessed 15 December 2021).

African Union (AU). (2021c). 'Infrastructure and Energy Development'. Available at: https://au.int/en/infrastructure-energy-development (Accessed 7 December 2021).

African Union (AU). (2020). 'Update on the African Integrated High-Speed Railway Network by AUDA-NEPAD'. Available at: https://www.au-pida.org/news/update-on-the-african-integrated-high-speed-railway-network-by-auda-nepad/ (Accessed 20 November 2021).

African Union (AU). (1980). 'Lagos Plan of Action or the Economic Development of Africa 1980–2000'. Addis Ababa: African Union.

Agbodo, E., MaharajInno, A. Adeyemo, B. and Davidson, I. (2017). *Transforming the West African Regional Electricity Market: Lessons and experiences*. Accra: IEEE Power Africa.

Agyei, J. and Clottey, E. (2007). *Operationalizing ECOWAS Protocol on Free Movement of People among the Member States: Issues of convergence, divergence and prospects for sub-regional integration*. Amsterdam: International Migration Institute.

Akale, C. Udegbunam, K.C. and Sanda, J. (2018). 'Assessment of ECOWAS Interventions in Guinea', *International Journal of Research and Innovation in Social Science*, II(IV): 138–42.

Akinterinwa, B. (2020). 'The Eco and the new Francophone–Anglophone rivalry: Addressing the impending dislocation of the ECOWAS', *This Day*, 18 November. Available at: https://www.thisdaylive.com/index.php/2020/07/05/the-eco-and-the-new-francophone-anglophone-rivalry-addressing-the-impending-dislocation-of-the-ecowas/ (Accessed 1 June 2022).

Akokpari, J. and Bimha, P.Z.J. (2021). 'The African Union as an interlocutor in European Union-Africa relations?' in T. Haastrup, L. Mah and N. Duggan (eds). *The Routledge Handbook of EU–Africa Relations*. London: Routledge.

Akokpari, J. (2016). 'Military intervention in Africa's conflicts as a route to peace: Strengths and pitfalls', *African Journal of Political Science and International Relations*, 10(12): 145–55. DOI: 10.5897/AJPSIR2016.0930.

Akokpari, J. (2008). 'Introduction: Human rights actors and institutions in Africa', in J. Akokpari and D. Zimbler (eds). *Africa's Human Rights Architecture*. Johannesburg: Fanele.

Akokpari, J. (2000). 'Globalisation and migration in Africa', *Africa Sociological Review*, 4(2): 72–92. Dakar: CODESRIA.

Al Jazeera. (2021). 'ECOWAS suspends Mali over second coup in nine months'. Available at: https://www.aljazeera.com/news/2021/5/31/ecowas-suspends-mali-over-second-coup-in-nine-months (Accessed 15 December 2021).

Aly, A.M. and Fatou, G. (2018). *Labor Markets and Jobs in West Africa*. AfDB Working paper Series, No. 297, June.

Ampomah, E. (2019). 'Examining the impediments to conflict management in West Africa: A study of the ECOWAS interventions in Liberia (1990) and Côte d'Ivoire (2010)'. Unpublished MA thesis, University of Cape Town.

Anokam, E. (2021). 'FG delegation to visit Ghana over Nigerian/Ghanaian traders' conflict', *The Guardian*, Nigeria, 10 May. Available at: https://guardian.ng/news/fg-delegation-to-visit-ghana-over-nigerian-ghanaian-traders-conflict/ (Accessed: 10 December 2021).

Asante, S.K.B. (2004). 'The travails of integration', in A. Adebajo and I. Rashid (eds). *West Africa's Security Challenges: Building Peace in a Troubled Region*. London: Lynne Rienner.

Bach, D. (2004). The Dilemmas of Regionalisation in A. Adebajo and I. Rashid (eds). *West Africa's Security Challenges*. Boulder, CO: Lynne Rienner.

Bala, M.T. (2017). 'The challenges and prospects for regional and economic integration in West Africa', *Asian Social Science*, 13(5): 24–34.

Bankole S.A., Olasehinde N. and Raheem A. (2012). 'ECOWAS Trade Liberalization Scheme (ETLS) and its impact on intra-regional trade', *Journal of West African Integration*, 1(1): 1–41.

Barka, H.B. and Ncube, M. (2012). *Political Fragility in Africa: Are military coups d'etat a never-ending phenomenon?* Abidjan: African Development Bank.

Bayane., M.B., Yanjun., Q. and Bekhzad, Y. (2020). 'A review and analysis of railway transportation system in the economic community of West

African States: Towards the development of sustainable regional goal', *Global Journal of Engineering and Technology Advances*, 2(2): 11–22.

Beecroft, I., Osabuohien, E., Efobi, U.R., Olurinola, I.O. and Osabohien, R. (2020). 'Manufacturing export and ICT infrastructure in West Africa: Investigating the roles of economic and political institutions', *Institutions and Economies*, 12(1): 1–36.

Bjornlund, V., Bjornlund H. and Van R.F. (2020). Why agricultural production in sub-Saharan Africa remains low compared to the rest of the world–a historical perspective. *International Journal of Water Resources Development*, 36(1).

Callaghy, T. (1994). 'Civil society, democratisation and economic change: A dissenting opinion about resurgent societies', in J. Harbeson, D. Rothchild and N. Chazan (eds). *Civil Society and the State in Africa*. Boulder, CO: Lynne Rienner, pp. 231–54.

Chete, N.L. and Adewuyi, A.O. (2012). *Dynamics of Trade between Nigeria and Other ECOWAS Countries*. Washington, DC: Brookings Institution.

ECOWAS. (2022). 'A parliamentary seminar aimed at taking ownership of ECOWAS Vision 2050'. Available at: https://parl.ecowas.int/a-parliamentary-seminar-aimed-at-taking-ownership-of-ecowas-vision-2050/ (Accessed 25 May 2022).

ECOWAS. (2016). 'ECOWAS Telecommunications'. Available at: https://www.ecowas.int/ecowas-sectors/telecommunications/ (Accessed 3 November 2021).

ECOWAS. (2010). ECOWAS Revised Treaty. Abuja: Economic Community of West African States (ECOWAS).

ECOWAS. (2010). *Towards a Democratic and Prosperous Community*. Abuja: ECOWAS Commission.

Efobi, R.U. and Osabuohien, S.E. (2016). 'Manufacturing exports, infrastructure and institutions in Africa: Reflections from ECOWAS', in D. Seck (ed.). *Accelerated Economic Growth in West Africa*. Cham: Springer International Publishing, pp. 157–79.

Egbuna, N.E. (2018). 'Evolution of monetary integration: Case of the West African Monetary Zone', *West African Journal of Monetary and Economic Integration*, 18(1): 1–20.

Engel, J. and Jouanjean, M. (2013). *Barriers to Trade in Food Staples in West Africa: An analytical review*, Washington, DC: World Bank Group.

Export–Import Bank of India. (2018). *Connecting Africa: Role of transport infrastructure*, Working Paper No. 27, 9. Available at: www. tralac.org/images/docs/12896/connecting-africa-role-of-transport-infrastructure-exim-bank-working-paper-march-2018.pdf (Accessed 10 December 2021).

GIZ, 2016. *The Common External Tariff (CET): Structure, Benefits, Challenges and the Way Forward of the CET.* Abuja: Deutsche Gesellschaft für Internationale Zusammenarbeit (GIZ) GmbH.

Hartmann, C. 2017. 'ECOWAS and the restoration of democracy in The Gambia', *Africa Spectrum*, 52(1). Hamburg: GIGA Institute for African Affairs. https://doi.org/10.1177/000203971705200104.

Human Rights Watch (HRW). (2018). 'Gambia: ex-president tied to 2005 murders of Ghanaian and Nigerian migrants', 16 May. Available at: https://www.hrw.org/news/2018/05/16/gambia-ex-president-tied-2005-murders-ghanaian-and-nigerian-migrants (Accessed 10 December 2021).

Ikome, F. (2006). 'The West African regional sub-system: myth or reality', in P. McGowan, C. Cornelissen and P. Nel (eds). *Power, Wealth and Global Equity: An international relations textbook for Africa*, 3rd edition. Cape Town: University of Cape Town Press.

Kajee, A. (2014). 'Beau Blaise: The peacebroker or warmonger of Burkina Faso?' *The Daily Vox*, 6 November. Available at: https://www. thedailyvox.co.za/beau-blaise-the-peacebroker-or-warmonger-of-burkina-faso/ (Accessed 4 June 2022).

Lucey, A. and Arewa, M. (2016). *Driving the African Peace and Security Architecture through ECOWAS*. Pretoria: Institute for Security Studies.

Mbaye A.M. and F.Gueye. (2018). Labor Markets and Jobs in West Africa, Working Paper Series No. 297, African Development Bank, Abidjan, Côte d'Ivoire.

Mutasa, C. (2008). 'The African Union's socioeconomic challenges', in T. Karbo and T. Murithi (eds). *The African Union: Autocracy, diplomacy and peacebuilding in Africa*. London: I.B Tauris.

Nossiter, A., Sayare, S. and Bilefsky, D. (2011). 'Leaders' arrest in Ivory Coast ends standoff', *The New York Times*, 11 April. Available at: https://www.nytimes.com/2011/04/12/world/africa/12ivory.html (Accessed 21 October 2021).

Okolo, J.E. (1983). 'The ECOWAS Defence Pact', *The World Today*, 39(5): 177–84.

Opanike, A., Aduloju, A.A. and Adenipekun, L.O. (2015). ECOWAS protocol on free movement and trans-border security in West Africa. *Covenant University Journal of Politics and International Affairs*, 3(1): 41-47.

Ranganathan, R. and Foster V. (2011). *ECOWAS's Infrastructure: A regional perspective*, Policy Research Working Paper No. WPS 5899. Addis Ababa: The World Bank Africa Region Sustainable Development Unit.

Reiss, K. (2015). 'Developing renewable energy sectors and technologies in West Africa'. Available at: https://www.wathi.org/developing-renewable-energy-sectors-and-technologies-in-west-africa-un-chronical/ (Accessed 9 December 2021).

Smith, D. (2011). 'Laurent Gbagbo appears before International Criminal Court', *The Guardian*, 5 December. Available at: https://www.theguardian.com/world/2011/dec/05/laurent-gbagbo-international-criminal-court1 (Accessed 10 December 2021).

Talabi, A. (2020). *ECO: The single currency agenda in West Africa*. Rochester: Social Science Research Network (SSRN).

Timetric, (2017). 'ECOWAS Trans-West African Railway – Nigeria: Project profile'. Available at: https://www.marketresearch.com/Timetric-v3917/ECOWAS-Trans-West-African-Railway-11200916/ (Accessed 3 November 2019).

Tornyi, E. (2015). '"Dumsor" causes 13,000 job cuts in four months'. Available at: http://pulse.com.gh/news/dumsor-unemployment-dumsor-causes-13-000-job-cuts-in-four-months-id3659185.html (Accessed 6 April 2017).

Torres C. and Seters J. (2016). *Overview of Trade and Barriers to Trade in West Africa: Insights in political economy dynamics, with particular focus on agricultural and food trade*, Maastricht: European Centre for Development Policy Management.

Traoré, D. (2021). 'Regional Integration and Scientific Research: The West Africa Institute's support proposal to the implementation of ECOWAS Vision 2050'. Praia: West Africa Institute. DOI:10.13140/RG.2.2.24635.34081

United Nations (UN). (2020). *International Migrant Stock 2020*. Geneva: United Nations. Available at: https://www.un.org/development/desa/pd/content/international-migrant-stock (Accessed 26 October 2021).

United Nations Conference on Trade and Development (UNCTAD).

(2019). *Economic Development in Africa Report 2019: Made in Africa: Rules of origin for enhanced intra-African trade.* Geneva: United Nations. Available at: https://unctad.org/es/node/20390 (Accessed 17 November 2021).

United Nations Conference on Trade and Development (UNCTAD). (2009). *Economic Development in Africa: Strengthening regional economic integration for Africa's Development.* Geneva: United Nations. Available at: https://unctad.org/en/Docs/aldcafrica2009_en.pdf (Accessed 10 January 2020).

United Nations Economic Commission for Africa (UNECA). (2021). 'ECOWAS –Harmonisation of sectoral policies'. Geneva: United Nations. Available at: https://archive.uneca.org/oria/pages/ecowas-harmonisation-sectoral-policies (Accessed 4 March 2021).

Vanheukelom, J. (2017). *Understanding the Economic Community of West African States.* Maastricht: European Centre for Development Policy Management.

World Bank. (2011). *ECOWAS's Infrastructure: A regional perspective*, Policy Research Working Papers. Washington, DC: World Bank. Available at: https://openknowledge.worldbank.org/handle/10986/3666?show=full (Accessed 10 December 2021).

Xuba, M. (2021). 'The Eco-currency: A new chapter for West Africa'. Available at: https://futureafricaforum.org/2021/01/14/the-eco-currency-a-new-chapter-for-west-africa/ (Accessed 10 November 2021).

Chapter Six

Synergy, ambition and challenges in the expanded East African Community

EMMANUEL MATAMBO

Introduction

The African Union (AU) recognises eight Regional Economic Communities (RECs) and the East African Community (EAC), on which this chapter is based, is one of them. The RECs are regional groupings of countries in the African Union. The 1980 Lagos Plan of Action set the tone for the establishment of the RECs. According to the African Union, RECs are regional groupings of African states the purpose of which is 'to facilitate regional economic integration between members of the individual regions and through the wider African Economic Community (AEC), which was established under the Abuja Treaty in 1991' (African Union, 1991). The Lagos Treaty, which has been in operation since 1994, is pointedly tailored to establish an African Common Market, with the RECs as building blocks.

Thus, RECs are a step towards continental integration. Even though regional integration has not borne the expected results historically, the African Union promotes it because it holds promise as a development strategy for Africa. Since the establishment of the Organisation of African Unity (OAU) in 1963, Africa has always called for 'the free movement of goods, services, people and capital between national markets' (Kayizzi-

Mugerwa, Anyanwu and Conceição, 2014: 1). However, regional integration has been slow, despite the patent benefits that the idea bears. A book by the World Bank, *Africa in the New Trade Environment: Market access in troubled times*, recommends that deepening regional trade integration can enhance Africa's market access to the current global trade environment (Coulibaly, Kassa and Zeufack, 2022).

This chapter focuses on the East African Community (EAC). The EAC has seven members, called partner states, comprising Burundi, Kenya, Rwanda, Uganda, Tanzania, South Sudan and the Democratic Republic of the Congo. Apart from the material and security motives and benefits of regional integration, common languages and cultures, some of which are spoken and found in several EAC partner states, are the intangible advantages that could reinforce integration.

Research conducted by Macharia (2013) noted the importance of Swahili, widely spoken across Africa, and how it could 'hasten the integration of the regional bloc [that is, the EAC], and form a firm foundation in preparation for a political federation'. It should be noted that while Swahili is not as popular in Rwanda and Burundi as it is in other members of the EAC, the two countries have increasingly introduced English, a language spoken in other member countries, as an alternative to French, which was previously dominant. This transnational interaction is a historical fact in Africa – not only in the EAC – and it was reinforced through intermarriages and trade, without regard to the borders that were later imposed by Europe. It is testament to East African cultural fluidity, which still prevails to the extent that 'some population groups are [still] oblivious of the existence of such boundaries' (Kibua and Tostensen, 2005: 1).

This chapter starts by exploring the concepts and moments that have defined the EAC in the late 20th century and the new millennium. To contextualise the contemporary EAC, the chapter starts with a historical narrative of colonial and immediate postcolonial attempts to integrate East Africa. It should be noted that the current EAC was preceded by the first EAC, established in 1967 and disbanded in 1977. The chapter then discusses the evolution of mandates, structures and infrastructure of the revived EAC, paying special attention to the key events, actors, drivers and processes. It presents the challenges that beset the EAC, before discussing the opportunities for better integration that exist in the EAC.

History of the EAC

For a more detailed history of East African integration, see Mngomezulu (2013), who offers a rich, archive-based study. This chapter merely provides a brief background to the EAC before independence came to its partners, then rushes to the independence era. It is noteworthy that the idea of an integrated East Africa preceded the independence of the partners that were to later form the EAC. For many years, the British Colonial Office sought to create a federation in East Africa that was to reach as far south as modern-day Zimbabwe (Kiano, 1959: 13; Nujoma, 2001: 121). They established an East African currency in 1905 and a postal union in 1911. An interesting fact is that after the discovery of minerals in South Africa in the second half of the 19th century, European mine owners used to source labour from as far as East Africa (Nujoma, 2001: 51).

The East African High Commission (EAHC) and the East African Central Legislative Assembly were established in 1948 by the British colonial administration, and the East African territories of Kenya, Uganda, Tanganyika and Sudan shared the fate of British imperialism. The colonial authorities believed that putting all British territories under one administration would be more efficient and would cut their administrative costs (Legum, 1967). Thus, the countries of the region shared many intersecting circumstances.

In 1963, prior to the formation of the EAC, the British Royal Office established the University of East Africa (UEA). The UEA was an amalgamation of Makerere University College in Uganda, the Royal College in Nairobi, Kenya, and (later) the University College in Dar es Salaam, Tanzania. At the time, Makerere was already an established institution with ties to the University of London (Hyslop, 1964: 286), thus, the UEA became an independent college of the University of London.

The EAC was first established in 1967, with the signing of the Treaty of East African Cooperation in Uganda. This was a historic moment for East Africa and the accompanying fanfare gave no hint that the EAC would be dissolved only a decade later in 1977. Kenya, Tanzania and Uganda were the founding members of the community. The establishment of the East African Currency Board, one of the main components of the EAC, hinted at a profound commitment to establishing a firm regional community in East Africa. It held much promise but was doomed because of the lack of logistical reconciliation among the three EAC members and national rather than regional moorings. When the UEA was established, Tanganyika (later called Tanzania) and Uganda had gained their independence, and Kenya followed later that year.

As mentioned earlier, when the UEA was envisaged, Makerere was an established institution, its Kenyan counterpart was in its nascent stages, and the Dar es Salaam College was not yet in existence. The UEA, therefore, was an amalgamation of colleges at markedly different levels of development. The disbandment of the UEA in 1970 was a portent of the bleak fate of the EAC.

However, the death of the initial EAC was to come seven years later and political fissures, economic nationalism and instability within member states made the existence of the community untenable, thus leading to its dissolution in 1977. The fall of Uganda's Milton Obote and the accession of Idi Amin to power in Uganda compounded an already fraught situation. Obote's ouster sundered the socialist consonance that Tanzania and Uganda had shared hitherto. Amin was not part of the signatories of the instruments that established the EAC, and his unconstitutional seizure of power repulsed the presidents of Kenya and Tanzania. It is telling as to how unsustainable the situation had become when Tanzania's Julius Nyerere offered the deposed Obote asylum in Tanzania, patently demonstrating that he was at variance with Amin's controversial presidency. In 1978, Amin and Nyerere's mutual resentment resulted in war, which eventually led to Amin's overthrow from power. Relations between Amin and Jomo Kenyatta, the then President of Kenya, were no better than those between Amin and Nyerere.

It should also be noted that Cold War politics were a factor because the EAC members were supported by opposing global players. Kenya was leaning towards the capitalist West, Tanzania with the socialist East such as China, and Uganda was the beneficiary of Soviet support. By adopting the Arusha Declaration in 1967, Tanzania embarked on a socialist trajectory or ideology that emphasised self-reliance over foreign investment (Nyerere, 1977). Milton Obote's *Common Man's Charter* was aligned to Tanzania's socialist path (Gershenberg, 1972). Kenya, on the other hand, crafted the 'African Socialism and its Application to Planning in Kenya' in Sessional Paper No. 10 (1965). This document was an oxymoron because, despite the nomenclature, it opened Kenya to a liberal economic system that attracted foreign investment, some of which would have gone to Uganda and Tanzania had the two countries not adopted frameworks that were not conducive to foreign investment. It is also noteworthy that Kenya had inherited better infrastructure from the colonial government, which was suitable for attracting foreign investment.

According to Adebajo (2020: 41), Tanzania and Uganda felt that among the EAC members, Kenya 'benefitted disproportionally from the inherited British institutions', especially in the area of industry. These ideological and material differences among the initial EAC trinity contributed heavily to weakening EAC synergy. It is difficult to establish a precise date for the formal demise of the community. However, failure to agree on the 1977/78 budget, Kenya's decision to set up its own airline early in 1977, and Tanzania's decision to close its border with Kenya effectively ended the EAC (Hazlewood, 1979). Notwithstanding the unfortunate end of the first EAC, its former members continued to explore the possibilities for future cooperation. They signed the Agreement for the Establishment of the Permanent Tripartite Commission for East African Co-operation on 30 November 1993 (Trans Africa Railway Corporation, 2022). The revived impetus for another EAC should also be seen from the perspective of human security as a pressing issue after the Cold War. Human security transcends national boundaries, and the transnational nature of conflict creates a firm premise for regional integration.

Full East African Co-operation operations started on 14 March 1996 when the Secretariat of the Permanent Tripartite Commission was launched at the headquarters of the EAC in Arusha, Tanzania. Considering the need to consolidate regional cooperation, the East African Heads of State, at their 2nd Summit in Arusha on 29 April 1997, directed the Permanent Tripartite Commission to start the process of upgrading the agreement establishing the Permanent Tripartite Commission for East African Co-operation into a treaty. The treaty-making process, which involved negotiations among the member states, as well as wide participation of the public, was successfully concluded within three years. It was signed on 30 November 1999 and entered into force on 7 July 2000 following the conclusion of the process of its ratification and deposition of the Instruments of Ratification with the Secretary-General by all three partner states. Article 5 of the treaty states that the objectives of the community shall be 'to develop policies and programmes aimed at widening and deepening co-operation among the Partner States in political, economic, social and cultural fields, research and technology, defence, security and legal and judicial affairs, for their mutual benefit'. Article 5(2) commits partner states to establish 'a Customs Union, a Common Market, subsequently a Monetary Union and ultimately a Political Federation'. The EAC has certain strengths that could immunise it from a difficult integration process. On entry into force of the treaty, the East African Community came into being in 2001. In 2004, the EAC signed its Customs Union Protocol, which came into force in 2005. That same year, presidents Yoweri Museveni of Uganda, Benjamin Mkapa of Tanzania, and Arap Moi of Kenya met and noted, with concern, the slow pace at which the EAC was moving towards integration. Thus, in 2006, the office of the Deputy Secretary General responsible for Political Federation was established. By 2022, with an expanded EAC, political federation has still not been achieved, but, as will be shown later, there are milestones that should be met before the envisaged federation is established.

In 2007, Burundi and Rwanda became members. One milestone was the adoption of the EAC Common Market Protocol in 2009, which allowed for the free passage of persons, capital and goods (Nugent and Soi, 2020: 437). This protocol came into force in 2010. South Sudan joined the EAC in 2016. The Democratic Republic of the Congo followed suit in April 2022, as the EAC's latest member. The EAC is very ambitious and unequivocal in its pursuit of political federation. It asserts its uniqueness as 'the only Regional Economic Community that has the objective to attain a Political Federation, in an incremental progression' (EAC, 2014: 9). It has set for itself milestones or stages that would lead to this goal. The Customs Union is the first stage, although important foundations, such as the East African Legislative Assembly (EALA) and the East African Court of Court of Justice (EACJ), had been laid in 2001. The establishment of these institutions 'can be seen as the earliest achievement of the Community towards Political Federation, providing fully functioning executive, legislative and judicial organs' (EAC, 2014: 11). The second stage is the monetary union, and political federation is the final milestone.

The next section will talk about the intricacies of the EAC customs Union.

Status of integration

Barney Walsh (2015: 75) recounts the contradiction of independent Africa's efforts to champion regional integration and the idea of Pan-Africanism, while maintaining the nation-state model left from colonialism. The erstwhile EAC evidently failed to cope with this legacy, and the current EAC is trying to avoid past mistakes. In August 2004, at the EAC Summit in Nairobi, Kenya, the then three EAC partners (Kenya, Tanzania and Uganda) expressed a common concern that integration in East Africa was slow. They appointed a committee that was tasked to find the means by which integration of the EAC could be expedited and the ultimate goal of political federation achieved through a fast-track mechanism. The 2017 EAC Summit suggested establishing a confederation before the ultimate goal of establishing a federation. Drafting of a confederation constitution, which was headed by retired Ugandan Chief Justice Benjamin Odoki, was expected to be finalised by 2021, 'in time for the proposed implementation of the confederation model by 2023' (Havyarimana, 2020). The process has been delayed; the accession of the DRC to the EAC could be a factor, as the DRC did not send its constitutional experts and draftsperson to the committee charged with framing the constitution.

Integration entailed moves such as a customs and monetary union and a common market. These are consistent with Article 75 of the EAC Treaty, which enjoins member states to establish a customs union, which includes the principle of asymmetry, the elimination of internal tariffs and other charges of equivalent effect, the elimination of non-tariff barriers, and rules of origin, among other measures. This has been in force since 2005. By this commitment, EAC countries 'agreed to establish free trade (or zero duty imposed) on goods and services amongst themselves and agreed on a common external tariff (CET), whereby imports from countries outside the EAC zone are subjected to the same tariff when sold to any EAC Partner State'.[1] Obviously the goods that are moved freely within the EAC must adhere to the rules of origin.

Infrastructure is one of the most crucial building blocks for regional and continental integration. At the AU Commission level, the Programme for Infrastructure Development in Africa (PIDA) is enjoined 'to develop a vision and strategic framework for the development of regional and continental infrastructure' (African Development Bank, 2022). The African Union Development Agency (AUDA-NEPAD) established the PIDA Quality Label (PQL) Award to recognise African institutions for excellence

---

1   Treaty for the Establishment of the East African Community (EAC) Customs Union Protocol and EAC Common Market Protocol. Wako Report. EAC Development Strategy.

in project preparation, especially feasibility studies and designs. At the inaugural award ceremony, held in Nairobi, Kenya, from 28 February to 2 March 2022, the EAC was one of the three recipients of the award. The award was for the proposed 256-kilometre, multinational Kisumu–Kisian–Busia/Kakira–Malaba–Busitema–Busia expressway project linking land-locked countries like Uganda with the port of Mombasa in Kenya.

This expressway will form a section of the Northern Corridor and will cover 115 kilometres in Kenya and 147 kilometres in Uganda. It also links to the proposed Rironi–Mau Summit Expressway in Kenya and the Kampala–Jinja Expressway in Uganda. 'When completed, the project will contribute to enhanced regional trade by reducing travel times, improve road safety and promote inter-modal transport services between road, rail and lake transport.' In an earlier study, Nugent and Soi (2020: 435) looked at the One-Stop Border Posts (OSPBs) of Busia between Uganda and Kenya, Malaba also between Uganda and Kenya, and the Mirama Hills and Kagitumba and Katuna/Gatuna (between Uganda and Rwanda). These OSBPs are found on the Northern Corridor which links the port of Mombasa to Uganda, Rwanda and the EAC's latest partner – the Democratic Republic of the Congo. The Northern Corridor is a crucial node of the EAC as it is the passage through which petroleum and basic consumer goods are supplied to the entire subregion. Thus, in terms of infrastructure coordination, the EAC seems to have done reasonably well thus far.

The establishment of the East African passport is another laudable step of integration in the EAC. In April 2017, the 35th EAC Council of Ministers 'directed Partner States to commence issuance of the New EAC e-Passport by 31st January 2018, after the consideration of the different status of preparedness by the Partner States' (EAC, 2017). By May 2022, Uganda was 'the first East African Country to fully shift to the new electronic passport, beating fellow East African Community members who have been deferring the implementation deadline for the new secure documents' (Andae, 2022).

Challenges and opportunities facing the EAC

The Sixth EAC Development Strategy spelt out seven priorities for the EAC, namely:

1. Full implementation of the Single Customs Territory (SCT)
2. Enhancing domestication and implementation of regional commitments

in line with the EAC Common Market Protocol

3.   Attainment of the EAC Single Currency
4.   Strengthening regional peace, security and good governance
5.   Development of quality multi-dimensional strategic infrastructure
6.   Institutional transformation of all EAC organs and institutions
7.   Increasing visibility of the EAC, stakeholder knowledge and awareness.

This section looks at the feasibility of achieving these priorities. The main question should be, how can the reconstituted REC avoid the fate of the first EAC? The ideological fissures that infected the first EAC seem to have been overcome, with all members adopting a liberal rather than statist stance on markets and the economy. This, of course, is hampered somewhat by the unbridled use of state or executive power in politics and, to some extent, the economy in countries such as Rwanda and Uganda.

The generational shift of leaders in the EAC is also an asset that can be used to fortify the community against implosion or inertia. Despite the longevity of leaders in power in Rwanda and Uganda, they all came to power after the collapse of the first EAC. The leaders of all partner states would naturally want to bequeath a better legacy than did the leaders of the first, ill-fated EAC. Uganda and Rwanda have been the strongest drivers of East African integration. President Museveni is the EAC Summit pivot for the work of the Odoki Committee and a champion for political federation. He is also the AU Champion for Regional Integration. The growth of the community is another asset that can be exploited for the good of all. The successful bid of the DRC to join the community attests to the notion that the EAC has some allure for countries in the region. Promoting stability in the DRC and South Sudan could lead to massive gains for the EAC. Due to chronic instability and economic debility, South Sudan has been a laggard. The three-year transitional period since its accession to the EAC ended in October 2019, but, since then, South Sudan has implemented neither the Customs Union Protocol nor the Common Market Protocol, as expected. Payment of its subscription fees have been seriously delayed, partly because it has not had a parliament to facilitate ratification.

The current EAC Treaty emphasises the tenets of democratisation, public participation and human rights. As will be seen, however, the behaviour of some EAC members is at variance with a thrust towards practising these tenets. On its website, the EAC reports that 'the process towards an East African Federation is being fast tracked, underscoring the serious determination of the East African leadership and citizens to construct a powerful and sustainable East African economic and political bloc'. For the EAC, transforming into a federation would be the ultimate stage of integration, but there are formidable hurdles to be surmounted before this can be attained. Some studies (for example, Bizuneh, Bulgut and Valev, 2018) have established that while larger and more stable countries are preferred in regional groupings, fragile and smaller states are not. The EAC, however, has to contend with the reality that it is mostly the big countries, such as the DRC and South Sudan, that seem to be chronically prone to instability. Dealing with massive challenges, as said elsewhere, will require the EAC to muster its resources, while lobbying for inter-REC coordination. In the case of the DRC, which is a member of both the EAC and the SADC, these communities have more chances of countering that country's protracted instability than if the effort were left to one REC.

The configuration of the EAC is such that it is a mixture of democratic, fragile, autocratic and notoriously unstable members. According to the 2021 Democracy Index, for example, the Democratic Republic of the Congo is one of the world's worst democracies (Democracy Index, 2021). Violence is always lurking within partner countries. Even Kenya, the biggest of the EAC economies with democratic promise, has shown a susceptibility to internal strife occasioned by ethnic violence and instability around times of elections. Kenya is also beset by Somali's state failure and instability, especially in the north-east regions that border with Somalia. In Rwanda and Uganda, the EAC has members who are saddled with long-serving or long-ruling regimes, reluctant to embrace political change and electoral credibility.

South Sudan, one of the more recent partners to join the EAC, has been dogged by civil war and internecine conflict almost since its inception in 2011. Magara (2022) argues that while colonial legacies play a part in South Sudan's instability, the death in 2005 of John Garang, who was the founding leader of the Sudan People's Liberation Movement (SPLM), and the accession of Salva Kiir Mayardit saw a sea change in leadership styles. Garang was a trade unionist while Kiir was a soldier, and his leadership style was tailored to catering for military needs at the expense of creating foundations conducive for nation-building. It is, indeed, logical to argue that a lack of national cohesion will, ipso facto, occlude regional integration.

Ethnic strife, a military orientation on state affairs and control of oil revenues have constituted what could be termed South Sudan's original and almost incurable sin. President Salva Kiir and his vice-president, Riek Machar, have been the main protagonists in South Sudan's internecine conflict.

Between 2013 and 2018, the South Sudanese civil war claimed about 400 000 lives and precipitated Africa's biggest refugee crisis since the 1994 Rwandan genocide. It is reported that the civil war spawned 1.7 million internally displaced persons and 2.5 million refugees (OCHA, 2018), and forced millions into extreme hunger (Buchanan, 2018: 5). UNESCO (2018) suggests that about 2.4 million South Sudanese children were out of school as a result. The Institute of Economics and Peace (2020) has thus named South Sudan as one of the world's most unpeaceful countries. Attempts to broker peace between Kiir and Machar have proved fitful, but received a fillip when, in April 2022, Kiir agreed to integrate some military officers loyal to Machar into the national army. As a demonstration of how South Sudan's instability and economic woes adversely impact regional integration, in 2021 the Intergovernmental Authority on Development (IGAD) suspended South Sudan's membership for failure to pay its annual contribution.

The most recent EAC partner, the Democratic Republic of the Congo, is another country that has a long history of instability, and presents one of the most complex and protracted humanitarian crises in Africa. The central government seems to have no control in certain parts of the country. Eastern DRC is mired in ongoing conflict, resulting in massive numbers of people requiring refugee assistance. According to the 2021 Regional Refugee Response Plan (RRRP), under the aegis of the UNHCR, 'by the end of 2020, some 940 421 Congolese refugees and asylum seekers were hosted across the African continent' (UNHCR, 2021). On 14 April 2022, Rwanda and the United Kingdom signed the Rwanda–UK Migration and Economic Development Partnership, which allowed the United Kingdom to send asylum seekers attempting to enter the United Kingdom to Rwanda. However, Rwanda announced that it would not welcome asylum seekers from its EAC partners of Burundi, Uganda, Tanzania and the DRC (Iliza, 2022). This, of course, is unlikely to stem the flow of migrants or asylum seekers across EAC borders, if the region is still stalked by insecurity. From this backdrop, the EAC is bound to encounter many difficulties, and crucial among these will be the human security of EAC citizens. The lack of candour at state level, which allows odious and long-ruling regimes to remain entrenched, shows that, while the EAC might claim to have a people-centred approach, this is more by declaration than by action, as citizens of authoritarian regimes do not enjoy the support of other EAC partners.

The simplified trade regime, modelled on the Common Market for Eastern and Southern Africa (COMESA) one, with a simplified certificate of origin, has had limited success, as has its COMESA prototype. This is because even though the EAC has simplified paperwork and formal customs clearance processes, certain domestic taxes and other border requirements have not been exempted. Implications of the regime remain generally incomprehensible to small-scale cross-border traders. 'In order to ease compliance by businesses and enhance the transparency of trade procedures, the East African Community trade information portal, an online platform linked to national trade facilitation portals in Kenya, Rwanda, Uganda and the United Republic of Tanzania, was launched in 2018' (UNCTAD, 2021: 79). Borders have proven to be particularly troublesome for the EAC. With limited industrial capacity, Rwanda and Uganda rely on receiving supplies of petroleum and consumer goods by roads. In the recent past, the two countries have had a complex border relationship. Tanzania has used food security as a justification for limiting food exports (Nugent and Soi, 2020: 437).

During the life of the initial EAC, sub-nationalisms played a part in occluding regional integration. Ethnic exclusivism, such as in Uganda, where King Mutesa II saw himself as separate from Uganda, weakened Uganda's own unity, let alone its integration with other countries. Mutesa and the Ugandan central government fought a civil war in 1966, which forced the King to go into exile in Britain. Coming a year before the establishment of the EAC, this civil war boded ill for East Africa's regional synergy and unity. Nationalist rather than regional thinking was thus a major hurdle in forging regionalism.

There should be studies into what caused the first EAC to collapse in 1977 and what the current players could do to prevent a similar fate. Kaburu and Adar (2020) argue that the founding treaties of EAC I and EAC II did not provide any avenues for the direct involvement of citizens in integration. As such, both took on a statist approach, which left out citizens who are the direct participants and beneficiaries of EAC initiatives. It is noteworthy, though, that Article 7(1) of the EAC Treaty states that the principles governing the EAC would include 'people-centred and market-driven co-operation'. Walsh (2015: 75) argues that the absence of a people-centred approach, in addition to nationalist tendencies, dealt a body blow to the first EAC. Following the same logic, Mulindwa (2020: 601) argues that the 'exclusion of strong actors such as [the] private sector and civil society from the Community's activities' was a factor in the demise of the first EAC. However, it should be taken into cognisance that at the time of the first EAC, the partner states were quite young, and might not yet have developed a formidable civil society base or a strong private sector. Kibua and Tostensen (2005: 3) argue that, unlike the situation during the first EAC, currently the private sector and civil society have become more assertive in the state affairs of EAC members. The private sector, appreciating how state-led economics hamper growth, have become important players in the EAC.

COVID-19 had a devastating impact on the EAC. From a decent regional growth rate of 5.4 per cent in 2019, the 2020 growth rate dropped to 2.3 per cent. According to the 2021/22 EAC budget, this contraction was a consequence of a reduction in exports, imports of intermediate goods, and the industrial sector. Lockdown measures taken to contain COVID-19 had adverse effects 'on tourism and aviation sectors, workers' remittances, foreign direct investment and loan disbursements' (Mohamed, 2021: 2). The EAC is plotting its economic recovery based on industrialisation and inclusive growth. The effectiveness of this strategy is yet to be seen.

Another factor that could hamper integration and stability in the EAC is the rise of extremist groups. Kenya has had to endure acts of terror as a result of, among other factors, 'politically unstable neighbouring countries like Somalia' (Otiso, 2009: 107). Tanzania should gird for similar instability across its border with the Mozambican province of Cabo Delgado. In October 2021, violent extremism also affected Uganda (in Kampala) and Tanzania (in Arusha). This problem requires a regional approach and offers a firm basis for deeper integration in East Africa, even beyond the EAC. In fact, this rising extremism calls for synergy across regional economic communities, across the EAC and the SADC in the case of Cabo Delgado. Ahlus Sunnah wal Jama'ah (ASWJ), locally known as al-Shabaab, has been conducting acts of terror in northern Mozambique, mainly since 2017. Reportedly, this group is sponsored by cross-border traders whose theatres of activity are in Tanzania (Zanzibar) and the Comoros (Casola and Iocchi,

2020). The Instituto de Estudos Sociais e Económicos (IESE), a Maputo-based research institute, argues that it was actually 'Tanzanian religious leaders [who] influenced the indoctrination and the recruitment of young Mozambicans into Al Shabaab's ranks' (Chichava 2022; see also Okunade, Faluyi and Matambo, 2021).

In both Tanzania and Mozambique, members of ASWJ are reported to be engaged in businesses such as timber logging and illegal poaching to fund their activities. This rise of extremism in Mozambique and Tanzania will cause further problems for the EAC and add to the insecurity that has already been wrought by the Somali-based al-Shabaab. Uganda has also endured violent extremism, which came to the fore in October 2021. Failure to deal effectively with this will arouse instincts of more border restrictions among countries of East Africa, thus undermining the gains that have already been made for the smooth passage of goods and services. To deal with this violent extremism requires not only deeper integration in the EAC, but also synergy among the different RECs, in this case the EAC and the SADC, whose member states, sharing borders as they do, have to contend with this cross-border violent extremism.

Conclusion

The EAC has an instructive history from which it could draw lessons for its current configuration. The first EAC failed due to the legacies of colonialism and instability, both within and among member states. This chapter argues that the EAC has certain advantages, despite being encumbered by daunting challenges. A common history, language and cultures – which were more apparent when Kenya, Tanzania and Uganda were the only Partner States – are advantages that could foster cohesion. These intangible advantages could then be used to achieve practical dividends in terms of political stability and economic gain.

The ambition and clarity of the EAC in what it wants to achieve in terms of creating a confederation and then a federation is a laudable characteristic in a region that, ultimately, seeks integration of the African continent. The challenges confronting the EAC include instability in countries such as the DRC and South Sudan, even though the EAC could actually be the solution to this instability. It is also noteworthy that Rwanda and Uganda, the leading drivers of East African integration, with Uganda being the champion of EAC political union, have entrenched regimes that have amended their constitutions in order to retain power. This scarcely bodes well for a region that seek to bolster the voice and participation of ordinary citizens in regional affairs. Extremist violence in non-EAC members, such as Somalia and Mozambique, which share borders with EAC members, also pose mortal danger to stability. These issues, compounded by the adverse effects of COVID-19, are the challenges with which the EAC has to contend.

References

Adebajo, A. (2020). 'Pan-Africanism: From the twin plagues of European locusts to Africa's triple quest for emancipation', in A. Adebajo (ed). *The Pan-African Pantheon: Prophets, poets and philosophers.* Johannesburg: Jacana Media, pp. 3–57.

African Development Bank (ADB). (2022). *Programme for Infrastructure Development in Africa (PIDA).* Available at: https://bit.ly/3igugW0 (Accessed 20 October 2021).

African Union. (1991). *Regional Economic Communities (RECs).* Available at: https://au.int/en/organs/recs (Accessed 10 October 2021).

Andae, G. (2022). 'Uganda leads East Africa in fully switching to e-passport', *The East African*, 24 May. Available at: https://bit.ly/3TzxyEf (Accessed 16 October 2021).

Buchanan, E. (2018). 'Hungry for peace: Exploring the links between conflict and hunger in South Sudan', reliefweb, Oxfam, 28 February.

Casola, C. and Iocchi, A. (2020). 'The "faceless evildoers" of Cabo Delgado: An Islamist insurgency in Mozambique? *ISPI Commentaries.* Oslo: Norsk Utenrikspolitisk Institutt. Available at: https://hdl.handle.net/11250/2711439 (Accessed 20 November 2022).

Chichava, S. (2022). 'Maulana Ali Cassimo: Insurgence in the north of Mozambique as seen from Niassa', *IDeIAS*, No. 147. Instituto de Estudos Sociais o Economicos. Available at: https://www.iese.ac.mz/wp-content/uploads/2022/03/ideias-147E-SC-1.pdf (Accessed 20 October 2021).

Coulibaly, S., Kassa, W. and Zeufack, A.G. (2022). *Africa in the New Trade Environment: Market access in troubled times.* Washington, DC: World Bank. Available at: https://openknowledge.worldbank.org/

handle/10986/36884 License: CC BY 3.0 IGO (Accessed 20 October 2021).

Democracy Index. 2021. Democracy Index 2021: The China challenge. Available at: https://www.eiu.com/n/campaigns/democracy-index-2021/ (Accessed 12 November 2021).

East African Community (EAC). (2022a). *Overview of EAC*. Available at: https://www.eac.int/overview-of-eac (Accessed 20 October 2021).

East African Community (EAC). (2022b). *Customs Union*. Available at: https://www.eac.int/customs-union. (Accessed 20 October 2021).

East African Community (EAC). (2022c). *EAC Secretariat receives top award during 7th PIDA Week held in Nairobi*. Available at: https://bit.ly/3JjxB2z (Accessed 20 October 2021).

East African Community (EAC). (2022d). Sixth EAC Development Strategy 2021/22–2025/26. Available at: https://www.eac.int/documents/category/strategy (Accessed 20 October 2021).

East African Community (EAC). (2017). *EAC to start issuing EA e-Passport January 2018*. Available at: https://bit.ly/3ElArCa (Accessed 20 October 2021).

East African Community (EAC). (2014). *Towards Political Federation in the East African Community: Achievements and challenges*. Available at: https://www.eac.int/component/documentmananger/category/political-federation (Accessed 20 October 2021).

Economist Intelligence Unit. 2021. 'Democracy Index, 2021'. London: Economist Intelligence.

Gershenberg, I. (1972). 'Slouching towards socialism: Obote's Uganda', *African Studies Review*, 15(1): 79–95.

Goto, J. (2012). 'Regional integration in East Africa diversity or economic conformity', Ethnic Diversity and Economic Instability in Africa: Policies for harmonious development. JICA-RI Working Paper No. 46, June. Tokyo: JICA Research Institute, pp. 1–26.

Havyarimana, M. (2020). 'Regional experts draft confederation constitution', *The East African*, 18 January. Available at: https://www.theeastafrican.co.ke/news/ea/East-africa-experts-draft-confederation-constitution/4552908-5422610-11fx1ge/index.html (Accessed 20 October 2021).

Hazlewood, A. (1979). 'The end of the East African Community: What are the lessons for regional integration schemes?' *JCMS: Journal of Common Market Studies*, 18(1): 40–58.

Hyslop, J.M. (1964). 'The University of East Africa', *Minerva*, 2(3): 286–302.

Iliza, A. (2022). 'Rwanda excludes refugees from neighbouring states in UK deal', *The East African*, 15 April. Available at: https://www.theeastafrican.co.ke/tea/news/east-africa/rwanda-excludes-refugees-from-neighbouring-states-in-uk-deal-3783834 (Accessed 18 October 2021).

Institute of Economics and Peace. (2020), 'Global peace index, 2020: Measuring peace in a complex world.' Available at: www.visionofhumanity.org/wp-content/uploads/2020/10/GPI_2020_web.pdf (Accessed 20 October 2021).

Kaburu, M.K. and Adar, K.G. (2020). 'Kenya citizens' sovereignty', in K.G. Adar, K.P. Apuuli, A.L. Lando, P-L. Masabo and J. Masabo (eds). *Popular Participation in the Integration of the East African Community: Eastafricanness and Eastafricanization*. Lanham, MD: Lexington Books, pp. 55–75.

Kayizzi-Mugerwa, S., Anyanwu, J.C. and Conceição, P. (2014). 'Regional integration in Africa: An introduction', *African Development Review*, 26(S1): 1–6.

Kiano, J.K. (1959). 'The Pan-African freedom of East and Central Africa?' *Africa Today*, vi (4).

Kibua, T.N. and Tostensen, A. (2005). *Fast-tracking East African Integration. Assessing the Feasibility of a Political Federation by 2010*, CMI Report R 2005: 14. Bergen: Chr. Michelsen Institute.

Legum, C. (ed). (1967). *Africa: A Handbook*. London: Anthony Blond.

Macharia, J.M. (2013). 'The role of a unitary language and communication in enhancing regional integration in the East African Community (EAC)'. Unpublished doctoral thesis, University of Nairobi. Available at: http://erepository.uonbi.ac.ke/handle/11295/60128 (Accessed 20 October 2021).

Magara, I.S. (2022). 'Complexities of international mediation at sub-regional levels in Africa: Lessons from South Sudan', *Journal of Aggression, Conflict and Peace Research*.

Mngomezulu, B.R. (2013). 'Why did regional integration fail in East Africa in the 1970s? A historical explanation'. Available at: https://phambo.wiser.org.za/files/seminars/Mngomezulu2013.pdf (Accessed 20 October 2021).

Mohamed, A. (2021). 'Presentation of the Budget of the East African Community for the Financial year 2021/22'. Available at: https://www.eac.int/documents/category/key-documents (Accessed 2 October 2021).

Mulindwa, P. (2020). 'The interstate border conflicts and their effects on region-building and integration of the East African Community', *African Journal of Governance and Development*, 9(2): 599–618.

Nugent, P. and Soi, I. (2020). One-stop border posts in East Africa: State encounters of the fourth kind. *Journal of Eastern African Studies*, 14(3): 433–454.

Nujoma, S. (2001). *Where Others Wavered: The autobiography of Sam Nujoma*. London: Panaf Books.

Nyerere, J.K. (1977). 'The Arusha Declaration ten years after', *African Review*, 7(2): 1–34.

Okunade, S.K., Faluyi, O.T. and Matambo, E. (2021). 'Evolving patterns of insurgency in Southern and West Africa: Refocusing the Boko Haram lens on Mozambique', *African Security Review*, 30(4): 434–50.

Otiso, Kefa (2009). 'Kenya in the crosshairs of global terrorism: Fighting terrorism at the periphery', *Kenya Studies Review*, 1(1): 107–32.

Trans Africa Railway Corporation. (2022). 'East African Community'. Available at: https://tarcltd.com/eac/ (Accessed 6 October 2021).

UNCTAD. (2021). Reaping the Potential benefits of the African Continental Free Trade Area for inclusive growth. Available at: https://unctad.org/system/files/official-document/aldcafrica2021_en.pdf (Accessed 16 October 2021).

United Nations Conference on Trade and Development (UNCTAD). (2022). UN list of least developed countries. Available at: https://unctad.org/topic/least-developed-countries/list (Accessed 21 October 2021).

United Nations Conference on Trade and Development (UNHCR). (2021). The Democratic Republic of Congo Regional Refugee Response Plan. Available at: https://data2.unhcr.org/en/documents/details/86008 (Accessed 20 October 2021).

United Nations Office for the Coordination of Humanitarian Affairs (OCHA). (2018). 'Humanitarian bulletin: South Sudan.' Available at: https://reliefweb.int/sites/reliefweb.int/files/resources/20180716_OCHA_SouthSudan_Humanitarian_Bulletin%236.pdf (Accessed 20 October 2021).

Walsh, B. (2015). 'Human security in East Africa: The EAC's illusive quest for inclusive citizenship', *Strategic Review for Southern Africa*, 37(1): 75–98.

Chapter Seven

The Intergovernmental Authority on Development and regional integration in the Horn of Africa

JOSEPH MAKANDA

Introduction

This chapter explores the role of the Intergovernmental Authority on Development (IGAD) in enhancing regional integration in the Horn of Africa. It assesses the IGAD's performance in promoting regional cooperation on important issues such as peace and security, research and development, infrastructure and food security. It takes stock of the progress that the IGAD has made thus far in harmonising the macroeconomic policies and development strategies of its member states.

The first section presents a historical overview of the IGAD, its formation and organisation, and features of the region. This is followed by a discussion of the IGAD's strategy and implementation plan to enhance regional integration in the Horn of Africa, which includes outlining its four main pillars. The third section highlights the challenges faced by the IGAD in attempting to enhance integration in a region that continues to be engulfed in struggles over economic and political power, marked by ethnic conflict and unstable peace and security. The author argues that through infrastructure development, the IGAD has been able to address, to some extent, the challenges of drought, access to markets, food and information, and promote integration and cooperation in the region.

Historical overview and the formation and organisation of the IGAD region

The quest for regional integration in Africa dates back to the early 20th century. According to Karangizi (2012), the inspiration for establishing and strengthening the regional integration institutions, also known as Regional Economic Communities (RECs), was the signing of the Abuja Treaty on 3 June 1991 by then Organisation of African Unity (OAU). Aniche (2020) and Mncube (2020) say that the Abuja Treaty contained a roadmap, comprising of six stages, to establish a full-fledged African economic community. The first stage entailed establishing regional economic blocs within five years of signing the Abuja Treaty into full effect (which was by 1999). The second stage involved strengthening the integration of the Regional Economic Community within another eight years, in other words, by 2007. Stage three entailed the establishment of a custom union and free trade agreements and zones at the level of the RECs, which was supposed to be achieved by 2017. This was to be followed by the harmonisation of customs and tariffs, and a common market in stage four, which was to be achieved by 2019. Stage five involved setting up of the continent's economic and monetary union (including the establishment of a single currency and a pan–African parliament) by 2023. The final stage was envisaged as being a transitional period for the full integration of political, economic and monetary policies on the continent by 2028 (Parliamentary Monitoring Group, 2000).

Tshimpaka, Nshimbi and Moyo (2021) contend that, 30 years after the signing of the Abuja Treaty, it is difficult to measure the successes and failures of the RECs in Africa because of the different processes of economic development and political conditions in each country. While the deadlines set in the Abuja Treaty have lapsed, with less than 10 years left to achieve full union by 2028, there is still some optimism about economic integration and achieving the objectives of the proposed union. For instance, Magu (2021) points out that much is still being invested in establishing the New Economic Partnership for Africa's Development (NEPAD), the eight RECs, the Economic Commission for Africa (ECA) and the African Development Bank (AfDB), among other institutions. Generally, the purpose of the RECs is to continue facilitating regional economic integration between members of the various regions and through the wider African Economic Community (AEC). According to Arthur (2017), the African Union (AU)

recognises the following eight RECS:
1. Arab Maghreb Union (UMA)
2. Common Market for Eastern and Southern Africa (COMESA)
3. Community of Sahel–Saharan States (CEN–SAD)
4. East African Community (EAC)
5. Economic Community of Central African States (ECCAS)
6. Economic Community of West African States (ECOWAS)
7. Intergovernmental Authority on Development (IGAD), and the
8. Southern African Development Community (SADC).

Among these RECs, the IGAD represents an interesting case in terms of its aspirations, objective realities, composition, contradictions and pressing demands for regional integration and cooperation. Some of the challenges facing the IGAD are persistent hunger and starvation, and both intrastate and interstate conflicts (Idris, 2019). In relation to human security in Africa, no other region is more plagued by protracted violent conflicts than the IGAD region. The presence of more than four United Nations and African Union peacekeeping operations in the region, involving over 50 000 troops (in Darfur, Abyei, Somalia and South Sudan), hundreds of Qatari military observers on the Djibouti–Eritrea border and thousands of Western military forces in Djibouti, attests to the peace and security challenges afflicting the region. A number of studies suggest that most IGAD member states, including South Sudan, which was sucked into a deeper political crisis and conflict at the end of 2013, are among the 35 most underdeveloped countries in the world (Mwenda, 2014; Back, 2016; Apuuli, 2020; Nwoko, 2021). The region is also faced with insurgents such as the Harakat al-Shabaab al-Mujahidden (al-Shabaab) operating mostly in Somalia and Kenya, and the Lord's Resistance Army (LRA) operating in Uganda, and South Sudan, the Central African Republic and the Democratic Republic of the Congo (DRC) (Apuuli, 2020; IGAD 2020). While these challenges continue to hamper the region, the IGAD remains resilient in facilitating economic integration among its member states.

The IGAD is the successor to the Intergovernmental Authority on Drought and Development (IGADD), which was founded in 1986 to address the recurring droughts and other natural disasters that had caused severe hardship in the East African countries of Djibouti, Ethiopia, Kenya, Somalia, Sudan and Uganda. On attaining its independence, Eritrea joined the IGADD in 1993 to become the seventh member state (Back,

2016; Desmidt, 2016; Berhanu, 2020). At its inception, Heally (2011) and Vhumbunu (2020) say that the IGADD had three focus areas. First, the IGADD was concerned with emergency and relief measures to alleviate the suffering of the victims of environmental disasters and drought. The IGADD's responses included assessing and determining the impact and extent of the disaster, and mobilising and coordinating relief measures. Second, the IGADD focused on short- to medium-term measures to deal with the effects of any crisis through resource and knowledge sharing, skill development and training, and infrastructural development. Specifically, the IGADD aimed to ensure the resilience of communities against drought; in other words, the IGADD ensured that food security was maintained, desertification was controlled, and natural resources (such as water, energy and marine resources) were rehabilitated and used effectively. Third, the IGADD aimed to develop long-term initiatives and projects to deal with the sustainability of the environment and development. In this regard, IGADD paid particular attention to the rural economy and the agricultural sector. From these main activities, it can be said that the IGADD was driven by the ultimate desire to not only improve food security, but also to deal with environmental challenges through regional cooperation.

However, in the 1990s, the Horn of Africa was faced with a series of peace and security challenges, such as the violent creation of Eritrea, the collapse of Somalia, the rise of cross-border terrorist threats and multiple political and security challenges. Driven by these new emerging political and socioeconomic challenges in the region, the Assembly of Heads of State and Government met in Addis Ababa in April 1995 and resolved to revitalise the IGADD as a response to the emerging political, economic and security challenges (Idris, 2019; Vhumbunu, 2020). Following the consensus built in these meetings, the regional states signed a Letter of Instrument to Amend the IGADD Charter/Agreement on 21 March 1996. As a result, the IGAD was born. The revitalised IGAD mandate increased to include promoting greater regional political and economic cooperation, as well as addressing peace and security issues. It also implemented a new organisational structure. Under Article 7 of the agreement establishing the IGAD, its aims and objectives include promoting joint development strategies; harmonising member states' policies; achieving regional food security; initiating sustainable development of natural resources; promoting peace and stability in the subregion; and mobilising resources for the implementation of programmes within the framework of subregional cooperation (IGAD, 2016b: 33; Ministers, 2020).

Organisationally, the IGAD is made up of four segments:

1. The Assembly of Heads of State and Government makes policy and directs and controls the functioning of the IGAD. It determines the main guidelines and programmes of cooperation and provides guidelines and monitors political issues especially on conflict prevention, management and resolution. It also appoints the executive secretary and approves the scale of contributions of member states to the budget.

2. The Council of Ministers comprises ministers of foreign affairs of member states, and one other focal minister who is designated by each member state (Article 10). This council is tasked with examining political and security affairs, including conflict prevention, management and resolution; post-conflict monitoring and enhancing humanitarian activities; promoting peace and security in the subregion and making recommendations to the Assembly of Heads of State and Government (Article 10).

3. The Committee of Ambassadors comprises assigned ambassadors from IGAD member states. The main functions and duties of this committee are, first, to 'advise the Executive Secretary on the promotion of his/her efforts in realizing the work plan approved by the Council of Ministers' and, second, to 'guide the Executive Secretary on the interpretation of policies and guidelines which may require further elaboration' (Article 11, point 2).

4. The Secretariat is an executive body of the IGAD (Article 12) tasked with following up on the resolutions of the assembly and council dealing with draft proposals and agreements, facilitating the economic and social development policy, arranging necessary resources to administer projects and programmes, and implementing regional projects and policies (Healy, 2011). In a nutshell, the Secretariat runs many of the activities of the IGAD such as the essential tasks of programme development, coordination, implementation and monitoring. In addition, the Secretariat deals with many national and regional policies and strategies at the national and regional levels (IGAD, 2016b).

For smooth operation of the Secretariat, Weldesellassie (2011) points out that there are four directors assisting the executive secretary, each with specific responsibilities:

1. agriculture and environment
2. economic cooperation and social development
3. peace and security, and
4. administration and finance.

The IGAD also has additional specialised institutions and programmes with their coordinators, such as the IGAD Security Sector Programme (ISSP), Conflict Early Warning and Response Mechanism (CEWARN), IGAD Centre for Pastoral Area and Livestock Development (ICPALD), IGAD Regional Aids Programme (IRAPP) and IGAD Climate Prediction and Applications Centre (ICPAC). The organisational structures are specifically designed to facilitate the regional strategy and implementation plan of the IGAD.

Features of the IGAD region

The IGAD region is one of the most strategic in Africa and covers an area of about 5.3 million square kilometres, straddling eight countries – Ethiopia, Djibouti, Eritrea, Somalia, South Sudan, Sudan, Kenya and Uganda. It is in the Red Sea Basin, thus linking Africa to the Middle East and the Nile Basin. Its coastline extends from the Red Sea to the Indian Ocean, including the Gulf of Aden and the Gulf of Toudjoura (with 6 960 kilometres of coastline). Inland, the region has 6 910 kilometres of international borders linking it to the Central African Republic, the Democratic Republic of the Congo, Rwanda, Egypt, Libya, Chad and Tanzania (Mwendwa, 2014; Nanni, 2016; Grant, Issa and Yusuf, 2020).

The IGAD region has a population of about 291 468 933 people (Hersi and Sharamo, 2020), and, by 2050, Bereketeab (2021) says that IGAD's population is estimated to rise to about 400 million. More than 55 per cent of this population will be under the age of 20 years. This might become a double-edged sword in that it could be an opportunity if they receive education and training and participate in the economy of these states, or it could be a source of instability if these economies fail to incorporate the youth into the economy and productive activity. Unfortunately, since the majority of the IGAD member states belong to the world's 'Least Developed Countries', unless the region can find a way to transform its economy, this certainly poses significant challenges to the regional bloc. In addition, a large percentage of the economic output of member states is dependent on natural resources (mining and agriculture) and most of the population is dependent on subsistence farming. This is aside from the recent mushrooming of flagship infrastructural projects and industrial parks across the region that are meant to usher in industrialisation and develop the manufacturing sector (Banerjee, 2021). The region's agriculture, comprising livestock and crop production, provides the basis for food supplies and export earnings, and employs over 80 per cent of the region's population (IGAD, 2016). This dependency on agriculture means that land and ecological corruption is a threat as it can influence and disrupt agrarian production and financial development and endanger food security and lead to starvation in the region. As a result, access to land and water remains one of the security and development concerns as ever-increasing population numbers and the urge to secure land create tensions within communities.

IGAD's regional strategy and implementation plan

In January 2016, the IGAD published the *IGAD Regional Strategy* as a way of assessing its 2011–2015 regional strategic programme. The *IGAD Regional Strategy, Volume 1, 2011–2015* was the first of its kind and set a foundation for strategic direction, planning and implementation by facilitating regional cooperation and integration. Prior to this document, for well over a decade, the regional body had been operating for the large part with programmes set on issues and on a sectoral basis and with very little strategic direction (IGAD, 2016). Later, IGAD published the *IGAD Regional Strategy, Volume 2: Implementation Plan 2016–2020* (IGAD, 2020; Ministers, 2020). Recently, the IGAD signed the regional strategy 2021–2025 (IGAD, 2021). All strategy documents reflect the specific strategic objectives of the IGAD to advance regional integration and cooperation, and envision a five-year action plan of implementation and monitoring in the Horn of Africa. While these areas of cooperation are extensive and detailed, they feature overlapping issues and themes.

Furthermore, all the IGAD's regional strategy documents (2011–2015, 2016–2020 and 2021–2025) focus on four key pillars:

- Pillar 1: Agriculture, natural resources and environment
- Pillar 2: Economic cooperation, integration and social development
- Pillar 3: Peace and security, and humanitarian affairs, and
- Pillar 4: Corporate development services.

These four pillars are meant to operationalise the objectives that IGAD has set out and turn them into concrete strategies and plans of action. For instance, in the strategic plan of 2011–2015, the IGAD identified institutional and wide regional capacity building by creating regional, continental and international partnerships to facilitate information and knowledge sharing in an early warning system. Similarly, in the 2016–2020 strategic plan, the IGAD sought new ways of promoting economic cooperation and social development in the region by enhancing regional capacity in agriculture, livestock development and food security. The main components of the implementation plans include funding the institutional capacity of security reform and the implementation of peace and sustainable development programmes, transitioning from medium-term to annual action plans, and monitoring and evaluation frameworks (IGAD, 2020). In IGAD's new 2021–2025 strategy document, intense reflections on the development of the new peace and security strategy are overemphasised. Arguably, in all regional strategy documents, the emphasis has been put on the specific strategic objectives of the IGAD in advancing regional integration and cooperation in that region. Hence, one cannot assess the IGAD's performance in promoting regional cooperation on such important issues as peace and security, research and development, infrastructure and food security, without taking cognisance of what each of the four pillars does and what it has achieved so far.

IGAD's four pillars

The IGAD's first pillar acknowledges the crucial role that agriculture plays in the region's economy. Over 80 per cent of the population in the region derive their livelihood from agriculture and, therefore, factors that directly affect land productivity 'constitute a continuous challenge to the welfare of the population' (IGAD, 2016c: 4). This pillar also acknowledges the region's perennial problem of hunger and starvation as a result of food insecurity. While agriculture remains a dominant means of livelihood, the regional strategy 2016–2020 admits that over '20 million of the region's 291 million population are chronically food insecure'. To alleviate the problem of food insecurity, the IGAD has a strong policy regarding access to sufficient food in Pillar 1, and encourages the effective management of the environment and natural resources. According to the IGAD (2016):

Member states recognize that a clean and healthy environment is a prerequisite for sustainable development and development activities in various productive and social sectors including agriculture and livestock, energy, industry and infrastructure may pose a negative impact leading to the degradation of the environment.

It is worth noting, therefore, that the regional body's major concern in Pillar 1 is the two interlocked problems of food insecurity and environmental degradation (IGAD 2016; Abebe, 2021). This is reflected succinctly in the organisation's heavy investment on Pillar 1, which was an initial mandate of the IGAD's predecessor, IGADD. In this regard, the IGAD has put in place the following programme areas: agriculture, livestock and food security, and natural resources management. Furthermore, the agriculture, livestock and food security programme has been split into five strategic programmes:

1. Agricultural production programme
2. Food security programme
3. Livestock development programme
4. Dryland development programme, and
5. Fisheries management programme.

The three main expected deliverables from the agriculture, livestock and food security programme are:

1. Improved and enhanced food security through the development of agriculture, fisheries and livestock, with which the region is well endowed. This is amidst the region's struggling agricultural development, which is dependent on erratic rainfall.
2. Improved livelihood and diminished poverty through agricultural development.
3. Enhanced resilience to natural disasters and economic shocks (IGAD, 2016).

Therefore, because of the high level of drought and starvation in the Horn of Africa, the IGAD has invested more resources in Pillar 1: agriculture, livestock and food security, than in all other programme areas. This is a clear sign that agriculture is a predominant sector, and it is linked to the argument that a lack of basic needs such as food is a key instigator of the region's conflicts (Abebe, 2021).

To address the problem of food insecurity as a result of drought and environmental degradation, the IGAD in conjunction with several other organisations like the FEWS-NET and the UN Food and Agriculture Organization's (FAO's) Global Information and Early Warning System (GIEWS) have instituted systems and mechanisms that have improved their weather forecast capabilities. While remote sensing and data processing technologies have continued to rapidly improve, it remains equally important for the IGAD's member states and development partners to recognise and react to these warnings (King-Okumu *et al.*, 2019; Tanui, 2020; Lung *et al.*, 2021). For instance, IGAD has made progress, especially in Kenya, largely through the collection of bottom-up information on vulnerability and responsiveness (Tanui, 2020).

The IGAD has also put in place some social protection schemes that have shown to be necessary and potentially effective against the severe impacts of drought, felt mostly by financially vulnerable people who are highly and directly dependent on natural resources. Del-Ninno, Coll-Black and Fallavier (2016) cite the Ethiopia Productive Safety Net Programme Phase III, which serves up to 8 million people, usually with food or cash-for-work/collective assets. Still, Mohamed (2017) says that this Ethiopian programme assists to a minor extent with direct household asset building, producing positive results for the poorest 20 per cent of the population. In Kenya, Song and Imai (2019) contend that the IGAD has come up with a Hunger Safety Net Programme that provides regular, unconditional electronic cash transfers of $25.00 per month to up to 100 000 households.

Infrastructure was found to be positively correlated with drought resilience and better drought management practices, which may be explained through better access to markets for inputs, outputs, food and information (King-Okumu *et al.*, 2020). As a result, food, feed and water can now be transported much faster than before over the main road axes in the regions, and populations go to urban centres to access assistance during drought and flooding seasons. In the context of drought, water resource management obviously needs attention. Water is essential for humans and for livestock, and is of key importance to agriculture, and there are many efforts all over the region to improve water access and quality (see, for instance, the IGAD's [2020] mapping of water resources in the transboundary Karamojong cluster).

Furthermore, the IGAD member states and the Secretariat have come up with various strategies to deal with the challenges posed by transhumance, including memoranda of understanding between countries, strategies on cross-border animal health, the mapping of transhumance routes, and integrated early warning systems on climate change. Studies have established that the initiatives and activities that have achieved the best results tend to be those that adopt a cross-border approach (Lung *et al.*, 2020; Tanui, 2020).

IGAD's Pillar 2 is anchored in economic cooperation, integration and social development. The main aim is to enhance and accelerate regional economic cooperation and social development for the region. This pillar is responsible for assessing the existing levels of trade integration in the region and on the continent. According to the IGAD (2016), intraregional trade and regional markets have remained stagnant and small, so Pillar 2 was established as a way of addressing these trade concerns. The IGAD's regional strategy for 2016–2020 (IGAD, 2016: 7) outlines three components that need to be enhanced if regional markets and relations are to be expanded. The broader key indicators of success for this pillar include:

- the number of cross-border trade agreements between all the member states
- the establishment of a functional free trade area
- a modified human development index and migration policy, and
- the strategies developed and adopted by member states (IGAD, 2016).

The first programme area of Pillar 2 is trade and investment, industry development and tourism. The main aim is to increase cross-border trade and interregional tourism in the Horn of Africa. The second programme area focuses on infrastructure development. This programme seeks to ameliorate the problem of 'physical and non-physical barriers' to interstate trade and investment in the region, by enhancing safety on the transport system, and mobilising and identifying potential funding sources to deal with issues related to socioeconomic integration. Lastly, the health and social development programme, which deals with education, health, employment, migration, culture and sport, is also key in advancing regional and economic cooperation (IGAD, 2016; Hersi and Sharamo, 2020; Ministers, 2020).

To address the issue of infrastructure development, the IGAD has proposed the development of the IGAD's Regional Infrastructure Master Plan (IRIMP). This master plan certainly offers an important regional strategic framework on transport connectivity, which would facilitate trade, economic relations and cost-effective and efficient transnational infrastructural development (Kicha, 2021). This plan focuses on four sectors that are necessary for regional connectivity: transport, energy, information and communications technologies (ICTs) and transboundary water resources. These are also expected to translate into sustained economic growth and poverty reduction. Under this programme, the regional strategy for 2016–2020 has proposed the development of:

1. IGAD Regional Transport Master Plan 2014–2040
2. IGAD's Regional Energy Master Plan 2014–2040
3. IGAD Regional ICT Master Plan 2014–2040, and
4. IGAD's Regional Transboundary Water Resources Master Plan 2014–2040 (Ministers, 2020).

There is also the infrastructural development programme that aims to address the region's transport development, and promote energy connectivity and ICTs. A typical example of this relates to ports, some of which are already operational (Djibouti, Sudan and Somalia) and others with the potential of serving (Ethiopia, Eritrea and Kenya), which exhibit subtle rivalry (Hersi and Sharamo, 2020). According to Hersi and Sharamo (2020), maritime trade in the IGAD region is poorly developed and lacks a regional mechanism. For that reason, in 2015 IGAD came up with an Integrated Maritime Strategy (2015–2030, IGAD IMS) to enhance the capacity of IGAD member states to deal with common regional maritime security challenges and threats. Kicha (2021) opines that the IGAD's IMS is intended to address the priorities of the regional maritime domain holistically, and goes far beyond a single focus on piracy. It addresses other maritime-related challenges, as well as opportunities for the region. According to Ministers (2020), the IGAD's IMS is a cross-sectoral framework formulated to anchor a sustainable regional maritime domain, as well as adhere to the overall objectives of the Blue Economy, taking into account regional and continental perspectives. In September 2021, the IGAD launched the Blue Economy Desk, which is tasked with promoting multisectoral maritime economic development.

Pillar 3 is concerned with peace, security and the humanitarian affairs of the region. As stated earlier, the IGAD region is prone to unending intra- and interstate conflicts. Therefore, all programmes under Pillar 3 are designed to address and respond to the root causes of conflicts and foster sustainable peace and stability in the region (IGAD, 2016). Pillar 3 focuses on three areas with six programmes and 21 specific projects. First, there is the conflict prevention, management and resolution programme area that addresses three different aspects of conflicts:

1. IGAD's Conflict Early Warning and Response Mechanism (CEWARN)
2. Enhancing IGAD's capacity for preventive diplomacy and mediation, and
3. Post-conflict reconstruction and development.

Second, the IGAD has the Transnational Security Threats (TST) programme that focuses on strengthening regional cooperation and coordination against existing, evolving and emerging transnational security threats. It also enhances the capacities of member states and institutions to address transnational conflicts.

Third, there is the governance, democracy, rule of law and human rights programme that seeks to strengthen the role of non-governmental organisations (NGOs) and community security organisations (CSOs on peace and security, as well as other stakeholders. This programme also assists member states in the areas of democracy, good governance, elections and rule of law (IGAD, 2016). It is commonly contended that most IGAD member states are marked by a lack of credibly elected national leaders and pervasive civil strives (Weldesellassie, 2011; IGAD, 2016: 44–45; Gutema, 2020; Massoud, 2020). For instance, it is unfortunate that almost all of the election results in the region have been disputed and have often led to violence and civil unrest. Political force has become a way of obtaining power and has eroded the legitimacy of elections and the outcome of results; for example, in Ethiopia (2005), in Kenya (2007), in Uganda (2010), and in Djibouti (2013) (IGAD, 2016).

To address the preceding problems, the IGAD is in the processes of ensuring that all its member states embrace democratic constitutional reforms and the empowerment of local communities through increased decentralisation, devolution and federalism (Mabera, 2020). Examples include diversity accommodation and the decentralisation of power in South Sudan, Kenya, Ethiopia and, to a varying degree, in Sudan and Uganda. This is evidenced by the surge of regular elections, for example, in Djibouti (2013), Uganda (2010), Kenya (2002, 2007, 2013, 2017) and Ethiopia (2018). This is a significant success and a trend that should be upheld (IGAD, 2020).

The IGAD has also become more active in facilitating and arranging conflict mediation. The authority and member states have come to realise that dealing with these persistent conflicts in the region is very difficult and cannot be left to the states alone, even if these appear to be intrastate issues (Pring, 2021). In line with this paradigm shift, it has been noticed that the authority has been involved in resolving decades-long conflicts in Sudan and South Sudan through extensive diplomatic means, and assisting with South Sudan's internal problems, as well as Somalia's longstanding statelessness and lawlessness. Despite these initiatives, Andemariam (2020) says that these tensions/conflicts have been some of the most formidable challenges in the region in recent years. Currently, Kenya is at the forefront of leading the IGAD member states in addressing the ongoing conflict between government forces and the Tigray People's Liberation Front in Ethiopia (Frazer and Devermont, 2021).

The IGAD has increased its utilisation of the regional policies and mechanisms for peace and security issues by ensuring that there is effective cooperation among member states to address both intra- and interstate conflicts (IGAD, 2016). One of the IGAD's key successes has been its partnership with the different member states and NGOs to detect early conflict warning signs, and implement prevention and response interventions in areas that experience the worst impacts of conflicts in the region (Tanui, 2020). In this regard, the IGAD has ensured that the governments of member states are alerted to any early warning signs, changing conditions and rising tensions so that preventive actions can be taken in good time.

In addition, the IGAD has also skilfully developed relationships with international partners to assist both financially and administratively to support its role as the security community for the Horn of Africa. For example, in the IGAD's peace negotiations in both South Sudan and Somalia, its international partners have been able to support and put pressure on the respective sides of the conflict (Ministers, 2020). This includes calling for the use of sanctions by the IGAD's partners to bring sustainable peace in its warring member states. For instance, Andemariam (2020) points out that the IGAD supported the US sanctions that forced Sudan back to the Comprehensive Peace Agreement (CPA) negotiations in 2000, and that the European Union has used institutional measures to support the ongoing Somali peace process.

In Pillar 4, the IGAD is concerned with corporate development and seeks to promote the overall corporate capacity of its member states (IGAD, 2016). In Pillar 4, the Secretariat focuses on two key programmes: (1) institutional strengthening, and (2) capacity building, research, science and technology (IGAD, 2016). Through Pillar 4, the IGAD wants to create a vibrant and more effective economy that is able to provide sustainable service delivery benefits to the region and, thus, increase the level of donor interest in 'basket funding' the IGAD's programmes and activities (IGAD, 2016).

IGAD's challenges in enhancing regional integration in the Horn of Africa

The preceding section revealed how the IGAD is attempting to bring about peace and security, on the one hand, and socio-economic collaboration, on the other hand. However, interstate conflicts have made it very difficult for the IGAD to focus on addressing regional integration and cooperation. For instance, border disputes have created distrust and instability, with wider regional implications for member states. In some instances, these border disputes have escalated into border wars and led to military invasions. For instance, the ongoing conflict between Kenya and Somalia over the disputed maritime boundary in the Indian Ocean is one such border conflict. Both countries claim the ownership of the coastline between Kenya and Somalia. There is also what is commonly known as the Ilemi Triangle, which is believed to contain substantial deposits of petroleum, which is on the borderline separating Kenya, Ethiopia and South Sudan. All three countries have claimed ownership of the small land mass (Shidane, 2020). There have also been instances where Kenya has accused Uganda and South Sudan of supplying arms to the Turkana ethnic group in the northern part of Kenya. It is alleged that these are used by Turkanas to carry out cattle rustling. The continuing uncertainties in Somalia and the current conflict between the government forces and the Tigray People Liberation Front in Ethiopia are other examples of conflict in the region, and all of these are jeopardising the relations among IGAD member states.

Shidane (2020) and Pring (2021) say that some of the IGAD's member states have a long history of interfering in each other's internal conflicts, either directly or by supporting oppositional militia groups. For instance, the relations between Sudan and Uganda remain fragile, largely because of Uganda's previous support of the Sudanese People Liberation Army, which led to Sudan's links to Ugandan rebel groups such as the Lord's Resistance Army (LRA) and the West Nile Bank Front (WNBF). Sudan's relations with Eritrea have also been marred by repeated border incidents since 1993. The Sudanese government has supported Eritrea's opposition groups like the Eritrean Islamic Jihad (EIJ), and, in turn, Eritrea used to provide assistance to the Sudan People's Liberation Army (SPLA). Sudan's relations with its neighbour, Ethiopia, are also characterised by conflict. Ethiopia accuses Sudan of exporting Islamic ideology to the region (Molla, 2002; Lawson, 2017). Ethiopia–Eritrea relations are still marred by conflict and tension, and both states support each other's oppositions. This has made it difficult to think of a genuine security policy and organised mutual peace strategy among the IGAD's member states. As a result, there is an air of uncertainty and non-cooperation rather than peaceful relationships and strengthening partnerships among the states. These ongoing conflicts have made collaboration a question of state interests and not those of the IGAD. Even though the IGAD has adopted many protocols and declarations on peace and security, their implementation has not been effective (Gebregeorgis, 2013) because of the interests of individual states in the region.

External interferences in the region have also made it very difficult for the IGAD to focus on addressing the issue of radical Islamism in the region. For example, although the IGAD has devoted considerable energy, time and money to deal with the crises in the region, the direct and indirect involvement of some Arab states continues to undermine the IGAD's ability to deal with ongoing intra- and interstate conflicts in the region (Mulugeta, 2009; Chan, 2019). According to Mulugeta (2009: 39), 'Al-Shabaab is said to be receiving financial support and weapons from supporters in Qatar and Saudi Arabia. Egypt and Libya also face similar accusations. Egypt has been repeatedly accused of spoiling the peace initiatives taken or endorsed by IGAD.' These states are well known for providing financial support to radical Muslim groups in the name of voluntary 'non-profit organisations', which remains problematic for the establishment of peace and security in the IGAD region (Mulugeta, 2009). As a result, terrorism has become a major obstacle to establishing peace and enabling development in the

IGAD region. Since the mid-1990s, Ethiopia, Kenya, Uganda and Somalia have faced terrorist attacks emanating from radical organisations based in Somalia (IGAD, 2016).

Overlapping regional memberships, a hindrance

The implementation of preferential trade between member states requires advanced and fair practices, such as the harmonisation of production and marketing, and import–export needs to be free of bureaucratic procedures, and rules and regulations need to be applied fairly (Desta and Gérout, 2018). Currently, an obstacle to the IGAD's regional integration and cooperation is that states have overlapping membership of various RECs in the region. For instance, all the IGAD member states, excluding Somalia, are members of the Common Market for Eastern and Southern Africa (COMESA). Djibouti, Somalia and Sudan are members of the Arab League, and Eritrea, Somalia, Sudan, Kenya and Djibouti are members of the Community of Sahel-Saharan States (CEN-SAD) (Healy, 2011; Gebregeorgis, 2013). Overlapping membership is a problem for three reasons. First, it is a challenge and constraint to the available economic and political resources of most IGAD member states and causes financial and administrative burdens. Second, overlapping membership sometimes leads to unnecessary conflicting commitments of member states to different RECs. Third, it causes conflicting political commitments and courses of action, and pressurising states to oppose the objectives of various subregional organisations on the continent at large.

Although regional institutions may have similar objectives, regional integration groups choose contradictory routes to achieve these. COMESA, for example, has a schedule for tax and tariff reductions (Mwale, 2017), which may not be similar to that of the IGAD. The implications and consequences of multiple memberships of regional groupings range from low-level participation in the IGAD's meetings to potential conflicts over mandates and divided loyalties. It also places heavy constraints on the integration process.

Poor communication infrastructures within member states

As a result of a lack of proper, organised communication and infrastructures, the IGAD region has been struggling with rapid growth and the expansion of market competitiveness among all the member states. Compared to the SADC region, the road, rail and air transport infrastructure is poor and this is hampering the free movement of goods and people. As a result, the IGAD's efforts at integration and cooperation have been rendered inefficient. The lack of technological advancement and poor infrastructure has also resulted in poor intrastate trade in the region.

Lack of powers to enforce

The IGAD has a high organ that comprises an Assembly of Heads of State and Government, a Council of Ministers, a Committee of Ambassadors and a Secretariat that are appointed by the heads of state and government. Most of these appointees' focus is on the interests of the appointing authority and not the interests of the region. Most of the IGAD officials are more loyal to their governments than to the institution. Hence, this structure could lead to (or create the appearance of) domination of the organisation by single heads of states, which may result in increased levels of politicisation of its programmes or, even worse, create a pattern of a single state-led organisation (Mwenda, 2014). In this regard, the follow-up of decisions taken at subregional meetings is left to the heads of state or a few ministers and to civil servants in the ministries dealing with cooperation matters without the involvement of the rest of the population.

This reveals how the IGAD's integration attempts in the region lack a strong supranational authority. The supreme policy and decision maker of the IGAD is the Assembly of Heads of State and Government. However, most decisions at the regional level allow governments to retain their sovereignty in the application of regional agreements. This is the greatest challenge to IGAD's integration and cooperation. As Mwendwa (2014: 95) puts it, '[t]he lack of political will on the part of the participating governments is also reflected in their reluctance to give executive independence to the secretariat in the running and management of the institution'.

Conclusion

The aim of this chapter was to assess the IGAD's performance in promoting regional cooperation on important issues such as peace and security, research and development, infrastructure and food security. It assessed not only the historical background of the IGAD but also its overall structure and strategies. It established that the IGAD's strategic plans of 2011–2015, 2016–2020 and 2021–2025 are organised along four fundamental pillars, with the aim of actively enhancing socioeconomic and political integration of the member states.

This chapter also highlighted some of the challenges and the achievements of the IGAD to date. The IGAD region continues to be engulfed in struggles over economic and political power marked by ethnic conflict and unstable peace and security. As a result, armed conflicts, famine, drought and external interference are immediate challenges that continue to hinder the IGAD's aspirations of promoting regional integration and cooperation in the Horn of Africa. These conflicts in the region have led to poor infrastructure and communications development.

What was established in this chapter is that integration and cooperation within the IGAD region (like the rest of Africa) is led by political and economic elites who lack the political will thus eroding confidence in the IGAD's capacity to address individual state's needs and interests. However, given that states in the region are weak with limited national economies and markets, they have no option but to work collaboratively. Still, although regional integration is a politically charged subject, there is a dire need for cooperation and collaboration, and a shift of focus to economic fronts and matters of trade, investment and joint infrastructural development.

Despite the challenges, the author maintains that the IGAD has been at the forefront of promoting integration and cooperation in the region. For instance, the IGAD has put much effort into developing the region's peace and security strategy through its policy and programmes of action, as stipulated in Pillar 1. Some of the IGAD's core peace and security success strategies are the African Peace and Security Architecture (APSA) and the Conflict Early Warning and Response Mechanism (CEWARN). These peace and security initiatives have assisted with regional cooperation and integration through conflict prevention and mitigation, and early warning responses of member states. For instance, the IGAD has also developed the distinctive use of international partners to assist, financially and administratively, to support its role as the regional security community in peace negotiations in both South Sudan and Somalia. In these states, the IGAD's international partners have been able to support and put pressure on the respective sides to put down their arms and return to peaceful negotiations.

The IGAD has made efforts to address infrastructural development in the region to promote trade and tackle the problem of famine. The author has found infrastructure development to be positively correlated with drought resilience and better drought management practices, which may be explained by better access to markets for inputs, outputs, food and information. A typical example in this regard are ports, which are already servicing Djibouti, Sudan and Somalia, and those with the potential to service Ethiopia, Eritrea and Kenya. In relation to famine, the IGAD has also put in place some social protection schemes to address the impact of drought and hunger in the region.

References

Abebe, W. (2021). 'Food insecurity in the Horn of Africa and its impact on peace in the region'. Pretoria: Institute for Peace and Security Studies (IPSS). Available at: https://www.africaportal.org/publications/food-insecurity-horn-africa-and-its-impact-peace-region/ (Accessed 19 November 2021).

Andemariam, S.W. (2020). 'The IGAD–Eritrea impasse: Future prospects in light of recent developments', in *Regional Economic Communities and Peacebuilding in Africa*. London: Routledge, pp. 123–37.

Aniche, E.T. (2020). 'Pan-Africanism and regionalism in Africa: The journey so far', in S.O. Oloruntoba (ed). *Pan-Africanism, Regional Integration and Development in Africa*. London: Palgrave Macmillan, pp. 17–38.

Apuuli, K.P. (2020). 'Uganda and the Intergovernmental Authority on Development (IGAD)', in V. Adetula, R. Bereketeab and C. Obi (eds). *Regional Economic Communities and Peacebuilding in Africa*. London: Routledge, pp. 161–73.

Arthur, P. (2017). 'Promoting security in Africa through regional economic communities (RECs) and the African Union's African Peace and Security Architecture (APSA)', *Insight on Africa*, 9(1): 1–21.

Back, I. (2016). 'IGAD, Sudan, and South Sudan: Achievements and setbacks of regional mediation', *The Journal of the Middle East and Africa*, 7(2): 141–55.

Banerjee, S. (2021). 'Horn of Africa emerging as a strategic pivot of the

Indian Ocean region: Need for repackaging SAGAR 2.0', *Journal of the Indian Ocean Region*, 17(2): 161–77.

Bereketeab, R. (2021). 'The COVID-19 pandemic in the IGAD region: Consequence and responses', *Economit Journal: Scientific Journal of Accountancy, Management and Finance*, 1(2): 110–21.

Bereketeab, R. (2012). 'Inter-governmental authority on development (IGAD): A critical analysis', in R. Bereketeab and K. Mengisteab (eds). *Regional Integration, Identity and Citizenship in the Greater Horn of Africa*. Woodbridge: James Currey, pp. 173–94.

Berhanu, K. (2020). 'Peacebuilding in the context of Ethiopia–IGAD relations', in V. Adetula, R. Bereketeab and C. Obi (eds). *Regional Economic Communities and Peacebuilding in Africa*. London: Routledge, pp. 174–86.

Chan, S.G. (2019). 'The development of IGAD as a distinctively African regional Security community for the horn of Africa with case studies of South Sudan and Somalia'. Master's dissertation, Department of Politics, University of Adelaide. Available at: https://digital.library. adelaide.edu.au/dspace/bitstream/2440/121595/1/Chan2019_MPhil. pdf (Accessed 20 November 2022).

Del Ninno, C., Coll-Black, S. and Fallavier, P. (2016). 'Social protection: Building resilience among the poor and protecting the most vulnerable', in R. Cervigni and M. Morris (eds). *Confronting Drought in Africa's Drylands: Opportunities for enhancing resilience*. Washington, DC: World Bank Group, pp. 165–84.

Desta, M.G. and Gérout, G. (2018). The challenge of overlapping regional economic communities in Africa: Lessons for the Continental Free Trade Area from the failures of the Tripartite Free Trade Area', in M.G. Desta and G. Gérout (eds). *Ethiopian Yearbook of International Law 2017*. Cham: Springer International Publishing, pp. 111–41.

Desmidt, S. (2016). *Peacebuilding, conflict prevention and conflict monitoring in the African Peace and Security Architecture*, European Centre for Development Policy Management No. 148. Available at: https:// ecdpm.org/wp-content/uploads/African-Peace-SecurityArchitecture- Background-Note-ECDPM-2016.pdf (Accessed 20 October 2021).

Frazer, J. and Devermont, J. (2021). 'Ethiopia Unravels: Fresh conflict in the Horn of Africa is more than a humanitarian crisis – it's a blow to regional security and US interests', *Hoover Digest*, (3): 94–98.

Grant, J.A., Issa, A. and Yusuf, B. (2020). 'Agential constructivism, shadow regionalisms and interregional dynamics in the Horn of Africa', in E. Lopez-Lucia and F. Mattheis (eds). *The Unintended Consequences of Interregionalism*. London: Routledge, pp. 165–84.

Gebregeorgis, A. (2013). 'Challenges to regional integration: The case of Intergovernmental Authority on Development (IGAD)'. Addis Ababa: Addis Ababa University.

Gutema, S. (2020). 'Re-examining the philosophy of constitutionalism and governance in the Gadaa Republic of the Oromo People in the Horn of Africa', *Journal of African Studies and Development*, 12(4): 115–27.

Healy S. (2011). 'Seeking peace and security in the Horn of Africa: The contribution of the Inter-Governmental Authority on Development', *International Affairs*, 87: 105–20.

Hersi, A. and Sharamo, R.D. (2020). 'How an IGAD Regional Maritime Council can boost trade'. Available at: https://media.africaportal.org/documents/How_an_IGAD_regional_maritime_council_can_boost_trade.pdf (Accessed 12 October 2021).

Idris, A.A. (2019). 'The role of IGAD (Intergovernmental Authority for Development) in facilitating civil war peace settlements in the Horn of Africa', *International Affairs and Global Strategy*, 78. DOI: 10.7176/IAGS/78-02.

International Authority for Development (IGAD). (2021). Regional Strategy for the Development of Statistics (2021–2025). Available at https://igad.int/download/regional-strategy-for-the-development-of-statistics-2021-2025/ (Accessed 27 October 2021).

Intergovernmental Authority for Development (IGAD). (2016). *IGAD Regional Strategy and Implementation Plan*. Available at: https://igad.int/documents/6-igad-rs-implementationplan-final-v6 (Accessed 10 November 2021).

Karangizi, S. (2012). 'The Regional Economic Communities', in A.A. Yusuf and F. Ouguergouz (eds). *The African Union: Legal and institutional framework*. Leiden: Brill Academic Publishers, pp. 231–49.

Kicha, L.H., 2021. 'Regional integration in the HOA: A critical reassessment of neo functionalism and intergovernmentalism'. Master's dissertation, Department of Economic History and International Relations, Stockholm University.

King-Okumu, C., Orindi, V.A. and Lekalkuli, L. (2019). 'Drought management in the drylands of Kenya: What have we learned?' in E. Mapedza, D. Tsegai, M. Bruntrup and R. Mcleman (eds). *Drought Challenges: Policy options for developing countries*, pp. 277–94. Current Directions in Water Scarcity Research Series, Vol. 2. Munich: Elsevier.

King-Okumu, C., Tsegai, D., Pandey, R.P. and Rees, G. (2020). 'Less to lose? Drought impact and vulnerability assessment in disadvantaged regions', *Water*, 12(4): 1136.

Lawson, F.H. (2017). 'Egypt versus Ethiopia: The conflict over the Nile metastasizes', *The International Spectator*, 52(4): 129–44.

Lung, F., Stutley, C., Kahiu, N., Vrieling, A., Zewdie, Y. and Fava, F.P. (2021). A regional approach to drought index-insurance in Intergovernmental Authority on Development (IGAD) countries. Vol. 1: Main report: Operational and technical feasibility assessment. The Drought Index-Insurance for Resilience in the Sahel and Horn of Africa (DIRISHA) project. Nairobi: International Livestock Research Institute (ILRI) Research Report.

Mabera, F. (2020). 'The Horn of Africa–Persian Gulf Nexus: Inter-regional dynamics and the reshaping of regional order in geopolitical flux', *Global Insight*, 136, April. Pretoria: Institute for Global Dialogue. Available at: https://docplayer.net/189859477-The-horn-of-africa-persian-gulf-nexus-inter-regional-dynamics-and-the-reshaping-of-regional-order-in-geopolitical-flux.html (Accessed 20 November 2022).

Magu, S.M. (2021). 'Region or continent: O/AU development and regional economic communities', in *Explaining Foreign Policy in Post-Colonial Africa*. Cham: Springer International Publishing, pp. 231–63.

Massoud, M.F. (2020). 'The rule of law in fragile states: Dictatorship, collapse, and the politics of religion in post-colonial Somalia', *Journal of Law and Society*, 47: S111–S125.

Ministers, C.O. (2020). 'Intergovernmental Authority on Development – IGAD', in *The Europa Directory of International Organizations 2020*, 22nd edition. London: Routledge. Organization.

Mncube, M. (2020). 'In Search of Pan-African Development Agency: A comparative analysis of the 1980 Lagos Plan of Action, the 1991 Abuja Treaty and the 2001 New Partnership for Africa's Development (NEPAD)'. Doctoral dissertation, University of Johannesburg.

Mohamed, A.A. (2017). 'Impact of Ethiopia's Productive Safety Net Programme (PSNP) on the household livelihood: The case of Babile

District in Somali Regional State, Ethiopia', *International Journal of Economy, Energy and Environment*, 2(2): 25–31.

Mulugeta, K. (2009). 'The role of regional and international organizations', in *Resolving the Somali Conflict: The case of IGAD*, FES Peace and Security Series. Addis Ababa: Friedrich Ebert-Stiftung. Available at: https://pdfs.semanticscholar.org/0641/88a68f8d97966bfff7f388fdece25a979b98.pdf (Accessed 10 October 2021).

Mwale, S.G. (2017). 'An historical background to the formation of COMESA', in V. Murinda (ed.). *The Free Trade Area of the Common Market for Eastern and Southern Africa*. London: Routledge, pp. 31–40.

Mwendwa, P.M. (2014). 'Weak states and regional integration in the inter-governmental authority on development (IGAD) region'. Doctoral dissertation, University of Nairobi.

Nanni, M. (2016). 'Water challenges in the IGAD region: Towards new legal frameworks for cooperation', *Water International*, 41(4): 635–51.

Nwoko, K.C. (2021). 'Regional peace and security: Can ECOWAS and IGAD contain mutating and emerging threats?' *AIPGG Journal of Humanities and Peace Studies*, 2(1).

Parliamentary Monitoring Group. (2000). Abuja Treaty Establishing the African Economic Community: Ratification. Available at: https://pmg.org.za/committee-meeting/67/ (Accessed 25 October 2021).

Pring, J. (2021). 'Towards a more integrated approach? Cooperation among the UN, AU and IGAD in mediation support',in C. Turner and M. Wahlisch (eds). *Rethinking Peace Mediation: Challenges of contemporary peacemaking practice*. Bristol: Bristol University Press, p. 261.

Shidane, J. (2020). 'The cross-border security challenges in the Horn of Africa Region: A case study of Kenya, Ethiopia Moyale Border'. Doctoral dissertation, Institute of Diplomacy and International Studies, University of Nairobi.

Song, S. and Imai, K.S. (2019). 'Does the hunger safety net programme reduce multidimensional poverty? Evidence from Kenya', *Development Studies Research*, 6(1): 47–61.

Tanui, C.C. (2020). 'Challenges and prospects of prevention and management of conflicts in Africa: The role of IGAD Early Warning Mechanism'. Doctoral dissertation, University of Nairobi.

The African Economic Community Treaty. (1991). Treaty Establishing the African Economic Community. Available at: https://au.int/en/treaties/

treaty-establishing-africaneconomiccommunity (Accessed 10 October 2021).

The Executive Secretary. (2020). 'IGAD charting its way for 2021–2025'. Available at: https://igad.int/executive-secretary/2594-igad-charting-its-way-for-2021-2025 (Accessed 15 November 2021).

Tshimpaka, L.M., Nshimbi, C.C. and Moyo, I. (2021). 'A historical background to regional integration in Africa and southern Africa', in *Regional Economic Communities and Integration in Southern Africa.* Singapore: Palgrave Macmillan, pp. 33–46.

Vhumbunu, H. (2020). 'The formation of the revitalized transitional government of national unity in South Sudan: Key priorities, tasks and challenges ahead', *Conflict Trends*, (2): 3–12.

Weldesellassie, K.I. (2011). 'IGAD as an international organization, its institutional development and shortcomings', *Journal of African Law*, 55(1): 1–29.

Chapter Eight

The Central African Economic and Monetary Community

TENIOLA TAYO AND MICHAEL ODIJIE

Introduction

The Central African Economic and Monetary Community (CEMAC)[1] was created in 1994 as a successor to the Customs and Economic Union of Central Africa (UDEAC),[2] which had been created in 1964 to liberalise tariffs and create a common market among six Central African countries, namely Cameroon, the Central African Republic, Chad, Congo, Equatorial Guinea and Gabon. The UDEAC was replaced by the CEMAC in 1994 after it was assessed as having failed in its mandate (Nono, 2014).

The CEMAC zone covers an area of 3 020 144 square kilometres, which is home to a population of 51 million people. Cameroon represents about half of the CEMAC population and also has the largest economy in the zone. Chad makes up about 30 per cent of the zone's population while each of the other four countries in the zone have less than 10 per cent of the region's population.

All the CEMAC countries, except for Cameroon, rely heavily on oil production and oil exports for foreign exchange and government revenues.

---

1 Acronym relates to its French name – Communauté Economique et Monetaire de l'Afrique Centrale.
2 Acronym relates to French name – Union Douanière et Économique de l'Afrique Centrale.

This has had implications for the stability of their economies, as dependence on oil has made the region vulnerable to shocks in the global oil markets (IMF, 2015).

Figure 8.1: The CEMAC member states

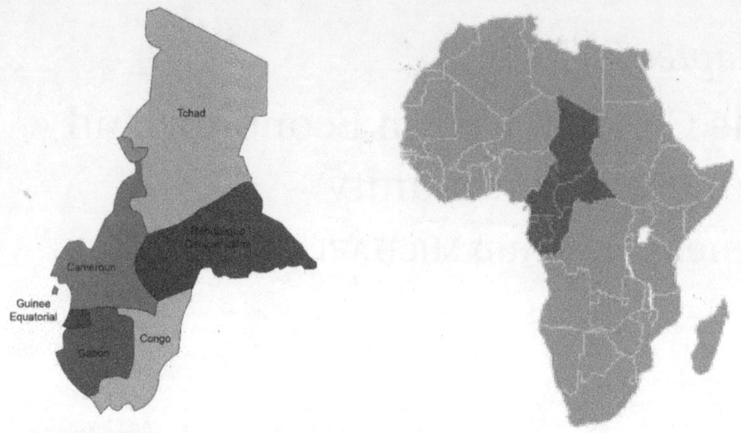

Source: cemac.int

The countries within this zone range from low-income economies Central African Republic (CAR) and Chad to lower middle income (Cameroon and the Republic of Congo) and upper middle-income economies (Gabon and Equatorial Guinea). The countries have varying socioeconomic indicators, with landlocked Chad and CAR being the worst off (World Bank, 2019).

The CEMAC is made up of two unions: the Central African Economic Union (UEAC), and the Central African Monetary Union (UMAC). On the one hand, the UEAC is charged with harmonising relevant regulations within member states to drive increased trade among them and facilitate the convergence of economic policies. On the other hand, the UMAC is responsible for managing the monetary convergence of member states, and its institutional architecture includes the Community Parliament, the Court of Justice and the Court of Auditors (Meyer, 2011). Its organs include the Conference of Heads of State; the Council of Ministers; the Ministerial Committee; the CEMAC Commission; the Bank of Central African States (BEAC); the Development Bank of Central African States (BDEAC); and the Banking Commission of Central Africa (COBAC) (Nono, 2014).

There are other institutions charged with the harmonisation of sectoral policies, including the Economic Commission on Cattle, Meat and Fishery Resources, the Interstate Committee on Pesticides, the Institute for Statistics and Applied Economics, the Subregional Multisectoral Institute for Applied Technology and the International Commission of the Congo–Ubangi Sangha Basin. There are also several schools and training facilities, such as an interstate school for customs officers, a tourism school, the Institute of Economy and Finance and an interstate centre for higher education on public health (Meyer, 2011).

All the CEMAC countries belong to the Economic Community of Central African States (ECCAS) – Chad and the CAR are also members of the Community of Sahel-Saharan States (CEN-SAD). The CEMAC has similar origins and mandates to ECCAS, as well as overlapping membership. However, although all the CEMAC member countries are part of ECCAS, ECCAS represents a wider group of 11 countries.[3] The CEMAC's predecessor, UDEAC, existed before the creation of ECCAS, but its lack of progress created a window for the creation of the latter. When UDEAC was transformed into the CEMAC, ECCAS was going through a period of dormancy, which lasted from 1992 to 1998 (Byiers, 2017), but it was revived in 1999 as part of the African Economic Community (AEC). Unlike the CEMAC, ECCAS is one of the eight Regional Economic Communities (REC) recognised by the African Union and there are concerns about the overlapping roles of the two RECs (Byiers, 2017). A distinguishing feature is that the CEMAC is made up of countries that share a common currency and colonial history, while ECCAS is made up of more diverse countries. This feature arguably gives the CEMAC more political legitimacy among its members although ECCAS might have more diplomatic legitimacy on the continental level (Byiers, 2017). Currently, this difference in membership allows both entities to coexist. Plans were announced to merge the two entities in 2022, but the merger has already been postponed once.[4]

The CEMAC treaty sets out a vision for the creation of a common

---

3   ECCAS members include Angola, Burundi, Cameroon, the Central African Republic, Chad, Congo, the Democratic Republic of the Congo, Equatorial Guinea, Gabon, Rwanda and São Tomé and Príncipe.
4   Africa Intelligence. (2023). 'ECCAS-CEMAC merger project in limbo'. Available at: https://www.africaintelligence.com/central-africa/2023/03/07/eccas-cemac-merger-project-in-limbo,109920977-bre (Accessed 7 March 2023).

Central African market predicated on the free movements of goods, services, capital and persons. The CEMAC's main objectives are to:[5]

- Ensure the stable management of the common currency (CFA franc);
- Secure the environment for economic activities and business in general;
- Harmonise the national sectoral policies for ever stronger integration;
- Establish an ever-closer union between the peoples of the member states to strengthen their geographical and human solidarity;
- Promote national markets by eliminating barriers to intracommunity trade;
- Coordinate development programmes and harmonise industrial projects; and
- Create a real common market.

Essentially, the main features of the CEMAC include its monetary union through the CFA franc; its customs union through the common external tariff (CET); and trade liberalisation through the generalised preferential tariff (GPT).

Although the CEMAC is considered to be more successful than ECCAS at driving economic integration in Central Africa, it has failed to reach several of its core integration objectives. This chapter analyses the successes and challenges of regional integration in the CEMAC and discusses some of the cross-cutting issues that could provide lessons for other integration efforts in Africa.

Integration successes

It can be argued that the areas in which the CEMAC has had more success with integration were those that had relatively fewer repercussions for some domestic policies. The establishment of a monetary union was an area with significant political support, most likely related to the shared colonial history of member countries. Other successes were hard won, such as the free movement of persons. These required the application of political and public pressure on countries that were not compliant with the agreement, and some of these negotiations are still ongoing.

---

5   Available at: https://www.cemac.int/node/32 (Accessed 20 November 2022).

Monetary union

The origins of the CEMAC can be linked to the African Financial Community (CFA),[6] a postcolonial arrangement created in 1945 by France in its former colonies, with the aim of deepening monetary integration through a common currency – the West African CFA franc and the Central African CFA franc. The issuance of the Central African CFA franc is guaranteed by the Bank of Central African States (BEAC),[7] an organ of the UMAC. This arrangement implies that monetary policy in the CEMAC is driven by the mandate of exchange rate stability through pegging the value of the CFA franc to the euro. To facilitate this, the CEMAC countries pool their foreign exchange reserves in the BEAC, after which some of the reserves are deposited in the French Treasury. The BEAC has recorded some gains in improving the transmission mechanism of the region's monetary policy, growing the regional reserves, and generally safeguarding the stability of the region's financial sector.

This system has allowed for monetary integration in the CEMAC zone with the single currency being shared by the six countries. On the one hand, this common currency is one of the pillars of trade and economic integration within the zone, but, on the other hand, it appears to have had little effect on trade within the CEMAC (Kangami and Akinkugbe, 2021). An additional issue is that the currency union has not led to the levels of macroeconomic convergence that one would expect from such an arrangement.

The free movement of persons

The free movement of people within a region is an important marker of integration as it helps drive intraregional investment, tourism and the establishment of market linkages. Labour mobility also supports the emergence of agglomeration economies, and is an important correcting mechanism for some of the effects of import exposure that can result from a free trade area (Marjit and Acharyya, 2003). The free movement of persons within a region also allows for levels of social and cultural integration, through mechanisms such as student exchanges.

Although the agreement providing for the free movement of persons

---

6   Acronym relates to French name – Communauté financière africaine, formerly Colonies françaises d'Afrique.
7   Acronym relates to French name – Banque des États de l'Afrique Centrale

within the CEMAC zone was signed in 2013, it was not until its complete ratification in 2017 that it truly came into force. The delay in ratification was the result of objections by Gabon and Equatorial Guinea, the smallest countries in the region, but also the ones with the highest GDP per capita. The eventual ratification of the agreement to abolish visas within the zone is considered a CEMAC success. There are, however, concerns about the persisting discrimination against CEMAC migrants by Gabon and Equatorial Guinea (Etahoben, 2020).

Related to the free movement of persons are other measures such as the integration of telecommunications infrastructure within the RECs. The CEMAC member countries successfully eliminated international roaming charges on mobile telecommunications within the zone in August 2021 (Atabong, 2021). Although this may not be considered highly significant, it has proven elusive to other RECs such as ECOWAS. Initiatives such as this form a part of the foundation for deeper economic integration.

The move towards supranationalism

The CEMAC is considered to have made some progress in supranationalism, or the surrender of some sovereignty by its member countries to allow it to take decisions on their behalf. This delegation of authority is an important feature of regional integration projects as it grants operational and sanctioning powers to the regional bodies. The organs that clearly have supranational powers are the CEMAC Commission, the regional banks, the Community Parliament, the Court of Justice, the Court of Auditors and other specialised bodies (Meyer, 2011). The supranational dimensions of some of CEMAC's governance structures presents a departure from the intergovernmentalism[8] (Schimmelfennig, 2018) that was the dominant approach of the UDEAC, its predecessor body (Meyer, 2011).

A key implication of this is the accountability mechanism that is created in situations where national governments fail to comply with the stipulations of regional policies. The CEMAC Parliament was officially inaugurated in April 2010, after several delays, and represents a democratic dimension to the CEMAC as its 30 members (five from each country) are elected by citizens to represent their interests. This allows the participation of citizens of the six member countries in the integration process. This is also unlike

---

8   Intergovernmentalism is a theory of regional integration that sees national governments as the key actors in integration projects.

some of the other African RECs, where regional parliamentarians are nominated by national governments (Jancic, 2019).

The Court of Justice provides a similar platform for accountability, where citizens of member states are allowed to bring cases, including those against the community or one of its agencies (Nono, 2014). An example of this is the case of *Mokamaned John Wilfrid v Inter-State School of Customs of CEMAC* brought to the court in 2006. The individual, Mokamaned, successfully disputed the decision of a director in the CEMAC agency to dismiss him.[9]

The CEMAC's governing treaties do not explicitly provide for the supremacy of community law over national laws, but it covers this to some degree in one of its addenda where it is stated that regulations are binding and applicable to all member states.[10] This is supposed to help disincentivise non-compliance of community regulations through sanctions. It also provides a mechanism for CEMAC citizens to hold their governments, and the governments of other member states, accountable for their actions. This has implications for governance and human rights issues within the CEMAC member countries (Nono, 2014).

Integration challenges

The uneven application of common external tariffs

The customs union created by the CEMAC includes a common external tariff on goods coming into the zone from third-party countries, considered one of the highest in Africa. There has been some success in negotiating and establishing the CET. However, although it is technically in place, there are deviations on the national level that have affected its effectiveness with the CEMAC member countries having differentiated tariffs on several hundred tariff lines. Some of these deviations include lower duties in Cameroon and Gabon for pharmaceuticals, as well as for tin and tin products in all countries except Chad (World Bank, 2019).

---

9   Mokamaned John Wilfrid v. L'École inter-État des Douanes de la CEMAC, Arrêt n° 02/CJ/ CEMAC/ CJ/06 du 30/11/2006.

10 Additif au Traité de la CEMAC relatif au système institutionnel et juridique de la Communauté (Addendum to the Treaty on The CEMAC Institutional and Legal System). Available at: <http://www.ehu.es/ceinik/tratados/11TRATADOSSOBRE-INTEGRACIONYCOOPERACIONENAFRICA/115CEMAC/IC1158FR.pdf> (Accessed 12 December 2022).

National-level variations are also driven by some additional charges that are imposed on imports from third-party countries into the CEMAC zone. Some luxury and durable goods, as well as beverages and tobacco, are faced with excise duties that may range from 20–50 per cent. In some CEMAC countries, a number of agricultural goods are charged a community preference levy of 0.44 per cent. These charges, including the applied value added tax (VAT), contribute to the unpredictability of charges on third-party country imports, contrary to the objectives of the CET.

There is also the issue of bilateral preferences applied to third parties, which sometimes deviates from the established most-favourable nation (MFN) protocol applied by the CET. One example of this is the reduction of duties by Cameroon on goods coming from the European Union, which is not consistent with the CET applied by the other countries in the zone (World Bank, 2019). This happened through the interim Economic Partnership Agreement[11] signed between Cameroon and the European Union, which came into effect in August 2014. A possible impact of this is trade deflection, where a product imported into a common market through a country with lower tariffs is then exported to other members of the bloc duty-free.

Stagnant trade

Increasing trade among the CEMAC member countries is a core objective of the arrangement, and it is one that has largely failed. The objective of increased trade was to be achieved through the tariff liberalisation that took place in 1998 (Nono, 2014). More precisely, the CEMAC implemented a generalised preferential tariff (GPT) for goods produced and traded within the zone. However, intraregional trade has remained quite low, estimated at between 2–5 per cent of the total trade of countries in the zone (World Bank, 2019). Intra-CEMAC trade also ranks poorly compared to other African RECs, as shown in Table 8.1. Trade levels have been highly inconsistent.

---

11 Available at: http://eur-lex.europa.eu/legal-content/EN/TXT/PDF/?uri=CEL-EX:22009A0228(01)&rid=2 (Accessed 20 November 2022).

Table 8.1: Share of intraregional exports in African RECs

	Share of intraregional exports			
	2000–2004	2005–2009	2010–2014	2015–2016
CEMAC	1.6	2.9	3.3	1
ECOWAS	9.4	9	7.4	8.1
COMESA	4.7	5	7.8	9
SADC	9	5.9	11.6	10.8
WAEMU	14.2	14.1	12.8	11.1
EAC	16	15.4	16.5	15.7

Source: World Bank

One of the obstacles facing increased trade within the CEMAC zone is the application of VAT and duties at the national level, which reduce the effects of tariff liberalisation. These include VAT rates that are not harmonised across the countries, despite the fact that common standards on VAT were introduced in 1999 (Doe, 2006). Duties are also applied to traded goods, notwithstanding the fact that the existing trade policy stipulates that only VAT is to be applied to goods traded within the CEMAC zone. These non-tariff barriers are particularly prominent in transactions involving agricultural products.

Contrary to what might be expected, the application of additional charges and high levies are often detrimental to national trade interests. In the case of the Congo, its restrictive trade practices, even within the CEMAC, have compromised its efforts to develop its non-oil sector and diversify its export base. The high charges and levies applied also did not lead to higher fiscal revenue as a result of exemptions and poor customs administration (Oliva, 2008).

Besides official taxes and levies, corruption within the member states has resulted in the application of other arbitrary charges and rents. Corrupt behaviours include small-scale harassments, referred to as *tracasseries*, that affect trade transactions, particularly those involving agricultural products. These informal payments are often unauthorised and are made to officials at the borders, thereby increasing trade and transport costs. Corruption and bribes have been found to increase trade costs by about 14 per cent (World

Bank, 2019). Consequently, transport costs along the CEMAC corridors are considered to be some of the highest in the world (Business in Cameroon, 2021). It has also been estimated that the elimination of these barriers could increase intra-CEMAC trade by 25 per cent, and subsequently add 1–2 per cent to CEMAC's GDP growth rate (World Bank, 2019).

Figure 8.2: CEMAC import sources, 2014–2021 – US$ thousands

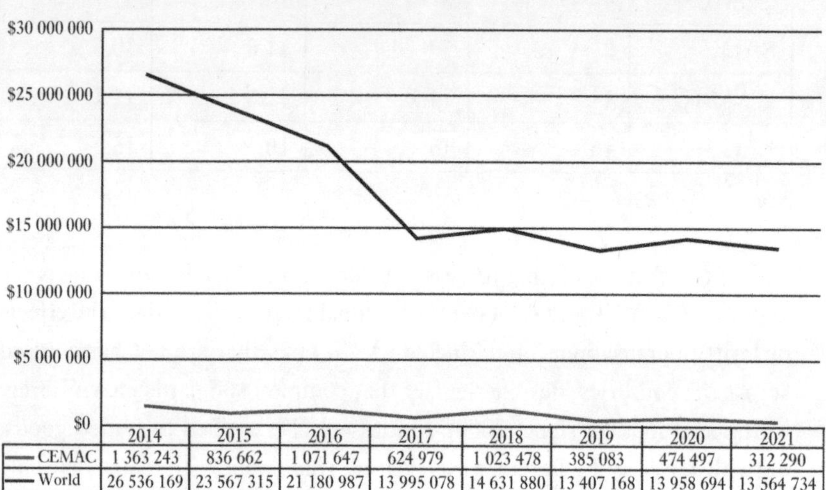

	2014	2015	2016	2017	2018	2019	2020	2021
CEMAC	1 363 243	836 662	1 071 647	624 979	1 023 478	385 083	474 497	312 290
World	26 536 169	23 567 315	21 180 987	13 995 078	14 631 880	13 407 168	13 958 694	13 564 734

Source: Trade Map

Corruption also contributes to supply-side trade constraints, as it has been listed as one of the top challenges to doing business within the CEMAC zone. The excessive taxation and bureaucratic red tape have contributed to the smuggling of goods across the borders. Products such as sugar, flour, pharmaceutical and petroleum products, and cement are disproportionately affected by fraud and counterfeiting (World Trade Organization, 2013). The Observatory of Abnormal Practices along the main Central African corridors (OPA-AC),[12] a platform for monitoring these corrupt practices, including the *tracasseries*, was launched in November 2021 (Business in Cameroon, 2021).

Some procedural issues are also affecting intra-CEMAC trade. One of these is the process for certifying the origins of goods to be traded to determine their eligibility for tariff-free import. The inefficiencies of this

---

12 Acronym relates to French name – Observatoire régional des pratiques anormales sur les principaux corridors de l'Afrique centrale.

process, as well as the inadequate capacity of issuing officers to carry out the assessment, leads to these certificates being rejected in some CEMAC countries. Other procedural issues include the insistence on the physical inspection of imported goods by most CEMAC countries. The embedded inefficiencies in these processes cause a further procedural bottleneck for intra-CEMAC trading.

Informal cross-border trade is considered to be quite significant in the CEMAC, as is the case in other African RECs. However, it has been argued that informal trade is driven by factors that are similar to those behind illicit trade, which include the taxes levied on goods and the challenges with customs procedures (World Bank, 2019).

In general, the poor harmonisation of policies and procedures at the national level presents a great challenge to regional trade. The policy variations at the national level are sometimes the result of a misalignment of national interests and regional agreements. These variations also create room for capture and exploitation, sometimes pushing trade transactions to illicit routes and channels. The overall impact of this has meant little or no growth in intraregional trade.

Finally, the poor levels of interconnecting infrastructure, which could facilitate trade, have also hindered intraregional trade growth. These include road and transport networks, as well as payment infrastructures. There are also supply-side constraints to intra-CEMAC trade. Countries in the CEMAC region have poor production structures and are unable to meet the demand of the regional market. The poor trade complementarity in the zone also creates a mismatch between demand and supply.

Assessment of performance

The performance of the CEMAC against its stated objectives can be summarised under the following points:

- The management of the common currency is relatively stable, but this is also the result of the support provided by the French Treasury. However, other expected outcomes of monetary integration, such as macroeconomic convergence, have not been as successful.
- Peace and security issues are a major rallying point for Central African countries. However, the ECCAS is considered to be more active in this domain than the CEMAC (Byiers, 2017).

- There have been significant attempts to harmonise sectoral policies, especially through the creation of supervising agencies. However, insufficient political will has challenged this process and made it largely unsuccessful.
- There is technically a free movement of citizens within the CEMAC zone but challenges remain with countries like Equatorial Guinea and Gabon, which continue to apply some discriminatory measures on CEMAC travellers and migrants.
- There continues to be quite significant barriers to intracommunity trade in the CEMAC zone, and trade volumes have not improved since the REC was established.
- The harmonisation of industrial policies and actions is also challenged by the issue of political will and the placement of national interests above regional cooperation.
- There is a general assessment that the CEMAC common market, although technically in place, is not quite the reality in practice.

What can we learn from the CEMAC integration issues?

The integration challenges faced by the CEMAC offer lessons that can be applied to other regional integration projects in Africa, including the African Continental Free Trade Area (AfCFTA).

Political will and policy differentiation

The creation of regional economic, monetary and trade policies in Africa sometimes does not sufficiently take into account the existing and evolving national interests. As one example, trade liberalisation policies – such as those within the CEMAC, ECOWAS and the African Union – are often at odds with national industrial policies. This dissonance creates situations where national governments commit to trade policies at the regional level, but find ways to distort the provisions of these policies at the national level. This leads to policy differentiation, which, at high levels, defeats the purpose of regional integration.

The political will to drive deeper integration in the CEMAC has been observed to fluctuate with the global oil prices. One explanation for this is that crashing oil prices create an urgency for economic reform, with a focus on regional markets for non-oil exports. However, a recovery of oil prices leads to a shift in national priorities, and a reduced interest in carrying out the reforms required to be in compliance with the regional policies.

At the core of this is the question of sovereignty and the general unwillingness to surrender national decision-making powers to a regional body (Kindzeka, 2014). This is despite the performance of political will at regional levels that leads to the signing – and even ratification – of key agreements (Tayo, 2020). Regardless of the provisions of regional agreements, many African governments consider national interests as supreme. The nature of many African democracies also means that these national interests may not necessarily reflect the needs of the majority of the population, but are the priorities of political and industrial elites (Odijie and Onofua, 2020). These priorities also change frequently, as a result of a lack of continuity of policy-making in some African countries.

One solution may be to pay greater attention to national policies and interests in the creation of regional policies. However, a challenge is presented in the choice of a method to coordinate national interests and policies into a coherent regional policy. The 'bottom–up' approach is, nevertheless, the preference for policy coordination (Byiers, Karaki and Woolfrey, 2018), as the reverse method of imposing regional policies on the national implementers is what leads to the issue of high levels of policy differentiation.

On the other hand, this is easier said than done, given the similarity of production and economic structures in some African countries and the poor trade complementarity. Deepening integration through measures like single markets sometimes creates the perception of direct export competition between African countries. Similar production structures and aspirations also drive the protection of similar industries (Odijie, 2019), sometimes with non–tariff measures that are in contravention of regional provisions. This also hinders the process of specialisation as it prevents the creation of regional value chains.

The political will to commit fully to the implementation of regional policies is sometimes also affected by historic links between some African countries, and European countries that served as former colonial governments. Colonial relationships often result in strong trade links that are sometimes more valued by African countries than growing trade links within regional communities. Breaking these trade or monetary ties is sometimes regarded as a risky economic decision that can lead to protracted instability.

The only way in which the valid concerns of national leaders can be taken fully on board is if their participation at the negotiation table focuses on being pragmatic about what national policies can be accommodated. Even after this, constant consultations will be required to evaluate the changes in circumstances at the national level.

These lessons ought to be applied to younger integration projects such as the AfCFTA, given that it is in its early stages of trade integration and there are plans to eventually create a customs union and a single currency. The political will exhibited by national governments needs to be interrogated carefully to determine its sustainability.

Compliance monitoring and enforcement issues

The periodic monitoring of compliance with regional treaty provisions will allow deviations to be caught early and possibly addressed. Enforcement powers can, therefore, be argued as prerequisites to compliance monitoring. However, in the case of the CEMAC, although the body has the powers to sanction member states, there is often an unwillingness to maximise these powers. This unwillingness is linked to the desire to protect the sovereignty of member states in fear that more invasive approaches could lead to the withdrawal of political support for the regional organisation.

In the CEMAC zone, there have been little to no sanctions applied to member countries that are in violation of the provisions of the regional treaties. The absence of consequences for non-compliant behaviour removes a major disincentive to engage in this behaviour. Improving integration outcomes within the zone will require the strengthening of the CEMAC Commission's regional enforcement capacities, and improved surveillance of data generated on the national level. Non-compliant behaviours that need to be monitored and discouraged include the indiscriminate use of non-tariff measures as a barrier to trade, the failure to implement the macroeconomic frameworks that can facilitate economic convergence, the repeated closure of borders, and the discrimination and harassment meted out to some CEMAC travellers within the zone.

There is also a tendency by members of African RECs to invoke the 'national security' clause as justification for non-compliant behaviour. While most treaties provide for this, it is essential that there are clearer guidelines for its use in order to prevent abuse.

On the one hand, the reluctance of African RECs to actively enforce the provisions of their guiding treaties is sometimes influenced by perceived legitimacy issues as far as supranational political power is concerned. African governments have been known to abruptly withdraw from regional arrangements when it is perceived that their absolute political power is being challenged. This brings to the fore the question of regional leadership mechanisms and the policy space available to them.

On the other hand, some regional arrangements, such as the AfCFTA, do not have any sanctioning powers, and depend mostly on diplomacy to negotiate compliance from member states. The reality, however, is that the sustainable success of integration projects requires a mechanism for discouraging a lack of compliance with key provisions. This is where citizen engagement comes in, as the democratic power of citizens can also be used as a countervailing mechanism to political leaders who may be more whimsical in their decisions to comply or not. Improved citizen engagement by RECs is crucial to secure a wider buy-in to integration processes, and increase the demand-side pressures for compliance and accountability on elected officials.

Managing bilateral agreements

As mentioned previously, existing and new bilateral agreements between third-party countries and a member of an African REC can sometimes pose challenges when not properly managed. A key issue is the ambiguity or insufficient clarity of the guidelines and procedures for engaging in third-party trade agreements within the context of a regional FTA. In the case of the CEMAC, the interim EPA between Cameroon and the European Union has put Cameroon in violation of the tariff liberalisation provisions of the CEMAC (World Bank, 2019). The AfCFTA is faced with a similar challenge, with the signing of bilateral trade agreements between AfCFTA member countries and non-member countries. An example of this is the bilateral trade agreement between Kenya and the United States, which risks putting Kenya in violation of some AfCFTA provisions (Ogutu, 2020).

Some third-party countries are exploring ways to take advantage of regional and continental trade agreements in Africa. It has been argued that the FTA between China and Mauritius is one of these initiatives, given that it could provide China with strategic access to the single African market, if properly managed. The Rules of Origin, however, may not provide similar access to the Chinese market for goods traded under the AfCFTA (Wigmore, 2020).

Generally speaking, the provisions for most RECs in Africa advocate for joint negotiations of trade agreements with external parties. However, a number of these provisions are ambiguous and unenforceable. There is also the reality that negotiations on the REC level are often stalled by the varying interests of the countries within them. The capacity and resources of the RECs to take charge of these negotiations is also in question.

Notwithstanding the above, it has been recommended that the negotiations of an EPA between the European Union and Central African countries should take place at the CEMAC level to avoid violations with the regional arrangement. It is also crucial that the issue of third-party treaties be dealt with more decisively in the provisions guiding Africa's RECs, with clear guidelines on how countries should proceed when faced with these.

Corruption and capture

Corruption at borders is a well-known feature of intra-African – as well as global – trade and is categorised as one of the major non-tariff barriers to trade. Traders are sometimes extorted by customs officials, and are forced to pay bribes that increase their trade costs. Corruption at borders includes theft from the misreporting of trade volumes (Widdowson, 2013). Corruption at borders affects the ability of the SMEs to trade easily as they can often not afford the trade cost implications of bribes (Klopp and Trimble, 2021). Some African trade integration projects have attempted to put in place mechanisms to monitor and address non-trade barriers like corruption, but these mechanisms have had varying success. This is because their effectiveness relies on the quality of reported data, and the capacity and political will of national governments to address the corruption allegations conclusively. There is a need for a more pragmatic approach to addressing corruption as a major barrier to intraregional trade in Africa.

Conclusion

The reform of the UDEAC to the CEMAC was expected to boost the economic and monetary integration of its member countries. However, the CEMAC has been largely unsuccessful on key indicators such as the volume of trade among its member countries. Its customs union is also plagued with several challenges, including the uneven application of its common external tariffs, as well as variations on levies and duties at the national level. Corruption and erratic political will appear to be the main causes of the failure of CEMAC's integration project and there is little expectation that this will change soon.

There are lessons that can be drawn from the CEMAC integration challenges for other African regional integration projects. This is because there are several parallels that can be drawn between the political and economic factors impeding the CEMAC integration and those in other West African regions.

References

Atabong, A.B. (2021). 'Free roaming now official in central Africa', *IT Web*, 10 November. Available at: https://itweb.africa/content/ j5alrvQajm8vpYQk (Accessed 10 October 2022).

Business in Cameroon. (2021). 'CEMAC launches Observatory of Abnormal Practices along the main Central African corridors', *Business in Cameroon*, 15 November. Available at: https://www. businessincameroon.com/public-management/1511-12054-cemac-launches-observatory-of-abnormal-practices-along-the-main-central-african-corridors (Accessed 10 October 2022).

Byiers, B. (2017). 'ECCAS and CEMAC: Struggling to integrate in an intertwined region', ECDPM Policy Brief, 9 December. Brussels: The Centre for Africa–Europe Relations.

Byiers, B., Karaki, K. and Woolfrey, S. (2018). 'The political economy of regional industrialisation strategies'. ECDPM Discussion Paper No. 237. Brussels: The Centre for Africa–Europe Relations.

Doe, L. (2006): *Harmonization of Domestic Consumption Taxes in Central and Western African Countries*, IMF Working Paper No. WP/06/8 (January). Washington, DC: International Monetary Fund.

Etahoben, C.B. (2020, April 25). 'CEMAC: Paying lip service to the Free Movement of Persons and Goods Agreement', *HumAngle*, 25 April. Available at: https://humanglemedia.com/cemac-paying-lip-service-to-free-movement-of-persons-and-goods-agreement/ (Accessed 10 October 2022).

International Monetary Fund (IMF). (2015). *Central African Economic and Monetary Community (CEMAC): Selected issues*. Available at: https://www.elibrary.imf.org/view/journals/002/2015/308/article-A004-en.xml (Accessed 10 October 2022).

Jancic, D. (2019). 'Regional parliaments and African economic integration', *The European Journal of International Law*, 30(1): 199–228. Available at: http://www.ejil.org/pdfs/30/1/2951.pdf (Accessed 10 October 2022).

Kangami, D.N. and Akinkugbe, O. (2021). 'Common currency and intra-regional trade in the Central African Monetary Community (CEMAC)', *Journal of African Trade*, 8(1). DOI:10.2991/jat.k.210521.001.

Kindzeka, M.E. (2014). 'Central Africa economic integration difficult after 20 years', *VOA*, 28 February. Available at: https://www.voanews.com/a/central-africa-economic-integration-difficult-after-20-years/1861181.html (Accessed 10 October 2022).

Klopp, J.M. and Trimble, M. (2021). *Corruption, Gender and Small-Scale Cross-Border Trade in East Africa: A review*, Global Integrity and Anti-corruption Project, Working Paper No. 10. Available at: https://ace.globalintegrity.org/wp-content/uploads/2021/03/Corruption-Gender-and-Small-Scale-Cross-Border-Trade-1.pdf (Accessed 10 October 2022).

Marjit, S. and Acharyya, R. (2003). *International Trade, Wage Inequality and the Developing Economy: A general equilibrium approach*. Berlin: Physica-Springer Verlag.

Meyer, A. (2011). 'Central African Economic and Monetary Union'. International Democracy Watch. Available at: http://www.internationaldemocracywatch.org/attachments/464_CEMAC-meyer.pdf (Accessed 10 October 2022).

Nono, G.M. (2014). *Integration Efforts in Central Africa: The case of CEMAC*. UNU-WIDER Working Papers No. W-2014/16. Available at: https://cris.unu.edu/sites/cris.unu.edu/files/W-2014-16.pdf (Accessed 10 October 2022).

Odijie, M.E. (2019). 'The need for industrial policy coordination in the African Continental Free Trade Area', *African Affairs*, 118(470): 182–93.

Odijie, M. and Onofua, A. (2020). 'Political origin and persistence of industrial policy in Africa', *Globalizations*, 17: 1–16.

Ogutu, M. (2020). 'Caught between Africa and the West: Kenya's proposed US free trade agreement', *Africa Portal*, 19 June. Available at: https://www.africaportal.org/features/caught-between-africa-and-the-west-kenyas-proposed-us-free-trade-agreement/ (Accessed 10 October 2022).

Oliva, M.A. (2008). *Trade Restrictiveness in the CEMAC Region: The case of Congo.* IMF Working Papers, No. 2008(015). Washington, DC: International Monetary Fund. Available at: https://doi.org/10.5089/9781451868777.001 (Accessed 10 October 2022).

Schimmelfennig, F. (2018). 'Regional integration theory' in *Oxford Research Encyclopedia of Politics.* Oxford: Oxford University Press. Available at: https://www.researchgate.net/profile/Frank-Schimmelfennig/publication/325392599_Regional_Integration_Theory/links/5b0af3560f7e9b1ed7f9c9e3/Regional-Integration-Theory.pdf (Accessed 10 October 2022).

Tayo, T. (2020). 'Economics alone isn't holding back West Africa's Eco', *ISS Today.* Pretoria: Institute for Security Studies. Available at: https://issafrica.org/iss-today/economics-alone-isnt-holding-back-west-africas-eco (Accessed 10 October 2022).

Widdowson, D. (2013). 'Bordering on corruption: An analysis of corrupt customs practices that impact the trading community', *World Customs Journal*, 7(2), 11–22.

Wigmore, S. (2020). 'Will Africa's first free trade agreement with China actually help Africa?' *Development Reimagined*, 2 October. Available at: https://developmentreimagined.com/2020/10/02/will-africas-first-free-trade-agreement-with-china-actually-help-africa/ (Accessed 10 October 2022).

World Bank. (2019). *CEMAC: Deepening regional integration.* Available at: https://documents1.worldbank.org/curated/en/491781560455916201/pdf/Deepening-Regional-Integration-to-Advance-Growth-and-Prosperity.pdf (Accessed 10 October 2022).

World Trade Organization (WTO). (2013). *Trade Policy Review: Report by the Secretariat – Countries of the Central African Economic and Monetary Community (CEMAC).* Available at: https://www.wto.org/english/tratop_e/tpr_e/s285_e.pdf (Accessed 10 October 2022).

PART 3

CONTINENTAL INTEGRATION MECHANISMS

Chapter Nine

The Pan-African Parliament:
A catalyst for African integration?

DAVID MONYAE AND SIZO NKALA

Introduction

This chapter analyses the role and impact of the Pan-African Parliament (PAP) on Africa's continental integration. It focuses on three areas that are part of its core mandate, namely peace and security, democratisation, and legislative and policy harmonisation. The PAP was inaugurated in March 2004 with high hopes that it was going to revitalise the continental integration project, which had largely stalled four decades after the inception of the Organisation of African Unity (OAU) in 1963. It was seen as an instrument of the democratisation of continental governance mechanisms, earmarked to promote public participation in continental institutions and programmes. However, this chapter argues that the continental legislature has had a mixed record in the aforementioned areas that fall under its jurisdiction. While this could be attributed to structural factors, such as a strong attachment to sovereignty and little progress in adopting democratic values across the continent, it also reflects the internal shortcomings of the PAP itself, such questionable democratic credentials, a lack of legislative powers and the low quality of parliamentarians, among other things.

The first section delves into the historical and theoretical context that led to and justified the formation of the PAP. The second section is a critical assessment of the institutional design of the PAP, as outlined in the 2001 Protocol to the Treaty Establishing the African Economic Community (the Abuja Treaty). The section that follows analyses the 2014 PAP Protocol, which engendered institutional reforms meant to improve the functionality and effectiveness of the continental parliament. The chapter then examines the PAP's activities in peace and security, democracy, and governance and legislative harmonisation with a view to understanding their impact on continental integration. The final section highlights and synthesises the main points.

A continental parliament: Historical and theoretical context

An adequate understanding of the PAP and its place in Africa's quest for continental integration necessitates a deep dive into the historical circumstances that culminated in its establishment. Such a historical context would stretch back to the founding of the Organisation for African Unity (OAU) in May 1963 by 32 newly independent African states. According to Article 2 of the OAU Charter, the organisation's founding purposes included promoting unity and solidarity, defending sovereignty and territorial integrity, and eliminating colonialism in territories where it continued to exist (OAU Charter, 1963). Kwame Nkrumah, the first president of independent Ghana, was one of the most forceful proponents of African unity, arguing that 'we must recognise that our economic independence resides in our African union … we have been too busy nursing our separate states to understand fully the basic need of our union, rooted in common purpose, common planning and common endeavour' (*New African*, 2012). The organisation comprised four principal organs, namely the Assembly of Heads of State and Government, the Council of Ministers, the General Secretariat, and the Commission for Mediation, Conciliation and Arbitration. Article 20 of the Charter established specialised commissions in the domains of defence, education and culture, and socioeconomic affairs. The original structure of the OAU was devoid of any legislative arm and was dominated by the executive in the form of the Assembly of Heads of State to an extent that every other organ was merely a derivative of the Assembly. Hence, it was very much a top-down and top-heavy organisation. Van Walraven (2004: 200) contends that the lack of a legislative organ in the OAU 'underlined the extent to which the organisation represented an organisation that catered almost exclusively to the interests of the state elites – often to the detriment of the majority of the unpriviledged and the powerless'. It was more committed to decolonisation, solidarity and mutual non-interference than continental integration. The

OAU was instrumental in eliminating colonialism and, by 1980, only South Africa and Namibia remained under white minority apartheid regimes. It also adopted a number of conventions such as the General Convention on the Privileges and Immunities of the OAU (1965), the Phyto-sanitary Convention of Africa (1967), the African Convention on the Conservation of Nature and Natural Resources (1968) and the OAU Convention Governing the Specific Aspects of Refugee Problems in Africa (1969), among others. If anything, these conventions exposed the paradox of a continental body keen on making international law without a legislative organ.

However, in the 1970s, Africa faced a devastating economic crisis which jolted the OAU into a reform mode. The economic crisis was caused by the 1973 Arab oil embargoes which sharply increased oil prices and landed most African countries in debt distress. In response, the OAU adopted the Lagos Plan of Action (LPA) in 1980 (Heidhues and Obare, 2011; Bawa and Ateku, 2020). The LPA stressed the need to enhance economic cooperation between African countries in industry, agriculture, infrastructure, transport and natural resources. This plan also intended to promote intracontinental trade and transform the structure of African economies from dependence on the exports of primary commodities to manufacturing and industrialisation. Thus, the LPA marked the beginning of the move by the OAU to intensify economic cooperation between member states to complement the original commitment to political cooperation (Navarro, 2008). However, the LPA was still just another agreement without any supranational institutions or treaties to make it binding on member states.

Alongside the economic crisis, Africa also faced pervasive political instability across the continent in countries such as Somalia, Mozambique, Angola, the Democratic Republic of the Congo (DRC), Liberia and Sudan, to mention a few (Ellis, 2000; Van Walraven, 2004). Military coups d'état were the order of the day as rule-based and democratic transfers of power proved elusive (Adejumobi, 2000; Posner and Young, 2007). The political instability in member states was partly a result of the OAU's failure or reluctance to call misbehaving state elites to order. Meanwhile, the economic crisis got worse through the 1980s. This grave situation was an indictment on the ineffectiveness and incompetence of the OAU as a continental body and provided the impetus for further reforms.

To that end, the OAU adopted the Treaty Establishing the African Economic Community in 1991 within which the idea of the Pan-African Parliament was first mooted. Article 14 of this treaty declared that 'in order to ensure that the peoples of Africa are fully involved in the economic development and integration of the Continent, there shall be established a Pan-African Parliament' (OAU, 1991). The treaty outlined six stages through which an African Economic Community (AEC) was going to be established. These stages included strengthening regional economic communities (RECs), speeding up economic integration of the RECs, establishing free trade areas within the RECs, establishing a continental Customs Union, an African Common Market and, finally, establishing institutions such as an African Monetary Union and a Pan-African Parliament, among others. The treaty was enforced in 1994 when the number of states that had ratified the treaty reached the required threshold. According to the timeline, the Pan-African Parliament was intended to be established by 2028, 34 years after the enforcement of the treaty. The enforcement of this treaty set in motion the process of institutional reforms in continental governance structures. In the 1999 Sirte Declaration, adopted at the 4th Extraordinary Session of the Assembly, African leaders declared their intention to form the African Union (AU) as a replacement of the OAU. The leaders claimed to be preparing the continental organisation for the new social, political and economic challenges of the 21st century. Paragraph 8(i) of the Sirte Declaration expressed the leaders' wish to 'establish an African Union, in conformity with the ultimate objectives of the Charter of our Continental Organisation and the provisions of the Treaty Establishing the African Economic Community'. In paragraph 8 (ii, b), the Sirte Declaration committed to ensuring:

> The speedy establishment of all the institutions was provided for in the Abuja Treaty, such as the African Central Bank, the African Monetary Union, the African Court of Justice and in particular, the Pan-African Parliament. We aim to establish that Parliament by the year 2000, to provide a common platform for our peoples and their grass-root organizations to be more involved in discussions and decision-making on the problems and challenges facing our continent.

Thus, the Sirte Declaration viewed the establishment of the PAP as a matter of urgency. The necessity of the PAP was re-emphasised in Article 17 of the African Union Constitutive Act, which was adopted in November 2000. Article 17 states that 'in order to ensure the full participation of African peoples in the development and economic integration of the continent, a Pan-African Parliament shall be established' (OAU, 2000). The PAP was finally established through the 2001 Protocol to the Treaty Establishing the African Economic Community Relating to the Pan-African Parliament. It was part of a coterie of organs established under the African Union, such as the African Court of Justice, the African Union Commission, the Economic, Social and Cultural Council (ECOSOCC), and the financial institutions (Mngomezulu, 2018). The adoption of the ECOSOCC opened up avenues of participation for a diverse range of civil society groups, thus further affirming the transformation of the continent from what Van Walraven (2004) labelled a trade union of tyrants to a people and grassroots-centred institution.

According to Van Walraven (2004: 199), 'the actual birth of the Pan-African Parliament could be interpreted as prima facie evidence that the OAU's transformation into the African Union has now progressed beyond mere renaming of institutions'. Similarly convinced of the potentially transformative impact of the PAP, Navarro (2008: 5) exclaims that the parliament is the most evident manifestation of the changing nature of the Pan-African project. The establishment of the PAP also more or less coincided with the increasing parliamentarisation of the RECs. Regional organisations, such as the East African Community (EAC), the Economic Community of West African States (ECOWAS), the Southern African Development Community (SADC), the Economic Community of Central African States (ECCAS) and the OAU (now the African Union) established parliamentary organs.

Table 9.1: Regional parliamentary institutions

Organisation	Parliamentary organ	Date established
ECOWAS	ECOWAS Parliament	1994
SADC	SADC Parliamentary Forum	1997
OAU/AU	Pan-African Parliament	2001
EAC	East African Legislative Assembly	2001
ECCAS	ECCAS Parliamentary Network	2002

However, it is important to note that the coming into existence of parliamentary structures at regional and continental levels did not unfold in a vacuum. It was a response to the shifting political winds that brought political transformation across Africa. Indeed, Jancic (2019: 2) rightly points out that, 'African regional parliamentarisation is a product of a specific set of politico-historical and socio-economic circumstances that are shaped by the post-colonial pursuit of a collective pan-African identity, the assertion of sovereignty and the recurring problems of maintaining peace and eliminating poverty'. According to Mpasane (2009: 1), the establishment of the PAP was the outcome of 'renewed confidence in the ability of parliaments to uphold good political governance'. The renewed confidence would have been inspired by the wave of democratisation that swept across the continent after the end of the Cold War in 1999, when political space was increasingly liberalised. Gibson (2002) notes that, by the end of 1994, 29 countries in sub-Saharan Africa had held a total of 54 elections with almost half of them declared 'free'. This round of elections got rid of 11 sitting presidents, including in countries such as Zambia, Cape Verde and Benin. Between 1995 and 1997, 16 countries in the region held elections, which meant that only four countries did not hold elections in the 1990s. This was a drastic improvement from the pre-1989 situation, when only Botswana and Mauritius held regular free and fair elections (Lynch and Crawford, 2011). The increasing significance of elections in Africa's political landscape meant that the African publics were asserting their voices in the governance of their countries. Hence, it is not far-fetched to assume that the shift towards public participation in national politics rubbed off on regional and continental politics, resulting in the establishment of parliamentary structures as a way of encouraging public participation in continental institutions. Nzewi (2009: 3) is of the view that, between 1990 and 2010, 'international pressure for governance reforms added impetus to the overhaul of the continental regional integration and regional economic efforts ... this created the opportunity for civil participation, responsive agency and accountability in the AU through its organs such as the PAP'.

The institutional architecture of the PAP

The PAP was formally established through the 2001 Protocol to the Treaty Establishing the African Economic Community Relating to the Pan-African Parliament (hereafter the Protocol), which entered into force in November

2003, paving the way for the inauguration of the PAP in March 2004.

The Protocol detailed the structure and functions of the PAP (OAU, 2001). Most importantly, Article 2(3i) states that: 'The Pan-African Parliament shall have consultative and advisory powers.' However, this Article also states that the aim of the PAP is to evolve full legislative powers based on universal continental suffrage for its elections in due course. Among the stated objectives of the PAP in Article 3 include:

- Facilitating the policies and initiatives of the African Union
- Promoting human rights, democracy, good governance, transparency and accountability
- Promoting public awareness of continental policies
- Promoting peace, security, stability and self-reliance
- Strengthening cooperation and solidarity at both continental and regional levels.

However, it has been argued that the powers of the PAP are fundamentally externally oriented in the sense that they are exercised more outside the African Union than in its internal functioning (Van Walraven, 2004). Each member state contributes five members, picked from their national parliaments. Jancic (2019) quips that having member states contribute equal numbers of parliamentarians to the PAP reflects the institution's prioritisation of sovereign equality rather than citizen representation. The provision that each national delegation represents the diverse political parties in their national parliaments provides an opportunity for the opposition parties that have been completely silenced, to articulate alternative visions on the continental stage (Navarro, 2008). Having been ratified by 51 countries thus far, the PAP has 255 members. Such a huge number of members imposes considerable logistics challenges and hefty financial costs on the African Union. The Democratic Republic of Congo (DRC), Eritrea, Guinea and Somalia are yet to ratify the Protocol. While members are seconded by their national parliaments, they vote on issues in their personal capacity. Cilliers and Mashele (2004) suggest that, as originally constituted, the PAP's lack of direct elections leaves little room for the participation of the African masses, which will not only limit its powers, but also ensures that establishment of the PAP does little to transform the elitist image of the African Union.

The Protocol also grants the PAP a range of powers and functions in Article 11. The PAP can deliberate on any issue independently or at the request of the AU Assembly. The institution is also empowered to make recommendations on the budget of the African Union, coordinate the harmonisation of laws among member states and make recommendations on resolving regional integration challenges. Further, the PAP can request the AUC staff to attend its sessions, promote the policies of the AUC in their respective national constituencies, and coordinate the activities and programmes of the RECs. However, the power of the PAP to hold the AUC and the AU Assembly accountable is severely constrained as it has no appointing power and its recommendations are not binding. Without budgetary or concrete supervisory powers, the PAP is a sham parliament, whose existence will have, at best, a marginal impact on the fundamentally intergovernmental nature of the African Union (see Van Walraven, 2004). According to Article 12(2), the PAP can elect its president, who is assisted by four vice-presidents from the different RECs that are recognised by the African Union. In terms of its operations, Article 14(2) directs that the PAP can meet in one-month-long sessions at least twice a year. This makes the PAP a semi-permanent institution with limited ability to respond to sudden developments on the continent. However, the AU Assembly or Council, and two-thirds of the PAP, have the power to request an extraordinary session. This option has not been exercised since its inception. The AU Assembly approves the budget of the PAP and this is set to remain the case until the PAP acquires full legislative powers. As such, the PAP lacks the vital budgetary power that is a fundamental function of national parliaments the world over (Ramet, 2017). The lack of budgetary authority greatly undermines the independence of the PAP and its ability to get adequate resources to develop its capacities and competencies (Nzewi, 2014). As per its Rules of Procedure and in accordance with Article 12(13) of the Protocol, the PAP has set up 11 permanent committees to help discharge its mandate effectively, as per Table 9.2.

The committees reflect the broad mandate of the PAP as it tackles diverse issues such as health, labour, trade, industrialisation, immigration, technology and gender, among others. The committees can comprise up to 30 members with each African region represented by at least three members (Dinokopila, 2013). To facilitate participation, the PAP embraces linguistic diversity by having African languages, Arabic, English, French and Portuguese as its official languages.

Table 9.2: Committees of the PAP

1.	Committee on Cooperation, International Relations and Conflict Resolution
2.	Committee on Justice and Human Rights
3.	Committee on Education, Culture, Tourism and Human Resources
4.	Committee on Health, Labour and Social Affairs
5.	Committee on Gender, Family, Youth and People with Disabilities
6.	Committee on Monetary and Financial Affairs
7.	Committee on Transport, Industry, Communications, Energy, Science and Technology
8.	Committee on Trade, Customs and Immigration Matters
9.	Committee on Rural Economy, Agriculture, Natural Resources and Environment
10.	Rules, Privileges and Discipline
11.	Committee on Audit and Public Accounts

Source: Pan-African Parliament Rules of Procedure

Towards a real parliament? – The 2014 PAP Protocol

In June 2014, the African Union adopted the Protocol to the Constitutive Act of the African Union Relating to the Pan-African Parliament (hereinafter the 2014 Protocol) as a review of the 2001 Protocol and to open the path towards the reform of the PAP. While it retains most of the provisions of the 2001 Protocol, the 2014 Protocol presents new provisions. First, unlike the 2001 Protocol, the 2014 Protocol recognises and incorporates the African Diaspora as part of its constituency (Article 2). Article 3(a) states that one of the objectives of the PAP shall be to 'give a voice to the African peoples and the Diaspora'. The recognition of the African Diaspora reflects a strategic posture by the African Union and the PAP to leverage the influence of African people residing in other regions of the world. In terms of membership, the 2014 Protocol kept the same quota of five parliamentarians per member state; however, there are important changes. While the old Protocol ordered that at least one of the five members from each state party be a woman, the 2014 Protocol increases that minimum to two. A member-state's PAP team is not recognised unless it reflects this balance (Article 4). The 2014 Protocol also makes important changes to the membership requirements of the PAP – members are not allowed to hold a seat in their national parliament. This is to ensure that members of the PAP devote themselves to discharging their PAP duties without having to attend to their duties in the national parliament (Article 5). This means that the national parliaments do not have the power to recall a PAP member. A parliamentary term is five years and it begins on the day on which the member is sworn in. Thus, it does not depend on the status of the representative's membership in national parliament. These reforms in the nature of the membership are intended to ensure a reduced turnover of members and an improvement in the stability and continuity of the PAP.

Perhaps the most significant part of the 2014 Protocol is Article 8, which describes the functions and powers of the PAP. The Protocol designates the PAP as the legislative organ of the African Union, which can draft model laws on subjects determined by the AU Assembly. The PAP can also propose subject areas to the AU Assembly for consideration. This is a significant change from the 2001 Protocol under which the PAP did not have any legislative role in the African Union, and was restricted to consultative and advisory roles on policy issues. Moreover, the PAP can receive and make recommendations on other organs of the African Union, and it can submit opinions on draft legal instruments, treaties and international agreements referred to it by the AU Council.

Despite these significant changes, the PAP does not have the power to enact laws; it still lacks a legislative function, which is the essence of a parliament. It also lacks budgetary independence and does not possess any effective budgetary oversight under the 2014 Protocol. Article 10 of the new protocol transfers the responsibility for the allowances of the PAP members to the member states, while in the old protocol, allowances were covered by the budget of the PAP. While this reduces budgetary pressures on the African Union, it means that PAP members are variously compensated as countries have varying abilities to compensate their delegates. Indeed, some countries may even fail to pay their delegates leading to non-attendance.

The 2014 Protocol proposes a Bureau of the PAP consisting of a president and four vice-presidents representing the five regions of the African Union (namely the Southern, East, North, West and Central Africa). At least two members of the Bureau should be women, reflecting the African Union's emphasis on gender equality. Members serve a two–and–a–half–year term and this can be renewed once (Article 12).

Among other changes introduced by the 2014 Protocol is the introduction of a secretary general to run the day–to–day administration of the PAP (Article 13). To enhance integration, the PAP is directed to convene an annual consultative conference with REC parliaments and national parliaments to deliberate on issues of common concern. However, the 2014 Protocol is still a long way from entering into force, having been signed by only 21 members and ratified by 12 members. At least 28 AU member states (simple majority) have to deposit the ratification instruments before the 2014 Protocol is enforced (AU, 2019).

However, not everyone is impressed with the changes in the new protocol. Fagbayibo (2017), for instance, has argued that the provisions of the 2014 Protocol do not give the PAP any meaningful law-making powers and the institution is set to remain a 'nominal platform', ill-equipped to advance African integration and development.

The performance of the PAP

Peace, conflict and security

Since its inception in 2004, the PAP has been a visible actor in the area of peace and conflict resolution, which is a fundamental prerequisite for successful African integration. Between 2004 and 2019, the PAP deployed fact-finding missions to numerous countries including the Great Lakes region, the Democratic Republic of the Congo, Sudan's Darfur region, the Central African Republic, Chad, Saharwi Arab Democratic Republic, Mali, Libya, South Sudan, Burundi and Niger (Pan-African Parliament, 2019). In 2004, the PAP embarked on fact-finding mission to Sudan in the wake of the Darfur crisis, which saw the extensive abuse of human rights (Sallah, 2007; Nwebo, 2019). The seven-person mission managed to speak to various stakeholders, including civil society, international organisations, government and the military, in a bid to resolve the conflict. A comprehensive report was produced and submitted to the relevant AU organs, which helped guide the continental body's intervention in the crisis (Nwebo, 2019).

The PAP also deployed fact-finding missions to Côte d'Ivoire in 2005, 2007 and 2011 tasked with resolving the conflict that had been raging since the 1990s. Its actions and reports helped to shed light on the conflict and encouraged the conflicting parties to reconcile (Tsegaye, 2020). Moreover, the PAP also responded to violent conflict in Libya, which had started in 2011, by issuing a strongly worded statement that reiterated the need for non-violence and the respect for human rights. The statement read that the PAP 'condemns the military aggression of NATO forces in the bombing of public facilities, infrastructure and residential sites and the targeted assassination of national leaders'.

Further, the PAP endorsed the efforts of the African initiative to resolve the Libyan conflict and called for an Extraordinary Session of the PAP to discuss and find solutions to the issue (Polity, 2011). It also reprimanded the government of Libya for excessive violence on its citizens and encouraged it to exercise restraint and respect the rights of the citizens (Tsegaye, 2020). A delegation of the PAP was later dispatched to Benghazi and Tripoli in Libya, and to Egypt and Tunisia in the wake of the 2011 Arab Spring uprisings in a quest to quell the violence and mediate a peaceful outcome (Jancic, 2019).

Another fact-finding mission was deployed to the Saharawi Arab Democratic Republic on the issue of its decolonisation in the same year. In a debate on the violence in South Sudan in 2017, a PAP member, who was part of the mission to that country, was quoted as saying, '140 000 people remain in refugee camps. The population of 9 million children are out of school or don't complete their education. The economy relies heavily on oil that accounts for 60% of conflicts' (SABC News, 2017).

In 2019, the PAP dispatched a mission to Niger to investigate the impact of climate change on security and terrorism in the Sahel region. The parliament has also engaged with the Somalian conflict that has been going on for decades. This conflict has been the subject of several of the PAP debates in an attempt to find lasting and sustainable solutions. Officials from other organs of the African Union, such as the AU Commission on Peace and Conflict, have been invited to make presentations before the PAP on the state of conflict on the continent.

The PAP has played an active role in the peace and security domain in Africa ever since it was inaugurated in March 2004. Even if its reports and recommendations on the various conflict zones are not binding, such activities are important in building the institutional presence of the parliament on the continent. As Nzewi (2014) rightly argued, the PAP should be using the non-legislative avenues afforded by the current PAP Protocol to gain influence and build a formidable profile for itself. The PAP's growing experience, expertise and knowledge about conflict dynamics in Africa will make it an indispensable and effective player in conflict prevention and resolution, thus creating favourable conditions for continental integration.

Elections and democracy

The PAP was established with a view to ensuring the effective and 'full participation of the African peoples in the economic development and integration of the continent' (OAU, 2001). It was an effort to democratise continental governance institutions, the control of which had been monopolised by the state elites. However, continental institutions can only be democratic when democracy thrives at the national level. The harmonisation of democratic norms and standards creates a firm foundation for further continental integration. Hence, improving the continent's democratic credentials has been one of the PAP's most visible activities. The parliament has been part of numerous election observation missions (EOMs) across Africa in a bid to ensure that African elections are conducted according to the standards set in the African Charter on Democracy, Elections and Governance (ACDEG), Declaration on the Principles Governing Democratic Elections in Africa, and the African Union Guidelines for Elections Observation and Monitoring. The PAP personnel make up 40 per cent of the AU election observation missions, which have observed elections in countries such as Burkina Faso, Comoros, Côte d'Ivoire, Congo, Djibouti, Chad, Senegal, Ghana, Kenya, Libya, Sierra Leone and Zimbabwe.

The validity of the EOMs' reports has come into question as they have endorsed some flawed elections. The PAP was part of the AU's 90-person election observer mission in Kenya's 2017 general elections. The mission pronounced the elections to be peaceful and satisfactory, meeting the standards for democratic elections in terms of Kenyan law and African Union requirements (AU, 2017). However, the elections were later nullified by the Kenyan Supreme Court on the grounds of irregularities (De-Freytas-Tamura, 2017). In another case, the AU observer mission endorsed the May 2019 tripartite elections in Malawi as 'generally peaceful and in accordance with the legal framework and international obligations for democratic elections' (African Union, 2019). However, Malawi's Supreme Court invalidated the outcome of the elections citing 'widespread, systematic and grave' irregularities that greatly violated the rights of the voters. The election had been won by the then incumbent, Peter Mutharika (Masina, 2020). The AU election observers also endorsed the disputed elections in Zimbabwe in 2018, even though other organisations such as the European Union, the Commonwealth Secretariat and the US Observer Mission declared the elections as not free and fair. This shows that the AU election observer missions, of which the PAP is a part, are not effective custodians of the democratic election standards in Africa. Without common political values and systems, the continental integration process will remain fragile.

The PAP's very own democratic credentials have been subject to debate (Gumede, 2017; Jancic, 2019). Gumede (2017) expressed concern that the continental parliament is made up of representatives who come from undemocratic countries. According to Freedom House 2020 metrics, only seven countries, home to 9 per cent of the continent's population, are classified as free (Freedom House, 2020). As a matter of fact, countries classified as unfree have increased from 14 in 2004, the same year PAP was inaugurated, to 20 in 2019. This means that most members of the PAP come from countries that are undemocratic and they may have acquired parliamentary seats through undemocratic means. Expecting PAP members, who have bogus democratic credentials, to lead the democratic regeneration of the continent seems like a big ask. Holding direct elections for PAP members, according to the continental guidelines, would go a long way in improving the democratic credentials of the institution. The first 22 years of the 21st century have seen 22 military takeovers and 26 failed attempts in Africa. While this represents a significant improvement from the 38 successful coups and 40 failed attempts in the 1980s and 1990s, Africa still has a long way to go in universalising democratic norms and standards (Mwai, 2022). This is despite the coming into force of the African Charter on Democracy, Elections and Governance in 2012, which sought to entrench democratic norms across the continent. As one of the institutions whose primary task is to lead the democratisation of the continent, the PAP has made little headway in its almost two decades of existence.

Legislative harmonisation

Legislative harmonisation is a crucial element of any integration process between sovereign states. The continental protocols and treaties can only be effective if they are domesticated and incorporated by national parliaments into national legal systems and regulations. Hence, one of the key functions of the PAP is to accelerate the process of the domestication of AU protocols, policies and treaties. The national parliaments are important partners in this respect as they have the power to make national laws, and they must accede to international treaties before they are ratified and domesticated. This is why the PAP has entered into strategic relationships with African national parliaments to speed up the process of legal and policy harmonisation. The PAP has organised the Annual Conference of Speakers of African Parliaments, which provides an opportunity for the PAP to interact and exchange ideas with national and regional parliamentary leaders. The conference is also a platform to provide feedback on the implementation of the African Union's policies and decisions, and the ratification of legal instruments. Moreover, the conference serves to create citizen awareness of the African Union's initiatives and policies through parliaments. Thus, the PAP is fulfilling its mandate of enhancing public participation in continental integration initiatives. The PAP also engages African parliaments individually. For example, in January 2022, the PAP Secretariat met with the Ghanaian parliament secretariat in a working mission, which resulted in the adoption of a collaborative framework to expedite the ratification and domestication of the African Union's decisions and treaties (Pan-African Parliament, 2022). However, the track record of the ratification of the African Union's treaties and other legal instruments has been mixed since the inauguration of the PAP in 2004. Table 9.3 lists the treaties that have been ratified since 2004.

Of the 40 treaties, conventions and protocols adopted by the African Union since 2004, only 12 have come into force, while 28 are still going through ratification. Some of the documents have been going through the ratification process for more than 10 years. While the PAP cannot be held entirely responsible for the slow rate of domestication of the continental agreements, such a dismal record reflects negatively on the effectiveness of the PAP as the organ with the explicit mandate to speed up the ratification of AU instruments. Without the domestic legislation of continental initiatives, integration will not be possible since the African Union relies on member states to implement its agreements.

Table 9.3: Ratified AU treaties, conventions, charters and protocols since 2004

Ratified treaties
Statute of the African Union Commission on International Law (AUCIL) (February 2004)
Convention on the African Energy Commission (December 2006)
The African Union Non-Aggression and Common Defence Pact (December 2009)
African Youth Charter (August 2009)
Revised Constitution of the African Civil Aviation Commission (May 2010)
African Charter on Democracy, Elections and Governance (February 2012)
African Union Convention for the Protection and Assistance of Internally Displaced Persons in Africa (December 2012)
African Charter on Statistics (February 2015)
Statute of the African Space Agency (January 2018)
Statute of the African Institute for Remittances (AIR) (January 2018)
African Charter on the Values and Principles of Decentralisation, Local Governance and Local Development (January 2019)
Agreement Establishing the African Continental Free Trade Area (May 2019)

Source: African Union

Conclusion

When it was inaugurated in 2004, the PAP became the symbol of the new continental project embodied by the formation of the African Union in 2002. It had been four decades since the inception of the OAU in 1963 with the intention of uniting the African continent. However, in those four decades, the African integration project was almost exclusively dominated by state elites to the exclusion of the African masses. Isolated from the masses, the project lacked the vital democratic grounding and legitimacy which, consequently, led to its stillbirth. Hence, the PAP was created to make continental integration people-oriented and people-centred. It was going to be the catalyst of African integration, which had made little headway in the previous four decades. However, 18 years after it came into existence, at the time of writing, one wonders whether the PAP is an institution fit for purpose.

One area in which the PAP seems to have performed exceedingly well is in promoting peace and security on the continent. The PAP has not shied away from the continent's hot spots, but has been active in providing comprehensive diagnoses of various conflicts and adding an important voice in calling for the peaceful resolution of conflicts. However, while peace and stability are fundamental for successful integration, they are not the only factors. The PAP was also mandated to promote democratic values and norms in Africa, as well as to accelerate the implementation of the African Union's decisions at the national level. Unfortunately, Africa has seen little improvement in democratic standards, with only seven countries, hosting 9 per cent of the continent's population, classified as free. The rest are either partially free or not free. Moreover, military coups are still in vogue, with 22 successful military takeovers and 26 failed coups across Africa in the last 22 years.

The PAP's election observation missions have repeatedly endorsed flawed elections in countries such as Malawi, Zimbabwe and Kenya. The lack of democracy means that the revitalisation of continental integration at the turn of the 21st century was a false start, since the voice of the masses is still suppressed. Moreover, the enforcement of the African Union's policies and decisions stands at just 30 per cent, with only 12 of the 40 treaties and conventions adopted having reached the ratification threshold since the PAP was established. Therefore, overall, the PAP seems to have had a minimal impact on continental integration in its 18 years of existence. While the idea of the PAP was valid, it has been undermined by the implementation of that idea. Major institutional reforms, such as direct elections and granting the PAP legislative powers, are needed to enhance the PAP's contribution to continental integration.

References

Adejumobi, S. (2000). 'Elections in Africa: A fading shadow of democracy?' *International Political Science Review*, 21(1): 59–73.

African Union (AU). (2019a). 'List of countries which have signed, ratified/acceded to The Protocol to the Constitutive Act of the African Union Relating to the Pan-African Parliament'. Available at: https://au.int/sites/default/files/treaties/7806-sl-PROTOCOL-5.pdf (Accessed 26 January 2022).

African Union (AU). (2019b). 'African Union Election Observation Mission to the 21 May Tripartite Elections in the Republic of Malawi'. Available at: https://au.int/sites/default/files/documents/38698-doc-report_of_the_african_union_election_observation_mission_to_the_21_may_2019_tripartite_elections_in_the_republic_of_malawi.pdf (Accessed 27 February 2022).

African Union (AU). (2017). 'Preliminary Statement, African Union Election Observer Mission to the 2017 General Elections in Kenya', *Press Statement*, 10 August 2017. Available at: https://au.int/en/pressreleases/20170810/preliminary-statement-african-union-election-observer-mission-2017-general (Accessed 20 January 2022).

African Union (AU). (2014). *The Protocol to the Constitutive Act of the African Union Relating to the Pan-African Parliament*, 27 June 2014. Malabo, Equatorial Guinea.

Bawa, J. and Ateku, A-J. (2020). 'After the Structural Adjustment Programme for Africa's economic crisis what next? A look at some immediate African Alternative Development Strategies', 30 May. Available at: SSRN, https://papers.ssrn.com/sol3/papers.cfm?abstract_id=3614173 (Accessed 20 February 2022).

Burke, J. and Pensulo, C. (2020). 'Malawi court annuls 2019 election results and calls for new ballot', *The Guardian*, 3 February. Available at: https://www.theguardian.com/world/2020/feb/03/malawi-court-annuls-2019-election-results-calls-new-ballot (Accessed 27 January 2022).

Cilliers, J. and Mashele, P. (2004). 'The Pan-African Parliament: A plenary of parliamentarians', *African Security Review*, 13(4): 73–84.

De Freytas-Tamura, K. (2017). 'Kenya Supreme Court nullifies presidential election', *New York Times*, 1 September. Available at: https://www.nytimes.com/2017/09/01/world/africa/kenya-election-kenyatta-odinga.html (Accessed 24 February 2022).

Dinokopila, B.R. (2013). 'The Pan-African Parliament and African Union human rights actors, civil society and national human rights institutions: The importance of collaboration', *African Human Rights Law Journal*, 13: 302–23.

East African Legislative Assembly (EALA). (2012). 'Pan-African Conference for speakers to take place in South Africa'. Available at https://www.eala.org/index.php/media/view/pan-african-conference-for-speakers-to-take-place-in-south-africa (Accessed 24 January 2022).

Ellis, S. (2000). 'Elections in Africa in historical context', in *Election Observation and Democratization in Africa*. London: Palgrave Macmillan, pp. 37–49.

Fagbayibo, B. (2017). 'Toothless Pan-African Parliament could have meaningful powers. Here's how', *The Conversation*, 23 November. Available at https://theconversation.com/toothless-pan-african-parliament-could-have-meaningful-powers-heres-how-87449 (Accessed 3 February 2022).

Freedom House. (2020). 'Democratic trends in Africa in four charts', 17 April. Available at: https://freedomhouse.org/article/democratic-trends-africa-four-charts (Accessed 27 February 2022).

Gibson, C.C. (2002). 'Of waves and ripples: Democracy and political change in Africa in the 1990s', *Annual Review of Political Science*, 5: 201–21.

Gumede, W. (2017). 'Policy Brief 15: Strengthening the Pan-African Parliament to deepen democracy in Africa', Democracy Works Foundation. Available at https://democracyworks.org.za/policy-brief-15-strengthening-the-pan-african-parliament-to-deepen-democracy-in-africa/ (Accessed 25 February 2022).

Heidhues, F. and Obare, G. (2011). 'Lessons from structural adjustment programmes and their effects in Africa', *Quarterly Journal of International Agriculture*, 50(1): 55–64.

Jancic, D. (2019). 'Regional parliaments and African economic integration', *European Journal of International Law*, 30(1): 199–228.

Lynch, G. and Crawford, G. (2011). 'Democratization in Africa 1990–2010: An assessment', *Democratization*, 18(2): 275–310.

Mngomezulu, B. (2018). 'Reflecting on the Pan-African Parliament: Prospects and challenges', *Journal African Foreign Affairs*, 7(2): 45–62.

Mpasane, S. (2009). *Transformation of the Pan-African Parliament: A path to a legislative body?* ISS Working Paper No. 181, March. Pretoria: Institute for Security Studies.

Mwai, P. (2022). 'Are military takeovers on the rise in Africa?' BBC News, 2 February. Available at https://www.bbc.com/news/world-africa-46783600 (Accessed on 24 February 2022).

Navarro, J. (2008). *Building of a Regional Parliamentary Assembly in an International Context: The creation and launching of the Pan-African Parliament*. 3rd GARNET Annual Conference, September, Pessac, France.

New African. (2012). 'Kwame Nkrumah – "The people of Africa are crying for unity"', *New African*, 26 July. Available at https://newafricanmagazine.com/3232/ (Accessed 13 February 2022).

Nwebo, O.E. (2019). 'The role of the Pan-African Parliament in promoting constitutionalism and democratic governance in Africa: Lessons from other supranational parliaments'. Unpublished Doctoral Thesis, University of Pretoria.

Nzewi, O. (2014). 'Influence and legitimacy in African Regional Parliamentary Assemblies: The case of the Pan-African Parliament's search for legislative powers', *Journal of Asian and African Studies*, 49(4): 488–507.

Nzewi, O. (2009). *The challenges of post-1990 regional integration In Africa: Pan-African Parliament*. Centre for Policy Studies Policy Brief No. 57, April. Johannesburg: Centre for Policy Studies.

Organisation of African Unity (OAU). (2001). *Protocol to the Treaty Establishing the African Economic Community Relating to the Pan-African Parliament*, 2 March 2001, Sirte Libya.

Organisation of African Unity (OAU). (2000). *Constitutive Act of the African Union*, 11 July, Lome, Togo.

Organisation of African Unity (OAU). (1999). *Fourth Extraordinary Assembly of Heads of State and Government: Sirte Declaration*, 8–9 September 1999, Sirte, Libya.

Organisation of African Unity (OAU). (1991). *Treaty Establishing the African Economic Community*, 3 June. Abuja, Nigeria.

Organisation of African Unity (OAU). (1963). *The OAU Charter*, 25 May, Addis Ababa, Ethiopia.

Pan African Parliament. (2019). 'Fact-finding missions'. Available at: https://pap.au.int/en/fact-finding-missions (Accessed 18 February 2022).

Polity. (2011). 'PAP: Statement by the Pan-African Parliament, on the security situation in Libya (20/05/2011)', 20 May. Available at: https://www.polity.org.za/print-version/pap-statement-by-the-pan-african-parliament-on-the-security-situation-in-libya-20052011-2011-05-20 (Accessed 20 February 2022).

Posner, D.N. and Young, D.J. (2007). 'The institutionalization of political power in Africa', *Journal of Democracy*, 18(3): 126–40.

Ramet, V. (2017). 'The Pan-African Parliament: Getting ready for the 2017 AU–EU Summit', European Parliament Policy Department, November 2017, Available at: https://www.europarl.europa.eu/RegData/etudes/BRIE/2017/570486/EXPO_BRI(2017)570486_EN.pdf (Accessed 27 February 2022).

SABC News. (2017). 'PAP seeks solutions on conflicts in Africa', 16 October. Available at https://www.sabcnews.com/pap-seeks-solutions-on-conflicts-in-africa/ (Accessed 21 February 2022).

Sallah, H. (2007). 'Rethinking conflict prevention and resolution: Lessons from the Pan African Parliament's mission to Darfur', *Conflict Trends*, 2007(1). Durban: Accord. Available at: file:///C:/Users/sizos/OneDrive/Documents/ACCORD-CT-2007-1.pdf (Accessed 20 February 2022).

Tsegaye, K.K. (2020). 'The role of regional parliaments in conflict resolution: The case of the Pan-African Parliament (2004–2011)', *African Journal of Political Science and International Relations*, 14(4): 168–79.

Van Walraven, K. (2004). 'From union of tyrants to power to the people? The significance of the Pan-African Parliament for the African Union', *Africa Spectrum*, 39(2): 197–221.

Chapter Ten

An appraisal of the AU's Peace and Security Council, 2003–2022

BHASO NDZENDZE AND ANSLELM W. ADUNIMAY

Introduction

The Peace and Security Council (PSC) was established by the African Union (AU) in 2003. Its main objective is to coordinate cooperation between the AU member states in promoting peace, security and stability in the continent by engaging in dispute and conflict resolution, peacekeeping and peacebuilding and intervening in member states in the event of war crimes, genocide and crimes against humanity. The PSC is tasked with promoting democracy, human rights, the rule of law and good governance among the member states, and is also is mandated to intervene in instances of unconstitutional changes of government. There is no doubt that peace and security are essential for successful regional and continental integration, hence the PSC has an important role to play in the integration agenda. This chapter assesses the performance of the PSC since it was established and suggests how this institution can perform better, with particular reference to its capacity for peacebuilding and conflict prevention.

In our assessment, the PSC had an impressive early record, owing to its proactiveness and willingness to act, but it has since become increasingly less effective. Statistically, there have been more conflicts initiated in the 15-year period after its formation than the preceding similar timeframe (see Figure

10.1). Moreover, while there has been a rise in the types of conflict for which it was not adequately trained, the majority of the conflicts are similar to those that persisted in its formative period. Most symbolic of all is that in 2020, a year designated by the African Union as the deadline for 'silencing the guns', Ethiopia – the home of the African Union's headquarters – became engulfed in a full-scale civil war and there have been about five successful coups in other African countries since. We argue that this lacklustre record is due to resource and political constraints. The political reasons include a lack of cooperation by the troubled countries, who also sit in the PSC, as well as the lack of coordination. Operating in this political economy, the PSC finds itself incapable of the sort of enablement required for it to fulfil its founding mission. The PSC's failure, therefore, is indicative of its structural limitations, as well as the broader problems plaguing the African Union in its current formation. This has left much of the response to the Regional Economic Communities (RECs), who have taken most of the initiative in recent years, especially in Southern and West Africa.

This chapter begins with a brief literature review and a discussion about the motivations behind the formation of the PSC, including the theoretical and historical underpinnings that led to its formation, its structure and functions. This is followed by an analysis of the PSC's performance, which seems to be declining as it is not living up to the contemporary challenges that have arisen since its entry into force. The chapter concludes with a discussion of the PSC's challenges and how these may be mitigated.

The literature

The African Union has placed particular emphasis on conflict resolution and management as a necessary prerequisite for its development. In its Agenda 2063, the continental body evokes, under the umbrella of Aspiration 4 ('A Peaceful and Secure Africa'), the peace–development nexus (4[32] and [33]): 'Africa will be a peaceful and secure continent, with harmony among communities starting at grassroots level. The management of our diversity will be a source of wealth, harmony and social and economic transformation rather than a source of conflict.' Practically, the document designates the event horizon of 2020, declaring that: 'Mechanisms for peaceful prevention and resolution of conflicts will be functional at all levels. As a first step, dialogue-centred conflict prevention and resolution will be actively promoted in such a way that by 2020 all guns will be silent' (African Union, 2013: 6).

The continent further links the attainment of peace as being conditioned on democracy (good governance and peaceful transfers of power): 'We recognize that a prosperous, integrated and united Africa, based on good governance, democracy, social inclusion and respect for human rights, justice and the rule of law are the necessary pre-conditions for a peaceful and conflict-free continent' (African Union, 2013: 6, section 4[35]). Both these links (security and development, and democracy and peace) are well established in the literature, with the scholarship establishing, though not without controversy (particularly around the question of causality, in other words, which causes which [Mross, 2019: 190]), a direct link between the absence of conflict and the presence of economic development. Similarly, the existence of democracy commonly correlates with stability, both within and between countries. The creation of the Peace and Security Council (PSC) stemmed from this understanding. It emerged out of the continent's diagnosis of the litany of issues confronting it, and sought to make use of the continent's collective capabilities to respond proactively and adequately to security (and thus developmental and governance) challenges. This has a basis in international law and state-making.

Historically, and in contemporary times, most countries find it difficult, if not impossible, to be assured of their security solely on the basis of their individual strength (Booth, 1987: 303; Jordaan, 2016: 160). In recognition of this, states have promulgated alliances, mutual defence pacts and international security organisations. These are examples of the concept of collective security in practice. As both a theory and a mechanism for action, the principle of collective security was consciously employed for the first time in the promulgation of the League of Nations, particularly Article 10 of its Covenant, which was initially cast in global terms. During the Cold War, it found expression in the transnational NATO and Warsaw Pact treaties. Since the 1990s, however, it has taken on a more regional form as well, because another change occurred: 'Collective security was intended to deal mainly with interstate conflict, yet most armed conflicts since the Cold War have been intrastate in nature' (Vogt, 2009: 253). The PSC was thus formed with both intra- and interstate conflicts in mind. Through the PSC, the continent committed itself to making available 'all possible assistances', including the deployment of the African Standing Force (ASF), for the purposes of foreign intervention.

As previously mentioned, the impetus for the PSC is also derived from international law, or, at the very least, is not explicitly barred by it. As the PSC was beginning to come into operation in 2004, the *Report of the Secretary-General's High-level Panel on Threats, Challenges and Change* was published. This lent further credence to the African Union's new interventionist approach and efforts. It stated that the use of military force for self-defence was justified, provided a threat was 'imminent' to a country's national security (United Nations, 2004: 63). The report further elaborated that 'the international community has a collective "responsibility to protect" (R2P) civilians in any state suffering gross human rights violations, even if their own government does not take responsibility to protect them, or is itself guilty of atrocities against them'. The UN Panel further affirmed that regional security structures had the right to 'fill the void in the UN's limited peace operations capacity and conduct peace operations within their regions, with UN approval and accountability to the UN' (United Nations, 2004: 69). More fundamentally, this was an assertion in support of Chapter VIII of the UN Charter, which grants a role to regional organisations in conflict management. Article 52 of the Charter states that:

> Nothing in the present Charter precludes the existence of regional arrangements or agencies for dealing with such matters relating to the maintenance of international peace and security as are appropriate for regional action, provided that such arrangements or agencies and their activities are consistent with the Purposes and Principles of the United Nations.

The PSC represented an African Union that, moving from its meek Organisation of African Union past, had taken a position that can be defined as 'interventionist' as far as peace and security matters in Africa were concerned (Murithi, 2012: 87–110). The PSC represents a more robust system for the early detection of crises or conflicts, and is vested with the powers to take steps to prevent these problems, itself an outgrowth of the AU's shift from 'non-interference' to 'non-indifference' (Sarkin, 2010). To complement its role in the promotion of peace and security, the PSC works in close collaboration with the AU Commission, the Panel of the Wise, the Continental Early Warning System (CEWS), an African Standby Force, and a Special Fund Trust (PSCAU Protocol, 2002: 4–5). According to Levitt (2010: 110), the Peace and Security Council forms a vital part of the African regional human rights system. As such, it is obligated to seek close collaboration with the African Union Commission on Human and People's

Rights, among other institutions (PSCAU Protocol, 2002: 26). While it can be argued that ensuring peace and security, per se, is not a new phenomenon in Africa, the establishment of the PSC ushered in a new era in the way in which peace, security and stability challenges were to be addressed on the continent by its internal actors. Of importance is the manner in which the AU's PSC Protocol called for the harnessing of forces between the council and other organisations/institutions, both within and outside the continent. We provide an overview of the PSC's structure and functions to enable an assessment of the PSC's track record since its formation.

Overview: Structure and functions of the AUPSC

The PSC comprises 15 member states, with each of the continent's five regions getting the following designated number of seats:
1. Central Africa: three seats
2. Eastern Africa: three seats
3. Northern Africa: two seats
4. Southern Africa: three seats
5. Western Africa: four seats.

Each of these 15 elected members enjoy equal rights (PSCAU Protocol, 2002: 7) and, for continuity, five members are elected for three-year terms and 10 for two-year terms. Despite there being no permanency, there are, nonetheless, no rules preventing member states from seeking and taking up consecutive successive re-elections. The PSC operates at the level of ambassadors, ministers and heads of state and government (Kioko, 2003: 817). Election of membership is also based on several criteria, as provided under the PSC Protocol and the Modalities for the Election of Members of the Peace and Security Council. The first criterion is equitable regional representation and rotation (PSCAU Protocol, 2002: 7). Article 5(2) of the PSC Protocol also stipulates prospective candidate countries have to fulfil a number of fundamental requirements to be eligible for election. These include a respect for constitutional governance, as well as the rule of law and human rights, a commitment to uphold the principles of the Union and a commitment to honour their financial obligations to the Union (PSCAU Protocol, 2002: 7). Nonetheless, these fundamental requirements are not being strictly observed because some states have experienced violent conflicts during their membership of the PSC, and others have failed in terms of constitutional governance and respect for the rule of law and human rights (Williams, 2009).

A question has been raised with regard to the criterion of 'respect for the rule of law' and how this may be measured in legal terms; further, 'if international standards are the means of measurement, how many African states genuinely would be entitled to AU membership' (Levitt, 2003: 116) and, consequently, membership of the PSC. The difficulty with this question is that the principle of the rule of law is an ideal, which many states fail to achieve. Despite the fact that respect for the rule of law is a fundamental requirement, it is possible to achieve at least the minimum criteria for its respect. In this regard, the African Union is best placed to decide whether a prospective member state qualifies, based on the minimum criteria for membership of the PSC. In true AU fashion, however, membership continues to rotate.

Table 10.1: Rotating Chair of the Peace and Security Council of the African Union from April 2022

No.	COUNTRY	MONTH OF CHAIRING	TERM	END OF MANDATE	REGION
1.	Burundi	April 2022	2	31 March 2024	Central Africa
2.	Cameroon	May 2022	3	31 March 2024	Central Africa
3.	Congo	June 2022	2	31 March 2024	Central Africa
4.	Djibouti	July 2022	2	31 March 2024	Eastern Africa
5.	Gambia	August 2022	2	31 March 2024	Western Africa
6.	Ghana	September 2022	2	31 March 2024	Western Africa
7.	Morocco	October 2022	3	31 March 2024	Northern Africa
8.	Namibia	November 2022	3	31 March 2024	Southern Africa
9.	Nigeria	December 2022	3	31 March 2024	Western Africa

No.	COUNTRY	MONTH OF CHAIRING	TERM	END OF MANDATE	REGION
10.	Senegal	January 2023	2	31 March 2024	Western Africa
11.	South Africa	February 2023	2	31 March 2024	Southern Africa
12.	Tanzania	March 2023	2	31 March 2024	Eastern Africa
13.	Tunisia	April 2023	2	31 March 2024	Northern Africa
14.	Uganda	May 2023	2	31 March 2024	Eastern Africa
15.	Zimbabwe	June 2023	2	31 March 2024	Southern Africa

The election for the 10 PSC Member States for two-year term will take place during the January/February 2024 Executive Council session, to be followed by the endorsement by the Assembly of the Union of the elected PDC Members. Following the election, the new members will take their seats on 1 April 2024.

Source: African Union (2022). Available at: https://www.peaceau.org/en/page/88-composition-of-the-psc (Accessed 28 November 2022).

It is also important to note that in addition to the 15 members, some other states and bodies may be invited to take part in certain PSC meetings, at least in the open session. These include the AU commissioner(s), interested heads of division within the commission, desk officers and other members of the AU secretariat, the AU legal counsel, delegations, and invited parties such as representatives of governments affected by conflicts and crisis situations, or outside entities such as representatives of Africa's subregional organisations, the United Nations and international non-governmental organisations (INGOs) (Williams, 2009).

The Peace and Security Council's performance, 2004–2022: An appraisal

As highlighted earlier, on one hand, the PSC has been established as a standing decision-making organ for the prevention, management and resolution of conflicts, and, on the other hand, as a collective and early-warning arrangement to facilitate a timely and efficient response to conflict and crisis situations in Africa (PSCAU Protocol, 2002: 4–5). The functions of the PSC are, therefore, aimed at fulfilling these objectives.

In line with Article 6 of the PSCAU Protocol, the areas in which the Peace and Security Council is authorised to function are:

> the promotion of peace, security and stability in Africa; early warning and preventive diplomacy; peace-making, including the use of good offices; mediation, conciliation and enquiry; peace support operations and intervention pursuant to Article 4(h) and 4(j) of the Constitutive Act; peace-building and post-conflict reconstruction; humanitarian action and disaster management; and any other function as may be decided by the Assembly (PSCAU Protocol, 2002: 8).

The functions of the council, as enumerated above, embrace the notions of conflict prevention, management and resolution, which are essential for peace maintenance on the continent. Nonetheless, the PSC's principal focus is to promote and ensure peace, security and stability in Africa. However, Levitt (2003) argues that, while the functions of the council are important, neither the Constitutive Act nor the PSCAU Protocol defines what the terms provided for in Article 6 of the PSCAU Protocol mean from an operational or a policy standpoint. It would seem that these instruments provide for the structures only, without giving an indication of how these are to operate in practice; a chronic culprit in the PSC's future aspirations, which will be visited in our analysis.

The adoption of the PSC-AU Protocol was a collective attempt to put into practice Article 1 of the African Charter, which compels member states of the AU to undertake legislative and other measures to realise the rights contained in the Charter – in this case, the right to peace and security. The PSCAU Protocol is, therefore, the central instrument of the AU's peace and security architecture on these grounds. As noted by Sands and Klein (2009), the creation of the PSC and the extent of its powers 'are clear evidence of the [AU] members' will to play a much more active role in the prevention of conflicts and in the maintenance of peace and security on the continent'. To perform its broad functions, the council is to be supported by the Commission of the AU (AUC) via its chairperson, a Panel of the Wise, a Continental Early Warning System (CEWS), an African Standby Force

(ASF), a Special Fund Trust and a Military Staff Committee. Each of these bodies is discussed separately.

An assessment of the PSC's performance

To establish and assess the performance of the PSC since the PSCAU Protocol entered into force in December 2003 and its launch on 25 May 2004 (Powell, 2005: 11), it is important that we examine some of the cases in which the PSC has been involved and the outcomes of these interventions. However, while it is important to assess the PSC's performance, it is relevant to diagnose the state of security in the continent. According to the African Union's PSC Report (2020), there is no region in Africa that is not facing instability. For instance, in Central Africa, the security situation in the DRC, particularly in the eastern region, remains very tense, and the security situation in the Republic of Cameroon has broken down along linguistic lines. Since October 2016 the two Anglophone regions (in the northwest and southwest) of Cameroon have been engaged in a secessionist war of independence (PSCAU Report, 2020: 8–14). The PSC has shown indecision and a lukewarm attitude towards taking any decisive steps to resolve the crisis. One can argue that this indecision is based on the fact that the PSC is of the opinion that not all local (national) remedies have been exhausted. This begs the question: how ready is the PSC to silence the guns in active conflicts, of which there are plenty?

In East Africa, Sudan's security situation also remains very tense. It should be noted that, on 21 November 2021, an agreement was signed between the Chairman of the Sovereign Council, Abdel Fatah Al Burhan and Prime Minister Abdalla Hamdok, which culminated in the reinstatement of the prime minister (PSCAU Communique, 2021). Nonetheless, calm is still to return on the ground. In South Sudan, the failure to unify the country's armed groups into a single force to foster national security has led to a continuation of the stand-off between warring parties (Woldemichael *et al.*, 2021), thereby rendering the security situation very volatile.

In Ethiopia, the civil war that has been ongoing since November 2020 continues unabated and the situation on the ground is extremely volatile. Both the Tigrayan forces and Ethiopian government (reportedly supported by their Eritrean neighbour), along with Amhara regional forces and Amhara militias, have been accused of carrying out transgressions such as extrajudicial killings, sexual violence and attacks on refugees (Dahir, 2021).

Most interestingly, since the outbreak of the crisis the AU has timidly reacted to the unfolding events, despite urging both parties to amicably silent the guns. In his capacity as the regional assembly chairperson, South African President Cyril Ramaphosa, in November 2020, dispatched an envoy of three former presidents – Mozambique's Joaquim Chissano, Liberia's Ellen Johnson Sirleaf and South Africa's Kgalema Motlanthe – with the mandate to mediate in the conflict (International Crisis Group, 2021). However, after months of talk, the trio were unable to obtain a ceasefire and bring the warring parties to dialogue. Moreover, Prime Minister Abiy 'made it clear that the Tigray operation is a law enforcement operation and efforts for mediation by the AU or anybody else would be rejected since Addis Ababa did not see itself at par with Mekelle, the capital city of the Tigray region' (Singh, 2021). In other words, this means that the involvement of any international body or entity would be considered as interference in Ethiopia's domestic affairs (Deleernsyder, 2021). In August 2021, the AU appointed the former Nigerian president, Olesegun Obasanjo, as a special envoy for the Horn of Africa in the hope that he would obtain a ceasefire and push for a political solution to end the crisis. After holding separate talks with the warring parties and engaging with various stakeholders, Obasanjo underscored that he was 'optimistic that common ground towards a peaceful resolution of the conflict can be secured' (African Union, 2021).

In North Africa, the situation in Libya is still marked by a continuous violation of the ceasefire by the forces allied to the Government of National Accord and those of the Libyan National Army (LNA) led by General Haftar. This has been compounded by the increased presence of foreign political and military interference in the country (PSCAU Report, 2020). In Southern Africa, despite the relative peace and stability in most member states, an atmosphere of uncertainty continues to loom over the political and security situation in states such as Lesotho, Zimbabwe, Eswatini and Mozambique (Tau, 2022). For instance, in Mozambique, and especially in the province of Cabo Delgado, the situation remains fragile, despite gains made by the Mozambican security forces and Rwandan and Southern African Development Community (SADC)-authorised troops (Sheehy, 2021).

In West Africa, the security situations in Mali and the Sahel remain very tense given that the country witnessed two coups d'état in less than a year (Lyammouri, 2021: 1). In Burkina Faso, reports from the United

Nations High Commission for Refugees (UNHCR) note that the security situation continues to be worrisome, given the continuous intimidation of armed groups (UNHCR, 2021). Faced with such high levels of insecurity and the deteriorating situation therein, Judd Devermont has stated that 'the governments of Burkina Faso, Mali, and Niger are ill-equipped to confront the worsening security crisis in the region', the reason being that their approach has been insufficient at best and counterproductive at worst (Devermont, 2021: 1).

Given the state of the security situation on the continent, it is worth asking how the PSC has performed. Apuuli (2021) notes that since the inception of the PSC, nine AU-mandated peace support operations have been deployed, including the African Union Mission in Burundi (AMIB, 2003–2004); the African Union Mission in Sudan (AMIS, 2004–2007); the African Union Mission Support to the Elections in Comoros (AMISEC, 2006); the African Union Electoral and Security Assistance Mission to the Comoros (MAES, 2007); the African Union Mission in Somalia (AMISOM, 2007 to today); the African-led International Support Mission in Mali (AFISMA, 2013); and the African-led International Support Mission in the Central African Republic (MISCA, 2013–2014) (Apuuli, 2021: 671). However, while some (such as the AMISEC and AMIB) have been credited with success, others have ended up in hybrid missions such as the AMIS (Apuuli, 2021: 671) or completely transformed into UN missions (Apuuli, 2021: 671). Moreover, there are some situations in which foreign external powers continue to intervene. This has been the case when, in the wake of the 9/11 attacks, the United States created the Africa Command (AFRICOM) 'to coordinate their military activities in the continent', while France has launched a succession of military operations, including in Mali since 2013, and in the CAR between 2013 and 2016 'to counter terrorism and anarchy in two collapsed states' (Kahombo, 2018: 17).

Based on the above analysis, one could agree with Juliana Abena Appiah who opines that the performance of the PSC is mixed. While some operations have been conducted fully, others have not (Appiah, 2018: 56). However, as the PSC grapples to fulfil its mandate of 'African solutions to African problems', challenges continue to hamper its efforts. These can be attributed to a number of factors. For instance, when it comes to the application of its norms, values and principles in its member states, one notes that these have not been applied evenly by the PSC. Examples include

Togo, Mauritania and Sudan where the PSC norms have been applied differently. In the case of Togo, it took the joint leadership of the ECOWAS and the AU to reverse the palace coup, which took place in February 2005 (Kwesi, 2008: 16). In Mauritania, however, 'a "blanket" application of sanctions after the coup d'état culminated in an inability to bring the desired change and a reversal of the military takeover' (Kwesi, 2008: 16), despite broader international efforts to encourage a return to democratic government. Nonetheless, Mauritania has managed to hold free and fair elections, with a democratic regime currently in place.

A declining record of effectiveness

Figure 10.1: African conflicts before and after the formation of the PSC

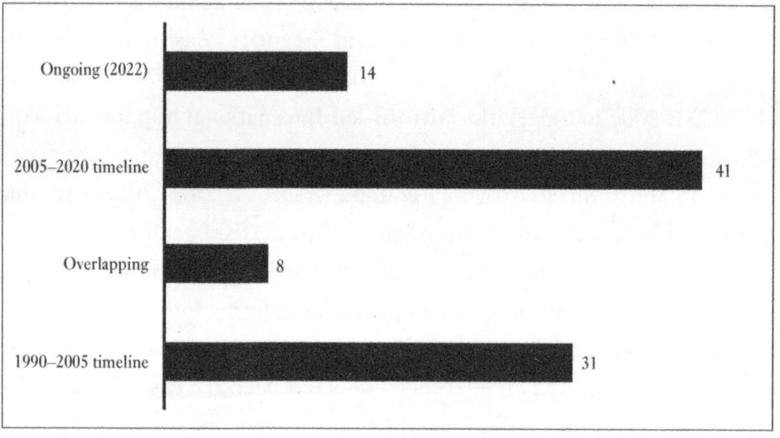

Source: Chart by authors. Data sourced from ACLEC (2022) and SIPRI (2022).

Between 2005 and 2020, there were 41 new conflicts on the continent, whereas over a 15-year period before the PSC, there were only 31 new conflicts. Thus, the record is clear: the PSC has had a poor record in anticipating and halting conflicts from escalating. Even accounting for the conflicts that the PSC 'inherited' (that is, those that occurred prior to its enactment and have persisted), we still find that more conflicts have occurred in the 15-year period since the PSC's formation than over a similar period before it. That is, the eight ongoing conflicts that began before 2005 (LRA activities in Uganda, the DRC, Sudan and South Sudan, the ADF insurgence in Uganda and the DRC, and the conflict in the Western Sahara), which the PSC 'inherited', account for fewer than the ten or more conflicts that would be sufficient to accurately assert that the PSC is mostly confronted with conflicts that precede its formation. In other words, it has failed to prevent new conflicts from breaking out, which is its mandate.

It may be asserted, moreover, that the PSC is confronted by new challenges it is incapable of managing. To be sure, the continental and global environment in which the PSC operates is mired in complexities emanating from an environment that has changed considerably since the late Cold War period and post-Cold War era of the 1990s. However, as the Institute for Security Studies (ISS) observes, the current wave of conflict is the latest resurgence after a period of decline. As the ISS notes, although conflict was high in the early 1990s, there were lower outbreaks and fatalities in Africa in the mid-2000s, but these have rebound once more since 2012. The major hotspots according to the database are Egypt, the CAR, the DRC, Libya, Mali, Nigeria, South Sudan and Somalia. Thus, it would appear that the major cause of conflict has shifted. Or, rather, the traditional forms of conflict (resource-based, communal, secessionist, anti-regime and civil wars) have remained but new forms of conflict have emerged in the form of terrorism, alongside escalated stakes with regard to increasingly limited resources amid growing populations. For example, the Boko Haram insurgency alone straddles multiple fronts and has affected at least five countries: Benin, Cameroon, Chad, Niger and Nigeria. Nonetheless, the insurgency is not as widespread as the spectacle of the terrorist would seem to imply. Plainly, the majority of the 41 new conflicts have been of the sort that the PSC is designed to anticipate and manage: disputes within countries between different formations, including the sitting governments. For example, the Tigray conflict, in a matter of about a year and a few months, has seen 2.5 million displaced, the same number reached by the Boko Haram insurgency after more than a decade in effect. Thus, the cases exemplify the 'typical' sort of conflict common in the early 21st century and which the PSC was formed to deal with. Indeed, they have been the most common form of conflict in the face of the PSC itself.

While issues of capacity abound, there is an insufficient supply of logistics, personnel and funds. For instance, the authorised target of 10 000 troops for the AMIS was not reached because of the reluctance of many states to contribute and expose their troops to grave security risks abroad (Kahombo, 2018). No doubt the United Nations remains the principal bidder of peace missions, such as the United Nations Operation in Burundi

(ONUB), the United Nations Organisation Stabilisation Mission in the DRC (MONUSCO), the United Nation Mission in South Sudan (UNMISS), the United Nations Multidimensional Integrated Stabilisation Mission in Mali (MINUSMA) and the United Nations Multidimensional Integrated Stabilisation Mission in the Central African Republic (MINUSCA) (Kahombo, 2018: 16–17).

Political interference has been equally noticeable, resulting in lethargy. Most notable is the case of Burundi in 2015 and 2016. On 17 October 2015, the PSC recommended the imposition of targeted sanctions and travel bans against Burundians who had played a role in that country's political violence. Exactly two months later, the PSC authorised the deployment of 5 000 peacekeepers to form the African Prevention and Protection Mission in Burundi (MAPROBU) intended 'to monitor the security situation, protect civilian populations under threat, create conditions for dialogue, to facilitate an agreement between parties as well as the disarmament of militias and the protection of political leaders' (African Union 2015c: 3). The Burundian government, however, refused the deployment, asserting that it would be considered an invasion. At the next PSC Summit on 29 January 2016, going against its earlier position, the organisation voted against peacekeeping deployment in Burundi and the imposition of sanctions.

A final challenge worth noting is that the interface between the PSC and similar organs in the RECs has been limited. Appiah notes that 'Institutional support to the PSC is also limited, although the set of activities has grown exponentially. The PSC Secretariat is overstretched because it supports both the PSC and some of its members with limited capacity in their embassies' (Appiah, 2018: 57).

Conclusion

This chapter has reviewed the impact of the African Union's Peace and Security Council and has found the entity failing fundamentally. Despite early promise and some initial effectiveness, it has become incapable of living up to the security problems emerging on the continent. The reasons are plenty, but fundamental reforms would need to be enacted for it to accomplish its lofty objectives. These include the removal or narrowing of political influence by interests in its operations. One such measure would be to institute majority or supermajority provisions in its operations to enable more precise decision-making, instead of each member state having an equal vote. This measure should also operate with stricter criteria for membership, taking into account the nature and conduct of the leaders of prospective member states. These criteria could include recommendations from the African Union's other major entity, the African Peer Review Mechanism (APRM), which is tasked with diagnosing the internal behaviour of states (including the treatment of their populations). In addition, the PSC could operate more through protocols and standing guidelines than through contingent developments. This would remove the potential politicisation of decision-making. Technologies such as artificial intelligence could also be utilised to improve early warning systems and improve combat against threats such as terrorist entities to render them more precise and minimise or eliminate potential civilian casualties. Scholarly effort should also be directed at understanding the success factors behind the number of cases in which the PSC has been able to be decisive and positively influential. These lessons could inform the reform process, in addition to broadening our theoretical understanding.

References

African Union. (2022). 'The Peace and Security Council'. Available at: https://au.int/en/psc (Accessed 20 November 2022).

African Union. (2021). 'Composition of the PSC'. Available at: https://www.peaceau.org/en/page/88-composition-of-the-psc (Accessed 1 November 2022).

African Union (2021). 'Statement on the prospects for peace in Ethiopia by H.E. Olusegun Obasanjo, High Representative of the Chairperson of the African Union Commission for the Horn of Africa'. Available at: https://au.int/sites/default/files/pressreleases/41152-pr-CP_STATEMENT_ON_THE_PROSPECTS_FOR_PEACE_IN_ETHIOPIA_BY_H.E._OLUSEGUN_OBASANJO.pdf (Accessed 20 November 2022).

African Union. (2020). 'Report of The Peace and Security Council on its Activities and the State of Peace and Security in Africa, for the Period from February 2019 to February 2020'. Addis Ababa: African Union.

African Union. (2013). Agenda 2063: The Africa We Want. Available at: https://au.int/sites/default/files/documents/33126-doc-01_background_note.pdf (Accessed 20 November 2021).

African Union. (2002). *Protocol Relating to the Establishment of the Peace and Security Council of the African Union*. Addis Ababa: African Union. Available at: https://au.int/sites/default/files/treaties/37293-treaty-0024_-_protocol_relating_to_the_establishment_of_the_peace_and_security_council_of_the_african_union_e.pdf (Accessed 5 November 2022).

African Union Peace and Security Council. (2021). 'Communique of the 1050th meeting of the AU Peace and Security Council (PSC) on the situation in the Sudan'. Available at: https://reliefweb.int/sites/reliefweb.int/files/resources/communique-of-the-1050th-psc-meeting-on-sudan-held-on-24-nov-2021.pdf (Accessed 20 November 2022).

Aning, K. (2008). The UN and the African Union's security architecture: Defining an emerging partnership? *Critical Currents*, 5: 17.

Appiah, J.A. (2018). 'Assessing the African Peace and Security Architecture (APSA) from an institutionalist approach and the difference it has made in Africa since 2002', *Brazilian Journal of African Studies*, 3(5): 47–64.

Apuuli, K.P. (2021). 'The African Union and peacekeeping in Africa: Challenges and opportunities', in A. Vasiliev, D. Degterev and T. Shaw (eds). *Africa and the Formation of the New System of International Relations: Rethinking decolonization and foreign policy concepts*. Cham: Springer Verlag, pp. 169–81.

Dahir, A.L. (2021). 'Tigray rebels executed dozens of civilians, report says', *The New York Times*, 10 December. Available at: https://www.nytimes.com/2021/12/10/world/africa/ethiopia-executions-rebels.html (Accessed 20 November 2022).

Deleernsyder, A.E. (2021). 'Ethiopia's Tigray conflict: Exposing the limits of EU and AU early warning mechanisms'. Brussels: Multinational Development Policy Dialogue and Konrad Adenauer Stiftung. Available at: https://www.readkong.com/page/ethiopia-s-tigray-conflict-exposing-the-limits-of-eu-and-3215626 (Accessed 20 November 2022).

Devermont, J. (2021). 'Politics at the heart of the crisis in the Sahel', CSIS Briefs, 6 December. Washington, DC: Center for Strategic and International Studies (CSIS).

International Crisis Group. (2021). 'Eight priorities for the African Union in 2022', Crisis Group Africa Briefing No. 177, 1 February. Nairobi/Brussels: International Crisis Group. Available at: https://d2071andvip0wj.cloudfront.net/b177-eight-priorities-for-the-au-2022.

pdf (Accessed 20 April 2022).

Kahombo, B. (2018). *The Peace and Security Council of the African Union: Rise or decline of collective security in Africa?* KFG Working Paper Series No. 23. Available at: https://publishup.uni-potsdam.de/opus4-ubp/frontdoor/deliver/index/docId/42286/file/kfg_wps23.pdf (Accessed 20 April 2022).

Kioko, B. (2003). 'The right of intervention under the African Union's Constitutive Act: From non-interference to non-intervention', *International Review of the Red Cross*, 85(852): 807–26.

Klein, P. and Sands, P. (2009). *Bowett's Law of International Institutions*, 6th edition. London: Sweet & Maxwell.

Kwesi, A. (2008). The United Nations, Security and Peacekeeping in Africa: Lessons and Prospects. Critical Currents, Working Paper No. 5. Available at: https://www.daghammarskjold.se/wp-content/uploads/2014/08/cc5_web.pdf#page=11 (Accessed 2 November 2021).

Levitt, J.I. (2003). 'The Peace and Security Council of the African Union: The known unknowns', *Transnational Law & Contemporary Problems*, 13: 109. Available at: https://commons.law.famu.edu/cgi/viewcontent.cgi?referer=&httpsredir=1&article=1111&context=faculty-research (Accessed 20 November 2022).

Lyammouri, R. (2021). 'For Mali and the Sahel, new tensions and an old – and worsening – security problem'. MEI Policy Centre. Washington, DC: Middle East Institute. Available at: https://www.mei.edu/sites/default/files/2021-11/For%20Mali%20and%20the%20Sahel%2C%20new%20tensions%20and%20an%20old%20—%20and%20worsening%20—%20security%20problem_4.pdf (Accessed 20 November 2022).

Mross, K. (2019). 'First peace, then democracy? Evaluating strategies of international support at critical junctures after civil war', *International Peacekeeping*, 26(2): 190–215. DOI: 10.1080/13533312.2018.1557052.

Murithi, T. (2012). 'Between reactive and proactive interventionism: The African Union Peace and Security Council's engagement in the Horn of Africa', *African Journal on Conflict Resolution*, 12(2): 87–110.

Powell, K. (2005). *The African Union's Emerging Peace and Security Regime: Opportunities and challenges for delivering on the responsibility to protect*, ISS Monograph Series, No 119. Pretoria: Institute for Strategic Studies.

Sands, P. and Klein, P. (2009). *Bowett's Law of International Institutions*.

London: Sweet and Maxwell.

Sarkin, J. (2010). 'The responsibility to protect and humanitarian intervention in Africa', *Global Responsibility to Protect*, 2(4): 371–87.

Sheehy, T.P. (2021). 'The need to build on security gains in Mozambique'. Washington, DC: United States Institute for Peace and Security.

Singh, G. (2021). 'The African Union and the Tigray crisis'. New Delhi: Observer Research Foundation. Available at: https://www.orfonline. org/expert-speak/the-african-union-and-the-tigray-crisis/ (Accessed 20 November 2022).

Tau, R. (2022). 'South Africa needs to play a stronger role in regional peace and security to help stem flow of migrants', *Daily Maverick*, 28 March. Available at: https://www.dailymaverick.co.za/opinionista/2022-03-28-south-africa-needs-to-play-a-stronger-role-in-regional-peace-and-security-to-help-stem-flow-of-migrants/ (Accessed 20 November 2022).

The Presidency of the Republic of South Africa. (2020). 'African Union Chairperson appoints AU Special Envoys to Ethiopia'. Available at: https://www.thepresidency.gov.za/press-statements/african-union-chairperson-appoints-au-special-envoys-ethiopia (Accessed 20 November 2022).

United Nations. (2004). 'The rule of law and transitional justice in conflict and post-conflict societies: Report of the Secretary-General'. Available at: https://www.un.org/ruleoflaw/blog/document/the-rule-of-law-and-transitional-justice-in-conflict-and-post-conflict-societies-report-of-the-secretary-general/ (Accessed 20 November 2022).

United Nations High Commission for Refugees. (2021). 'Burkina Faso: UNHCR Operational Update'. Available at: https://reliefweb.int/sites/reliefweb.int/files/resources/UNHCR%20BKF-%20External%20Operational%20Update%20September-October%202021.pdf (Accessed 20 November 2022).

Williams, P.D. (2009). 'The Peace and Security Council of the African Union: Evaluating an embryonic international institution', *The Journal of Modern African Studies*, 47(4): 603–26.

Woldemichael, S., Sirengo, E., Louw-Vaudran, L., Matungadura, C., Mahdi, M. and Maunganidze, O.A. (2021). 'Deadly cost of South Sudan's delayed security reforms', ISS Peace and Security Council Report No. 2021 (139), pp. 9–10.

Chapter Eleven

The Africa Centres for Disease Control and Prevention

KINGSLEY STEPHEN ORIEVULU

Introduction

On 1 February 2021, the now ex-director of the Africa Centres for Disease Control and Prevention (Africa CDC), Dr John Nkengasong, celebrated the fourth anniversary[1] of this relatively new technical agency of the African Union (AU). He also applauded the 35 pioneers[2] drawn from the African Union Youth Volunteer Corp (AUYVC) programme, who supported the establishment of different arms of the agency to promote health security in Africa. This celebration marked the birth of a vital regional (multilateral) institution in Africa, charged with public health surveillance, response and implementation. It also represents a shift towards a concerted institutional approach to identifying, tackling and responding to health security issues (or threats) through professional and technical engagements, training and leadership in policy and implementation.

31 January 2022 was the fifth anniversary of the Africa CDC, an agency of the African Union, which marked half a decade since this institution was born and plunged straight into the task of safeguarding health security on the continent. In 2020, President Cyril Ramaphosa of South Africa

---

1   https://twitter.com/JNkengasong/status/1356195047365091329
2   https://twitter.com/JNkengasong/status/1356995560721551360

handed over the role of chairperson of the African Union to President Félix-Antoine Tshisekedi Tshilombo of the Democratic Republic of the Congo (2021), then in 2022 this role was filled by the President of Senegal, Macky Sall, who, until recently, led the work on the continent – especially during the recent COVID-19 pandemic (African Union, 2022). In addition, new commissioners were elected to various departments within the AU structures, and the chairperson of the AU Commission, Moussa Faki Mahamat, was re-elected for a second term in 2021. This anniversary importantly coincided with a dire crisis period in the global (but especially African) public health arena. The continent was threatened by the rampaging COVID-19 pandemic, a continuing battle with resurgent Ebola and other diseases outbreaks, the challenges posed by a growing vaccine nationalism, as exhibited by wealthy – mostly Western – nations, as well as the departure of the pioneer Executive Director of Africa CDC, recalled by the US Government. Indeed, all these factors pointed to a fifth anniversary filled with many challenges, and some prospects.[3] What this implied was that the task at hand for this novel, yet indispensable, African public health institution was enormous, especially as it charted the path to the future establishment and consolidation of a strong public health system, which Africa could be proud of.

This chapter identifies and examines some pertinent issues as the Africa CDC moves past its fifth anniversary. It examines the immediate future of the Africa CDC – possibly the next five years of its existence and work on the continent – and situates its place and role within the context of the African Union's quest to re-emphasise regional integration and the role of its institutions to lead Africa's quest to actualise the 'Africa We Want'. The following section provides an overview of discussions on regional integration in Africa, especially as it pertains to tackling different development challenges in Africa. It provides a basis on which to explore how the Africa CDC contributes to this integration through its New Public Health Order agenda, which is intended to contribute to the quest for African solutions to African problems. It also discusses some of the issues with which the agency has to grapple, and finally puts forward some recommendations.

---

3   In addition to all these events, the Africa CDC gained its autonomy, which was approved by the Heads of State during the 35th Africa Union Summit in Addis Ababa (February 2022). Available at: https://healthpolicy-watch.news/africa-cdc-gets/ (Accessed 21 November 2020).

Regional integration and Africa's development challenges: A literature overview

Regionalism or regional integration are important concepts in international relations, especially when issues of peace, security and development are discussed. Conceptually, regionalism remains a contested concept. A major outlook on regionalism and regional integration focuses on economic interdependence. According to Akinyemi (2019), it entails 'an arrangement where countries of the same subregion enter into an agreement to enhance economic cooperation through agreed institutions and rules, focused on removing barriers to free trade, free movement of people and capital within the specific region' (Akinyemi *et al.*, 2019). This perspective places regionalism within the ambits of economic interdependence and cooperation involving countries with shared economic interests, hence establishing multilateral systems and supranational institutions to guard against default from these economic agreements. Essentially, therefore, regionalism promotes the processes of economic globalisation – the movement of goods, services, people and technologies, among others – and it is consolidated by means of multilateral networks (Barbieri, 2019).

The idea that regionalism and regional integration can or should be narrowly conceptualised from an economic interdependence purview was not accepted by Börzel and Risse (2019). They drew on a comparative analysis of 10 regional organisations across the world to buttress the argument that this paradigm of regional integration centred on economic interdependence was only truly applicable in Europe (Börzel and Risse, 2019). These authors contend that economic interdependence is not the sole driver of regionalism, and that there are other issues such as political and human security, as well as ideas of a unified common identity popularised by elites (such as a pan-African identity). These factors contribute to the idea of integration becoming popular and acceptable to the public (Börzel and Risse, 2019). In fact, these authors suggest that the concept of regional integration should be broadened to encapsulate issues beyond economic interdependence, including security, as well as a desire for regime security by state actors (Börzel and Risse, 2019). This view is also captured by Barbieri, who emphasised the complexity and dynamism of the concept of regionalism beyond a simple outlook on economic interdependence (Barbieri, 2019). This complexity ensures that regionalism transcends the promotion of 'market liberalisation' or the prevention of 'state conflict' and represents a 'tool to address the broad set of problems arising in various fields' (Barbieri, 2019: 436).

In defining regionalism as a process that entails establishing multilateral institutions to aid or facilitate different categories of engagement and collective action between states in areas such as political, security and economic action, Gilbert Khadiagala (2008) points to the transnational context of interstate relations based on cross-cutting issues of concern. In the globalisation debate, especially with regard to the liberal critique of the realist state-centric approach to security and sovereignty, the existence or emergence of different transnational issues, ranging from terrorism and cross-border crimes to climate change impacts, as well as the threat of cross-border pandemics, all contribute to a global or regional order that requires unique and collaborative action to understand and manage them (Hettne and Söderbaum, 2006; Hay, 2013). Although regionalism differs from globalisation, one thing is clear – it is definitely a response to the prospects and challenges linked to globalisation, one of which is the current global COVID-19 pandemic, in addition to the constant problem of cross-border terrorism and the impacts of climate change (Oloruntoba, 2021).

Edward Best and Thomas Christiansen explain regionalism as akin to different types of special relationships existing between countries that are neighbours – a relationship that transcends the obvious diplomatic ties but retains every element of these states in terms of their juridical status in the Weberian sense (Best and Christiansen, 2011). They show how regional cooperation and integration – two fundamental dimensions of regionalism – are crucial to understanding the interdependence and emergent perceptions of common interests and identity associated with the concept of regionalism (Best and Christiansen, 2011; Barbieri, 2019). By distinguishing between the limited arrangements and mutual support and dependence in various aspects of interstate relations, without harmonised rules in regional cooperation – vis-à-vis the structured adoption of or harmonisation of policy structures and rules – with a view to developing a uniform and united position on transnational (economic, security and political) issues characteristic of regional integration, these scholars bring to the fore the view that regionalism also entails a striving that transcends the state, despite having the state as its foundation (Adetula, 2004; Khadiagala, 2008; Best and Christiansen, 2011).

As scholars have contended, regionalism – strides for cooperation and integration – in low- and middle-income countries (LMICs), including those in Africa, have been centred on development, state-promoted industrialisation and nation-building, first and foremost through protectionism and import substitution (Söderbaum, 2015). Oloruntoba shows that, in Africa, the subject of regionalism has generally been studied in the context of market or economic integration, developmental cooperation and integration, new regionalism, open regionalism and African citizenship (Oloruntoba, 2021). The role of the Pan-African agenda in the colouring of regionalism and regional integration and cooperation has been emphasised by many scholars as well (Adetula, 2004; Best and Christiansen, 2011; Söderbaum, 2015; Oloruntoba, 2021). This is rooted in the ideals of collective self-reliance, as well as strides towards protectionism, bearing in mind the impact of colonialism, and neocolonial systems of international trade (Söderbaum, 2015).

With Africa facing myriad problems, regional integration has been one modality within international relation parlance in the attempt to manage and address these challenges. Regionalism provides a framework for understanding the collective action approach advocated in many quarters with regard to dealing with various transnational issues within and about the continent. Consequently, regionalism in Africa has seen the formation of various continental or regional mechanisms or institutions, such as the African Union (formerly the Organisation of African Unity), the Regional Economic Communities (RECs), and the regional or subregional custom areas, as well as other continental mechanisms designed to pursue and actualise a collective African (or at least African regional) interest in various areas, namely development, security and economics (Adetula, 2004). However, achieving the goals of regional integration in Africa has been a subject of debate, with many scholars contending that this has been a failure mainly because of the interests at play and the fact that regionalism is somewhat antithetical to the desires of the (ruling) political elites (Adetula, 2004; Gibb, 2009).

Despite these observations, the centrality of a collective approach to addressing socioeconomic, political and health security issues cannot be downplayed in the context of the ongoing coronavirus pandemic – and in the light of many other public health or health security challenges facing Africa – the place of a supranational institution like the African Union and, more specifically, its technical agency, the Africa CDC, becomes crucial. From a regionalism and regional integration point of view, these institutions are vital in charting the course of advancing the interest of the collective. This is where the Africa CDC comes to the fore. Indeed, some early outlook on the COVID-19 situation, relative to Africa and Africa's management of the pandemic, have highlighted the importance of the collaborative effort of African countries – through intranational collaborative efforts – to ensure that Africa did not become the graveyard that many analysts and doomsayers had expected and predicted (Oloruntoba, 2021; Happi and Nkengasong, 2022). Regionalism in Africa was, therefore, crucial in achieving low infection and mortality rates on the continent compared to other regions, such as Latin America and the Caribbean (Oloruntoba, 2021).

The place of the Africa CDC in leading the charge in public health surveillance, preparedness and response cannot be taken for granted. This is why this chapter's outlook on this crucial technical agency situates it within the stride towards an African-led collective approach to actualising the African health security agenda, which is exemplified in the Africa CDC's concept of the 'New Public Health Order' (Nkengasong *et al.*, 2017a; Nkengasong and Tessema, 2020). The following section situates the Africa CDC in the context of the last five years (2017–2022) and its New Public Health Order mantra. This is followed by a look at some of the issues pertaining to the institution, especially with regard to achieving its goals in the next five years.

Africa CDC in the last five years (2017–2022)

The statute of the Africa CDC was adopted by the 26th Assembly of Heads of State on 31 January 2016 (African Union, 2016). This situated the agency at the AU headquarters in Addis Ababa, until the institution could move to its own headquarters. Since January 2017, when the Africa CDC commenced its activities, it has had to grapple with myriad challenges but has managed to surmount many of these with relative success. Much credit in this regard goes to the previous chairperson of the African Union Commission (AUC), Nkosazana Dlamini-Zuma, who assumed her leadership role in the difficult context of the 2014–2016 Ebola pandemic (response). She lobbied the heads of state (and other partners) to establish an African institutional approach to public health challenges (Tikum,

2016) and this eventually gave birth to this unique, specialised technical institution of the African Union (Nkengasong *et al.*, 2017b).

Since then, the Africa CDC has responded to and managed about three waves of Ebola virus outbreaks in Africa. The institution has mobilised bilateral, multilateral and multi-stakeholder partnerships (and funds) to respond to these health crises – initially under the AUC Chairperson Dlamini-Zuma, and later in 2019 under Moussa Faki Mahamat. These engagements culminated in resource mobilisation running into millions of US dollars for the Ebola responses in the DRC and within the broader African context (African Union, 2019).

The establishment of five regional coordinating centres (RCCs) – Southern, Eastern, Central, Western and Northern African regions – and the subsequent mobilisation of (youth) volunteers and young professionals across the continent to set-up and run these centres, set in motion a system of cross-country surveillance and planning to build a strong regional presence (Nkengasong *et al.*, 2017b; Happi and Nkengasong, 2022). It signalled an intention to respond effectively and efficiently to current and potential public health threats on the continent. This led to the establishment of numerous programmes – antimicrobial resistance (AMR), one-health, health information systems (data sharing and situation room platforms on various diseases), ECHO, laboratory and national public health institutes (NPHIs) and public health workforce development and saving livelihoods programmes (among others) – to support member states' efforts. The Africa CDC's workforce development programme also assists with training their public health workforce (Nkengasong *et al.*, 2017a, 2017b). All these programmes and more recent initiatives were made possible through partnerships and resource mobilisation led by the team.

Partly as a result of its nascent nature and the positive prospects for driving health security agenda(s) in Africa, the Africa CDC has attracted (and keeps attracting) many 'suitors', donors, partners and funding opportunities. Suffice it to say that this has made it an attraction point for 'a new scramble for Africa' as far as the global health security agenda(s), discourse and/or competition is concerned. In the few years of its existence, this organisation has attracted resources – including technical assistance and collaborations – running into billions of US dollars for its programmes, including staff recruitment, programme development, technical assistance and training (Happi and Nkengasong, 2022). Indeed, prominent among these partners are the United States Centre for Diseases Control (USCDC), the (now defunct) Public Health England (PHE), the European Union (EU), Canada, Japan and China, among others. In fact, like the United States, Chinese experts from the China CDC have been drafted as part of the technical team supporting the work of the institution and training the workforce. Foundations and philanthropic organisations, including MasterCard, the Bill and Melinda Gates Foundation and the Suzan Thompson Buffett Foundation have also not been left out (Happi and Nkengasong, 2022). The same can be said of multilateral organisations such as the United Nations agencies, including the United Nations Populations Fund (UNFPA), the World Health Organization (WHO) and the United Nations Development Programme (UNDP). These partnerships, funds and technical expertise have been crucial in different responses to communicable and non-communicable diseases across Africa, such as the emergence of the Rift Valley fever in Kenya (2018), Ebola in parts of Eastern and Southern Africa (2018–2020), Lassa fever in Nigeria (2018 and 2019), among others (Nkengasong and Tessema, 2020).

These partnerships have not been solely international. In addition to the statutory responsibilities of member states to contribute to the funding of the Africa CDC, the organisation has collaborated with African non-state actors. The Ebola and the COVID-19 response forums in 2018 and 2019 saw collaborations with the Dangote Foundation, the Patrice Motsepe Foundation, MTN and many other players on the continent. These partnerships and funding streams were important in supporting activities and programmes run by the institution to address and manage public health crises across countries on the continent.

In the face of the plethora of public health challenges and the task of managing these crises in Africa, this institution, through its former director, John Nkengasong – under the AUC leadership of Moussa Faki Mahamat – has achieved admirable successes in its response to Ebola and the recent COVID-19 pandemic. These efforts were rewarded in 2021, when Dr Nkengasong was recognised as one of the 100 African Personalities (together with the likes of Dr Adesina Akinwunmi, President of the African Development Bank (AfDB), and Dr Tedros Adhanom Ghebreyesus, Director of the WHO). This award demonstrated the recognition of the achievements of the Africa CDC in safeguarding Africa's health. One of the major achievements involved its efforts, in collaboration with the

AU leadership and the WHO, to secure vaccines for poorer countries – the majority of which are in Africa – to tackle the rampaging COVID-19 pandemic. These efforts continue to solidify the centrality and importance of this crucial public health institution in Africa to achieve an Africa-driven and focused health (policy) agenda. This is exemplified in the New Public Health Order of the Africa CDC – a framework that aims to establish a robust African public health system for the future; a framework further popularised by the successes of the 2nd International Conference on Public Health in Africa (CPHIA) in Rwanda, 2022, under the auspices of the acting Director Dr Ahmed Ogwell Ouma, ushering in the new public health order in Africa.[4]

Africa CDC and the New Public Health Order for Africa

In an interview published on YouTube on 9 November 2021, the current acting director of the Africa CDC, Dr Ahmed Ogwell Ouma, described the New Public Health Order as 'a vision for Africa to be able to handle its health security agenda locally; where we set our priorities, we set the direction, and we guide the pace at which we deliver for health security on the continent' (Hwenda, 2021a). Going further, he stated: 'We want to be in charge of our [African] destiny and we want to be in charge of prioritisation of our activities. This is the essence of the New Public Health Order' (Hwenda, 2021a). This description of the New Public Health Order summarises the core of the vision and objectives of the Africa CDC, especially as envisioned by the AU's Assembly of Heads of States[5] – a vision for Africa to drive its own health security agenda, bearing in mind the needs of the continent and understanding that its global partners may not always put the needs of the African continent as a priority in the event of a global public health emergency. The COVID-19 pandemic demonstrated this point.

This New Public Health Order is tied to the imperative to address crucial barriers to optimal public health in Africa as they pertain to 'health systems and systems for health' within the context of the implementation of the International Health Regulation (IHR)[6] to which African leaders committed themselves (Nkengasong *et al.*, 2017a). This means that addressing

---

4   https://cphia2022.com/
5   https://africacdc.org/news-item/call-to-action-africas-new-public-health-order/
6   The IHR is a global legal agreement that aims to prevent and respond to the spread of diseases to avoid them becoming international crises (Nkengasong et al., 2017a).

these barriers to achieve the desired goal will require skills, personnel, infrastructure, systems of accountability to measure progress, a professional and motivated workforce, data sharing mechanisms, commitment and political will, robust legal systems and instruments, country ownership and leadership of initiatives and strategies, reliable and committed bilateral and multilateral partnerships, including private sector actors, and indeed, an AU-specific health diplomacy strategy to guide efforts at the supranational level. These are all components that will support health systems and ensure that there are effective and accountable systems for health on the continent (Nkengasong *et al.*, 2017a).

The New Public Health Order is therefore built around these components of the health system as its four pillars suggest: (1) strengthened public health institutions (PHIs) on the continent; (2) local manufacturing of vaccines, therapeutics and diagnostics; (3) a strengthened public health workforce; and (4) respectful local and international partnerships (Nkengasong *et al.*, 2017b; Nkengasong and Tessema, 2020; Hwenda, 2021a). Achieving the health security agenda requires a strong public health system on the continent, which means that national and regional public health institutions have to be developed first. The Africa CDC therefore encourages member states to establish national public health institutes (NPHIs) if these are not already in existence. These NPHIs become the platform upon which the Africa CDC can provide technical support and expertise where the country lacks these.

The second pillar's emphasis on the local manufacturing of vaccines, therapeutics and diagnostics is the result of Africa's ongoing experience of vaccine nationalism, which has seen wealthier countries hoarding vaccine supplies, making it difficult for many LMICs to access enough for their populations. The dearth of local manufacturing industries, infrastructure and partners working to ensure the local production of vaccines has made the Africa CDC focus on leveraging the Africa Continental Free Trade Area (AfCFTA) secretariat to mainstream the local production of vaccines and to bolster the distribution of health products. In this way, a component of the 'systems of health' can be achieved by persuading private-sector actors to see health systems support as an investment rather than a cost by drawing on the devastating effects that the ongoing Coronavirus pandemic has had on business (Nkengasong *et al.*, 2017a).

The last two pillars – a strengthened public health workforce and respectful partnerships – point to other important aspects of the effort to ensure public health security. In the former, the focus is on ensuring that the workforce is professional, skilled, motivated and accountable within the different national, regional and continental public health institutions operating to actualise the New Public Health Order. Respectful partnerships include bilateral and multilateral engagements at local or regional levels – including those with the private sector, foundations and charities. These partnerships are often characterised by resource provision – funds and technical expertise (Hwenda, 2021a) – but they may also entail conflicting interests or alternative agendas. Thus, under this pillar, the focus lies on ensuring meaningful partnerships that respect the vision of an African-led health security agenda that focuses on advancing and achieving the health needs within the continent (Hwenda, 2021a).

This New Public Health Order's agenda, bolstered by its four pillars, signals the task that the Africa CDC has been given to pursue a safer Africa. The ongoing COVID-19 pandemic makes it even more urgent to ensure that this agenda is achieved. As an institution dependent on resources from AU member states and partners, Africa CDC's challenge is to chart a course of action that reflects the values of the founders of the AU in this drive to achieve its set objectives in the next half decade.

Matters arising: Africa CDC's post-2022 key issues

This chapter now turns to some key issues to consider relative to this institution and the broader African health security agenda in the next four to five years. There are some pertinent issues that need to be navigated, managed and/or sorted out as this institution grows and as its responsibilities, partnerships and reach increase (or broaden). These issues range from *stability* to *autonomy* (independence) to circumvent varying bureaucracies; and the management of partnerships (donors and strategic partners) and agenda(s). The latter also entails issues involving the discursive 'new scramble for Africa' or 'war of dominance between the US and China', as exemplified in the discussions around siting the Africa CDC's headquarters. All these issues are discussed in light of the central idea, which is to achieve the Africa Health Strategy (2030) at the core of the mandate of the Africa CDC.

Stability

The Africa CDC has the major task of achieving the objectives of the Africa Health Strategy. The key ingredient is maintaining a stable and smooth-running institution. As a relatively young institution – less than six years old – achieving this mandate is linked to the nature of its leadership and the messaging this leadership sends to partners and to the broad spectrum of stakeholders. Indeed, even the morale of the workforce and its productivity are tied to the leadership. It is therefore crucial to maintain a structure that has been relatively productive within a very short time of the organisation's existent for the stability of this important institution. This means that the current leaders – as far as they have demonstrated effectiveness – should be maintained and encouraged to build on their achievements and further the cause of the Africa Health Strategy.

There is always the danger, however, that the success of this organisation under its current leadership could encourage other organisations to poach some of the workforce that have worked tirelessly to build the institution. For instance, institutions such as the USCDC, the World Bank, the WHO and even the Africa Development Bank (AfDB) are known to 'poach' bright candidates emerging from important African institutions. The cases of the former director of the Nigeria Centre for Diseases Control (NCDC) who moved to the WHO, and the nomination of Dr Nkengasong by President Joe Biden are recent examples (Princewill, 2021). Similarly, the former AU Legal Counsel is now the Secretary General of the AfDB. While these are upward trajectories for individuals, sometimes it can take the organisation or institution a long time to identify suitable replacements, which does not bode well for continuity and the effective consolidation of institutional achievements. Thus, the 'recall' of the Africa CDC director due to his achievements and the WHO appointment of the NCDC director are not in the long-term interest of the Africa CDC, which is still in its infancy.

The argument for stability is also tied to the fact that the current leadership of the organisation has been working on strategies and building networks of partners aligned to their vision and modus operandi. This is coupled with the hard work of building trust through organisational mechanisms that ensure a smooth-running organisation. In fact, the AU's ability to tackle the coronavirus situation and the challenges of vaccine nationalism, and their success in securing vaccines for African countries, all signal the importance of a stable organisation and leadership working together to achieve African interests. As the 'New Public Health Order' envisions an African Health Security agenda centred on strong PHIs, the local manufacturing of vaccines, therapeutics and diagnostics, a strong public health workforce and respectful partnerships, a stable Africa CDC with strong, visionary leadership cannot be overemphasised. Efforts to galvanise an African approach to a COVID-19 vaccine through initiatives such as the AU's African Vaccine Acquisition Trust (AVAT). The Africa CDC's leaders played an integral role in engaging with AU member states and other partners – especially in the wake of the 'failures of multilateralism' in the management of the pandemic (McNair, 2021). Indeed, while Africa was dealt the short straw in the vaccine acquisition race (Moodley *et al.*, 2021) and faced numerous difficulties in its attempts to buy vaccines – as Mr Strive Masiyiwa,[7] the vaccine envoy to the African Union, observed – stability in leadership and messaging was crucial in this institution's proactive management of this and other public health emergencies on the continent.

Autonomy

The position of the Africa CDC as an institution mandated to steer the continental health security mandate implies the necessity of a level of autonomy to achieve its mandate. A number of institutions linked to the African Union operate by virtue of their mandates under a level of autonomy. The Africa Union Development Agency (AUDA–NEPAD) and the Africa Peer Review Mechanism (APRM), as well as the Pan-African Parliament (PAP), among others, are able to operate drawing on the AU agenda to actualise their unique mandates. Similarly, the Africa CDC with its special focus on safeguarding the health of the continent is able to exercise these levels of autonomy because of its position and the urgency with which it needs to operate in certain circumstances. Central to this issue is the availability of resources, both financial and technical. This is a point clearly made in 2021 by the Rwandan President, Paul Kagame:

Excellencies, I would like to take this opportunity to emphasise the importance of our domestic health financing agenda, particularly in light of the COVID-19 pandemic. Without strong national health

---

7   https://www.theguardian.com/global-development/2021/jun/24/rich-countries-deliberately-keeping-covid-vaccines-from-africa-says-envoy

> systems in every country, our continent will remain vulnerable
> to pandemics. We need to strengthen our commitment to increase
> domestic resource mobilisation and improve health outcomes. I also
> urge the strengthening of Africa CDC to allow its autonomy and
> effectiveness (Kagame, 2021).

Funding is a necessary tool for the actualisation of the mandate of the Africa CDC. It is also central to the framework of the New Public Health Order as far as achieving its four pillars is concerned. Sustainable financing is identified by Dr Ouma as a major challenge for the future of the New Public Health Order and, indeed, the autonomy of the institution itself (Hwenda, 2021). As an AU agency striving for a pan-African approach to health security, domestic financing is its main source of resources. AU member states committed to spending at least 15 per cent of their annual budget on health (security) in the 2001 Abuja Declaration – a target to improve their health sectors (African Union, 2001). At the same time, these countries, through their contributions to the African Union, spearhead the funding of the Africa CDC. Inadequate and unpredictable financing for the Africa CDC would mean instability, while dependence on external actors or funders for the execution of the mandates of the institution runs the risk of negatively impacting its capacity and ability to chart a course that represents an African health security agenda.

An important point relative to the need for autonomy is linked to efficiency and effectiveness. Many public service institutions in Africa are known to struggle with efficiency due to myriad bureaucratic hurdles and red tape that stifle innovation and ingenuity. Although bureaucracy may not be terribly dangerous to an organisation, many of these public institutions have suffered from a lack of motivation among the workforce, a lack of competition, insufficient skills and capacity building, and the preponderance of bureaucrats instead of technocrats and technical professionals. The New Public Health Order's emphasis on strengthening the public health workforce on the continent – including its internal workforce – is instructive in this light.

An additional challenge in terms of the autonomy of the Africa CDC involves interactions and engagements with fellow multilateral institutions with a similar mandate at a global or regional level or within specific areas of interest. For example, institutions such as the WHO, the UNFPA and AU agencies such as AUDA-NEPAD have cross-cutting mandates and work on similar areas of public health. As the 'new kid on the block', the question of autonomy in developing and driving Africa's health agenda may also require clearer demarcation between the role the Africa CDC plays and areas of collaboration and cooperation in achieving the mandate of health security on the continent. While there is the potential for a tug-of-war between the Africa CDC, its collaborators and partner institutions about who leads or controls the African health agenda or its implementation, this may not augur well for Africa in the long run and, therefore, demands continuous engagement and clear communication, especially from the purview of the leadership of the AU Assembly. In fact, at the recent 35th Ordinary Session of the AU Assembly, member states affirmed the autonomy of the Africa CDC, which provides the basis on which to consolidate all the work of the institution.

Managing partnerships and agendas

Another point of interest is the burgeoning partnerships that the Africa CDC has been building since its emergence in its quest to build strong public health systems in Africa. As the fourth pillar of the New Public Health Order demonstrates, the Africa CDC seeks to build respectful partnerships with bilateral, multilateral, private sector and philanthropic actors, within Africa and internationally. These partnerships are crucial for much needed resources – funds and technical expertise – to enable the institution to actualise its objectives. During the COVID-19 pandemic, actors such as the AfDB, UNECA and the African Export–Import Bank (Afreximbank) have been working with the Africa CDC and providing resources to tackle the pandemic on the continent. This is in addition to resources and technical support from the USCDC, EU-CDC, PHE, China CDC and other partners.

In such circumstances, institutes always have to navigate the murky waters of partners' strategic interests in providing resources and be aware of any potential attempts to steer or influence the course of their operations and policy direction. Being an African institution, the Africa CDC pursues an African health security agenda. However, the challenges of insufficient or unpredictable regional financial and technical commitments or the failure to invest adequately in the Africa CDC puts the institution in a position of having to act wisely to manage the excesses of partners without unnecessarily antagonising them. For example, the tussle relating to the placement of the Africa CDC headquarters demonstrates a level of strategic squabbling between the Chinese, who want to build the headquarters in Addis Ababa, and Morocco, who want to build it in Morocco. At the same time, other interested parties have pressured South Africa to prevent the Chinese from building the headquarters in Addis Ababa (Fabricius, 2020). Such squabbles put the leadership of the African Union and the Africa CDC in difficult positions because they depend on technical and financial assistance from these donors. This brings into focus the challenges of partnerships and the importance of a strong regional base to drive the agenda of the institution.

Driving the manufacturing of vaccines in Africa

A major lesson from the COVID-19 pandemic experiences relates to personal protective equipment (PPEs), diagnostics and vaccine acquisition and the importance of local manufacturing, production and distribution platforms on the continent. As pillar two of the New Public Health Order stipulates, ensuring local manufacturing and distribution of vaccines, therapeutics and diagnostics has become a major focus of the Africa CDC. This important goal requires financial commitment and political will from the AU member states, and the Africa CDC's role in galvanising collective action to achieve this is instructive. One mechanism has remained the continuous encouragement of countries to invest in the health sector in line with the 2001 Abuja Treaty. Another is leveraging the AfCFTA secretariat to engage all actors, whose contributions remain crucial, to achieve the goal of manufacturing vaccines and therapeutics in Africa.

Under this platform, the Africa CDC launched the AVAT target 2040 to establish manufacturing hubs across the continent. Establishing these hubs hinges on governments investing in health and infrastructure, and financial investments from the AfDB and Afreximbank. It also involves galvanising private-sector actors to be part of public–private partnerships (PPPs) to facilitate the processes of funding, etc. In addition, the policy and legislative environment must be designed to facilitate intra-Africa trade and the free movement of goods, hence Africa CDC's engagements with state actors to leverage the AfCTA as a mechanism to drive the New Public Health Order.

While this is commendable, the challenges that abound include the inadequate or inconsistent commitment and political will among state parties to provide the necessary resources. Problems of credible commitment and a lack of trust in governments can disincentivise the private sector from participating in this vision. Consequently, the Africa CDC's engagement with member states and partners such as the AfDB to re-emphasise their commitments remains crucial in the long run.

Conclusion

Following the achievements of the Africa CDC, irrespective of its rocky beginnings more than five years ago and some of the concerns raised, it is imperative to reiterate its centrality in the drive to strengthen health systems in Africa. This chapter has demonstrated that in the context of advancing an Afro-focused public health security agenda, the Africa CDC has been faced with different challenges, but it has demonstrated its potential to drive this agenda forward. As a relatively new player in the African health arena with many public health challenges, it has remained focused on the task at hand, and has adequate mechanisms and processes to facilitate the work that is currently underway. Currently the Africa CDC still has issues of leadership independence and empowerment, training and capacity building, and requires partnerships to ensure the development of public health infrastructure in the continent and reduce its dependency on foreign aid.

On the question of leadership in the context of 'losing' its pioneer director, Dr John Nkengasong, who departed to lead the US global AIDS response, the question of stability arises. This notwithstanding, the institutional framework established under his leadership, the strong work carried on by the acting director (Dr Ogwell), the recent appointment of a new Director General,[8] and the workforce who built the systems at the Africa CDC provide a strong base on which to continue the task of achieving its vision, especially the Africa Health Strategy (2030). There is an urgent need to maintain the organisational sense of responsibility and commitment to this vision across all levels of leadership and to consolidate the systems within the organisation so that it can function effectively.

According to Dr Nkengasong, Africa needs about 3 000–6 000 or more epidemiologists (and biostatisticians) to run its public health system effectively and efficiently, but the continent has barely 1 000 of these experts in the system (Hwenda, 2021b). To bridge this gap, the Africa CDC

---

8   https://au.int/en/pressreleases/20230222/au-assembly-appoints-dr-jean-kaseya-director-general-africa-centers-disease

has partnered with the European and Developing Countries Clinical Trials Partnership (EDCTP) to train 150 epidemiologists and statisticians over a period of three years. Establishing a system of skilled professionals with the expertise needed to oversee the public health situation and manage future emergencies as opposed to having to seek foreign aid to help curtail public health issues in Africa is a step in the right direction. Although this move is commendable, more should be done to train personnel to bridge the deficit of over 2 000 epidemiologists and biostatisticians alone, not to mention other relevant stakeholders in the public healthcare delivery system.

In an attempt to manage the COVID-19 pandemic, the African Union reached an agreement with member states to devote resources to increase the rate of testing, because several sources had cited the low-rate testing as the reason for the low number of recorded coronavirus cases across the continent. In the next half decade, it will be important for the Africa CDC to look beyond the COVID-19 pandemic and foster more of these partnerships to consolidate surveillance and testing for other public health emergencies and infectious diseases that are endemic across the continent, such as the Ebola virus disease, yellow fever, Lassa fever, cholera and HIV/AIDS. With proper surveillance systems in place to enhance monitoring – testing, treatment and tracing – the Africa CDC would be empowered with data to make informed decisions and deploy relevant measures to tackle the challenges.

In line with the point on the role of leadership and vision in the sustainability of the Africa CDC, it is salient to note that the most effective way to achieve this is by increasing the capacity of regional centres to tackle the public health situations within their regions, while the headquarters focuses on strategy, fostering partnerships and resource management. The regional centres should oversee the training of public health experts to ensure that they are absorbed into the system and not 'lost' to poaching or the ambition to look for 'greener pastures' outside the continent. The regional centres should also work closely with the different national health departments within the region to develop a more effective method of handling their particular challenges. In addition, regional centres need to be empowered to handle important tasks like monitoring and surveillance, and taking prompt action in the case of emergencies, while making relevant recommendations to the 'centre' for a more comprehensive approach to the situation.

In the face of the COVID-19 pandemic, one major challenge that forestalled the global effort against the virus was the shortage of personal protective equipment (PPE). This was the result of a form of 'PPE nationalism' – developed countries hoarding materials even though they had more than enough or buying entire production batches despite limited supplies, leaving other (developing) nations with nothing but money in their hands. Inasmuch as the African Union has made an effort to curtail the unavailability of PPE across the continent, with the launch of the Africa Medical Supplies Platform in partnership with member countries and the Afreximbank, the need for a sustainable, long-term solution begs attention.

To conclude, in the next five years, the Africa CDC should leverage its leadership position to promote the local manufacturing of PPEs in Africa. Although this would require the involvement of stakeholders, the aim is to reduce the time, cost and protocol spent in procuring these materials in the event of a public health emergency. To achieve this, indigenous manufacturers should be supported financially and with relevant regulations, while agreements could also be reached with foreign manufacturers to establish factories across the continent to boost the availability of materials and provide employment, with a resultant positive effect on the economy.

References

Adetula, V.A. (2004). 'Regional integration in Africa: Prospect for closer cooperation between West, East and Southern Africa'. Paper presented at the IDASA/FREDSKORPSET Research Exchange Programme, Johannesburg, 2–4 May.

African Union Commission. (2022). 'Press release: President Macky Sall of Senegal, takes over as the new Chairperson of the African Union (AU) for 2022'. Available at: Available at: https://au.int/en/pressreleases/20220205/president-macky-sall-senegal-takes-over-new-chairperson-african-union-au-2022 (Accessed 7 February 2022).

African Union Commission. (2019). 'Africa Against Ebola: A Private Sector and Partners Forum'. Available at: https://au.int/en/africa (Accessed 7 February 2022).

African Union Commission. (2016). 'Statute of the Africa Centres for Diseases Control and Prevention (Africa CDC)'. Available at: https://au.int/sites/default/files/treaties/36439-treaty-0055_-_africa_cdc_e.

pdf (Accessed 7 February 2022).

African Union Commission. (2001). 'Abuja Declaration on HIV/AIDS, Tuberculosis and Other Related Infectious Diseases'. African Summit on HIV/AIDS, Tuberculosis and Other Related Infectious Diseases, Abuja, Nigeria, 24–27 April 2001. Available at: https://au.int/sites/default/files/pages/32894-file-2001-abuja-declaration.pdf (Accessed 7 February 2022).

Akinyemi, O., Efobi, U., Osabuohien, E. and Alege, P.J. (2019). 'Regional integration and energy sustainability in Africa: Exploring the challenges and prospects for ECOWAS', *African Development Review*, 31(4): 517–28. https://doi.org/10.1111/1467-8268.12406.

Barbieri, G. (2019). 'Regionalism, globalism and complexity: A stimulus towards global IR?' *Third World Thematics: A TWQ Journal*, 4: 424–41.

Best, E. and Christiansen, T. (2011). 'Regionalism in international affairs', in J. Baylis, S. Smith and P. Owens (eds). *The Globalization of World Politics: An introduction to international relations*, 5th edition, Chapter 26. Oxford: Oxford University Press.

Börzel, T.A. and Risse, T. (2019). 'Grand theories of integration and the challenges of comparative regionalism', *Journal of European Public Policy*, 26: 1231–52.

Fabricius, P. (2020). 'SA urged to stop China building Africa disease control centre HQ in Addis Ababa', *Daily Maverick*, 9 June. Available at: https://www.dailymaverick.co.za/article/2020-06-09-sa-urged-to-stop-china-building-africa-disease-control-centre-hq-in-addis-ababa/ (Accessed 7 January 2022).

Gibb, R. (2009). 'Regional Integration and Africa's Development Trajectory: meta-theories, expectations and reality', *Third World Quarterly*, 30: 701–21.

Happi, C.T. and Nkengasong, J.N. (2022). 'Two years of COVID-19 in Africa: Lessons for the world', *Prevention Web*, Updates, 3 January. Nature Publishing Group.

Hay, C. (2013). Chapter 15: International relations theory and globalization', in D. Tim, K. Milja and S. Steve (eds). *International Relations Theories: Discipline and diversity*, 3rd edition. Oxford: Oxford University Press.

Hettne, B. and Söderbaum, F. (2006). 'Regional cooperation: A tool for addressing regional and global challenges', in *Meeting Global Challenges: International cooperation in the national interest*. International Task

Force on Global Public Goods, pp. 179–244.

Hwenda, L. (2021a). 'Africa has a bold new public health order: Interview with Dr Ahmed Ogwell Ouma, Deputy Director Africa CDC', in I. Hwenda (ed.). *The HSS Podcast – Let's Talk about Health in Africa: Titans of Industry Episode*. YouTube. Available at: https://www.youtube.com/watch?v=sBLp3E9qf1o (Accessed 7 January 2022).

Hwenda, L. (2021b). 'Why public health institutes are the military barracks for fighting disease: Interview with Dr John Nkengasong, Executive Director Africa CDC', in L. Hwenda (ed). *The HSS Podcast – Let's talk about health in Africa: Titans of Industry Episode*. YouTube. Available at: https://www.youtube.com/watch?v=0O0LDL36cXAandlist=PLGSk-3mupm2GJY5UXVOOmlDdcD9MHV_u_3 (Accessed 7 January 2022).

Kagame, P. (2021). 'Progress report on the institutional reform of the African Union and on domestic health financing'. Statement by President Paul Kagame at the 34th Ordinary Session of the AU Assembly. Available at: https://au.int/en/speeches/20210206/statement-president-paul-kagame-34th-ordinary-session-au-assembly (Accessed 7 January 2022).

Khadiagala, G.M. (2008). *Governing Regionalism in Africa: Themes and debates*. Centre for Policy Studies Policy Brief, No. 51. Available at: https://media.africaportal.org/documents/polbrief51.pdf (Accessed 7 January 2022).

McNair, D. (2021). 'Multilateralism's failure to tackle our biggest challenges is compounding them'. European Council on Foreign Relations (ECFR Council). Available at: https://ecfr.eu/article/multilateralisms-failure-to-tackle-our-biggest-challenges-is-compounding-them/ (Accessed 7 January 2022).

Moodley, K., Blockman, M., Pienaar, D., Hawkridge, A.J., Meintjes, J., Davies, M.A. and London, L. (2021). 'Hard choices: Ethical challenges in phase 1 of COVID-19 vaccine roll-out in South Africa', *South African Medical Journal*, 111(6): 554–58.

Nkengasong, J., Djoudalbaye, B. and Maiyegun, O. (2017a). 'A new public health order for Africa's health security', *The Lancet Global Health*, 5: e1064–e1065.

Nkengasong, J.N., Maiyegun, O. and Moeti, M. (2017b). Establishing the Africa Centres for Disease Control and Prevention: Responding to Africa's health threats', *The Lancet Global Health*, 5: e246–e247.

Nkengasong, J.N. and Tessema, S.K. (2020). 'Africa needs a new public health order to tackle infectious disease threats', *Journal of Cell Biology*, 183: 296–300.

Oloruntoba, S.O. (2021). 'Unity is strength: COVID-19 and regionalism in Africa', *The International Spectator*, 56: 56–71.

Princewill, N. (2021). 'Two of Africa's COVID experts are leaving the continent. Is this a brain drain or gain for Africa?' *CNN*. Available at: https://edition.cnn.com/2021/10/16/africa/africa-health-experts-brain-drain-intl-cmd/index.html (Accessed 7 February 2022).

Söderbaum, F. (2015). *Early, Old, New and Comparative Regionalism: The scholarly development of the field*, KFG Working Paper Series. Available at: https://papers.ssrn.com/sol3/papers.cfm?abstract_id=2687942 (Accessed 9 January 2022).

Tikum, N. (2016). 'Prejudice disguised as critique: The legacy of AU Commission Chair Dlamini-Zuma', *Pambazuka News*. Available at: https://www.pambazuka.org/pan-africanism/prejudice-disguised-critique-legacy-au-commission-chair-dlamini-zuma?fbclid=IwAR2jhi2iUE-o0pDHY5bKBXGO7NjkHPzkwEkHcXMHEoyBexGK34JyDmvQALw (Accessed 7 February 2022).

Chapter Twelve

The free movement of persons and African integration

Khabele Matlosa

Introduction

Human migration globally, and in Africa specifically, is a fact of life. Migration has consistently been part of human life and it still is today. It is no surprise, then, that Cohen aptly proclaims that 'human beings were, from the beginning, a migrating species. As they sought food, warded off enemies and explored their landscape, humans ranged far off their origins in Africa eventually populating the world's land mass' (Cohen, 2019: 12). Human migration, therefore, cannot be wished away (Shimeles, 2010) and is set to remain a factor of human life in the future (AU/IOM, 2020).

This chapter discusses migration with a special focus on the free movement of persons. It presents the current state of play and highlights its prospects for success. The idea of the free movement of persons is not new in Africa – it predates the African Union (AU). It was part and parcel of the integration agenda of the Organisation of African Unity (OAU). The 1991 Treaty Establishing the African Economic Community, adopted by the OAU in Abuja, Nigeria, called for accelerated continental integration, including the free movement of persons. When the OAU transformed into the African Union, the latter inherited this agenda and accelerated efforts towards its realisation by, inter alia, developing normative frameworks and their implementation modalities.

The biggest impetus that saw the African Union rekindle the momentum towards the free movement of persons was the celebration of the 50th Anniversary of the OAU/AU in 2013 under the theme, Pan-Africanism and African Renaissance. This Golden Jubilee celebration witnessed the adoption of the 50th Anniversary Solemn Declaration reaffirming the commitment of African leaders to a common African identity and a common African citizenship. This ideal was further recalibrated and infused into the Agenda 2063 as one of its seven aspirations (see footnote 5). Furthermore, the free movement of persons and the African Passport became one of the 14 flagship projects of Agenda 2063.[1]

This chapter is divided into four substantive sections. The first section is the conceptual and theoretical exploration of migration to set the stage for subsequent discussions. Functionalist paradigms of migration include the neoclassical and the new economics of migration theories. The structuralist paradigms include the dual labour market and world system theories. The second section discusses migration in the African context. It illustrates that Africa is a closed space to African migrants. At the very heart of this problem lies the restrictive visa regimes on the continent. Section three provides justification for the free movement of persons as a way of opening up Africa to African migrants. Benefits and challenges of free movement of persons are highlighted. The fourth section reviews the experience of the free movement of persons and regional passports within the five regions of the continent, namely Central, East, North, Southern and West Africa. It demonstrates that while some regions have advanced considerably, others still lag behind.

Conceptual and theoretical exploration

Human migration is the movement of people from one region of a country to another (internal migration) or from one country to another (external migration). The International Organization for Migration (IOM) defines

---

1   The 14 flagship projects of Agenda 2063 are the (1) Integrated High Speed Train Network; (2) Grand Inga Dam; (3) Continental Free Trade Area; (4) Pan-African Virtual and e-University; (5) African Economic Platform; (6) Single African Air Transport Market; (7) Free Movement of Persons and the African Passport; (8) Continental Financial Institutions; (9) Pan-African E-Network; (10) Silencing the Guns by 2020; (11) Outer Space Policy and Strategy; (12) Great Museum of Africa; (13) African Commodities Strategy; and (14) Cyber Security.

migration as 'the movement of persons away from their place of usual residence either across an international border or within a State' (IOM, 2019: 137). It may be either permanent, as in the case of a migrant who moves to reside in another region/country, or semi-permanent, in the case of a person who oscillates between their home region/country and another region/country for work purposes. Migration, therefore, is 'a permanent or semi-permanent change of one's residence or site of labour. As a process, it involves an origin, destination and intervening factors' (Matlosa, 2001: 24–25).

Other related concepts are emigration, immigration and displacement. Emigration is a component of migration, denoting movement out of a given country. It denotes 'the act of moving from one's country of nationality or usual residence to another country, so that the country of destination effectively becomes his/her new country of usual residence' (IOM, 2019: 64). Conversely, immigration refers to a component of migration into a given country. It denotes 'the act of moving into a country other than one's country of nationality or usual residence, so that the country of destination effectively becomes his/her new country of usual residence' (IOM, 2019: 103).

Displacement is a component of migration that is involuntary or forced on persons due to circumstances beyond their control. It denotes 'the movement of persons who have been forced to flee or leave their homes or places of habitual residence, in particular as a result of, or in order to avoid, the effects of armed conflict, situations of generalized violence, violations of human rights or natural or human-made disasters' (IOM, 2019: 55). It is this component of migration that De Haas refers to as 'distress migration' (De Haas, 2021: 29).

Recent literature also points to climate change as a factor forcing people to migrate and this is referred to as environmental migration (Hocheleithner and Exner, 2018; AU/IOM, 2020). Environmental migration denotes 'the movement of persons who, predominantly for reasons of sudden or progressive changes in the environment that adversely affect their lives or living conditions, are forced to leave their places of habitual residence, or choose to do so, either temporarily or permanently, and who move within or outside their country of origin or habitual residence' (IOM, 2019: 65).

The concept of migration inextricably intersects with migration theories. Theories are a way of understanding and explaining phenomena:

(1) What is migration? (2) Why does it happen? (3) How does it happen? (4) What factors drive it? (5) What are its possible consequences and impact? According to Bueno and Prieto-Rosas, migration theories,

> seek to understand the reasoning behind and motivations for the decisions of individuals and households to move from one location to another – domestically or internationally – as well as factors that explain the maintenance of migration flows over time. Different theories employ different concepts, assumptions and frames of reference depending on their discipline of origin and the time in which they were formulated (Bueno and Prieto-Rosas, 2019: 1).

There are two main paradigmic/ideational frameworks that have informed and shaped discourses on migration. First, the functionalist paradigm/ideation propounds a thesis that migration is propelled and sustained by a person's (individual agency) or a household's (family agency) rational choice. Two theories in this paradigm are (1) the neoclassical economics, and (2) the new economics of migration. Of these, the neoclassical economics is the oldest theoretical model, which is traceable to the works of Arthur Lewis (1954), and later refined by Ranis and Fei (1961), Todaro (1969), Harris and Todaro (1970) and Todaro (1976). The structuralist theories posit that economic structures at national (that is, uneven capitalist penetration) and global (unequal globalisation) levels are more important in influencing people to migrate (Matlosa, 2001).

The principal thesis of this theory is that migration 'is caused by geographic differences in the supply and demand for labor' (Massey *et al.*, 1993: 433). Individuals, therefore, make rational cost–benefit calculations before deciding to either migrate or stay (De Haas, 2021: 4). According to Massey *et al.* (1993: 434), the five main assumptions of this theory are as follows:

1. International migration of workers is caused by differences in wage rates between countries.
2. The elimination of wage differentials will end the movement of labour.
3. The international movement of highly skilled workers responds to differences in the rate of return to human capital, leading to a fairly distinct pattern of migration that may be opposite to that of unskilled workers.

4. Labour markets are primary mechanisms by which migration is induced.
5. The way for governments to control migration flows is to regulate labour markets in countries of origin and/or countries of destination.

While the neoclassical economics confines the agency for migration to individuals, the new economics of migration identifies households or families as the key decision-makers for individuals to either migrate or stay. This theory was pioneered by Stark (1978), Stark (1984), Stark and Boom (1985) and Stark (1991). It propounds the idea that migration occurs 'in contexts of relative poverty and constraints as a household's or family's (instead of an individual's) co-insurance strategy aimed at diversifying (instead of maximising) income through risk-spreading' (De Haas, 2021: 5). The decision to migrate, therefore, is taken by larger units of related people in the form of a household or family and not just the individual 'to minimize risks and loosen constraints associated with a variety of market failures, apart from those in the labour market' (Massey *et al.*, 1993: 436).

Massey *et al.* (1993: 440) note the following key assumptions of the new economics of migration:
1. Families, households or other culturally defined units of production and consumption are appropriate units of analysis for migration research.
2. A wage differential is not a major factor for migration as households or families have strong incentives to diversify risk through cross-border human movement.
3. International migration does not stop with the elimination of wage differentials as long as other markets are either absent, imperfect or in disequilibrium.
4. Governments can influence migration rates not only through policies that influence labour markets, but also through those that shape insurance markets, capital markets and futures markets.
5. Government policies and economic changes that shape income distribution will also change the relative deprivation of some households or families, thereby altering their incentives to migrate.

The structuralist paradigm of migration offers a different set of perspectives. There are two main theories within this paradigm, namely: (1) the dual labour market theory, and (2) the world system theory. Pioneered by Piore

(1979), the dual labour market theory propounds the idea that migration 'is not caused by push factors in sending countries (low wages or high unemployment), but by pull factors in receiving countries (a chronic and unavoidable need for foreign workers)' (Massey *et al.*, 1993: 441).

The five main assumptions of the labour market theory are as follows:

1. International migration is primarily demand-driven and propelled by employers, recruiters or governments acting on behalf of employers.

2. The demand for migrant workers grows out of structural factors and manifests through recruitment practices – employers have incentives to recruit while at the same time holding wages constant.

3. The low level of wages in migrant supply countries does not rise as a result of shifts in supply and demand, as wages are held down by social and institutional mechanisms.

4. Low-level wages may fall, however, as a consequence of an increase in the supply of immigrant workers, given that the social and institutional checks that keep low-level wages from rising do not prevent them from falling.

5. Governments are unlikely to influence migration patterns through policies that produce small changes in wages or employment changes (Massey *et al.*, 1993: 444).

The world systems theory of migration builds on the notion of the dualism or bifurcation of the labour market at national, regional and global levels. It is inspired by the works of Emmanuel Wallenstein (1974) and other subsequent works (Petras, 1981; Sassen, 1988; Morawska, 1990; Castles, 2007, 2010) to make a case that 'structures have, in fact, a tendency to reproduce or even reinforce inequalities, both "vertically" between social groups (such as classes) and "horizontally" across space (i.e. between peripheral rural areas and the cities or between the rich and the poor countries)' (De Haas, 2021: 7). The primary thesis of this theory is that factors that drive migration are not premised on agency of individuals and/or households, but are predicated on the structural foundation of the production. Capitalism, perforce, survives on the existence of a large and cheap labour force that services the labour demands of the industrial sector. The penetration of capitalism in developing countries was also accompanied by the creation of labour reserves within countries and between countries (Matlosa, 2001). Migration within and between countries, therefore, follows this logic.

Influenced principally by the neo–Marxist political economy perspective, the radical assumptions of this theory include the following five:

1. International migration is a natural consequence of capitalist market formation in developing countries, which has catalysed human movement to the developed countries.
2. Globally, the flow of labour, as a rule, tends to follow the flow of goods and capital, albeit in the opposite direction.
3. International migration is more likely between past colonial powers and their former colonies than the other way round.
4. Migration flows from the dynamics of market creation and the structure of the global economy and, therefore, has little to do with wage or employment differentials.
5. Political and military interventions by developed countries in developing countries have the net effect of leading to forced displacement in the form of both refugees and internally displaced persons (Massey *et al.*, 1993: 448).

Since the recent past, some migration scholars have begun to question the exclusive utility of these theories in total isolation from each other as if they are polar opposites representing a bifurcated world. Consequently, they have made a case for a synthesis of these theoretical explanations if we are to have a comprehensive understanding and explanation of the migration phenomenon. Massey *et al.* argue that,

> it is possible that individuals engage in cost–benefit calculations; that households act to diversify labor allocations; and that the socio-economic context within which these decisions are made is determined by structural forces operating at the national and international levels. Thus, we are sceptical both of atomistic theories that deny the importance of structural constraints on individual decisions, and of structural theories that deny agency to individuals and families (Massey *et al.*, 1993: 455).

The critique for theoretical exclusivism and the call for conceptual eclecticism is corroborated by De Haas, who argues that, instead of perceiving migration theories as 'exclusive truth claims', there is a need for

> a vision in which the validity of theoretical assumptions is contingent

on the specific conditions under which migration occurs, the specific social and class groups concerned as well as on levels of analysis. This implies that both the functionalist and historical–structural paradigms can have explanatory power and relevance and can, therefore, to a certain extent, be combined and integrated in a wider meta-theoretical framework which is able to simultaneously incorporate agency and structure in explaining migration and which acknowledges that the vast majority of migrants face some level of constraint yet also have some level of choice (De Haas, 2021: 9).

The analysis in this chapter resonates with this call for an eclectic and integrated theoretical approach or framework in our understanding and explanation of migration. The following section discusses migration in the African context.

Migration in the African context

Africa is the second most populous continent after Asia. Its total population was estimated at 1.3 billion in 2019 (AUC, 2021: 7). West Africa accounts for the largest share of the population at 30.4 per cent, followed by East Africa at 27.7 per cent. The percentage share of the total population in the Northern, Southern and Central African regions was 15.5 per cent, 13.7 per cent and 12.8 per cent, respectively (AUC, 2021:7). A considerable proportion of this population comprises African international migrants.

Current trends suggest that intra-Africa migration by Africans outstrips their migration to other continents. Available data for 2010 show that there were 17.2 million African international migrants in Africa, which increased to 26.3 million in 2019, which translates to a 4.8 per cent average annual growth rate (AUC, 2021: 1). Shimeles reminds us that '79 percent of Sub-Saharan African migrants move within the same region. Less than 22 percent of migrants from Africa emigrate outside Africa, with less than 15 percent of African migrants emigrating to Europe and North America' (Shimeles, 2018: 2).

These facts are important to dispel the myth of an exodus of irregular migrants on dangerous journeys across the Mediterranean Sea to Europe, suggesting that outward migration from Africa outweighs intra-Africa migration. Popular and sensational narratives tend to focus on irregular migration from 'North Africa to Europe, often in exaggerated ... terms.

In reality, available data show that most African migrants generally move within the continent, and that migration from key countries in Africa to the European Union in recent years has been mostly regular' (AU/IOM, 2020: 27). This mythology of a poverty-driven and conflict-propelled exodus of hopeless, helpless and desperate Africans to Europe is 'influenced by media images of massive refugee flows and "boat migration", and alarmist rhetoric of politicians suggesting an impending immigrant invasion' (Flahaux and De Haas, 2016: 1).

Migration rate (migration-to-population) in Africa is 2.9 per cent, the lowest in the world, 'only higher than that of Asia and North America. Over time, the migration rate in Africa has declined while the global average rate increased from 2.9 percent of total population to about 3.4 percent' (Shimeles, 2018: 1). Intra-Africa migration is largely accounted for by sub-Saharan African migrants, while migrants from North Africa tend to emigrate to other continents, notably Europe. The situation is a rather mixed bag when we consider human movement within, between and outside the five regions of the continent, as Table 13.1 illustrates.

Table 12.1: Migration patterns within and from Africa (percentage of migrants by origin and destination)

Destination							
Origin	Africa	East Africa	Central Africa	North Africa	Southern Africa	West Africa	Outside of Africa
Africa	78.54	30.33	13.1	5.99	3.33	25.79	21.33
Eastern Africa	88.67	64.75	13.67	9.34	0.75	0.16	11.33
Central Africa	84.09	11.11	48.82	10.55	1.38	12.23	15.91
Northern Africa	49.56	29.93	4.56	13.36	0.05	1.67	50.44
Southern Africa	55.78	33.22	4.6	0.38	16.43	1.16	44.22
Western Africa	89.17	0.06	2.29	0.83	0.02	85.97	10.83

Source: Shimeles, 2018: 3

Two regions that exhibit high levels of intraregional migration are West Africa at 85.97 per cent and East Africa at 64.75 per cent. The performance of West and East Africa is partly explicable by reference to the advanced visa-open policies in these two regions. Intraregional migration in Central Africa is below 50 per cent at 48.82 per cent. Intraregional migration rates in Southern Africa and North Africa are even lower at a paltry 16.43 per cent and 13.36 per cent, respectively. Interestingly, North Africa and Southern Africa rank highest on the continent in terms of volumes of outward African migration to other continents. While a total of 50.44 per cent of Africa's outward migration emanates from North Africa, 44.22 per cent of Africa's outbound migration originates from Southern Africa.

One of the factors inhibiting greater and freer human movement of Africans in Africa has to do with the selective application of visa regimes. A visa is 'an endorsement (through a certificate or stamp in a travel document) showing a visitor is allowed to enter the country for a specific length of time and for specific activities' (AfDB, 2021: 6). Thus, the biggest elephant in the room in respect of Africans moving freely within their own continent is the visa. Some African countries have open visa regimes, the top 10 being Benin, Seychelles, The Gambia, Senegal, Ghana, Rwanda, Nigeria, Uganda, Guinea Bissau and Cabo Verde (AfDB, 2021: 17). A more visa-open country is the one that has 'a liberal or relaxed visa for visitors, meaning that visitors either do not need a visa when they enter its territory or can get a visa upon arrival' (AfDB, 2021: 6). Others have restrictive visa regimes, such as South Sudan, Guinea, Djibouti, Libya, Equatorial Guinea, Sudan, Eritrea, Egypt, Burundi and Algeria (AfDB, 2021: 17). A more visa-restrictive country 'requires visitors to get a visa before they travel. Visitors might obtain the visa from an embassy, a consulate or another source' (AfDB, 2021: 6).

The inaugural African Development Bank's (AfDB's) Visa Openness Report of 2016 illustrated the impact of the problem of visa restrictiveness in terms of intra-Africa human movement. That report showed that Africans required a visa to travel to 55 per cent of other African countries. Africans could get a visa on arrival in 25 per cent of other African countries, and they did not need a visa to travel to 20 per cent of other African countries (AfDB, 2016:13). It is instructive to compare this with travel by North Americans in Africa. North Americans required a visa to travel to 45 per cent of African countries, they could get a visa on arrival in 35 per cent of African countries, and they did not need a visa in 20 per cent of African countries (AfDB, 2016: 13). Alongside a prohibitive visa regime, there is a fairly permissive visa regime that facilitates the relatively easy movement of migrants from other continents, such as North America.

To promote the free movement of Africans within Africa, visas have to be gradually relaxed (and ultimately abolished) to allow easy entry of migrants into the countries of destination. Progressive relaxation and gradual abolition of visas is not a pipe dream. For instance, the Seychelles has abolished visas. This explains, in part, why it ranks number one on the 2021 AfDB Visa Openness Index (together with Benin and The Gambia). Before visas are abolished, they need to be incrementally relaxed through measures such as the introduction of e-visas, the acquisition of visas on arrival, the granting of gratis visas, etc. One African country that has relaxed its visa regime at a phenomenal speed and on the road towards its abolition is Rwanda.[2] Visa relaxation and abolition constitute the first step towards the implementation of the free movement of persons in Africa. According to the Implementation Roadmap of the Protocol to the Treaty Establishing the African Economic Community Relating to Free Movement of Persons, Right of Residence and Right of Establishment (the subject of the next section), four key steps are critical for the effective realisation of the letter and spirit of this protocol, namely visa relaxation, the right of entry, right of residence and right of establishment.

Towards the free movement of persons

Simply defined, the free movement of persons in Africa means unrestricted mobility or migration of African citizens across borders for various livelihood needs. The notion of the free movement of persons, as used in this chapter, denotes travel across borders of African countries on the basis of an open visa policy as opposed to a restrictive visa policy.

The idea of free movement of persons in Africa is as old as the ideal of Pan-Africanism[3] itself (see Mandaza and Nabudere, 2002; Mathews, 2018). There are essentially 10 steps that have marked the historical evolution of this idea thus far. First, the 1963 Charter of the OAU had as one of its goals

---

2   Rwanda ranks number six on the 2021 Africa Visa Openness Index developed by the African Development Bank covering 54 African countries. Rwanda is the first African country to ratify the Protocol on Free Movement of Persons, Right of Residence and Right of Establishment.

3   Pan-Africanism denotes a set of ideas and a worldview 'expressing the desire for political and psychological liberation and unity of all Africans on the continent or those in the diaspora' (Mathews, 2018: 15–16).

the promotion of unity and solidarity of African states and the coordination of efforts to achieve a better life for Africans in the spirit of Pan-Africanism (OAU, 1963). Although the OAU Charter did not explicitly make reference to the free movement of persons, it is implied by reference to unity and solidarity.

Second, in 1981 the OAU adopted the African Charter on Human and Peoples' Rights. This charter provided for the promotion and protection of the rights of African citizens to leave their countries of origin and reside in other African countries with the right to return to their countries of origin. Six years later, the African Commission on Human and Peoples' Rights, based in Banjul, The Gambia, was established to oversee the implementation of this charter. Article 12 of the African Charter on Human and Peoples' Rights provides that (1) every individual shall have the right to freedom of movement and residence within the borders of a State provided s/he abides by the law, and (2) every individual shall have the right to leave any country including his/her own, and to return to his/her country. This right may only be subject to restrictions, provided for by law, for the protection of national security, law and order, public health or morality (OAU, 1981: 4–5).

Third, exactly 10 years later, in 1991 the OAU adopted the Treaty Establishing the African Economic Community (AEC) – the Abuja Treaty. Article 43 of the Abuja Treaty provides that: (1) Member States agree to adopt, individually, at bilateral or regional levels, the necessary measures, in order to achieve progressively the Free Movement of Persons, and to ensure the enjoyment of the right of residence and the right of establishment by nationals within the Community; and (2) For this purpose, Member States agree to conclude a Protocol on Free Movement of Persons, Right of Residence and Right of Establishment (OAU, 1991: 31).

Fourth, with the transformation of the OAU to the African Union, the latter committed to accelerate the implementation of the 1991 Abuja Treaty (AU, 2000: 3), including the free movement agenda from the former. One of the key objectives of the African Union is to 'achieve greater unity and solidarity between the African countries and the peoples of Africa' (AU, 2000: 5). Towards this objective, the African Union adopted the Minimum Integration Programme (MIP) in 2009. Article 2.1.2, subsection 93 of the MIP provides for the elaboration and ratification by the Regional Economic Communities (RECs) and member states of protocols on the free movement of persons, rights of residence and establishment as a priority of the MIP.

Subsection 94 of Article 2.1.2 provides that certain priority actions at the continental level, like visa exemption for Africans holding diplomatic and service passports, could facilitate the free movement of persons among the RECs in Africa (AU, 2009: 31).

Fifth, during the celebrations of the Golden Jubilee of the OAU/AU in 2013, under the theme 'Pan-Africanism and African Renaissance', AU member states adopted the 50th Anniversary Solemn Declaration. In this declaration, African leaders committed themselves to the African identity and Renaissance and they proclaimed their 'unflinching belief in our common destiny, our Shared Values and the affirmation of the African identity; the celebration of unity in diversity and the institution of the African citizenship' (AU, 2013: 2). It was on the basis of this Solemn Declaration that Agenda 2063 – The Africa We Want[4] was developed in 2013.

Step six was the adoption of Agenda 2063 in 2014. The vision of African Union, as articulated in Agenda 2063, is 'an integrated, prosperous and peaceful Africa, driven by its citizens, representing a dynamic force in the international arena' (AU, 2015: 1). Aspiration 2 of Agenda 2063 envisions 'an integrated continent, politically united and based on the ideals of Africa's Renaissance' (AU, 2015: 1). By 2063, Africa shall be: (1) A continent with seamless borders, and cross-border resources will be managed through dialogue; and (2) A continent where the free movement of people, capital, goods and services will result in significant increases in trade and investments among African countries. Thus, to realise the free movement of persons idea, African leaders agreed to 'introduce an African Passport, issued by Member States, capitalizing on the global migration towards e-passports, and with the abolishment of visa requirements for all African citizens in all African countries by 2018' (AU, 2015: 4–5). It was

---

4   Agenda 2063 is the long-term development blueprint of the African Union which was developed between 2013 and 2015 through an inclusive and consultative process culminating in seven aspirations on the Africa We Want. These are: (1) A prosperous Africa based on inclusive growth and sustainable development; (2) An integrated continent, politically united and based on the ideals of Pan-Africanism and the vision of Africa's Renaissance; (3) An Africa of good governance, respect for human rights, justice and the rule of law; (4) A peaceful and secure Africa; (5) An Africa with a strong cultural identity, common heritage, shared values and ethics; (6) An Africa whose development is people-driven, relying on the potential of its women and youth, and caring for children; and (7) Africa as a strong, united, resilient and influential global player and partner (AU, 2015: 1)

in the context of this commitment that African leaders adopted the free movement of persons and the African Passport as one of the 14 Flagship Projects of Agenda 2063 (see footnote 2).

Seventh, during the 2015 Summit of the African Union held in Johannesburg, South Africa, a Declaration on Migration was adopted, calling for AU member states to accelerate the free movement of persons and the development of the African Passport. In January 2016, African Ministers of Foreign Affairs met in Mekelle, the capital of the Tigray region in Ethiopia, as part of the implementation of the Johannesburg Declaration on Migration. The ministers recommitted the African Union to the free movement of persons, imploring AU member states to relax visa regimes to allow for this. The ministers urged the African Union Commission (AUC) to develop the protocol on free movement of persons to be adopted in January 2018.

Eighth, building on the Mekelle decision, during the AU Summit in Kigali, Rwanda, in July 2016, the AU Assembly adopted a decision on the African Passport and identified the free movement of persons as a crucial element for deepening continental integration and unity in the spirit of Pan-Africanism, the African Renaissance and the realisation of Agenda 2063. During that summit, the African Union Diplomatic Passport was issued to various leaders in a symbolic gesture of political commitment towards the development, production and issuance of the African Passport.

Ninth, the Protocol to the African Economic Community Relating to Free Movement of Persons, Right of Residence and Right of Establishment was adopted by the African Union Policy Organs in January 2018. During the development of this protocol, the AUC worked closely with the RECs and member states with the technical support of the International Organization for Migration (IOM). Significantly, the protocol was adopted together with a comprehensive 'implementation roadmap' with clear milestones and time-frames as its annexure. The protocol has been signed by 33 of the 55 AU member states. It requires 15 ratifications to come into force. So far, four member states have ratified the protocol, namely Rwanda, Mali, Niger, and São Tomé and Príncipe. With the protocol and its implementation roadmap adopted, the requisite normative framework for the advancement of free movement of persons now exists at the continental level through the African Union. What now remains is demonstration of political commitment and leadership towards concrete action in the form of the ratification, domestication and effective implementation of the protocol and the issuance of the African Passport to African citizens. But, as the saying goes, it is easier said than done. The fact that only 33 countries have signed this protocol and only four have ratified it shows that a huge gap still exists between declarations and concrete action on the part of African leaders.

Tenth, both the Protocol on Free Movement of Persons and the African Continental Free Trade Area (AfCFTA) were launched in Kigali, Rwanda, in 2018. It is worth noting that the latter has progressed faster than the former, illustrating more commitment of African leaders to free trade in capital, goods and services and less appetite for the free movement of persons. The AfCFTA is aimed at facilitating free intra-Africa trade and investment. It came into force on 30 May 2019 following its ratification by the requisite number (22) of AU member states. Trading was supposed to commence on 1 July 2020, but, due to COVID-19, it was moved to 1 January 2021. AfCFTA has been signed by 54 of the 55 AU member states, and it has 36 ratifications. Further progress on the AfCFTA is demonstrated by the establishment and operationalisation of the AfCFTA secretariat based in Accra, Ghana, headed by Wamkele Mene from South Africa. Free trade and free movement are flipsides of the same coin: the cross-border movement of capital, goods and services goes together with the movement of business people and workers, as well as small cross-border traders, who are mainly women. Thus, it is well-nigh impossible for the AfCFTA to achieve its intended socioeconomic advancement of Africa without the free movement of persons being pursued with the same vigour as that invested in free trade.

The Protocol to the Treaty Establishing the African Economic Community Relating to Free Movement of Persons, Right of Residence and Right of Establishment adopted by the African Union Summit in January 2018 provides for the development of the African Passport. Article 10 of the Protocol provides that:

- State Parties shall adopt a travel document called 'African Passport' and shall work closely with the Commission to facilitate the processes towards the issuance of this Passport to their citizens;

- The Commission shall provide technical support to Member States to enable them to produce and issue the African Passport to their citizens; and

- The African Passport shall be based on international, continental and national policy provisions and standards and on a continental design and specifications (AU, 2018: 9).

To facilitate the issuance of the African Passport to African citizens, the AUC has facilitated the development of guidelines for the design, production and issuance of the African Passport working closely with the RECs and member states. During the development of these guidelines, the AUC received considerable technical support from the International Civil Aviation Organisation (ICAO). These guidelines were completed and adopted by the AU Summit of 2019 as an additional enabler for the free movement of persons. Once the Protocol on Free Movement of Persons comes into force, facilitated by the African Passport, a visa-free Africa is likely to be within reach. A solid foundation for a borderless Africa will be firmly in place. A common African identity and citizenship will evolve, thereby shattering the myth of a divided Africa balkanised through colonially imposed borders. This will go a long way in cementing Pan-Africanism, the African Renaissance, and continental integration and unity, as espoused in Agenda 2063. Africa will then be widely open to its own citizens, while still open to migrants from other continents. It is highly possible that the free movement of persons in Africa could reduce the outward migration of Africans to Europe – risking their lives through the Sahara Desert and the Mediterranean Sea. The easy movement of Africans within Africa may also reduce migration to North America.

As part of the advocacy for the ratification, domestication and implementation of the 2018 Protocol, it is important to identify the benefits and challenges of the free movement of persons in Africa (AU and IOM, 2018). The expected benefits of the protocol include 'integration, pan-Africanism, enhance science, technology, education, research and foster tourism, facilitate inter-African trade and investment, increase remittances within Africa, promote mobility of labour, create employment, improve the standards of living of the people of Africa and facilitate the mobilisation and utilisation of the human and material resources of Africa in order to achieve self-reliance and development' (Hirsch, 2021: 498).

All of the noble objectives of the protocol are achievable, but the actual implementation of these objectives faces enormous practical challenges at the continental level. There are several hurdles that impede ratification, domestication and implementation of the protocol and its implementation roadmap. The first hurdle is that the idea of free movement of persons is generally not understood by government officials, the private sector or the general populace (Adepoju, 2009). This is particularly the case for government officials who are charged with initiating and effecting the the protocol. The free movement of persons is often misconstrued as the sudden abolition of visas and borders and is thus perceived as the onset of anarchy. This perception is incorrect. The implementation of the protocol is expected to follow a sequence of four main stages, as highlighted earlier, and within the framework of laws and regulations in place in all the 55 member states, thus ensuring that chaos and anarchy are avoided.

Second, it is also evident that narrow national sovereignty stands in the way of its effective implementation. According to the 2020 AU/IOM report, this manifests in 'the desire of states to maintain their sovereignty by having control over those who enter their territory and protection of the labour market within countries. In reality, the porous natural boundaries of African states make it difficult to control entrances and exits throughout an entire territory' (AU and IOM, 2020: 82).

Third, the dilemma of narrow national sovereignty (as opposed to pooled sovereignty at regional and continental levels) is reinforced in some regions and countries by the upsurge of xenophobia and Afrophobia, as has been evident in South Africa since 2004 (Claassen, 2017). Of the five regions of the African continent, Southern Africa exhibits the highest intensity of xenophobia and Afrophobia. This, in part, explains why the region is ranked a distant third in terms of the pursuit of the free movement of persons, according to the AfDB Visa Openness Index. In fact, South Africa, as the regional hegemon, has resisted efforts towards free movement of persons. Its position was articulated early in its post-apartheid days by Mangosuthu Buthelezi, then Minister of Home Affairs: 'South Africa is faced with another threat and that is SADC ideology of free movement of people, free trade and freedom to choose where you live or work. Freedom of people spells disaster for our country' (Hirsch, 2021: 507). Given South Africa's overwhelming dominance over the region, it is no wonder that many countries in Southern Africa have severe visa restrictions and only a few (Madagascar, Mauritius, Mozambique and Namibia) have ratified the protocol.

Hirsch has identified four additional hurdles to the implementation of the protocol, namely inadequate systems of civil registration and identity documentation; weak administration of the criminal justice systems, including the poor exchange of civil and criminal data and data standards; unreliable and corruption-ridden border management systems; contagious security threats, including terrorism; and a general lack of regional and/or continental repatriation systems (Hirsch, 2021: 509–10).

These problems are not insurmountable if there is the political commitment at the highest level of the state to implement the protocol. Bilateral arrangements are enough proof of this. A notable example here is the bilateral visa-free movement of people across the border separating the towns of Rusizi in Rwanda and Goma in the Democratic Republic of the Congo. It is estimated that 30 000 people criss-cross this border daily, about 75 per cent of them are women traders, with a small proportion of tourists. They do not face any visa restrictions or use passports, but only an electronic card for identification (AU and IOM, 2020: 2).

The latest impediment to the free movement of persons was the onset of COVID-19 in 2020. Measures adopted by African states to halt the spread of COVID-19 included many that curtailed human movement within and across countries, with deleterious effects for the implementation of the protocol. These measures included: (1) declaration of states of emergencies/disasters; (2) lockdowns; (3) border closures; and (4) tightening visa requirement to include COVID-19 tests. The net effect of these measures included the decline in all forms of travel (by air, land and sea): international travel in Africa dropped by 95 per cent in 2020; tourism in Africa declined by 57 per cent in 2020; and, consequently, hotel occupancy dropped by 73 per cent (AfDB, 2020: 10).

In order for the free movement of persons to be fully realised at the continental level, important lessons should be learned from the rich experiences (both positive and negative) of the RECs, which are discussed in the following section.

Regional trends

It is appropriate to reflect on the regional trends in the free movement of persons for three main reasons. First, the African continent is divided into five regions (Central, East, North, Southern and West), all of which are organised into RECs, with varying experiences of the free movement of persons. Second, Africa's RECs are the building blocks of the African Union to their experiences with the free movement of persons idea are bound to form the foundation for the continental effort to implement the 2018 protocol on the free movement of persons. Third, while all the RECs have adopted a variety of normative frameworks[5] towards the free movement of persons, the Economic Community of West African States (ECOWAS) and East African Community (EAC) have gone a step further by introducing regional passports.

The RECs are far more advanced than the African Union on the free movement of persons and the regional travel documents. This is a testimony to the English aphorism that 'charity begins at home'. Be that as it may, it is worth noting that some regions are far more advanced than others on both fronts. According to the AfDB's Visa Openness Report of 2021, of the top 20 most visa-open countries, 45 per cent are in West Africa and 30 per cent are in East Africa (AfDB, 2021: 20).

In essence, throughout the African continent, ECOWAS and the EAC

---

5   EAC: Article 2(4)(b) of the 2009 Protocol on the Establishment of the East African Community Common Market Protocol (CMP) provides for the free movement of persons across borders of partner states. ECOWAS: Article 2(3) of the 1979 Protocol Relating to Free Movement of Persons, Residence and Establishment commits ECOWAS members to facilitate the free movement of persons through three main phases: phase I: right of entry and abolition of visas, phase II: right of residence and phase III: right of establishment. COMESA: Article 3 of the 1998 Protocol on the Free Movement of Persons, Labour, Services and Rights of Establishment and Residence encourages COMESA member states to relax visa requirements, while Article 5 calls for their abolition six years after the coming into force of the protocol. IGAD: the 2012 Regional Migration Policy Framework of the Inter-Governmental Authority on Development (IGAD) deals broadly with the imperative for its member states to harmonise their migration policies while leaving the issue of the free movement of persons and labour mobility to bilateral arrangements. SADC: Article 2 of the 2005 Protocol Facilitation of Movement of Persons (FoMP) commits SADC state parties to progressively eliminate obstacles to the movement of persons into and within their territories. ECCAS: Chapter V of the 1983 Treaty establishing the Economic Community of Central African States (ECCAS) provides freedom of movement, residence and establishment of nationals of its member states. Article 3 (f) of the 2013 revised Treaty Establishing the Community of Sahel-Saharan States (CEN-SAD) commits its member states to promote the free movement of persons, goods and services. AMU: Article 1 of the 1989 Treaty Instituting the Arab Maghreb Union (AMU) calls for the progressive realisation of the free movement of persons and transfer of services, goods and capital among its member states. The development of the AU Protocol on Free Movement of Persons drew enormous inspiration from these regional normative instruments by RECs. In general, these are impressive and progressive instruments, but they hardly ever reflect the situation on the ground in respect of the free movement of persons, with the exception of the ECOWAS and EAC experiences so far.

are the trailblazers in terms of advancing the free movement of persons, using the EAC Passport and ECOWAS Passport as major catalysts. In fact, currently efforts are underway to introduce a regional electronic Identity Document for EAC and ECOWAS citizens to complement their regional passports.

Of the top 20 most visa-open countries, the Southern African and North African regions account for only 20 per cent and 5 per cent, respectively (AfDB, 2021: 20). This means that both the Southern African Development Community (SADC) and the Arab Maghreb Union (AMU) still have a long way to go to catch up with the EAC and ECOWAS. Even more serious than the worrisome situations in Southern and North Africa, is the fact that there is no single country from Central Africa in the top 20 most visa-open countries (AfDB, 2021: 20). There are no regional identity documents and/or travel documents in Southern Africa and North Africa. In the Economic Community of Central African States (ECCAS), some countries have introduced a regional travel document but its effectiveness is unclear.

This regional snapshot has implications for the pursuit of the free movement of persons at the continental level. For starters, it is evident that for the protocol to be effectively implemented, it is imperative that East Africa and West Africa lead the way and champion this idea, even in terms of ratification of the protocol. Taken together these two regions comprise 21 countries (15 in ECOWAS and 6 in the EAC). If all of these countries ratify the protocol, it will easily come into force, given that only 15 ratifications are required for this.

The other implication of the regional snapshot is that, given the disparities among the five regions, the regions and various countries cannot be expected to move at the same pace. Each region and country should be allowed to move at its own pace, on the basis that the coalition of the willing (in this case, the EAC and ECOWAS) lead the way and the laggards (the SADC, UMA and ECCAS) play a catch-up game at their own pace.

Another important factor here relates to the appetite for the free movement of persons among African countries that cuts across the five regions. Interestingly, Africa's economic powerhouses or regional hegemons have a low appetite for the free movement of persons compared to small, landlocked and island states. This observation is corroborated by the findings of the 2016 AfDB Visa Openness Index. This study found that 'many of the continent's regional and strategic hubs have restrictive visa policies. Africa's upper middle-income countries as a group have low visa-openness scores. Africa's small, landlocked and island states are more open, promoting trade links with their neighbours; eight out of nine of Africa's upper middle-income countries have low visa-openness scores' (AfDB, 2016: 13).

The 2018 Protocol on Free Movement of Persons has to be popularised in regions that are still lagging behind, as well as in Africa's economic powerhouses. These regional hegemons have to embrace the free movement of persons and the African Passport if progress is to be made towards a people-centred integration in Africa. What is incontrovertible is the reality that the African Passport will act as a major catalyst for the free movement of persons.

Conclusion

Migration in general, and in Africa in particular, has consistently been a key feature of human life. It remains one of the most pressing development issues on the continent. It is bound to characterise Africa's future development trajectory within the framework of Agenda 2063 – The Africa We Want.

In the classical and contemporary discourse, there are various theories of migration, chief among which are categorised into two main schools of thought: (1) the functionalist paradigm, and (2) the structuralist paradigm. The former includes two main theories, namely the neoclassical economics and the new economics of migration. The latter also includes two theories, namely the dual labour market and the world system theories.

Although there is a plethora of literature on migration in Africa, little has been researched and written about the free movement of persons. This chapter contributes to a few recent efforts (AU/IOM, 2020; Hirsch, 2021) to fill this policy and academic lacuna in migration discourse. The chapter has demonstrated that in its efforts to accelerate regional integration, the African Union is pursuing various initiatives linked to Agenda 2063, notably the AfCFTA and the free movement of persons. It has focused mainly on the free movement of persons, arguing that it is inextricably intertwined with the free trade idea.

This chapter discussed the benefits and challenges of the free movement of persons. It demonstrated that benefits are achievable, given a conducive environment, and the challenges are not insurmountable. At the very heart of the free movement of persons rests the African Passport – a major catalyst for the realisation of this Pan-Africanist dream. The African Passport is bound to accelerate the four main stages of achieving the free movement of persons, namely a gradual relaxation of visas, the right of entry, the right of residence and the right of establishment.

The chapter has explored the experience of Africa's five regions, namely Central, East, North, Southern and West Africa. It reaffirms the findings of the 2020 AU/IOM *African Migration Report* and the 2021 AfDB *Visa Openness Report* that West and East Africa have relatively more visa open countries and are fairly advanced on the free movement of persons and regional travel documents. The other three regions (Southern, North and Central) are far behind as they are marked by relatively more restrictive visa regimes. Be that as it may, the principle of variable geometry applies here: the more advanced regions and countries should lead the way towards the free movement of persons, while the laggards should follow at their own pace.

References

Adepoju, A. (2009). 'Migration management in West Africa within the context of ECOWAS Protocol on Free Movement of Persons and the common approach on migration: challenges and prospects', in M. Tremolieres (ed). *Regional Challenges of West African Migration: African and European perspectives*. Paris: OECD.

African Development Bank (AfDB). (2021). *Africa Visa Openness Report, 2021*. Abidjan, Côte d'Ivoire.

African Development Bank (AfDB). (2020). *Africa Visa Openness Report, 2020*. Abidjan, Côte d'Ivoire.

African Development Bank (AfDB). (2016). *Africa Visa Openness Report, 2016*. Abidjan, Côte d'Ivoire.

African Union (AU). (2018). 'Protocol to the Treaty Establishing the African Economic Community Relating to Free Movement of Persons, Right of Residence and Right of Establishment'. Addis Ababa, Ethiopia.

African Union (AU). (2015). *Agenda 2063 – The Africa We Want. Popular Version*. Addis Ababa, Ethiopia.

African Union (AU). (2013). '50th Anniversary Solemn Declaration'. Addis Ababa, Ethiopia.

African Union (AU). (2009). 'The Minimum Integration Programme'. Addis Ababa, Ethiopia.

African Union (AU). (2000). 'Constitutive Act of the African Union'. Addis Ababa, Ethiopia.

African Union (AU) and International Organisation for Migration (IOM). (2020). *Africa Migration Report: Challenging the Narrative*. Addis Ababa, Ethiopia.

African Union (AU) and International Organisation for Migration (IOM). (2018). *Study on the Benefits and Challenges of Free Movement of Persons in Africa*. Geneva, Switzerland: International Organization for Migration.

African Union Commission. (2021). *Report on Labour Migration Statistics in Africa*. Addis Ababa, Ethiopia.

Bueno, X. and Prieto-Rosas, V. (2019). 'Migration theories', in D. Gu and M. Dupre (eds). *Encyclopedia of Gerontology and Population Aging*. Cham: Springer, pp. 1–11.

Castles, S. (2007). 'Twenty-first century migration as a challenge to sociology', *Journal of Ethnic and Migration Studies*, 33(3): 351–71.

Claassen, C. (2017). *Explaining South African Xenophobia*, Afrobarometer Working Paper No. 173. Accra, Ghana: Afrobarometer.

Castles, S. (2010). Understanding global migration: A social transformation perspective', *Journal of Ethnic and Migration Studies*, 36(10): 1565–86.

Cohen, R. (2019). *Migration: The movement of humankind from prehistory to the present*. London: Andre Deutsch.

De Haas, H. (2021). 'A theory of migration: the aspiration-capability framework', *Comparative Migration Studies*, 9(8): 1–35. https://dol.org/10.1186/s40878-020-00210-4.

Harris, J. and Todaro, M. (1970). 'Migration, unemployment, and development: A two-sector analysis', *The American Economic Review*, 60: 126–42.

Hirsch, A. (2021). 'The African Union's Free Movement of Persons Protocol: Why has it faltered and how can its objectives be achieved?' *South African Journal of International Affairs*, 28(4): 497–517.

Hochleithner, S. and Exner, A. (2018). *Theories of Migration in and from Rural Sub-Saharan Africa: Review and critique of current literature*. Swedish International Centre for Local Democracy, Working Paper No. 14, Stockholm.

International Organisation for Migration (IOM). (2019). *Glossary on*

Migration. International Migration Law, No. 34. Geneva, Switzerland: IOM.

Lee, E. (1966). 'A theory of migration', *Demography*, 3(1): 47–57.

Lewis, A. (1954). 'Economic development with unlimited supplies of labour', *The Manchester School of Economic and Social Studies*, 22(2): 139–91.

Mandaza, I. and Nabudere, W. (eds). *Pan-Africanism and Integration in Africa*. Harare: SAPES Books.

Massey, D., Arango, J., Hugo, G., Kouaouci, A., Pellegrino, A. and Taylor, J. (1993). 'Theories of international migration: A review and appraisal', *Population and Development Review*, 19(3): 431–66.

Mathews, K. (2018). 'The African Union and the Renaissance of Pan-Africanism', in T. Karbo and T. Murithi. (eds). *The African Union: Autocracy, diplomacy and peacebuilding in Africa*. London: I.B. Tauris.

Matlosa, K. (2001). 'Introduction', in K. Matlosa (ed.) *Migration and Development in Southern Africa*. Harare: SAPES Books.

Morawska, E. (1990). 'The sociology and historiography of immigration', in V. Yans-McLaughlin (ed). *Immigration Reconsidered: History, sociology, and politics*. New York: Oxford University Press, pp. 187–240.

Organisation of African Unity (OAU). (1991). Treaty Establishing the African Economic Community. Addis Ababa, Ethiopia.

Organisation of African Unity (OAU). (1981). The African Charter on Human and Peoples' Rights. Addis Ababa, Ethiopia.

Organisation of African Unity (OAU). (1963). The Charter of the Organisation of African Unity. Addis Ababa, Ethiopia.

Petras, E. (1981). 'The global labor market in the modern world-economy', in M. Kritz, C. Keely, and S. Tomasi (eds). *Global Trends in Migration: Theory and research on international population movements*. New York: Centre for Migration Studies, pp. 44–63.

Piore, M. (1979). *Birds of Passage: Migrant labour in industrial societies*. Cambridge: Cambridge University Press.

Ranis, G. and Fei, J. (1961). 'A theory of economic development', *The American Economic Review*, 51: 533–65.

Sassen, S. (1988). *The Mobility of Labour and Capital: A study in international investment and labour flow*. Cambridge: Cambridge University Press.

Shimeles. A. (2018). 'Foresight Africa Viewpoint: Understanding the patterns and causes of African Migration: Some facts', *Africa in Focus*, Thursday, 18 January. Washington, DC: Brookings Institution.

Shimeles, A. (2010). *Migration Patterns, Trends and Policy Issues in Africa.* AfDB Working Papers Series No. 119. Tunis: African Development Bank.

Stark, O. (1984). 'Migration decision making: A review article', *Journal of Development Economics,* 14: 251–59.

Stark, O. (1991). *The Migration of Labour.* Cambridge: Basil Blackwell.

Stark, O. and Bloom, D. (1985). 'The new economics of labor migration', *The American Economic Review,* 75: 173–78.

Todaro, M. (1969). 'A model of labor migration and urban unemployment in less-developed countries', *The American Economic Review,* 59: 138–48.

Todaro, M. (1976). *Internal Migration in Developing Countries: A survey.* Geneva: International Labor Office.

PART 4

THE AFRICAN CONTINENTAL FREE TRADE AREA: CHALLENGES AND PROSPECTS

Chapter Thirteen

Who trades what with whom in Africa? Mapping intraregional trade

ROD ALENCE

Introduction

Economic integration through intraregional trade has long been a central aim of African leaders. Greater trade among African countries would address colonial legacies of internal fragmentation and external dependence in the region's international economic relations. The design of integration initiatives has evolved over time – from the inward-looking 'collective self-reliance' of the Lagos Plan of Action of 1980, to the African Economic Community outlined in the Abuja Treaty of 1991, to the 'open regionalism' of the African Continental Free Trade Agreement of 2018. This evolution has reflected changes in prevailing ideas about economic development, as well as in the rules and institutions of the global trade regime. What all major initiatives to promote regional economic integration in Africa have shared is a commitment to expanding intraregional trade.

Yet, for all these efforts, results on the ground have been disappointing. As of 2019, trade among African countries accounts for only about one-eighth of the continent's total trade, and Africa's trade with the rest of the world remains skewed in ways that echo the colonial era. Primary products (minerals, fuels and cash crops) continue to dominate the region's exports, while manufactured goods continue to dominate its imports. After decades of initiatives to promote regional integration, internal fragmentation and external dependence continue to characterise African trade.

Structural obstacles grounded in Africa's economic geography and history are important reasons for the difficulty expanding intraregional trade. Gravity models of trade illuminate geographical obstacles, and the concept of trade complementarity illuminates historical ones. Gravity models portray trade between any two countries as a function of the sizes of their economies and their geographical proximity. Influential economic studies have found that simple 'gravitational' forces fit the observed patterns of bilateral trade within the region: African national economies are small and the African continent is large, which helps to explain why intraregional trade flows are modest (Foroutan and Pritchett, 1993; Elbadawi, 1997; Redding and Venables, 2004; Geda and Seid, 2015). The concept of trade complementarity emphasises the 'fit' between potential trading partners, with trade more likely to emerge when the products exported by one country match the import demands of another (Schiff, 2011). Since the colonial era, however, most African countries have exported mainly primary products and imported mostly manufactured products, making them unlikely 'natural trading partners' (Yeats 1999; Geda and Yimer 2019). Weak gravitational forces due to Africa's geography, coupled with weak trade complementarities due to historical patterns of specialisation, have hindered the expansion of intraregional trade.

Economic studies of these structural obstacles are useful, but they also contain blind spots with respect to assessing Africa's intraregional 'trade potential'. Methodologically, they rely on a 'wide-angle lens' well-suited to capture systematic deviations between intra-African and global trade patterns, rather than a 'zoom lens' that reveals features of bilateral trade within Africa. For example, economic studies that employ the gravity model estimate statistically 'predicted' bilateral trade flows between countries, using data sets that span several regions. The key gravitational predictors are the sizes of each country's economy and the geographical distance between them. They are augmented by other structural and policy-related variables, sometimes including measures of trade complementarity (see, for example, Van Beers and Linnemann 1988; Turkson 2015; Olney 2022). Such studies can determine whether Africa possesses unexploited intraregional trade potential (in the sense that it underperforms its statistically predicted level), and whether unfavourable structural or policy variables explain Africa's disappointing performance (if its actual level aligns with predictions, once its unfavourable features are 'controlled for' statistically). Yet the wide–angle focus on deviations between African and global patterns neglects questions that call for a zoom lens, to observe the more nuanced details about who trades what with whom in Africa.

My aim in this chapter is to zoom in on neglected features of the geography and product composition of existing trade within Africa to provide new insights into the potential for expanding intraregional trade. Drawing on detailed bilateral trade data, I proceed in three steps. The first clarifies geographical patterns of trade, using network cartograms to visualise empirical trade flows. Network cartograms are stylised maps that incorporate key features of gravity models: the sizes of economies and the value of trade between them. They address the 'with whom' question of intra-African trade. The second step turns to the product composition of trade, using the notion of 'regional orientation' to identify products with revealed complementarities within Africa. (These products turn out to be quite different from those that dominate Africa's exports to the rest of the world.) It addresses the question of 'what' is traded internationally within Africa. The third step leverages the first two, mapping the geography of trade flows, specifically in those products oriented toward intraregional trade. It simultaneously addresses questions about 'what' African countries trade and 'with whom'. Zooming in on intra-African trade patterns makes it possible to assess trade potential in a way that adds value to wider–angle economic studies.

Before proceeding to the analysis, let me briefly clarify terminology. Given that this chapter (like this volume) focuses on 'regional integration' across the continent of Africa, when I refer generically to 'region', I mean the entire continent. I use 'subregion' specifically to refer to five geographical subdivisions of the continent, as defined by the African Union (AU). (These are listed in Table 13.1.) Two potential sources of confusion emerge: first, the African Union formally refers to these units as geographical 'regions' (not 'subregions'); second, the African Union also recognises 'regional economic communities' (RECs) whose memberships overlap and do not conform strictly with the five geographical subdivisions. For the purposes of the data analysis in this chapter, it makes sense to define subregions geographically, so that each country can be assigned unambiguously to one, and only one, subregion.

Measuring African trade

The trade data I analyse captures goods exchanged between country dyads (exporter and importer) according to a detailed product classification, for the 2019 calendar year. They originate from official national trade statistics reported to the United Nations Statistical Division, which compiles them in the Comtrade database (United Nations, 2021). Comtrade records each trade transaction twice: when goods move from one country to another, they are recorded as exports in the statistics of one country and as imports in the statistics of the other. These 'mirrored' values do not match exactly – partly because import values include transport costs, while export values do not, and partly because national statistics are not perfectly reliable. To address these discrepancies, French researchers developed a statistical procedure to harmonise the mirrored Comtrade values (Gaulier and Zignago, 2010). Their Database for International Trade Analysis is known by its French acronym, BACI. It assigns a single value to each trade flow – by first deducting transport costs from imports, then weighting the adjusted values according to the reliability of each country's data. All trade estimates in this chapter are my calculations from BACI data.

BACI gives values of bilateral trade flows within detailed product categories, but has limitations, mainly due to the source data. The completeness and accuracy of official trade data are far from perfect anywhere in the world, and data quality in Africa is particularly weak (Yeats, 1990; Jerven, 2014). An obvious gap in coverage is that BACI omits any transaction that is not recorded by either partner, as such transactions are invisible in official statistics. Some trade is unrecorded because it is concealed from authorities – for example, the trade in illegal goods or smuggling of legal goods. Other unrecorded trade, such as informal local trade in foodstuffs and livestock, may cross unpoliced and unmarked national borders (Golub, 2015). Data problems also arise where trade is recorded, but details are incorrect. The deliberate misinvoicing of trade, with or without the connivance of corrupt officials, is a way of evading trade taxes or concealing illicit financial flows. Errors may also reflect technical deficiencies of customs administration, which can lead to products being placed in the wrong category, or to misrecording the origin or destination country of trans-shipped goods. Despite these limitations, BACI provides useful ballpark estimates of Africa's international trade, specifying exporting and importing countries and product categories.

Africa's recorded intraregional trade in 2019 was worth US\$66.5 billion (single-counting the values, which appear as one partner's exports and another partner's imports), according to BACI. The comparable figure for African countries' total trade with the world (averaging the values of exports and imports) was US\$525.4 billion. Intraregional trade thus accounted for about 13 per cent of Africa's total trade. The composition of Africa's trade with the rest of the world reflected a persistent historical pattern: 81 per cent of Africa's exports to the rest of the world were 'primary commodities', and 71 per cent of its imports from the rest of the world were 'manufactured goods' (using the United Nations Conference on Trade and Development [UNCTAD] product classifications). Lucrative fuels and minerals enhance Africa's export proceeds. Even counting these, the region's ratio of total trade to economic output in 2019 (measured using 2021 World Bank estimates of gross domestic product [GDP]) is 43 per cent, roughly equal to the global average of 42 per cent.

Step 1: Mapping the geography of intra-African trade

To visualise data on the geography of intra-African trade, I begin with a network cartogram of country-to-country flows. Figure 13.1 highlights the central determinants in gravity models: economic size and geographical distance. Each country is a circle whose size is proportional to its GDP, labelled with a three-letter code (listed in Table 13.1). The centre of each circle approximates its geographical location, but the larger circles 'bounce' nearby smaller circles from their true locations. The algorithm used to draw the cartograms minimises these distortions, preserving the impression of a map (Dorling, 1996: 32–36; Jeworutzki, 2020). Network lines connect pairs of circles (drawn using graphics tools from Butts, 2022; 2008) that represent the top 100 largest bilateral flows. Together they account for more than 90 per cent of Africa's intraregional trade. The thickness of each line is proportional to the value of two-way trade between the two countries.

Gravity models predict larger trade flows between larger economies that are located closer to each other, all else being equal. The pattern in Figure 14.1 broadly conforms with this prediction. South Africa's prominence in intra-African trade is striking. As the second-largest economy in Africa in 2019, the country was party to 28 per cent of intraregional trade and was the largest intraregional exporter. Although it exported about twice as much to the region as it imported, it was also the leading intraregional importer. It was also a party to nine of the top 10 flows (the exception being Algeria-Tunisia, the ninth-largest flow). Of the top 10, only two spanned major subregions of the continent, South Africa's flowed with Nigeria and Ghana. A large share of Africa's intraregional trade depends on South Africa, which was only fully integrated into the continental economy after its transition to democracy in 1994. Conversely, South Africa depends on intraregional trade to an extent that is often overlooked, even among South Africans themselves (Alence, 2015).

Figure 13.1: Network cartogram of intra-African trade in goods (all products), 2019 (Circles are sized proportional to GDP based on World Bank data; the thickness of the connecting lines are proportional to the value of two-way trade based on BACI data, and only the top 100 trade values are shown).

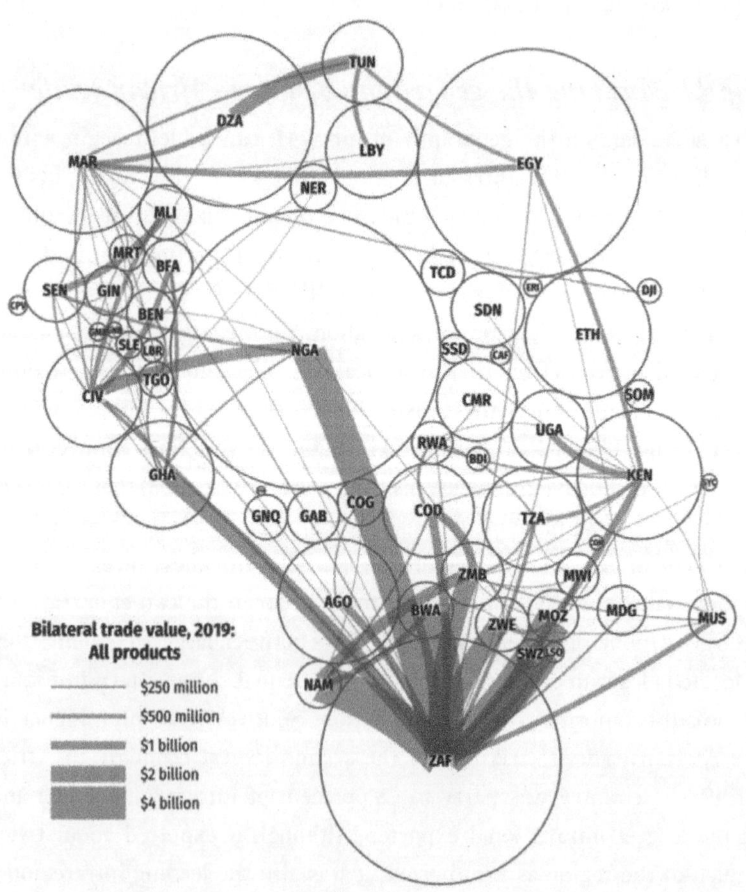

Table 13.1: Five geographical (sub)regions of Africa, as defined by the African Union

North
Algeria (DZA), Egypt (EGY), Libya (LBY), Mauritania (MRT), Morocco (MAR), Sahrawi Arab Democratic Republic* (ESH), Tunisia (TUN)
West
Benin (BEN), Burkina Faso (BFA), Cabo Verde (CPV), Côte d'Ivoire (CIV), Gambia (GMB), Ghana (GHA), Guinea-Bissau (GNB), Guinea (GIN), Liberia (LBR), Mali (MLI), Niger (NER), Nigeria (NGA), Senegal (Sen), Sierra Leone (SLE), Togo (TGO)
Central
Burundi (BDI), Cameroon (CMR), Central African Republic (CAF), Chad (TCD), Congo (COG), Democratic Republic of the Congo (COD), Equatorial Guinea (GNQ), Gabon (GAB), São Tomé and Príncipe (STP)
East
Comoros (COM), Djibouti (DJI), Ethiopia (ETH), Eritrea* (ERI), Kenya (KEN), Madagascar (MDG), Mauritius (MUS), Rwanda (RWA), Seychelles (SYC), Somalia (SOM), South Sudan (SSD), Sudan (SDN), Tanzania (TZA), Uganda (UGA)
Southern
Angola (AGO), Botswana (BWA), Eswatini (SWZ), Lesotho (LSO), Malawi (MWI), Mozambique (MOZ), Namibia (NAM), South Africa (ZAF), Zambia (ZMB), Zimbabwe (ZWE)
Note: * Means BACI data on bilateral trade is not available. Three-letter country codes are in parentheses.

For a clearer subregional summary, Figure 14.2 aggregates flows within and across the five major geographical subregions of Africa defined by the AU and listed in Table 14.1. Each country belongs to one, and only one, geographical subregion. The design of Figure 14.2 is like that of Figure 14.1, but with circles representing subregional totals rather than individual countries. The circles' sizes are proportional to each subregion's GDP, and the thicknesses of the connecting lines are proportional to trade values. Additionally, the thickness of the circles themselves varies to represent the value of international trade within each subregion (on the same scale as the connecting lines). Comparing them shows, for example, that trade within the Southern African subregion far exceeds levels within each other subregion, as well as levels of trade between each pair of subregions.

Figure 13.2: Network cartogram of intra-African trade by subregion (all goods), 2019

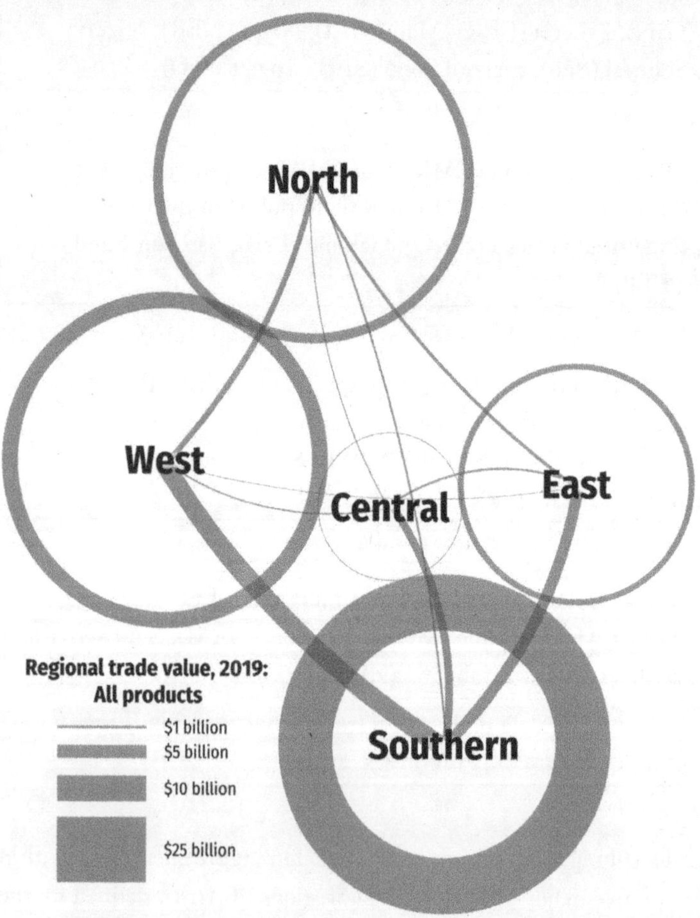

The subregional trade pattern in Figure 13.2 highlights challenges to achieving truly continental economic integration. Trade between the East and West subregions is negligible, as is trade between the Northern and Southern subregions. Meanwhile, the Central subregion does not trade much with any subregion other than Southern Africa, much of which consists of the Democratic Republic of the Congo's trade with neighbouring Zambia and South Africa. Two notable flows across subregions connect South Africa with the East African hub of Kenya and with the Anglophone West African hubs of Nigeria and Ghana. More modest flows connect the large economies of North Africa with the East and West subregions. The Egypt–Kenya dyad dominates North African links to East Africa; links to the West involve Morocco and several, mainly Francophone, West African countries. (Bilateral national trade networks within each subregion can be seen by referring back to Figure 13.1.) The East African subregion has a clear hub-spoke pattern centred on Kenya, a miniature version of the Southern African subregion's pattern centred on South Africa. The West African pattern is more of a patchwork, reflecting Anglophone and Francophone networks, as well as Nigeria's modest role as a subregional hub, despite having the subregion's largest economy by far.

Step 2: Identifying the product composition of intra-African trade

Identifying the products traded within Africa helps to reveal the potential for expanding intraregional trade. Intraregional trade accounts for only about one-eighth of Africa's total international trade. The region's trade with the rest of the world – to which it exports mainly primary products and from which it imports mainly manufactured goods – therefore dominates the product composition of its total trade. Trade within the region cannot exhibit the same structural imbalance between products exported and imported because, in intraregional trade, every export for one African country is an import for another. Logic dictates that the product composition of intraregional exports must exactly match that of intraregional imports. It also dictates that neither can match the unbalanced composition of trade with the rest of the world.

Detailed classifications in BACI make it possible to disaggregate trade by product. UNCTAD (2021) defines a hierarchy of product groupings, which I use to create five categories: 'food', 'agricultural raw materials', 'ores and metals', 'fuels' and 'manufactured goods'.[1] Applied to all of Africa's international trade, the data confirm the structural mismatch between the composition of exports and imports. More than two-thirds (69 per cent) of Africa's exports are primary products, consisting of fuels (37 per cent), ores and metals (27 per cent), and agricultural raw materials (5 per cent). In contrast, manufactured goods alone account for more than two-thirds (67 per cent) of its imports.

The concept of 'regional orientation' distinguishes export products that are more likely to be exported to other African countries, rather than being exported to the rest of the world. A simple measure is the percentage of a region's total exports of a product whose final destination lies within the region.[2] At the extremes, if all exports of a product end up outside the region, regional orientation for the product would be 0 per cent; if all exports of the product were to end up inside the region, regional orientation for the product would be 100 per cent. Intervening percentages, loosely speaking, are the probability that the product will, if exported, contribute to intraregional trade. Data from BACI show that the regional orientation for Africa's exports across all products in 2019 was 13 per cent. We have already seen that it is the value of intra-African exports expressed as a percentage of the value of the region's total exports.

The regional orientation of Africa's exports varies considerably over the five major product groupings. The horizontal dimension of Figure 13.3 shows that the regional orientations of classic primary exports – ores and metals, agricultural raw materials, and raw materials – range from 6 to 9 per cent. The corresponding shares for manufactured goods and food are much higher, at 27 per cent. The vertical dimension shows the 'importance' of the five product groups in terms of their shares of Africa's total exports. The

---

1   I modify the UNCTAD groups in two ways: I include tea, coffee, cocoa and spices in 'agricultural raw materials' (reflecting their status as export 'cash crops'); and I include precious stones and non-monetary gold in 'ores and metals' (reflecting their common origins in the mining sector). To apply the (slightly modified) UNCTAD product groups required an intervening step: converting the Harmonized System (HS, revision 5 [2017]) product codes in the BACI data to the Standard Industrial Trade Classification (SITC, revision 3) codes UNCTAD used to define their product groups, through concordance matching (Liao et al., 2020). About half of 1 per cent of Africa's total recorded trade is 'unclassified' in the UNCTAD product groupings.

2   Yeats (1998: 8–9) presents and discusses a similar measure, though the scale of his index differs.

area of the rectangle for each product group has a useful interpretation: it is the extent to which the product group 'pulls' the average regional orientation of African exports up or down. Primary exports, we already know, account for about two-thirds of the region's total exports, and for this reason they occupy about two-thirds of the vertical space in Figure 13.3. Because their regional orientation falls well below the average of 13 per cent, these product groups pull the regional average down. Manufactured goods and food, in contrast, account for about one-third of total exports, but because of their much stronger regional orientation, they pull the average up.

Figure 13.3: Contribution to the regional orientation of African exports, by product group (based on BACI trade data)

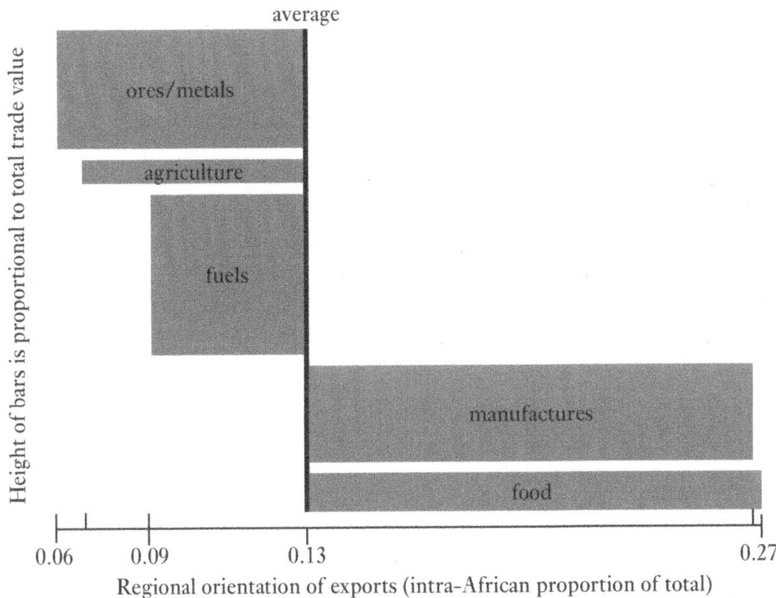

Within the food and manufacturing sectors, specific products contribute more than others to the regional orientation of Africa's exports. My measure of these contributions is similar to the area of the rectangles in Figure 13.3. It is the percentage points by which the product's regional orientation exceeds the African average (13 per cent) multiplied by the total value of exports of the product. This gives the contribution in dollar terms. Table 13.2 lists the products (defined at the four-digit HS classification) with the top five contributions. The bigger the 'excess contribution', the more the product pulls up the regional average. Precise rankings of products are sensitive to the details of the classification criteria. Still, the products listed in Table 13.2 contribute substantially to intra-African trade. The top five food products account for about three-tenths of total intra-African trade in food, while the top five manufactured goods account for about one-eighth of the trade in their category. Several products, such as maize and cement, are exported almost exclusively within the region – as evidenced by regional orientation scores of 90 per cent and above – while the value of their exports in 2019 ran into hundreds of millions of dollars.

Table 13.2: Top five manufacturing and food products contributing to the regional orientation of African trade, 2019

Product group	Short description	Regional orientation (%)	Total exports ($ millions)	'Excess contribution' ($ millions)	HS code (Rev. 5)
Food	Fish	52	2124	824	0303
	Sugar	55	1986	823	1701
	Palm oil	92	539	426	1511
	Maize	90	429	328	1005
	Tobacco products	86	379	277	2402
Manufactures	Cement	91	838	649	2523
	Odoriferous substances*	92	817	640	3302
	Transport vehicles	26	3999	509	8704
	Plastic packaging	82	578	399	3923
	Fertilizers	25	3216	372	3105

Notes: Calculated from BACI data, at the four-digit HS level; see HS documentation for full descriptions of products. Total exports include intra-African exports and exports to the rest of the world. 'Excess contribution' to intraregional trade refers to the excess of the product's regional orientation above the average regional orientation (13%), multiplied by the total value of exports of the product.

*Refers mainly to food and beverage additives.

Unpacking the regional orientation of African trade by product clarifies how intraregional trade differs from Africa's trade with the rest of the world. While primary products (fuels, minerals and cash crops) dominate its exports to the rest of the world, manufactured goods and food are much more crucial to trade within the region. The regional orientation of Africa's overall trade may seem disappointing, but closer inspection of exports reveals some products that contribute significantly to elevating the intraregional share.

Step 3: Identifying intra-African trade potential

What are the prospects for expanded intraregional trade in Africa? The previous two steps of the analysis have focused successively on geographical patterns and on product composition. The first illustrated key insights from the gravity model, such as the general tendencies for trade flows to concentrate within subregions and for longer-distance trade links to connect larger economies. The second illustrated key insights from the notion of economic complementarity, with intra-African trade tending to concentrate in product groups like manufactured goods and food, which find a 'natural' match between African exporters and African importers. The third and final step in the analysis considers geographic and economic patterns simultaneously, to gain greater insight into the potential for expanded intraregional trade.

The approach here is to revisit the geography of bilateral trade flows from the first step, filtering to focus exclusively on the product groups that exhibited the strongest regional orientation (food and manufactured goods) in Step 2. If progress in expanding intraregional trade is most likely to occur in places and for products that are already being traded widely, this exercise will help us to zoom in on the potential for trade growth. The rationale is that change tends to be incremental – not necessarily to say that it must be slow or fast, just that it is reasonable to expect it to happen one step at a time. More profound changes may accumulate over time, but even ambitious policy initiatives cannot erase geographical and economic factors that structure current trade patterns.

Figure 13.4 includes only trade in food and manufactured goods, which makes all the network lines thinner than in Figure 13.1. These 'high-potential' products account for about three-fifths of total intraregional trade, and other exports fall away. Yet some patterns look similar in both figures, these being flows in which food and manufactured goods account for a large share of total trade. South Africa's status as a major hub within an active Southern African trade network survives, for example, as does Kenya's position as the hub of a smaller East African network. The most striking change is in Nigeria's position once its trade in primary products (especially fuels) is stripped away. Its importance as a trade partner within the West African subregion, and as an economic bridge to Southern Africa, are further diminished. Nigeria had the largest economy in all of Africa in 2019, yet its contribution to intraregional trade in food and manufactured products – as an exporter and as an importer – is surprisingly meagre.

Figure 13.4: Network cartogram of intra-African trade in goods (food and manufactured goods only), 2019 (see Figure 14.1)

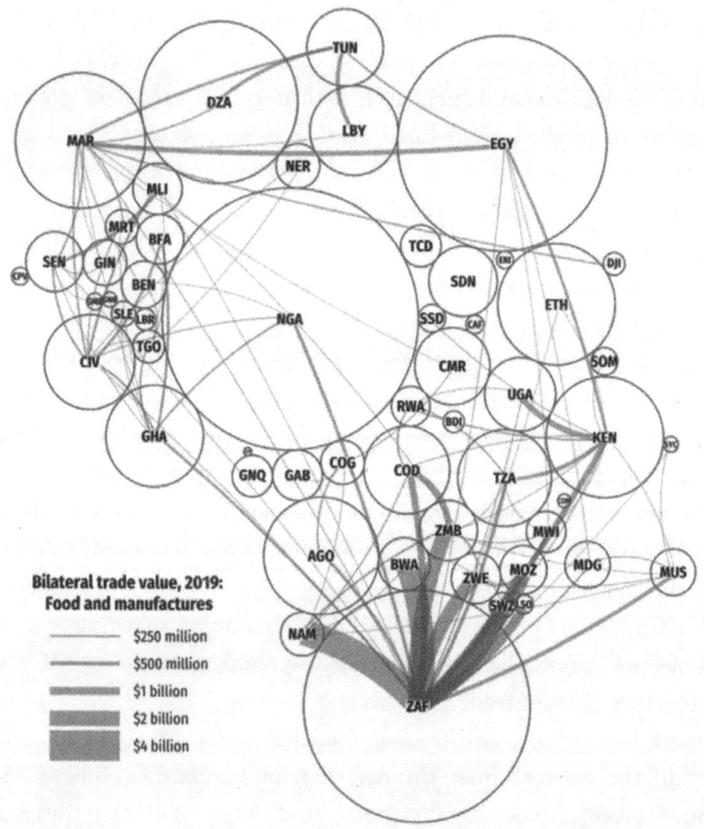

Figure 13.5 shows trade in food and manufactured goods by subregion. Compared with Figure 13.2, the circle representing Southern Africa becomes thinner but remains the thickest overall, as it trades more food and manufactured products internally than any other subregion. East Africa's trade, internally and with other subregions, resembles that shown in Figure 13.2, as its intraregional trade is less dependent on primary products. The biggest differences emerge for West Africa, where excluding Nigeria's resource trade predictably cuts significantly into the value of trade within the subregion and with Southern Africa.

Figure 13.5: Network cartogram of intra-African trade by subregion (food and manufactured goods only), 2019 (see Figure 13.2)

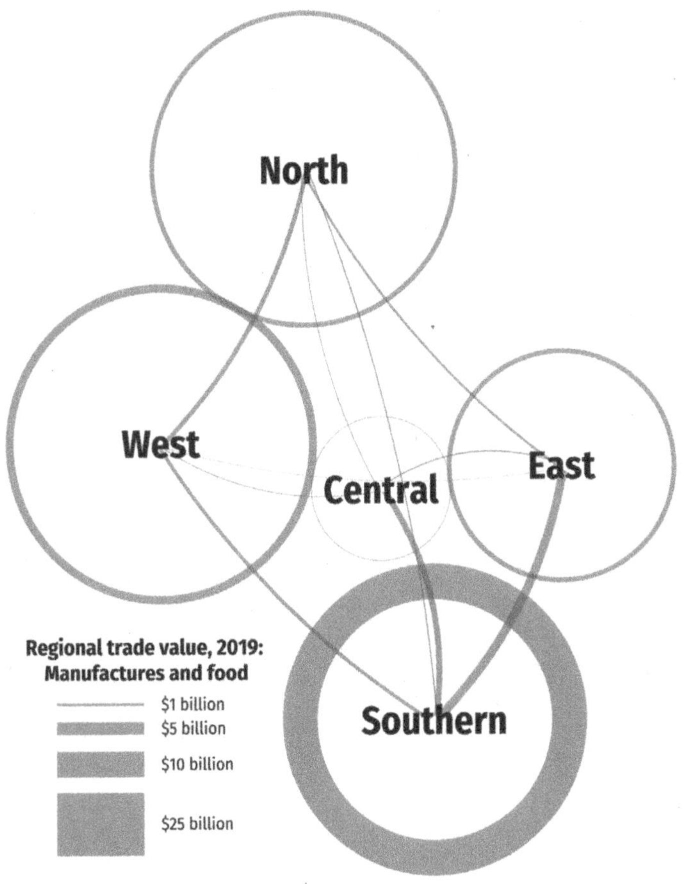

In sum, food and manufactured goods have had a proven record of contributing to the regional orientation of African trade, and this section has focused on the geographical pattern of these flows. The realised potential for intraregional trade in food and manufactured goods is most evident in Southern Africa, and to a lesser extent in East Africa. The picture in the rest of the continent is of modest flows within, and especially across, subregions. The limited involvement of Africa's largest economy, Nigeria, in intraregional trade in these high-potential products is especially striking. Zooming in on who trades what with whom in Africa helps to identify challenges to achieving economic integration on a continental scale.

Conclusion

In this chapter, I have sought to clarify the potential for expanded intraregional trade in Africa. I have explored the geography and product composition of intra-African trade flows, using bilateral trade data from 2019. In contrast to economic studies that take a wide-angle perspective, which compares African trade with statistical expectations estimated using data from several regions, I have zoomed in on the details of bilateral trade within Africa. The analysis has centred on data visualisations that represent important patterns of variation in who trades what with whom.

Gravity models offer the important insight that expanding intraregional trade is difficult in Africa because it is a large continent populated by small economies. Small economies, located far from one another, are unlikely to achieve high levels of trade. The network cartograms in this chapter confirm this tendency. The largest trade flows are between big economies and their neighbours. Hardly any large flows connect countries in different subregions. Flows between the North and Southern subregions and between the West and East subregions are negligible. Yet the pattern is far from uniform. The sharpest contrast is between the Southern and West subregions, which are home to the two biggest economies in Africa: South Africa and Nigeria. Southern Africa has by far the highest level of subregional trade, firmly linked to its South African hub. By comparison, the network cartograms of subregional trade in West Africa look like a thin cobweb, with Nigeria playing a small role, despite the impressive size of its economy.

The concept of trade complementarity offers the insight that intraregional trade is difficult in Africa because its countries are not 'natural trading partners'. The historical specialisation of most economies, so that they export mainly primary products and import mainly manufactured goods, creates economic mismatches. This characterisation is broadly accurate, but overlooks the kinds of products that African countries do trade with each other. Unpacking the regional orientation of African trade in various product groups revealed intraregional flows that look very different from flows between Africa and the rest of the world. Specifically, African exports of food and manufactured goods are, on average, about four times more likely to be consumed within Africa than are African exports of primary products. Some food and manufactured products have export values running into several hundred million dollars annually, in fact, and are destined almost exclusively for other African markets – products that include maize and cement.

These findings about the geographical patterns and product composition of intra-African trade can stimulate clearer thinking about initiatives to promote regional economic integration. Given the region's difficult geography, efforts to reduce barriers to trade need to go beyond stroke-of-the-pen trade policy reforms. They must also include sustained efforts to invest in transport infrastructure and improved customs administration. Current patterns of intra-African trade suggest that the food and manufacturing sectors are well positioned to benefit from real reductions in trade barriers and costs. Making trade easier within Africa will favour diversification to 'non-traditional' exports, at least marginally and admittedly from a small base. The chapter shows that levels of intra-African trade vary subregionally, with some subregions faring much better than others. Southern Africa has so far outpaced other parts of the continent, most notably West Africa. Given the gravitational drag on trade development and limited trade complementarities, achieving grand visions of continental integration will depend on first taking incremental steps to remove practical barriers to trade between neighbouring countries.

References

Alence, R. (2015). 'Trading with the frenemy: How South Africa depends on African trade', in G. Khadiagala, P. Naidoo, D. Pillay and R. Southall (eds). *New South African Review 5*. Johannesburg: Wits University Press, pp. 284–97.

Butts, C.T. (2022). 'network: Classes for relational data', The Statnet Project. R package version 1.17.1.

Butts, C.T. (2008). 'network: A package for managing relational data in R,' *Journal of Statistical Software*, 24(2): 1–36.

Dorling, D. (1996). 'Area cartograms: Their use and creation', in *Concepts and Techniques in Modern Geography*, Series 59. Norwich: School of Environmental Sciences, University of East Anglia.

Elbadawi, I. (1997). 'The impact of regional trade and monetary schemes on intra-sub-Saharan Africa trade', in A. Oyejide, I. Elbadawi and P. Collier (eds). *Regional Integration and Trade Liberalization in Sub-Saharan Africa*, Vol. 1, *Framework, Issues and Methodological Perspectives*. London: Macmillan, pp. 210–55.

Foroutan, F. and Pritchett, L. (1993). 'Intra-sub-Saharan African trade: Is it too little?' *Journal of African Economies*, 2: 74–105.

Gaulier, G. and Zignago, S. (2010). *BACI: International Trade Database at the Product-Level: The 1994–2007 Version*, CEPII Working Papers No. 2010–23. Paris: Centre d'Etudes Prospectives et d'Informations Internationales.

Geda, A. and Seid, E.H. (2015). 'The potential for internal trade and regional integration in Africa', *Journal of African Trade*, 2: 19–50.

Geda, A. and Yimer, A. (2019). 'The trade effects of the African Continental Free Trade Area (AfCFTA): An empirical analysis'. Department of Economics, Addis Ababa University.

Golub, S. (2015). 'Informal cross-border trade and smuggling in Africa', in O. Morrissey, R. López and K. Sharma (eds). *Handbook of Trade and Development*. Cheltenham, UK: Edward Elgar, pp. 179–209.

Jerven, M. (2014). 'On the accuracy of trade and GDP statistics in Africa: Errors of commission and omission', *Journal of African Trade*, 1(1–2): 45–52.

Jeworutzki, S. (2020). 'cartogram: Create Cartograms with R', R package version 0.2.2. Available at: https://cran.r-project.org/web/packages/cartogram/index.html (Accessed 20 October 2021).

Liao, S., Kim, I.S., Miyano, S. and Zhu, F. (2020). 'concordance: Product Concordance.' R package version 2.0.0. Available through CRAN.

Olney, W.W. (2022). 'Intra-African trade', *Review of World Economics*, 158: 25–51. DOI:10.1007/s10290-021-00421-6.

Redding, S. and Venables, A. (2004). 'Geography and export performance:

External market access and international supply capacity', in R.E. Baldwin and L.A. Winters (eds). *Challenges to Globalization: Analyzing the economics.* Chicago, IL: University of Chicago Press, pp. 95–127.

Schiff, M. (2001). 'Will the real "natural trading partner" please stand up?' *Journal of Economic Integration*, 16(2): 245–61. Available at: https://www.e-jei.org/upload/B5510HKA0VAVU6KE.pdf (Accessed 25 October 2021).

Turkson, F.E. (2015). 'Integration and regional trade in sub-Saharan Africa', in O. Morrissey, R.A. Lopez and K. Sharma. *Handbook on Trade and Development.* Cheltenham, UK: Edward Elgar, pp. 210–31.

United Nations. (2021). *UN Comtrade.* Online trade database. Available at: http://comtrade.un.org/ (Accessed 25 October 2021).

UNCTAD. 2021. Classifications. Available at: https://hbs.unctad.org/classifications/ (Accessed 12 October 2021).

Van Beers, C. and Linnemann, H. (1988). 'Commodity composition of trade in manufactures and South–South trade potential', *Journal of Development Studies*, 27(4): 102–22.

World Bank. (2021). *World Development Indicators.* Online database (as updated 15 September 2021). Available at: https://databank.worldbank.org/source/world-development-indicators (Accessed 25 October 2021).

Yeats, A.J. (1999). *What Can be Expected from African Regional Trade Arrangements? Some empirical evidence*, Policy Research Working Papers, No. WPS2004. Washington, DC: World Bank.

Yeats, A.J. (1998). 'Does Mercosur's trade performance raise concerns about the effects of regional trade arrangements?' *World Bank Economic Review*, 12: 1–28. doi.org/10.1093/wber/12.1.1.

Yeats, A.J. (1990). 'On the accuracy of economic observations: Do sub-Saharan trade statistics mean anything?' *World Bank Economic Review*, 4(2): 135–56. Available at: https://EconPapers.repec.org/RePEc:oup:wbecrv:v:4:y:1990:i:2:p:135-56 (Accessed 25 October 2021).

Chapter Fourteen

Building continental institutions: The African Continental Free Trade Area

SIZO NKALA

Introduction

On 21 March 2018, 44 African heads of state and government signed the Agreement Establishing the African Continental Free Trade Area (AfCFTA) in Kigali, Rwanda. This paved the way for the establishment of the largest free trade area in the world – a bold undertaking by any measure. It was a watershed moment in what has been a long and arduous journey towards the realisation of the Pan-African aspiration of continental economic integration. On 30 May 2019, the Agreement entered into force having been ratified by more than 22 countries. The AfCFTA was officially launched in January 2021, a little over a year from the time of writing. As of March 2023, 46 countries had ratified the Agreement. The new trade regime seeks to eliminate barriers to trade, expand the market size and economies of scale for African firms and, thus, stimulate productivity, investment and economic growth in the long run. Article 3 of the Agreement states that the general objectives of the AfCFTA include creating a single liberalised market for goods and services, contributing to the movement of capital, goods and natural persons, and laying the foundation for the establishment of a Continental Customs Union in the future. This is to be done through the gradual elimination of tariffs and the implementation of trade facilitation measures aimed at reducing the stifling transaction costs. It is an ambitious task and, for a project of its magnitude, it is still too early to pass a judgement on the performance of the AfCFTA. Neither is this what this chapter intends to do.

This chapter proceeds from the view that the performance of the AfCFTA will hinge directly on the success or lack thereof of the institutionalisation of the rules, practices, procedures and routines that will mediate and structure intra-African trade relations under the AfCFTA. Indeed, regional integration is an exercise in building a viable and cross-border institutional infrastructure that will shape the choices and interactions of the concerned regional actors (Khadiagala, 2011). Through the various protocols on trade in goods, trade in services, dispute settlement and e-commerce, the AfCFTA trading regime brings into play new norms and standards to which state parties and businesses will have to adhere as they trade with one another across Africa. In other words, the AfCFTA is primarily a systematic corpus of rules and regulations designed to govern the intracontinental exchange and flow of goods and services. Hence its very existence and effectiveness depends on the adherence to those rules by the relevant actors. This submission problematises the challenges and opportunities for the institutionalisation of the system of rules that constitute the new free trade area. It discusses factors and conditions that may undermine or promote the institutionalisation of the AfCFTA. This is important because the lack of respect for and adherence to the rules under the new trade regime will render the AfCFTA non-consequential.

Institutionalisation: A conceptual analysis

The pervasiveness of institutions in every aspect of modern society has made them an object of sustained academic interest. Institutions can be understood as widely recognised, stable and accepted systems of rules, routines, procedures and practices that structure human interactions and relations across the political, social and economic spheres (Searle, 2005; Hodgson, 2007). They have also been conceived of as a set of formal and informal constraints, norms, traditions and conventions that influence action, choices and policy through a system of incentives and disincentives (North, 1990). Breaking away from the dominant structuralist view, Dequech (2009) emphasises the ideational dimension of institutions pointing out that institutions shape the identity of social agents by providing ways of organising, selecting and interpreting information. Hence, institutions are much more than rules that structure interaction but are also co-constitutive of the agents themselves who activate and reproduce the institutions. Since time immemorial, humans have deliberately and consciously invented and developed institutions to govern their relations and create orderly and sustainable societies. The process by which institutions (rules, procedures and norms) become a central, fundamental, valued and stable element of any sphere of human interaction is known as institutionalisation (Huntington, 1968; Judge, 2003; Palanza *et al.*, 2016). Thus, institutionalisation denotes the increasing significance of a specific set of rules and norms in structuring the choices and behaviours of agents and actors, be it in politics, economics, culture, sport or any other spheres. For Judge (2003: 501), institutionalisation is 'a general concept illuminating a process of institutional change' in the sense of institutions playing an increasingly important role in structuring and shaping social life. Mainwaring and Torcal (2006) and Ufen (2008) define institutionalisation as the process by which a practice becomes widely known and well established, if not universally accepted. Therefore, the institutionalisation of the AfCFTA means the growing acceptance of and compliance by the member states and other actors trading under the rules that make up the trade agreement establishing the new free trade area.

In his seminal work *Political Order and Changing Societies*, Huntington (1968) cited the level of political institutionalisation as the major determinant of the degree of political stability and violence. He contended that widespread political violence in the developing postcolonial countries in the Global South could be attributed to the low level of political institutionalisation. Huntington argued that 'without strong political institutions, society lacks the means to define and to realise its common interests' (Huntington, 1968: 10). To paraphrase Huntington, without strong trade institutions, Africa will struggle to form a stable trading community envisaged under the AfCFTA Agreement. Berman (1997) noted that effective and legitimate political institutions can serve as a common and trusted platform to resolve sectoral grievances. Thus, institutions can serve as an infrastructure that binds the society together. Palanza *et al.* (2016) were of the view that the importance of the US Congress, as an arena on which policy and political battles were decided, contributed to its high level of institutionalisation. This means that the rules and outcomes of congressional deliberation are accepted as legitimate by political players of opposing parties.

On the institutionalisation of political power in sub–Saharan Africa, Posner and Young (2007: 129) observed how 'formal institutional rules are coming to matter much more than they used to and have displaced violence as the primary source of constraints on executive behaviour'. This implies that political actors and agents in Africa have come to respect and accept the authority of formal rules in accessing and relinquishing political power. Other scholars have contributed to the understanding of institutionalisation by applying it to the analysis of political parties (Selznick and Broom, 1955; Levitsky, 1998; Randall and Svasand, 2002; Basedau and Stroh, 2008). The level of institutionalisation of political parties, as entities that are made up of a set of rules and procedures, is indicated by the soundness of the design of those rules and the extent to which the rules and procedures are valued by both party members and supporters. Moreover, Levitsky (1998) and Basedau and Stroh (2008) point out that an entity made up of procedures and rules is highly institutionalised if it is recognisable and differentiated from its environment. Systems of rules and procedures that achieve high levels of institutionalisation have been found to share certain fundamental qualities. Some of the widely cited qualities include complexity, boundedness, coherence, adaptability and utility, among others (Huntington, 1965, 1968; Polsby, 1968; Judge, 2003; Palanza *et al.*, 2016). Thus, the extent to which entities that consist of systems of rules and procedures can thrive and flourish is determined by their possession of these qualities.

Regional integration and institutionalisation

In the pursuit of regionalism or regional integration, systems of rules and procedures are indispensable. Regionalism and regional integration schemes – whether in the form of regional organisations, free trade areas or monetary unions – have succeeded or failed on the basis of the quality of their systems of rules and procedures (institutions) (Mistry, 2000; Jetschke, 2009; Rattanaseeve, 2014; Beeson, 2018). Regional integration arrangements or organisations are only as good as their level of institutionalisation. That is, the degree to which the rules and procedures that make up the regional entities are respected and complied with by the relevant regional actors, which is itself a function of the possession of qualities such as complexity, coherence, autonomy, boundedness and utility (see Huntington, 1965, 1968; Polsby, 1968). Beeson (2018) asserts that regional integration is not simply a result of geographical contiguity or cultural affinities. Instead, the crucial factor behind regional integration 'is the degree of institutionalisation that occurs at the regional level' (Beeson, 2018: 7). African regional integration schemes have all too often succumbed to a still birth due to severely low levels of institutionalisation. Noting the central role of institutions in driving continental integration, Fagbayibo (2018) bemoans the defective institutional capacity of the African Union Commission (AUC), which is characterised by a dysfunctional organisational system, poor recruitment process and low staff morale. This results in the failure to implement the African Union's policies and non-compliance by member states. The institutional design of the African Union has been criticised as limiting continental integration; it is said to be a fundamentally intergovernmental rather than a supranational organisation. Being an intergovernmental entity means that it possesses no legal or independent power so it is limited to issuing statements and agreements, which are not binding (Grimm and Katito, 2010; Fagbayibo, 2018). The limited powers of the African Union, Qobo (2007) argues, has led to its failure to impose standard rules on democratic and human rights norms and standards on its members. This lack of uniform political standards has thwarted the prospects of political institutionalisation at the regional level, which makes it difficult to coordinate and implement regional policies among countries with diverse political systems.

Lewis (2020) problematised the institutionalisation of regional conflict prevention mechanisms in the West African region. For him, the institutionalisation of conflict prevention involves a complex network of state, regional and non-state organisations. The historical and social commonalities between these organisations provide the foundation for cooperative institutionalisation. Lewis identifies commitment capacity and domestication of commitment, mobilisation capacity, vertical and horizontal partnership, harmonisation of policies and programmes, and multidimensional actors as the essential conditions for successful institutionalisation of regional conflict prevention mechanisms. Mistry (2000) laments that between 1960 and 2000, African attempts at regional economic integration have failed largely because regional agreements have not been translated into domestic policies and regulations, there has been a reluctance to cede national sovereignty for common interests, and a lack of effective enforcement of trade agreements. Hartzenberg (2011) is of the view that high trade transaction costs and poor regulatory frameworks have undermined the growth of intracontinental trade under regional integration schemes. Thus, the poor qualities of regional institutions lead to low levels of compliance among regional actors, which renders regional initiatives moribund. Factors that degrade the quality of regional institutions in Africa include the lack of human resource capacity and a lack of sufficient funding. Dependence on foreign development partners has also been cited as an important obstacle to the realisation of regional integration (Olaniyan, 2008; Parshotam, 2018).

Jetschke's (2009) analysis of the failure of the Association of Southeast Asian Nations (ASEAN), which was formed in 1967, also highlights the centrality of institutions in regional initiatives. The author points out that the ASEAN is characterised by 'light institutionalisation', which is defined as a lack of centralisation, formalisation, broad scope and broad membership that defined the organisation from the beginning. Rattanaseeve (2014) emphasises that the development of institutions is central to driving regional integration. The growth and development of the ASEAN institutions has been stunted by excessive informality and a strong commitment to national sovereignty and non–interference in the internal affairs of member states. The limited powers of the ASEAN Secretariat, its lack of resources and professional staff make it weak and dependent on the decisions of the heads of state. It therefore has limited autonomy, which is a key aspect of institutionalisation (see Polsby, 2003; Palanza, 2016). That said, this chapter examines the institutionalisation prospects and challenges of Africa's milestone continental integration initiative – the AfCFTA.

AfCFTA: A rules–based trading regime

At its core, the AfCFTA is a rules-based regional initiative. The rules are set to structure the behaviour of state parties as they engage in trade in order to achieve the goals and objectives of the agreement. The rules are outlined in a set of six protocols, namely the trade in goods, trade in services, dispute settlement mechanism, intellectual property rights, investment and e-commerce. In addition to the six protocols, the AfCFTA is also underpinned by operational instruments such as the Rules of Origin and the Schedules of Tariff Concessions, which detail further rules to be adhered to in the implementation of the agreement. The Protocol on Trade in Goods outlines the rules that will govern the trade in goods between state parties with a view to creating a single liberalised market for the flow and movement of goods between member states. The protocol has rules on non-discriminatory practices, including the application of the 'most favoured nation' treatment, national treatment and special and differential treatment. On the liberalisation, the protocol outlines rules on import and export duties, quantitative restrictions, schedules of tariff concessions, and the rules of origin principles. There are rules on customs cooperation, trade facilitation measures and trade remedies that are meant to expedite and reduce trade transaction costs. These include the application of anti-dumping and countervailing measures, and global and preferential safeguards. Part 6 of the protocol gives directions on the application of product standards and regulations within the AfCFTA, while part 7 deals with the treatment of special economic zones and how member states can protect infant industries in their territories. Further, part 8 outlines the conditions under which exceptions to the provisions of the protocol may be granted. These include the maintenance of public order; the protection of human, animal and plant life; the trade in gold and silver; products of prison labour; the protection of natural resources; and ensuring adequate domestic supplies of essential products. States are also allowed to take measures to protect their essential security interests and to remedy their critical balance of payments. According to part 10 of the protocol, a committee will be put in place to monitor, implement and evaluate the protocol. The AfCFTA Rules of Origin, which will determine the goods that can be traded under the terms of the agreement, is almost complete, with agreements having been reached on the criteria for conferring originating status on almost all tariff lines, save for a few. The Annex to the Rules of Origin has been published on the AfCFTA website.

The Protocol on Trade in Services outlines the rules governing the supply of services between member states, which includes the production, distribution, marketing, sales and delivery of services. The main objective of the protocol is to create a single and liberalised market for the supply and consumption of services between the AfCFTA state parties. Among the principles which are to govern the trade in services within AfCFTA include the 'most favoured nation' treatment, which means that a member state should treat services and service suppliers from a fellow member state no less favourably than it treats services and service suppliers from a third party (non-member state). State parties are obliged to be transparent and publish any information affecting the provisions of the protocol, except confidential information. Compatibility between the domestic regulations and terms of trade in services is emphasised and member states are tasked with establishing institutions to review any issues and disputes around trade in services. The protocol also elaborates on rules regarding the mutual recognition of standards, licences and certifications, the treatment of monopolies and exclusive service suppliers, the avoidance of anti-competitive business practices and restrictions on international payments and transactions. These measures are intended to grow intracontinental trade in services. However, states are permitted to apply restrictions to trade in services to protect their balance of payments, albeit in a non-discriminatory manner and in ways that do not negatively affect the financial and commercial interests of another state party. Trade in services will also be guided by principles such as progressive liberalisation, the promotion of market access, and the application of national treatment. Each member state is expected to provide a Schedule of Specific Commitments relating to its commitments on market access and national treatment. A Trade in Services Committee will be responsible for overseeing the implementation, monitoring and evaluation of the protocol.

The Protocol on Rules and Procedures on the Settlement of Disputes provides the basis for the administration of the Dispute Settlement Mechanism (DSM). This protocol will be critical to the institutionalisation of the AfCFTA. It outlines the rules and procedures to be followed in the resolution of disputes or conflicts between member states regarding the provisions of the AfCFTA. The administration of the DSM will be important in clarifying the rules and procedures of the AfCFTA, which, if done well, will promote trust and adherence among member states. The protocol spells out how complaints can be lodged by aggrieved parties, the adjudication of cases, the review of decisions and the implementation of the outcomes of adjudication. Other protocols on investment, intellectual property rights and e-commerce were still being negotiated at the time of writing. However, once the negotiations are complete, they will add greater scope to rules-based multilateral trading under the AfCFTA. This chapter considers how the rules and regulations of the AfCFTA, outlined in various protocols, can – to borrow the words of Huntington (1968) – 'gain stability and value'.

Opportunities and challenges for the institutionalisation of the AfCFTA

The value of the AfCFTA

One of the fundamental prerequisites for the effective institutionalisation of an organisation or set of rules is that it must be valuable to its members (Levitsky, 1998; Randall and Svasand, 2002; Basedau and Stroh, 2008). In the same manner, for the AfCFTA to be effective and develop as an institution, it must be valuable to the people and entities that have to comply with its rules. Palanza *et al.* (2016) found that the high level of institutionalisation attained by the US Congress was attributable to its effectiveness as a platform for determining policy options and achieving political objectives. Hence, the AfCFTA can also accomplish high levels of institutionalisation if member states deem it an effective platform for pursuing economic and political objectives. Businesses will also find it valuable if it reduces transaction costs, increases economies of scale and, thus, boosts profits. The establishment of the AfCFTA is a huge step towards the fulfilment of the Pan-Africanist goal of establishing an African Economic Community and, ultimately, a political union (Gumede, 2020). According to Manboah-Rockson (2020: 2), the launch of the AfCFTA 'marked the re-dedication of [the] Africa Union (AU) towards the attainment of the Pan-African vision'. If the African leaders' rhetoric is anything to go by, the AfCFTA holds immense ideological value, and its aim is to unite the African continent. The South African president, Cyril Ramaphosa, declared that the commencement of the AfCFTA was a 'clearest affirmation yet that Africa is determined to take charge of its own destiny' (The Presidency, Republic of South Africa, 2020). His Rwandan counterpart, Paul Kagame, noted that 'the Continental Free Trade Area symbolises our progress toward the ideal of African unity' (African Union, 2018a). At the time of writing, 36 out of 55 African countries had signed the trade agreement, indicating their willingness to adopt it and align their domestic rules and regulations for its implementation. However, this still leaves one third of African countries who are yet to ratify the agreement, over a year after it came into force. Perhaps its ideological value does not hold universal appeal on the continent, which may undermine its full institutionalisation.

Beyond the ideological value, the AfCFTA has also been shown to hold significant value in terms of its economic potential. Numerous studies have been conducted to show the economic impact of the AfCFTA in Africa. According to the African Development Bank (2019), the removal of tariffs and non-tariff barriers (NTB) and the implementation of the trade facilitation agreement (TFA) would add US$100 billion (3.5 per cent) to the African GDP, increase total exports by US$295 billion and imports by US$293 billion by 2035. A 2020 study by the World Bank noted that, by 2035, the full implementation of the AfCFTA could increase real income gains by 7 per cent or US$450 billion. However, it warned that these gains would not be distributed equally, with countries such as the Ivory Coast and Zimbabwe likely to see bigger gains at 14 per cent, while Malawi, Madagascar and Mozambique would average only 2 per cent. Intracontinental exports would increase by 81 per cent, and manufacturing exports in intra-African trade would increase by 110 per cent, and 62 per cent overall (World Bank Group, 2020). Saygili *et al.* (2018) also found that the removal of tariffs would grow Africa's GDP by 0.97 per cent and increase its exports and imports by 2.5 per cent and 1.8 per cent, respectively. The economic value of the AfCFTA trade agreement seems to be immense. According to the institutionalisation theory, the economic value attached to the AfCFTA should translate to high levels of institutionalisation (Palanza *et al.*, 2016). However, as the World Bank report observed, the economic gains accruing from the AfCFTA deal will not be evenly distributed. Hence, the countries that stand to gain the least are unlikely to fully comply with the trade agreement. Pasara (2019) urged the AfCFTA to devise an equitable model of redistributing the benefits of the AfCFTA to avoid bias towards certain countries.

Complexity and internal organisation

Complexity is one of the most widely adopted indicators of the level of institutionalisation in the literature (Huntington, 1968; Polsby, 1968; Judge, 2003; Basedau and Stroh, 2008). In this chapter, the analysis of the complexity of the AfCFTA will focus on its internal organisation and structure, which includes its functional divisions and departments and how they relate to one another. The more complex an organisation or system, the more likely it is to be stable and secure and thus attain high levels of institutionalisation. AfCFTA's institutional framework consists of four organs: the Assembly, the Council of Ministers, the Committee of Senior Trade Officials and the Secretariat. According to the AfCFTA Agreement, the Assembly, which is the supreme decision-making organ of the African Union, consisting of heads of state and government, is the ultimate authority for the AfCFTA. It is responsible for interpreting the provisions of the agreement. The final interpretation of the agreement is done by consensus.

Figure 14.1. The institutional framework of the AfCFTA

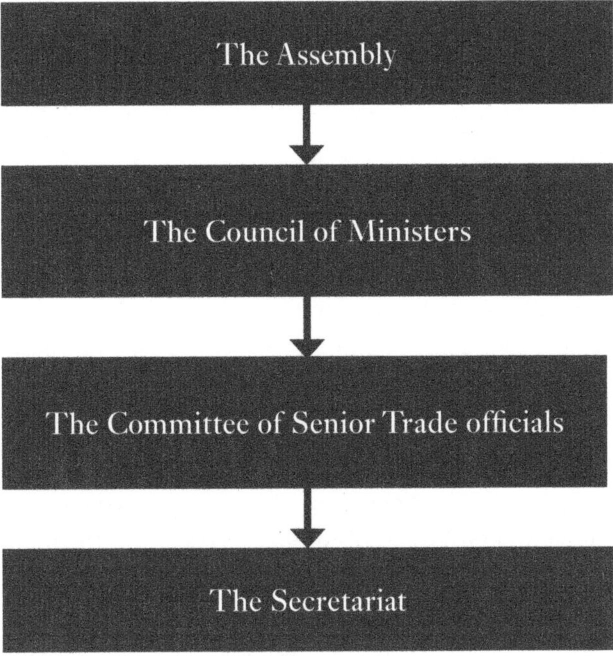

Source: African Union, 2018b. Agreement Establishing the African Continental Free Trade Area.

Below the Assembly is the Council of Ministers, which reports to the Assembly. The Council of Ministers is made up of state parties' ministers of trade or any official authorised by a state party. This council monitors the implementation and enforcement of the agreement. Its duties include overseeing the harmonisation of policies, supervising all committees, delegating responsibilities to committees, supervising the Secretariat, determining the organisational structure and budgets of the Secretariat and making recommendations to the Assembly. Scheduled to meet twice a year, the decisions of the Council are binding on state parties. Coming third in the chain of authority is the Committee of Senior Trade Officials, which is made up of permanent secretaries or senior bureaucrats designated by state parties. This organ is responsible for implementing the decisions of the Council of Ministers, developing action plans for implementation, and ensuring the proper functioning of the AfCFTA, including directing the Secretariat to perform specific assignments. This committee meets at least twice a year and reports the proceedings of the meetings to the Council. It is concerning that the decision-making organs of the AfCFTA meet only a few times a year. The Secretariat is embedded within the AU system and enjoys functional autonomy with an independent legal personality. Its budget is drawn from the annual budget allocation of the AU, while its responsibilities are decided by the Council of Ministers. The Secretariat is also mandated to work with state parties in the implementation of the various protocols making up the AfCFTA Agreement. Further, the Secretariat has its headquarters in Accra, Ghana. All decisions in the AfCFTA framework are adopted by consensus; however, issues of procedure can be settled by a simple majority. Each of the Protocols on Trade in Goods and Services have been assigned specific committees, which are conduits through which the Council of Ministers implements, monitors and evaluates the AfCFTA provisions. The protocol committees are also responsible for producing annual reports for state parties' consideration. The Protocol on Rules and Procedures on the Settlement of Disputes is administered by the Dispute Settlement Body (DSB) established under Article 5 of the protocol. The DSB oversees the appointment of panels to adjudicate on matters brought before it and ensures the implementation of rulings.

Although the AfCFTA has an elaborate and clear organogram, it falls short on several fronts, thus undermining the prospects of the institutionalisation of the free trade area. First, the organisational structure is excessively top down as it is dominated by the state parties, with no presence of private sector or civil society actors. Businesses are ultimately responsible for implementing the rules of the AfCFTA, so their representation in the organisation's structures would provide an opportunity for them to make an input in the decisions and give feedback to the authorities for better implementation (Grant and Byers, 2021). For example, in Ghana, the host of the AfCFTA Secretariat, a report showed that only 26.2 per cent of the firms knew about the AfCFTA (World Bank, Ghana Statistical Service and the UNDP, 2020). Compliance with the rules will be very low or very costly if the business community is not part of the AfCFTA initiative. Grant and Byers (2021) further highlight that businesses can even decide not to use the AfCFTA when moving goods across borders if they are not sure about its implications or if they find compliance costly. Civil society organisations come in handy in spreading public awareness of the AfCFTA rules and safeguarding public interests. As Fagbayibo (2019) rightly notes, the reduction of tariffs and the operation of the new trade regime will have implications for public welfare, which need to be taken into consideration. This will also enhance the democratic legitimacy and acceptance of the AfCFTA, thus contributing to its institutionalisation (see Berman, 1997; Judge, 2003). Without the involvement of civil society in the AfCFTA processes, it will be difficult to spread information about the body. One of the commonly identified characteristics of effectiveness is the public recognition and perception of the organisation (Levitsky, 1998; Randall and Svasand, 2000). If civil society's participation in the AfCFTA is limited, the organisation will struggle to gain a public image of its own, which will limit the extent of its development as an institution. Moreover, the Secretariat, which is responsible for running the operations of the AfCFTA, seems to be too dependent on political structures such as the Assembly and the Council of Ministers. In an analysis of the failed institutionalisation of the ASEAN, Rattanaseeve (2014) argued that one of the causes of the failure was that the ASEAN Secretariat was too dependent on the decisions made by the political leaders. The Secretariat had no power to make its own decisions, which weakened the regional institutions. It will be difficult for the AfCFTA Secretariat to set itself apart from the AU and form an independent and recognisable identity, which has been widely cited as an essential element of effective institutionalisation (Palanza *et al.*, 2016). Moreover, the AfCFTA Secretariat's dependence on the political organs of the AU will affect its recruitment of qualified and professional staff. Politically motivated appointments will negatively affect the professionalisation, and, consequently, the effectiveness of the Secretariat in discharging its mandate. Palanza *et al.* (2016) and Polsby (1968) argued that professionalisation was an important indicator of the institutionalisation of the US legislature. Another major weakness is the thin presence of the AfCFTA Secretariat beyond its headquarters in Ghana. Being present in only one location makes it difficult for the Secretariat to coordinate a continent-wide implementation of the AfCFTA rules. The AfCFTA Secretariat must be visible across Africa to ensure the enforcement of the agreement (Basedau and Stroh, 2008).

The autonomy of the AfCFTA

Autonomy is an indispensable quality for successful institutionalisation (Levitsky, 1998; Mistry, 2000; Judge 2003). A free trade area with the magnitude and scope of the AfCFTA is certainly no exception. Article 13 of the AfCFTA Agreement emphasises that the Secretariat will be an autonomous body with an independent legal personality. Article 14(5) goes on to state that 'the funds of the Secretariat shall come from the overall annual budgets of the African Union'. Ensuring that the Secretariat is not dependent on any external sources for funding is important to protect it from undue influence and to maintain its autonomy. However, it is doubtful that the AU, itself heavily dependent on external finance and unreliable contributions from member states, will be able to fully fund the AfCFTA Secretariat to execute its ambitious mandate. A staggering 70 per cent of the AU Commission's budget is sourced from external donors (Louw-Vaudran, 2016). In October 2020, 18 countries, about one third of the AU membership, were under sanctions for defaulting on their payments (The Conversation, 2020). This funding gap is filled by powerful external actors whose interests and influence may jeopardise the autonomy of the AfCFTA Secretariat. China, a country with vast economic and political interests in Africa, pledged to provide cash assistance to capacitate the Secretariat (Mwareya and Bhobho, 2021). China is estimated to have more than 10 000 enterprises in Africa, with many Chinese manufacturers moving to the continent to take advantage of cheap labour. Hence, the AfCFTA tariff elimination is likely to benefit Chinese firms located in Africa more than it will benefit African businesses since the majority of African citizens do not have the capital to start businesses in their own countries (see Adeshokan, 2021). Other external, corporate actors, such as the African Development Bank (AfDB) and the African Export Import Bank (Afreximbank), have also chipped in to cover the funding shortfalls. The AfDB signed a US$4.8 million institutional support grant for the AfCFTA Secretariat in 2019. The Afreximbank has pledged a US$1 billion contribution to the AfCFTA Adjustment Fund, which is intended to help state parties and private-sector players adjust to the systemic changes that have been brought about by the advent of the AfCFTA. These funds will certainly go a long way to strengthen the institutions of the new free trade area. However, countries such as China, Japan, the United States and the European Union are major shareholders in these banks, so it is not far-fetched to doubt if the funding from the aforementioned banks makes the AfCFTA immune from undue influence. If the AfCFTA is to execute its mandate effectively in the interests of continental integration, its Secretariat must have an independent source of funds.

Moreover, the interest in the AfCFTA's autonomy is not only linked to its sources of funding. The AfCFTA is an ambitious scheme that depends on the cooperation of a vastly diverse set of actors with different and highly sensitive interests. The AfCFTA has to reconcile the interests of big business and small businesses operating in different sectors, least developed, developing and middle-income countries, labour and consumers. This is a challenging task. As Pasara (2019) has observed, some state parties are unwilling to eliminate tariffs because of the polarisation of benefits, with a few large and coastal countries reaping the most benefits, while small and landlocked countries are likely to suffer welfare losses. According to some estimates, the elimination of tariffs will result in fiscal losses of over US$4 billion in the short term (Oramah, 2021). Some countries, especially poor countries who have no significant domestic industrial base or tax base and depend on tariffs for revenue, will lose more than others. Ndonga *et al.* (2020) point out that countries such as South Africa, Kenya and Egypt, with a robust manufacturing capacity, will benefit more than countries like Malawi, with negligible manufacturing capacities, who depend on exports of primary commodities and import most of the things they need. Least developed countries such as Malawi get 27 to 65 per cent of their government revenues from trade taxes, so eliminating tariffs will significantly erode the government's revenue base. Odijie (2019) argues that the AfCFTA will produce winners and losers among different stakeholders such as governments, manufacturers, consumers and labour. For example, the removal of tariffs on some products may result in governments losing revenue, domestic industries being outcompeted and workers losing their jobs. The loss of revenue and the protection of domestic industries are some of the reasons why free trade areas in regional economic communities have largely failed (Ndonga *et al.*, 2020). As Akeyewale (2018) argues, 50 per cent of Africa's GDP is controlled by South Africa, Egypt and Nigeria, while the continent's six island states control just 1 per cent of Africa's GDP. It is apparent that the AfCFTA is a trading bloc characterised by excessively high levels of income disparity. This is perhaps why, more than a year since its launching at the time of writing, very little trade has taken place under the new trade deal (Fabricius, 2021). It is very difficult for highly unequal countries to agree on a single trading regime without the weaker parties having to make substantial sacrifices. The question is whether the AfCFTA will be able to protect its autonomy from the powerful countries and act in a manner that advances continental and not national interests. Moreover, the AfCFTA should strive to consider the divergent interests of diverse actors in its rules of origin, which determine the eligibility of products to be traded under the AfCFTA terms and conditions. Depending on how they are designed, the rules of origin can advance the interests of some sectors and regions at the expense of others. Therefore, it is important for the AfCFTA to maintain its autonomy and act impartially when considering the interests of the actors involved. A continental integration scheme such as the AfCFTA can only succeed if its members believe they are being treated fairly. Ajibo (2019) is pessimistic about the capacity of Africa's least developed countries to implement the rules of origin requirements and trade facilitation measures. He writes that these countries are already struggling to implement the World Trade Organization (WTO) trade requirements, so they do not have the technical capacity to administer the terms of the AfCFTA Agreement.

Supranationalism and national sovereignty

Africa's past and current regional integration initiatives have been severely stunted by the chronic tension between supranationalism and national sovereignty (Qobo, 2007; Hartzenberg, 2011). Continental institutions such as the African Union, the Pan-African Parliament, the Peace and Security Council and now the AfCFTA are by no means supranational institutions. As Grimm and Katito (2010) noted, they are fundamentally intergovernmental enterprises that have no identity outside their constituents. When it comes to regional and continental integration arrangements, national sovereignty still takes precedence over regional and continental sovereignty. This leaves regional and continental institutions without the legal power to enforce their mandates and agreements. The implementation of their initiatives depends on the goodwill and political will of member states, which is not there in most cases. Nyirabu (2004) argues the same point, noting that supranationalism is yet to take root in Africa with African states unwilling to transfer their sovereignty to regional and continental institutions.

Chingono and Nakana (2009) also observed that the failure of regional integration in southern Africa under the Southern African Development Community (SADC) is due to the dominance of nationalism. 'Not only is the celebration of nationalism likely to cause more hostility than unity between and among the countries and peoples of the sub-region, but it also leads to incompatible policies which are difficult to harmonize' (Chingono and Nakana, 2009: 402). It is unfortunate that the AfCFTA does not have any legal powers. The implementation and legality of the Agreement Establishing the AfCFTA depends on its ratification by member states. It is up to the member states to align their domestic laws and regulations to the terms of the agreement and to enforce them. Thus, instead of a single and centralised authority responsible for monitoring and enforcing the agreement, the AfCFTA will potentially have 55 sovereign centres of power. Without the centralisation of authority, the AfCFTA rules and regulations will not be applied uniformly. This will make trading under the AfCFTA come with prohibitively cumbersome and costly compliance requirements for businesses. In the end, the trading rules will lose their universality, which is a fundamental element of high levels of institutionalisation. Hence, the AfCFTA's potential to achieve substantial institutionalisation is greatly undermined by the subordination of supranationalism to national sovereignty.

Conclusion

Africa has a long history of regional and continental integration initiatives. The AfCFTA is the latest in a long line of regional integration arrangements. However, the continent has enjoyed limited success when it comes to regional integration with most of the schemes becoming neglected and moribund before they are even implemented. This has set the regional integration programme back significantly. Existing scholarship has widely attributed the failure of these initiatives to institutional deficiency. If care is not taken, the AfCFTA is likely to suffer the same fate. Therefore, this chapter has problematised the dynamics of the institutionalisation of regional integration schemes with a view to mapping out the opportunities and challenges of the institutionalisation of the AfCFTA. Such factors as the AfCFTA's instrumental (economic) and ideological value, its complex internal organisational structure and the level of its autonomy will have a positive impact on its institutionalisation. However, the unequal distribution of benefits of free trade, the undermining of the AfCFTA's autonomy by powerful interests, both inside and outside the continent, and the underfunding of the AfCFTA Secretariat threaten the successful institutionalisation of the AfCFTA Agreement. Moreover, the excessively top-down structure of the AfCFTA, which is characterised by state domination to the exclusion of other actors such as the business community, think tanks and civil society organisations, will militate against the realisation of high levels of institutionalisation of the AfCFTA.

References

Adeshokan, O. (2021). 'China is the biggest winner from Africa's New Free Trade Bloc', *Foreign Policy*, 19 August 2021. Available at: https://foreignpolicy.com/2021/08/19/africa-china-afcfta-free-trade-economy-investment-infrastructure-competition/ (Accessed 27 January 2022).

Afreximbank. (2022). 'AfCFTA Secretariat and Afreximbank sign an agreement for the management of the AfCFTA Adjustment Fund'. Available at: https://www.afreximbank.com/afcfta-secretariat-and-afreximbank-sign-an-agreement-for-the-management-of-the-afcfta-adjustment-fund/ (Accessed 23 February 2022).

African Development Bank Group. (2019). 'AU, African Development Bank sign $4.8 million grant earmarked for continental free trade secretariat'. Available at: https://www.afdb.org/en/news-and-events/au-african-development-bank-sign-48-million-grant-earmarked-continental-free-trade-secretariat-28574 (Accessed 19 February 2022).

African Development Bank. (2019). *African Economic Outlook 2019*. Abidjan, Côte d'Ivoire: ADB.

African Union. (2018b). 'Agreement Establishing the African Continental Free Trade Area.' Available at: https://au.int/sites/default/files/treaties/36437-treaty-consolidated_text_on_cfta_-_en.pdf (Accessed 27 January 2022).

African Union. (2018a). 'Keynote Address by President Paul Kagame, Chairperson of the African Union, at AfCFTA Business Forum, 20 March 2018'. Available at: https://au.int/en/speeches/20180320/keynote-address-president-paul-kagame-chairperson-african-union-afcfta-business (Accessed 24 January 2022).

Ajibo, C.C. (2019). 'African continental free trade area agreement: The euphoria, pitfalls and prospects', *Journal of World Trade*, 53(5).

Akeyewale, R. (2018). 'Who are the winners and losers in Africa's Continental Free Trade Area?' Geneva: World Economic Forum. Available at: https://www.weforum.org/agenda/2018/10/africa-continental-free-trade-afcfta-sme-business/ (Accessed 15 January 2022).

Basedau, M. and Stroh, A. (2008). Measuring Party Institutionalization in Developing Countries: A New Research Instrument Applied to 28 African Political Parties. GIGA Research Programme: Legitimacy and Efficiency of Political Systems, No. 69, February 2008.

Beeson, M. (2018). 'Institutionalizing the Indo-Pacific: The Challenges of Regional Cooperation', *East Asia*, 35: 85–98. https://doi.org/10.1007/s12140-018-9288-3.

Berman, S. (1997). 'Civil society and political institutionalization', *American Behavioral Scientist*, 40(5): 562–74.

Chingono, M. and Nakana, S. (2009). 'The challenges of regional integration in Southern Africa', *African Journal of Political Science and International Relations*, 3(10): 396–408.

Dequech, D. (2009). 'Institutions, social norms, and decision-theoretic norms', *Journal of Economic Behavior & Organization*, 72(1): 70–78.

Fabricius, P. (2021). 'The apparent false start of Africa's free trade deal may be the first of several to come', *Daily Maverick*, 3 December 2021. Available at: https://www.dailymaverick.co.za/article/2021-12-03-the-apparent-false-start-of-africas-free-trade-deal-may-be-the-first-of-several-to-come/ (Accessed 12 February 2022).

Fagbayibo, B. (2019). A Case for Democratic Legitimacy of the AfCFTA Process. Afronomics Law, 17 January 2019. Available at: https://www.afronomicslaw.org/2019/01/16/a-case-for-democratic-legitimacy-of-the-afcfta-process/ (Accessed 21 January 2022).

Fagbayibo, B. (2018). 'Nkrumahism, Agenda 2063, and the role of intergovernmental institutions in fast-tracking continental unity', *Journal of Asian and African Studies*, 53(4): 629–42.

Grant, C.M. and Byiers, B. (2021). 'The AfCFTA: From institutional structures to private sector engagement', The Centre for Africa–Europe Relations (ECDPM), 12 April 2021. Available at: https://ecdpm.org/talking-points/afcfta-institutional-structures-private-sector-engagement/ (Accessed 24 January 2022).

Grimm, S. and Katito, G. (2010). *African Developments: Continental integration in Africa – AU, NEPAD and the APRM*, Briefing Paper, No. 4/2010. Bonn: Deutsches Institut für Entwicklungspolitik (DIE).

Haftel, Y.Z. and Wajner, D.F. (2018). 'Linking economic performance and regional institutionalization: more local, less global?' in G. Press-Barnathan, R. Fine and A.M. Kacowicz (eds). *The Relevance of Regions in a Globalized World*. London: Routledge.

Hartzenberg, T. (2011). *Regional Integration in Africa*, WTO Staff Working Paper, No. ERSD-2011-14. Geneva: World Trade Organization (WTO). http://dx.doi.org/10.30875/fad9df15-en.

He, K. and Feng, H. (2020). 'The institutionalization of the Indo-Pacific: problems and prospects', *International Affairs*, 96(1): 149–68.

Hodgson, G.M. (2007). 'Institutions and individuals: interaction and evolution', *Organization Studies*, 28(1): 95–116.

Huntington, S.P. (1968). *Political Order and Political Decay. Political order in changing societies.* New Haven, CT: Yale University Press.

Huntington, S.P. (1965). Political development and political decay', *World Politics*, 17(3): 386–430.

Jetschke, A. (2009) 'Institutionalizing ASEAN: Celebrating Europe through network governance', *Cambridge Review of International Affairs*, 22(3): 407–26. DOI: 10.1080/09557570903107688.

Judge, D. (2003). 'Legislative institutionalization: a bent analytical arrow?' *Government and Opposition*, 38(4): 497–516.

Khadiagala, G. (2011). *Institution Building for African Regionalism*, ADB Working Paper Series on Regional Economic Integration No. 85, August 2011. Abidjan: African Development Bank.

Levitsky, S. (1998) 'Institutionalization and Peronism: The concept, the case and the case for unpacking the concept', *Party Politics*, 4(1): 77–92.

Lewis, R.B.J. (2020). 'West Africa: Cooperative institutionalization of conflict prevention mechanisms in regional subsystems', *Conflict Studies Quarterly*, 30: 55–71.

Louw-Vadran, L. (2016). 'A new financing model for the AU: Will it work?' *ISS Today*. Pretoria: Institute for Security Studies. Available at: https://issafrica.org/iss-today/a-new-financing-model-for-the-au-will-it-work (Accessed 19 January 2022).

Mainwaring, S. and Torcal, M. (2006). 'Party system institutionalization and party system theory after the third wave of democratization', in R.S. Katz and W. Crotty (eds). *Handbook of Party Politics*. London, Thousand Oaks, CA: SAGE Publications, pp. 204–27.

Manboah-Rockson, J.K. (2020). 'Launch of the African Continental Free Trade Area (Afcfta) within Agenda 2063: An assessment of the "actorness" of the African Union (AU) in international relations (IR)'. Available at: http://dx.doi.org/10.2139/ssrn.3535518 (Accessed 6 February 2022).

Mistry, P.S. (2000). 'Africa's record of regional integration and cooperation', *African Affairs*, 99: 553–73.

Mwareya, R. and Bhobho, N. (2021). 'Will China help or hurt the AfCFTA?' *The Africa Report*, 2 February 2021. Available at: https://www.theafricareport.com/61451/will-china-help-or-hurt-the-afcfta/ (Accessed 13 January 202).

Ndonga, D., Laryea, E. and Chaponda, M. (2020). 'Assessing the potential impact of the African continental free trade area on least developed countries: A case study of Malawi', *Journal of Southern African Studies*, 46(4): 773–92.

North, D.C. (1990). A transaction cost theory of politics', *Journal of Theoretical Politics*, 2(4): 355–67.

Nyirabu, M. (2004). 'Appraising regional integration in southern Africa', *African Security Studies*, 13(1): 21–32.

Odijie, M.E. (2019). 'The need for industrial policy coordination in the African Continental Free Trade Area', *African Affairs*, 118(470): 182–93.

Olaniyan, O. (2008). 'Challenges in achieving regional integration in Africa'. Keynote address at the Southern African Development Forum on progress and prospects in the implementation in Southern Africa. Organized by UNECA-SA, Lusaka, Zambia, 29–31 May 2008.

Oramah, B.O. (2021). 'Facilitating the transformational AfCFTA: Tools for eliminating bottlenecks'. Brookings, 11 March 2021. Available at: https://www.brookings.edu/blog/africa-in-focus/2021/03/11/facilitating-the-transformational-afcfta-tools-for-eliminating-bottlenecks/ (Accessed 20 January 2022).

Palanza, V., Scartascini, C. and Tommasi, M. (2016). 'Congressional institutionalization: A cross-national comparison', *Legislative Studies Quarterly*, 41(1): 7–34.

Parshotam, A. (2018). *Can the African Continental Free Trade Area offer a new beginning for trade in Africa?* Occasional Papers, Trade and Investment, SAII Programme. Available at: https://saiia.org.za/research/can-the-african-continental-free-trade-area-offer-a-new-beginning-for-trade-in-africa/ (Accessed 10 October 2022).

Pasara, M.T. (2020). 'An overview of the obstacles to the African economic integration process in view of the African continental free trade area', *Africa Review*, 12(1): 1–17.

Polsby, N.W. (1968). 'The institutionalization of the US House of Representatives', *American Political Science Review*, 62(1): 144–68.

Posner, D.N. and Young, D.J. (2007). The institutionalization of political power in Africa', *Journal of Democracy*, 18(3): 126–40.

Qobo, M. (2007). 'The challenges of regional integration in Africa: In the context of globalisation and the prospects for a United States of Africa'. Institute for Security Studies Papers, No. 145, p. 16.

Randall, V. and Svåsand, L. (2002). 'Political parties and democratic consolidation in Africa', *Democratization*, 9(3): 30–52.

Rattanasevee, P. (2014). 'Towards institutionalised regionalism: The role of institutions and prospects for institutionalisation in ASEAN', *SpringerPlus* 3(556): 1–10. https://doi.org/10.1186/2193-1801-3-556.

Saygili, M., Peters, R. and Knebel, C. (2018). 'African Continental Free Trade Area: Challenges and opportunities of tariff reductions.' UNCTAD Research Paper No. 15. Geneva: United Nations Conference on Trade and Development.

Selznick, P. and Broom, L. (1955). *Sociology: A text with adapted readings.* New York: Harper & Row.

Searle, J.R. (2005). 'What is an institution?' *Journal of Institutional Economics*, 1(1): 1–22.

The Conversation. (2020). 'How member states and partners impede the African Union's quest for financial autonomy', *The Conversation*, 22 December 2020. Available at: https://theconversation.com/how-member-states-and-partners-impede-the-african-unions-quest-for-financial-autonomy-151115 (Accessed 13 January 2022).

The Presidency, Republic of South Africa. (2020). Opening statement by African Union Chairperson President Ramaphosa at the 13th Extraordinary Session of the AU Assembly on AfCFTA, 5 December 2020. Available at: https://www.thepresidency.gov.za/speeches/opening-statement-african-union-chairperson-president-ramaphosa-

13th-extraordinary-session-au-assembly-afcfta (Accessed 13 January 2022).

The World Bank, Ghana Statistics Service and UNDP. (2020). 'How COVID-19 is affecting firms in Ghana: Results from the Business Tracker Survey – Wave 2'. Available at: https://www.gh.undp.org/content/ghana/en/home/library/poverty/ghana-covid-19-business-tracker-wave-2.html (Accessed 23 January 2022).

Ufen, A. (2008). Political party and party system institutionalization in Southeast Asia: Lessons for democratic consolidation in Indonesia, the Philippines and Thailand', *The Pacific Review*, 21(3), 327–50.

World Bank Group. (2020). *The African Continental Free Trade Area: Economic and distributional effects*. Washington DC: International Bank for Reconstruction and Development. Available at: http://localhost:14773//entities/publication/1c04980c-dcd8-5bd9-9abc-a028630500db (Accessed 21 November 2021).

Chapter Fifteen

The AfCFTA Protocol on Trade in Goods
TENIOLA TAYO AND MICHAEL ODIJIE

Introduction

The Protocol on Trade in Goods is one of the most important parts of the agreement establishing the African Continental Free Trade Area (AfCFTA), because it lays the foundation for the rest of the trade Agreement. This protocol (which is laid out in 32 articles from pages 17 to 30 of the Agreement; see AfCFTA Agreement 2019) deals with the terms for trading in physical items. Trade in physical goods is distinct from trade in services; the latter involves the sale and delivery of intangible products and is covered in a different protocol. The Protocol on Trade in Goods deals with the terms for trading goods under the AfCFTA. The main objective of this protocol is to create a free trade area (FTA) in the form of a liberalised African market for the exchange of goods, which will help to lay the foundation for the establishment of a Continental Customs Union (UNCTAD, 2021: 15; AfCFTA Agreement, 2019: 17–30). This protocol specifies a set of six related objectives to realise the principal goal of boosting intra-African trade in goods by reducing tariff and non-tariff hindrances to trade; progressively eliminating tariffs; progressively eliminating non-tariff barriers (NTBs); enhancing the efficiency of customs procedures, trade facilitation and transit; enhancing cooperation to overcome technical barriers to trade and sanitary and phytosanitary measures; developing and promoting regional and continental value chains; and enhancing socioeconomic development, diversification and industrialisation across Africa (AfCFTA Agreement, 2019: 19).

This chapter discusses the Protocol on Trade in Goods within the framework of the six abovementioned objectives. This protocol also has nine annexes, all of which will be alluded to in the objectives,[1] a most favoured nation clause and four provisions for trade remedy and safeguard measures.

The six objectives/measures of the protocol

The first stated objective to bring about the vision of the Protocol on Trade in Goods is the progressive elimination of tariffs. The schedule for tariff concessions on trade in goods is part of Phase I of the AfCFTA negotiation process (Lunenborg, 2019). According to the agreed modalities, the AfCFTA seeks to liberalise 97 per cent of tariff lines and 90 per cent of imports by the end of the implementation period, which is between five and 15 years. This means that duties will remain at most 3 per cent of tariff lines and 10 per cent of imports.

This liberalisation plan acknowledges differences in the sizes of the economies and development levels of African countries, leading to the following categorisation: non–Least Developed Countries (non-LDCs), Least Developed Countries (LDCs), and G6 countries. The non–LDCs are required to liberalise 90 per cent of tariff lines within five years and 97 per cent of tariff lines within 10 years. The LDCs have 10 years to liberalise 90 per cent of tariff lines, with 97 per cent to be liberalised within 13 years. The G6 countries have 15 years to liberalise 90 per cent of tariff lines (Hartzenberg, 2019). Table 17.1 summarises the schedule for eliminating tariff lines. These distinctions are necessitated by the recognition that tariff concessions present higher opportunity costs for some LDCs and G6 countries, as tariffs are an important source of government revenue for these countries. However, it is estimated that the total tax revenue for African countries under the full implementation of the AfCFTA will decrease by less than 1 per cent in the short term (Arenas and Vnukova, 2019). Similarly, the World Bank research into the economic and distributional effects of the AfCFTA estimated that tariff revenues would decline by less than 1.5 per cent for most countries and more than 1.5 per cent for the Republic of Congo (3.4 per cent), The Gambia (2.7 per cent), the Republic of Congo

---

1   'Annexes' in this case means an instrument attached to a protocol; each of these instruments forms an integral part of the AfCFTA Agreement. The nine annexes cover tariff concession schedules; rules of origin; customs cooperation and mutual administrative assistance; trade facilitation; non-tariff barriers; technical barriers to trade; sanitary and phytosanitary measures; transit; and trade remedies (AfCFTA Agreement, 2019:19).

(2.1 per cent) and Zambia (1.6 per cent) (World Bank, 2020).[2]

Table 15.1: Schedule for eliminating tariff lines for LDCs, non-LDCs and G6 countries

	LDCs	Non-LDCs	G6 countries[3]
Full liberalisation	90% of tariff lines	90% of tariff lines	90% of tariff lines
	10-year phase down	5-year phase down	15-year phase down
Sensitive products	7% of tariff lines	7% of tariff lines	Not yet determined
	13-year phase down (current tariffs can be maintained during first 5 years, with phase down mandatory from year 6)	10-year phase down (current tariffs can be maintained during first 5 years, with phase down mandatory from year 6)	
Excluded products	3% of tariff lines	3% of tariff lines	Not yet determined

Source: United Nations (2022)

The progressive elimination of tariffs is expected to help integrate the AfCFTA signatory countries gradually into the free trade area by preventing the sudden inflow of goods from one country to another. A progressive approach is needed to allow countries to adjust to the AfCFTA, because there are instances where sudden changes in trade could have negative social and even political consequences. Countries are also permitted to completely exclude 3 per cent of goods from the FTA, provided this does not make up more than 10 per cent of the goods traded. These allowances

---

2   The World Bank study also showed that the AfCFTA would lead to an increase in real income, an increase in the volume of total exports (with manufacturing exports gaining the most), boosting regional output by US$211 billion by 2035, all of which would lead to a reduction in poverty and boost Africa's income by $450 billion by 2035 (a gain of 7 per cent) while adding US$76 billion to the income of the rest of the world.

3   G6 countries: Ethiopia, Madagascar, Malawi, Sudan, Zambia and Zimbabwe.

are indented to allow countries to pursue industrial policies or protect domestic sectors of social importance (Odijie, 2019). Apart from the three categories of differentiation adopted in the schedule for the elimination of tariff lines, most countries have very specific local political and economic processes that give rise to vested interests that may not be in line with the trade initiatives. Some of these political processes are informal and, therefore, cannot be represented in trade negotiation positions, especially in an agreement such as the AfCFTA, the form of which is agreed at the continental level.[4] Such state-level interests may frustrate the implementation of the planned elimination of tariff lines and introduce other barriers that are non-tariff in nature. Indeed, the above framework is similar to the Regional Economic Communities (RECs) in Africa, which have not been successfully implemented due to local circumstances. For example, in the East African Community (EAC), different countries have arbitrarily refused to institute trade liberalisation because of local circumstances. For many years, Savannah Cement, which is produced in Kenya, was not accorded preferential treatment when exported to Uganda because of Uganda's local cement industry; likewise, Del Monte Kenya's exports of pineapple juice in Tetra Paks were not accorded preferential treatment in Rwanda because of a domestic producer of juice with links to the government (EAC NTB, 2015). In 2016, Tanzania arbitrarily imposed a high tariff rate on Kenyan plastic products (EAC NTB, 2015). A reporting and monitoring mechanism could help to solve this problem.

The second of the six related objectives/measures under the Protocol on Trade in Goods, is the progressive elimination of non-tariff barriers (NTBs). While tariffs are a kind of formal taxation that is imposed on imported goods, NTBs comprise several procedures, prohibitions and conditions that function to hinder trade (WTO, 2020). In the context of trading in Africa, NTBs pose a bigger obstacle than tariff barriers (Knebel, 2020; Njiteu, 2021; Zongo and Oyelami, 2021). Standard NTBs can range from administrative to bureaucratic obstacles to trade, and they may also be unjustified and improper applications of non-tariff measures (Erasmus, 2020). Non-tariff measures are policy instruments that are designed primarily to protect public health or the environment

---

4   Theoretically, even if such political interests could be represented in negotiation positions, most African countries lack the political, legal and economic expertise required to undertake such trade negotiation. They also lack proper channels for communication between vested interests capable of blocking the implementation of trade agreements and trade negotiators.

(such as sanitary and phytosanitary standards), but, in the process, they can affect trade considerably through compliance and procedural costs. NTBs include (but are not limited to) pretexts for non-tariff measures. These could be bureaucratic obstacles, corruption (including demands for bribes), restrictive licensing processes, certification challenges and many more. In the AfCFTA Protocol on Trade in Goods, NTBs are defined as any 'barriers that impede trade through mechanisms other than the imposition of tariffs' (AfCFTA Agreement, 2019: 18), and Annex 5 to this protocol deals specifically with NTBs (Compiled Annexes on AfCFTA, 2020: 26). The NTB Annex provides a conceptual categorisation of what are considered NTBs as well as a mechanism for identifying, categorising and progressively eliminating NTBs in practice (AfCFTA, 2020, Article 3).

Article 4 of the NTB Annex calls for the creation of a subcommittee (under the Committee on Trade in Goods) composed of designated representatives of state parties to establish a procedure for the implementation of Annex 5, as well as monitor its implementation and undertake periodic reviews regarding its elimination. The state parties shall also establish an NTB Coordination Unit (to coordinate the elimination of NTBs, working with the NTB subcommittee, the National Focal Points and the RECs); a National Monitoring Committee (to identify, resolve and monitor NTBs); and National Focal Points (to facilitate the removal of NTBs and report on their elimination). All of these efforts are focused on the creation of NTB monitoring mechanisms responsible for identifying, reporting and monitoring NTBs within the AfCFTA. An NTB reporting mechanism is a platform enabling traders to submit complaints about NTB-related issues experienced while trading. These complaints are taken up by National Focal Points, appointed specifically to resolve the problems reported. These mechanisms currently exist in some forms in different regions as part of the regional integration project. For example, the ECOWAS Borderless Alliance allows individuals in trading chains (transporters, forwarding agents, traders, trade and transport stakeholders, private companies, policy-makers, etc.) to register barriers to trade online with their country's Focal Point (Borderless Alliance, 2020; Vhumbunu and Rudigi, 2021). Similarly, the East African Community (EAC) has a Time-Bound Programme for the Elimination of NTBs, which is based less on day-to-day NTBs than that of ECOWAS (Argent, 2011). A tripartite mechanism has also been established by the Common Market for Eastern and Southern Africa (COMESA), the East

African Community (EAC) and the Southern African Development Community (SADC).

The AfCFTA NTB Reporting, Monitoring and Eliminating Mechanism builds on these regional initiatives.[5] Annex 5 (Appendix 2) explains the *Procedure for Elimination and Co-operation in the Elimination of Non-Tariff Barriers;* accordingly, state parties must exhaust online reporting mechanisms at the regional level before escalating complaints or trade concerns to the AfCFTA level. Indeed, the AfCFTA monitoring mechanisms are closely linked to those of the RECs, which is a problem because the REC mechanisms have been an unmitigated failure. For example, the focus of the ECOWAS mechanism has drifted away from more structural NTB issues that require high-level consultation to petty issues such as police stops (Odijie *et al.*, 2022). This drift is because of a lack of political buy-in, which has led corporate traders to ignore the mechanism due to insufficient political interest. Given that disputes arising from the implementation of Annex 5 are to be settled by states in accordance with the AfCFTA Protocol on Dispute Settlement, and that private parties have no standing (Erasmus, 2020), a strong political buy-in is needed for the AfCFTA NTB mechanism to be effective. This is problematic because some NTBs are deeply political. However, one advantage of the AfCFTA NTB Reporting, Monitoring and Eliminating Mechanism is that it is a member-driven arrangement, with no supranational institution to impose requirements on the states involved. Therefore, the effectiveness of this mechanism will be based on what states make of it. This is a far better approach than creating a legal instrument or supranational institution to act on behalf of the states or to request compliance. Such a supranational institution is bound to fail to the degree that it cannot enforce compliance at the state level. With the current formula, states will negotiate and implement NTBs according to their trade needs with political buy-in, as is currently the case. There is a direct link between NTBs and trade facilitation, as well as customs procedure and transit, which are covered under the third specific objective of the Protocol on Trade in Goods.

The third specific objective of this protocol is to enhance the efficiency of customs procedures, trade facilitation and transit. The third objective is specified in multiple overlapping annexes. Annex 3 contains mainly provisions on customs procedures (Compiled Annexes on AfCFTA,

---

5 As of 13 January 2020, anyone can report an NTB to intra-African trade via the AfCFTA NTB Reporting, Monitoring and Eliminating Mechanism. Available at: https://tradebarriers.africa/resolved_complaints (Accessed 20 November 2022).

2020), and calls for the harmonisation of customs tariff nomenclatures and customs procedures, the automation of customs operations, cooperation on information exchanges, and technical cooperation. Annex 4, on trade facilitation, calls for the simplification and harmonisation of international trade procedures, as well as logistics to expedite the processes of importation, exportation and transit. This is to be done through the state publication of trade processes, the establishment of Enquiry Points, advance rulings on trade applications, pre-arrival processing, electronic payments, the quick release of goods, and much more. A key trade facilitation structure is the Designated Competent Authorities (DCAs), the state organisations whose primary task is to issue the Certificate of Origin needed for countries to trade under the AfCFTA.

The Certificate of Origin is proof that a particular product complies with the rules of origin applying in the AfCFTA. Rules of origin (RoO) are legal criteria used to determine the national source of a product in the context of international trade. Within the AfCFTA, the RoO specify the conditions under which a product traded between parties to the agreement can claim local origin status and, therefore, benefit from the preferences offered by the AfCFTA. This prevents countries outside of the AfCFTA from benefitting from the preferences through re-exportation. Products that cannot demonstrate compliance to local origin will be traded outside of the AfCFTA free trade area. The AfCFTA follows an approach to RoO that is similar to the one used in various African RECs – preferences are given to products only if it can be demonstrated that they originated from one or more of the economic parties of the AfCFTA. This approach entails that trading products have to be wholly produced in AfCFTA states; furthermore, in cases where non-originating inputs are used in the production of a product, that these are substantially transformed within the AfCFTA state party (or parties, under the cumulation provisions).

The Protocol on Trade in Goods and its relevant annexes leave much room for manoeuvre in their stipulations regarding the make-up and duties of the DCAs. In most countries, the DCAs are now seen as a focal point for trading under the AfCFTA, especially for coordinating other parts of the AfCFTA (such as Enquiry Points and Focal Points for NTB mechanisms, and much more). A successful trade transaction under the AfCFTA requires the interaction of the DCAs in the trading countries involved. Although most countries are locating their DCAs in local customs, few are seeking to create distinct entities that will bring together stakeholders beyond their customs agencies. For example,

Ghana located its DCA in a customs division of the Ghana Revenue Authority (GhanaWeb, 2021), but this is potentially a problem because revenue generation is sometimes at odds with trade facilitation. This challenge illustrates the political negotiations that are accompanying the domestication of the AfCFTA at the national level. Related to this are the varying levels of capacity and transparency of agencies within countries and the challenges that may arise as they begin to interface with each other to jointly ensure the efficiency of customs procedures. A country with an inefficient public service is likely to exhibit the same inefficiency in the context of the AfCFTA implementation. However, very little can be done about this at the regional level, as the AfCFTA is country-led. The AfCFTA Secretariat could offer training to national agencies after determining their specific needs and weaknesses; however, some of these weaknesses are political rather than technical problems that require training to solve.

The fourth objective of the Protocol on Trade in Goods is to enhance cooperation in the areas of technical barriers to trade and sanitary and phytosanitary measures, as explicated in Annex 6 and Annex 7. Annex 6 covers issues relating to standards, technical regulations, conformity assessment procedures, accreditation and metrology in the state parties. The state parties have agreed that the World Trade Organization's technical barriers to trade agreement (as well as sanitary and phytosanitary measures) shall form the basis of the AfCFTA. This objective is related directly to NTBs because states sometimes interpret technical barriers to trade (non-tariff measures) as NTBs; hence, one of the objectives of this annex is to 'facilitate trade by the elimination of unnecessary and unjustifiable technical barriers to trade' (Compiled Annexes on AfCFTA, 2020). This is done by adopting international best practices, as well as strengthening cooperation between states. Due to their protectionist tendencies, many African countries may rely on technical barriers as a form of protectionism when direct tariffs cannot be imposed. This may be the case for countries with large consumer markets but low productive capacity and a strong protectionist tendency, such as Nigeria (McCulloch *et al.*, 2017). A classic example of this is the trade war over milk in the EAC (Wakabi, 2020). This started when Kenya decided to protect its milk sector from imports from Uganda, which seemed to have a comparative advantage in milk production. Kenya first raised doubts about Uganda's milk production capacity, due to its price advantage, but these doubts were debunked through a fact-finding mission in 2019. Kenya then effectively banned the importation of milk from Uganda, insisting that it was suspicious about the quality of Ugandan exports and uncertain that the country met food safety control standards. In essence, Nairobi said that it had found Ugandan imports to contain levels of aflatoxins that were consistently higher than safety limits (Blanshe, 2021). In essence, given that health and safety organisations are positioned at the state level, states can easily use these pretexts to protect their local industries. Increased cooperation on technical barriers to trade and sanitary and phytosanitary measures would prevent states from using safety as a pretext to impose protection and disrupt trade.

The fifth objective is to develop and promote regional and continental value chains. Indeed, this objective is one of the overarching aims of the AfCFTA, as it has the potential to expand the input market for producers in Africa. Regional and continental value chains are also crucial for the inclusion of small and medium-sized enterprises (SMEs) in the AfCFTA, as they can be embedded in the supply chains of large-scale producers that can afford the costs of cross-border trade. One of the premises of the AfCFTA is that freer trade between African countries will function to boost productive activities and industrialisation because producers have potential sources of inputs and market for their products (Luke, 2019). The development of new value chains through the AfCFTA is also predicated on the rules of origin, which stipulate the minimum criteria for determining the eligibility of goods for preferential trade under the AfCFTA. Goods can be considered to have originated from an AfCFTA state party if they were wholly obtained in the corresponding state or if they have undergone substantial transformation in that state.[6] Currently, the AfCFTA RoO require traded goods to have 40 per cent local content, but with wide variations. The imported content of traded goods can be up to 60 per cent.[7] The RoO further clarify the transformation processes that cannot be considered as conferring origin. These include simple processes that do not require special skills, machines or tools, granted that these skills, machines or tools do not contribute to the product's essential characteristics or properties. These processes are detailed in Table 15.2.

6   Compiled Annexes to the Protocol on Trade in Goods on the Establishment of the Continental Free Trade Area. Available at: https://www.tralac.org/documents/resources/cfta/1999-compiled-annexes-to-the-afcfta-agreement-legally-scrubbed-signed-16-may-2018/file.html (Accessed 18 November 2021).

7   Update on Rules of Origin of the African FTA. Presentation by Francis Mangeni, Head of Trade Promotion and Programmes, AfCFTA Secretariat. Available at: https://na.eventscloud.com/file_uploads/7a357c7b3ff61107cdb579c24aac44d1_FrancisMangeniEN.pdf (Accessed 18 November 2021).

Table 15.2: Working or processing not conferring origin

(a) operations exclusively intended to preserve products in good condition during storage and transportation;

(b) breaking-up or assembly of packages;

(c) washing, cleaning or operations to remove dust, oxide, oil, paint or other coverings from a product;

(d) simple ironing or pressing operations;

(e) simple painting or polishing operations;

(f) husking, partial or total bleaching, polishing or glazing of cereals and rice;

(g) operations to colour sugar or form sugar lumps, partial or total milling of crystal sugar;

(h) peeling, stoning or shelling of vegetables of Chapter 7, fruits of Chapter 8, nuts of Heading 08.01 or 08.02 or groundnuts of Heading 12.02, fruits, nuts or vegetables;

(i) sharpening, simple grinding or simple cutting;

(j) simple sifting, screening, sorting, classifying, grading or matching;

(k) simple packaging operations, such as placing in bottles, cans, flasks, bags, cases, boxes or fixing on cards or boards;

(l) affixing or printing marks, labels, logos, and other like distinguishing signs on the products or their packaging;

(m) simple mixing of materials, whether or not of different kinds which does not include an operation that causes a chemical reaction;

(n) simple assembling of parts of articles to constitute a complete article;

(o) a combination of two or more operations specified in sub-paragraphs (a) to (n); and

(p) slaughter of animals.

Source: Compiled Annexes to the Protocol on Trade in Goods on the Establishment of the Continental Free Trade Area

Complementary production policies may require an assessment of the competitive advantages of firms in the context of the political interests of state parties, thereby teasing out possible areas for production specialisation aided by direct state-to-state negotiation. Harmonisation alone – without direct negotiation – would create several problems with coordination. Many African countries have similar production structures and interests, leading to a collective focus on a narrow set of goods and, consequently, competition for markets and foreign investment in the same goods (Byiers *et al.*, 2018). Fragmented and disjointed production strategies in the context of a free trade area are a flaw for which the AfCFTA has been criticised (Odijie, 2019). The core assumption of those framing the AfCFTA – namely that freer trade will create better value chains in Africa – is deeply problematic. It may be self-evident that freer trade will lead to better trade in the textbook sense; however, domestic interests render this difficult. In areas of Africa in which successful value chains are developing, such as that of cement production in West Africa (see Dangote Cement, 2021), there has been direct negotiation between states according to their political realities. For example, Dangote Cement negotiated with the governments of Benin and Togo, paying a fee to both (Adeshokan, 2020), to allow its cement to be exported. It also negotiated different deals with Senegal, Cameroon and Ghana, according to their local realities (Dangote Cement, 2021). Although cement is supposed to be freely traded in the West African region, no countries abide by this rule. Had Dangote Cement assumed that the region's free trade rule would allow the company to export its products, it would have faced real political challenges from neighbouring countries. Indeed, the development of regional value chains faces major challenges in relation to legitimacy and enforcement by regional bodies (which do not have the political basis required to impose implementation), as well as inconsistencies in political will between national governments, which is where actual power resides (Tayo, 2021).

The final objective of the Protocol on Trade in Goods is to enhance socioeconomic development, diversification and industrialisation across Africa. This enhancement is expected to be the outcome of some of the other objectives; that is, better trade between African countries will lead to the creation of new production chains, which will then provide the bases for industrialisation and diversification (Signé, 2019; AfDB, 2021). This objective requires no further explication, but the idea that freer trade among

African countries will lead to industrialisation is somewhat ahistorical. Industrialisation, by which we mean the development of industries in a country, has historically been brought about through industrial policies. Industrial policies are deliberately structured to generate the development and growth of industries or promote structural transformation within a country (Whitfield and Zalk, 2020). Indeed, one of the main historical arguments against free trade is that it is inimical to the use of industrial policies because it takes away the policy space needed for states to institute the kinds of industrial policies used by now-developed countries during their development (Chang, 2006). Those framing the AfCFTA have acknowledged this. The excluded list (comprising the 3 per cent of products that will not be liberalised) is in essence an attempt to give countries policy space to exclude the products that they wish to protect using industrial policies. However, as in the RECs, the exclusion list creates new problems of coordination because most African countries tend to have industrial policies in similar industries, which thus closes down the regional/continental market for exports (Odijie, 2019).

Historically, there has been a sequential relationship between the building of domestic productive capabilities in a product line (production) and the pursuit of freer trade in the same product (looking for a market for products). As in Nigeria, which protected its cement industry for over a decade (Akinyoade and Uche, 2018) and turned to promoting freer trade when the industry became strong enough to compete, free trade negotiations are dependent on what states sell to other states. Countries that have already gone through the process of industrialisation (such as South Africa) stand a chance of gaining more from the AfCFTA. Likewise, countries with developed sectors (such as cement in Nigeria) also stand a chance of gaining from the AfCFTA. However, the problem of linking the AfCFTA with automatic industrialisation is that very few such cases exist. Although the geographical fragmentation of global production processes (explicated through global value chains) means that open trade can promote an industrial policy through a cheaper supply of inputs, it does not render the historical mode of industrialisation obsolete.

Conclusion

The Protocol on Trade in Goods is a major pillar of the AfCFTA Agreement that will guide the implementation of the AfCFTA. Its main objective is to boost intra-African trade for collective African development through measures such as trade liberalisation and the elimination of NTBs, as well as other possible barriers created by customs procedures and technical barriers to trade. It is envisioned that this protocol, when implemented, will lead to the development of regional and continental value chains, and promote diversification and industrialisation. Although the agreement generally adopts a continent-level discourse, it is essentially a member-driven arrangement without a supranational institution to impose requirements on the states. This is an advantage, because some of the main problems with existing trade agreements in African countries, such as the Economic Partnership Agreement between several African regions and the European Union, arise from the disconnection between the terms of the agreement at the regional level and their feasibility at the level of the state (Interview with a trade negotiator, 2021). Some groups at the state level have the political power to block regional agreements and they use this power accordingly if the agreements go against their interests. Ideally, such domestic 'interest groups' should be factored into the process of negotiating the AfCFTA, because it is member-state driven. However, most African countries lack proper channels of communication between domestic vested interests and the negotiators of trade agreements. Such interests will block certain policies after they have been negotiated.

Furthermore, there are several other obstacles to tariff elimination for the broader objective of increasing intra-African trade and industrialisation. High trade costs, such as transport costs and compliance costs, along with on-the-ground constraints, are some of the main hindrances to intra-African trade (World Bank, 2012). More trade in goods between African countries would require transport infrastructure that is currently lacking, leading to high transport costs. High transport costs would also make it harder for SMEs to participate in the AfCFTA, as they do not have the benefits of economies of scale. Some measures have been put in place to address these high transport costs, such as the Single African Air Transport Market (SAATM). The SAATM seeks to liberalise intra-African air transport, resulting in lower air transport costs for goods traded within the continent (Abate, 2016; Lubbe and Shornikova, 2017; Njoya, 2017). In addition, the African Development Bank has committed to investing US$2 billion in AfCFTA-enabling infrastructure (Ukpe, 2021). However, this falls short given the bank's estimation that the continent's infrastructure financing needs will reach US\$170 billion a year by 2025, with an estimated gap of around US\$100 billion a year (Kato, 2021). A more pragmatic approach to reducing transport costs in the short term would involve expanding on the routes already established by large exporters. Logistics firms would also enjoy economies of scale as a result of specialising in transport and handling. Another type of trade infrastructure that is currently lacking is marketplaces to connect African buyers and sellers. These marketplaces are crucial for connecting demand with supply within the continent. The rise of marketplaces such as Alibaba has helped to increase trade between African countries and China (Peiyue, 2020). Linked to this is the need for payment systems to ease the interaction between currencies within the continent. A Pan-African Payment and Settlement System has been set up by the AfCFTA Secretariat and the AfreximBank (Peiyue, 2020).

References

Abate, M. (2016). 'Economic effects of air transport market liberalization in Africa', *Transportation Research Part A: Policy and Practice*, 92: 326–37.

African Development Bank (AfDB). (2011) 'African Development Bank and AfCFTA Secretariat partner to stimulate industry'. Available at: https://www.afdb.org/en/news-and-events/press-releases/african-development-bank-and-afcfta-secretariat-partner-stimulate-industry-46499 (Accessed 15 April 2022).

Adeshokan, O. (2020). 'Border closures will not stop Dangote expansion', *The Africa Report*, 19 June. Available at: https://www.theafricareport.com/30461/border-closures-will-not-stop-dangote-expansion/ (Accessed 15 April 2022).

Akinyoade, A. and Uche, C. (2018). Development built on crony capitalism? The case of Dangote Cement. *Business History*, 60(6): 833–858.

Arenas, G. and Vnukova, Y. (2019). *Short-Term Revenue Implications of Tariff Liberalization under the African Continental Free Trade Area (AfCFTA)*. Washington, DC: World Bank.

Blanshe. M. (2021). 'Kenya's ban of Ugandan milk points to flaws in soft diplomacy', *The Africa Report*, 30 March. Available at: https://www.theafricareport.com/71198/kenyas-ban-of-ugandan-milk-points-to-flaws-in-soft-diplomacy/ (Accessed 20 November 2021).

Byiers, B., Karaki, K. and Woolfrey, S. (2018). *The Political Economy of Regional Industrialisation Strategies*, ECDPM Discussion Paper No. 237. Brussels: The Centre for Africa-Europe Relations. Available at: https://ecdpm.org/publications/the-political-economy-of-regional-industrialisation-strategies/ (Accessed 15 April 2022).

Chang, H.J. (2006). 'Policy space in historical perspective with special reference to trade and industrial policies', *Economic and Political Weekly*, 627–33.

Compiled Annexes on AfCFTA. (2020). Available at: https://afcfta.au.int/en/documents/2020-12-28/compiled-annexes-establishment-afcfta (Accessed 20 November 2021).

Dangote Cement. (2021). 'Operations'. Available at: https://www.dangotecement.com/operations/#:~:text=Dangote%20Cement%20is%20Africa's%20leading,across%20Africa%20as%20at%202020 (Accessed 15 April 2022).

EAC NTB. (2015). 'Status of elimination of non-tariff barriers in the East African Community as of December'. Available at: http://repository.eac.int/bitstream/handle/11671/1620/NTB%20December%202015-%20V1.pdf?sequence=1&isAllowed=y (Accessed 15 April 2022).

Erasmus, G. (2020). 'Does the AfCFTA have a formula to tackle Africa's non-tariff barriers?' tralac Blog, 28 July. Available at: https://www.tralac.org/blog/article/14801-does-the-afcfta-have-a-formula-to-tackle-africa-s-non-tariff-barriers.html (Accessed 15 April 2022).

GhanaWeb. (2021). 'Customs Division of GRA designated to issue rules of origin certificates'. Available at: https://www.ghanaweb.com/GhanaHomePage/business/Customs-Division-of-GRA-designated-to-issue-rules-of-origin-certificates-1148654 (Accessed 15 April 2022).

Golub, S.S. (2012). 'Entrepôt trade and smuggling in West Africa: Benin, Togo and Nigeria,' *The World Economy*, 35(9): 1139–61. https://doi.org/10.1111/j.1467-9701.2012.01469.x.

Hartzenberg, T. (2019). The African Continental Free Trade Area Agreement – what is expected of LDCs in terms of trade liberalisation? Available at: https://www.un.org/ldcportal/afcfta-what-is-expected-of-ldcs-in-terms-of-trade-liberalisation-by-trudi-hartzenberg/ (Accessed 15 April 2022).

Kato, R.L. (2021). 'What will it take to fill Africa's growing infrastructure deficit?', *Africa News*, 5 October. Available at: https://www.africanews.

com/2021/10/05/what-will-it-take-to-fill-africa-s-growing-infrastructure-deficit//#:~:text=The%20African%20Development%20Bank%20estimates,finance%20to%20complement%20public%20resources (Accessed 15 April 2022).

Knebel, C. (2020). 'Breaking down non-tariff barriers' Great Insights Magazine, 26 March. Brussels: The Centre for Africa–Europe Relations ECDPM. Available at: https://ecdpm.org/great-insights/african-continental-free-trade-area-agreement-impact/breaking-down-non-tariff-barriers/ (Accessed 15 April 2022).

Lubbe, B. and Shornikova, S. (2017). 'The development of African air transport', in K. Button, G. Martini and D. Scotti (eds). *The Economics and Political Economy of African Air Transport*. London: Routledge, pp. 16–39.

Luke, D. (2019). 'Making the case for the African Continental Free Trade Area' in D. Luke and J. Macleod (eds). *Inclusive Trade in Africa: The African Continental Free Trade Area in comparative perspective*. London: Routledge, pp. 5–12.

Lunenborg, P. (2019). '"Phase 1B" of the African Continental Free Trade Area (AfCFTA) Negotiations', South Centre, Policy Brief, No. 63(4).

McCulloch, N., Balchin, N., Mendez-Parra, M. and Onyeka, K. (2017). *Local Content Policies and Backward Integration in Nigeria*. ODI SET Paper. Available at: https://set.odi.org/local-content-backwardintegration-in-nigeria (Accessed 15 April 2022).

Njoya, E.T. (2016). Africa's single aviation market: The progress so far', *Journal of Transport Geography*, 50: 4–11.

Njiteu, R.R.L. (2021). 'Assessing the impacts of eliminating Non-Tariff Barriers in the framework of the African Continental Free Trade Area on Cameroon's economy', Global Trade Analysis Project, GTAP Resource No: 6329. Available at: https://www.gtap.agecon.purdue.edu/resources/res_display.asp?RecordID=6329 (Accessed 15 April 2022).

Odijie, M.E. (2019a). 'The need for industrial policy coordination in the African Continental Free Trade Area', *African Affairs*, 118(470): 182–93.

Odijie, M.E. (2019b). 'Africa should focus on industrialisation. Free trade will follow', *The Conversation*. Available at: https://theconversation.com/africa-should-focus-on-industrialisation-free-trade-will-follow-127142 (Accessed 15 April 2022).

Peiyue, C. (2020). 'China's African traders confront a formidable new foe: Alibaba', *Sixth Tone*. Available at: https://www.sixthtone.com/news/1006459/chinas-african-traders-confront-a-formidable-new-foe-alibaba (Accessed 15 April 2022).

Prag, E. (2013). 'ASR Forum: Engaging with African informal economies: Mama Benz in trouble: Networks, the state, and fashion wars in the Beninese textile market', *African Studies Review*, 56(3): 101–21.

Prag, E. (2010). *Entrepôt Politics: Political struggles over the Dantokpa marketplace in Cotonou, Benin*, DIIS Working Paper No. 2010: 03.

Sai-wing, H. (2005). 'Distortions in the trade policy for development debate: A re-examination of Friedrich List', *Cambridge Journal of Economics*, 29(5): 729–45.

Signé, L. (2019). *Africa's Industrialization Under the Continental Free Trade Area: Local strategies for global competitiveness*. Washington, DC: Brooking Institute. Available at: https://www.brookings.edu/blog/africa-in-focus/2019/06/04/africas-industrialization-under-the-continental-free-trade-area-local-strategies-for-global-competitiveness/ (Accessed 15 April 2022).

Tayo, T. (2021). 'Africa's free trade agreement: Great expectations, tough questions', *ISS Today*. Pretoria: Institute for Security Studies. Available at: https://issafrica.org/iss-today/africas-free-trade-agreement-great-expectations-tough-questions (Accessed 15 April 2022).

Tralac Factsheet. (2021). Available at: https://www.tralac.org/documents/resources/infographics/4378-afcfta-roo-factsheet-2-july-2021/file.html (Accessed 15 April 2022).

Ukpe, W. (2021). 'AfCFTA: African Development Bank to spend $2 billion on infrastructure', *Nairametrics*. Available at: https://nairametrics.com/2021/06/26/afcfta-african-development-bank-to-spend-2-billion-on-infrastructure/ (Accessed 15 April 2022).

United Nations. (2022). 'The African Continental Free Trade Area Agreement: What is expected of LDCs in terms of trade liberalisation?' Available at: https://www.un.org/ldcportal/content/african-continental-free-trade-area-agreement-what-expected-ldcs-terms-trade-liberalisation (Accessed 15 April 2022).

United Nations Conference on Trade and Development (UNCTAD). (2021). Implications of the African Continental Free Trade Area for Trade and Biodiversity: Policy and regulatory recommendations'. Available at: https://unctad.org/system/files/official-document/ditctedinf2021d3_

en.pdf (Accessed 15 April 2022).

Vhumbunu, C.H. and Rudigi, J.R. (2021). 'Eliminating non-tariff barriers in the African Continental Free Trade Area: Lessons and experiences from African Regional Economic Communities', *Journal of African Foreign Affairs*, 8(2): 129.

Wakabi, M. (2020).'Uganda–Kenya milk war boils over with no end in sight of regional trade tiffs', *The East African*, 19 January Available at: https://www.theeastafrican.co.ke/tea/business/uganda-kenya-milk-war-boils-over-with-no-end-in-sight-of-regional-trade-tiffs-1435138 (Accessed 15 April 2022).

Whitfield, L. and Zalk, N. (2020). 'Phases and uneven experiences in African industrial policy', in A. Oqubay, C. Cramer, H-J. Chang, & R. Kozul-Wright (eds). *The Oxford Handbook of Industrial Policy*. Oxford: Oxford University Press, pp. 842–66.

World Bank. (2020). *The African Continental Free Trade Area: Economic and distributional effects*. Washington, DC: The World Bank.

World Bank. (2012). *De-fragmenting Africa: Deepening regional trade integration in goods and services*. Washington, DC: World Bank Group. Available at: http://documents.worldbank.org/curated/en/245181468009603809/De-fragmenting-Africa-deepening-regional-trade-integration-in-goods-and-services (Accessed 15 April 2022).

World Trade Organization (WTO). (2020) 'Non-tariff barriers: Red tape, etc.' Available at: https://www.wto.org/english/thewto_e/whatis_e/tif_e/agrm9_e.htm (Accessed 15 April 2022).

Zongo, A.M.I. and Oyelami, L. (2021). *Modelling the Impact of Non-Tariff Barriers in Services on Intra-African Trade: Global trade analysis project model*. Bordeaux Economics Working Paper No. 2022-08, Bordeaux School of Economics. Available at: SSRN 3854631.

PART 5

INFRASTRUCTURAL INTEGRATION IN AFRICA

Chapter Sixteen

Regional electricity integration in Africa: The case of the African single electricity market

EKEMINIABASI EYITA-OKON

Introduction

Electricity sectors across Africa have undergone significant reforms over the years to address the access problem and overall electricity poverty in Africa. These reforms include (but are not limited to) privatisation, restructuring the national electricity supply industry to enable horizontal (instead of vertical) integration, and 'pooling' resources at a regional level. Despite these efforts, access to an available, affordable and secure electricity supply remains challenging to households and businesses in the region. In the latter part of the 21st century, the energy challenge has transcended issues of access to include the deployment of renewable energy technologies and the expansion and modernisation of the electricity sector. Against the backdrop of the uneven distribution of energy resources in the region, regional electricity cooperation and integration are critical to address the electricity crisis in Africa. As a result, efforts at collective action have been on the cards since the late 1980s through the establishment of regional power pools (RPPs), such as the Southern African Power Pool (SAPP), the West African Power Pool (WAPP), the East African Power Pool (EAPP), and the Central African Power Pool (CAPP).

On a continental level, the African Union (AU) has been coordinating the harmonisation of African electricity markets since 2015. This effort culminated in the launching of the African Single Electricity Market (AfSEM) in June of 2021 – a project under the Continental Master Plan (CMP) aimed at linking Africa's regional energy infrastructure to address the growing imbalance between the demand and supply of electricity (AU-PIDA, 2021). The main objective of the AfSEM is to 'improve access to reliable and sustainable energy, to promote industrialisation, economic development, and job creation' (AU-PIDA, 2021). While this initiative is promising – particularly against the backdrop of the 'net zero emission' and 'decarbonisation' and 'just transition' debate – increasing the share of renewable energy in the region's electricity mix, and improving electrification rates, access and affordability is imperative to attaining sustainable and just development in Africa. Considering that the AfSEM would be in collaboration with existing African Power Pools, it is necessary to probe the successes and challenges of these pools and draw lessons from them to ensure that the AfSEM achieves its set goals.

Integrating the existing electricity markets into a single continental market presents a coordination problem, because, despite the shared interest in integrating the market, certain factors undermine the ability of actors to commit with any credibility. These factors range from the dynamics of existing national and regional markets to the quality of physical infrastructure, capital and political will. Thus, drawing on lessons from existing RPPs in Africa, this chapter seeks to explore the challenges of achieving the AfSEM. It probes why governments in African continue to choose integration as a pathway to development, despite uneven successes in past attempts. Using the electricity sector as a case study, it looks at how to overcome cooperation problems to ensure the success of the AfSEM. We argue that despite the projected benefits (and costs) of the initiative, its success is predicated on addressing the coordination problem.

The analysis draws on game theory models on the strategic foundations of cooperation and integration. A key insight from game theory on regional electricity integration is that the mere prospects of mutual gains is insufficient to entice strategically rational actors to cooperate and coordinate their strategies to achieve collective outcomes. Thus, how effective regional institutions are in monitoring compliance – and rewarding cooperation and punishing defection – is crucial in translating economic interests into commitment that is credible over time. To this end, the following section presents a discussion on game theory and its relevance to the political economy of regional electricity integration in Africa. Thereafter, an overview of the electricity situation in the region is presented to provide a context for the emergence of regional power pools in Africa. Finally, the chapter discusses the challenges of achieving the AfSEM, drawing on lessons learned from the RPPs.

The political economy of regional electricity integration: A game theoretic assessment

Often dubbed as the 'science of strategies', game theory provides an insightful way of thinking about conflict and cooperation in social interactions. Snidal (1985) argues that the theory is elaborated as a theoretical approach to international politics by contrasting it with metaphorical and analogical uses of games. Thus, it captures important contextual features of the international system that affects prospects for international cooperation. The key assumption of the theory is that actors are rational and strategic. Rationality implies utility maximisation, while strategic implies taking actions that would help maximise the actor's gains while minimising losses. It aims to deduce likely outcomes, such as what moves a player will make, taking into consideration the player's preferences and possible moves open to them. In game theory, each combination of moves by all players results in a set of payoffs or utility to each player (Goldstein, 2004). 'Rationally, each actor tries to maximise gains or minimise losses under conditions of uncertainty and incomplete information, which requires each actor to rank order of preferences, estimate probabilities, and try to determine and predict what the other actor(s) will do' (Tema, 2014).

Game theory is rooted in the rationalist assumptions on human behaviour. Rational choice theory assumes that an actor chooses an alternative course of action believed to result in a social outcome that optimises their preference under subjectively conceived constraints. This theory has made immense contribution to the question of how to establish social order among people with varying interests. The problem characterising social order reflects in various forms such as mutual cooperation, as depicted in the 'prisoners' dilemma' (PD) game, social dilemma (with N players), collective action and the provision of public goods, social norms and social movements (Sato, 2013). Critiques of rational choice theory have questioned the explanatory power of the theory, citing that it is overly focused on 'maximising utility' rather than questioning the origins of the actor's preferences. Such critics have argued for the place of culture theory in providing context to understanding an actor's decision-making process (Satyo, 2013). But actors are faced with various options in any social interactions. Their preferences and the quest to prioritise individual over collective gains (or vice versa) is shaped by a combination of factors, including past experiences, culture, beliefs and traditions, perceptions and the threat factor, among others.

The PD game has largely been the focus of social contract theory while coordination games such as the stag hunt or the battle of the sexes receive less attention (Camerer, 1997). A one-shot PD game emphasises the challenges of prioritising individual rationality over collective gains. In this game, each player is better off choosing an alternative path to the other player (non-cooperative behaviour). Thus, the dominant strategy for each player is to pursue their respective individual interests and confess to the crime. However, this pursuit creates a sub-optimal collective outcome, as both end up confessing and serving a medium sentence for bank robbery. In this game, non-cooperative behaviour is an optimal strategy with collateral damage on collective gains. While this game mirrors key issues in social interaction, coordination games tease out another dimension to the cooperation problem.

Over the years, African governments have agreed to pursue many ambitious, yet beneficial, regional integration initiatives, but rarely have these agreements been implemented. Why have governments expended so much energy identifying potential benefits from integration, yet had so little success cooperating in reaping the said benefits? The electricity industry is characterised by sunk cost; that is, once investments are made it is difficult/impossible to reverse them. Thus, integrating the electricity supply infrastructure of an entire region requires that participating actors cooperate (that is, choose collective gains over individual self-sufficiency) to achieve the mutually desirable outcomes of addressing electricity insecurity in the region. Beyond cooperation, these actors need to intentionally coordinate local, national and subregional strategies to achieve the collective continental goal of a single electricity market. A game-theoretic perspective helps to clarify why governments often struggle to achieve mutually desirable outcomes. It provides tools for analysing strategic interaction among rational actors – that is, situations in which actors' choices are guided by their own preferences, but where achieving one's own preferred outcomes depends on the ability to anticipate the choices of others.

The challenges of regional electricity integration are underpinned by the coordination problem, as depicted by the 'stag hunt or assurance of trust' game, which describes a conflict between safety and social cooperation. 'The problem of coordination arises when two or more individuals can reach some mutually desired outcome or avoid a mutually undesired one, only by combining their actions in a certain way, but where more than one possible combination will suffice. The presence of multiple ways to combine actions requires that individuals coordinate on *the same* combination' (McAdams, 2009).

The stag hunt game theory is a story of two hunters, who have the option of individually pursuing/hunting a hare, or collectively hunting a stag (Skyrms, 2001). The benefit associated with pooling their resources (hunting skills, expertise and materials) to pursue/hunt the stag is a bigger portion of meat for each hunter. Thus, cooperation ensures collective gains, leaving both hunters better off (3, 3). If each one hunts the hare, they will have some meat for dinner, albeit smaller portions (in comparison to the stag) (2, 2). However, if both opt to hunt the stag but one hunter unilaterally defects in pursuit of the hare, there is a risk of neither having meat for dinner (0,1 or 1,0). As the day gets darker, both hunters consider the easier option (that is, hunting the hare) rather than going home with no meat. In this game, maximum gains (the stag) are possible through collective action; any other type of action (unilateral defection) yields suboptimal gains (the hare or nothing). Thus, the dominant strategy is to cooperate and coordinate strategies in hunting the stag (3, 3) as it yields a higher payoff than unilateral defection (0, 1 or 1, 0). The payoffs are depicted in Table 16.1.

The payoff matrix supports the theoretical case for regional electricity integration. Existing literature emphasises the benefits of integrating electricity markets in Africa. The arguments include improvement in the supply conditions, efficiencies through the economies of scale, improved access to electricity, a reduced cost burden on state coffers owing to the participation of the private sector, increased interdependence among neighbouring countries and an improvement in the politico-legal frameworks in cooperating countries (Ebehard, 2003; World Energy Council, 2005; Economic Consulting Associates, 2010).

Table 16.1: Stag hunt payoff matrix

Hunter I	Hunter II	
	Hunt stag	*Hunt hare*
Hunt stag	3 3	0 1
Hunt hare	1 0	2 2

The logic of the game is premised on the importance of cooperation, characterised by coordinating strategies to reap the benefits of collective action, which is to hunt the stag (3, 3). In relation to efforts at regional electricity integration, it is insufficient for governments to merely agree to the rules, agreements and institutions that make integration possible. The failure to coordinate strategies – develop infrastructure such as interconnectors and cross-border transmission lines, reconfigure the national electricity industry and market to align with regional goals and establish a supranational institutional infrastructure to effectively monitor and oversee the integration process – will lead to a suboptimal outcome (1, 0 or 0, 1). Subsequently, as defection become visible in the N-player arrangement, countries could default to national utilities and markets over regional markets, leading to the outcome (2, 2) and continued monopolising of the electricity supply chain at a country level.

Regional electricity markets in Africa: An overview

Electricity is an important driver of economic and human development. It is central to the functioning of the industrial and service sectors in any economy (Eyita, 2014). In addition, the link between electricity and human welfare has been adequately established in the literature (Saadi, Miketa and Howells, 2015; Bezerra *et al.*, 2017; Pascale, 2017; World Bank, 2018).

A market, in layperson's term, is a place where the exchange of goods and services takes place. Thus, an electricity market is a place where producers of surplus electricity supply their commodity to end-users at a given price margin. Harris (2006) argues that a complete market is key to the success of regional electricity integration, where producers can capture signals from end-users, such as the impact of the commodity and its costs (to the environment, for instance), and these are taken into consideration to improve efficiency. A complete market (with information) also creates an enabling environment for producers to make profits. This has proven to be a strong incentive for continued efficiency to aid the inflow of profits. According to Harris (2006), the nature of electricity causes the microeconomics of power generation to change at an extraordinary frequency. Thus, coordination and uninterrupted communication or signals between suppliers, end-users and intermediaries are crucial to the efficiency of (regional electricity) markets. Such features are characteristic of a competitive market, as opposed to the traditional (and state-run) 'command and control' method of planning, and management proves. These value judgements require the signals – such as energy price, capacity price and emission cost – to be monetised and efficiently communicated so that the net cost and revenue can be quickly maximised.

Electricity markets across the globe have evolved over time. Traditionally, each country had its own electric utility that would solely run the supply-side: generation, transmission on high-voltage lines, and distribution to end-users on low-voltage lines. However, since the 1980s, electricity markets have become increasingly deregulated across the globe, enabling the trade in electricity under competitive rules. A key feature of deregulation is the creation of power pools to manage the workings of the organised market, where producers with surplus electricity and end-users or consumers can readily buy and sell electricity. In a power pool, several neighbouring utilities are interconnected through a transmission network which allows energy to be traded across the (sub)region. A high number of suppliers in the market leads to a low cost of electricity for end-users, and the reverse is the case if the number of producers (and amount of supply) is less than the demand for the commodity. Beyond the technicalities, power pools or any effort at regional electricity integration requires coordination of strategies by the cooperating parties.

The African Single Electricity Market (AfSEM) and the coordination problem

The AfSEM project is in its infancy, having been launched in June 2021 by the African Union (AU) in partnership with the European Union (EU) and other key industry actors. The project emerges under the framework of the Continental Harmonisation Agenda aimed at harmonising policies, legislation, and regulatory and institutional frameworks at the regional and continental levels to deepen cooperation, while eradicating barriers to cross-border energy trade and investments (EU Technical Assistance Facility (TAF) for the Sustainable Energy for ALL [SE4ALL] Initiative – East and Southern Africa, 2021). The justification for the integration of energy markets in the region stems from the inability of national capacity to adequately address electricity insecurity in the region. The World Energy Council (2005), the World Bank and the AU note the importance of transcending the traditional approach of limiting energy planning and service provisions to the national level, which has so far produced poor results in addressing the access, availability, reliability and affordability problems in Africa (World Energy Council, 2005).

A regionally integrated electricity market is believed to enhance the quality and security of supply at both national and regional levels, while incentivising private-sector participation and investments. A regional market will create a haven for, and boost, electricity trade, enabling the full recourse of Adam Smith's notion of comparative advantage with respect to countries endowed with energy resources. Thus, the cost and benefits associated with 'pooling' resources are shared among participating member states. The benefits of harmonisation, according to the AU, include the long-term stability of the power sector; catalysing investments through commitments at both the regional and continental levels; increasing cross-border trading and power pooling, while enhancing access to electricity; enhancing continental initiatives and influence in terms of network regulation, the electricity market, design and coordination; improving learning from the 'best practice' regulation through pooling of regulatory resources; and creating a competitive market system for the effective operation of the supply chain process – generation, transmission, distribution and sale, among other processes (African Union, 2021).

To this end, the AU and its partners devised two major documents to facilitate/guide the process of integration, namely the *Strategy for the Development of a Harmonized Regulatory Framework for the Electricity Market in Africa* and the *Action Plan for the Harmonised Regulatory Framework for the Electricity Market in Africa*. This strategic document outlines six key objectives that would accelerate Africa's development and improve electricity access. These strategic objectives include: (1) developing effective regional and continental electricity markets; (2) improving the operational efficiency and performance of the electricity supply industry (ESI); (3) creating a stable, transparent and predictable environment to attract investment; (4) enhancing electricity market frameworks to increase access; (5) enhancing renewable energy frameworks (in light of the global calls for a transition to green and clean energy sources); and (6) establishing norms, standards and frameworks for energy efficiency (African Union, 2021). These objectives holistically tackle core issues plaguing the ESI in Africa, such as investments, infrastructure, policy (and implementation), institutional capacity, and diversifying and transitioning to greener energy sources.

In addition to these objectives, the strategy document outlines five pillars around which the regulatory harmonisation process can revolve at the national, regional and continental levels. These pillars are (1) to create a robust economic regulatory framework; (2) establish a solid technical regulatory framework; (3) create an enabling electricity market; (4) enhance renewable energy frameworks; and (5) establish norms, standards and frameworks for energy efficiency (EU Technical Assistance Facility (TAF) for the Sustainable Energy for All (SE4ALL) Initiative, 2021).

Pursuant to these strategies, the action plan was developed to identify the target areas and pillars of the harmonisation process. Since 2015, the African Union Commission (AUC) through the Department of Infrastructure and Energy (DIE), in association with the EU Technical Assistance Facility (TAF) on Sustainable Energy for All (SE4ALL), have been working on a programme designed to integrate national and regional electricity markets in Africa into a single continental market (African Development Fund, 2021). Thus, during the Specialised Technical Committee meeting on Infrastructure (transport, energy and tourism) held in Nouakchott and Cairo in 2018 and 2019, respectively, the Africa Energy Ministers directed the African Union Development Agency (AUDA-NEPAD) and the African Union Commission to pioneer the design and development of a Continental Master Plan (CMP) for transmission to guide efforts at continental integration through the AfCFTA project (African Development Fund, 2021).

The CMP, as the blueprint for the AfSEM, was designed to be developed in two phases. The first phase focused on baseline studies, which reviewed the existing five African power pool plans, identified power demand and generation capacity to the year 2063, and mapped key transmission corridors and priority generation and transmission projects (Climate Parliament, 2022). The first phase was completed in October 2020. The findings showed that the WAPP and the SAPP power system master plans were up to date, the EAPP and CAPP master plans were outdated and required critical updates to serve as the base for the CMP, while the Comité Maghrébin de l'Electricité (COMELEC) had no master plan in place. The second phase of the CMP is dedicated to developing the Integrated Continental Transmission Network Master Plan. In January 2020, the AUDA-NEPAD submitted a formal request to the African Development Bank for financial assistance to support the development of the plan. The request was approved and the project development will be financed through the bank's Regional Operations Envelope (ROE). This envelope is part of the African Development Bank's and the African Development Fund's commitment to support regional operations in member countries. As a result, 25 per cent of the group's replenishment (or funding) is set aside for this purpose, while 15 per cent of the ROE is used to support the development of regional public goods in member states (African Development Fund, 2021).

Against the backdrop of the global call for transitions to green and clear energy solutions, the regional electricity integration plan seeks to deliver on this goal while meeting other strategic commitments. However, we argue that the success of the AfSEM is predicated on overcoming the coordination problem, without which the project becomes another ambitious and unfulfilled development agenda. Next, we examine the challenges facing existing African power pools as lessons for the AfSEM initiative.

Challenges of coordination for AfSEM: Lessons from existing regional power pools in Africa

In sub-Saharan Africa, there are four major regional power pools, namely the Central African Power Pool (CAPP), the East African Power Pool (EAPP), Southern African Power Pool (SAPP) and West African Power Pool (WAPP). Table 16.2 provides a summary of each power pool.

Table 16.2: Summary of power pools in sub-Saharan Africa

Member states	Angola Burundi Cameroon Central Africa Republic (CAR) Democratic Republic of the Congo (DRC) Equatorial Guinea Gabon Republic of Congo São Tomé & Príncipe Chad	Burundi Democratic Republic of the Congo Djibouti Egypt Ethiopia Kenya Libya Rwanda Sudan Tanzania Uganda	Benin Burkina Faso Côte d'Ivoire Gambia Ghana Guinea Guinea-Bissau Liberia Mali Niger Nigeria Senegal Sierra Leone Togo	Angola Botswana Democratic Republic of the Congo Lesotho Malawi Mozambique Namibia South Africa Swaziland Tanzania Zambia Zimbabwe
Date of formation	2003	2005	1999	1995
Institutional bodies	ECCAS	COMESA	ECOWAS	SADC
Existing market types/nature of trade agreements			Bilateral contracts	Short-term electricity market Day-ahead market

Across all four subregions, the existence of the power pool has had a varied impact on the energy poverty or electricity insecurity problems. Access to an affordable and reliable supply of electricity remains a challenge as power outages have been on the rise over the years. A report by the Infrastructure Consortium for Africa (ICA) shows that power trade remains relatively low in Africa, with less than 1 per cent for CAPP and EAPP, but relatively higher in SAPP and WAPP combined (Infrastructure Consortium for Africa, 2011). Figure 17.1 depicts the rate of power outages across four major economies in sub-Saharan Africa.

Figure 16.1: Number of power outages in a typical month

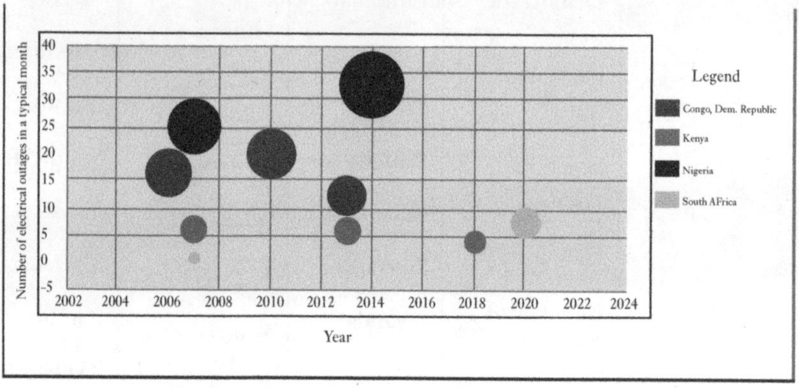

Data source: World Bank (2022)[1]

The graph depicts an increase (rather than a decrease) in power outages, despite the existence of power pools. There was a notable increase in the number of power outages in Nigeria (between 2006 and 2014) and South Africa (2007 and 2020). Power outages also increased in the DRC in 2006, 2010 and 2013, and in Kenya in 2007, 2013, and 2018.

Key lessons

The coordination problem in existing power pools (and by extension, AfSEM) emerge in key areas like infrastructure development, finance/capital and the politics of national energy utilities. Infrastructure remains

---

1   The data was sourced from the World Bank Data Bank on Power Outages in Firms in a Typical Month (number). Available at: https://data.worldbank.org/indicator/IC.ELC.OUTG (Accessed 10 November 2021).

a key challenge to the effective functioning of existing regional power pools. Installed generation capacity in most parts of the region, except in South Africa, remain at a staggering 70 gigawatts (GW), accounting for the continued and growing gap in access to electricity. Poor maintenance of existing infrastructure and failure to develop new ones, owing to a lack of funding, explain the low generation capacity in the region. South Africa's power infrastructure is in stark contrast to its counterparts in the region. With the full exploration of coal-fired plants, its generation capacity sits at about 40 000 megawatts, while Nigeria generates close to 4 000 megawatts of electricity – insufficient for its population of 206.1 million people. Thus, efforts at regionalism, especially under the auspice of the African Continental Free Trade Agreement (and AfSEM), would incentivise states to actively invest in improving domestic generation capacity. For one, the profits likely to be generated from the sale of surplus electricity on the regional grid would reduce the cost to the end-user, arguably endorsing the political salience of the commodity. The AU, through its subsidiaries like the Programme for Infrastructure Development in Africa (PIDA) and external partners like the World Bank and the EU, recognise the infrastructure deficit as a sectoral priority to attain the successful harmonisation of the energy market, with implications for other sectors of the economy.

The political economy of energy resources provides insight into the coordination problem as far as regional electricity integration is concerned. Government-owned enterprises or national electric utilities in several member states across the region are cognisant of the politically salient nature of electricity and the possible implications on domestic politics. National utilities often supply power at a subsidised rate to domestic consumers, which inadvertently ensures their monopoly over the industry, while deterring private-sector investments and participation. On a regional scale, most governments fear the loss of sovereignty and dependence on intermediaries, such as transit states, for the supply of a commodity considered to be strategic to national security. This position reflects the realist ideology in self-sufficiency, especially where goods that are intrinsically linked to a nation's security are concerned. Thus, the uncertainty in the behaviour of cooperating actors and the unpredictability of future events further serve as deterrents to cooperation and the coordination of strategies.

Finally, power pools (and the AfSEM) underperform due to a lack of capital and investments. Budgetary constraints in most countries in the region, especially small, land-locked states, have undermined investments in infrastructure development to meet the requirements of regional power pools. In most parts of the region, private capital is unwilling to participate in the market because of the nature of the industry – characterised by sunk cost – and the overall political and economic climate. While the AfSEM (and AfCFTA) provides an opportunity for expansive energy markets, in which the supply and demand of electricity could evolve without market barriers, the onus falls on each member state to capitalise on the opportunity to build and increase capacity, while making their respective environments conducive for investments.

References

African Development Fund (ADF). (2021a). *Project: Continental Power System Master Plan Project (CMP) – Technical Assistance*. Project Appraisal Report, African Development Bank Group. Available at: https://www.afdb.org/en/documents/multinational-continental-power-system-master-plan-project-cmp-technical-assistance-project-appraisal-report (Accessed 10 November 2021).

African Development Fund (ADF). (2021b). *Regional Operation Envelope*. Available at: https://adf.afdb.org/adf/the-enveloppes/regional-operation-envelope/ (Accessed 10 November 2021).

African Union. (2021). *Strategy for the Development of a Harmonised Regulatory Framework for the Electricity Market in Africa.* June. Available at: https://au.int/en/documents/20210618/strategy-development-harmonised-regulatory-framework-electricity-market-africa (Accessed 10 November 2021).

AU-PIDA. (2021). *High-level EU and AUDA-NEPAD Officers Report Progress on Africa's Continental Power Master Plan, Towards the African Single Electricity Market (AfSEM)*. Available at: https://www.au-pida.org/news/high-level-eu-and-auda-nepad-officers-report-progress-on-africas-continental-power-master-plan-towards-the-african-single-electricity-market-afsem/ (Accessed 10 November 2021).

Bezerra, P.B.D.S, Callegari, C.L., Ribas, A., Lucena, A.F.P., Portugal-Pereira, J. Koberle, A. and Schaeffer, R. (2017). 'The power of light: Socio-economic and environmental implications of a rural electrification program in Brazil', *Environmental Research Letters,* 12(9)(095004): 1–14.

doi:https://doi.org/10.1088/1748-9326/aa7bdd.

Camerer, C.F. (1997). 'Progress in behavioral game theory', *Journal of Economic Perspectives* 11(4): 167–88.

Climate Parliament. (2022). *African Continental Power System Masterplan.* Available at: https://www.climateparl.net/post/african-continental-power-system-masterplan (Accessed 10 November 2021).

Cramton, P. (2017). 'Electricity market design', *Oxford Review of Economic Policy*, 33(4): 589–612. doi:https://doi.org/10.1093/oxrep/grx041.

Ebehard, A. 2003. 'The political, economic, institutional and legal dimensions of electricity supply industry reform in South Africa', *Political Economy of Power Market Reform Conference.* 1–46.

Economic Consulting Associates. (2010). *The Potential of Regional Power Sector Integration.* Briefing Note, Energy Sector Management Assistance Program (ESMAP). Available at: https://www.esmap.org/sites/esmap.org/files/BN004-10_REISP-CD_The%20Potential%20Regional%20Power%20Sector%20Integration-Literature%20Review.pdf (Accessed 10 November 2021).

EU Technical Assistance Facility (TAF) for the Sustainable Energy for ALL (SE4ALL) Initiative – East and Southern Africa. (2021a). 'Strategy for the development of a harmonised regulatory framework for the electricity market in Africa', *African Union,* 18 June. Available at: https://au.int/en/documents/20210618/strategy-development-harmonised-regulatory-framework-electricity-market-africa (Accessed 10 November 2021).

EU Technical Assistance Facility (TAF) for the Sustainable Energy for All (SE4ALL) Initiative. (2021b). *Action Plan for Harmonised Regulatory Framework for the Electricity Market in Africa.* Action Plan, African Union. Available at: https://au.int/sites/default/files/documents/40437-doc-ActionPlan_HarmonisedRegulatoryFrameworkElectricityMarket.pdf (Accessed 10 November 2021).

Eyita, E.K. (2014). 'Energy security through transboundary cooperation: Case studies of the Southern African Power Pool (SAPP) and the West African Power Pool (WAPP).' Masters thesis, University of the Witwatersrand.

Eyita-Okon, E.K. (2020). 'The political economy of regional hydropower investments in Africa.' Doctoral dissertation, University of the Witwatersrand.

Goldstein, JS. (2004). 'Game Theory', in J.S. Goldstein. *International Relations*. London: Longman, pp. 86–89.

Harris, C. (2006). *Electricity Markets: Pricing, structures and economics*. Hoboken, NJ: John Wiley & Sons.

Infrastructure Consortium for Africa. (2011). *Regional Powere Status in African Power Pools*. Tunisia: Infrastructure Consortium for Africa (ICA)/African Development Bank. Available at: https://www.icafrica.org/fileadmin/documents/Knowledge/Energy/ICA_RegionalPowerPools_Report.pdf (Accessed 10 November 2021).

McAdams, R.H. (2009). 'Beyond the prisoners' dilemma: Coordination, game theory and law', *Southern California Law Review*, 82(209): 209–58.

Pascale, A. (2017). 'The links between energy and human welfare.' Doctoral Dissertation, University of Queensland.

Saadi, N., Miketa, A. and Howells, M. (2015). 'African clean energy corridor: Regional integration to promote renewable energy fueled growth', *Energy Research and Social Science*, 5: 1–3. DOI:10.1016/j.erss.2014.12.020.

Sato, Y. (2013). 'Rational choice theory', *Sociopedia.isa*, pp. 1–10. DOI: 10.1177/205684601372.

Skyrms, B. (2001). 'The stag hunt', *Proceedings and Addresses of the American Philosophical Association*, 75(2): 31–41. doi:https:doi.org/10.2307/3218711.

Snidal, D. (1985). 'The game theory of international politics', *World Politics*, 38(1): 25–57. doi:https://doi.org/10.2307/2010350.

Tema, M. (2014). 'Basic assumptions in game theory and international relations', *International Relations Quarterly* 5(1): 1–4. Available at: http://www.southeast-europe.org/pdf/17/dke_17_a_e_Malvina-Tema_Game-Theory-and-IR.pdf (Accessed 10 November 2021).

World Bank. (2018). *Access to Energy at the Heart of Development*, 18 April. Available at: https://www.worldbank.org/en/news/feature/2018/04/18/access-energy-sustainable-development-goal-7 (Accessed 20 November 2021).

World Energy Council. (2005). *Regional Energy Integration in Africa*. London: World Energy Council.

Chapter Seventeen

Transport infrastructure and regional integration in Africa

SIKANYISO MASUKU

Introduction

The idea of fostering cooperation and economically integrating the African continent goes as far back as 1963, when the Organisation of African Union (OAU) was established. Actual attempts to make this a reality only gained momentum in 1991 through the Treaty Establishing the African Economic Community (the Abuja Treaty) as well as the Sirte Declaration of 1999, which reinvigorated the now rechristened African Union's (AU's) mandate to accelerate the process of integration. The Constitutive Act of the African Union, signed in 2000, was emphatic on the need to accelerate integration around a continental free trade area (AU, 2000). However, it was the Abuja Treaty (which entered into force in May 1994) that had more practical implications for the foundation of such integration, with Article 28 of the treaty envisioning integration on the continent as being achievable through a form of decentralisation – to be done in six stages over a period of 34 years. This decentralisation was to entail the establishment of eight Regional Economic Communities (RECs), that is, the Arab Maghreb Union (AMU), the Community of Sahel-Saharan States (CEN-SAD), the Common Market for Eastern and Southern Africa (COMESA), the East African Community (EAC), the Economic Community of Central

African States (ECCAS), the Economic Community of West African States (ECOWAS), the Intergovernmental Authority on Development (IGAD) and the Southern African Development Community (SADC). These RECs were, in essence, the building blocks on which a new African economic community was to be founded. The RECs have since made inroads towards overall integration, particularly in the areas of infrastructure (the SADC and EAC), trade liberalisation and facilitation (ECOWAS and COMESA), the free movement of people (ECOWAS), and peace and security (ECOWAS and the SADC) (Jerome and Nabena, 2016). The establishment of an Africa Continental Free Trade Area (AfCFTA) commencing in 2021 (the largest free trade area since the establishment of the World Trade Organization) and a Continental Customs Union (CCU) was also all in keeping with the ideals of cooperation and economic integration on the African continent.

If the goods and services traded between the envisioned economic communities was the blood and lifeline to inclusive development, a competent transport infrastructure was the capillary network through which it would traverse for the collective benefit of the continent. However, even though there are a few cases where regional trade has been successfully instituted (through effective transport infrastructure development), fragile regions have, unfortunately, lagged behind. Proof of this is seen in the African Infrastructural Development Index, which showed a consistent trend in the average index improvements for the year 2020, with North Africa having consistently experienced the most development in information and communications technology (ICT), power, transport, water and sanitation, followed by Southern Africa, East Africa and Central Africa (AfDB, 2020). In the Central African Economic and Monetary Community (CEMAC), roads carry nearly 90 per cent of domestic passengers, as well as goods. This, however, is not without its challenges given the low road density in the region (compared to the rest of the continent) (AfDB, 2019).

The AfDB (2019) estimates that only 15.7 per cent of a network of 147 314 kilometres of road links between CEMAC countries are paved (and there are no two capitals that are linked by a fully paved road). The uneven infrastructural development across regions (a function of not only historical factors, but also variations in political and security risks between regions) reflects the limited progress of the RECs in delivering on their regional harmonisation and monitoring effort (SASSTP, 2019). This status quo has only increased through the years and, along with it, implications on how far the principles of the Abuja Treaty (Article 61G) can be adopted; that is, organising, structuring and promoting (at regional and community levels) passenger and goods transport services (Dumitru and Hayat, 2015). Where political and security risks (due to conflict) have impeded private sector participation in infrastructure construction projects, intracontinental trade has also suffered, for example, the civil war in the Democratic Republic of the Congo (DRC) has led to the destruction of critical routes linking East and West Africa (Tamosaitiene *et al.*, 2021). As a result of these issues, despite Africa having more RECs than any other region in the world, intra-African trade is the lowest of all global regions (see AfDB, 2018).

The uneven development of transport infrastructure and the adverse impact this has had on Africa's trade networks is not only an attribute of political and security risk indices (discussed earlier), and their variation between regions – but also other political and economic factors. For instance, after the attainment of independence by most African states, a lack of cohesion was partly informed by political realism, with each state pursuing its own national interests by abrogating on calls for regional economic integration, choosing instead to protect internal trade by tightening national borders (Bell, 2017). This type of red tape and protectionism were counterintuitive to the vision of an integrated Africa, and, in undoing this, the Abuja Treaty (Article 61) encouraged a harmonisation of rules and regulations relating to transport and communications on the continent. Regardless of such pan-Africanist rhetoric and the anticipation of a new era, little has changed, with regional fragmentation being proliferated by long delays and cumbersome procedures at national borders, punitive and arbitrary transit tariffs, transport restrictions, etc. (SSATP, 2019). Yang and Gupta (2007) concur with these assertions and argue that high external trade barriers and low resource complementarity between member countries has limited both intra- and extra-regional trade in Africa, making the existing regional trade arrangements (RTAs) obsolete.

Where formal trade networks have been either inefficient, over-bureaucratised or redundant, informal cross-border trading (ICBT) has endeavoured to fill the void; for example, in 2020 ICBT amounted to 30–40 per cent of total intraregional trade in the SADC region and 40 per cent in the COMESA region (Stuart, 2020). Although heavily linked to food security, economic development and other factors, ICBT's contribution to the macroeconomics (at both the exit and entry points) has either been low or hard to quantify, given its informality and the illegality it is often associated with. Only seven years away from the year 2028 – when a single customs union, common currency and central bank, as well as the Pan-African Parliament were envisioned to have been in place – the AECs remain a pipe dream with little coordination between the eight RECs (Jerome and Nabena, 2016).

Although not exhaustive, the abovementioned issues constitute a necessary background into some of the existential politics surrounding the cooperation and economic integration discourse on the African continent. Amid such threats/opportunities, of more importance and significance to this chapter is the feasibility of instituting cross-regional transport infrastructure networks and accelerating integration around a continental free trade area. To contribute to this ongoing debate, this chapter argues that independent Africa not only carries the burden of a redundant colonial transport infrastructure (which cemented regional inequities and disunity), but it has also fallen under the trappings of structuralist economics – further proliferating infrastructural development that is uneven, at both sectoral and country group levels.

Neoliberalist principles as an antithesis to regional integration: Theorising the growth of protectionism in contemporary Africa

The pursuit of political and economic interests to the benefit of individual states is a basic manifestation of political realism in international relations (Bell, 2017). This, of course, is to the disservice of the spirit with which economic regions were conceived; that is, the expectation that they would function as a collective force. Instead of such an idealised unity of purpose to work towards the economic regional integration of Africa, we have seen a regression towards neoliberalism and an observance of comparative advantage principles. These principles (theorised around the mobility of capital transfers and realism) are conceptualised in this chapter as having led to an overreliance on private and foreign capital in the transfer of industrial know-how and equipment.

In the wake of this regression, the situation that now obtains is one in which participation in the global production system (particularly with industrialised countries) is prioritised as a means to accrue much needed foreign exchange earnings (McMichael, 1996). Such foreign exchange in Africa (and the rest of the developing world) is prioritised as key to purchase capital equipment technologies, which are essential for continued industrialisation. Apart from the ensuing Western-centric focus on trade by African states (as opposed to strengthening intracontinental trade first), the specialisation and exchange with developed economies also demands the removal of market restrictions as the only viable means to earn a greater share in the wealth of nations (Street, 1967: 46).

The downsides of this equation are critiqued in this chapter as having had adverse impacts on African regional integration, with some apparent consequences, including (1) the imposition of red tape and protectionist policies by individual states in abrogation of intracontinental trade and (2) the arising challenges African states now face in shielding domestic economies from those of the developed world. The following sections examine the two subsectors of transport infrastructural development (roads and railways) to see how their development has been pursued to realise the AfCFTA.

Strides towards high-capacity and efficient transport corridors

In operationalising the vision of an integrated Africa, certain inroads have been made in prioritising the expansion and refurbishment of transport infrastructure. While some of the initiatives are development oriented, others have been reactionary and designed as corrective measures in areas perceived to be stumbling blocks to regional integration. For instance, after noting a deterioration of road infrastructure in sub-Saharan Africa (SSA), the Africa Region Infrastructure Department of the World Bank and the United Nations Economic Commission for Africa (UNECA) became part of an initiative known as the Africa Transport Policy Programme (SSATP). Established in 1987, the SSATP initiative also comprised African countries, Regional Economic Communities (RECs), continental institutions such as the African Union Commission, public and private-sector organisations, and international development agencies and organisations (SSATP, 2019). Since its most recent Annual General Assembly held at Victoria Falls in Zimbabwe on 29 November 2019, the SSATP's membership has grown to an impressive 42 countries. Further determined by how the deterioration of road infrastructure on the continent continued unabated (despite substantial capital investments by governments and donors), the SSATP championed several action plans, which included the Road Management Initiative (RMI) – formerly known as Road Maintenance Initiative. The initiative entailed having a dedicated Road Fund (RF), that is, a separate fund outside the central government's general budget, charged with promoting integration, connectivity and cohesion through financing road maintenance services (Potter, 1997). It also entailed commercialising the African corridors, in other words, putting road maintenance on a sustainable long-term basis and financing it wholly or in part from user charges rather than general revenues (Brushett, 2005).

Since 1987, the SSATP has been working towards promoting effective policy and strategy formulation/implementation for corridor development at the country and regional levels. This has included integrated corridor development and performance-based monitoring mechanisms that support regional integration through evidence-based decision-making. Regardless, the SASSTP still faces several challenges to achieving its many objectives, particularly its current Third Development/DP3, which is a multi-year work programme (2015–2020) consistent with the framework for action of the 2014 Africa Sustainable Transport Forum (ASTF). The DP3 is focused primarily on regional integration, urban mobility and road safety. Among its many challenges, one of the most prominent (discussed in greater detail later) has been the non-implementation of the SSATP's trade-facilitation measures and transport-sector policies by the 42 member states. Non-compliance (partly an outcome of poor enforcement of existing treaties) has been noted as constituting a bigger impediment to regional integration than the actual suboptimal physical condition of the infrastructure. Recently, Beitbridge border post – a passage to the whole continent and thus one of Africa's busiest border posts with over 25 000 people crossing it daily – succumbed to crippling logistical nightmares, which were mostly owing to Zimbabwe's unilateral introduction of a new commercial terminal and the imposition of exorbitant access fees (in cash) for commercial trucks to the tune of US$200 (Ndlovu, 2021). Such a total disregard for existing treaties and non-tariff barriers exemplify why there continue to be challenges to the free movement of goods, services and persons across African borders (Ravenhill, 2016). Non-compliance to regional treaties is also appositely tied to the issue of sovereignty as only a few governments in Africa have been willing to relinquish their sovereignty by permitting the requisite transfer of authority to regional institutions (Ravenhill, 2016).

To further consolidate the aspirations of an economically integrated Africa, the African Heads of State and Government 12th Assembly in Uganda, Kampala adopted declaration /AU/Decl. 1 (XII) in 2010. This declaration requested the African Union Commission to establish the Programme of Infrastructure Development for Africa (PIDA). In terms of the interregional and continental integration drive, the PIDA has since become the single most vital programme with ambitious hopes to facilitate the interconnection of transport networks, not only between landlocked and island countries, but also across the generality of African states. The overall objective in facilitating such interconnection has been to support Africa's global competitiveness through territorial, economic and social cohesion (SSAPT, 2019). To date, PIDA has had success in many areas, including the transboundary and intraregional infrastructure development brokered in 2012 in partnership with the AU, the United Nations Economic Commission for Africa, and the African Development Bank. PIDA's transport vision encompasses an African continent where transportation services enable the free movement of not only goods/freight but also people, through efficient, safe, affordable and reliable transportation services. These transportation services are envisioned by PIDA as being tenable through (1) connecting African cities through modern roads and railways; (2) developing modern African Regional Transport Infrastructure Network (ARTIN) corridors; and (3) developing world–class ports and air transport services on the continent (PIDA, 2012).

In theory, these initiatives (in so far as the ARTIN is concerned) stand as the medium through which the regional economic cooperation agenda is to be operationalised. However, several challenges continue to stand in the way of the Constitutive Act of 2002 and the Abuja Treaty's noble aspirations of an economically integrated Africa. The SSATP's 2019 annual report summarises these issues as including but not confined to: (1) the continued inadequate institutional capacity to lead the execution of the action plan; (2) the limited and uneven progress of the RECs in delivering on their regional harmonisation and monitoring effort; (3) inadequate funding; and (4) weak technical leadership at a continental level. Cumulatively, these issues have partly accounted for why the economic cost of inefficiencies on the African regional transport infrastructure network is estimated at US$140 billion

(SSATP, 2019). In the wake of these realities, economic solidarity and development – that is, the establishment of an African Continental Free Trade Area (AfCFTA) – cannot be said to be remotely feasible without the availability of requisite transport infrastructure. This being the case, the proceeding sections proffer a discussion into some of the factors simultaneously proliferating regional fragmentation while encumbering the realisation of a cross-border and integrative transport network on the continent, which would guarantee a more reliable, faster and cheaper movement of both cargo and people.

Long-term interconnectivity and development: The impact of colonial rail transport investments

The World Bank's global statistics on goods transported by rail since the 1900s (one million tonnes per kilometre) show a significant increase in the preferred use of this cost-efficient and environmentally friendly option for carrying freight (World Bank, 2019). In comparison to road transport, this growth is the result of the greater efficiency gains from rail transport in terms of energy consumption and carbon emissions per traffic unit. The reduction in transport costs per tonne/kilometre realised from rail transport have also been estimated to be as high as 75 per cent compared to road transport (AfDB, 2015). The importance of rail infrastructure in linking Africa's eight RECs – and thereby establishing an African economic community – therefore cannot be understated.

Although roads can most certainly link the rural agricultural producer to the urban centres, cross-country and, indeed, intra-Africa trade requires a well-functioning rail network that is joined to strategic seaports and manufacturing zones. In the past, corridor improvement that failed to link national and rural networks was blamed for limiting the potential for sustainable economic growth because it provided little benefit for national producers, nor did it promote the trade of regional products (SSATP, 2019). Noting not only the importance of corridor development but also the rail transport network, the 2009 Declaration on the Development of Transport and Energy Infrastructure in Africa (within the framework of PIDA) sought to speed up the development of infrastructure as well as energy and transport services on the continent (African Union, 2009). The expansion of Africa's railway network is also part and parcel of the AU's objective to meet the aspirations of its agenda by 2063 (African Union, 2015). Despite these efforts, however, there has continued to be an underinvestment in the African railway network (relative to the amounts poured into other types of infrastructure such as roads or energy) by international financial institutions. Not only is the funding for rail infrastructure development insufficient but (as the following sections will show) it is also often unevenly distributed and thus contributes little to regional integration by reducing the interconnectivity inefficiencies in Africa's trade networks.

Although there is an unarguably minimal presence of the private sector in the construction of Africa's transport and utility infrastructure, this has applied predominantly to the investment component and not the actual use of that infrastructure. This is particularly true when it comes to the African rail network infrastructure where, currently, through the SSATP promoted concessions, over 70 per cent of the available rail network on the continent is being operated by private operators (SSATP, 2019). Public–private partnerships and the demand for model bidding documents in the selection of concessionaires has achieved the successful transference of operating rights to private enterprises, but this has done little to enforce the rehabilitation or maintenance of the already dilapidated rail infrastructure by respective concessionaires. Just as most African roads are underserviced and dilapidating, the rail network (totalling a low 90 320 kilometres) is succumbing to the same vices, becoming increasingly limited with a network that stood at just 3.1 kilometres of rail for every 1 000 square kilometres in 2005 (Jerome and Nabena, 2016: 92). While the obsolescence and non-functionality of Africa's rail transport infrastructure gets worse (due to the huge financing needs impeding any developmental or corrective programmes), some of the challenges in the sector can be traced back to the colonial era (Jedwab and Moradi, 2016; Graff, 2019).

During the colonial era, rail penetration (as well as the location of the infrastructure) was often motivated by the need to extend colonial control and, most importantly, to facilitate natural resource exploitation. These two needs often necessitated the construction of rail networks that were purpose built as feeders (see Figure 18.4), strategically linking African ports to the hinterland (Mouhamed and Qiu, 2020). In constructing rail networks, the colonial system often considered the territorial delimitations of the time – factoring in how the mainland of Africa was fragmented between the different colonial superpowers. The outcome (which was wholesomely inherited by independent African states) has been a severely sparse rail network with both limited length and quality (Jerome and Nabena, 2016: 92). The effects of this have been far-reaching, especially when one considers how the majority of rail transport infrastructure still in use in modern-day Africa was built by colonial empires – 88 per cent of the total railway mileage in sub-Saharan Africa was built before independence (Jedwab and Moradi, 2012). This has had a profoundly negative impact on Africa's desire to operationalise the much-needed intracontinental trade; for example, in some economic regions, the reduced quality of the line has decreased the freight volumes that cargo trains can bear, while the limited length has meant less ease of doing business due to a greater reliance on road transport in finishing off an increasingly longer last mile (Mouhamed and Qiu, 2020). Given these issues, Africa's competitiveness has thus continued to be asphyxiated by the high costs of energy and, in this case, inefficient rail transport services.

These limited positive economic outcomes (economic cooperation and regional integration) are also argued in Graff's (2019) study on Africa's trade network, as being consequences of colonial planning – its legacy being a redundant railway infrastructure with an outdated purpose of supporting extractive economies and facilitating military manoeuvrability. Jedwab *et al.* (2017) describe the colonial railway network as one that was not predicated on linking the predominantly small and landlocked economies of Africa into a cohesive trading ecosystem. It is also equally important to note how the spatial organisation of economic activity during the colonial era adversely contributed to a situation in which the areas with a high density of colonial railway networks often attracted/lured the further development of other forms of transportation infrastructure (such as roads) at relatively the same locations (see Figures 17.5 and 17.6). As a result, regions with railway lines characteristically developed a higher density of road infrastructure compared to those without railway lines, while also becoming more urbanised; that is, urbanisation not only became uneven, it also became clustered around rail networks (Jedwab and Moradi, 2016). While contemporary economic activity still huddles around these colonial railway lines (constructed between 1890 and 1960), they now constitute a disservice to modern-day Africa's vision of a continental free trade area.

Spatial inefficiencies (a legacy of the colonial planning) have thus had far-reaching implications on the establishment of an efficient transport network, often making intracontinental trade in Africa not only costly but also slow. While Graff (2019) notes how most planned rails during the colonial era were never constructed or completed, it is the built rail infrastructure (rather than the planned railways) that is the focus of this chapter, given its role in proliferating interconnectivity inefficiencies within Africa's trade networks. Southern Africa had an unfairly high rail density, with the overall network being of a limited length, that is, in keeping with its utility in natural resource exportation/extraction through the peripheral ports, thus largely underserving other landlocked parts of Africa. As illustrated in Figures 17.1 and 17.3, the uneven nature of the infrastructural development across regions in modern-day Africa still follows this colonial precedent, displaying similar spatialised patterns.

The existential failures in establishing and coordinating various new modes of transport, increasing the rail/road accessibility of previously disenfranchised areas, boosting intracontinental trade and socioeconomic cooperation (thereby reversing the colonially imposed spatial inequities) has had far-reaching implications on trade in modern-day Africa. One of the effects has been the limited spatial diversity of foreign aid-funded projects on the African continent (as depicted in Figures 17.2 and 17.3); in other words, the colonial rail infrastructure projects in Africa have not only skewed trade networks towards a suboptimal equilibrium, but they have also influenced a form of regional preferentialism and inefficient aid provision (Graff, 2019). In essence, just like a viscous fluid, international development aid has pursued a path of least resistance – often clamouring around areas where there is some form of pre-existing transport infrastructure. For instance, between 25–33 per cent of international aid from the World Bank and China have been directed at the same geographic destinations, that is, regions that already possessed a surplus of road infrastructure development (with the Chinese aid being by far the most constricted in terms of spatial diversity) (Graff, 2019). The implications of this aid for transport infrastructure in Africa have been quite pronounced – there is certainly a positive relationship between the World Bank and Chinese aid and an overabundance of roads (Holtz and Heitzig, 2021). This has been counterintuitive to any regional integration efforts and the systematic optimisation of Africa's transport infrastructure facilities for the benefit and interconnectivity of multiple countries on the continent.

Although over 4 500 kilometres of colonial railway lines were rehabilitated by Uganda, Kenya, Ethiopia and Nigeria between 2016 and 2017 – these were mostly individual country efforts and, thus, not necessarily tied to intracontinental connectivity (Jerome and Nabena, 2016: 93). Apart from the limited length and spatial distribution of Africa's rail infrastructure, other factors that are of great disservice to the consolidation of regional trade include the technical outdatedness of the existing rail infrastructure (most of which is over a century old). This has meant many problems conterminous with ageing tracks – for example, insufficient ballast, rail wear and deteriorating earthworks – all of which have lowered the total share of rail freight in intra-African trade (Jerome and Nabena, 2016: 93).

Figure 17.1: World Bank aid, spatial distribution

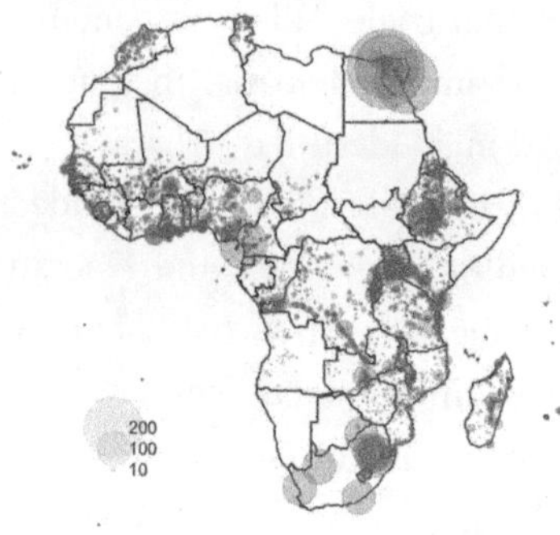

Source: Graff (2019: 43)

Figure 17.2: Chinese aid, spatial distribution

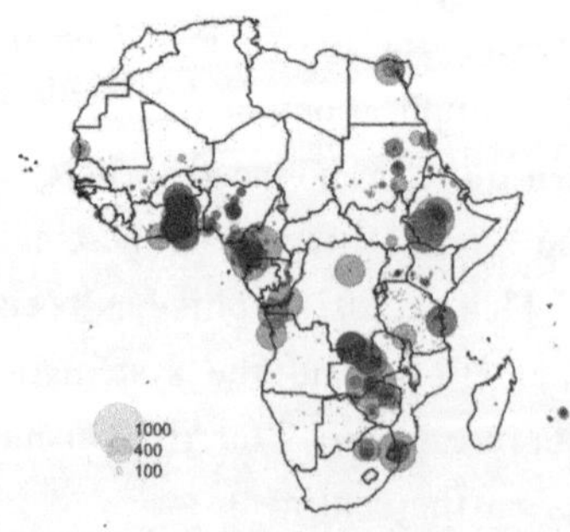

Source: Graff (2019: 43)

The historical issues outlined here have contextualised the origins of some of the imbalances/inefficiencies in Africa's transport networks, which are in themselves outcomes of (1) the spatialised development of colonial rail infrastructure and (2) the uneven patterns of international development aid that unfolded thereafter. Even in the case of aid for transport infrastructural development, its limited spatial diversity has only deepened Africa's imbalanced transport networks. These factors have adversely deepened regional segmentation, in the process delaying intra-Africa trade and stifling potential efficiency gains from what is supposed to be the systematic optimisation of transport infrastructure facilities that serve multiple African countries. Having shown the connection between rail networks and the subsequent development of road infrastructure in independent Africa, this chapter now discusses the current state of Africa's road network, and the extent to which it is functioning as an apparatus for regional connectivity.

Interconnectivity inefficiencies and Africa's road infrastructure

Africa's trade and transport corridors stem from four subregional seaports: in East Africa (Mombasa and Dar es Salaam), West Africa (Abidjan, Tema, Lomé, Cotonou and Dakar), Central Africa (Douala) and Southern Africa (Durban, Maputo and Beira). In a continent characterised by mostly small and landlocked economies, the importance of reliable road and railway transport networks to access those subregional seaports cannot be overstated; but of even more importance is the extent to which such a transport network facilitates intracontinental cooperation and economic integration. Although roads carry at least 80 per cent of goods and 90 per cent of passengers across Africa, only 53 per cent of the continent's entire road network is paved (Jerome and Nabena, 2016). As already mentioned, there is an uneven distribution of that paved portion, with some regions being over supplied and others underdeveloped (Graff, 2019).

Apart from the said intraregional differences in transport infrastructure, it is also important to note how the best performers in Africa – countries with relatively well developed transport infrastructure – still lag considerably behind international averages (see Figure 17.3).

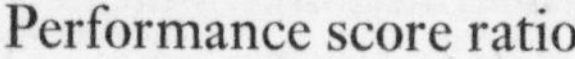

Figure 17.3: Gaps in Africa's infrastructure

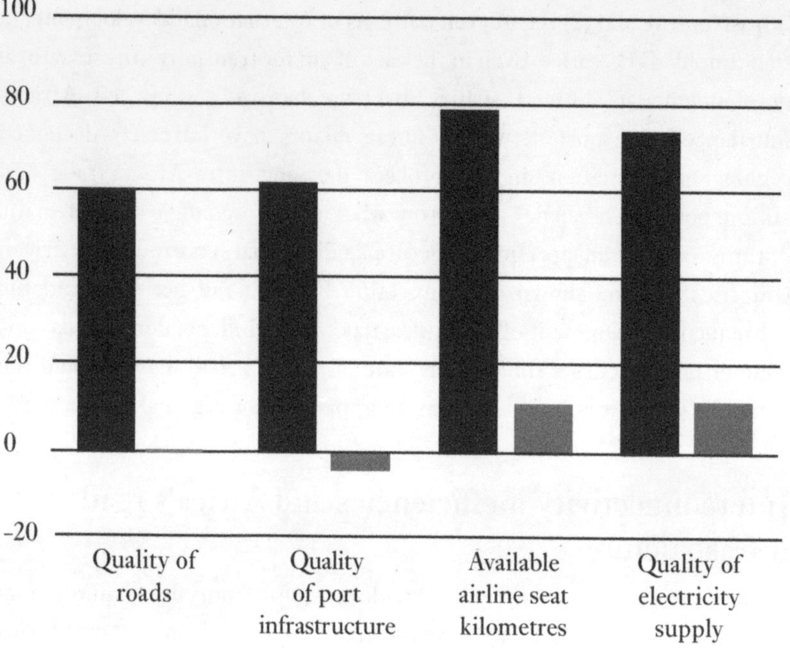

Key

■ Least African performer to bext Africn performer score ratio

■ Best African performer to OECD Average score ratio

Source: World Economic Forum (2017)

The inconsistencies illustrated in Figure 17.3 not only account for why transport costs in Africa are between 50 per cent and 175 per cent higher than in other developing parts of the world (Hall, 2018), but they are also indicative of the existential challenges that stand in the way of cross-country economic collaborations and the optimisation of facilities serving multiple countries. For instance, although the 1971 Trans-African Corridor (a partnership between the African Development Bank, the AU and the international community, and coordinated by UNECA) was intended as a road-based means to connect African capitals to all centres of production, ports and markets, it has encountered several challenges. With nine primary highway routes totalling 60 000 kilometres (listed in Figure 17.4) and the longest leg running from Tripoli to Cape Town (9 610 kilometres) – the 'unity highway' was idealised as 'the circulatory system of a developing technocracy through which Africans would become economic producers' as well as consumers (Cupers and Meier, 2020: 64). Needless to say, however, after the 1980s when most African states started attaining independence, the Trans-African Corridor became a largely forgotten phenomenon. For most African countries, the period after independence was not only characterised by a country-specific inward focus (leaving little room for continental obligations/expectations), but also the burgeoning of novel civil conflicts, mostly waged in response to the limited scope of effective political and economic reforms (UNCHR, 1993, 1995, cited in Kalipeni and Oppong, 1998: 1637). In some instances, peace took time to be restored and, when it eventually prevailed, what resulted were fragile states with security, capacity and legitimacy challenges. In this context, the biggest threat to Article 61 of the Abuja Treaty (the need to expand, modernise and maintain transport and communications infrastructure) (see OAU, 1991: 54) was a deficit of strong institutions. Without these, African states could not implement national developmental policies, let alone the expectations of regional treaties such as the Trans-African Corridor.

Figure 17.4: The Trans-African Corridor primary highway routes

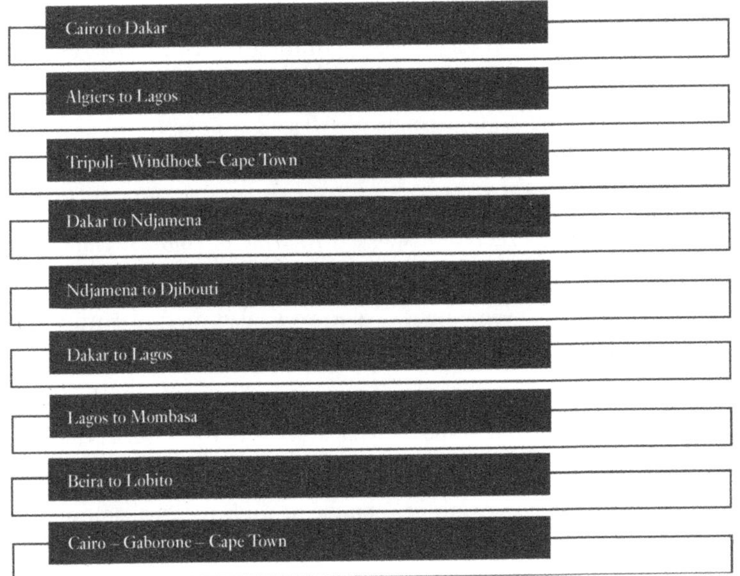

Source: African Development Bank (AfDB) (2019)

Although the Trans-African Corridor has begun to reappear in plans for contemporary African infrastructure, progress has been slowed by civil wars, cross-border tensions and terrorism in Nigeria (where some parts are Boko Haram infested), Libya, the Horn of Africa, Central Africa and parts of East Africa. Further to this, a serious lack of financial resources and the politics/complexities around developing new vehicle/road standards, regulations, visa requirements (one-stop border posts with joint customs and immigration offices from adjoining countries) and international vehicle insurance systems for the corridors have also stalled the Trans-African Corridor development (Cupers and Meier, 2020). To date, although a few developments have occurred on the nine highways (listed in Figure 18.5), the completion of the 4 400-kilometre stretch across the Sahel, connecting Senegal to Chad, is the most significant; the other routes are inundated with significant missing links (Jerome and Nabena, 2016). Over 40 years after the Trans-African Corridor idea was conceived, of the highway's 60 000 total kilometres, approximately 20 per cent remains unconstructed, with some regions experiencing less development than others; for example, in landlocked Central Africa, 65 per cent of the highway remains unconstructed, with only 3 891 kilometres of the planned 11 246 kilometres having been paved (Whitehead, 2014; AfDB, 2017). These connectivity issues have had far-reaching implications for the realisation of the AfCFTA; that is, intra-Africa trade currently sits at between 13 and 14 per cent of the continent's total global trade, severely limiting the full realisation of a potential market of 1.2 billion people (Johnson, 2019). Figure 18.6 illustrates some of the far-reaching repercussions of Africa's connectivity challenges (suboptimal transport infrastructure) on the ease of carrying out business, that is, intracontinental bilateral trade.

Whereas the previous section discussed the role of colonial empires in the spatialisation of Africa's rail infrastructural development, independent Africa's infrastructural development discourse is also marred with a new calibre of foreign characters. Pursuing what Max and Angels (1976) predicted as a 'more thorough exploitation of old markets', those foreign characters are no longer potentates nor imperial states (as was the case during and before colonialism), but rather industrialists and multinational companies (MNCs) that emerged as a result of a boom in multinationalism and the establishment of the global production system (McMichael, 1996; Burgis, 2016; Eyssen, 2018). Their presence and the penetration of private investment, private capital and technologies from abroad has been opportunistically necessitated by African countries, lack of capacity to fully exploit and maximise the natural resource wealth in their respective territories despite their indispensable position in the global extractive industry. Along with this penetration has been a commensurate extracontinental focus on the orientation of Africa's transport infrastructure – it has become a means in itself to maximise foreign entities' own economic returns, without any focus on expanding, modernising or maintaining the African transport infrastructure for the benefit of sustainable intracontinental trade. These reasons partly account for the little effort shown by global capital and host governments to ensure that strategic investments in extractive sectors also encompass long-term infrastructure development within host states, in other words, spatial linkages.

Figure 17.5: Regional fragmentation and its impact on economic integration

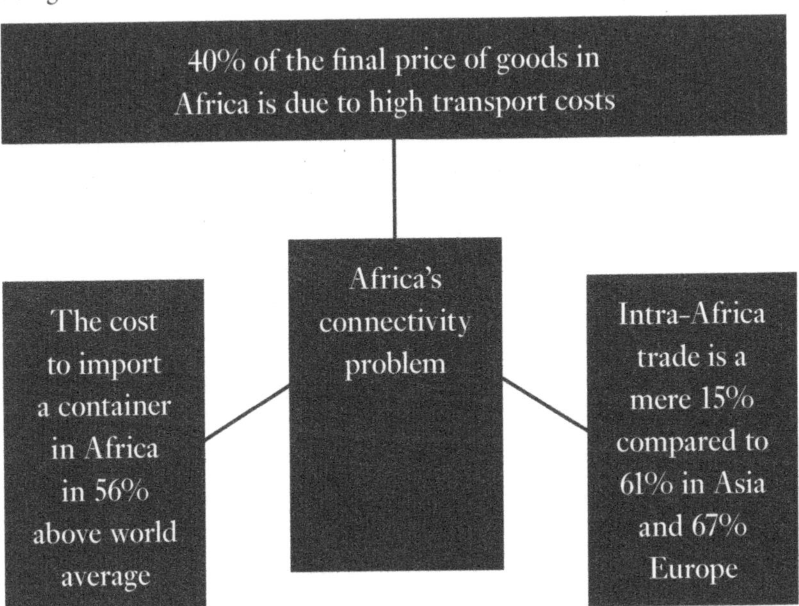

Source: Sub-Saharan Africa Transport Policy Programme (2015)

One such threat to the feasibility of spatial linkages has been lax regulatory regimes, which have adversely promoted the proliferation of 'crony capitalism' and its many constituents, for example, thin capitalisation and structured investment contracts, as well as the use of debt rather than aid by developing and developed economies to establish/consolidate their dominant positions in the international development finance market (Wooley, 2021). While serving the individualistic interests of corporate behemoths and African politicians, the accrued debts still benefit from explicit or implicit forms of host government liability (despite them not appearing on government balance sheets), which then not only introduces major public financial management challenges, but also blurs the distinction between private and public debt (Malik *et al.*, 2021). These factors have come at the expense of the common vision/unity of purpose required to operationalise the regional economic integration agenda (Enderwick, 2005; Otusanya *et al.*, 2009). They also account for why, despite Africa receiving more aid than Europe, Central Asia, Latin America and the Caribbean combined – most of which is designated for infrastructural development projects – there is still no link between foreign aid and positive economic outcomes, nor a commensurate construction of roads, railways and other transport infrastructural development in recipient countries (Clemens and Kremer, 2016; World Bank, 2017; Graff, 2019).

While cronyism and lax regulatory regimes certainly do account for why, despite the considerable outpouring of foreign direct investment (FDI) in the African continent (almost US$12 billion in lending commitments annually), this capital continues to be detached from any meaningful transport infrastructural developments (especially over the last 10 years – see Figure 17.4), there are also other contributing factors. One of these factors is the lack of effort that has gone into tailoring external support (including World Bank lending) to Africa's very specific circumstances (Harral and Faiz, 1988). Just as we have seen the limited spatial diversity of infrastructural development aid in railway transport, there has been a reduced function of private-sector investment and public–private partnerships in developmental areas (World Economic Forum, 2017) as well as a constricted focus by international financial institutions (IFIs) on funding the construction of new corridors at the expense of ensuring that the existing road infrastructure is diligently maintained. With poor governance, corruption and other structural factors, the neglect of the existing transport infrastructure has resulted in both losses to its value and functionality, reducing the ease and safety of regional interconnectivity, which that infrastructure is intended to facilitate. For instance, a preventive road maintenance expenditure of US$12 billion in the 1970s and 1980s could have easily averted infrastructure losses to the tune of US$45 billion (Harral and Faiz, 1988). The ensuing dilapidation of the road infrastructure and its eventual loss due to poor – or in some cases, non-existent – maintenance, has consequently made African roads very dangerous with an unacceptably high incidence of road accidents. According to the SSAPT annual report for 2019, despite having a low road network density of 0.08 kilometre per square kilometre and a vehicle fleet that accounts for only 2 per cent of the world's total, Africa's road-related fatality rate is currently the highest in the world standing at 24.1 per 100 000 (SSATP, 2019). These factors are important to note when considering Africa's poor development trajectory and contrasting this with the missing transport infrastructure and its importance in the long-term sustainability of not just the extractive industry but also the functioning of local markets (UNCTAD, 2017; Renwick *et al.*, 2018).

Although the previous paragraph discussed an absence of strong institutions on the continent and the adverse impact of this on the coordination of transport infrastructural development projects, the broader implications of this – such as dissuading private-sector participation in transport and utility infrastructure development projects – should be noted. For instance, the SSATP in its 2019 annual report also noted weak technical, institutional and financial capacity, as well as poor governance (weak leadership/corruption) as some of the key challenges facing Africa's transport sector. When we consider China's Belt and Road Initiative (BRI) infrastructure project – apart from the labour violations, environmental hazards, and public protests – corruption has been reported as the most notable challenge, with 35 per cent of the project facing implementation challenges (Malik *et al.*, 2021). The inability to implement policies and maintain autonomy (Tyagi, 2012) has not only promoted rife conditions for crony capitalism (as illustrated in the previous paragraph), it has also delayed the uptake of available loans and grants from financial institutions. For instance, only 93.8 per cent of the total funds allocated in 2012 were disbursed by the AfDB that year, with a further decline in disbursements to 70.1 per cent in 2014, that is, over half of that designated for infrastructure development (see AfDB, 2014). Cumulatively, as evidenced by an Africa competitiveness report compiled by the World Economic Forum in 2017, these issues have had wider implications on regional and continental efficiency gains (see Figure 17.5).

The World Economic Forum report shows that, over the last 10 years, the quality of transport infrastructure and energy supply in Africa has declined by 6 and 3 per cent respectively. In fact, only the quality of roads has improved modestly over the past 10 years, while the quality of ports, airports and electricity infrastructure has remained poor.

Figure 17.5: Average trends in selected infrastructure indicators

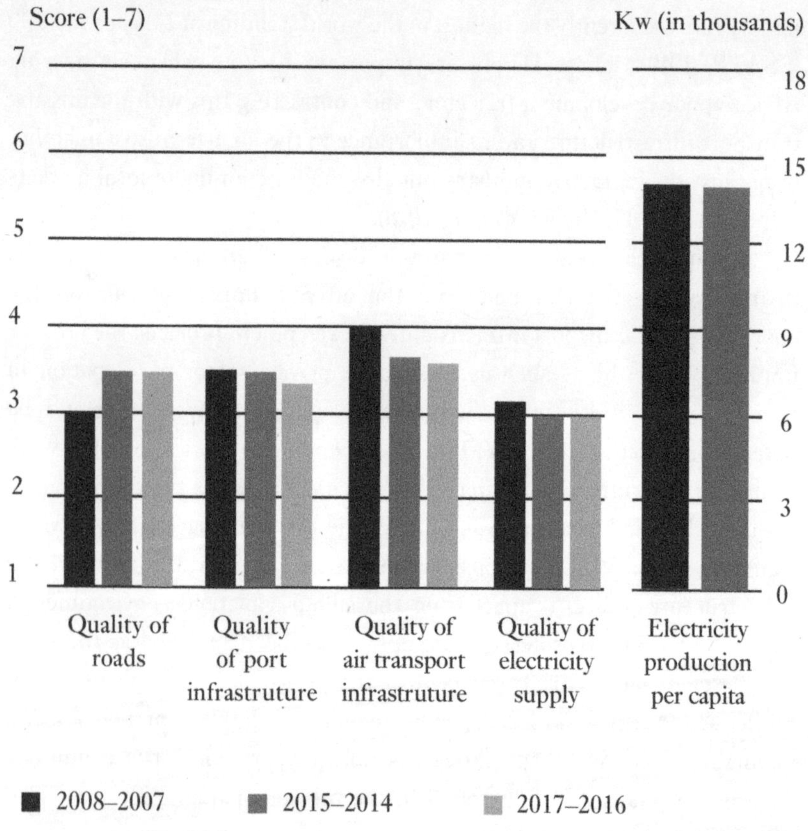

Source: World Economic Forum (2017)

Although the involvement of public–private partnerships and private-sector investment in the construction of transport and utility infrastructure is only minimal on the African continent, this is not to say that these partnerships do not exist. Where they do exist, however, it is not unusual to find a lack of transparency and unfavourable commercial loan terms (threats to debt sustainability). As a result of debt acceleration, China's cumulative loans to Africa from 2000 to 2016 had already amounted to US$124 billion, with oil-related loans to countries like Angola constituting a quarter of cumulative Chinese loans to the entire continent (Eyssen, 2018). While Chinese collateralised loans against future commodity export receipts come with the challenge of relatively high interest rates (nearly 6 per cent), the collateralisation of strategic economic assets (for acquisition in the event of debt-repayment challenges) is also a principal cause of concern (Malik *et al.*, 2021). A good example of this is China's Belt and Road Initiative (BRI) projects. AidData, a research institute that seeks to make development finance more transparent, analysed 13 427 aid and debt-financed projects in 165 countries (worth US$843 billion) and found that the BRI had left many lower and middle-income countries with undeclared/hidden debts totalling US$385 billion (Malik *et al.*, 2021).

Although the BRI was initially hailed as a potential catalyst for African regional economic integration, resource-secured infrastructure finance by China has led to a loss of national assets and the sovereignty/agency of African states to participate in the regional and continental cooperation agenda (Nantulya, 2019; Brautigam *et al.*, 2020). A preference for the collateralisation of liquid assets is evidenced by a 2020 study, which also found that over 40 per cent of Chinese state-owned lenders' financial portfolio was collateralised (Acker *et al.*, 2020). In Zambia, for instance, as a result of the country's failure to repay loans of up to US$8.7 billion, the national airport, electricity company and major road projects are all at risk of a Chinese takeover. Furthermore, where transport infrastructure is funded by foreign lenders, the need to expedite the returns on their investments (in line with their own geo-economic strategies) can also mean an export revenue-oriented focus, with the constructed transport networks being purpose built for exporting minerals/agricultural commodities and the importation (into the host country) of processed/manufactured goods (Burgis, 2016: 62). Max and Angels (1967: 83–84) express the same sentiments:

> The need of a constantly expanding market for its products causes the bourgeoise over the whole surface of the globe. It must nestle everywhere, settle everywhere, establish connexions everywhere ... with new industries that no longer work up indigenous raw material, but raw material drawn from the remotest zones.

A particularly good example of an export revenue-oriented focus on infrastructural development is provided by PIDA. PIDA's priority projects (which include the Brazzaville–Kinshasa Bridge, Algiers–Lagos Trans-Saharan Highway, the Lagos–Abidjan Transport Corridor and hundreds of others) have been accused of focusing on infrastructure investment that serves corporate greed without furthering regional integration, that is, mutual growth based on development linkages (PIDA, 2018; WRM, 2019). Whereas a fairly distributed road transport network can promote the trade in regional products by connecting rural areas and national producers – foreign-funded infrastructural development projects tend to shy away from such a focus. The arising road network connectivity challenges have thus not only delinked rural agricultural producers from urban centres, but they have also marginalised them from cross-country trade and, in the long run, are impeding the development of regions where the majority of the population is rural bound, for example, in least developed countries (LDCs), land-locked developing countries (LLDCs) and small island developing states (SIDS) (Avery *et al.*, 2017).

Conclusion

The importance of sound transport infrastructure and logistics to connect African countries in order to achieve the envisioned goal of regional integration is a topic that has been in the public domain for a long time. Known and documented challenges have included, but have not been confined to, the issue of low resource complementarity between member countries, limited funding, low institutional capacity and a deficit of technical leadership on the continent. Apart from examining the challenges to the synergies between governments, the private sector, and institutional investors in transport infrastructure development, this chapter has contributed to the ongoing discourse on regional integration in Africa. This was done by focusing on two transport subsectors (roads and railways), and juxtaposing the declarations and treaties canvassing regional integration in Africa against their tenability into actual solutions to the interconnectivity inefficiencies affecting the continent. In addition, the practical strides made by regional institutions towards ensuring the development of high-capacity and efficient transport corridors on the continent were discussed. These included the institutionalisation of the SSATP and PIDA, along with the efficacy of their subsequent action plans to solve regional segmentation (and the arising connectivity challenge) in Africa's trade networks. In doing so, this chapter drew relevant parallels between the contemporary challenges facing the road and rail transport infrastructure network in accelerating economic integration, as well as the historical factors that resulted in a heavily segmented continent, that is, the uneven and spatialised development of the colonial transport infrastructure.

While the policies and continental treaties for promoting regional interconnectivity are certainly there – with bold and ambitious declarations for a future Africa that is economically integrated – the reality is that there are massive gaps in theory versus praxis, which are in themselves a reflection of unmet financing needs and a poor enforcement of existing treaties. Some of the implementation gaps, discussed in this chapter, are the result of (1) the spatialised development of the colonial rail infrastructure on the continent and (2) its subsequent influence on the uneven patterns of international development aid that materialised thereafter. But an even bigger stumbling block to regional integration (more than the suboptimal physical condition of the transport infrastructure) has been the reluctance/ inability of African states to abide by the continental treaties and other transport sector policies. Concomitantly tied to this has been a normative absence of peace and political stability; for example, in West Africa alone, there have been three coups d'état in a space of only five months (Campbell, 2021). Without peace and political stability, it is impossible to integrate the African continent economically, as these two are key prerequisites for economic and infrastructural development. The arising uneven and limited progress in transport infrastructure development between regional economic communities (with subsequently high transaction costs for intra-African trade) has made the possibility of an African economic community less feasible. The factors, which are stumbling blocks to cooperatively building cross-border and integrative transport infrastructure to ensure the safer, cheaper and faster movement of goods and people, pose considerable threats to the establishment of an African Continental Free Trade Area.

Whereas the expectation has always been that African countries (within their respective regional economic communities) would take steps to correct the spatialised orientation of historical/colonial transport infrastructure – which is by its very nature at great odds with the contemporary goal of an integrated continent – this has been far from the case. Crony capitalism, lax regulatory regimes and a low technical capacity (which has led to a poor uptake of available loans/grants from financial institutions) have also been discussed as some of the precipitating factors behind a poor compliance (at country level) to continental treaties on regional integration, urban mobility and road safety. These factors have also been partly responsible for why (1) strategic investments in Africa's extractive sectors have failed to incorporate commensurately long-term transport infrastructure development/maintenance in their plans and (2) little enforcement has been made for concessionaires to include the rehabilitation, maintenance or transport infrastructure in their model bidding.

References

Acker, K., Bräutigam, D. and Huang, Y. (2020). Debt relief with Chinese characteristics. China–Africa Research Initiative Research Paper, No. 39. Available at: https://papers.ssrn.com/sol3/papers.cfm?abstract_id=3745021 (Accessed 29 September 2021).

African Development Bank (AfDB). (2020). 'Economic brief – The Africa Infrastructure Development Index (AIDI) 2020–July 2020'. Available at: https://www.afdb.org/en/documents/economic-brief-africa-infrastructure-development-index-aidi-2020-july-2020 (Accessed 12 August 2021).

African Development Bank (AfDB). (2019). 'Cross-border road corridors: The quest to integrate Africa'. Available at: https://www.afdb.org/fileadmin/uploads/afdb/Documents/Publications/Cross-border_road_corridors.pdf (Accessed 28 August 2021).

African Development Bank (AfDB). (2018). 'Importance of regional and continental integration for Africa's development'. Available at: https://www.afdb.org/en/news-and-events/importance-of-regional-and-continental-integration-for-africas-development-18773 (Accessed 10 August 2021).

African Development Bank (AfDB). (2017). 'Integrating Africa: Completing Cape-to-Cairo road'. Available at: https://www.afdb.org/en/news-and-events/multimedia/video/integrating-africa-completing-cape-to-cairo-road-1408 (Accessed 6 September 2021).

African Development Bank (AfDB). (2015). 'Rail Infrastructure in Africa: Financing Policy Options'. Available at: https://www.afdb.org /fileadmin/uploads/afdb/Documents/Events/ATFforum/Rail_

Infrastructure_in_Africa_-_Financing_Policy_Options_-_AfDB.pdf (Accessed 25 August 2021).

African Development Bank (AfDB). (2014). 'Annual Report'. Available at: https://www.afdb.org/fileadmin/uploads/afdb/Documents/Publications/AR2014/AR2014-Executive_Summary_-EN.pdf (Accessed 20 August 2021).

African Union. (2015). *Agenda 2063: The Africa We Want*. Addis Ababa: African Union Commission.

African Union. (2009). 'Declaration on development of transport and energy infrastructure in Africa'. Declaration Assembly/AU/Decl, 1. Addis Ababa: African Union. Available at: http://archives.au.int/handle/123456789/267 (Accessed 20 November 2022).

Avery, L.J., Regmi, M.B., Joshi, G.R. and Mohanty, C.R.C. (2017). 'Rural–urban connectivity in achieving sustainable regional development'. Background paper for Intergovernmental Tenth Regional Environmentally Sustainable Transport (EST) Forum, 14–16 March 2017, pp. 14–16.

Bell, D. (2017). 'Political realism and international relations', *Philosophy Compass*, 12(2): e12403.

Brautigam, D., Huang, Y. and Acker, K. (2020). 'Risky business: New data on Chinese loans and Africa's debt problem', *Briefing Paper*, (3): 1–20.

Brushett, S. (2005). *Management and Financing of Road Transport Infrastructure in Africa*. World Bank Sub-Saharan Africa Transport Policy Program, Discussion Paper No 4, Road Management and Financing (RMF) Series.

Burgis, T. (2016). *The Looting Machine: Warlords, oligarchs, corporations, smugglers, and the theft of Africa's wealth*. London: HarperCollins.

Campbell, J. (2021). 'Coups are back in West Africa'. Available at: https://www.cfr.org/blog/coups-are-back-west-africa (Accessed 15 September 2021).

Clemens, M.A. and Kremer, M. (2016). 'The new role for the World Bank', *Journal of Economic Perspectives*, 30(1): 53–76.

Cupers, K. and Meier, P. (2020). 'Infrastructure between statehood and selfhood: The Trans-African Highway', *Journal of the Society of Architectural Historians*, 79(1): 61–81.

Dumitru, A. and Hayat, R. (2015). 'Sub-Saharan Africa: Politically more stable, but still fragile', *Economic Research*. Available at: https://economics.rabobank.com/publications/2015/december/sub-saharan-africa-politically-more-stable-but-still-fragile/ (Accessed 12 August 2021).

Enderwick, P. (2005). 'What's bad about crony capitalism?' *Asian Business and Management*, 4(2): 117–32.

Eyssen, B. (2018). 'Double debt risk for African countries that turn to China'. Available at: https://www.dw.com/en/double-debt-risk-for-african-countries-that-turn-to-china/a-44819336 (Accessed 7 September 2021).

Graff, T. (2019). *Spatial Inefficiencies in Africa's Trade Network* (No. w25951). Pretoria: National Bureau of Economic Research. Available at: https://www.nber.org/papers/w25951 (Accessed 12 August 2021).

Hall, J. (2018). 'In fits and starts: The Trans-African Highway extends its reach'. Available at: https://www.inonafrica.com/2018/07/10/in-fits-and-starts-the-trans-african-highway-extends-its-reach/ (Accessed 6 September 2021).

Harral, C. and Faiz, A. (1988). *Road Deterioration in Developing Countries: Causes and remedies* (No. 13370, pp. 1–76). Washington, DC: The World Bank.

Holtz, L. and Heitzig, C. (2021). 'Figures of the week: Africa's spatial distribution of road infrastructure'. Available at: https://www.brookings.edu/blog/africa-in-focus/2021/03/17/figures-of-the-week-africas-spatial-distribution-of-road-infrastructure/ (Accessed 1 September 2021).

Jedwab, R. and Moradi, A. (2012). 'Colonial investments and long-term development in Africa: Evidence from Ghanaian railways'. Unpublished manuscript, George Washington University and Sussex University.

Jedwab, R., Kerby, E. and Moradi, A. (2017). 'History, path dependence and development: Evidence from colonial railways, settlers and cities in Kenya', *The Economic Journal*, 127(603): 1467–94.

Jedwab, R. and Moradi, A. (2016). 'The permanent effects of transportation revolutions in poor countries: Evidence from Africa', *Review of Economics and Statistics*, 98(2): 268–84.

Jerome, A. and Nabena, D. (2016). 'Infrastructure and regional integration in Africa', in D.H. Levine and D. Nagar (eds). *Region-building in Africa: Political and economic challenges*. New York: Palgrave Macmillan, pp. 89–108.

Johnson, M.A. (2019). 'The Cairo–Cape Town Highway: What you need to know'. Available at: https://www.linkedin.com/pulse/cairo-cape-town-highway-what-you-need-know-mark-anthony-johnson/ (Accessed 6 September 2021).

Kalipeni, E. and Oppong, J. (1998). 'The refugee crisis in Africa and implications for health and disease: a political ecology approach', *Social Science and Medicine*, 46(12): 1637–53.

Malik, A., Parks, B., Russell, B., Lin, J., Walsh, K., Solomon, K., Zhang, S., Elston, T. and Goodman, S. (2021). *Banking on the Belt and Road: Insights from a new global dataset of 13,427 Chinese development projects.* Williamsburg, VA: AidData at William & Mary.

Marx, K. and Engels, F., 1967. *The communist manifesto.* 1848. Trans. Samuel Moore. London: Penguin.

McMichael, P. (1996). *Development and Social Change: A global perspective.* Thousand Oaks, CA: Pine Forge Press.

Mouhamed, B.B. and Qiu, Y. (2020). 'Past, present and future development of West African railways', *Journal of Sustainable Development of Transport and Logistics*, 5(1): 103–14.

Nantulya, P. (2019). 'Implications for Africa from China's One Belt One Road Strategy'. Available at: https://africacenter.org/spotlight/implications-for-africa-china-one-belt-one-road-strategy/ (Accessed 18 August 2021).

Ndlovu, R. (2021). 'Beitbridge chaos: Zimbabwe forms crisis team to ease 10 km queues at border', *Times Live*, 22 October. Available at: https://www.timeslive.co.za/news/africa/2021-10-22-beitbridge-chaos-zimbabwe-forms-crisis-team-to-ease-10km-queues-at-border/ (Accessed 28 October 2021).

OAU. (1991). *Treaty establishing the African economic community.* Addis Ababa: Organization of African Unity. Available at: https://au.int/sites/default/files/treaties/37636treaty0016__treaty_establishing_the_african_economic_community_e.pdf (Accessed 11 August 2021).

Otusanya, A.J., Lauwo, S. and Bakre, O.M. (2009). 'Extractive Industry Transparency Initiative: A utopia in oil and mining industry in developing country'. Conference paper. Available at: URI: studylib.net/doc/7584475/extractive-industry-transparency-initiativehttp://ir.unilag.edu.ng:8080/xmlui/handle/123456789/2716 (Accessed 16 October 2022).

Programme for Infrastructure Development in Africa (PIDA). (2012). 'Programme for Infrastructural Development in Africa: Vison'. Available at: https://www.au-pida.org/pida-vision/ (Accessed 30 August 2021).

Programme for Infrastructure Development in Africa (PIDA). (2018). 'PIDA Progress Report'. Available at: https://www.tralac.org/documents/

resources/african-union/2509-2018-pida-progress-report-summary-update/file.html (Accessed 17 August 2021).

Potter, M.B.H. (1997). *Dedicated road funds: A preliminary view on a World Bank initiative.* International Monetary Fund.

Ravenhill, J. (2016). 'Regional integration in Africa: Theory and practice', in D.H. Levine and D. Nagar (eds). *Region-building in Africa.* New York: Palgrave Macmillan, pp. 37–52.

Řehák, V. (2019). 'Region-Building in Africa. Political and Economic Challenges', *Archiv Orientální*, 87(1): 214–16.

Renwick, N., Gu, J. and Hong, S. (2018). 'China and African governance in the extractive industries', *Revue internationale de politique de développement*, (10.1). https://doi.org/10.4000/poldev.2547.

SSATP. (2019). 'Third Development Plan'. Available at: https://www.ssatp.org/sites/ssatp/files/SSATP-DP3%20Document%202018.pdf (Accessed 30 August 2021).

Street, J.H. (1967). 'The Latin American "structuralists" and the institutionalists: Convergence in development theory', *Journal of Economic Issues*, 1(1–2): 44–62.

Stuart, J. (2020). 'Informal cross-border trade in Africa in a time of pandemic'. Available at: https://www.tralac.org/blog/article/14487-informal-cross-border-trade-in-africa-in-a-time-of-pandemic.html (Accessed 16 August 2021).

Tamosaitiene, J., Sarvari, H., Chan, D.W. and Cristofaro, M. (2021). 'Assessing the barriers and risks to private sector participation in infrastructure construction projects in developing countries of Middle East', *Sustainability*, 13(1): 153.

UNCTAD. (2017). Establishing development linkages in the extractive industry: Lessons from the field. Available at: https://unctad.org/system/files/official-document/tdb64d3_en.pdf (Accessed 16 August 2021).

Whitehead, E. (2014). 'How we made it in Africa: Trans-African Highway remains a road to nowhere'. Available at: https://www.howwemadeitinafrica.com/trans-african-highway-remains-a-road-to-nowhere/39863/ (Accessed 6 September 2021).

Wooley, A. (2021). 'China Development Finance Program'. Available at: https://www.aiddata.org/blog/aiddatas-new-dataset-of-13-427-chinese-development-projects-worth-843-billion-reveals-major-increase-in-hidden-debt-and-belt-and-road-initiative-implementation-problems

(Accessed 30 September 2021).

World Economic Forum. (2017). *The Africa Competitiveness Report, 2017.* Available at: http://www3.weforum.org/docs/WEF_ACR_2017.pdf (Accessed 20 August 2021).

World Bank. (2019). 'Railways, goods transported (million tonne-km): Data'. Available at: https://data.worldbank.org/indicator/IS.RRS.GOODMT.K6?-contextual=region&end=2019&name_desc=false&start=1995&view=chart (Accessed 25 August 2021).

World Rainforest Movement (WRM). (2019). 'Infrastructure in Africa for extractive industries and corporate profits: What about community needs?' Available at: https://wrm.org.uy/articles-from-the-wrm-bulletin/section1/infrastructure-in-africa-for-extractive-industries-and-corporate-profits-what-about-community-needs/ (Accessed 17 August 2021).

Yang, Y. and Gupta, S. (2007). 'Regional trade arrangements in Africa: Past performance and the way forward', *African Development Review*, 19(3): 399–431.

Chapter Eighteen

Digital infrastructure: Creating the backbone for development

ODILILE AYODELE

Introduction

The dream of African continental integration is pinned not only on normative conceptions of integrative integration, but also on material considerations. Adequate soft and hard infrastructure is key to Africa's ambitions and is linked to positive developmental outcomes. Soft infrastructure refers to all the services that contribute to a country's economic, social, health and cultural wellbeing, such as postal, financial and health services, all of which are key for growth and prosperity. Still, soft infrastructure is one of the continent's areas with acute deficiencies. Hard infrastructure, which refers to physical infrastructure such as roads, railways, ports, and electricity and broadband connections, is also an area of concern.

If Africa is to be prosperous, it cannot rely solely on its natural resource wealth. Instead, it must improve the conditions for entrepreneurship and develop efficient public administration for a healthy social economy, which entails ensuring a healthy mix of hard and soft infrastructure. The growing digital economy also needs a solid blend of infrastructures. The African Union's (AU's) Digital Transformation Strategy (DTS) is based on the understanding that Africa's ability to transform digitally requires digital infrastructure, enabling policies and a regulatory environment, digital skills, and innovation and entrepreneurship.

The promise of a Single Digital Market (SDM) for Africa gives breath to the aspirations of millions of Africans to transform their economies. However, the actualisation of these aspirations hinges on the ability of African countries to digitally transform their economies, which in turn is dependent on digital infrastructure and having the appropriate skills and systems that allow citizens to benefit.

In this chapter, I argue that, without concerted efforts to improve digital infrastructure on the continent quickly, any hope of enhanced cross-border trade or benefit from the digital economy is a pipe dream. I lean on Atkinson *et al.*'s (2016: 2) conception of infrastructure as being the 'systems that societies use to transport goods, people, or information'. They specifically describe digital infrastructure as 'those where at least a portion contains information technology' (Atkinson *et al.*, 2016: 2).

Increased access to digital infrastructure underpins Africa's vision for continental integration, not only because it improves the continent's economic prospects, but also because it pushes African countries to a collective agreement on regulatory standards and contracts on developing physical infrastructure. I bolster my arguments with primary and secondary data, including trade statistics, academic literature, newspaper articles and official documents.

This chapter contributes to scholarship on the transformative power of infrastructure and is a preliminary reflection on the implications of the African Continental Free Trade Area (AfCFTA). I illustrate that narrowing the digital divide and improving Africa's cross-border flows are linked directly to its ability to enhance and harness the benefits of its digital infrastructure. I do not approach the discussion on digital infrastructure from the large technical systems view. Instead, I take a more holistic, sociotechnical approach and examine the interconnectedness of people, technological artefacts and systems. Moreover, I do not discuss digital infrastructure at a granular level but look at the more prominent connectivity indicators. I consider infrastructure such as broadband connectivity rates, particularly undersea cables because these metrics speak to the ability of a state or region to access the modern economy. It is not within the scope of this chapter to speak to the public administration, education and skills or governance effectiveness that also form part of a state's ability to capitalise on the digital economy.

My argument is laid out in four steps:

1. What is digital infrastructure and why it is essential?
2. What is the state of Africa's digital infrastructure environment and who are the primary providers and funders?
3. What is Africa's Digital Transformation Strategy and what are the stumbling blocks to developing a digital single market (DSM) for Africa?
4. Some preliminary ideas for Africa's digital future.

Digital infrastructure

Digital infrastructure is the key feature of our society and the economy in the 21st century. Its existence is undoubtedly multifaceted but also characterised by multiple endogenous and exogenous tensions (Edwards, 2003). These include issues of ownership, control, management and data sovereignty. These tensions are felt more acutely in African countries because of the vast digital divide. Africa has the lowest internet penetration rate globally and, because of its poor access to financial resources and low state-level investment, it is struggling to narrow this divide.

What is digital infrastructure?

Digital infrastructure has to be approached from two perspectives because there are physical and non-physical aspects. Atkinson *et al.* (2016) describe digital infrastructures as being hybrid or dedicated, both using information technology. Dedicated digital infrastructure is purely digital, for instance, broadband cables transferring digital data (Atkinson, 2021: 3). In contrast, hybrid digital infrastructure combines both physical and digital components (Atkinson, 2021: 3), for example, smart water meters that use wireless technology to collect and transmit water billing information.

Hard or dedicated, digital infrastructure in Africa still lags behind the rest of the world. In 2018, approximately 30 per cent of Africa's population had access to the Internet, and less than 40 per cent had access to smartphones (Dannouni *et al.*, 2020). Now 4G networks cover nearly 60 per cent of Africa's population (OECD, 2021). Financial technology (Fintech), the integration of technology into financial services, has become almost ubiquitous across the continent, with people in Africa having more mobile money accounts than in any other developing region (AUC/OECD, 2021).

Interpreting these numbers, however, needs a degree of nuance as Africa is not 'homogenous'. Southern Africa, for instance, has an internet penetration rate of 55 per cent while Central Africa has a penetration rate of only 12 per cent (Dannouni *et al.*, 2020). There is a further divide between those who live in rural and urban areas, with internet usage statistics sitting at 26 per cent and 47 per cent respectively (AUC/OECD, 2021). Moreover, according to the 2021 UNCTAD Digital Economy Report, fixed broadband penetration has increased in developed and developing countries. Although the average number of subscriptions per 100 people between 2005 and 2020 was meagre in the least developed countries (LDCs), these countries leapfrogged into using mobile broadband. According to the UNCTAD connectivity report, there were 351 million mobile broadband subscriptions in 2020, which is 26 times the subscription rate of fixed broadband (UNCTAD, 2021: 8; ITU, 2021: 10).

Although the adoption rate of mobile broadband and the smartphone, or internet-enabled phones, was relatively high, it has the lowest adoption rate (although this is predicted to increase exponentially). The barriers to adoption include the cost of data and smartphones; in 2019, the estimated cost of a device represented as much as 30 per cent of monthly GDP (UNCTAD, 2021: 10). Any plans for infrastructure growth, and maturation, must keep these differences in mind. However, there are several challenges in building physical digital infrastructure that should also be considered.

Challenges to building digital infrastructure

Developing digital infrastructure is not only about designing and building technical systems that meet a need; there are also sociopolitical implications of making infrastructures available or withholding them (Von Schnitzler, 2013; Boyer, 2018). For instance, during apartheid, the availability and deployment of telecommunications infrastructure were closely linked to race-based politics (Horwitz, 1997). Therefore, one would assume that closing fissures and improving development prospects would mean creating an attractive regulatory environment for investment, building networks and employing suitable policy instruments. Yet, the solution is not that simple.

On the one hand, having solid regulations and policies are essential. On the other hand, there are dangers inherent in regulatory capture and reinforcing inequity (Sutherland, 2006). Specifically, the policies and regulatory environment can support (or create) societal fissures between the haves and the have-nots. Huawei (2015: 6) warns that the digital divide will intensify if issues such as the quality of networks and devices, and the quality of applications and services, are not addressed. In essence, they argue that those with 2G connections, or basic mobile phones, are at a distinct disadvantage compared to those with a 4G connection or a new generation mobile phone that allows the user a more comprehensive array of options, thus enabling them to take full advantage of digital technologies. They describe this phenomenon as digital enablement, which is 'the result of benefitting from ICT with the purpose of overcoming the gap between the individuals, communities and economies that are digitally enabled and those who are not' (Huawei, 2015: 6).

Efforts to close the digital divide and digitally enable populations on the margins means that states, the private sector, and regional bodies need to think broadly about their policy interventions and the possible ramifications of merely adding to increasing access without providing the ability to utilise it. Possible interventions include revamping the basic education curriculum to include digital literacy. Countries like South Africa and Rwanda have already begun implementing such programmes with varying degrees of success. The private sector and regional bodies could participate by funding grassroots educational initiatives that focus on basic and advanced digital literacy programmes for poor communities.

Moreover, for the African continent, narrowing the digital divide by increasing digital infrastructure goes beyond attracting financing for infrastructural development projects; it includes setting up a responsive and flexible regulatory environment to deal with technologies that evolve faster than the laws and policies can accommodate. Commerce in the digital era is complex, owing to the unfixed nature of data; in other words, data in one country may be stored on servers outside the country's borders. Therefore, creating the infrastructure (material and non-material) to support e-commerce on the continent would mean developing regulatory frameworks that respond to data localisation and ownership questions, as well as privacy and security. African countries cannot finance infrastructure development, let alone build it, but all states are precarious.

Focusing on the role of individual states or championing politicians, in stimulating infrastructure development is easy, particularly in the developing country context. For instance, Thabo Mbeki, Olusegun Obasanjo and Paul Kagame are often heralded as the progenitors of mobile telephony in their respective countries. They were often at the forefront of increased communications infrastructure investment. However, a full appreciation of the challenges to creating a positive infrastructure investment environment necessitates looking beyond the state level. In other words, regulatory responses must be external and domestic; as Plantin and De Seta (2019: 262) highlight, '[t]the development of an infrastructure is never a standalone project. It depends on networks that build on and grow in relation to the existing infrastructure.' This begs the question: what role do global, continental and regional bodies play in galvanising infrastructure building, particularly on the African continent?

There are several international frameworks around internet governance, and, by extension, e-commerce, such as the World Intellectual Property Organisation (WIPO), but individual states are still responsible for shaping their regional and domestic regulatory environments. However, the 21st-century digital ecosystem relies on regulatory harmonisation and interoperability, including the digital economy.

Competing for internet and data governance is complicated by having to deal with highly contested issues such as cross-border electronic trade, data privacy and cyber security. This is further complicated by competing internet and data governance approaches. The standard-bearers are the European Union (EU), China and the United States, all with divergent approaches. African countries must navigate these complexities and ensure their regional and national policies are development orientated. This means that African companies and states are inadvertently tasked with ensuring that underserved communities are serviced and networked. This stands in contrast to the information and communications technology (ICT) development paths of more developed countries.

Broadband connectivity

Broadband refers to the transmission of data over a high-capacity internet connection; there are several types of broadband, including fibre-optic cables, mobile broadband and satellite services. New technologies have necessitated increased access to undersea fibre-optic cables to increase capacity. Most broadband access is via satellite services and mobile broadband, but these are no longer sufficient. Since the early 2000s, there have been simultaneous moves in the private and public sectors to ensure that more people are connected to the internet. With assistance from the World Bank Group, the African Union (AU) aims to connect every individual, business and government on the continent by 2030. Improving capacity by building physical infrastructures, such as undersea cables and sea-to-land fibre optic cables, has seen private and public-sector entities move at breakneck speed to connect the continent. Figure 19.1 illustrates all the undersea fibre-optic cables that have been built, or are currently being built, around the African continent.

Figure 18.1: African undersea cables (July 2021)

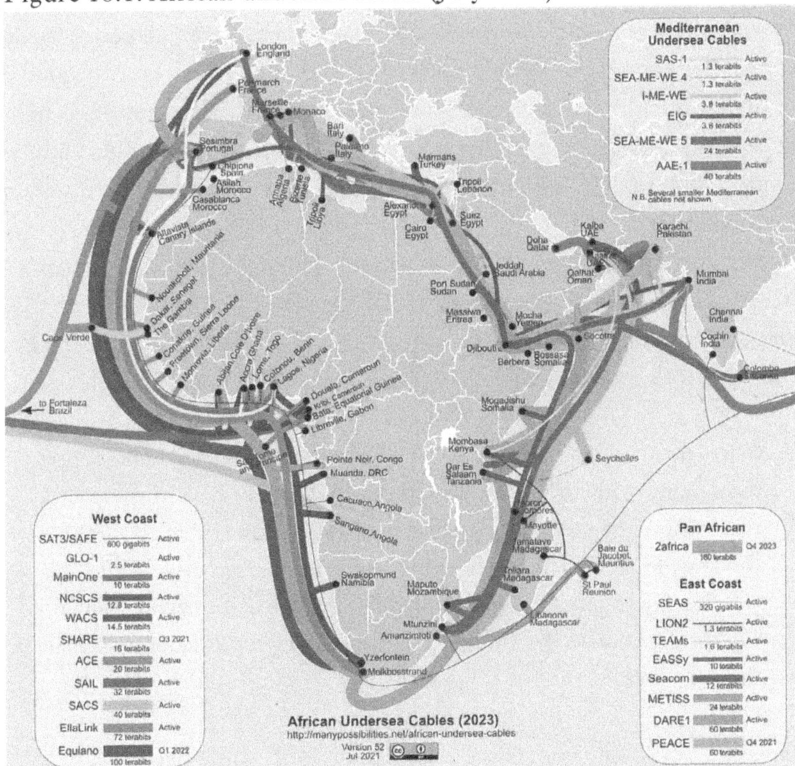

Source: Song (2021)

The improvement of physical infrastructure undergirds all efforts to harness the benefits of the digital economy. Affordability and connectivity targets are primarily government concerns. Individual governments are finding various ways to influence pricing and connectivity, directly or indirectly, in line with their country's laws and economic dogma. In many parts of the continent, history has not been promising with regard to meeting targets. An illustrative example is the failure of the Common Market for Eastern and Southern Africa's (COMESA's) COMTEL regional connectivity project. COMTEL, launched in 2005, was meant to improve broadband connectivity across eastern and southern Africa, but, by 2017, it had not met its mandate (Malakata, 2017) and, by 2021, the project was abandoned (Gakunga, 2021). Many issues plagued COMTEL, from national telecom operators being reluctant to participate to the project's inability to secure financing. All challenges point to the fact that without private sector buy-in and intense lobbying internally by states, there is little to no chance of regional, let alone pan-African connectivity, projects succeeding. This leaves African states at the mercy of digital infrastructure funders and puts states at risk of getting caught in the geopolitical struggles between China, the European Union and the United States (all of whom have technology firms vying for primacy on the continent).

Big technology firms, such as Apple, Huawei, Facebook, Amazon, Microsoft and Google, have set their sights on the continent (Quartz, 2021) and are investing heavily in infrastructure. Much of the investment has been put into undersea cables. As Steve Song (2019) points out:

> these new cables also represent a new generation of fibre optic technology with the result that these cables may have the capacity that is more than ten times greater than any existing cable. Add to this the knowledge that the greater part of all undersea cable traffic are bits flowing to refresh the far-flung data caches of Google, Facebook, Microsoft, et al. What we see is nothing less than a tectonic shift in the very architecture of the internet.

Google's cable, Equiano, is set to go live in 2022, while Facebook's cable, 2Africa, is set to be completed in 2023. Several other consortiums have also laid down cables – some of which are already active. Table 18.1 details the consortiums that own the various undersea cables illustrated in Figure 18.1.

Table 18.1: Undersea cable ownership consortiums in Africa

Undersea cables	Ownership
Seacom	Industrial Promotion Services (25%), an arm of the Aga Khan Fund for Economic Development VenFin Limited (25%) (Kenya – founded by Prince Karim Aga Khan IV of Pakistan) Herakles Telecom LLC (backed by Blackstone) (25%) Convergence Partners (12.5%) Shanduka Group (12.5%)
Eassy	90% African-owned. African ownership is largely underwritten by development financial institutions including: World Bank/IFC, the European Investment Bank, the African Development Bank, Agence Française de Développement and the KfW Development Bank. South African investors in Eassy include Telkom/Vodacom, MTN and Neotel.
TEAMS	85% of the cable is owned by TEAMs (Kenya) Ltd and Etisalat of the United Arab Emirates (UAE) owns 15%. The Kenyan government holds 20% of the TEAMS (Kenya) Ltd holding.
Glo-1	Globacom (Nigeria)

Source: Majority African owned undersea cables. Adapted from Song (2001 and 2008)

What does this mean for Africa?

On its face, it would appear that additional investment in material infrastructure would benefit the continent. The AU's DTS and the vision of an SDM will be buoyed by all this investment. Africa has not yet realised the dream of cross-border integration, which is necessary to deal with negotiating landing rights and capacity allocations. Moreover, as much of the infrastructure is built by the private sector, how much agency do African governments have to ensure digital enablement in rural areas? There is a danger of the focus being primarily on urban centres.

China in Africa

Any discussions of Africa's hard/physical infrastructure cannot ignore the extra-regional investment by China. The China–Africa relationship attracts a lot of scrutiny because of the apparent asymmetry between the African continent and the Chinese. However, China's Belt and Road Initiative (BRI), which includes the Digital Silk Road (DSR), interfaces comfortably with the stark infrastructure requirements across the African continent. As a result, Chinese companies are the largest investors in Africa's digital infrastructure. Even the 2Africa cable is partially owned by China and runs on Chinese hardware.

The leading companies in Africa are Huawei and the state-owned ZTE (Zhongxing Telecommunication Equipment) Corporation. In 2010, ZTE had over 300 million users across the continent (Marshall, 2011). Over a decade later, Africa's infrastructure backbone is primarily Chinese, which is understandable as most are Chinese-funded. Consequently, 50 per cent of Africa's 3G systems are built by Huawei, and ZTE builds approximately 30 per cent. Huawei has also built 70 per cent of the 4G networks on the continent (Wright, 2020).

As Africa digitally transforms, the need for other infrastructure, such as pan-African data centres, has become more acute. The engine of digital infrastructure is data centres – online services, such as web hosting, etc., need data centres to function. Beard (2021) aptly points out that Africa has less than 1 per cent of data centre capability, even though it has 17 per cent of the world's population, which is set to grow to 60 per cent. This observation is important because it means a broader market and access to sensitive state information. Most of Africa's data goes through data centres outside the continent, specifically France. Beard further observes that as 4G and 5G are rolled out at a faster rate, data centres will be even more profitable (Beard, 2021). These developments ensure that geopolitical tensions between the three leading players in the technology space – the European Union, the United States and China – would intensify, particularly on the African continent. Huawei has already fired the first salvo, including data centres, as part of its offering. In 2021, the Senegalese government commissioned a new data centre to be built, which will handle local data, including government data (Van den Made, 2021). The data centre and much of its infrastructure backbone is underpinned by Chinese technology.

Two days before the 2021 Forum on China–Africa Cooperation

(FOCAC), the Chinese state council released a white paper, *China and Africa in the New Era: A partnership of equals*, which detailed the vision of China's ongoing relationship with Africa. Interestingly, the paper details the initiatives of the DSR, such as closer ties between Africa and Chinese consumers via e-commerce platforms. The paper notes explicitly that:

> China is helping African countries to eliminate the digital divide. Rapid development and fruitful results have been achieved in this field – building digital infrastructure, transition towards a digital society, and the application of new technologies such as the Internet of Things and mobile finance. Chinese companies have participated in a number of submarine cable projects connecting Africa and Europe, Asia, and the Americas. They have cooperated with major African operators in achieving full basic coverage of telecommunications services in Africa. They have built more than half of the continent's wireless sites and high-speed mobile broadband networks. In total, more than 200,000 km of optical fiber has been laid, giving broadband Internet access to 6 million households, and serving more than 900 million local people. To date, more than 1,500 companies in 17 cities in 15 African countries have selected Chinese corporate partners on their digital transformation path. Twenty-nine countries have selected smart government service solutions provided by Chinese companies. China and Africa have jointly established a public cloud service in South Africa that covers the entire African region. The two sides also released the first 5G independent networking commercial network in the region (for full text, see Xinhuanet, 2021).

Understanding China in Africa (and elsewhere, for that matter) goes beyond profit-driven motivations. Johnathan Hillman explains it perfectly: the BRI is 'also a vehicle for China to write new rules, establish institutions that reflect Chinese interests and reshape "soft" infrastructure' (Africa Business, 2019). Such a move puts China at direct loggerheads with the European Union.

European Union–Africa

The European Union, like the United States, has been forced to rethink how it engages with Africa as a counter to Chinese influence. However, the Chinese dominate ICT hardware globally; for instance, Huawei is the world's largest telecom equipment manufacturer, operating in 170 countries (Capri, 2019). The European Union attempts to counter the Chinese dominance of hard infrastructure by increasing the power of its soft infrastructure. Specifically, it has developed data protection standards (the GDPR), among other 5G and 6G technologies.

The creation of the EU–US Transatlantic partnership speaks powerfully to Brussels' desire to hinder the Chinese influence, as their relationship shapes the world economy. This is further evidenced by the creation of the EU–US Trade and Technology Council (TTC) in June 2021.

At the inaugural meeting in September 2021, the TTC agreed to work collectively to regulate global semiconductor supply chains and adopt a unified approach to technology standards, while respecting each other's regulatory autonomy (European Commission, 2021). The implications of this deeper partnership on technology between the European Union and the United States is that African countries are being forced further into taking up positions in the battle between the EU–US and China.

Parallel to shifts in power in the digital ecosystem, relations between the European Union and Africa are also changing. The language around Europe's relationship with Africa has changed significantly, moving from the idea of development cooperation to partnerships. However, this is further complicated because the European Union has several relationships with various AU member states and RECs. Africa's digital infrastructure landscape is also heavily shaped by the regulatory power of the European Union and it is set to be shaped further as Africa's planned SDM interfaces with the European Union's SDM (which has a market of over 50 million people). There are important implications for this evolving relationship on their partnership on the digital economy.

Ultimately, the European Union is proposing that Africa model its digital environment on the EU model. By dominating the regulatory climate and through tight development partnerships, the European Union is directly influencing the shape of Africa's digital ecosystem.

The danger in isomorphic mimicry of the EU's model, including the regulatory environment, is that Africa's digital development is at a very different stage from that of the European Union. Zlalina Georgieva points out that the rollout of infrastructure varies across the continent, and the regulatory environment for the digital economy is not as robust as that in the European Union. Specifically, the author suggests that 'the simultaneous adoption of protectionist telecommunications regulation (for infrastructural roll out) and digital regulation (for guarding local digital rights) might be the step in the right direction in a developmental context' (Georgieva, 2021). The pressure for liberal market conditions, often from the global North, would continue to be an issue as Africa tries to find workable solutions.

The ultimate hope for the continent is the development and implementation of a solid digital transformation framework that is cognisant of the contextual challenges and is ultimately implemented.

The African Union's digital transformation

Africa is blessed with a young population, and the potential for innovation and commercial success is relatively high (Geiger and Bamba, 2021). It is these dynamics that have made it increasingly attractive for investors. However, the continent is still held down by a high commercial failure rate and weak infrastructure (Liu, 2019). As the world rapidly transforms, digital transformation on the African continent has been hobbled by the lack of material infrastructure and affordability constraints (Sumatra and Lanvin, 2020). As the Executive Secretary of the United Nations Economic Commission for Africa (UNECA), Vera Songwe, points out, 'digitalisation is a critical component to trade easily within Africa's borders and reaching a global marketplace requires significant progress in Africa's digital infrastructure, as well as a focus on regulations that protect and enhance digital trade' (Songwe, 2020). For instance, Rwanda has been able to use digital technologies to increase annual revenue by over 6 per cent, and South Africa has reduced the cost of tax collection significantly (Songwe, 2019).

The scaffold of Africa's digital transformation – on paper at least – starts with the strategic plan, Agenda 2063. Complementing Agenda 2063 are connectivity targets within the Sustainable Development Goals (SDGs), the EU project, the International Telecommunications Union (ITU) and UNICEF's Giga Project.

The African Union's Digital Transformation Strategy (DTS), 2020–2030 supports the continent's vision for digital transformation. The purpose of this framework is to harmonise continental efforts to close the digital divide by improving affordability and increasing access to the internet. The objective of Africa's digital transformation strategy is:

> [t]o harness digital technologies and innovation to transform African societies and economies to promote Africa's integration, generate inclusive economic growth, stimulate job creation, break the digital divide, and eradicate poverty for the continent's socio-economic development and ensure Africa's ownership of modern tools of digital management (AU, 2020).

The DTS does not function independently; it builds on existing international frameworks, as well as the AU's existing frameworks such as the Policy and Regulatory Initiative for Africa (PRIDA), the Programme for Infrastructure Development in Africa (PIDA), the African Continental Free Trade Area (AfCFTA), the Single Air Transport Market (SAATM), and the Free Movement of Persons (FMP), including the plan to develop a Single Digital Market (SDM). As much as all these plans seem promising, there is a specific implementation gap, evidenced by the failure to adopt Africa's cybersecurity and digital identity framework, the Malabo Convention (AU, 2014). This convention was meant to be the cornerstone of Africa's digital governance. The building blocks of the convention date back to the Oliver Tambo Declaration in 2009 (AU, 2009) and the 2010 Abuja Declaration (AU, 2010). These two instruments fed directly into Agenda 2063, ensuring that Africa's digital presence is part of its developmental agenda and not just the domain of the private sector.

The African Heads of Government Assembly's decisions assume a continental approach to digital governance and the digital economy (AU, 2018). Yet not all African countries have adopted national ICTs and digital technology plans.

The major challenge for digitisation on the African continent relates to insufficient ownership of the process of digital transformation – particularly in the public sector. In other words, many digitisation efforts are led by external actors. Under normal circumstances, this should not be an issue, but the African context necessitates these states be developmentally focused. The result is that the profit-driven private sector often owns the hard infrastructure, and the regulatory framework to support the digitisation process is ill-equipped for the task. Meghan Kathure (2021) correctly points out that too many bilateral and multilateral agreements work outside the ambit of a pan-African strategy and the lack of a concluded e-commerce protocol. Kathure eloquently states that the 'fissures' in pan-African solidarity are apparent in the 'expressed interests by six countries to the Joint Statement Initiative on e-commerce negotiations and the proposed Kenya–USA Free Trade Agreement constituting e-commerce provisions' (Kathure, 2021).

The AU developed a digital technology and ICT framework to support digitisation on a continental level. However, it runs the risk of suffering the same fate as the AU's 2014 Malabo Convention, which, at the time, was the most wide-ranging cybersecurity framework in existence. By the end of 2021, most AU member states had still not adopted or ratified the Malabo Convention. This is of great import for the plans for an SDM. More importantly, the slowness in negotiating and implementing an AfCFTA protocol on e-commerce jeopardises the feasibility of an African SDM.

Regulatory impulse

The promise of an SDM works on the assumption that Africa's digital landscape can be transformed enough to allow African countries to leapfrog technological stages, but two significant factors – alongside the basic infrastructure, such as electricity – would have to be in place.

First, African countries have to create an attractive regulatory environment – regionally and nationally – that is developmentally responsive and not just market-driven. The reality in many African countries is that a critical mass of private investment is necessary to build up infrastructure and distribution capabilities. However, if the regulatory impulse is geared only towards serving the private sector rather than accommodating populations at the base of the pyramid, the digital divide would deepen further. In other words, as broadband becomes ubiquitous, poorer people cannot access or enjoy the benefits of increased access because their communities are not connected. They don't have advanced smartphones and do not have the appropriate skills to benefit from the digital age.

Second, public institutions are essential. Paul Edwards explains best: 'building regional to world-scale infrastructures require large institutions with long lifespans, enormous political, economic, and social power; and (on the private-sector side) great wealth' (Edwards, 2003: 200). What does this mean in the African context and our institutions? As the AU and the Regional Economic Communities (RECs) continue to reform and adapt to bring the AfCTA to life, the dream of an SDM relies heavily on African regional institutions to ensure that the building blocks are in place.

Why is regulation so controversial?

Improving digital infrastructure is related to the ability to exploit the digital economy, but it is also about improving efficiency and resiliency. A prosperous Africa is one where the economy is integrated and robust. The latter can be achieved only if access to the economy is made possible for most of its citizens and not only those who are well resourced or politically connected.

Affordability and improving access to the digital economy are PRIDA's driving force, one of the building blocks of Africa's DTS. PRIDA is a joint initiative of the AU, the European Union and the ITU. One of the three tracks of PRIDA is the harmonisation of spectrum utilisation and regulation. However, there is still a challenge in getting countries to harmonise their regulations. Part of the problem may be that individual states have different approaches to the digital economy and telecommunications infrastructure.

The concept of regulation remains contentious due to fears of the potential stifling of innovation and growth. Gugu Resha cites South Africa's former Director-General of Communications, Andile Ngcaba, who warns that, '[w]e need to move away from regulation to enabling growth and the future. Regulating too early may stunt the development of digital economies, especially in Africa. We need to rather think of models and systems to enable innovation and investment' (Resha, 2021: 6).

Regulatory harmonisation still poses a challenge across various issues, including cross-border data flows, digital security and personal data protection. The AUC and OECD report that:

> [m]ost national strategies aim at turning a country into a 'regional digital hub' but do not prioritise regional and continental cooperation. National regulatory agencies cannot deal with technology-related challenges in isolation. If governments do not fix the issues at the regional and continental levels, they may not be able to realise the full potential of digital transformation for African firms and job creation (AUC/OECD, 2021: 30).

Across the continent, there have been various approaches to legislation and regulation of the digital economy. For instance, only 61 per cent of states have legislation that deals with electronic legislation (UNCTAD, 2021). Table 18.2 presents the state of e-commerce legislation in e-transactions, consumer protection, data protection/privacy and cybercrime adoption in the 54 African UNCTAD member states.

Table 18.2: Adoption of e-commerce legislation in Africa

Privacy and data protection	28 (52%)
Cybercrime	39 (72%)
Electronic transactions	33 (61%)
Consumer protections	28 (52%)

Source: Author

Doing business on the African continent is further complicated by several logistical hurdles. Dupoux *et al.* (2018) estimate that retail e-commerce will only be commonplace on the continent in five to ten years, as e-commerce currently stands at about 2 per cent, but it is hoped that this will improve to around 4 to 6 per cent in five years. There are several reasons for this, one of which is that the AU, unlike the European Union, is fragmented into 16 trade zones. The cost of conducting business is further intensified due to the poor road and rail networks, which means that distributing goods is significantly impacted. The authors estimate that the average cost of getting goods to the market in Africa is 320 per cent of their value (Dupoux *et al.*, 2018).

To bridge the digital divide, Africa needs to implement a transformation strategy. However, there is a distinct danger of underinvesting in next-generation digital networks. The fact that much of the investment comes from external sources, particularly multinational cooperation – and regulatory harmonisation is slow – makes it unlikely that African countries themselves would invest considerably in building the infrastructural capacity. For instance, PRIDA is funded by the European Union. The private sector funds the Smart Africa Alliance. Companies such as Hewlett Packard Enterprise (HPE), Google, Microsoft, Facebook, Inmarsat, Liquid Telecom, Orange, Intel, Ericsson, Huawei and Tata Communications and Transformation Services put considerable resources into Smart Africa.

The Alliance also partners with the ITU, the World Bank, the GSMA and the African Development Bank.

Despite the risks, the private sector is not the enemy. The embrace of digital technologies has forced the lines to be blurred between the private and public sectors, with various partnership arrangements being explored. One such arrangement is public–private partnerships (PPP) which are a regular feature of government policy and practice in many parts of the world. Models range between a simple build finance agreement, where the private finance partner finances the cost of the material infrastructure, and long-term lease agreements. PPP offers a potentially viable counter to the challenges developing countries face in digital transformation, such as the lack of financial, technical or human resource capacity (Twizeyimana *et al.*, 2018; Palaco *et al.*, 2019). Although there is fair criticism about the value of PPPs, there is also concern about PPPs entrenching a culture of external dependency in African countries.

A precise definition of PPP does not exist because the concept remains contentious. For instance, the idea of partnership gives the impression of a somewhat equal relationship. However, traditional PPP typology is varied and includes lateral and top-down models. A lateral model posits public and private actors on an equal footing, whereas top-down models position private actors arguably more advantageously. There has been increasing evidence-based research that conventional PPPs are not necessarily beneficial for the countries that pursue them or even for the private sector partners; the costs do not always result in the expected outputs.

More contemporary models are 'hybrid' with many variations: finance packages subsidised by development partners or the state itself; the government is heavily involved in project development and preparations; or the government provides substantial guarantees to the private-sector actors.

Conclusion

The dream of an economically integrated Africa is underpinned by success in transforming its economy digitally; improving digital infrastructure is the cornerstone of Africa's digital future. The AfCFTA plays a significant role in advancing Africa's digital agenda. Still, the real test would be how member states treat digitisation efforts in the first five years of the agreement. Would African countries take the reins regarding digitisation, or would they leave all actions to the private sector? Success lies in the middle – robust private–public sector partnerships are the key.

When the focus is on PPPs, the question will always arise as to whether the private sector is driving the relationship or whether the states (and regional institutions) deliver on their developmental mandate. A case in point is the lack of flexibility in delivering low-cost broadband services in Africa through options such as Television White Spaces (TVWS). This describes 'the unused, broadcasting frequencies in the analogue spectrum' (Axiz, 2020). TVWS is less expensive than mobile broadband. South Africa is one of the few African countries that have developed a regulatory framework around its usage (McLeod, 2021; Mzekandaba, 2021). TVWS is pervasive on the continent but less utilised. Spectrum availability needs solid regional plans and the willingness to use available spectrum for other uses.

Africa has also failed to implement a framework on digital security. This is a crucial element in ensuring that the continent benefits from the increasing digital capacity. Not implementing the Malabo Convention and not having data protection legislation or cybercrime laws in many countries is hurting Africa terribly. In 2017, the cost of cybercrime in Africa was approximately US\$3.5 billion (Serianu, 2017, cited in AUC/OECD, 2021: 30).

Ultimately, African countries need to develop a new way of interacting with their traditional partners – the European Union and China, and to a lesser extent the United States – while working on closing the digital divide. At the embryonic stages of the AfCFTA, the AU has a perfect opportunity to negotiate new terms of engagement, but this will succeed only if the continent works collectively and quickly. The potential success will depend on whether the e-commerce protocol is expedited so that the rules of engagement are clear before any other rules become the standard of operation. Most importantly, if Africa intends to succeed in the digital age, frameworks and legislation must be coordinated.

References

Africa Business. (2019). 'China's Global Vision: *Africa Business book* review', *African Business*. Available at: https://african.business/2019/06/trade-investment/chinas-global-vision/ (Accessed 15 October 2022).

African Union (AU). (2018). 'Declaration on Internet Governance and Development of Africa's Digital Economy', Assembly/AU/Decl.3(XXX), 30th Ordinary Session of the AU Assembly in Addis Ababa, 28–29 January. Available at: https://archives.au.int/bitstream/handle/123456789/8149/Assembly%20AU%20Decl%203%20XXX%20_E.pdf?sequence=1andisAllowed=y (Accessed 15 October 2022).

African Union (AU). (2014). *Convention on Cyber Security and Personal Data Protection*, 27 June. Available at: https://au.int/sites/default/files/treaties/29560-treaty-0048-african_union_convention_on_cyber_security_and_personal_data_protection_e.pdf (Accessed 15 October 2022).

African Union (AU). (2010). 'Abuja Declaration, Third Conference of African Ministers in Charge of Communication and Information Technologies', AU/Citmc-3/Min/Decl.(III), 3–7 August. Available at: https://au.int/sites/default/files/documents/30944-doc-citmc-3_2010_abuja_declaration_final_verision_eng_0.pdf (Accessed 15 October 2022).

African Union (AU). (2009), Oliver Tambo Declaration, Extra-Ordinary Conference of African Union Ministers in Charge of Communication and Information Technologies, Johannesburg, 2–5 November. Available at: https://africainonespace.org/downloads/TheOliverTamboDeclaration.pdf (Accessed 15 October 2022).

African Union (AU). *The Digital Transformation Strategy for Africa (2020–2030)*. Available at: https://au.int/sites/default/files/documents/38507-doc-dts-english.pdf (Accessed 15 October 2022).

Atkinson, R.D., Castor, D., Ezell, S., McQuinn, A. and New Joshua (2016). 'A policymaker's guide to digital infrastructure', Information Technology and Innovation Foundation, May. Available at: https://www2.ititf.org/2016-policymakers-guide (Accessed 15 October 2022).

Atkinson, R.D. (2021). 'Building back better' requires building in digital', Information Technology and Innovation Foundation, May. Available at: https://www2.itif.org/sites/defaulst/files/2021-build (Accessed 15 October 2022).

AUC/OECD. (2021). *Africa's Development Dynamics 2021: Digital transformation for quality jobs*. AUC, Addis Ababa/OECD Publishing, Paris.

Axiz. (2020). 'Connecting Africa using TVWS'. 20 May. Available at: https://axiz.com/tvws/ (Accessed 15 October 2022).

Beard, S. (2021). 'Data centres are a growing investment opportunity in Africa', *Knightfrank.Com*, 7 April. Available at: https://www.knightfrank.com/research/article/2021-04-07-data-centres-are-a-growing-investment-opportunity-in-africa (Accessed 15 October 2022).

Boyer, D. (2018). '9. Infrastructure, potential energy, revolution', in N. Anand, A. Gupta and H. Appel (eds). *The Promise of Infrastructure.* New York: Duke University Press, pp. 223–44.

Cohen, T. (2003). 'Rethinking (reluctant) capture: South African telecommunications and the impact of regulation', *Journal of African Law*, 47(1): 65–87.

Dannouni, A., Maher, H., Gildemeister, J., Dupoux, P., Ivers, L., Ngambeket, G. and Vaganov, I. (2020). 'The race for digital advantage in Africa', *BCG Global*, 9 March. Available at: https://www.bcg.com/publications/2020/race-digital-advantage-in-africa (Accessed 15 October 2022).

Dupoux, P., Ivers, L., Niavas, S. and Chraïti, A. (2018). 'Pioneering one Africa', *BCG Global*, 4 April. Available at: https://www.bcg.com/publications/2018/pioneering-one-africa-companies-blazing-trail-across-continent (Accessed 15 August 2022).

Edwards, P. (2003). 'Infrastructure and modernity: Force, time, and social organization in the history of sociotechnical systems' in T.J. Misa, J.P. Brey, and A. Feenberg (eds). *Modernity and Technology.* Cambridge, MA: MIT Press.

European Commission (2021). 'EU–US Trade and Technology Council inaugural joint statement', 29 September. Available at: https://ec.europa.eu/commission/presscorner/detail/e%20n/statement_21_4951 (Accessed 15 October 2022).

Gakunga, M. (2021). 'COMESA Telecoms Project dropped, 20 years later after failing to take-off – Common Market for Eastern and Southern Africa (COMESA)', *Comesa.Int.* Available at: https://www.comesa.int/comesa-telecoms-project-dropped-20-years-later/ (Accessed 15 October 2022).

Geiger, M. and Moulaye, I.B. (2021). 'What Hong Kong and Singapore can teach Africa on how to become an economic powerhouse', *World Economic Forum*, 5 January. Available at: https://www.weforum.org/agenda/2021/01/hubs-africa-growth-potential-economics/?utm_source=sfmcandutm_medium=emailandutm_campaign=2739507_Agenda_weekly-8January2021andutm_term=andemailType=Newsletter (Accessed 15 October 2021).

Georgieva, Z. (2021). 'How (not) to regulate digital markets: Lessons from the EU', *Afronomicslaw.Org*, 26 August. Available at: https://www.

afronomicslaw.org/category/analysis/hownot-regulate-digital-markets-lessons-eu (Accessed 15 November 2021).

Huawei (2015). 'Connecting the future, digital enablement: Bridging the digital divide to connect people and society'. Available at: https://www.huawei.com/minisite/digital-enablement/download/Digital+Enablement_ENGLISH+online.pdf (Accessed 15 October 2021).

Horwitz, R.B. (1997). 'Telecommunications policy in the new South Africa: Participatory politics and sectoral reform', *Media, Culture and Society*, 19(4): 503–33.

International Telecommunications Union (ITU). (2021). *Connectivity in the Least Developed Countries: Status report 2021*. Available at: https://www.un.org/ohrlls/sites/www.un.org.ohrlls/files/21-00606_1e_ldc-digital_connectivity-rpt_e.pdf (Accessed 15 October 2021).

Kathure, M. (2021), 'Africa's digital sovereignty: Elusive or a stark possibility through the Afcfta?' *Afronomicslaw.Org*, 16 June. Available at: https://www.afronomicslaw.org/category/analysis/africas-digital-sovereignty-elusive-or-stark-possibility-through-afcfta (Accessed 15 October 2022).

Liu, A. (2019). 'Africa's Future Is Innovation Rather Than Industrialization', *World Economic Forum*, 1 September. Available at: https://www.weforum.org/agenda/2019/09/africa-innovation-rather-than-industrialization/ (Accessed 15 October 2022).

Malakata, M. (2017). 'Comesa seeks to revive dormant US$30M Comtel Project,' *ITWEB Africa*, 6 June. Available at: https://itweb.africa/content/WnpNgM2KbERqVrGd (Accessed 15 October 2022).

Marshall, A. (2011). 'China's mighty telecom footprint in Africa', *Newsecuritylearning.Com*, 14 February. Available at: http://www.newsecuritylearning.com/index.php/archive/75-chinas-mighty-telecom-footprint-in-africa (Accessed 15 November 2021).

McLeod, D. (2021). 'TV white spaces in South Africa is now ready for commercial lift-off', *Techcentral*. Available at: https://techcentral.co.za/tv-white-spaces-in-south-africa-is-now-ready-for-lift-off/169579/ (Accessed 15 October 2021).

Mzekandaba, S. (2021). 'TV white space connectivity gains ground in South Africa', *Itweb*. Available at: https://www.itweb.co.za/content/PmxVE7Kl6mgMQY85 (Accessed 15 August 2022).

OECD. (2021). 'Percentage of inhabitants that live within 4G mobile technology coverage in Africa as of 2020, by region' [Graph]. Statista. Available at: https://www.statista.com/statistics/1231983/share-of-4g-coverage-in-africa-by-region/ (Accessed 15 October 2022).

Palaco, I., Park, M.J., Kim, S.K. and Rho, J.J. (2019).'Public–private partnerships for e-government in developing countries: An early stage assessment framework', *Evaluation and Program Planning*, 72: 205–18. DOI: 10.1016/j.evalprogplan.2018.10.015.

Plantin, J-C. and De Seta, G. (2019). 'WeChat as infrastructure: The techno-nationalist shaping of Chinese digital platforms', *Chinese Journal of Communication*, 12(3): 257–73.

Quartz. (2021). 'Beyond Silicon Valley'. Available at: https://qz.com/on/ beyond-silicon-valley/ (Accessed 24 October 2021).

Resha, G. (2021). 'Governance to facilitate inclusive development: Rights, rules and revenues', Brenthurst Foundation Discussion Paper, No. 013/2021, November. Available at: https://www.thebrenthurstfoundation.org/ downloads/gr-discussion-paper-_-final-draft.pdf (Accessed 24 October 2021).

Song, S. (2021). 'African undersea cables', *Many Possibilities*. Available at: https://manypossibilities.net/african-undersea-cables/ (Accessed 24 October 2022).

Song, S. (2020). 'Africa's Telecoms Infrastructure in 2019', *ManyPossibilities. Net*, 3 January. Available at: https://manypossibilities.net/2020/01/ africa-telecoms-infrastructure-in-2019/ (Accessed 24 October 2021).

Song, S. (2008). 'GLO-1 added to undersea cables', Shuttleworth Foundation. Available at: https://web.archive.org/web/20090624032755/http:// www.shuttleworthfoundation.org/our-work/blogs/glo-1-added- undersea-cables (Accessed 24 October 2021).

Songwe, V. (2020). 'The role of digitalisation in the decade of action for Africa,' *UNCTAD*, 7 September. Available at: https://unctad.org/news/role- digitalization-decade-action-africa (Accessed 24 November 2021).

Songwe, V. (2019). 'A digital Africa', *Finance and Development*, 56: 2. Available at: https://www.imf.org/external/pubs/ft/fandd/2019/06/ digital-africa-songwe.htm (Accessed 24 October 2022).

Soumitra, S. (2007). 'Exploring best practices in public–private partnership (PPP) in e-government through select Asian case studies', *International Information and Library Review*, 39(3–4): 203–10.

Steijn, B., Klijn, E.-H. and Edelenbos, J. (2011). 'Public private partnerships: Added value by organizational form or management?' *Public Administration*, 89(4): 1235–52.

Sutherland, E. (2006). 'Quis Custodiet Custodes? In the digital society who will regulate the regulators?' *ITU Telecom World*, 4–8 December 2006. Available at https://ssrn.com/abstract=1752447 (Accessed 24 October 2021).

Twizeyimana, J.D., Larsson, H. and Grönlund, Å. (2018). 'E-government in Rwanda: Implementation, challenges and reflections.' *Electronic Journal of e-Government* 16(1): 219–31.

UNCTAD. (2021*). Cross-border Data Flows and Development: For whom the data flow*, 29 September, Digital Economy Report, UNCTAD/DER/2021.

UNCTAD. (2021). Summary of Adoption of E-Commerce Legislation Worldwide. UNTAG Global Cyberlaw Tracker. Available at: https://unctad.org/topic/ecommerce-and-digital-economy/ecommerce-law-reform/summary-adoption-e-commerce-legislation-worldwide (Accessed 25 November 2021).

Van den Made, J. (2021).'Chinese tech, ignored by the West, is taking over Africa's Cyberspace', *RFI Science and Technology*, 22 July. Available at: https://www.rfi.fr/en/science-and-technology/20210722-chinese-tech-ignored-by-the-west-is-taking-over-africa-s-cyberspace (Accessed 24 November 2021).

Von Schnitzler, A. (2013). 'Traveling technologies: Infrastructure, ethical regimes, and the materiality of politics in South Africa', *Cultural Anthropology*, 28(4): 670–93.

Wright, B. (2020). 'Africa's reliance on Chinese ICT backbone sparks debate'. *CIO*, 23 March. Available at: https://www.cio.com/article/3533435/made-in-china-africas-ict-infrastructure-backbone.html (Accessed 24 October 2021).

Xinhuanet. (2021). 'Full text: China and Africa in the new era: A partnership of equals', *News.Cn*, 26 November. Available at: http://www.news.cn/english/2021-11/26/c_1310333813.htm (Accessed 24 October 2021).

Chapter Nineteen

Africa's Blue Economy infrastructure and its potential for continental integration

THOKOZANI SIMELANE AND FRANCIS MWAIJANDE

Introduction

The concept of the Blue Economy, as a developmental paradigm, has been embraced and analysed in different ways. The concept initially emerged during the Earth Summit in Rio de Janeiro in Brazil in 1992 (Pauli, 2010; World Bank, 2021). It featured again in the international development agenda during the 2012 Rio+20 Summit. As per the widely adopted definition, the Blue Economy entails economic development that uses aquatic and marine resources as a springboard for human development. Its main sectors include fishing, shipbuilding, marine transport, coastal tourism, energy extraction from the oceans and other economic activities that are directly or indirectly linked to aquatic and marine ecosystems (Kabil *et al.*, 2021). As with other economic sectors, the full potential of the Blue Economy and its contribution to human development requires a purpose-built infrastructure. In this chapter this is referred to as the Blue Economy infrastructure. As this is a new concept, no specific definition exists. Hence it can be hinted that the Blue Economy infrastructure refers to all physical prerequisites that must be developed to successfully exploit aquatic and marine resources under the notion of the Blue Economy.

For Africa, investing in Blue Economy infrastructure would yield many benefits that have the potential to promote regional integration. Of the 54 member countries of the African Union (AU), 38 are coastal states (Karani and Failler, 2020; Nagy and Nene, 2021). This indicates that Africa is well endowed with aquatic and marine assets or Blue Economy resources. These include oceans, seas, rivers and lakes, with the associated flora, fauna and energy. Africa's lake zones cover approximately 240 000 square kilometres, while 64 per cent of the land area is covered by transboundary river basins (Nagy and Nene, 2021). These constitute a reliable source of ocean-based economic activities that can be used to promote economic integration if the infrastructure is developed to exploit these aquatic and marine natural resources. The coastal countries of Africa should seriously consider working together to develop the necessary infrastructure that will advance the Blue Economy on the continent.

It is argued in this chapter that, for Africa to fully realise the benefits of the Blue Economy, it must avoid its past mistakes of neglecting the importance of developing and maintaining infrastructure. For decades, a call for investment in Africa's infrastructure has prioritised roads, housing, telecommunications and railways. Little has been said about the infrastructure needed to integrate the Blue Economy into Africa's development. This is despite the fact that the AU has developed a Blue Economy strategy at the continental level, which seeks to guide African countries on how to integrate the Blue Economy into their economic plans and strategies. Infrastructure for the Blue Economy includes the development of processing and storage warehouses, cold storage rooms, harbours, maritime transport, road networks, ships, distribution centres, human capital and technology. As infrastructure is a very broad concept, arguments presented by the authors might not cover all facets of the infrastructural development required to kick start the Blue Economy in Africa.

This chapter focuses on what can be considered as the critical foundations of Blue Economy infrastructure. Within the constraints of this chapter, it merely presents an overview, providing opportunities for other scholars to extend the scope of the required infrastructure, such as estimating the investment required to integrate the Blue Economy into Africa's economies and determining the human capital investment needed to support it.

The chapter draws on secondary data and literature. Qualitative empirical methods were employed to provide a situational analysis, tracing information and integrating data from various sources. For the benefit of a wider readership, the authors have been concise and have limited the theoretical or philosophical analyses of how the development of Blue Economy infrastructure can be linked to existing economic theories.

However, the authors seek to develop a sense of urgency among policy-makers, developers and politicians about the importance of investing in the infrastructure to sustainably exploit the aquatic and marine resources in Africa. The chapter begins by tracing the origins of the Blue Economy, how it has been evolving and how Africa sees the Blue Economy as an opportunity for human and economic development. To support the argument for the need to invest in the required infrastructure, the chapter focuses on sectors that are central to the development of the Blue Economy, such as technological innovations. The potential for Africa's economic integration through investment in Blue Economy infrastructure has also been emphasised by highlighting opportunities for collaboration. The chapter concludes by putting forward various considerations needed to integrate the Blue Economy into the mainstream economic sectors in Africa.

Literature review

Any economic opportunity, such as the exploitation of minerals, the exploration of space or the development of vaccines, requires purpose-built infrastructure. The basic infrastructural requirements for the Blue Economy include electricity, road and rail networks, ports, warehouses and cold-storage rooms. Electricity is key to the operations of the various processes of the Blue Economy, such as running cold storage rooms and warehouses to keep and extend the shelf life of resources like fish. However, much of Africa has electricity issues and people still rely on traditional methods of preserving fish through drying. The state of energy infrastructure in Africa, therefore, is a potential impediment to fully realising the potential benefits of the Blue Economy (AUC, 2020).

Another essential infrastructural requirement necessary for the exploitation of aquatic and marine resources are road networks (Burgess *et al.*, 2015). Fortunately, this has been fairly well researched. The total road networks in Africa amount to 204 kilometres per 1 000 square kilometres of land area compared to the world average of 966 kilometres per 1 000 square kilometres of land area. As cited in the literature, the road networks in Africa require urgent attention and upscaled investment. The general condition of African roads and the funding required to improve them may directly compete with investments needed to develop other infrastructure for the Blue Economy, as some nations may prefer to expand their investment in road networks in an effort to bring them up to international standards.

The financing requirement for Africa's infrastructure is estimated at US$93 billion annually (Mafusire *et al.*, 2010). Ports are another key element of the Blue Economy infrastructure. They are the primary hubs for importing and exporting commodities on a large scale. Maritime transport is the cheapest mode of bulk transportation, and globally over 90 per cent of all goods are transported by ship, which accounts for up to 70 per cent of total global sales revenue. There are over 100 functioning ports in Africa, but their performance rate is 20 container moves per hour compared to 25–30 moves in other parts of the world.

The 2030 Agenda for Sustainable Development highlights the role of seaborne trade as an engine for inclusive and sustainable growth and development (Aschauer, 1993). The important role of maritime transportation is recognised in developed economies and has attracted huge investments in infrastructure and operations. This has also encouraged emerging economies to build the necessary capacity to raise their level of participation. Little of this investment in maritime infrastructure has found its way to Africa.

The literature on infrastructure emphasises the importance of rail linkages between coastal and inland areas. Rail networks are the least developed in Africa. Many countries have not invested in their rail infrastructure (Mikou *et al.*, 2019) and there have been very few additions to the systems since the colonial era (Mafusire *et al.*, 2010). The 1 067-kilometre-long Tazara Railway, developed in the 1970s, is an interesting point of reference (Mafusire *et al.*, 2010). The lack of good road and rail infrastructure is thus a limiting factor, which the African Development Bank has acknowledged as requiring attention (Mafusire *et al.*, 2010).

The challenge with transport infrastructure in Africa is not only limited to the physical deficit but also the lack of linkages between roads and rail lines, and their poor connectivity to ports (Mafusire *et al.*, 2010). This relationship has been explored by authors like Cisneros-Montemayor *et al.* (2020) who, using a fuzzy logic model, identified stark differences in outlook on the capacity for establishing a Blue Economy, and on its potential outcomes. The authors studied indicators from multiple disciplines and evaluated their current capacity to contribute to establishing an equitable, sustainable and viable ocean sector, consistent with a Blue Economy approach (Cisneros-Montemayor *et al.*, 2020). They found that the key differences in the capacity of regions to achieve a Blue Economy are not based solely on available natural resources, but include other factors such as national stability, corruption and infrastructure, which can be improved through targeted investments and cross-scale cooperation (Cisneros-Montemayor *et al.*, 2020). From a human capital point of view, knowledge gaps can be addressed by integrating historical, natural and social science information on the drivers and outcomes of resource use under the notion of a Blue Economy.

To attract investment for infrastructure development post COVID-19, the Organisation for Economic Co-operation and Development (OECD, 2021) put forward the following three priorities for consideration by Africa:

1. Increase domestic resource mobilisation through peer learning and the exchange of information.
2. Strengthen institutions to attract private investment and enhance the effectiveness of public investment and services.
3. Create an African infrastructure ecosystem and grow pipelines of bankable quality infrastructure projects.

As authors such as Crafts (2009) have indicated, underdeveloped infrastructure in Africa is a binding constraint, which affects most African countries (AfDB/OECD/UNDP, 2016). Unfortunately, various studies on the state of infrastructure in Africa have revealed that the infrastructure gap has been widening rather than closing (Briceño-Garmedia and Foster, 2009; Ramakgopa, 2021).

Despite the body of knowledge on the state of Africa's infrastructure, there is an obvious gap in research on the investment required to develop infrastructure so that Africa can realise the economic potential of the Blue Economy (AU, 2014). Generally, Africa's relative lack of infrastructure indicates investment opportunities that could be exploited by scaling up investments in various economic sectors, including the Blue Economy (Mafusire *et al.*, 2010).

Assessment of the state of infrastructure in 32 African countries by Afrobarometer shows that, despite some progress, infrastructure still remains the biggest challenge (Mitullah *et al.*, 2016). The lack of energy infrastructure stands out as a key constraint, as also noted by Owusu-Sekyere (2018). Afrobarometer (Mitullah *et al.*, 2016) reported that while some countries have achieved universal electricity coverage, more than 70 per cent of the population in sub-Saharan Africa has limited or no access to electricity (Blimpo and Cosgrove-Davies, 2018).

Africa has been identified as a continent with enormous potential for a Blue Economy, yet converting from a resource-based economy that solely exploits raw materials (Forje, 2018) to one that incorporates its oceans, seas and coasts will require substantial investment in infrastructure (Rozenburg and Fay, 2019). It is well documented that infrastructure development promotes economic growth and fosters regional integration (Bhattacharyay, 2010).

The strategic framework for the socioeconomic transformation of Africa over the next 50 years refers specifically to the Blue and Ocean Economy as the main goal for accelerated economic growth, especially for the priority areas of marine resources and energy, and port operations and marine transport. It also identifies the Blue Economy as having an influence on priority areas such as sustainable natural resource management, biodiversity conservation, sustainable consumption and production patterns, water security, climate resilience, natural disasters preparedness and prevention, and renewable energy.

From the literature reviewed for this chapter, it is apparent that the body of knowledge on Blue Economy infrastructure is lean. Much has been written about the need for investment in Africa's infrastructure. What is clear is that Africa will require large investments to attain the desired levels of infrastructure, comparable to developing and developed countries. While this may mean that the Blue Economy infrastructure is not prioritised, it may benefit indirectly. However, if a country considers the Blue Economy to be a critical component of economic development, it has to be incorporated into its national development plan and strategy.

Africa's Blue Economy resources and their state

Since its conception, references to Blue Economy have been changing (Pauli, 2010). Some authors refer to it as the sector that comprises the oceans, seas and coasts, which covers a wide range of interlinked established and emerging sectors (Mohanty *et al.*, 2015). Established sectors include coastal tourism, ports, transport, ship building, oil and gas industries, while emerging sectors range from marine renewable energy to blue biotechnology. A selection of Africa's Blue Economy resources (for instance, rivers and fisheries) and infrastructure (such as ports and technology) are discussed. The aim is to highlight their state and how their exploitation can be improved through regional integration.

Natural resources

The Blue Economy resources of Africa cover both aquatic and marine spaces, including oceans, seas, coastlines, lakes, dams and rivers, as well as marine and freshwater flora and fauna (Figure 19.1). Thirty-eight countries in Africa are coastal (Nagy and Nene, 2021) states, and there are a number of island states such as Mauritius, Seychelles, the Comoros, Sao Tomé and Principe and Cape Verde, all with large aquatic ecosystems. Others have access to major rivers such as the River Nile (the longest river in Africa) and its tributaries, which connect north (Egypt) and east (Ethiopia and Sudan) Africa; the Congo River (the second longest and world's deepest river), which flows through Angola, Cameroon, the Central African Republic, the Democratic Republic of the Congo, and the Republic of the Congo; the Niger River, the principal river of West Africa that flows through Algeria, Burkina Faso, Benin, Cameroon, Chad, Côte d'Ivoire, Guinea, Mali, Niger and Nigeria; the Zambezi River, which traverses Angola, Botswana, Malawi, Mozambique, Namibia, Tanzania, Zambia and Zimbabwe; and then there are others such as the Limpopo and Orange rivers in southern Africa; and the Senegal, Niger and Volta rivers in central Africa. These rivers are a natural source of regional integration as they pass through more than one country so their management requires regional collaboration.

Figure 19.1: Africa's rivers and lakes

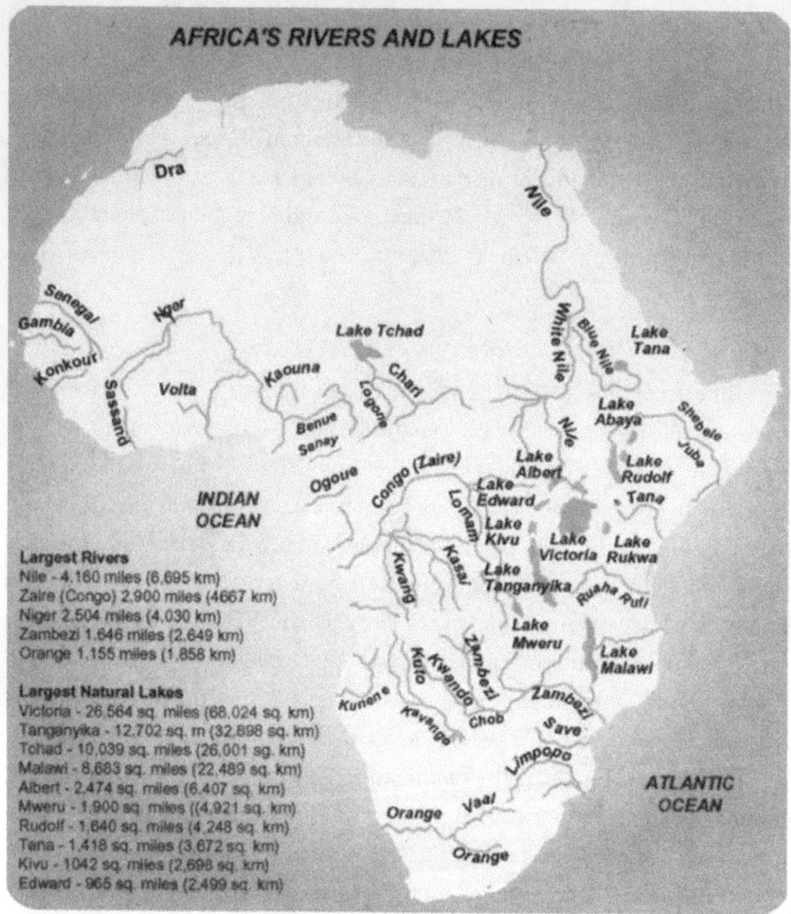

Source: www.za.pinterest.com

The Blue Economy encompasses a range of economic activities that utilise these ecosystems, including fisheries, aquaculture, tourism, transport, shipbuilding, energy, bioprospecting and underwater mining (Pelc and Fujita, 2002) (Figure 19.2). Currently, the largest aquatic and ocean-based economies in Africa are fisheries, aquaculture, tourism, transport, ports, coastal mining and energy.

The Blue Economy emphasises the interconnectedness with other sectors so it is important for regional integration. It is responsive to emerging and frontier sectors, and supports important social considerations such as gender mainstreaming, food and water security, poverty alleviation, wealth retention and jobs creation (UNECA, 2016). The Blue Economy, therefore, plays an influential role in Africa's regional economic integration and structural transformation (UNECA, 2016).

Figure 19.2: Economic sectors linked to the Blue Economy

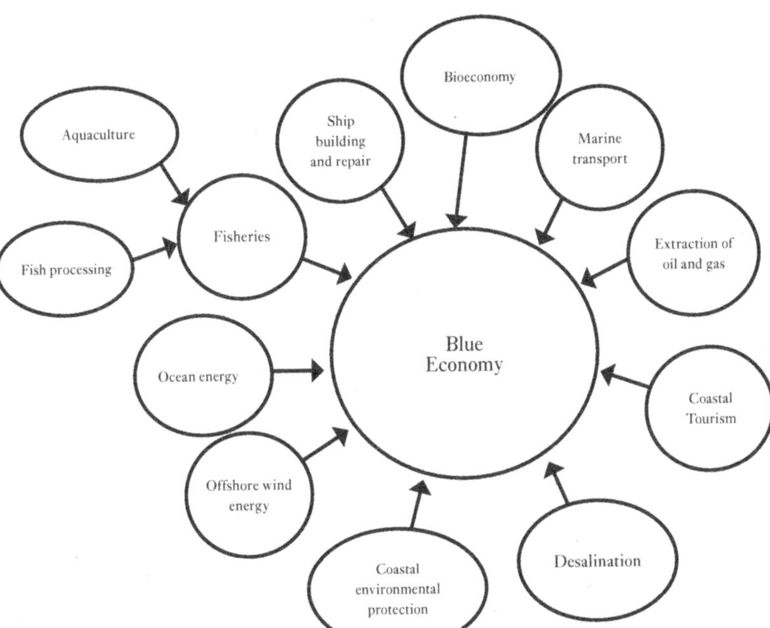

Source: author

Translating this influence into quality growth, through the generation of inclusive wealth, requires new perspectives on regional integration (UNECA, 2016). The Blue Economy provides this opportunity. For example, the International Energy Agency estimates that renewable energy from the ocean has the potential sufficient to provide up to 400 per cent of the current global energy demand (UNECA, 2016). This, if exploited successfully in Africa, has the potential to provide the entire continent with electricity, thus promoting continental integration.

The economic worth of all maritime-related activities in Africa was estimated to be €1.5 trillion annually as early as 2010 (UNECA, 2016). By 2020, it was predicted that this would grow to €2.5 trillion annually. Although it is unclear whether these estimations and expectations have come to pass, they show that Africa needs comprehensive, cogent and integrated plans to fully realise the benefits of the Blue Economy (UNECA, 2016).

From the human capital development and benefits perspectives, it was estimated that in 2018, the African fisheries sector employed approximately 13 million people, 7 million of whom were fishers and 6 million were processors (UNECA, 2016). More than half of the fishers were employed in inland fisheries, but most of the processors worked in marine artisanal fisheries (UNECA, 2016). Fisheries production in Africa currently stands at about 10 million tonnes per annum and this is expected to remain constant until 2063 due to, inter alia, overfishing, overcapacity and poor governance (UNECA, 2016). This is exacerbated by the lack of Blue Economy infrastructure to promote the efficient exploitation of aquatic resources.

The gross value-added of all the fisheries in Africa is estimated at US$21 billion per annum, or 1.26 per cent of the GDP (US$1.9 trillion) of all African countries (UNECA, 2016). Marine artisanal fisheries contribute the most at US$8.1 billion, followed by marine industrial fisheries at US$6.8 billion and inland fisheries at US$6.3 billion (UNECA, 2016). As indicated, the full realisation of the potential for fisheries and other economic activities linked to the Blue Economy in Africa is constrained by a lack of infrastructure, such as the cold-storage facilities and warehousing needed for storing fish stock.

Ports

Ports are important water–land interfaces in the logistics chain for many maritime economic activities, such as:

- Fishing
- Oil drilling
- Cruise vessels
- Coastal shipping
- Passenger ferries
- International shipping
- Mining of marine minerals
- Other offshore economic activities.

There are approximately 100 ports in Africa, 52 of which handle containers and transnational trade, which is important for the continent's economy. It is estimated that the output of these ports will increase from 265 million tonnes in 2009 to 2 billion tonnes by 2040.

The maritime industry in Africa is valued at approximately US$1 trillion a year. Port efficiency and connectivity can unlock or undermine the economic potential of a country. Today, ports are enhancing their efficiency with the overall goal of becoming transhipment hubs, which would raise port earnings, attract frequent feeder services, create opportunities for coastal shipping and generate cost savings from economies of scale.

Although Africa has a relatively small impact on international trade (3 per cent of world volumes), African shipping shows an upward trend. As a result, traffic in African container ports has grown at an average rate of 8 per cent per annum over the past five years, compared to a global average of 5 per cent. The traffic in African harbours should exceed 2 billion tonnes by 2063 from 500 million tonnes in 2018. This increase will be facilitated by the modernisation of the ports to accommodate the latest generation of large ships (more than 21 000). The creation of subregional maritime shipping and cabotage companies, and the development of transport corridors and the application of freight rates will allow African shippers to transport their cargoes at a reasonable cost.

Technology and innovation

Recent developments in technology and innovation have highlighted the need for scientific collaboration among countries because technological capability is unequally distributed. The globalisation process has driven countries to assimilate and transfer technologies at a much higher rate than ever before. Major technological breakthroughs happen only in the developed part of the world, either at national or at major company level. The developing countries always lag behind – and this is true for Africa. Science and technology will play a critical role in determining the fate of the continent, and this is what is needed in Africa's Blue Economy strategy.

There is always a technology gap and some countries and regions are always technologically more advanced than others. The more developed countries are increasingly exploiting their technological capacities to their advantage, while developing countries, especially those in Africa, are left on the margins of scientific breakthroughs. The main target in Africa must be the development of a knowledge base and the subsequent development of infrastructure that will allow good marine research and the exchange of knowledge across countries. This can be referred to as integration through knowledge development and exchange.

Countries at the technology frontier are constantly upgrading their knowledge base and implementing incremental or radical innovation. Developing or less developing countries always face difficulties, even in absorbing the latest technologies. Many of them still rely on technology that is already outdated in developed countries (Archibugi and Coco, 2004). An integrated Africa sharing science, technology and innovation has many benefits, the critical one being the strengthening of a knowledge base to enhance competences to generate scientific knowledge that could be assimilated by the global system of innovation. This could help the continent to solve problems that are endemic to Africa, while contributing to the international knowledge system. Through participation in the global system of innovation, Africa may attain the targets set in Agenda 2063.

Neoclassical economics assumes that technology is a 'public good' and freely available in the global market. As technology is a 'public good' and freely available, anyone and everyone interested in that technology can use it without any restriction. This assumption has not emphasised the development of 'absorptive capacity' through the technological learning process and the initiatives (through education, and institution or infrastructure building) behind the 'technological learning' and adaptation.

The Blue Economy's potential for Africa's continental integration

The Blue Economy features strongly in several regional strategies aimed at attaining the UN's 2030 Agenda for Sustainable Development. There are challenges, however, that limit countries' ability to realise the full potential of the Blue Economy. These include a lack of infrastructure, human capacity, financial capability, the relevant technology and a policy-enabling environment.

To ameliorate these challenges, countries need to forge integration that promotes economic transformation. Africa has some excellent examples of maritime, riparian and river-based cooperation and dispute settlement, including instances of maritime and transnational aquatic boundary delimitation and demarcation. A collaborative approach to the Blue Economy would create the foundation for the formulation of shared visions.

The development of the Blue Economy is an integral part of Agenda 2063, which seeks to promote economic integration in the exploitation of marine resources. Marine resources will enable Africa to expand its fishing, aquaculture and mariculture sectors and foster the emergence of vibrant pharmaceutical, chemical and cosmetics industries. The extraction of mineral resources and the generation of new energy resources through the Blue Economy will provide the feedstock for resource-based industrialisation and place Africa at the centre of global trade in value-added products.

Central to this is the need to modernise Africa's maritime transport and logistics infrastructure, and processing industries, and improve its reliability and efficiency with the view to linking the continent's economies to national, regional and global value chains, as well as facilitating tourism and recreation activities, to name a few.

Building on the experience of implementing the Green Economy for transitioning to low-carbon development, an increasing number of African member states are formulating Blue Economy strategies to diversify their economic base and catalyse socioeconomic transformation. There is no doubt that the Blue Economy offers numerous opportunities for collaboration among African countries.

Possible areas for collaboration

Development of infrastructure for fisheries

Improving the infrastructure for fisheries is key to harnessing marine resources under the Blue Economy strategy. The main fishing activity is capturing fish in both marine and fresh waters. In 2010, Africa contributed 7 597 427 million tonnes of fish (FAO, 2021), which was 9 per cent of the total global catch. Africa's contribution to world fishery production has grown from 5.9 per cent in 2011 to 8.1 per cent in 2021 (FAO, 2021). This increase is accredited to the extension of national exclusive economic zones (EEZs), a higher fishing capacity and technological progress, the creation of national industrial fleets, a higher rate of motorisation of artisanal canoes (61 per cent in Africa) and fishing agreements signed between African countries and others, especially the European Union (FAO, 2021). Uganda and the United Republic of Tanzania are the leading fishing countries in the African Great Lakes region, while Nigeria and Egypt, with their river fisheries, remain the main producers in Africa (FAO, 2021).

The top 10 African exporters account for 89.5 per cent of the total value of fish and fishery product exports from the continent. Morocco (29 per cent), Namibia (15.8 per cent), South Africa (12.3 per cent), Mauritius

(7 per cent) and Senegal (6.3 per cent) are among the top 50 global fish exporters (FAO, 2021). Exports from Africa grew from 3.5 per cent in 1980 to approximately 4 per cent during the early 1990s, and then stabilised around 4.6 per cent (FAO, 2021). In 2010, Africa's top 10 exporters received between 46 per cent and 92 per cent of their fishery export revenues from the European Union (FAO, 2021).

To safeguard Africa's stock from depletion due to overexploitation, the conservation of stock in the wild must be intensified, and aquaculture technologies must be deployed to countries where overfishing is eminent. This requires a coordinated effort and collaboration among African countries.

Critical infrastructure needed in the fisheries sector are fishing vessels that are capable of exploiting marine resources on a large scale. Despite many opportunities for collaboration in this sector, the commercial fishing vessel capacity in most African countries is not well developed, so most countries rely on leased fishing vessels.

The development of infrastructure for processing marine products

Given that Africa is a significant contributor to the world fish market, the infrastructure to process marine products is critical and Africa needs to catch up with the world. This requires the development of world-class processing areas for marine products. Collaboration to develop this sector needs to take place under the African Continental Free Trade Area (AfCFTA).

There is a need to construct cold storage warehouses for fish processing at Indian Ocean ports. This is a promising economic development area for the Blue Economy on the continent. There is little available literature on the state of marine product processing infrastructure, but it can be assumed that, given the general state of infrastructure on the continent, this sector is also suffering, so due consideration should be given to its development under the aegis of the Blue Economy.

Development of marine transport and port infrastructure

Marine transport infrastructure is offered by local and international shipping and marine transport corporations. The major international shipping lines include Maersk, a Danish company shipping line with the largest fleet, followed by the Mediterranean Shipping Company (MSC) and Compagnie Générale Maritime (CGM) (BMI Research, 2016). Africa's participation in this sector is non-existent so collaborations are needed.

Ports are the gateways for various commodity exports. Globally, ports handle 80 per cent of merchandise trade by volume and 70 per cent by value. Investment in ports and their related transport infrastructure to advance trade and promote overall economic development and growth is vital. Africa needs to take advantage of the economic potential of its ports and shipping sector if it is to realise its growth ambitions.

Development of infrastructure for tourism

The tourism sector is going to be the main contributor to the Blue Economy in many African countries. The continent is known for its pristine beaches, but tourism requires the necessary infrastructure to attract tourists. This includes clean and sustainably managed beaches and well built and maintained hotels and facilities. Such infrastructure attracts more tourists, which brings in foreign exchange.

The major Blue Economy tourism activities along coastal beaches including maritime archaeology, surfing, cruises, ecotourism and recreational fishing. Both the public and private sectors are engaged in marketing the Blue Economy. Countries need to collaborate and formulate African standards for this sector to create harmony in the expectations of tourists.

An issue in coastal regions is pollution by plastics. Countries must collaborate to solve this problem under the promotion of the Blue Economy in Africa.

Integrating Africa through the Blue Economy value chains

Globalisation has changed the way Africa trades and engages with the rest of the world. Staritz and Reis (2013) say that 'the global economy is increasingly structured around global value chains that account for a rising share of international trade, global gross domestic product, and employment'. Within this context, the Blue Economy value chain offers opportunities to integrate Africa's innovation platform. The structure of the global economy is such that transnational corporations break down their operations and locate them in different regions (Staritz and Reis, 2013). When the allocation of operations is made, Africa is often left out of the global value chain system, so the continent remains a supplier of many of the natural resources used in goods produced elsewhere in the world. Weak infrastructure and limited intra-Africa trade mean that the prospects for an integrated Blue Economy in Africa are weak (Del Prete, Giovannetti and Marvasi, 2018). Despite this, the Blue Economy offers Africa an opportunity to integrate infrastructural operations and value chains, and this should not be missed.

To enhance the prospects of competitiveness, the infrastructure and intra-Africa trade must be reinforced by value chains designed to promote trade and support all opportunities provided by the Blue Economy sectors. This can be linked to the AfCFTA.

The concept of value chains is desirable to bridge the fragmentation of marine production in Africa. Value chains are needed to connect the geographically fragmented production processes into interlinked production processes that are shared among African countries. Through this, Africa would derive the full benefits of developing high-quality goods that would compete successfully in both local and international markets.

Conclusion

Although the Blue Economy is considered to hold unlimited opportunities for Africa, as spelled out in the AU's Blue Economy strategy, the reality is that the continent needs a plan to develop its infrastructure requirements for the Blue Economy. This must be developed in all sectors of the Blue Economy – some of which have been highlighted here – that have the potential to contribute to the GDP of the continent.

It must be acknowledged that Africa's aquatic and marine natural resources have remained underexploited (Obi, Okeyo and Simelane, 2018). These are now attracting attention for their potential contribution to regional integration, inclusive economic growth and sustainable development. This has prompted the AU (2012) to develop Africa's Blue Economy strategy as a framework to guide the exploitation of aquatic and marine resources across Africa.

As reflected in the literature review, there is a varying degree of assimilation of the Blue Economy. Some countries have successfully embraced the concept and have started to integrate their marine and freshwater resources into their mainstream economies. Others are lagging behind. To ensure that Africa is not left behind, countries need to collaborate in all sectors of the Blue Economy.

One significant objective of the AU's Blue Economy strategy is that it seeks to steer development that promotes inclusive growth through the sustainable exploitation of aquatic and marine resources, so that the Blue Economy becomes a fundamental component of continental integration, growth and transformation through:

- advancing knowledge on marine and aquatic biotechnology
- enhancing marine environmental sustainability
- strengthening the growth of an Africa-wide shipping industry
- promoting the development of sea, river and lake transport
- enhancing the management of fishing activities in Africa's aquatic spaces, and
- promoting the efficient exploitation and beneficiation of Africa's marine and deep-sea minerals and other resources to provide an enabling environment for a sustainable Blue Economy.

The Blue Economy is seen as one of the pillars of Agenda 2063. It seeks to achieve an inclusive and sustainable growth that will contribute significantly to Africa's integration and socioeconomic transformation from a resource-based economy to one that is inclusive and embraces sustainable development and prosperity. If developed to its full potential, the Blue Economy will promote integration both at regional and continental levels and contribute to the diversification of African economies (Lee, Noh and Khim, 2020). The AU's (2012) strategy presents African countries with an alternative road map that will marshal African countries to recognise and exploit Blue Economy opportunities to achieve their national development objectives, improve their infrastructure, and participate in African value chains.

Most countries in Africa have been sluggish in developing their Blue Economy strategies and road maps. This has delayed the implementation of the AU's Blue Economy strategy, which is also integrated into Agenda 2063 and 2050 Africa's Integrated Maritime Strategy. What can be highlighted is that more than 90 per cent of Africa's imports and exports are transported by sea, with some of the most strategic gateways for international trade directly linked to Africa (UNECA, 2016). Maritime zones under Africa's jurisdiction total about 13 million square kilometres, including territorial seas, and approximately 6.5 million square kilometres of the continental shelf (UNECA, 2016). Even small countries like Mauritius have a larger share of the continental shelf. Mauritius is one of the smallest countries in Africa but with its territorial waters, it becomes a country of 1.9 million square kilometres, the size of South Africa (UNECA, 2016).

Investing in the development of the Blue Economy infrastructure would, therefore, help many African countries to utilise their marine and coastal resources to improve their economic positions. This would further assist Africa to improve its maritime transport, energy, water, and e-connectivity through Blue Economy investments. In addition, the development of infrastructure like ports, roads and technology linked to the Blue Economy would lead to the realisation of the benefits of regional and continental connectivity. This can be achieved only through regional and continental integration where limited resources for development, such as finance, are effectively deployed to develop purpose-built infrastructure to unlock all facets of the Blue Economy (Erokhin, 2018).

From transport systems to power-generation facilities and water and sanitation networks, infrastructure provides amenities that enable societies to function and economies to thrive (Wenhai *et al.*, 2019). This makes infrastructure a catalyst for integrating countries at regional and continental levels (Keen, Schwarz and Wini-Simeon, 2018). This chapter introduces the concept of Blue Economy infrastructure to outline how this could be done. Policy-makers must realise that, although Africa has the potential to harness its aquatic and marine resource under the notion of the Blue Economy, this will remain a dream unless the necessary infrastructure is provided. This emphasises a need for the AU, through AUDA-NEPAD, to move beyond the strategy to how the Blue Economy infrastructure could be developed through integration and collaboration.

Areas of collaboration include the development of fisheries infrastructure and associated industries; the improvement of the operations of ports; the development of standards that will improve the competitiveness of the tourism sector in Africa; and the development of Blue Economy value chains that would link African countries.

The concept of Blue Economy infrastructure is relatively new in the literature. This chapter introduces the concept to make authorities aware of the importance of planning and investing in the infrastructure needed to promote the integration of the Blue Economy into the mainstream economies of Africa. This will, in turn, promote the integration of the continent at regional and continental levels.

References

African Development Bank (AfDB). (2010). 'Closing the gap: Infrastructure deficit and opportunities in Africa', *Economic Brief*, 1(September). Senegal: The African Development Bank Group Chief Economist Complex. Available at: https://www.afdb.org/fileadmin/uploads/afdb/Documents/Publications/ECON%20Brief_Infrastructure%20Deficit%20and%20Opportunities%20in%20Africa_Vol%201%20Issue%202.pdf (Accessed 10 October 2022).

AfDB/OECD/UNDP. (2016). *African Economic Outlook 2016: Sustainable cities and structural transformation*. Paris: OECD Publishing. Available at: https://doi.org/10.1787/aeo-2016-en (Accessed November 2021)

African Union. (2014). 'Financing Agenda 2063: First ten-year plan'. Available at: https://au.int/sites/default/files/documents/33126-doc08_financing_agenda_10_year_palan.pdf (Accessed 29 November 2021).

African Union. (2012). '2050 Africa's Integrated Maritime Strategy'. AU, Addis Ababa, Ethiopia. Available at: https://au.int/sites/default/files/newsevents/workingdocuments/33832-wd-african_union_3-1.pdf (Accessed 29 November 2021).

African Union Commission. (2020) 'Elaboration of the 2021-2030 Priority Action Plan for the AU Program for Infrastructure Development in Africa (PIDA)'. Available at: https://pp2.au-pida.org/wpcontent/uploads/2020/04/English-Analytical-Report-Integrated-Corridor-Approach-andSelection-Criteria.pdf (Accessed 29 November 2021).

Aschauer, D.A. (1993). 'Genuine economic returns to infrastructure investment', *Policy Studies Journal*, 21(2): 380–90.

Attri, V.N. and Bohler-Muller, N. (eds). (2018). *The Blue Economy Handbook of the Indian Ocean Region*. Pretoria: Africa Institute of South Africa.

Bhattacharyay, B. (2010). *Estimating Demand for Infrastructure in Energy, Transport, Telecommunications, Water, and Sanitation in Asia and the Pacific: 2010–2020*. ADBI Working Paper No. 248. Tokyo: Asian

Development Bank Institute.

Blimpo, M. and Cosgrove-Davies, M. (2018). *Electricity Uptake for Economic Transformation in Sub-Saharan Africa*. Washington, DC: World Bank.

Booz Allen Hamilton. (2007). 'The global infrastructure investment deficit'. McLean, VA: Booz Allen Hamilton.

Briceño-Garmendia, C.M. and Foster, V. (2009). *Africa's Infrastructure: A time for transformation*. Africa Development Forum. Washington, DC: World Bank.

Burgess, R., Jedwab, R., Miguel, E., Morjaria, A. and Padró I Miquel, G. (2015). 'The value of democracy: Evidence from road building in Kenya', *American Economic Review*, 105(6): 1817–51.

Cadot, O., Röller, L.-H. and Stephan, A. (2006). 'Contribution to productivity or pork barrel? The two faces of infrastructure investment', *Journal of Public Economics*, 90 (6–7): 1133–53.

Crafts, N. (2009). 'Transport infrastructure investment: Implications for growth and productivity', *Oxford Review of Economic Policy*, 25(3): 327–43.

Erokhin, V. (2018). 'Northern Sea Route as an infrastructure framework of the Russia–China Arctic Blue Economic Corridor', *Marketing and Logistics*, 15(1): 12–29.

Food and Agriculture Organisation of the United Nations (FAO). (2021). 'GLOBEFISH – Information and analysis on world fish trade'. Available at: https://www.fao.org/in-action/globefish/fishery-information/resource-detail/en/c/338418/ (Accessed 10 November 2021).

Forje, E. (2018). 'Unblocking Africa's underdevelopment through the One Belt One Road Initiative', in T. Simelane and L. Managa, (eds). *Belt and Road Initiative-Alternative Development Path for Africa*. Pretoria: Africa Institute of South Africa, Human Science Research Council.

Gurara, D.l, Klyuev, V., Mwase, N., Presbitero, A., Xu, X.C. and Bannister, G. (2017). *Trends and Challenges in Infrastructure Investment in Low-income Developing Countries*. IMF Working Paper No. 2017/233, 7 November. Available at: https://www.imf.org/en/Publications/WP/Issues/2017/11/07/Trends-and-Challenges-in-Infrastructure-Investment-in-Low-Income-Developing-Countries-45339 (Accessed 10 November 2022).

Kabil, M., Priatmoko, S., Magda, R. and Dávid, L.D. (2021). 'Blue Economy and coastal tourism: A comprehensive visualization bibliometric analysis', *Sustainability*, 13: 3650. https://doi.org/ 10.3390/su13073650.

Karani, P. and Failler, P. (2020). 'Comparative coastal and marine tourism, climate change, and the Blue Economy in African large marine ecosystems', *Environmental Development*, 36: 100572.

Keen, M.R., Schwarz, A-M. and Wini-Simeon, L. (2018). 'Towards defining the Blue Economy: Practical lessons from Pacific Ocean governance', *Marine Policy*, 88: 333–41. doi: 10.1016/j.marpol.2017.03.002.

Lee, K-H.; Noh, J. and Khim, J.S. (2020). 'The Blue Economy and the United Nations' Sustainable Development Goals: Challenges and opportunities', *Environmental International*, 202(137): 105528.

Mafusire, A., Anyanwu, J., Brixiova, Z. and Mubila, M. (2010). 'Infrastructure deficit and opportunities in Africa', *The African Development Bank Economic Policy*, Vol. 1, September Issue.

Mikou, M., Rozenberg, J., Koks, E., Fox, C. and Peralta-Quiros, T. (2019). 'Assessing rural accessibility and rural roads investment needs using open source data'. Background paper prepared for this report. Washington, DC: World Bank.

Mitullah, W., Samson, R., Wambua, P.M. and Balongo, S. (2016). 'Building on progress: Infrastructure development still a major challenge in Africa', *Dispatch* No 69. January.

Mohanty, S.K., Dash, P., Gupta, A. and Gaur, P. (2015). *Prospects of Blue Economy in the Indian Ocean*. New Delhi: RIS.

Nagy, H. and Nene, S. (2021). 'Blue Gold: Advancing Blue Economy governance in Africa', *Sustainability*, 13: 7153. https://doi.org/10.3390/su13137153

Obi, A, Okeyo, D and Simelane, T. (2018). Marine and Bioresources in the Indian Ocean RIM. Association', in V.N. Attri and N. Bohler-Muller (eds). *The Blue Economy Handbook of the Indian Ocean Region*. Pretoria: Africa Institute of South Africa.

Organisation for Economic Development and Cooperation (OECD). (2021). 'Improving public finance, boosting infrastructure: Three priority actions for Africa's sustainable development after COVID 19'. Paris: OECD.

Owusu-Sekyere, E. (2018). 'Attracting investment for infrastructure development in Africa', in T. Simelane and L. Managa (eds). *Belt and Road Initiative: Alternative development path for Africa*. Pretoria: Africa Institute of South Africa.

Pauli, G. (2010). *The Blue Economy: 10 years, 100 innovations, 100 million jobs*. New Mexico: Paradigm Publications.

Pelc, R. and Fujita, R.M. (2002). 'Renewable energy from the ocean', *Marine Policy*, 26(6): 471–79.

Ramakgopa, D. (2021). Tackling South Africa's infrastructure deficit: the role of development finance institutions. *Policy Insights*, 102. Johannesburg: South African Institute of International Affairs.

Rozenberg, J. and Fay, M. (eds). (2019). *Beyond the Gap: How countries can afford the infrastructure they need while protecting the planet*. World Bank sustainable infrastructure series. Washington, DC: International Bank for Reconstruction and Development.

Staritz, C., & Reis, J. H. (2013). *Global value chains, economic upgrading, and gender: Case studies of the horticulture, tourism, and call center industries*. Washington, DC: The World Bank.

United Nations Economic Commission for Africa (UNECA). (2016). *Africa's Blue Economy: A policy handbook*. Addis Ababa, Ethiopia: UNECA.

Wenhai, L., Cusack, C., Baker, M., Tao, W., Mingbao, C., Paige K., Xiaofan, Z., Levin, L., Escobar, E., Amon, D., Yue, Y., Reitz, A., Neves, A.A.S., O'Rourke, E., Mannarini G., Pearlman, J., Tinker, J., Horsburgh, K.J., Lehodey, P., Pouliquen, S., Dale, T., Peng, Z. and Yufeng, Y. (2019). 'Successful Blue Economy examples with an emphasis on international perspectives', *Frontiers in Marine Science*, 6: 261. doi: 10.3389/fmars.2019.00261.

World Bank. (2021). 'What is the Blue Economy?' Available at: http://www.worldbank.org/en/news/infographic/2017/06/06/blue-economy (Accessed 16 November 2021).

PART 6

THE MEDIA AND EXTERNAL ACTORS IN REGIONAL INTEGRATION

Chapter Twenty
The role of the media in driving Africa's regional integration
BOB WEKESA

Introduction

This chapter focuses on the African integration and media nexus. As will become evident in the following discussions, one is hard put parachuting into this largely unexplored nexus, thus warranting a circuitous entry. At its fundamental conception, African regional integration is understood as the free movement of people, goods, services and ideas across the continent. In Africa, as in other regions of the world, regional integration is both an ideal and a process aimed at overcoming divisions between nations occasioned by geography and history, politics and policies, economics and nationalities, cross-border infrastructure, and culture and institutions (Sako, 2006; Qobo, 2007; Ancharaz *et al.*, 2011; Khadiagala, 2011; Mbekeani, 2013; Pasara, 2019). How communications broadly, and the media and journalism more specifically, are implicated in attempts at harnessing or overcoming these factors are examined in this chapter.

Regional integration often takes the form of region-building with activities ranging 'from integration and cooperation within regional institutions, to more informal or ad hoc processes and practices' (Fawcett, 2016: 21). We can think of region-building as nation-building on a continental scale. Indeed, some of the literature on Africa, broadly speaking, generalises and treats region-building and nation-building synonymously (see Emerson, 1961; Orji, 2012; Bandyopadhyay and Green, 2013). For instance, the core thesis in a recent book chapter is that media ought to play a developmental role 'within the state and, *ipso facto*, the continent' (Isike and Omotoso, 2017: 210). However, an argument can be made for the distinction between media and nation-building and media and region-building for the sake of clarity. In this scheme of things, media and nation-building should be seen as those activities that lead to integration within specific nation states, for instance, media and societal integration in the Democratic Republic of the Congo or South Sudan. Media and region-building would denote the integration of African countries in line with continental goals, such as the African Union's (AU's) Agenda 2063 and the African Continental Free Trade Area (AfCFTA). This contrast helps to separate media and nation-building within a singular nation-state, and the idea of media and what we may refer to as nations-building (note 'nations' – plural – rather than 'nation'). This chapter deals with media and region-building rather than media and nation-building within specific, national territorial boundaries. As Khadiagala (2011: 1) argues, 'attempts to build regional integration schemes in Africa have oscillated between subregional and continental domains, raising profound questions about the geographical reach of regionalism'. In this context, the focus is on continental rather than specific subregions – what Khadiagala (2011: 1) labels 'continentalism and sub-Regionalism' – except for when regional perspectives intersect with the continental integration dynamics.

Two interlinked, yet distinguishable, typologies have emerged in extant regional integration literature. One is formal region-building, ideated as 'regionalism', aimed at developing 'formally agreed to arrangements between groups of countries intended to express a common sense of identity while achieving common goals and improving quality of life' (Longley, 2021). Ravenhill (2016: 37) points out that 'regionalism reflects purposive action by states ... [an] institutional form which coordinates relations among three or more states based on generalized principles of conduct'.

The second strand in the typology revolves around the concept of regionalisation. Regionalisation is understood as 'a process of increased integration within a given geographical area ... [often in] "spontaneous or undirected" ways and driven not just by formal institutions but increasingly by nonstate actors' (Fawcett, 2016: 21; Ravenhill, 2016: 37). Khadiagala (2011: 1–2) defines regional cooperation as 'a more flexible form of regionalism, denoting the coordination and coalescence of policies around common objectives'. Regional cooperation can, therefore, be conceptualised as close to regionalisation.

Another layer of concepts in the regional integration scholarship differentiates 'inter-governmentalism' and 'neofunctionalism' (see Schimmelfennig, 2018). The former is proximate to the concepts of government-led formality or regionalism, the latter close to non-state actor interventions driven largely on the informal plane or regionalisation. Thus, regional integration as a region-building dynamic in Africa takes formal regionalism dimensions with governments in control, and informal regionalisation driven by functional impulses with non-state actors on the forefront.

Commentators have noted two contradictory trends in Africa's pursuit of integration, whether from the standpoint of regionalism or regionalisation. On one side of the spectrum is the optimistic picture. Optimists argue that African integration has garnered successes, for instance, in tapping into the notion and practice of African agency to shape agendas in multilateral organisations (Shaw, 2016). In the same breath, Ravenhill (2016: 38–39) argues that 'the AU [African Union] has excelled in […] political roles. It facilitates and institutionalises a collective voice for African states that far exceeds that which an individual state might achieve.'

On the other side, pessimistic views emphasise failures due to a surfeit of obstacles that stand in the way of bringing African countries together. A key stumbling block is the disinterest by African nations to cede sovereignty to the collective whole, arising out of the contradictions of regional integration goals, while upholding territorial integrity and national sovereignty (see Wachira, 2007). Most scholars of African integration fall on the pessimistic end of the spectrum, as evident in works that latch on terms such as 'obstacles', 'impediments' and 'barriers' to African integration in their titles (Sako, 2006; Qobo, 2007; Ancharaz *et al.*, 2011; Mbekeani, 2013; Pasara, 2019). Media perspectives on regional integration and region-building in Africa equally take optimistic and pessimistic directions, as we shall see in this chapter.

Broad media perspectives

Against this background and in the context of scholarship around African region-building, regional integration, regionalism and regionalisation, this chapter deals with the media–integration nexus. Media is an umbrella term under which a multiplicity of practices and platforms nest. In this chapter, we concentrate on news media, commonly referred to as the gathering, packaging and dissemination of information to publics through traditional and digital print and broadcast platforms. In its role of educating, informing and entertaining, the media normatively plays either a positive or negative role in African regional integration. This chapter does not focus on the broader field of African communications, which includes practices such as corporate communication (see Mersham *et al.*, 2011), organisational communication such as works analysing the internal workings of AU communication structures and mechanisms, and cross- and inter-cultural communication such as the seminal work by Webb and Sure (2000) on African languages and linguistics (indigenous-language media). These are included only to the extent that they intersect with news media and journalism. As explained later, the focus on news media and journalism responds to extant gaps in African communication scholarship.

It is evident that continental organisations are cognisant of the need to use news media and journalism in the pursuit of the integration ideal and processes. The embeddedness of communication architectures and structures in media strategies and officials responsible for media work speaks to the intergovernmental-led regionalism. For instance, the AU and subregional organisations have comprehensive communication strategies, in which the roles of news media and journalism are well articulated (East African Community, 2014; Common Market for Eastern and Southern Africa, 2016; Southern African Community, 2016; African Union, 2018). In terms of neofunctional regionalisation, many non-state media organisations either promote and accelerate the integration agenda or serve as impediments to it.

Drawing on African integration literature, this chapter operationalises media and regionalism versus media and regionalisation to provide a new analytical framework through which the new media and journalism aspects of Africa's integration can be studied.

Fundamental factors impacting the media–integration nexus

Across traditional and digital media, the African landscape is one of great asymmetries, diversity, unevenness and extremes. It is thus important to make a passing comment on the fundamental factors impacting the African landscape before analysing the media–integration nexus. These factors impose constraints while also portending opportunities for news media-led integration.

The continent is home to 54 nations, amounting to over 3 000 ethnic communities, characterised by a wide range of cultures and over 2 000 indigenous languages (see Atienza, n.d.; Webb and Sure, 2000; Tshabangu and Salawu, 2021), as well as the colonial languages of English, French and Portuguese. A palpable problem arises for media-led integration, given the great diversity of languages, even though the colonial European languages partially address the veritable Tower of Babel. The population of the continent amounted to over 1.4 billion people in 2022 (Statista, 2022), with widely varying demographic profiles and population sizes across countries. For instance, Nigeria, with over 200 million people, has a completely different media ecology from the Seychelles, which has a population of less than 100 000. In economic terms, Nigeria, South Africa and Egypt, with gross domestic products (GDPs) of over US$400 billion each, have far bigger media markets than Burundi, Somalia or the Central African Republic, which are less than US$2 billion (Kamer, 2022; World Population Review, 2022). On the political end of things, Mauritius, Cape Verde, Botswana, Seychelles and South Africa, which are ranked as democratic, have more liberal press freedoms, while the Democratic Republic of the Congo (DRC), Central African Republic, Chad, Egypt and Djibouti, ranked as the least democratic, have restricted press freedoms (Freedom House, 2020; Kamer, 2022; Saleh, 2022). All these factors are further complicated by the equally complex country-by-country statuses in the digital media sphere, discussed below.

Gaps in the media: Africa integration scholarship

The question is, has the media served as an impediment to or a facilitator of African integration, region-building, regionalism and regionalisation? Divergent positions and debates about African integration have been ventilated, more in the fields of economics and broader political science than in the communications fields allied to the disciplines of journalism and the media. While literature on Africa's integration has increased over the past few years, the theme of media and African integration is greatly understudied.

Among the reasons for the low levels of scholarship on the media is probably because the role of the media is often taken for granted. While the media feature at the level of strategy and policy, political and economic integration agendas take centre stage (see Didiugwu, 2013). An internet search using keywords such as 'media and African integration', 'economics and African integration', 'politics and African integration' confirms how politics and economics trump the media in all manner of literatures.

The media have certainly been used instrumentally, as indicated earlier, by the communication mechanisms of continental and subregional organisations. It is also valid to argue that the media make up a subset of political and economic integration, a point that makes sense when you think of 'media and political integration' and 'media and economic integration'. However, even searches on the 'media and political/economic integration' do not yield much literature, reinforcing the under-research on the theme. Given the use of the media as an instrument for the promotion of the integration ideal, it is reasonable to hypothesise that scholarship currently trails woefully behind practice. This chapter presents an opportunity to include media perspectives, thereby redressing a few extant gaps.

Given this lack of scholarship, a disclaimer is necessary. Because the media and African integration theme has not been studied much, it is rational to treat the matter in broad strokes in lieu of more targeted studies. Perspectives on the media and African integration must be coaxed from academic works on policy. One approach is to examine how the media feature in the many policy documents by the AU, and other subregional and policy organisations. The other is to tease out integration tropes in extant media and journalism studies. Collectively, these approaches speak to a theory–praxis strategy as a means of building knowledge – indeed theory-building – on the media-integration nexus (see Mersham *et al.*, 2011; Tamba *et al.*, 2012; Karam and Mutsvairo, 2022: 1–2). While these approaches provide pathways for grasping the media–integration nexus, they require innovative research methodologies to enable the role of the media to emerge more clearly. This chapter draws on both strategies to contribute to the African integration scholarship.

Application of integration concepts

The two conceptual paths in African integration and region-building were differentiated earlier. This can be nuanced by considering two media perspectives. The first is the state-led regionalism in which states play dominant roles. The formal integration of the media as a facilitator of the real and aspirational yearnings for African regionalism can be analysed at the supranational level in the AU's Agenda 2063. When discussing regionalism and the media, it is important to begin with historical accounts of the efforts to establish intergovernmental media institutions and mechanisms. The historical base helps to bring the discussion full circle to the present (Orji, 2012).

Second is regionalisation in which both states and non-state actors seek to boost regional integration. This is the more informal leveraging of non-state media actors as agents of African integration aspirations. For convenience, we shall treat the concept of regionalisation as applying to non-state actors and not state actors. Here, discussions revolve around the place and role of private or commercial media acting independently or in concert with formal continental organisations.

The two dimensions are ideationally and pragmatically connected. The policies, strategies and practices of organisations such as the AU and Regional Economic Communities (RECs) that pursue regionalism may incentivise non-state media actors to promote regional integration imperatives, namely, regionalisation. Analogously, as Ravenhill (2016: 38) emphasises, the 'processes of regionalization, often led by nonstate actors, may indeed increase the incentive for governments to collaborate'. In the media context, privately owned media may advocate for African integration to the extent that governments and leaders are encouraged, if not constrained, to pursue regionalism goals.

Regionalism and the media for African integration

The regionalism and media-for-African-integration dimension is the agential dynamic in which formal institutions seek to tap news media to drive region-building. One of the seven aspirations of Agenda 2063 is for 'an integrated continent, politically united and based on the ideals of Pan-Africanism and the vision of Africa's Renaissance' (African Union, 2015: 4). The ambition is to create a federal or confederate union. Literature on

African integration understands RECs as the building blocks of region-building (for instance, Erasmus and Hartzenberg, 2022). Indeed, the Agenda 2063 recognises the role of communications as an enabler through the 'continuous mobilisation of the African people and the diaspora in various formations, effective communication and outreach, and sustained and inclusive social dialogue' (African Union, 2015: 19). Ideally, formal media institutions managed by the AU, RECs and other bodies should be effective in spreading the integration agenda. But are they?

Regionalism and media for African integration goes back to the pre-independence era. One example is the Central Broadcasting Services established during the 1940s, which broadcast radio and film content in Zambia, Malawi and Zimbabwe (Banda, 2007: 78). It is, however, more appropriate to concentrate on the postcolonial efforts, where media went hand in hand with the decolonisation process. For instance, the revolutionary Ghanaian leader, Kwame Nkrumah, in pursuing the creation of a continental African state in the late 1950s to the early to mid-1960s, intoned thus:

> Our revolutionary African press must carry out revolutionary purposes. This is to establish a progressive political and economic system upon our continent that will free men from want and every form of social injustice and enable them to work out their social and cultural destinies in peace and at ease. [In this respect] the African newspaper is a collective educator – a weapon, first and foremost to overthrow colonialism and imperialism, and to assist total African independence and unity (cited in Domatob, 1988: 82).

Efforts by leaders such as Nkrumah inspired the establishment of formal media institutions. These plans and strategies experienced chequered and uneven trajectories in the decades that followed. However, plotting a fine line of intergovernmental media dynamics is beyond the remit of this chapter. It is sufficient here to point out some of the key developments.

The cases of URTNA/AUB and PANA Press

In the broadcasting sector, an exemplar of regionalism was the Union of National Radios and Televisions of Africa (URTNA), which was established in 1962 (see Organisation of African Unity, 1969; 1975). URTNA changed its name to the African Union of Broadcasting (AUB) at a general assembly in Abuja, Nigeria, in October 2006, discussed later.

URTNA was seen as 'Africa's answer to reduce the high levels of dependency upon foreign program sources' (Holmes 1985: VIII). Among other aims, it sought to serve as a link for inter-Africa programme exchange, formulate projects for promoting programme exchange, make African programmes accessible around the globe and encourage initiative (see Holmes, 1985: 5; Eko, 1991: 3; Paterson, 1998: 579–80).

The links between URTNA and the Organisation of African Unity (OAU) were only formalised in the 1970s, however, leading to the broadcast of OAU meetings via the national broadcasters of member organisations, essentially most of the African public or state broadcasters. URTNA's model was forged in the exchange of content between African public or state broadcasters, first with radio programme exchanges and eventually with television programme exchanges. This was because, in the 1960s, only a few African countries had television broadcasting infrastructure (see Holmes, 1985). However, as far back as the mid-1980s, URTNA was already facing serious challenges. Holmes (1985: 41) points out the problems at the time as '[not] being able to establish regular and more frequent program exchange among member organizations ... continuous use of imported television programs by URTNA members, the need for a mechanism to harmonise similar or interdependent projects in program exchange, limited finances ... lack of highly trained and experienced manpower, the reliance on outmoded and poorly maintained equipment, and the lack of standardized broadcasting equipment.'

It has been noted that URTNA and its successor, the AUB, did not have 'enormous effect' in the exchange of radio and television programmes (Berger, 2007: 165). Paterson (1998: 579) points out that one of the impediments to the success of URTNA was the unwillingness of African governments to cooperate on sensitive (political) issues, and that URTNA was 'an organization that is very political, totally incompetent, and politics makes all the decisions ... all you're getting is propaganda'. In other words, sovereignty over media control tramped any impulses towards an integrated African broadcast media.

As mentioned, the AUB took over the operations of URTNA in 2006. On its website, the AUB states its vision as that of 'an Africa that works and succeeds, [and] a catalyst of African integration'. Its mission is 'overcoming clichés and stereotypes on Africa and projecting the image of a continent on the move'. However, it appears that the problems that dogged URTNA persisted even after the organisation rebranded as AUB. Apart from the distribution of the FIFA World Cup and the Confederation of African Football broadcasts, there isn't much evidence of widespread success in AUB's media-based region-building vision and mission. We shall return to the factors that stymied state-led broadcast media and regionalism projects in Africa later. For now, it is important to turn to the intergovernmental, regionalism dynamic in the print media sector.

In the print media sector, progress towards an African news agency with any semblance of continental reach, led by governments – the essence of regionalism – was slow from the early days of independence in the 1960s. A proposal for the establishment of a news agency was first probed in the late 1950s as African countries – beginning with Ghana – gained independence and sought to establish their own news and information mechanisms (see Akuta, 2001). Literature indicates that the more concerted 'idea to establish PANA [Pan-African News Agency] was the result of a 1961 regional conference that African news media professionals and political leaders hosted' (Cavanagh, 1989; Akuta, 2001; Ndangam, 2006: 251; Biodun, Johnson and Kamaldeen, 2014). Significantly, one of the resolutions of the inaugural African Heads of State and Government Summit held in Addis Ababa, Ethiopia in May 1963 was the need to establish an African news agency. A month earlier, in April 1963, the precursor of the African news agency, the Union des agences d'informations Africaines (African Information Agency), had commenced operations in Tunis, Tunisia (Ba, 2017). This, however, was a heavily Francophone-North Africa inclined agency. It was not until July 1979 that African ministers of information signed an agreement for the establishment of the PANA, the media organisation that came closest to a multilateral pan-African platform. It would take another four years before PANA started its news dissemination activities in May 1983, as a specialised organ of the OAU from its headquarters in Dakar, Senegal, with regional offices in Sudan, Zambia, the Democratic Republic of the Congo, Nigeria and Libya (Ba, 2017; Cavanagh, 1989: 353).

The regionalism factors that motivated the establishment of URTNA were similar to those that encouraged the establishment of PANA. Key among these was the drive to counteract an ostensibly distorted image of Africa at the hands of Western media (Cavanagh, 1989: 353; Akuta, 2001). Thus, the integrative mission of PANA was undergirded by a collective

African inclination to liberate the continent from Western media agencies, which were considered imperialistic in a postcolonial setting. However, African governments failed to follow through on their motivations and resolutions to establish the agency, made in the first two decades of the independence of most African nations.

The roll out of PANA's news dissemination activities was made possible by the United Nations Educational Science and Cultural Organization (UNESCO) in its heyday of supporting media development in the Global South under the New World Information and Communication Order (NWICO) campaign of the 1970s and 1980s (Cavanagh, 1989: 354; Akuta, 2001). In African communications and media studies, the NWICO advocacy and debates with the UNESCO report of 1980 at the core (see McBride, 1980) have been a mainstay of discourses on global news and information flows that place the Global South at a great disadvantage. In this third decade of the 21st century, however, UNESCO's role as a voice for equitable media flows and a prop to the interests of Africa and the Global South has waned considerably. Moreover, that it took the involvement of UNESCO for PANA to get off the ground demonstrates the continent's reliance or dependency on external efforts and funding for intra–Africa projects.

A big challenge is that there is little coverage of Africa by journalists from one country to another. Most of the stories are sourced from international news agencies, particularly Reuters (UK), Associated Press (USA), France's Agence France-Presse (AFP) and foreign broadcasters (Bunce, 2017: 4, 19; Article 19, 2003: 3–4). With the overreliance on feeds from news agencies, the idea of an integrated African media, indigenous to the continent, remains a pipe dream. Even in the otherwise liberating digital media sphere, no less than the AU itself has noted that 'the vast majority of content accessed by users in Africa is hosted overseas' (African Union, 2020: 37). To date, lamentations of the negative impact of foreign media continue. Indeed, research has shown that Africa is reported on more by international media corporations (Western and emerging economies) and correspondents than by African media, a running theme in an instructive volume edited by Bunce *et al.* (2017).

Even with UNESCO's financial and technological support, PANA was beset by many challenges from the beginning. These included financial solvency, the rise of democratisation at the end of the Cold War and media liberalisation in the early 1990s, advances in technologies and increased competition in the global media ecology. All these problems were worsened by African governments' incapacity to match their interests in setting up the continental news agency with requisite financial commitments (Cavanagh, 1989; Akuta 2001). As the agency faced certain demise, the OAU approached UNESCO once more in 1992, with a call for a rescue plan (Akuta, 2001: 5). The restructuring that followed eventually led to PANA's privatisation in 1997 after it had failed to meet the Pan-African public media roles for which it had been established. Essentially, it was realised that the running of an intergovernmental media establishment needed financial sustainability and that the continental governing body and its member states were ill-placed to ensure this financial imperative.

Today, PANA is a private, for-profit media organisation with information on its website vaguely indicating that it is 'the fruit of committed African investors who decided to endow the continent with an efficient means of communication'. Although an important communication avenue for African news in Arabic, English, French and Portuguese, the agency is a far cry from what its founders envisaged. Indeed, the fact that it is privately owned means that it plays more of a regionalising than a regionalism role, in line with the definition of the two concepts in this chapter. The chapter now examines the non-state regionalising dynamic of the media in African integration.

Regionalisation and African media integration

The second broad dimension in the media-for-African-integration thesis is the extent to which non-state African media organisations incorporate the integration agenda into their operations. The concept of regionalisation may be a relatively new one, but it is observable at play in Africa's non-state media history. The early colonial period (roughly the late 19th century) lay the foundation for modern African commercial media. Western-style print media outlets emerged in the late 19th century. They were used firstly by imperial and colonial powers for sociopolitical control and, secondly, by Africans for decolonisation (see Shaw, 2016: 494–98). Media outlets often took subregional forms due to the control of the subregions by British, French and Portuguese colonists, and the Pan-African nature of the decolonisation struggles. Thus, the relationship between the media and regionalisation has a long history.

As discussed earlier, the intergovernmental initiatives of PANA and URTNA/AUB failed. Internal factors such as poor commitment by African governments to these two entities played a decisive role in their failure. At the same time, however, there were also external factors that impeded these continental attempts at building regionalism. Two of the most significant factors were the liberalisation of the media sector and the information and communication technology revolution, which led to the rise of digital media. These two forces gained steam in the 1990s, coinciding with the headwinds that PANA and URTNA/AUB were experiencing.

In the 1990s, and continuing into the 2000s, African broadcast and telecommunications sectors underwent rapid deregulation, commercialisation and privatisation. The resultant freeing up of broadcast frequency spectrums and airwaves, and the licensing of new broadcasters, saw the arrival of numerous new radio and television channels – both local and international (Article 19, 2003: 3). As Paterson (1998: 575) puts it, 'broadcast liberalisation … [came] quickly to most countries on the continent, the result of the influx of satellite channels, external pressures for economic restructuring and democratisation, and increasing commercial interest in Africa as a television market'. By 2010, there were reportedly 600 television stations (Nwulu *et al.*, 2010), where there had been only 60 or so stations in the late 1980s (Paterson, 1998: 577). Citing the advocacy NGO, Article 19, Myers (2014: 2) states that Africa had only 10 private broadcasters in 1985, rising to over 2 000 private radio stations and over 300 independent television stations. Article 19 (2003: 2) states that 'by 2002, direct to home satellite TV had reached 41 countries in Africa', this being a higher quality television reception technology.

The result was the emergence of a private broadcasting sector, which supplanted the dominance of state broadcasters. The defining point is that these independent broadcasters did not have the same continental integration mandates and motivations as the public or state broadcasters (radio and television) unless integration developments had commercial benefits. In other words, the liberalisation of the broadcast sector in Africa, essentially a commercialisation trend, led to the explosion of private media outlets within African countries without a commensurate rise in 'regionalising' content (see Eko, 1991). In fact, many of the new broadcasters ended up relying on content from the same Western news sources (see Paterson, 1998: 578) that had inspired the media and regionalism plans from the 1960s through the 1980s.

Private media and regionalisation

As we have seen, private or commercial media have risen in importance over the past three decades. Pursuing a profit model, bereft of the region-building agenda, the commercial media that emerged did not have to actively propound integration messages, such as those embedded in Agenda 2063, unless they had strong news elements. This means that the integration and region-building narrative does not get purchase at the African citizen level, the target audience often being elites in policy, academic and corporate circles. Thus, these failures mean that African media are not providing platforms for the participation of populaces in the integration discourses.

A case in point is the coverage of one of the major integration projects, the African Continental Free Trade Area (AfCFTA). When the operations of the AfCFTA were launched in January 2021, there was much media coverage, most of it tending towards region-building. This coverage has fizzled out, however, less than two years later. This author's web search in June 2022 of three African general readership news magazines showed that the *Mail & Guardian* had last published on the matter in February 2022, AllAfrica.com in January 2022, and the *New African* in August 2020. This is a case of low levels of media-driven regionalisation, given the acknowledged potential for the AfCFTA to accelerate continental integration.

Most of the major African news media outlets are confined to their own countries, rarely pursuing a continental agenda, especially an integration agenda. However, there are a few cases of continental regional integration through the media. For instance, the Africa Press Organisation (APO), established in 2007, distributes press releases from governments, non-governmental organisations and the private sector, and remains a leading source of information on happenings around the continent. The APO has forged partnerships with both public and private organisations around the continent.

A recent example of a media partnership is that of the African Media Agency (AMA), a Pan-African PR and communications firm, and Smart Africa Media news house. AllAfrica.com reports that 'the partnership aims to share stories of economic development and opportunity on the African continent and in the African diaspora to encourage increased development and investment' (AllAfrica.com, 2022). AllAfrica.com is itself an example of a media partnership platform as it republishes hundreds of stories daily on African developments by media organisations from around the continent.

The AU is one of many organisations that partner with AllAfrica.com for continental news dissemination. It started a web service in the early 1990s and has gone on to become a news aggregator drawing on news productions from over 140 African news organisations.

Another example is that of the Nairobi-based A24. In 2015, for example, A24 partnered with the AU for 'the distribution of news and information on the implementation of the Year of Peace and Security to its vast African and international networks through its online portal' (African Union Development Agency, 2015). In yet another example, the AU's Information and Communication Directorate partnered with the Germany's Gesellschaft für Internationale Zusammenarbeit's (GIZ) Citizens Engagement and Innovative Data Use for Africa's Development programme in 2022 to inaugurate a journalistic fellowship focused on social and digital media (African Union, 2022). Equally, the AU has tapped into journalists working for private media to disseminate advocacy messages about many of its programmes. A case in point is the 2020 virtual meeting during which the AU lobbied journalists to provide coverage for its 'Silencing the Guns in Africa' project, intended to reduce the number of armed conflicts on the continent (African Union, 2020a).

Overall, partnership between the continental integration organisations and the media as a potential means of regionalisation has not reached an optimum level. Researchers from the South African Institute of International Affairs analysed why this was the case, and offered some reasons using the case of the African Peer Review Mechanism (APRM), a governance agency of the AU. These include the poor packaging of content for use by journalists; a lack of elucidation of the technicalities of the mechanism; and inadequate attempts to reach the media through APRM structures (Turianskyi and Grey-Johnson, 2014; see also Nyarota, 2004; Allison, 2013; Afrobarometer, 2015; Africa No Filter, 2021). These findings may well apply to many other formal integration agencies. Often the integration story is told from the point of view of high-level officials, with little interpretation for laypeople.

The digital media sphere

Media liberalisation in the early 1990s went hand in hand with the global rise in information and communication technologies. The internet – the key technology that enables digital media – emerged on the continent in the early 1990s. By the mid-1990s, only about 11 African countries had internet access, but by 2000, all African countries had internet access (Jensen, 2000; Adomi, 2005: 257). The information and communications technology (ICT) revolution gained steam throughout the first decade of the 2000s, accompanied by an explosion in what came to be referred to as digital media, new media and social media. This was both a boon and a bane for African integration and region-building.

Esipisu and Kariithi (2007) observe that 'in many African countries, as the new media entities have emerged, state-owned media … has stagnated in the face of competition and diversity'. Given that the state-led approach to media-driven region-building was predicated on an intergovernmental media model, the rise of independent digital media – particularly social media – lessened the importance of state actors. Instead, there was a proliferation of the so-called many-to-many forms of communication, which were not invested with the integration imperative. Indeed, digital media have been nothing short of disruptive, resulting in dwindling newsroom revenues and staff cutbacks across established media (see Cheruiyot *et al.*, 2022). This has meant less appetite for continental reporting projects in favour of domestic news, often stories that do not require large financial outlays to undertake. At the same time, African audiences are sucked into the global digital sphere, due to factors related to the preponderance of digital media flows from the West to the Global South.

There are many examples where social media have served to drive a wedge between countries, thus serving as an impediment rather than a facilitator of regional integration. This has been the case particularly when conflicts between countries arise. A recent example of social media serving a splintering rather than integration role was the dispute between Uganda and Rwanda over alleged military and espionage intrusions either side of the border (Bisiika, 2021). Another example is the conflict between Ethiopia and Egypt over the use of the Nile River waters (France24, 2020).

On the positive side, digital media could aid the region-building ideals and processes in, for instance, spreading continental integration messages. This is a good example of media playing a regionalisation role. The building and deployment of ICT infrastructures and digital connectivity within and between countries has addressed some of the information-flow deficits. The continent has made appreciable strides in adopting and using mobile technology and the internet for communication and commercial purposes.

The digital revolution has placed communication capabilities in the hands of millions of Africans and has meant that many more can now access media from around the continent. Social networking sites such as Instagram, Facebook, Twitter, Snapchat and LinkedIn have been appropriated by citizens as a means of communication.

A good example of viral regionalisation is that of the annual Africa Day events on 25 May, celebrating the establishment of the OAU in 1963. Social media – Facebook, Twitter, LinkedIn and Instagram – have been used heavily, particularly by the youth, in these annual events, helping to connect African populaces around Agenda 2063. With active social media users standing at over 215 million in 2019 (African Union, 2020b: 37), the Africa Day/Week activities illustrate some of the discreet ways in which digital media are leading the way in regionalisation.

Conclusion

Except for a few cases, various media initiatives to cover Africa by Africans have not been successful. This means that a comprehensive African story is not being told.

Thus, the intersection of media and African integration must be approached with a huge dose of realism. On the pessimistic front, continental media projects and initiatives have not lived up to their promise. Yet, on the optimistic side, we see several African media organisations plying their trade on the continent, and we see digital media flattening information flows continentally.

It is evident that across the economic, political and cultural pillars of African integration, there are many gaps that require dedicated initiatives if African media are to report seamlessly for the benefit of audiences across the continent. This would have to be done on a grand and impactful scale to increase information on the opportunities of integration, while addressing the challenges. It would require more dedicated initiatives in which AU negotiates agreements with both private and public media in each of the African countries to cover the integration story as a matter of principle. Unbundling the seven aspirations of Agenda 2063 and tracking their implementation through stories at the community level could prove particularly rewarding.

The digital revolution on the continent should also be tapped as a means of enhancing communication within and between the countries. Individuals and communities are already leveraging, appropriating and using various digital infrastructure and gadgets for everyday communication, education, business, financial transactions and entertainment. The relevant bodies charged with advancing continental integration would have to partner with digital media companies to create bespoke applications for the promotion of regional integration events and developments.

References

Adomi, E.E. (2005). 'Internet development and connectivity in Nigeria', *Program*, 39(3): 257–68.

Africa No Filter. (2021). *How African Media Covers Africa*. Johannesburg: Africa No Filter. Available at: http://dc.sourceafrica.net/documents/121016-Africa-No-Filter-How-African-Media-Covers-Africa.html#:~:text=The%20 'How%20Africa%20covers%20Africa,Council%20and%20the%20 Hilton%20Foundation (Accessed 2 July 2022).

African Union (AU). (2022). 'Call for applications open for the inaugural AU Media Fellowship'. Available at: https://au.int/en/newsevents/20220418/ call-applications-open-inaugural-au-media-fellowship (Accessed 5 June 2022).

African Union (AU). (2020a). 'Virtual conference on the role of the media in Silencing the Guns in Africa'. Available at: https://au.int/en/ newsevents/20201008/virtual-conference-role-media-silencing-guns-africa (Accessed 5 June 2022).

African Union (AU). (2020b). *The Digital Transformation Strategy for Africa (2020–2030)*. Available at: https://au.int/en/documents/20200518/ digital-transformation-strategy-africa-2020-2030 (Accessed 2 July 2022).

African Union (AU). (2015). *Agenda 2063: The Africa We Want*. Available at: https://au.int/sites/default/files/documents/36204-doc-agenda2063_ popular_version_en.pdf (accessed 26 June 2022).

African Union and European Union. (2018). Global Monitoring for Environment and Security and Africa: Communications and engagement strategy, 24 May. Available at: https://au.int/sites/default/ files/pages/34807-file (Accessed 24 October 2022).

African Union Development Agency. (2015). 'African Union, A24 Media in Make Peace Happen Partnership'. Available at: https://www.nepad.

org/news/african-union-a24-media-make-peace-happen-partnership (Accessed 5 June 2022).

Africa Union of Broadcasting. (2016). *A Road Map, 2016–2020: The transformation agenda*. Available at: https://fr.uar-aub.org/road-map-2016-2020 (Accessed 2 July 2022).

Afrobarometer. (2015). 'Is media playing its role in regional integration?' Available at: https://afrobarometer.org/blogs/media-playing-its-role-regional-integration (Accessed 2 July 2022).

AllAfrica.com. (2022). 'African Media Agency (AMA) and Smart Africa Media Join forces to deliver quality content for the Africa and diaspora audience'. Available at: https://allafrica.com/stories/202204220339.html (Accessed 5 June 2022).

Allison, S. (2013). 'African journalism is being stifled by a lack of resources', *The Guardian Africa Network*. Available at: https://www.theguardian.com/world/2013/mar/01/african-journalism-stifled-lack-resources (Accessed 18 June 2022).

Akuta, N.C. (2001). 'The Pan-African News Agency: A historical analysis of Africa's voice in the global news flow'. PhD. dissertation, Graduate School of Howard University. Ann Arbor, MI: Bell & Howell Information and Learning Company.

Ancharaz, V., Mbekeani, K. and Brixiova, Z. (2011). 'Impediments to regional trade integration in Africa', *Africa Economic Brief*, 2(11), September. African Development Bank. Available at: https://www.afdb.org/fileadmin/uploads/afdb/Documents/Publications/AEB%20VOL%202%20Issue%2011_AEB%20VOL%202%20Issue%2011.pdf (Accessed 20 October 2022).

Atienza, E. (n.d.). 'Meet the tribes in Africa'. Available at: https://whileinafrica.com/meet-the-tribes-inafrica/#:~:text=With%20around%203%2C000%20tribes%20and,with%20fascination%20around%0Every%20corner (Accessed 5 June 2022).

Article 19. (2003). *Broadcasting Policy and Practice in Africa*. Johannesburg: Article XIX, University of the Witwatersrand. Available at: https://www.article19.org/data/files/pdfs/publications/africa-broadcasting-policy.pdf (Accessed 2 July 2022).

Ba, M.A. (2017). 'The role of African media in regional integration', *AllAfrica.com*. Available at: https://allafrica.com/stories/201711010232.html (Accessed 3 March 2022).

Banda, F. (2007). 'Central Africa: 50 years of media', in E. Barratt and G. Berger (eds). *50 Years of Journalism: African media since Ghana's Independence*. Johannesburg: The African Editors Forum.

Bandyopadhyay, S. and Green, E. (2013). 'Nation-building and conflict in modern Africa', *World Development,* 45(C): 108–18. DOI: 10.1016/j.worlddev.2012.09.012.

Berger, G. (2007). 'Looking ahead: What next for African media?' in Barratt and Berger (eds). *50 Years of Journalism*. Johannesburg: The African Editors' Forum.

Biodun, H.S., Johnson, W.A. and Kamaldeen, B. (2014). Mobilising Pan African News Agency participation in global news flow', *International Journal of Innovative Research and Development*, 3(1). Available at: http://52.172.159.94/index.php/ijird/article/viewFile/46561/37791 (Accessed 3 March 2022).

Bisiika, A. (2021). 'Rwanda, Uganda still at war, but this time on social media', *Daily Monitor*, 23 October. Available at: https://www.monitor.co.ug/uganda/oped/commentary/rwanda-uganda-still-at-war-but-this-time-on-social-media-3592682 (Accessed 2 July 2022).

Bunce, M. (2017). 'The international news coverage of Africa: Beyond the 'single story', in M. Bunce *et al.* (eds). *Africa's Media Image in the 21st Century: At the 'Heart of Darkness' to 'Africa Rising'*. London and New York: Routledge.

Bunce, M., Franks, S. and Paterson, C. (eds). (2017). *Africa's Media Image in the 21st Century: From the 'Heart of Darkness' to 'Africa Rising'*. London and New York: Routledge.

Cavanagh, K. (1989). 'Freeing the Pan-African News Agency', *The Journal of Modern African Studies*, 27(2): 353–65.

Cheruiyot, D., Wahutu, J.S., Mare, A., Ogola, G. and Mabweazara, H.M. (2022). 'Making news outside legacy media: Peripheral actors within an African communication ecology', *African Journalism Studies*, 4(4). https://doi.org/10.1080/23743670.2021.2046397.

Common Markets for Eastern and Southern Africa. (2016). *COMESA Policy and Strategy 2016–2020*. Available at: https://www.comesa.int/wp-content/uploads/2019/02/COMESA-Communication-Strategy.-_final_web_email.pdf (Accessed 2 July 2022).

Didiugwu, F.I. (2013). 'The mass media and the challenges of regional integration in Africa'. Paper presented at the 5th European Conference on African Studies, *African Dynamics in a Multipolar World*, 27–29 June 2013, Lisbon, Portugal.

Domatob, K.J. (1988). 'The challenge before African media', *India International Centre Quarterly*, 15(1) (Spring): 79–94.

East Africa Community. (2014). 'The East African Community Communication Policy and Strategy'. Available at: http://repository. eac.int/bitstream/handle/11671/339/EAC%20Communication%20 Policy%20and%20Strategy.pdf?sequence=1&isAllowed=y (Accessed 2 July 2022).

Eko, L.S. (1991). 'An African response to the media explosion', *Wajibu*, 6(4).

Emerson, R. (1961). 'Crucial problems involved in nation-building in Africa', *The Journal of Negro Education*, Summer, 1961, 30(3): 193–205.

Erasmus, G. and Hartzenberg, T. (2022). 'The meaning of building blocks for African integration is defined by the applicable legal instruments and subsequent practice'. Trade Law Centre (Tralac), 6 March. Available at: https://www.tralac.org/blog/article/15546-the-meaning-of-building-blocks-for-african-integration-is-defined-by-the-applicable-legal-instruments-and-subsequent-practice.html (Accessed 18 June 2022)

Esipisu, I and Kariithi, N. (2007). 'New media development in Africa', *Global Media Journal: Africa Edition*, 1(1). https://doi.org/10.5789/1-1-45.

Fawcett, L. (2016). 'Region-building debates in a global context', in H.D. Levine and D. Nagar (eds). *Region-Building in Africa: Political and economic challenges*. New York: Palgrave MacMillan.

France24. (2020). 'Nile Dam dispute spills onto social media'. Available at: https://www.france24.com/en/20200709-nile-dam-dispute-spills-onto-social-media (Accessed 2 July 2022).

Freedom House. (2020). 'Democratic trends in Africa in four charts'. Available at: https://freedomhouse.org/article/democratic-trends-africa-four-charts (Accessed 25 June 2022).

Holmes, P.A.H. (1985). 'The role of URTNA's Programme Exchange Centre in Nairobi to mass media development and broadcast sharing in Africa with emphasis on Kenya: Case study'. PhD Dissertation, Northwestern University.

Isike, A.C. and Omotoso, A.S. (2017). 'Reporting Africa: The role of the media in (un)shaping democratic agenda', in A. Olokotun and A.S. Omotoso (eds). *Editors Political Communication in Africa*. Cham: Springer Verlag.

Jensen, M. (2000). Making the Connection: Africa and the Internet. *Current History*, 99(637): 215–20. https://doi.10.1525/curh.2000.99.637.215.

Kamer, L. (2022). 'GDP of African countries 2021, by country', *Statista*. Available at: https://www.statista.com/statistics/1120999/gdp-of-african-countries-by-country/ (Accessed 5 June 2022).

Karam, B. and Mutsvairo, B. (2022). 'Reframing African ontologies in the era of decolonization', in B. Karam and B. Mutsvairo (eds.) *Decolonizing Political Communication in Africa: Reframing ontologies*. Routledge: London and New York.

Khadiagala, M.G. (2011). *Institution Building for African Regionalism*. ADB Working Paper Series, August 2011.

Longley, R. (2021). 'Regionalism: Definition and examples', ThoughtCo. Available at: https://www.thoughtco.com/regionalism-definition-and-examples-5206335 (Accessed 5 June 2022).

Mbekeani, K.K. (2013). *Understanding the Barriers to Regional Trade Integration in Africa*. Tunis: African Development Bank Group.

McBride, S. 1980. *One World, Many Voices*. Paris: UNESCO.

Mersham, G., Skinner, C. and Rensburg, R. (2011). 'Approaches to African communication management and public relations: A case for theory-building on the continent', *Journal of Public Affairs*, 11(4): 1–13.

Myers, M. (2014). *Africa's Media Boom: The role of international aid*. Washington DC: Center for International Media Assistance (CIMA).

Ndangam, N.L. (2006). 'It's not all Africa @ allafrica.com.', *Global Media and Communication*, 2(2): 251–56.

Nyarota, G. (2004). 'Africa through the eyes of African reporters', *Nieman Reports*. Available at: https://niemanreports.org/articles/africa-through-the-eyes-of-african-reporters/ (Accessed 18 June 2022).

Nwulu, N.I., Adekanbi, A., Oranugo, T.L. and Adewale, Y.Y. (2010). 'Television broadcasting in Africa: Pioneering milestones', *2010 Second Region 8 IEEE Conference on the History of Communications*, pp. 1–6.

Organisation of African Unity (OAU). (1975). 24th Ordinary Session Council of Ministers, 13–21 February 1975. Available at: https://archives.au.int/handle/123456789/9406?show=full&locale-attribute=ar (Accessed 2 July 1975).

Organisation of African Unity (OAU). (1969.) Twelfth Ordinary Session of Ministers, Addis Ababa, 17–24 February 1969. Available at: https://archives.au.int/bitstream/handle/123456789/7380/CM%20249%20

Add.%203_E.pdf?sequence=1&isAllowed=y (Accessed 2 July 2022).

Orji, E.K. (2012). 'Historical research and nation-building in Africa', *LWATI: A Journal of Contemporary Research*, 9(3): 80–89.

Pasara, M.T. (2019). 'An overview of the obstacles to the African economic integration process in view of the African continental free trade area', *Africa Review*, 12: 1–17. DOI:10.1080/09744053.2019.1685336.

Paterson, A.C. (1998). 'Reform or re-colonisation? The overhaul of African television', *Review of African Political Economy*, 25(78): 571–83. https://doi.org/10.1080/03056249808704344.

Qobo, M. (2007). 'The challenges of regional Integration in Africa in the Context of Globalisation and the Prospects for a United States of Africa', ISS Paper No. 145, June. Pretoria: Institute for Security Studies.

Ravenhill, J. (2016). 'Regional Integration in Africa: Theory and practice, in D.H. Levine and D. Nagar (eds). *Region-Building in Africa*. New York: Palgrave MacMillan.

Sako, S. (2006). *Challenges Facing Africa's Regional Economic Communities in Capacity Building*, The African Capacity Building Foundation (ACBF) Occasional Paper No. 5. Available at: https://opendocs.ids.ac.uk/opendocs/bitstream/handle/20.500.12413/2966/op005-2006-222014.pdf?sequence=1&isAllowed=y (Accessed 18 October 2022).

Saleh, M. (2022). 'Press freedom index in Africa 2022, by country', Statista. Available at: https://www.statista.com/statistics/1221101/press-freedom-index-in-africa-by-country/ (Accessed 5 June 2022).

Schimmelfennig, F. (2018). 'Regional integration theory', in *Oxford Research Encyclopaedias*. Available at: https://oxfordre.com/view/10.1093/acrefore/9780190228637.001.0001/acrefore-9780190228637-e-599 (Accessed 3 July 2022).

Shaw, M.T. (2016). 'African agency post-2015. The roles of regional powers and developmental states in regional integration', in D.H. Levine and D. Nagar (eds). *Region-Building in Africa*. New York: Palgrave MacMillan.

Shaw, I.S. (2009). 'Towards an African Journalism Model: A critical historical perspective', *The International Communication Gazette*, 71(6): 491–510. https://doi.org/10.1177/1748048509339792.

Southern African Development Community (SADC). (2016). *Revised SADC Communication and Promotional Strategy, 2016–2020*. Available at: https://www.sadc.int/files/1215/2525/6435/SADC-Communications__

Promotions_Strategy_2016-2020.pdf (Accessed 26 June 2022).

Tamba, R.M., Oloruntola, S. and Ifeoma, A. (2012). 'Intellectual poverty and theory building in African mass communication research', Journal of African Media Studies, 4(2): 139–55.

Tshabangu, T. and Salawu, A. (2021). 'Indigenous-language media research in Africa: Gains, losses, towards a new research agenda', *African Journalism Studies*, 43(1): 1–16. https://doi.org/10.1080/23743670.202.1998787.

Turianskyi, Y. and Grey-Johnson, J. (2014). *APRM and the Media: Getting the Story Right*, SAIIA Occasional Paper No. 171. Johannesburg: South African Institute of International Affairs.

Wachira, M.G. (2007). *Sovereignty and the 'United States of Africa' Insights at the EU*, ISS Paper No. 144, June 2007.

Wainaina, B. (2011). 'How to write about Africa', *Granta Magazine*. Available at: https://granta.com/how-to-write-about-africa/ (Accessed 20 May 2017).

Webb, V. and Sure, K. (eds). (2000). *African Voices: An introduction to the languages and linguistics of Africa*. Cape Town: Oxford University Press.

World Population Review. (2022). *Poorest Countries in Africa 2022*. Available at: https://worldpopulationreview.com/country-rankings/poorest-countries-in-africa (Accessed 5 June 2022).

Chapter Twenty-one

The impact of external actors in Africa's regional integration

DAVID MONYAE

Introduction

The forefathers of African politics recognised integration on the continent as a concrete foundation on which to address developmental challenges and as a tool to realise Pan-Africanism. The ideological underpinnings of Pan-Africanism were pertinent to the formation of the Organisation of African Unity (OAU) in 1963, from an anti-colonial focus on the African continent. The call for integration was echoed by prominent African leaders at various conferences around the world, years before the wave of decolonisation reached the shores of the African continent (Aworaro, 2015). Integration was also seen as a viable mechanism for addressing heterogeneous partitions among African countries, which was evident during the establishment of the OAU charter as the Casablanca and Monrovia groups supported two different ideological approaches to integration. After a necessary compromise, the OAU adopted a micro-nationalistic approach to integration, which was the one advocated by the Casablanca bloc.

However, the OAU lacked significant powers to address the complex political, security and economic issues that faced the continent as a result of the loosely formulated integration strategy in its charter. By the late 1990s, it became evident that it was necessary to revisit and redesign the organisation into a modern and effective institution. The failures and/or inability to achieve the intended objectives of the development strategies such as the Lagos Plan of Action and structural adjustment programmes (SAPs), the end of apartheid in South Africa, the amplification of globalisation, and the rise of regional integration agreements in Europe and Asia called for the OAU mandate to be re-examined in a changing global environment.

The founding of the African Union (AU) in 2002 was aimed at rectifying the pitfalls and challenges that had constrained the work of the OAU. It signalled a new era of Africa's integration based on a macro-nationalism approach, which addressed a broader range of issues. Since its formation, the AU has strengthened integration on a range of diverse issues on the continent. The inauguration of the New Partnership for Africa's Development (NEPAD) in 2001 signalled a new era in Africa's approach to socioeconomic development through the implementation of an African-conceived and controlled development plan. NEPAD shifted the focus away from an inward-looking strategy of self-reliance to an outward-looking strategy of integrating African economies into the global market and redefined the scope of dealing with external actors. However, despite its transformation and change of structure, the AU faces several issues, both internally and externally. Internally, one of the main problems is the issue of implementing the resolutions that are passed by the member states. The organisation also experiences budget deficits to support its projects and operations because a significant proportion of its member states default or do not pay full annual fees (Luqman and Zekeri, 2015). There is also a lack of policy coherence between the organisation and its member states (Vanheukelom, 2017).

Externally, the AU faces several powerful old and new actors who are driven by diverse interests and objectives, which has brought both opportunities and challenges to the desire for continentalism. The powerful external actors that are competing for influence include the European Union (EU), the United States of America, Japan and China, who have different ideologies and motivations for their interaction with the continent. This chapter examines the role these external actors play within the framework of Africa's regional integration. It focuses on their initiatives to improve integration by looking at the role they play in terms of trade, health, investment, and peace and security. The chapter begins with a theoretical framework which is key to understanding the different strategic partnerships the AU has forged with different external partners. After a brief background into how the AU evolved, its strategic partnerships with the EU, the United States, China and Japan are analysed.

Theoretical framework: Summitry

The international political landscape has always been characterised by competing global powers, who use both diplomacy and hard power to achieve their national objectives and influence over nations. As the world has become more interconnected and interdependent as a result of globalisation, the use of diplomacy has ascended into an accepted feature of international relations in the 21st century. In addition, the rise of multipolarity, as new non-traditional players with significant military and economic resources compete for influence in the global political arena, and the collective international solidarity against states that divert from internationally acceptable norms and practices has made the use of hard power undesirable (Cornago, 2008). Diplomacy is now one of the main drivers of foreign policy, as states have opted to use it over hard power, which has become increasingly unattractive in an interconnected and multipolar global political landscape.

One of the ways in which states have used diplomacy to engage with one another is through the use of 'summits' also known as 'summitry' or 'summit diplomacy'. Summits such as the AU summit, the G20 or the Forum on China–Africa Cooperation (FOCAC) have become a dominant practice in modern diplomacy (Reynolds, 2009). As domestic problems have become supranational in nature, cooperation with other states has become an important feature of foreign policy. Summits afford states, through their main decision-makers, an opportunity to have a one-on-one dialogue and jointly address issues that affect or benefit them as a collective, which might otherwise be difficult to resolve if a single state took the initiative. According to Dalton (2018), summitry offer 'powerful symbols' of alliance and some form of reconciliation.

There is no universally agreed definition of a summit by international relations scholars. The definition of the term has been subject to debate. Abbott (2012) suggests deriving a definition by categorising the different types of summits that occur, while Mace *et al.* (2016: 3) provide typologies of summitry such as 'ad hoc/serial, bilateral/multilateral, regional/ global'. Despite debates on its definition, the central tenet of summitry is the direct interaction of political leaders, whether physically or through digital telecommunication devices, to discuss underlying national, regional or global issues. The rise of summitry has been made possible by myriad technological developments in the 20th and 21st centuries, for example, information and communication technologies (ICTs) and air travel.

On the other hand, summits circumvent the use of ambassadors and embassies, which are formal and traditional diplomatic practices. It is very difficult to find a leader in the 21st century who has relegated all matters of foreign affairs to his ambassadors or ministers/secretaries of foreign affairs. Diplomatic practice has become one of the primary responsibilities of state leaders, whether by default or construction. Supporters of summits argue that global leaders can negotiate better and faster on difficult issues when they engage in a one-on-one interaction (Mellisen, 2002). Summits allow leaders to assess and evaluate the personalities of their peers and how they deal with their domestic issues, which in turn helps them to weigh up the best way in which to approach these peers when negotiating supranational policies (Agwor, 2021). Summits are also vital in terms of legitimising internationally adopted policies and practices, and getting leaders to adopt these as domestic policies for implementation in their respective nations.

On the other hand, some scholars do not approve of the use of summitry – they think that global leaders are ill-equipped to deal with the rigorous diplomatic processes. Dalton (2018) argues that leaders lack the necessary expertise in many issues that are dealt with at summits, and they pay little attention to the finer details of the deals they make compared to career diplomats, who are experts in several fields. Critics contend that leaders consistently make blunders that change the direction of the summits and sometimes even harm state-to-state relations (Caramerli, 2012).

Despite the different schools of thought, summits continue to be on a growth trajectory in modern diplomacy. It is important to point out that not all summits have been successful. For instance, the North Korea–US summit in 2018 failed to bring any significant diplomatic progress between the United States and North Korea. In contrast, other summits have led to the fruition of successful diplomatic progress. For instance, the Malta Summit led to the eventual end of the Cold War between the United States and the Soviet Union, and the normalisation of diplomatic processes between the two superpowers at the time.

From the OAU to the African Union

The struggle of the Pan-African movement led to the establishment of the OAU in 1963. The Pan-African movement emerged outside the African continent in the 19th century, initiated by intellectuals of African descent in the United States. The first three Pan-African conferences were organised in Europe (London and Paris) and the United States (New York) (Bujra, 2002). It was only at the fifth congress in Manchester that prominent Pan-African nationalist leaders, such as Kwame Nkruma from Ghana and Julius Nyerere from Tanzania, platformed against colonial rule and its shackles on the continent. The independence of Ghana in 1957 gave a significant boost and renewed hope to the Pan-African movement on the continent. The All African People's Conference held in Accra, Ghana in December 1958 gave African leaders a new perspective: that to tackle the shackles of colonialism and achieve sustainable economic development, it was paramount for independent African states to be unified politically.

The OAU was formed in 1963, a few years after the conference in Accra. However, the establishment of the OAU was not a straightforward process, as ideological differences regarding the nature of integration took centre stage during the consultation meetings before its formulation. Kwame Nkruma and Julius Nyerere advocated for two different approaches to regional integration, which threatened to divide the Pan-African movement into two groups, namely the Casablanca and Monrovia groups. The Casablanca group, led by Kwame Nkruma, supported the federalist political unification approach, while Monrovia advocated for a pragmatic approach to integration (Mangwende, 1984). Nkruma later compromised his position of federalism, which opened the door for the two groups to combine and form the OAU in 1963. About 32 representatives from newly liberated African countries signed the OAU Charter, which aimed to promote the unity and solidarity of African countries, to cooperate and fight colonialism (Yihdego, 2011).

The adoption of a gradual integration process by the OAU challenged its effectiveness to address the number of crises that rose in subsequent years, which later threatened its existence. After gaining independence, the majority of African countries faced serious economic crises and political instabilities. The 1970s oil crisis, accompanied by poor economic policies, a lack of domestic financial capital and the introduction of the SAPs by the International Monetary Fund (IMF) and the World Bank, brought a significant number of African countries close to a complete collapse. On the political spectrum, instability and insecurity rose in several countries, and unconstitutional changes of power and inter- and intrastate conflicts occurred frequently (Schalk *et al.*, 2005).

The founding principles of non-interference and respect for the sovereignty and territorial integrity in the OAU Charter made the organisation unable to respond effectively and decisively to the issues facing the continent. It was criticised for being a 'club of authoritarian regimes … it failed to deliver in the key areas of governance, and development' (Yihdego, 2011: 569). It became increasingly clear that something concrete had to be done to deter the imminent catastrophe that was on the horizon. The OAU responded by hosting various summits aimed at mitigating the multifaceted problems the continent was facing. The 1980 Lagos Plan of Action for the Economic Development of Africa and the Treaty Establishing the African Economic Community, signed at a summit in Abuja, Nigeria in 1991, which came into force in 1994, led to the formation of the African Economic Community (AEC) and Regional Economic Communities (RECs) such as the Economic Community for West Africa (ECOWAS) and the Southern Africa Development Community (SADC). This signified the organisation's move to an alternative development approach, aligned to the Casablanca integration ideology.

The African Union and its institutions

The changes in the political and economic environment in the late 1990s called for the OAU to revisit its mandate and modernise to respond to the contemporary continental and global issues. By the mid-1990s, Namibia and South Africa, which were the last countries to be liberated, had gained their independence. Furthermore, the success of the European Union and the rise of regional economic blocs, such as the North American Free Trade Agreement (NAFTA) and the Association of Southeast Asian Nations (ASEAN), convinced African leaders to reform the OAU so that it could tackle the sociopolitical and economic challenges faced by the continent.

The attempt to form the African Union (AU) commenced at a summit in Libya in 2001, when African leaders lamented the need for a continental union with a structure and function similar to that of the European Union. The AU Charter retained some of the principles articulated in the OAU Charter.

The most important feature of the AU was the transformation of its economic approaches, the adoption of different policy actions such as the Lagos Plan of Action (LPA) and the Structural Adjustment Programme (SAP) and the launch of Economic Cooperation Agreements (ECAs) to accelerate economic growth, cooperation and development on the continent. However, these plans failed to achieve their objectives and neither did they manage to gain sufficient political support. The New Partnership for Africa's Development (NEPAD) was thus formed to address the shortfalls of the previously implemented policy actions and as a strategy to tackle African problems with home-grown solutions (Luqman and Zekeri, 2015). At NEPAD's core is the call for democratic principles and good governance as the foundation for creating an environment for sustainable development. The African Peer Review Mechanism (APRM) is a structure created within NEPAD, where member states can meet voluntarily to discuss issues around the best governance practices necessary for the consolidation of integration (ISS, 2022).

Another key feature of the AU is the African Peace and Security Architecture (APSA), an institution equipped to prevent, address or anticipate conflicts on the continent by working together with the RECs such as the SADC and ECOWAS. Before the establishment of the APSA, peace and security issues were conducted by the OAU and the RECs, but their influence was less effective because of the legally binding principles of non-interference and state sovereignty that were enshrined in the OAU Charter. The APSA has five pillars that work together to drive Africa's peace and security initiative. The Peace and Security Council (PSC) is the core institution and it implements the decisions of the entire APSA (Vanheukelom, 2017). NEPAD and the APSA are the two institutions the AU has used to implement strategic partnerships with external actors on issues related to socioeconomic development and peace and security.

The strategic partnership of the African Union and the European Union

The relationship between Africa and Europe has existed for hundreds of years, even before colonisation, which commenced in the 15th century. The postcolonial independence of African states and the intensification of intercontinental relations in the late 20th century created the need for new economic and political relations. During the decolonial period, the European Economic Community (EEC), the precursor of the European Union, formed the 1975 Lomé Convention to initiate economic cooperation with developing countries in the Global South (Gordon, 2021). The Lomé Convention went through a series of renegotiations in terms of aid provision and the scope of preferential trade agreements. The formation of a common market in Europe in the early 1990s, and the subsequent complaint logged by the United States to the World Trade Organization (WTO) that the Lomé convention contravened the WTO rules, led to the end of this convention.

The Lomé Convention was replaced by the Cotonou Partnership Agreement (CPA), which ran for 20 years from the year 2000, but has since been extended to 2023. The EU and AU partnership commenced in 2000, when the two regional organisations held their first summit in Cairo, Egypt, to establish strategic partnerships on various issues aimed at boosting economic growth and sustainable development through the intensification of trade and economic integration (Resty, 2021).

Another framework that has coordinated AU–EU relations is the Joint Africa–EU Strategy (JAES), which has been in force since 2007. According to Africa-EU Energy Partnership (AEEP) (2007), the JAES was initially formulated to handle EU–Africa relations on a continent-to-continent basis away from the CPA, and to ensure that the cooperation between the two partners evolves from one of donor–recipient to one of equal partnership on several mutually beneficial issues. However, the JAES has failed to achieve this. As Resty (2021) argues, the EU also has an existing partnership with North African countries under the Neighbourhood Policy and numerous bilateral relations with African countries outside the existing frameworks, which have complemented and sometimes complicated AU–EU relations. AU–EU relations have seen a transformation over the years and have diverted from their primary objectives.

AU–EU cooperation on trade, health and development

Historically, North and sub-Saharan Africa have been treated differently in EU trade policies towards the continent. Since the 1990s and 2000s, the EU has established bilateral free trade agreements (FTA) with Algeria, Egypt, Morocco and Tunisia. The AU and EU have worked together on a variety of trade and development initiatives through the CPA. Before China, India and the United States, the EU is by far Africa's greatest export market and its top trading partner. The trade between the two areas is evenly distributed, with a little excess in the EU's favour. The data below show how much commerce the EU has with Africa compared to external players.

The CPA has been central in establishing numerous preferential trade agreements between the EU and African countries. These agreements export African commodities into EU markets on favourable terms. The EU has several economic partnerships agreements (EPAs) with several sub-Saharan and North African countries through the CPA. The EPAs have been implemented on a multilateral basis through AU-recognised RECs to drive regional integration and a bilateral basis. Currently, multilateral EPAs include the EU–East Africa Community (EAC) and the EU–SADC EPA. On a bilateral basis, the EU has the EU–Ghana and EU–Ivory Coast EPAs.

The EU–AU partnership has also transcended into the health sector. In 2020, during the peak of COVID-19, the EU launched Team Europe as a strategy to provide the necessary support to tackle the pandemic around the world and in Africa. According to the European Commission (2022), the EU has committed, '€100 million EU humanitarian support to COVID-19 vaccination rollout in Africa'. Furthermore, the COVID-19 pandemic exposed Africa's over-reliance on externally produced medication and the need for the continent to have a medical regulator to improve and boost drug production (Donor Tracker, 2022).

In December 2021, the EU launched an ambitious Global Gateway as a strategy to mitigate infrastructure shortfalls that have been seen in the wake of the COVID-19 pandemic. The EU has set aside funds worth about €150 billion as an investment package aimed at supporting and boosting Africa's sustainable and inclusive development (EU, 2022). The funds were announced at the 2022 EU–AU Summit and they are to be invested in different economic sectors to transform Africa's economic environment (Deutsche Welle, 2022).

AU–EU peace and security partnership

The EU has prioritised intercontinental collaboration on peace and security, to a certain extent over trade, in its partnership with the AU.

This decision was in part influenced by the rise of conflicts and terrorist cells in Africa which threatens European security to a larger extent. Due to a lack of financial resources and capacity-building mechanism, the AU petitioned for the establishment of the African Peace Facility (APF) in 2003 through the CPA in an attempt to find secure funding for its peace and security operations under the APSA. The finances for the APF were disbursed by the European Development Fund (EDF), which is funded by member states in parallel to their EU yearly budget obligations to the EU. The APF supported various AU–Peace Support Operations (AU-PSOs) in fragile states on the continent, for example, in the Central African Republic and the African Mission to Somalia (AMISOM).

Recently, the AU has formulated different policies aimed at reducing its financial dependency on the EU for the operation of the APSA. In 2021, the APF was replaced by the European Peace Facility (EPF), which analysts have argued could undermine Africa's peace and security efforts, and lead to the militarisation of the continent (Woldemichael, 2022). The EPF, as an instrument of funding peace and security efforts, will cover various regions, not only the African continent, as demonstrated earlier. While the AU has led the peace and security initiative and directed how and where funds should be allocated under the APF, under the EPF there is currently a complete overhaul of this practice (Hauck and Shiferaw, 2021). The overall impact that EPF will have in terms of peace and security in Africa is yet to be fully realised as the project has just been implemented by the EU.

Africa–China relations

Africa–China relations witnessed a rejuvenation at the turn of the millennium as Beijing adopted the 'Going out' strategy to ease domestic overcapacity and find new markets for its industries, as well as to reassert itself as a dominant global political power. Although Africa–China relations have seen a significant expansion in cooperation in the last 22 years, the relationship between the two dates back to the 1400s when the Chinese explorer Zheng He first contacted the eastern part of the African continent. Unlike dominant political powers from the West (except for the United States), China does not carry the burden of being a former colonial master, so its relationship with Africa is conducted on an equal

South–South partnership aimed at addressing or achieving mutually aligned interests. In 2000, China formed the Forum on China–Africa Cooperation (FOCAC) as a framework to advance Africa–China relations. Since its formation, cooperation between China and Africa has seen a significant rise in areas of trade, aid, foreign direct investment (FDI), health and development (Thomas, 2021).

In addition to robust economic and development ties, Africa and China have also formed strong diplomatic relations through the FOCAC. The Johannesburg FOCAC VI summit in 2015, which saw the participation of the AU as a full member for the first time, was significant as China acknowledged and supported the adoption of Agenda 63 for the first time, and in addition made a financial pledge to support the implementation of the continent's development ambitions. The signing of the Memorandum of Understanding (MoU) called 'The Promotion of Cooperation in Railway, Road, Regional Aviation Networks and Industrialisation Fields' in 2015, further solidified efforts between the two players to engineer Africa's development trajectory. Building on the MoU, the AU and China signed an agreement in 2016 focusing on the construction of Africa's High-speed Railway Network. China also constructed Nigeria's first and only standard gauge railway line between the capital city, Abuja, and the gateway city to Northern Nigeria, Kaduna, which commenced operation in 2019 (Adogo, 2018).

In addition, it complements the development of road and railway networks across the continent. China has also been involved in the construction and development of industrial parks/economic development zones (EDZs) in several African countries to boost Africa's industrial and manufacturing capacity. At the summit in Johannesburg, the AU and China stressed the need to implement industrial cooperation in line with the indigenous environment laws of host nations. Currently, China has constructed industrial parks in Ethiopia, notably the Eastern Industrial Zone, and the Suez Economic and Trade Cooperation Zone (SETC) in Egypt and signed MoUs to construct additional industrial parks in Mozambique and Angola. At the recent FOCAC summit in Dakar, Senegal, the 2025 Vision for China–Africa Cooperation was adopted, which outlines areas of cooperation by the two parties for the next 15 years (Sun, 2021). In addition, China made commitments to increase trade cooperation with Africa, especially in importing more African goods to China to reduce the trade deficit that exists.

In the health sector, China has increased the level of cooperation with the AU. It has been one of the leading partners in the health sector on the continent for decades. The first cooperation dates back to the early 1960s, when Beijing sent its first team of medical personnel to Africa. The COVID-19 pandemic has rejuvenated and opened new avenues for cooperation (Nantulya, 2021). During the 2020 FOCAC summit in Dakar, President Xi announced a set of policy actions to assist African governments in the fight against the COVID-19 pandemic. These include the provision and production of COVID-19 vaccines through joint ventures, the construction of Africa's Centre for Disease Control and Prevention (CDC) in Ethiopia, and the delivery of medical equipment (Thomas, 2021).

Peace and security

Over the years, there has been a shift in China's foreign policy in Africa in terms of peace and security. While China has always championed itself as a pacifist state and adopted a policy of non-interference in the domestic affairs of its partners, as the core pillar of its diplomacy, recently this approach is being diluted, especially in Africa. As Ryder and Eguege (2022) argue, investments in hard infrastructure that have been made through the FOCAC and the Belt and Road Initiative (BRI), and the desire to protect these and see a return on investment in these projects – bearing in mind the history of insecurity in Africa – could explain this sudden shift in foreign policy by Beijing (Debelo, 2017).

In 2008, China started to engage in peace and security operations in Africa with the deployment of its naval forces along the African coast in the Gulf of Aden. China was also actively involved in the peace process between Sudan and South Sudan in 2005, and has continued to be an active external player in maintaining peace in South Sudan with the approval of the AU and the United Nations (UN) (Debelo, 2017). China is now one of the paramount players in the UN Peacekeeping Operations (UNPKOs) on the continent. As Bayes (2020) points out, China opened a military base beyond its territory for the first time in Djibouti (2017) in an attempt to tackle insecurity on the continent. The military base is located in the Horn of Africa, close to the Suez Canal, which is one of the most important maritime passages for global trade and the area is synonymous with maritime piracy due to insecurity in the surrounding countries. By opening the military base, Beijing was able to portray its unilateral military presence as part of the international effort to combat piracy and protect global trade passing through the Suez Canal (Tanchum, 2021). Other scholars are of the view that the Chinese military base in Djibouti is aimed at protecting and securing China's economic interests in the region (Debelo, 2017; Caliskan, 2021). Subsequently, China is also one of the biggest arms exporters to African countries at relatively affordable prices and it has also provided both lethal and non-lethal military hardware to support multilateral and bilateral missions on the continent.

AU–US relations

To encourage economic growth and development, and strengthen political relations in sub-Saharan Africa, the United States adopted the African Growth and Opportunity Act (AGOA) in 2000 and, since its inception, the programme has been the keystone of US–Africa economic collaboration. The AGOA is the brainchild of former president Bill Clinton, who introduced the programme to enhance and strengthen USA–Africa trade cooperation. In 2015, after consultation, Congress extended the AGOA to 2025, in part this was due to rising competition from China and the EU, which also have trade agreements on the continent. The programme permits participating member states to export both primary commodities and manufactured goods to the US market. It also boosts US investors' confidence about investing in participating member states, as eligibility to participate in the programme requires member states to meet the US's strict criteria. When a country fails to meet the criteria, its eligibility is revoked, or it is not accepted in the programme. For instance, the Biden Administration recently removed Mali from the AGOA after a coup d'état in May 2021. Ethiopia and Guinea have also been removed from the programme as a result of allegedly violating the criteria.

Several countries have benefitted greatly from the AGOA. For instance, South Africa is one of these, having enjoyed the benefit from exports and industrial investments. Due to the removal of tariffs on imports into the US market, the automotive industry in South Africa has seen an increase in investments by global car manufacturing giants, such as Mercedes-Benz and Toyota, into local car manufacturing plants that are able to export cars into the US market. The AU recognises the AGOA as one of the continent's strategic partnership agreements and has taken various steps to ensure that African countries maximise their benefits. However, the AGOA has failed to meet its intended objectives. Since the financial crisis, trade between the US and the AGOA participants has been on a downward trend, failing to achieve maximum benefits. The US's push for supposedly democratic values has also inclined other eligible countries towards China, with its non-interference policy.

Health

The US is one of the most important players in the African health sector. For the past two decades, it has been the leading player in tackling health-related issues in Africa, such as tuberculosis (TB), HIV/AIDS, Ebola and, recently, the COVID-19 pandemic. South Africa, Rwanda, Nigeria and Botswana are the biggest recipients of the President's Emergency Plan for AIDS Relief (PEPFAR) funding on the continent (Adepoju, 2022).

In addition, the US extended its health assistance coverage to support countries in Africa against the COVID-19 pandemic. A report by USAID says that the funds are meant to assist African countries to reinforce their response systems to the pandemic. For instance, the US donated millions of COVID-19 vaccines through the African Union's African Vaccine Acquisition Trust (AVAT). The cooperation is also set to increase the number of health workers on the continent and open the door to the private sector as partners in the manufacturing of health-related products, including vaccines and medical equipment.

Africa–Japan relations

Africa–Japan relations have passed through multiple phases since their inception in 1961. In the beginning, Japan's interaction with Africa was based on its unwavering support against communism on the African continent, through its alliance with the United States. According to Adem (2015), the creation of the Tokyo International Conference on African Development (TICAD) in 1993 signalled Japan's new era and ambitions to become a responsible and influential global player in the field of development and security. The TICAD is the platform through which Africa and Japan interact on diplomatic, development and peace and security issues (Nakamura, 2022). The TICAD is a collaboration between

Japan and the AU, plus other external stakeholders such as the UN. The ICAD was hosted on African soil for the first time in 2016 for for the first time its sixth summit.

It was at the third TICAD summit in 2003 that there was a massive change in relations between Japan and Africa. The number of heads of state attending the summit increased from 15 at the second summit in 1998 to 28 at the third. The summit articulated new strategies for engagement with Africa, which have continued to dictate Japan–Africa relations to date. The emphasis on 'ownership' and 'partnership' inclusion in the TICAD process is accompanied by the belief in putting the African continent in charge of its own development approach and relegating external players to the role of complementary supporters of this approach.

The Shinzo Abe administration revived Japanese interest in the continent as it launched an outward-looking economic strategy as a way of reviving the Japanese economy (Pajon, 2020). Official development assistance (ODA) through the TICAD has been channelled to African countries through the official Japanese development vehicle, the Japanese International Cooperation Agency (JICA). JICA, through the directive of the TICAD, is responsible for directing and implementing different ODA activities on the continent. These range from healthcare initiatives and refugee-relief programmes to industrial and infrastructural development. In Southern Africa, it has invested in the Nacala Corridor, which consists of a railway line that stretches from Zambia through Malawi to Mozambique. In West Africa, it has invested in the West Africa Growth Ring, and in East Africa in the Northern Corridor. The goal of these investments is to promote and develop regional integration and investments and to increase trade in these regions, which consist of several landlocked countries, through the construction of good quality railway infrastructure.

The TICAD has faced numerous challenges. Domestically Japanese private businesses have shown reluctance to participate in the practice. In 2016, the former president, Shinzo Abe, hosted the TICAD support in Kenya and demonstrated a clear path to divert from ODA-driven foreign policy to one that focuses on private investments to compete effectively with other global powers on the continent. Compared to the investment outflows of other global powers, Japan's FDI is below par and not competitive (Ngila, 2022). The economic challenges in Japan, which have contributed to the decline of funds allocated to its ODA programme and the unwillingness of private Japanese companies to enter the African market, have made the TICAD less attractive to African leaders. At the eighth TICAD summit in 2022, which was hosted by Tunisia, the number of African heads of state who attended declined significantly and the financial commitments that were made were mainly from the Japanese government.

Peace and security

According to Tariku (2019), Japan has collaborated with the AU and the UN, as well as individual African countries, to address insecurity on the continent. In 2009, Japan joined the multilateral efforts to combat insecurity off the coast of Somalia, which was hampering the free movement of maritime trade in the Horn of Africa. Despite reduced insecurity off the coast of Somalia, Japan has taken the position of extending its military presence on the continent. This could be a response to its regional rival, China, which opened its military base in Djibouti in 2017. Moreover, the military bases in Djibouti have been used for other military operations, including acting as a logistic hub for Japanese ground troops who were in South Sudan from 2012 to 2017.

Japan has invested extensively to ensure peace and security on the continent. At the beginning of 2012, Japan deployed ground troops for a peacekeeping mission in South Sudan. This was to support UN peacekeeping under the UN Mission in South Sudan (UNMISS). The deployed Japanese troops were to work in non-combatant roles by the post-WWII Japanese Constitution, which restricts combat military involvement, so they were deployed to rebuild vital infrastructure such as roads, bridges and boreholes. These forces were also involved in capacity-building efforts in South Sudan, which included facilitating national dialogue to ensure sustained peace, and training police officers to equip them with the necessary skills to deal effectively with the fragile security environment.

Conclusion

The AU and other external actors are drivers of regional integration on the African continent. Over the past two decades, the AU has signed numerous continent-to-continent and bilateral partnerships with external actors, which have brought positive outcomes in the health sector, infrastructure, investment and peace and security. Indeed, external actors have been vital in the provision of the necessary resources to fuel integration and fund key programmes that have brought numerous development benefits, including mitigating the HIV/AIDS and COVID-19 pandemics, infrastructure deficits and insecurity on the continent. Despite their positive impacts, the different approaches have not been entirely constructive on the continent. While some actors have tried to work with Africans as equal partners, for instance, Japan, others have dictated the terms of engagements for continued investment, such as what gets priority and the ways to achieve it, which has to an extent limited and negatively affected the work of the AU, especially in the field of peace and security. Of course, this has also been accompanied by AU member states' inability to pay their annual financial dues to the continental institution. The increased role of external players has contributed to the AU's lack of prioritisation and agency. For instance, it has entered into multiple partnerships on the same issues with different actors who have different goals and objectives, some of which overlap and conflict with each other. To utilise its strategic partnership with external players effectively, the AU needs to develop a coherent plan on how to engage external players, which is supported by a binding legal framework and enforcement mechanisms, to achieve its pan-African ambitions for the continent.

References

Abbott, L.C. (2013). 'Networked governance and summit diplomacy: Shaping the maternal, newborn and child health agenda'. Available at: https://uwspace.uwaterloo.ca (Accessed 15 September 2022).

Adem, S. (2015). 'Sino–Japanese rivalry in Africa?' *Asia Pacific World*, 6(2): 90–102.

Adepoju, P. (2022). 'Nkengasong's PEPFAR prospects and hopes for Africa CDC'. Available at: https://healthpolicy-watch.news/nkengasong-pepfar-africa-cdc/ (Accessed 23 September 2022).

Adogo, H. (2022). 'The African Union cannot go to Beijing without an action plan'. Available at: https://www.dailymaverick.co.za/article/2022-03-07-the-african-union-cannot-go-to-beijing-without-an-action-plan/ (Accessed 20 September 2022).

Agwor, O.N.D. (2021). 'Summitry: The ancient and modern of diplomatic dialogue', *International Journal of Innovative Legal & Political Studies*,

9(2): 39–50.

Aworaro, F. (2015). 'Regional integration and development in Africa: Between the present realities and overcoming future challenges', *African Journal of Governance and Development*, 4(2): 5–16.

Bayes, T. (2020). 'China's growing security role in Africa: Suggestions for a European response'. Available at: https://www.kas.de (Accessed 19 September 2022).

Bujra, A. (2002). 'Africa: From AOU to AU'. Available at: https://www.academia.edu/27579091 (Accessed 10 September 2022).

Caliskan, G. (2021). 'The only place in the world China has a military base: Djibouti'. Available at: https://www.ankasam.org/the-only-place-in-the-world-china-has-a-military-base-djibouti-v/?lang=en (Accessed 21 September 2022).

Caramerli, A. (2012). 'Summitry diplomacy: Positive and negative aspects', *Relationes Internationales*, 5(1): 23–30.

Cornago, N. (2008). 'Diplomacy', in L. Kurtz (ed.). *Encyclopedia of Violence, Peace, and Conflict*. Oxford: Elsevier.

Dalton, Y. (2018). 'The future of summit diplomacy'. Available at: https://www.researchgate.net/publication/331262257_The_Future_of_Summit_Diplomacy (Accessed 11 September 2022).

Debelo, R.A. (2017). 'The African Union's peace and security partnership with China'. APN Briefing Note, No. 12. New York: African Peacebuilding Network, pp. 1–2.

Deutsche Welle. (2022). 'Africa: EU reveals €150 billion investment plan for Africa', *AllAfrica*, 10 February. Available at: https://allafrica.com/stories/202202110089.html (Accessed 11 September 2022).

Donor Tracker. (2022). 'EU, Belgium, France, Germany, Gates Foundation commit US$113 million for health product regulatory strengthening in Africa'. Available at: https://donortracker.org (Accessed 17 September 2022).

Geda, A. and Kibret, H. (2002). 'Regional Economic Integration in Africa: A review of problems and prospects with a case study of COMESA', Working Papers 125, Department of Economics, SOAS University of London. Available at: https://www.soas.ac.uk/sites/default/files/2022-10/economics-wp125.pdf (Accessed 15 December 2022).

Hauck, V. and Shiferaw, L.T. (2021). 'Continuity and change in European Union–Africa relations on peace and security'. Durban: ACCORD. Available at: https://www.accord.org.za/analysis/continuity-and-change-in-european-union-africa-relations-on-peace-and-security/ (Accessed 18 September 2022).

Luqman, S. and Zekeri, M. (2015). 'New Partnership for Africa's Development (NEPAD) and development in Africa', *The International Academic Conference for Sub-Sahara African Transformation & Development*, 3(6): 1–10.

Mace, G., Thérien, J., Dabène, O. and Tussie, D. (2016). 'Introduction. Summitry and governance in comparative perspective', in Summits and Regional Governance. The Americas in comparative perspective, Global Institutions Series. London: Routledge. Available at: https://www.researchgate.net/publication/315794751 (Accessed 10 September 2022).

Mangwende, W. (1984). 'The OAU: An analysis of the function, problems and prospects of the organization', *Zambezia*, 12(1). *The African e-Journals Project*, 21–38. https://journals.co.za/doi/abs/10.10520/AJA03790622_28.

Mellisen, J. (2002). 'Summit diplomacy coming of age', Netherlands Institute of International Relations 'Clingendael', Discussion Papers in Diplomacy. Available at: https://www.clingendael.org/publication/summit-diplomacy-coming-age (Accessed 11 September 2022).

Nakamura, H. (2022). 'Japanese foreign policy toward Africa: Towards a middle power diplomacy', *Journal of Inter-Regional Studies: Regional and Global Perspectives*, 6: 1–15.

Nantulya, P. (2021). 'China's Role in COVID-19 in Africa: Tuánjié (solidarity) or zhànlüè (strategy)?' Durban: ACCORD. Available at: https://www.accord.org.za/analysis/chinas-role-in-covid-19-in-africa-tuanjie-solidarity-or-zhanlue-strategy/ (Accessed 20 September 2022).

Ngila, F. (2022). Japan is changing its approach to Africa', *Yahoo! Finance*, 25 August. Available at: https://finance.yahoo.com/news/japan-changing-approach-africa-080200901.html (Accessed 26 September 2022).

Pajon, C. (2020). 'Japan's Economic Diplomacy in Africa: Between strategic priorities and local realities', *Notes de l'Ifri*, December: 1–28.

Pajon, C. (2017). 'Japan's security policy in Africa: The dawn of strategic approach?' *Notes de l'Ifri*, 93: 1–30.

Resty, N. (2021). 'The EU–AU trade and development partnership: Towards a new era?', FEPS Policy Brief, October. Brussels: Foundation for European Progressive Studies, pp. 1–28. Available at: https://www.researchgate.net/publication/356087173_THE_EU-AU_TRADE_

AND_DEVELOPMENT_PARTNERSHIP_TOWARDS_A_NEW_ ERA (Accessed 21 January 2023).

Reynolds, D. (2009). 'Summitry as intercultural communication', *International Affairs*, 85(1): 115–27.

Ryder, H. and Eguege, O. (2022). 'Africans welcome China's role in peace and security, but are pushing for greater agency and responsibility'. Durban: ACCORD. Available at: https://www.accord.org.za/analysis/ africans-welcome-chinas-role-in-peace-and-security-but-are-pushing- for-greater-agency-and-responsibility/ (Accessed 21 September 2022).

Schalk, B., Auriacombe, C.J. and Brynard, D.J. (2005). 'Successes and failures of the organization for African unity: Lessons for the future African Union', *Journal of Public Administration*, 40(3.2): 496–511.

Sun, Y. (2021). 'An examination of the 2035 Vision for China–Africa cooperation'. Available at: https://www.brookings.edu/blog/africa-in- focus/2021/12/27/an-examination-of-the-2035-vision-for-china-africa- cooperation/ (Accessed 19 September 2022).

Tanchum, M. (2021). 'China's new military base in Africa: What it means for Europe and America'. Available at: https://ecfr.eu/article/chinas- new-military-base-in-africa-what-it-means-for-europe-and-america/ (Accessed 21 September 2022).

Tariku, Y. (2019). *Africa–Japan Relations in the Context of Global Peace and Security: The need for a well-tailored policy*, IPSS Policy Brief, 13(9): 1–10. Addis Ababa: Institute for Peace and Security Studies.

Thomas, D. (2021). 'What did FOCAC 2021 deliver for Africa?' Available at: https://african.business/2021/11/trade-investment/what-can-africa- expect-from-focac-2021/ (Accessed 21 September 2022).

Vanheukelom, J. (2017). 'Understanding the African Union: How to become fit for purpose?' Available at: https://ecdpm.org/wp-content/ uploads/African-Union-Background-Paper-PEDRO-Political- Economy-Dynamics-Regional-Organisations-Africa-ECDPM-2017. pdf (Accessed 12 September 2022).

Woldemichael, S. (2022). 'Africa should be better prepared for Europe's security funding shift'. Available at: https://issafrica.org/iss-today/ africa-should-be-better-prepared-for-europes-security-funding-shift (Accessed 19 September 2022).

Yihdego, Z. (2011). 'The African Union: Founding principles, frameworks and prospects', *European Law Journal*, 17(5): 568–94.

Regional integration: Mission impossible?

SIZO NKALA AND DAVID MONYAE

It is fair to conclude that after six decades of trying, the regional integration project in Africa has met with limited success. Africa's regional integration approach has evolved from the import-substitution-based approached of the 1970s and 1980s, which sought to achieve self-sufficiency, to one based on open regionalism with an emphasis on enhancing Africa's participation in the global economy adopted in the 1990s. Nonetheless, the Pan-African goal of a united and integrated Africa remains elusive despite sustained efforts to make it a reality. After about 17 Regional Economic Communities (RECs) and numerous regional and continental initiatives, such as the African Economic Community (AEC), the New Partnership for Africa's Development (NEPAD) and the Programme for Infrastructure Development in Africa (PIDA), to mention a few, regional integration has failed to register significant inroads. This volume took stock of the performance of some of the African Union-recognised RECs such as the SADC, ECOWAS, EAC, COMESA and IGAD since their inception. These RECs were founded or revived with the intention of making them the building blocks of the AEC envisaged under the 1991 Abuja Treaty. As the various contributions in this volume have shown, almost every index of regional integration, namely trade integration, productive integration, macroeconomic integration, infrastructural integration and the free movement of persons, retains a disappointingly low score.

Table 22.1: Scores of different dimensions of regional integration in Africa

Dimension	Score
Trade integration	0.382
Productive integration	0.201
Macroeconomic integration	0.399
Infrastructural integration	0.22
Free movement of people	0.441

Source: Africa Regional Integration Index. Available at: https://www.integrate-africa.org/ (Accessed 21 December 2022).

The average integration index across all dimensions is only 0.32. This means that Africa has achieved only 32 per cent of its potential regional integration. One of the most cited indicators of regional integration, the level of intra-African trade, tells a similar story. In 2021, intra-African trade was only 14 per cent (US$71 billion) of Africa's total trade. In some AU-recognised regional economic communities such as the AMU, IGAD, ECCAS and the EAC, intraregional trade was lower than 6 per cent of their total trade. This despite two of the regional organisations, ECCAS and the EAC, having established free trade areas to facilitate the movement of goods, people and capital across borders. The best-performing subregion in terms of intraregional trade was the SADC with 32 per cent internal trade. The low levels of trade are a manifestation of the legacy of colonialism, which created a fragmented and disconnected continent populated by small and dysfunctional states with barely any lines of communication with one another (Uzodike, 2009). Moreover, almost all of the six deadlines set out in the stages of the 1991 Treaty Establishing the African Economic Community have not been met. For example, the Treaty promised that, by 1999, RECs would have been established in regions where they do not exist and all would have been strengthened.

While RECs have been established in all regions – with some regions having even more than two RECs – it is debatable whether these have been strengthened. If the regional integration indices are anything to go by, it seems that the various RECs are still fragile institutions. Moreover, according to the 1991 Treaty, by 2017 every REC should have established a free trade area and a customs union. However, only five (SADC, COMESA,

ECOWAS, EAC and ECCAS) of the eight African Union-recognised RECs have established free trade areas, albeit all are works in progress. Even more concerning is that none of the RECs have a functioning customs union except for the Southern African Customs Union (SACU) comprising South Africa, Lesotho, Namibia, Botswana and Swaziland. However, the SACU is not one of the eight AU-recognised RECs. ECOWAS, COMESA and the EAC have mulled the prospects of a customs union. In the case of COMESA, a customs union was launched in 2009 but it is yet to be fully operational; and the SADC missed the 2010 and 2015 deadlines to establish a customs union. Overlapping memberships of different RECs, narrow political interests and insufficient trade complementarity continue to hamper the full implementation of customs unions. The establishment of a Continental Customs Union was supposed to happen in 2019, while 2023 was earmarked for the creation of the African Common Market. None of these milestones have been reached and it seems that none of them will be realised any time soon.

It is no wonder that there is an air of despondency around the discourse on regional integration. The assessment of the RECs in this volume (ECOWAS, SADC, IGAD, EAC and CEMAC) has revealed how difficult it is for member states to reach an agreement, let alone implement such an agreement on macroeconomic policy. As a result of their different levels of economic development and the need to respond to unique socioeconomic and political-economic circumstances, it can be very challenging to coordinate a regional monetary or fiscal policy.

Khabele Matlosa's contribution on the state of the free movement of persons in the continent, which is a vital element of regional integration, paints a disappointingly bleak picture. Only four countries, namely Rwanda, Niger, São Tomé and Príncipe and Mali have ratified the Protocol on the Free Movement of Persons, Right of Resident and Right of Establishment in Africa, which was adopted by the African Union in 2018. This protocol is part of the initiatives that are central to the realisation of the AEC. However, most African states' visa policies are still very restrictive. This makes it difficult for Africans to travel to other African countries, thus undermining tourism, the movement of goods and capital and the mobility of labour.

Moreover, as emphatically stated in four contributions in this volume, infrastructure is key to the success of the regional integration project in Africa. Yet Africa's infrastructure is either in a state of serious disrepair or non-existent altogether. Africa's roads, railways, power systems, airports, seaports, rivers and telecommunications have proven inadequate to provide a stable basis for regional integration. The poor state of infrastructure is one of the main reasons behind the failure of several free trade areas (FTAs) established in different RECs. The African Development Bank (AfDB) estimated that Africa has an infrastructure funding deficit of US$100 billion against its infrastructure funding needs of up to US$170 billion annually. It has been highlighted that the continent's transport costs are the highest in the world, which makes its products less competitive on the world stage. Power systems, which are mostly designed to serve national markets, have been deemed inefficient and too expensive. This has left hundreds of millions of Africans without access to power. Regional power pools in Africa's various regions, such as the Southern African Power Pool and the West African Power Pool, meant to alleviate power shortages, have been slow to materialise. Equally important has been the deleterious impact of the disparate soft infrastructure, which makes trading and cooperation immensely difficult. A melting pot of regulations, protocols, standards, customs administration and lingua franca, which do not speak to one another, add to the costs of cross-border trade (Kayizzi-Mugerwa, Anyanwu and Conceicao, 2014).

This book also cast the spotlight on continental institutions such the Pan-African Parliament (PAP), the Peace and Security Council (PSC), the Africa Centre for Disease Control and Prevention (Africa CDC) and the African Continental Free Trade Area (AfCFTA). These institutions were established with a view to creating an environment conducive to regional integration in the continent. The PAP and the PSC have had a longer existence as they were created at the beginning of the 21st century (in 2004 and 2003, respectively). While there was much hope that these institutions would brighten Africa's prospects of regional integration, an analysis of their record shows that they have fallen short of the expectations imposed on them. Their lack of supranational authority, which is a result of the high premium most African countries have placed on national sovereignty, has greatly undermined their operational effectiveness. The PAP does not possess fundamental parliamentary powers such as making laws and budgetary control. In addition, it lacks democratic legitimacy as it is not elected directly by the African masses, making it an elite institution. As argued in this book, the PAP has not succeeded in its mandate to bring the people into Africa's integration processes and to hold African leaders accountable for their policies. The PSC has also left a lot to be desired in terms of addressing peace and security issues on the continent. Africa's security situation remains precarious with new conflicts erupting at a rapid rate, while the PSC seems unable to intervene. The acute shortage of financial and human resources, and the reliance on the consent of the nation-states for an intervention to proceed, have rendered the PSC ineffective.

The Africa CDC and the AfCFTA are relatively new institutions, having been established in 2015 and 2019, respectively. The Africa CDC is meant to coordinate the continent's approach to pandemics which, as the COVID-19 pandemic has shown, can set the regional integration agenda back significantly. The AfCFTA was created with a view to boosting intra-African trade by eliminating tariff and non-tariff barriers to trade. It has been estimated that, if implemented fully, the AfCFTA has the potential to raise income by US$450 billion and lift about 30 million people out of poverty by 2035. Further, the implementation of the new trade regime is forecast to increase Africa's exports by US$560 billion with most of the gains coming from manufacturing. However, if the performance of the FTAs at the subregional level is anything to go by, it will be very difficult to implement a free trade agreement on a continental scale with so many countries and interests to coordinate. The contributions on the AfCFTA in this book have highlighted the importance of building strong institutions to support the new FTA. The AfCFTA Secretariat and the state parties must ensure that the trading rules underpinning the AfCFTA are respected by all parties.

The chapters in this volume have also examined the RECs' performance in the regional security dimension. Most RECs found themselves having to get involved in conflict resolution and prevention in their member states as the conflicts were seriously hampering the economic integration process. For example, the IGAD created the Peace and Security Division in 2003 in the wake of political instability in some of its member states. ECOWAS has the Department of Political Affairs, Peace and Security (PAPS), which has played an integral role in coordinating the organisation's intervention in conflict areas in countries like Sierra Leone, Liberia and Côte d'Ivoire. As discussed in this volume, more than any other REC, ECOWAS has been effective in conflict resolution in the region. The SADC, ECCAS and the EAC have all invested resources and created departments charged with maintaining peace and security in their regions. It is not only at the subregional level that peace and security have assumed an important place. The African Union created the Peace and Security Council (PSC) to address peace and security issues on the continent. Operating through the African Peace and Security Architecture (APSA), the PSC has intervened in some of Africa's hotspots, including Somalia, Sudan and the Democratic Republic of the Congo (DRC). However, as observed, the PSC's effectiveness has been undermined by the chronic lack of financial and human resources and its lack of supranational powers since it can intervene only at the invitation of the concerned countries. Most member states have been reluctant to contribute their troops for the PSC's peacebuilding and peacemaking missions. While the African Union has created the African Standby Force (ASF), comprising soldiers, police and civilians in their countries of origin, to coordinate the rapid deployment of troops in the case of a peace and security emergency, the ASF is yet to be deployed to a conflict zone. The African Union and the RECs have preferred to create ad hoc security coalitions to intervene in violent conflict. In some cases, member states have rejected the intervention of the ASF on the principle of respect for sovereignty and non-intervention in internal affairs.

The way forward

Notwithstanding the false starts over the last 60 years, regional integration remains firmly on the agenda of the African Union, as expressed in the Agenda 2063. Numerous studies have shown how regional integration is indispensable if Africa is to realise the goals it set for itself in the Agenda 2063. The challenges facing Africa and the world in general cannot be dealt with successfully at the national level. No single country can fight climate change and environmental deterioration, contain pandemics of highly contagious diseases, suppress transnational terrorist networks, or produce everything its people need on a competitive and sufficient scale. More than ever before, countries depend on cross-border trade, the free flow of ideas, information and technology for the security and welfare of their citizens and their territorial integrity. The trend towards interconnectedness and interdependence is therefore intensifying across the political, security and economic spheres. However, interconnectedness and interdependence cannot occur on their own. For these processes to thrive, deliberate and careful intervention is needed from African leaders.

The foundation of any successful regional integration scheme is political will and commitment from the leaders entrusted with the implementation of regional integration initiatives. Africa has produced tonnes of well thought out regional integration programmes, which have been undermined by the reluctance or inability of African leaders to allocate resources and energy to see them through. In most cases, powerful sectoral interests – who have little to gain from regional integration – work through their access to and influence over the political elite in their countries to ensure that these programmes suffer a still birth. Hence, as Mkandawire (2014) rightly pointed out, it is fundamentally important that regional integration is anchored on a thorough and adequate understanding of national and sectoral interests. Regional integration initiatives that are detached from and insensitive to the realities of the political economy of member states will be greeted only with hostility and indifference and no efforts will be expended to implement them.

The lack of appreciation for the political economy dynamics of member states stems from the design of the regional integration arrangements. The negotiation of these arrangements tends to be the exclusive territory of state executives, with little to no consultation with non-state actors such as the private sector, civil society organisations and independent research institutes, among others (Tavares and Tang, 2011). The result is that the integration schemes amount to an 'elite pact' with little grounding in or connection to the grassroots constituencies. What is usually overlooked is that it is generally private sector actors that are expected to use these regional integration agreements. If the signed agreements do not align with the interests of the business community, they will simply be ignored. Moreover, the civil society organisations are important in building narratives and disseminating information about regional integration initiatives. This is vital in promoting public awareness and consciousness of the regional integration, which will encourage public feedback and ownership of the processes and grant them a veneer off democratic legitimacy. Unfortunately, African publics have little knowledge of these regional integration initiatives, which, ironically, are meant to improve their welfare. Without any input from the masses, the political elite, who are the signatories to these regional agreements, are shielded from public accountability and, thus, are not compelled to implement them. It is imperative that regional integration efforts be more participatory and inclusive going forward to make them more resilient, especially in the face of hostility from special interests.

The failure of regional integration in Africa has also been rightly attributed to inherently weak regional institutions, whose structure militates against their effectiveness in promoting regional integration. Regional institutions such as the African Union, the Pan-African Parliament, the Peace and Security Council and the various RECs are devoid of any supranational authority. This means that their operations depend on the consent of their member states as they do not have the power to independently enforce regional agreements. For example, the treaties adopted by the African Union are nominally binding, the PAP has no power to make continental legislation and the PSC only intervenes in conflict situations at the invitation of the affected member state. It is a classic case of the whole not being bigger than the sum of its constituent parts. As has been widely highlighted, African leaders are still unwilling to lose absolute sovereignty over their countries to supranational institutions. However, without empowered regional institutions, regional integration will not make any significant progress (Thonke and Spliid, 2012). Therefore, there needs to be a paradigm shift on the part of the African political elite which would make them amenable to relinquishing part of their sovereignty over the territories they govern for the sake of regional integration.

References

Kayizzi-Mugerwa, S., Anyanwu, J.C. and Conceicao, P. (2014). 'Regional integration in Africa: An introduction', *African Development Review*, 26(1): 1–6.

Mkandawire, T. (2014). 'On the Politics of Regional Integration'. Tralac Annual Conference, 15–16 May 2014, Cape Town, South Africa.

Tavares, R. and Tang, V. (2011). 'Regional economic integration in Africa: Impediments to progress?' *South African Journal of International Affairs*: 18(2): 217–33.

Thonke, O. and Spliid, A. (2012). 'What to expect from regional integration in Africa?' *African Security Review*, 21(1): 42–66. https://doi.org/10.108 0/10246029.2011.629452.

Uzodike, U.O. (2009). 'The role of regional economic communities in Africa's economic integration: Prospects and constraints', *Africa Insight*, 39(2): 26–42.

Contributors

ANSLEM W. ADUNIMAY is a researcher and Postdoctoral Fellow at the University of Johannesburg (UJ), in the 4IR and Digital Policy Unit within the Department of Politics and International Relations. He is also a Junior Research Fellow within the Research Department at the African Centre for the Constructive Resolution of Disputes (ACCORD). He holds a BA from the University of Douala, Cameroon, in the field of Law and Political Science. He moved to South Africa where he obtained his MA in Politics and International Relations at UJ, with a focus on conflict and security dynamics in the Great Lakes Region, using the International Conference on the Great Lakes Region (ICGLR) as a case study. His PhD at UJ focused on the mediation and leadership nexus in the Democratic Republic of the Congo (DRC) and Burundi.

JOHN AKOKPARI is Emeritus Professor of Politics. He obtained his BA, MA and PhD from the University of Ghana, the International University of Japan and Dalhousie University (Canada), respectively. He taught at St Mary's University (in Nova Scotia, Canada), and at the National University of Lesotho before joining the University of Cape Town (UCT). Professor Akokpari was a former head of the Department of Political Studies, and a former director of the interdisciplinary research institute, the Institute for Democracy, Citizenship and Public Policy in Africa (IDCPPA) at UCT. His research interests are African studies, with a focus on civil society, democratisation, international relations, international migration, regionalism and conflict studies.

ROD ALENCE is Associate Professor in International Relations at the University of the Witwatersrand (Wits) in Johannesburg. At Wits, he developed and coordinates an interdisciplinary postgraduate programme in computational social science. His research focuses on the international and comparative political economy of development and democracy in Africa. He received an AB degree from Columbia University and MA and PhD degrees from Stanford University. While doing his doctoral research, he was a Fulbright scholar at the University of Ghana, and his thesis won the American Political Science Association's annual award for best in the field of political economy.

EMMANUEL AMPOMAH is a Young African Research Fellow with the Equitable Education and Economies unit of the Human Sciences Research Council (HSRC) and a graduate student at the University of Cape Town. His research interests are in the fields of conflict mediation and resolution, African politics and youth livelihoods.

ODILILE AYODELE heads up the Digital Africa Research Unit at the Institute for Pan-African Thought and Conversation at the University of Johannesburg. She holds an MA in International Relations from the University of the Witwatersrand and a PhD in Political Studies from the University of Johannesburg. She teaches Pan-African Thought and Leadership and guest lectures in Conflict Resolution in Africa, Critical Development Studies and Research Methodology at the post-graduate level. Her research focuses on the international relations of technology, the political economy of communications technology and digital diplomacy.

ROB DAVIES is an Honorary Professor at the University of Cape Town's Nelson Mandela School of Public Governance and a member of the Advisory Council on Trade and Industrial Development appointed by the Secretary General of the African Continental Free Trade Area. Between 2009 and 2019, he served as South Africa's Minister of Trade and Industry and was a Member of Parliament between 1994 and 2019.

EKEMINIABASI EYITA-OKON is a Postdoctoral Research Fellow at the Centre for Africa–China Studies. She holds a PhD in International Relations from the University of the Witwatersrand. Her research interests include international and African political economy and development, focusing on the food–water–energy–environment nexus. She is the founder of two book clubs, namely African Girls Do Read (AGDR) and African Women in Political Economy and Development (AWIPEAD).

GILBERT M. KHADIAGALA is the Jan Smuts Professor of International Relations and Director of the African Centre for the Study of the United States (ACSUS) at the University of the Witwatersrand, Johannesburg, and he was the head of department of International Relations at Wits (2007–2017). Professor Khadiagala obtained a BA in Political Science from the University of Nairobi, Kenya; an MA in Political Science from McMaster University, Hamilton, Ontario, Canada; and a PhD in International Studies from the School of Advanced International Studies (SAIS) at the Johns Hopkins University in Washington, DC. He has taught for over 30 years in Kenya, Canada, the United States and South Africa. His research focuses on African politics, mediation and conflict resolution. He was the founding director of the Africa Program at the Woodrow Wilson Centre for International Scholars in Washington, D.C. (1999–2002) and has been a consultant to various international organisations.

JOSEPH MAKANDA is an upcoming social sciences scholar with a keen interest in conflict analysis, post-conflict peacebuilding and development, forced migration and identity politics, governance and political transformation in Africa. He holds a PhD in Conflict Transformation and Peace Studies from the University of KwaZulu-Natal, and he currently works as postdoctoral research fellow at the Johannesburg Institute of Advanced Study at the University of Johannesburg. Makanda also holds a BA in Philosophy from St Joseph's Theological Institute, a BSocSci (Hons), and an MSocSci in Conflict Transformation and Peace Studies from the University of KwaZulu-Natal.

RICH MASHIMBYE is a Postdoctoral Research Fellow at the Institute for Pan-African Thought and Conversation at the University of Johannesburg where he undertakes research in a variety of areas encompassing politics, security and socio-economic matters. He has published various journal articles, book chapters and newspaper opinion pieces on issues that affect Africa or are located on the continent.

SIKANYISO MASUKU holds a PhD in Conflict Transformation and

Peace Studies from the University of KwaZulu-Natal. He is currently a Research Fellow at the Thabo Mbeki African School of Public and International Affairs at the University of South Africa. He is a published author in international, peer reviewed journals and monographs. His particular research interests include social protection and welfare, poverty and inequality, the politics of belonging/citizenship, human mobility and migration.

EMMANUEL MATAMBO is the Research Director at the Centre for Africa–China Studies. He holds a PhD in Political Science from the University of KwaZulu-Natal, South Africa. His research interests include Africa–China relations, terrorism in Africa, subnational politics and constructivism in international relations. In 2019, he was a Fall Scholar in the Africa Program at the Woodrow Wilson International Center for Scholars in Washington, D.C., and, in 2020, he was appointed as a Fellow of the Atlantic Council's Millennium Leadership Program.

KHABELE MATLOSA is a visiting professor at the Wits School of Governance, University of Witwatersrand, Johannesburg. He is the former Director of the Department of Political Affairs at the African Union Commission in Addis Ababa, Ethiopia.

DAVID MONYAE is Associate Professor of Political Science and International Relations at the University of Johannesburg, and Co-Director of the Centre for Africa–China Studies. Professor Monyae is an international relations and foreign policy expert, with a PhD in International Relations from the University of the Witwatersrand. He previously served as Section Manager: International Relations Policy Analysis at the South African Parliament, providing strategic management, parliamentary foreign policy formulation, and monitoring and analysis services. He has published widely and is a respected political analyst who features in the national and international media.

FRANCIS MWAIJANDE holds a PhD from the University of Arkansas, and an MA from the University of Wolverhampton. He is a senior lecturer of Public Policy and Social Science Research at Mzumbe University in Tanzania. He worked as an adjunct instructor in the Department of Political Science, University of Arkansas, in 2008 where he taught Comparative African

Politics focusing on social policy and public sector reforms, democracy and the Millennium Development Goals. He was also a principal investigator for the Food Price Trends Analysis for Policy Options for Enhancing Food Security in Eastern Africa through the Association for Strengthening Agricultural Research in the Eastern and Central Africa (ASARECA).

BHASO NDZENDZE is an Associate Professor and Head of Department of Politics and International Relations at the University of Johannesburg (UJ). He is also Head of the 4IR and Digital Policy Research Unit at UJ. He completed his PhD at the University of the Witwatersrand with a thesis that put forth a typological theory of interstate war in Eastern Africa, drawing on case studies occurring between 1977 and 2000. His work – on conflict, democracy, technology and trade – has been published in numerous international journals and featured in the popular press. His most recent book is *Artificial Intelligence and International Relations Theories* (Palgrave, 2023).

SIZO NKALA is a Postdoctoral Research Fellow at the University of Johannesburg's Centre for Africa–China Studies, where he produces academic publications, manages commissioned research projects, organises seminars and interacts with the media. He holds a PhD in Political Science from the University of KwaZulu-Natal, where he also lectured for three years. He worked as an external consultant for In On Africa (formerly Consultancy Africa Intelligence) and is a Laureate of the Council for Social Science Research in Africa (CODESRIA) and the Center for African Studies Basel (CASB) Summer School. Dr Nkala's research interests include China–Africa relations in the technology, media and economic spheres, African political economy, immigration and global politics.

MUXE NKONDO is a social policy, national strategy development, and discourse analysis scholar and practitioner. He was former Deputy Vice-Chancellor (Academic Affairs) at the University of the North (now Limpopo) and Vice-Chancellor of the University of Venda, South Africa. He is a Harvard Andrew Mellon Fellow in English, and was a volume editor for the 2013/14 and 2015/16 *State of the Nation* published by the HSRC Press.

MICHAEL ODIJIE is a Research Fellow in the Department of History at University College London (UCL). He is currently part of the EU-funded

AFRAB project which studies African abolitionism. Prior to this he was a Research Fellow at the Centre for African Studies at the University of Cambridge. Dr Odijie has a BA (Hons) in History and International Studies from the Ambrose Alli University in Nigeria and an MA and PhD from the University of Sheffield in the United Kingdom.

KINGSLEY ORIEVULU holds a PhD in Development Studies and International Relations from the University of the Witwatersrand. Dr Orievulu specialises in development interventions involving development partnerships, governance, human rights, livelihood security, inclusive development planning and implementation, climate change and sustainable development at the Africa Health Research Institute.

TENIOLA TAYO is a policy adviser, focusing on regional integration issues in Africa, including the African Continental Free Trade Area and wider trade, investment and development policies. She is currently the Trade Policy Fellow at the Africa Policy Research Institute. She also runs Aloinett Advisors, a policy research and advisory firm. She previously worked as a consultant with the Institute for Security Studies, Supply Chain Africa, the United Nations Development Programme, and the West Africa Think Tank (WATHI). She has also worked as a senior legislative aide with the Nigerian Senate and as a consultant with the Office of the Vice President. She has an MA from the London School of Economics, and recently completed a fellowship at the European University Institute's School of Transnational Governance.

THOKOZANI SIMELANE holds a PhD in Philosophy (PhD) and D. Eng in Industrial Engineering. He is a Professor of Practice at the Faculty of Engineering and the Built Environment, Department of Urban and Regional Planning, University of Johannesburg, and is a principal investigator of South Africa's National Food and Nutrition Security Survey. Among other positions, he served as an Interim Research Director at AISA, when it was being incorporated into the Human Sciences Research Council (HSRC), a departmental manager at the Council for Scientific and Industrial Research (CSIR) and the South African Bureau of Standards (SABS). He has published extensively in international scientific journals and has co-edited nine books.

Bob Wekesa is Deputy Director at the African Centre for the Study of the United States at the University of the Witwatersrand, South Africa, and interim chairman of the Africa–US Universities Network. He is secretary to the Governing Board of the US Business in Africa Awards (USBAA). Since 2015, Wekesa has been a senior lecturer at the Wits Centre for Journalism. He holds an MA and a PhD from the Communication University of China. His interest is international communication, focusing on the intersection of media and international affairs. He has published extensively on Africa–China and Africa–US relations and is currently leading a 'US–Africa Cities' conference and publication project.

Siphamandla Zondi is Professor in the Department of Politics and International Relations and Acting Director of the Institute for Pan-African Thought and Conversation at the University of Johannesburg. He chairs the South African BRICS Think Tank, which facilitates the participation of researchers in BRICS policy development processes. He is the editor of the *International Journal of African Renaissance Studies*, the *African Journal of Political Science* and the *Journal of BRICS Studies*.

Index